HANDBOOK OF NICHE TOURISM

T0317653

RESEARCH HANDBOOKS IN TOURISM

Series Editor: Robin Nunkoo, *University of Mauritius*

This timely series brings together critical and thought-provoking contributions on key topics and issues in tourism and hospitality research from a range of management and social science perspectives. Comprising specially- commissioned chapters from leading authors, these comprehensive *Research Handbooks* feature cutting-edge contributions written with a global readership in mind. Equally useful as reference tools or high-level introductions to specific topics, issues, methods and debates, these *Research Handbooks* will be an essential resource for academic researchers, practitioners, undergraduate and postgraduate students.

Titles in this series include:

Handbook of Niche Tourism

Edited by

Marina Novelli

Professor of Tourism and International Development, School of Business and Law, University of Brighton, UK

Joseph M. Cheer

Professor of Sustainable Tourism and Heritage, School of Social Sciences, Western Sydney University, Australia

Claudia Dolezal

Senior Lecturer and Researcher, Institute of Tourism, Wine Business and Marketing, IMC University of Applied Sciences, Austria

Adam Jones

Principal Lecturer of Strategy and Enterprise, School of Business and Law, University of Brighton, UK

Claudio Milano

Adjunct Professor, Department of Social and Cultural Anthropology, Autonomous University of Barcelona, Spain

RESEARCH HANDBOOKS IN TOURISM

Cheltenham, UK • Northampton, MA, USA

Published by
Edward Elgar Publishing Limited
The Lypiatts
15 Lansdown Road
Cheltenham
Glos GL50 2JA
UK

Edward Elgar Publishing, Inc.
William Pratt House
9 Dewey Court
Northampton
Massachusetts 01060
USA

Paperback edition 2024

A catalogue record for this book
is available from the British Library

Library of Congress Control Number: 2022941073

This book is available electronically in the **Elgar**online
Geography, Planning and Tourism subject collection
http://dx.doi.org/10.4337/9781839100185

ISBN 978 1 83910 017 8 (cased)
ISBN 978 1 83910 018 5 (eBook)
ISBN 978 1 0353 3733 0 (paperback)

Printed and bound by CPI Group (UK) Ltd, Croydon, CR0 4YY

Contents

Acknowledgements

Several people have significantly contributed to the realization of this *Handbook of Niche Tourism*. First of all, we are grateful for the enthusiastic and professional support of each contributor, as without them, this collection would not have become a reality.

We are particularly grateful to all those that believed in this project, contributed general comments and constructive reviews and offered feedback, making this *Handbook* a platform for further discussion on niche tourism.

As academics, practitioners and activists, we would like to acknowledge the challenges that all those involved in tourism have been facing during the on-going COVID-19 pandemic and we hope that this *Handbook* will provide some useful food for thoughts for the future.

About the editors

Marina Novelli (PhD) is Professor of Tourism and International Development at the University of Brighton (UK) and a global authority in the field of tourism and sustainable development. With a background in economics, she has written and covered advisory roles for International Development Agencies (World Bank, UNESCO, UNIDO, Millennium Challenge Corporation and European Union), as well as governments and businesses in the field of international tourism policy, planning, development and management in Africa, Europe and Asia. Her work has had a demonstrable impact far beyond tourism by contributing to more effective economic growth, improved environments and more inclusive societies. She is the author of the first comprehensive edited collection on *Niche Tourism – Contemporary Issues, Trends and Cases* (Elsevier, 2005). She is committed to generating new knowledge on ways in which tourism can play a key role in sustainable development by stimulating local economies, conserving the environment, developing people and changing lives.

Joseph M. Cheer (PhD) is Professor in the Center for Tourism Research at Wakayama University, Japan; board member of PATA (Pacific Asia Travel Association); and Co-Editor-in-Chief of the journal *Tourism Geographies*. He is an Adjunct Professor at Aukland University of Technology, New Zealand and a Visiting Professor at UCSI University, Malaysia. His recent collaborative book projects include: *Global Tourism & COVID-19: Implications for Theory and Practice* (2022) and *Recentering Tourism Geographies in the Asian Century* (2022). He has published in *The Conversation* and *World Economic Forum*, and commentates for Nikkei Asia and Channel News Asia. He is board member of the International Geographical Union (IGU) Tourism Commission; Critical Tourism Studies – Asia Pacific; and the American Association of Geographers, Recreation, Tourism and Sport (AAG-RTS). Joseph is an *Australian Research Council* (ARC) *Linkage Project* grant recipient with colleagues at the University of Melbourne, examining Aboriginal futures through tourism. He is a recent *Australia–Japan Foundation* grant recipient, benchmarking rural tourism for community resilience in Australia and Japan.

Claudia Dolezal (PhD) is a Senior Lecturer and Researcher in Tourism in the Institute of Tourism, Wine Business and Marketing at the IMC University of Applied Sciences in Austria. Her background is in tourism, international development and social anthropology with research conducted in Southeast Asia, Latin America, London and Austria. Her research focuses on regional, rural and sustainable tourism development, specifically on the role that tourism plays in the achievement of the UN Sustainable Development Goals. Claudia has published particularly on the topics of community-based tourism, sustainable development and social change in tourism. She is regularly engaged in capacity-building programmes and courses, such as for the UNWTO (World Tourism Organization) in Mexico, and delivers international keynotes and guest lectures. Claudia has edited special issues for various journals, while also acting as editorial board member of the *Austrian Journal of South-East Asian Studies* (ASEAS) and *Tourism Planning and Development* and has co-edited the book *Tourism and Development in Southeast Asia*, published by Routledge.

Adam Jones (PhD) is a Principal Lecturer of Strategy and Enterprise in the School of Business and Law at the University of Brighton (UK). Adam recently was awarded his PhD from the School of Applied Social Science at the University of Brighton, with a thesis on 'How are carbon-light holidays possible? A social practice analysis of no-flight holidays'. He started his career in the travel industry working as a tour guide and rising to the position of Head of Marketing. It was during his time as Head of Marketing, Research and Product Development that he developed an expert understanding of the issues around strategic direction and the challenges applying the principles of strategic marketing to an extremely competitive and challenging commercial environment within a sustainable context. Adam's work included developing the company's strategy for Corporate Social Responsibility (CSR) and setting industry-wide reporting standards on CSR issues with the United Nations Environmental Programme.

Claudio Milano (PhD) is Adjunct Professor in the Department of Social and Cultural Anthropology at the Autonomous University of Barcelona. PhD in Social and Cultural Anthropology and a Master's degree in Social and Cultural Anthropology (Cultural Differences and Transnational Processes), both awarded by the Autonomous University of Barcelona (Spain). Master's degree in Tourism Economics and a Bachelor's degree in Tourism, both from the Faculty of Economics at the University of Naples Federico II (Italy). Currently Visiting Research Fellow at the Center for Tourism Research, Wakayama University and a Visiting Professor at Tor Vergata University of Rome. He is the Co-Deputy Chair of the Commission on Anthropology of Tourism at the International Union of Anthropological and Ethnological Sciences (IUAES).

Contributors

António D. Abreu (PhD) is a biologist, PhD in Marine Biology, researcher and manager in the UNESCO Chair in Biodiversity and Conservation for Sustainable Development at the University of Coimbra. He is a specialist in the environment, developing scientific activity in the areas of marine biology and ecology, protected areas, environmental impact assessment, environmental management and biodiversity. He has extensive international work experience, having worked in the last 20 years for UNESCO, African Development Bank, World Bank, IFAD, and other agencies and governments of different countries in Africa, Asia, South America and Europe. He worked at UNESCO as Programme Specialist in the Division of Ecological and Earth Sciences as well as consultant for UNESCO Biosphere Reserves. He currently is the Coordinator of the EEAGrants project: Portuguese Biosphere Reserves – sustainable territories – resilient communities. He is Vice-President of the European Network of Environment Councils representing the Portuguese National Council for Environment and Sustainable Development.

Cristina Abreu is a biologist, with the title of Environmental Specialist of the Biologists' Portuguese Chamber. She has a Master's degree in Sustainable Tourism Destinations and Tourism Territory Planning from the University of Lleida/Barcelona and is a PhD student in Tourism Management at ISCTE. Her professional activity includes university teaching, including supervising postgraduate theses in biodiversity, nature conservation and sustainable tourism. She is an environmental consultant, with experience in environmental impact studies and environmental monitoring, and has been a team member of several applications to UNESCO Biosphere Reserves in Portugal and abroad. She is a senior auditor of the Environmental Management Systems and Sustainable Tourism Certification. Her main interests focus on innovation, nature conservation and environmental management in nature tourism, particularly in classified areas.

Manisha Agarwal is a full-time Associate Lecturer at James Cook University Singapore. She is also enrolled in the PhD programme at the College of Business, Law and Governance at the James Cook University, Townsville, Australia. Her research interests include tourist behaviour and understanding underlying psychological processes in tourists, in particular motivation, experience, satisfaction and loyalty. She is also interested in understanding and using different methodologies to learn more about tourist behaviour and the phenomenon of tourism in general.

Joanne Ailwood (PhD) is an Associate Professor at the University of Newcastle, Australia. Her research sits within the fields of early childhood education, children and families using poststructural theoretical perspectives. Joanne has worked with teachers and schools in Zimbabwe and has published in the fields of history and policies of education, early childhood education and international teacher education. Joanne's most recent work investigates how we account for the work of care in the early years. Her research is underpinned by the theoretical perspectives of Michel Foucault and Rosi Braidotti.

Clive Allanso is a Visiting Lecturer and Doctoral candidate at the University of Brighton whose research involves developing a critical understanding of the 'value of arts' beyond the commercial meaning of the term, and the role of art champions in the development of creative sector SMEs (i.e. galleries, fairs, museums, studios) and value chain connection with the tourism sector in West Africa.

Simona Azzali (PhD) is an Assistant Professor at the Department of Architecture at Prince Sultan University (PSU), Riyadh, where she teaches urban and architectural design studios, urban theory and research methods modules. Prior to commencing her appointment at PSU, she worked and researched for various renowned academic institutions as James Cook University Singapore, the National University of Singapore, UCL London, Politecnico di Milano and Qatar University. She is passionate about cities and a strong advocate of a people-oriented and participatory design approach to build better cities by design.

Martine Bakker (PhD) is a tourism development expert, trainer and researcher with over 25 years of extensive international experience in tourism-driven inclusive and sustainable development. Martine is currently a research scholar at the International Institute of Tourism Studies at George Washington University in Washington DC.

Maria Pia Bernardoni is a contemporary arts' curator, international project facilitator and art events' organizer. Since 2015 she has been the curator of international exhibitions for the African Artists' Foundation and LagosPhoto festival. Since 2020 she has, alongside Prof. Novelli, been facilitating Building Bridges through Contemporary Arts, a network of arts professionals aimed at fostering mutually beneficial collaborations between sector operators in Europe and Africa.

Ernest Cañada (PhD) holds a PhD in Geography and is a postdoctoral researcher at the University of the Balearic Islands (UIB) under the Margarita Salas programme. He has been the coordinator of Alba Sud, an independent research centre based in Barcelona special-izing in tourism from critical perspectives since 2008. He lived in Central America for 10 years. During his three-year postdoctoral fellowship (2022–2024) Cañada will work with Wageningen University, The Autonomous University of Barcelona and the University of the Balearic Islands, under the Margarita Salas grant programme. His main areas of research about tourism are the analysis of labour, socio-ecological conflicts and post-capitalist alternatives. Cañada's research has been focused on both Spain and Latin America. His latest publications include: *Turismos de proximidad, un plural en disputa* (Icaria Editorial, edited with Carla Izcara), *#TourismPostCOVID19. Lockdown touristification* (Alba Sud Editorial, 2021, edited with Ivan Murray), *Turistificación global. Perspectivas críticas en turismo* (Icaria Editorial, 2019, edited with Ivan Murray).

Jaeyeon Choe (PhD) is an interdisciplinary researcher at the School of Management at Swansea University, UK; and a Visiting Professor in the School of Hospitality and Tourism at Hue University, Vietnam. She is a fellow of the Royal Geographical Society and co-editor of a book *Pilgrimage Beyond the Officially Sacred: Understanding the Geographies of Religion and Spirituality in Sacred Travel* (Routledge, 2020). She has written and spoken about spiritual and wellness tourism primarily in Southeast Asia, including Indonesia, Thailand and Vietnam. She gave the keynote address at the Sustainable Tourism Development for Southeast Asia Conference in Vietnam in December 2019. She runs 'Tea Time Chat Series' on YouTube, which addresses wellness and spiritual tourism, religious tourism, pilgrimage and Southeast Asian tourism with key authors and practitioners in the area. She also produces monthly stakeholder reports entitled 'Asia Pacific Travel and Tourism Report' with industry partners.

Fabio Corbisiero (PhD) is based at University of Naples Federico II, Department of Social Sciences, Italy. His research draws from the literatures on urban sociology, tourism studies, gender and LGBT studies, and focuses on understanding how the spatial organization creates and reproduces inequality for vulnerable social categories. His current research agenda investigates (1) how the urban context, particularly the experience of European cities, determines the life chances of vulnerable people; (2) how tourism forms emerge and evolve in urban contexts; and (3) how places and geographies structure socio-economic opportunity in Italy and elsewhere. He has been a Visiting Fellow at CUNY University – Graduate Center, New York and a Visiting Professor at the KTH Royal Institute of Technology, Stockholm, and University College Dublin.

Cassie Perpetua Forsythe is Communications and Digital Manager for Sabah Tourism Board, Malaysia. She has been employed with the tourist board since 2012 and for several years managed the Australian inbound sector. Cassie assisted in organizing the annual ANZAC and Sandakan Day Memorial ceremonies in Sandakan, which piqued her interest to further study the Sandakan–Ranau Death Marches. Over the years, she has developed a sense of camaraderie with a group of Australians who visit Sabah annually to commemorate their fallen soldiers.

Carla Fraga is an Associate Professor at the Department of Tourism, Universidade Federal de Juiz de Fora (UFJF), Brazil. She holds a D.Sc. in Transport Engineering from the Programa de Engenharia de Transportes of the Instituto Alberto Luiz Coimbra de Pós-Graduação e Pesquisa em Engenharia, Universidade Federal do Rio de Janeiro (PET/COPPE/UFRJ), Brazil. She is currently undertaking a specialization course in Neuroscience and Applied Psychology at Universidade Presbiteriana Mackenzie (2020 – in progress), Brazil. She leads the Grupo de Pesquisa Transportes e o Turismo (GPTT). Her research interests are tourism, transportation and neuroscience. She is a member of the International Academy for the Development of Tourism Research in Brazil (ABRATUR), and of the Associação Nacional de Pesquisa e Pós-Graduação em Turismo (ANPTUR).

Francesc Fusté-Forné (PhD) holds a PhD in Tourism (University of Girona) and a PhD in Communication (Ramon Llull University). He is a lecturer and researcher at the Department of Business, University of Girona. He is undertaking research on culinary and rural heritages from a marketing and travel perspective. Particularly, he focuses on the food tourism phenomcna, making connections among food identities, landscapes, regional development, rural activities, street food and tourist experiences. He also conducts research on the role of gastronomy in relation to mass media and as a driver of social change.

Maria Gebbels (PhD) is a Senior Lecturer in Hospitality Management, University of Greenwich, UK. Her latest research focuses on gender issues and women's career advancement in hospitality, hospitality professionalism and career development, prison fine dining, hospitality in adventure tourism and critical hospitality.

Ulrike Gretzel (PhD) is a Senior Fellow at the Center for Public Relations, University of Southern California. Her research spans the design and evaluation of intelligent systems, as well as the development and implications of artificial intelligence. Her work in tourism addresses ways in which tourists engage with each other and with tourism organizations through websites, mobile apps and social media, and she has analysed how tourism experiences are represented and marketed online. She studies social media marketing, influencer marketing and the emerging reputation economy. She has also researched smart tourism development, technology adoption and non-adoption in tourism organizations, and the quest for digital detox experiences. She has published over 100 peer-reviewed journal articles. She is frequently acknowledged as one of the most cited authors in the fields of tourism and persuasion and is a Fellow of the International Academy for the Study of Tourism.

Jayni Gudka is CEO of the social enterprise Unseen Tours and a community-based tourism consultant, a role through which she creates opportunities for genuine interactions between tourists and host communities via projects in West Africa and South-East Asia. With the belief that that the tourism, heritage and events industries have much to gain by employing people from marginalized communities, her work and research focuses on creating opportunities for them to collaborate. Unseen Tours is a not-for-profit social enterprise which offers unique and eye-opening experiences of London to both tourists and long-time London residents. The organization not only ensures benefits to the host communities by hiring local guides who are knowledgeable about specific areas of London, but also provides work opportunities to homeless and vulnerably housed individuals who are often excluded from the tourism sector.

Tracy Harkison (PhD) is an Associate Professor at the School of Hospitality and Tourism, Auckland University of Technology, New Zealand. Her research interests include co-creating luxury accommodation experiences, hospitality education, hospitality human resource management and the hospitableness of hospitality.

Stefan Hartman is Head of Department of the European Tourism Futures Institute (ETFI – www.etfi.eu) at NHL Stenden University, Leeuwarden, the Netherlands. At the ETFI he helps actors in the leisure and tourism industry to develop strategies and actions that allow them to manage continually changing business environments. To do so, he uses his knowledge of transition management, resilience and adaptive capacity building. Stefan obtained his PhD at the University of Groningen, the Netherlands. His research focuses on the development, strategic (spatial) planning and governance issues related to spaces and places that are in the process of becoming destinations for tourism and leisure.

Jasper Hessel Heslinga works as Senior Researcher–Lecturer at NHL Stenden University of Applied Sciences, Leeuwarden, the Netherlands, and is currently based at the European Tourism Futures Institute (ETFI). He obtained his PhD from the University of Groningen. Heslinga also works as Programme Manager for the Centre of Expertise Leisure, Tourism and Hospitality (CELTH), Breda, the Netherlands.

Jesper Holm is an Associate Professor at Roskilde University, Denmark, researching transdisciplinary studies in environmental and health innovations and the various pathways for sustainable transition. In recent years, his focus has been on different approaches to greening tourism: by destination management, ecotourism niches, guiding entrepreneurship and the development of sustainable tours.

Montserrat Iglesias (PhD) is Senior Lecturer of English as a Foreign Language and Head of Studies at CETT Language School, CETT-UB Barcelona School of Tourism, Hospitality and Gastronomy (affiliated to the University of Barcelona, Spain). With a background in languages and education, she is a global authority in the field of language tourism. Her research has also focused on academic tourism and on the development of communicative competence in English for Specific Purposes. As well as delivering webinars and publishing book chapters, journal articles, encyclopaedia entries and conference papers related to her research topics, she is a co-author of *Ready to Order* (Pearson, 2002), an English language course for hospitality students.

Grzegorz Iwanicki is an Assistant Professor of Socio-Economic Geography at Maria Curie-Skłodowska University in Lublin, Poland. He has published articles related mainly to urban tourism, nightlife economy, city breaks, astro-tourism, and light pollution and its impact on the socio-economic sphere. His current work and recent scientific projects focus specifically on dark sky parks, astro-tourism, and initiatives against light pollution and their impact on local communities. In 2021 he took part in the project *Development of National Just Transition Plan (NJTP) setting the framework for Territorial Just Transition Plans*, financed by the Polish National Fund for Environmental Protection and Water Management on behalf of the Ministry of Climate and Environment.

Lee Jolliffe is a Visiting Professor at Ulster University, UK. She has a research interest in heritage tourism and, in particular, on niche areas of rural and culinary tourism, including tea-related tourism.

Zilmiyah Kamble (PhD) is currently working with James Cook University, Singapore, as a Senior Lecturer in Hospitality and Tourism. She has a wealth of experience both in the tourism industry and academia, spanning across five different countries (the UK, Seychelles, India, Malaysia and, currently, Singapore). She runs events and hospitality management courses at both undergraduate and postgraduate level. Her diverse research interests include tourism planning and development, tourism's social and cultural impacts, responsible tourism, sustainable tourism, social cohesion and social capital through tourism. She has also consulted for the Seychelles Ministry of Tourism, and published research pertaining to tourism's impacts, tourism development and policy reviews of tourism development post-war in Sri Lanka.

Balvinder Kaur Kler (PhD) is a Senior Lecturer in Tourism at the Faculty of Business, Economics and Accountancy, Universiti Malaysia Sabah. She has taught the Special Interest Tourism module to final year students since 2008. Born and raised in Sabah, Malaysian Borneo, her research explores meanings and attachments to place from both a resident and a tourist perspective. She was introduced to the term 'topophilia' by the late Professor Dick Braithwaite, who she met in 2002 on his many visits to Sabah. She continues to apply this framework to understand niche tourist experiences. Balvinder received her PhD in Tourism from the University of Surrey.

Heather Kennedy-Eden (PhD) is an Instructional Assistant Professor at Texas A&M University teaching hospitality and tourism classes, and acts as the internship coordinator. Her research focuses on technology's impacts on family tourism and personal heritage tourism. Her work covers topics from how smart phones affect family bonding in everyday life and on vacation, to how technology has impacted personal heritage tourism through the use of smart phones and apps, to how DNA results affect travel destinations of personal heritage tourists.

She studies social media, social media groups and how people who work on building family trees travel and engage with others while researching their personal family history.

Joanna Kosmaczewska is an Associate Professor at the University of Life Sciences of Poznań, Poland. Her research encompasses tourism economics and tourism behaviour. She has authored around 75 publications and a number of expert assessments and projects in the field of tourism. She is a member of CITUR (Centre for Tourism Research, Development and Innovation) – Tourism Research Unit of IPLeiria (Portugal), co-owner of a travel agency and an Executive Partner at the Polish Market for Oestetur touroperator – Destinos ao Rubro, Portugal (2015–2019).

Joanna Kowalczyk-Anioł is an Assistant Professor at the Institute of Urban Geography, Tourism Studies and Geoinformation at the University of Lodz (Poland). Her research interests include urban tourism (hypertrophy), heritage cities, cultural tourism, tourist behaviour, generations (BB, X, Y, Z) in tourism, sustainable tourism development, social resilience to tourism pressure and social conflicts in tourism.

Viltė Kriščiūnaitė is a graduate of the Culture and Tourism Management programme at Vytautas Magnus University, Agriculture Academy, Faculty of Bioeconomy Development, Study programme Culture and Tourism Management, Universiteto str. 10, Akademija, Kaunas distr., Lithuania. Her scientific interests include culture and tourism management, nature tourism, dark tourism and niche tourism.

Magdalena Kubal-Czerwińska is an Assistant Professor in the Department of Tourism and Health Resort Management, Institute of Geography and Spatial Management, Faculty of Geography and Geology at the Jagiellonian University in Krakow (Poland). Her background is in socio-economic geography and tourism; she holds both an MSc and a PhD in Tourism Geography. She is an active and involved researcher with research interests revolving around topics such as entrepreneurial behaviour in hospitality on rural areas, gender in tourism, cultural tourism, sustainable development in tourism and hospitality, and attitudes and behaviours towards the problem of reducing food waste. She has been involved as a researcher in national and international projects, such as the Visegrad Funds, Twinning (H2020), National Science Centre (Poland).

Josef Kunc (PhD) is an Associate Professor at Masaryk University, Faculty of Economics and Administration, Brno, Czech Republic. He is an economic geographer and regionalist specializing in the transformation of the current socio-economic and spatial environment of cities and regions. Other areas of scientific interest include consumer preferences, shopping behaviour and special interest tourism. He has written over 80 research publications, including articles in peer-reviewed scientific journals, books and book chapters. He has experience as a leader of national research projects and a team member of national and international projects (i.e. EU FP7 Collaborative Project).

Lea Kužnik (PhD) earned her doctorate in 2007 from University of Ljubljana, Faculty of Arts, Department of Ethnology and Cultural Anthropology. She has interests in museology, children's museums and interactive learning environments. Her doctoral thesis, 'Interactive Learning Environments and Children's Museums: Theoretical Model and Its Planning' presents novel scientific research on children's museums in Slovenia. She is currently employed at Biotechnical Educational Centre Ljubljana, Vocational College as an Assistant Professor for

Tourism and Cultural Heritage. Her latest research is focused on dark tourism, a topic which is very poorly developed in Slovenia. She has proposed a typology of dark tourism in Slovenia which can serve as a basis for further efforts in the design of new dark tourism products based on Solvenia's dark heritage.

Dominic Lapointe is a Professor in the Department of Urban and Tourism Studies at Université du Québec à Montréal. He holds the Chaire de recherche sur les dynamiques touristiques et les relations socioterritoriales and leads the Groupe de recherche et d'intervention tourisme territoire et société (GRITTS) at UQAM. His work explores the production of the tourism space, its role in the expansion of the capitalist system and its biopolitical dimensions. His latest research looks at climate change, social innovations, indigeneity and critical perspectives in tourism studies.

Alison McIntosh (PhD) is a Professor of Tourism and Hospitality at Auckland University of Technology, New Zealand. Her main research interests are in social justice, inclusion and advocacy through tourism and hospitality. She leads the Tourism For All New Zealand research group, which aims to make tourism accessible for all.

Salvatore Monaco (PhD) is a Researcher in Sociology at the Faculty of Education, Free University of Bozen – Bolzano (Italy). He obtained a PhD in Social Sciences and Statistics at the Department of Social Sciences, University of Naples Federico II. He is also a researcher at Osservatorio LGBT and OUT (Osservatorio Universitario sul Turismo), University of Naples Federico II. His research interests concern social exclusion, tourism, urban contexts, technologies and new media.

Markéta Novotná (PhD) is an Assistant Professor at Masaryk University, Faculty of Economics and Administration, Brno, Czech Republic. She is a regionalist specializing in tourism and sustainable development. In her research, she focuses on regional tourism planning, destination governance and consumer behaviour concerning responsibility and pro-environmental attitudes. She has been involved in both basic and applied research projects contributing to the decision-making process of politicians and policymakers. As a member of the Czech Association of Scientific Experts in Tourism, she has participated in an analysis for the Tourism Development Strategy of the Czech Republic 2021–2030. She is the author of over 30 research publications, including research articles, conference papers and book chapters.

Daniel H. Olsen (PhD) is an Associate Professor in the Department of Geography at Brigham Young University. His research interests revolve around the intersections of religion, spirituality, heritage and tourism. He has published over 75 book chapters and articles on these topics, and is the co-editor of *Tourism, Religion, and Spiritual Journeys* (Routledge, 2006), *Religious Pilgrimage Routes and Trails* (CABI, 2018), *Dark Tourism and Pilgrimage* (CABI, 2020), *Religious Tourism and the Environment* (CABI, 2020) and *The Routledge Handbook of Religious and Spiritual Tourism* (Routledge, 2022).

Robert Pawlusiński is a Senior Lecturer in the Department of Tourism and Health Resort Management, Institute of Geography and Spatial Management at the Jagiellonian University in Krakow (Poland). He holds a PhD in Tourism Geography (Jagiellonian University) and Master's degrees in Tourism Geography (Jagiellonian University) and Management (Krakow University of Economics). His research interests include urban tourism with a focus on night-time economy and tourism development policies, heritage tourism and sustainable development in tourism. He has been involved as a researcher in national and international projects, including for the Visegrad funds, the UN Environment Programme and the National Science Centre (Poland).

Senthilkumaran Piramanayagam is a Professor at the Department of Allied Hospitality Studies, Welcomgroup Graduate School of Hotel Administration, Manipal Academy of Higher Education (University), Manipal, India. He has authored many book chapters, case studies, articles, reports and conference papers on consumer behaviour in tourism and hospitality. He has been selected as a Research Director for a research project funded by the Indian Council of Social Science Research (ICSSR), Government of India, on employing people with disabilities to manage high employee attrition in hospitality firms in India. He has also contributed as a statistician and data analyst in many collaborative research projects within the field of management and health science. His current main areas of interest include consumer behaviour in tourism and hospitality, branding of tourism services and hospitality educational administration.

Enrico Porfido (PhD) is a PhD Architect and Urban Planner with studies and working experiences in Italy, Albania, Norway, Portugal, Brazil and Spain. His research focuses on the relationship between tourism, landscape and local communities, investigating its effect on coastal and urban landscapes. A former lecturer at the Universiteti Polis in Tirana, he is now based in Barcelona where he collaborates with public and private institutions. Today he is a lecturer at Ostelea – Tourism Management School, CETT – Barcelona School of Tourism, Hospitality and Gastronomy, and Fundació Politècnica de Barcelona. He is a member of the Institute Habitat, Territory, Tourism (Polytechnic University of Catalunya) and the Sealine Research Centre (University of Ferrara), and he co-founded the independent research group 'paisviagem'. In this framework, he recently started a collaboration with the Gulbenkian Foundation of Lisbon. He regularly publishes in international scientific journals and magazines.

Yash Prabhugaonkar is a graduate from James Cook University Singapore.

Rasa Pranskūnienė (PhD) is based at Vytautas Magnus University, Agriculture Academy, Faculty of Bioeconomy Development. He is a committee member of the study programmes in a) Tourism Industries and b) Culture and Tourism Management, and Director of Vytautas Magnus University Agriculture Academy Museum, Universiteto str. 10, Akademija, Kaunas distr., Lithuania, e-mail: rasa.pranskuniene@vdu.lt. His scientific interests include overtourism, degrowth, heritage and tourism, niche tourism, critical theory, grounded theory and qualitative research methods.

Ricardo Nicolas Progano (PhD) is a Lecturer at the Center for Tourism Research of Wakayama University, Japan. His research interests include religious tourism, heritage management and cross-cultural studies. He has carried out fieldwork on the recent tourism development of Japanese pilgrimage sites, such as Kumano Kodo and Koyasan. His research publications include: Progano, R. N. (2021). The Impact of COVID-19 on Temple Stays: A Case Study from Koyasan, Japan'; Progano, R. N. et al. (2020). 'Visitor Diversification in Pilgrimage Destinations: Comparing National and International Visitors through Means-end'; Progano, R. N. (2018). 'Residents' perceptions of socio-economic impacts on pilgrimage sites: How does the community perceive pilgrimage tourism?'; and Kato, K. & Progano, R. N.

(2017). 'Spiritual (walking) tourism as a foundation for sustainable destination development: Kumano-kodo pilgrimage, Wakayama, Japan'.

Helena Reis (PhD) in Tourism, is an Assistant Professor at the School of Management, Hospitality and Tourism of Algarve University and a member of the Research Centre for Tourism, Sustainability and Well-being (CinTurs). With a Master's in Women's Studies, her interests relate to consumer behaviour, gender and tourism. She has published in the *Journal of Travel Research*, *Journal of Hospitality and Marketing Management* and *The International Journal of Tourism Policy*, among others. Her recent research interests are connected to nightscapes, perceptions of darkness and how we are attracted to night skies that are not possible to enjoy any more due to increasing light in cities.

Tanja Ostrman Renault is presently a PhD candidate at the University of Primorska, Faculty of Tourism Studies – Turistica, Slovenia. Tourism has always represented an important part of her interests and became a way of life during six years spent in Mozambique. When she returned to Europe, she decided to dedicate her academic career to tourism. Tanja is self-employed, and besides being a teacher and translator, she is also a member of the national committee of tourist guides at the Tourism and Hospitality Chamber of Slovenia, as well as a Tourism Informant at the Slovenian Tourism Board. Academically, she has been researching dark tourism and, in particular, cemetery tourism; lately, she has been working on apitourism in Slovenia.

Áurea Rodrigues (PhD) holds a PhD in Tourism from the University of Aveiro, and is an Assistant Professor in Tourism Studies at the Department of Sociology and Associate Member of the Interdisciplinary Centre for History, Culture and Societies – CIDEHUS, University of Évora, Portugal. Her current research interests include astro-tourism, consumer behaviour in tourism and sustainable tourism development in rural destinations. Her papers have been published in the *Journal of Vacation Marketing*, *International Journal of Tourism Research*, *Tourism Analysis*, *European Countryside*, and *Anatolia*, among others. ORCID 0000-0002-4989-5365.

Anthea Rossouw, Founder of Dreamcatcher South Africa NPC, is a globally recognized stakeholder engagement and social change management specialist practitioner. Anthea follows an inclusive, pluralistic approach with sustainability as the key outcome, constructively addressing the UNSDG's since their launch in 2000. Working with communities across South Africa, into Africa and beyond, Anthea innovates challenges into solutions which affirm diversity; address poverty, gender and youth inequality; and tackle environmental degradation. Harnessing tourism enterprise development and environmental rehabilitation as vehicles for change, Anthea has pioneered and implemented award-winning community-driven waste behaviour change (including developing a botanical garden on a former waste dump) and sustainable community-based tourism models across South Africa, and is currently working across Africa to contribute to change for sustainable tourism futures. Anthea and Dreamcatcher South Africa NPC were the 2020 recipients of the Africa Tourism Leadership Forum Awards for: Woman in Leadership; Championing Sustainability and Outstanding Entrepreneurship.

Dionisia Russo Krauss (PhD) is based at Universita' Degli Studi di Napoli Federico II, Italy. She is a tenured professor (Geography and Economic–Political Geography) and coordinator of the three-year degree programme in Tourism Sciences with a managerial orientation. She graduated with honours in Political Sciences in 1997, at the University of Naples 'Federico II', with a thesis on Political and Economic Geography, and in 2002 she obtained her PhD in Political Geography at the University of Trieste. As part of her research activity, she has dedicated herself in particular to the study of the immigration phenomenon, focusing attention on issues related to gender, religion and urban transformations produced by immigration. She has also studied various aspects of tourism geography and cultural geography concerning, in particular, issues relating to the regions of southern Italy, and focused on the analysis of some issues falling within the field of investigation of the geography of languages.

Emmanuel Salim (PhD) is postdoctoral researcher at the University of Lausanne (Switzerland) and Co-President of the Collectif Perce-Neige (France), which aims to promote trans-disciplinarity in mountain territories. He holds a PhD in Geography from the University Savoie-Mont-Blanc (France) and works in an interdisciplinary perspective on the evolution of the cryosphere in the face of climate change and its impact on glacier tourism. His work integrates glaciology, geography (physical and human), environmental psychology and, more recently, territorial economics. Emmanuel is also an associate member of the LABEX ITTEM (Univ. Grenoble-Alpes, France), which addresses issues of innovation and transition in mountain territories. Beyond the academic world, his work allows stakeholders to better adapt to global changes. He also has a strong commitment to the dissemination of knowledge, notably through numerous public lectures and his activity on social media.

Partho Pratim Seal (PhD) has more than two decades of experience in academia and hospitality. He is an alumnus of IHM Chennai and a postgraduate in Hotel Management and Management, pursuing a PhD in Hotel and Tourism Management. An avid wordsmith who believes that writing is the most influential and resourceful medium to disseminate information, he has authored three books: *Computers in Hotels: Concepts and Application* (Oxford University Press, 2013), *Food & Beverage Management* (Oxford University Press, 2017) and *How to Succeed in Hotel Management Job Interviews* (Jaico, 2015). His interests are in human resource management, entrepreneurship and food anthropology. He has published research papers in indexed international journals and is a reviewer for international journals.

Kathleen Smithers (PhD) is a Lecturer at Charles Sturt University, Australia. Her research sits within the fields of tourism, higher education and sociology of education, and uses a poststructural theoretical perspective. Kathleen has worked across a number of projects, including Virtual Reality in Schools, school improvement and precarity in higher education. With a focus on equity in all her projects, her doctoral thesis investigates developmenttourism in schools in Zimbabwe.

Marta Soligo works at a Postdoctoral Research Faculty at the University of Nevada, Las Vegas's (UNLV) International Gaming Institute, focusing on themes such as medical tourism, corporate social responsibility and problem gambling. At UNLV, Soligo teaches Sociology of Leisure. She is also a Visiting Professor of Sociology of Tourism at the Università degli Studi di Bergamo (Italy), for the Master's course in Planning and Management of Tourism Systems. Her most recent interests centre around a variety of key topics in today's travel market, such as sustainable development, heritage preservation and popular culture. She received her PhD in Sociology from UNLV and her Master's degree in Planning and Management of Tourism Systems from the Università degli Studi di Bergamo. Soligo's doctoral dissertation was an ethnographic study of the representations of Italian culture in Las Vegas's themed resorts, centring on topics such as immigrant labour in hospitality and the experience economy. Moreover, she is currently investigating sustainable entrepreneurship within the hospitality industry, focusing on gastronomic and wine tourism in Italian rural contexts and cultural landscapes. In 2013, she was a visiting scholar for the Center for Research in Engineering, Media and Performance (REMAP) at the University of California, Los Angeles (UCLA), investigating film-induced tourism in Hollywood.

Andrzej Stasiak (PhD) holds a PhD in Earth Sciences and works at the Institute of Urban Geography, Tourism and Geoinformation, University of Łódź (Poland). Since 2019, he has been the editor-in-chief of *Turyzm/Tourism* – the oldest Polish scientific journal on tourism. From 2000 to 2012, he was Vice-Rector for Research and the Rector of the College of Tourism and Hotel Industry (WSTH) in Łódź, and from 2002 to 2011 was the science editor of the WSTH Publishing House and of the scientific journal *Tourism and Hotel Industry*. He has also managed and is an expert in numerous EU tourism projects. He has lectured courses in tourist products, coached on courses for tour guides and is a member of the Provincial Examining Board for Tour Guides in Łódź, as well as a member of a group working on legal regulations regarding tourist trails in Poland, at the Ministry of Sport and Tourism. He was co-originator and co-organizer of a series of conferences entitled 'Culture and Tourism' (2006–2015), and has authored or co-authored over 120 publications on tourism marketing, cultural tourism (including open air museums, culinary tourism, movie tourism) and social tourism. In recent years, he has been involved in research on tourism in the experience economy.

Frédéric Tardieu is the founder and President of Sulubaaï Environmental Foundation, Philippines SMILO (Small Islands Organization), Director Delegate for Asia Pacific, Member of the Ocean Platform Climate and Director of Pangatalan. Sulubaaï is a Philippine non-profit organization dedicated to conserving, protecting and restoring the natural resources of Palawan Island through environmentally sustainable practices and restoration of active eco-systems in partnership with the local community. This is a private initiative funded through eco-tourism. Pangatalan island in Palawan, Philippines, is the first sustainable island in the Asia Pacific region, with five goals focusing on energy, water, waste, landscape and biodiversity. It has been awarded the title Zero Carbon Resort of Palawan. Frédéric is former real estate developer who undertook a radical change of life. He is a self-taught person and has lived in the Philippines since 2011. He wanted to prove that everything that man has destroyed can be returned to nature.

Faye Taylor (PhD) is Digital Learning Manager and Programme Director for the Online MBA at Nottingham Business School, Nottingham Trent University, UK. Her research interests centre on the political economy of sustainable tourism in the context of crisis. Commencing with her doctoral research, which explored the influence of political economy and conceptualizations of sustainability upon the post-tsunami redevelopment of Koh Phi Phi, Thailand, she has continued to research the field of backpacker tourism, island tourism, film tourism impacts and vulnerability. Her future research aspirations lie in uncovering sources of destination vulnerability and working with destination stakeholders towards developing crisis mitigation strategies.

K Thirumaran (PhD) received his PhD from the National University of Singapore. He worked in the tourism industry for over 10 years both in Singapore and the United States. At James Cook University Singapore, Thiru specializes in business and tourism management.

He coined the term 'affinity tourism' which refers to the propensity of guests to partake in 'familiar' and 'similar' cultural experiences to those of their hosts. He volunteers his time as a reviewer for a number of high-quality tourism and hospitality journals. His research focuses on service excellence and cultural and luxury tourism.

Jane Widtfeldt Meged is an Associate Professor at Roskilde University, Denmark. Jane Meged is a tourism researcher whose research interests are guided tours, network innovation, the sharing economy, sustainability, urban ecotourism and precarious working life. She has published several articles and book chapters, which focus on sustainable tourism transformations, applying a critical perspective on the tourism economy.

Ben Wielenga (MSc) works as researcher for the European Tourism Futures Institute (ETFI). He is also involved as lecturer in the Tourism Management programme of NHL Stenden University of Applied Sciences, Leeuwarden, the Netherlands. He obtained his Master's degree in Cultural Geography at the University of Groningen, the Netherlands. Ben has a strong interest in nature tourism research.

Paul Williams is currently Academic Director at Regent College, London. Following a career in higher education spanning 25 years where he taught, researched and undertook consultancy work focused on tourism marketing, place-making, ceramics and cultural-led regeneration, he was seconded to champion Stoke-on-Trent's UK City of Culture bid. Through his tourism advisory and ceramics connections work and as chair of an externally funded Cultural Destinations Partnership, he continues to shape cultural and creative sector policy developments and visitor economy strategies nationally and internationally.

Introduction to niche tourism – contemporary trends and development

Marina Novelli, Joseph M. Cheer, Claudia Dolezal, Adam Jones and Claudio Milano

NICHE TOURISM: NATURE, PURPOSE AND EVOLUTION

The term *niche tourism* has its origins in the fields of ecology (Hutchinson, 1957; Hannan and Freeman, 1977) and marketing (Claycamp and Massy, 1968; Johnson, 1971; Lambkin and Day, 1989; Kotler, 1994). Hutchinson (1957) is credited for the introduction of the term *niche* from a biology/ecology perspective, broadly referring to a region in a multidimensional space, an optimum location that a creature can exploit, leveraging extant environmental conditions in the presence of competitors. The *niche concept* is also derived from market segmentation theories initiated by Smith (1956) and based on economic theories of imperfect competition and demand-side-oriented and short-term strategies. It has also become accepted as a fundamental concept in business strategy (Porter, 1980).

In marketing terms, employment of the term niche assumes that there is market potential for a product or service (Lambkin and Day, 1989). In tourism terms, this can be furthered by referring to a specific product tailored to meet the needs of a particular market segment. The clear premise is that the market should not be seen as homogeneous, but rather, characterised by individuals with specific needs and wants (Novelli, 2005). When looked at from a historical perspective, Marson (2011: 3) suggests that 'the basic foundations of niche tourism existed before the modern conventions of mass tourism'. For instance, while the *Grand Tour* of the 16th to 18th centuries is often referred to as an early form of mass tourism and associated with the relatively large number of young European men of the upper classes travelling as a part of their education, it provided early connotations of what constitutes niche tourism. This manifested as likeminded individuals travelling independently with a specific purpose, well before travel and tourism was accessible to a wider socioeconomic spectrum, with the first Thomas Cook excursion not taking place until 5 July 1841. Additionally, Marson's (2011) reference to Francis Galton's 1872 textbook, *Art of Travel*, epitomises his experiences and provides insight into how early literature described what today would be classified as adventure travel and tourism.

In modern times, niche tourism was preceded by alternative travel paradigms, including special interest tourism and other forms of creative tourism (Read, 1980; Getz, 2000a, 2000b; Richards and Raymond, 2000; Hall, 2003, 2004; Richards and Wilson, 2007; Ohridska-Olson and Ivanov, 2010). This set the context for new debates in tourism studies and the spurring of novel forms of special interest tourism products and markets. These were primarily associated with the diversification and expansion of tourism motivation, consumption and production patterns, overseeing shifts from commodified mainstream types of tourism into tailor-made and unique alternative options (Read, 1980).

Niche tourism as a concept was not fully examined until 2002, when the Crichton Tourism Research Centre at the University of Glasgow held a one-day conference on the theme *Niche Tourism in Question: Interdisciplinary Perspectives on Problems and Possibilities*. This led to published proceedings edited by Macleod (2003), constituting one of the first attempts to reach a consensus on the use of the term and to investigate its application. Subsequently, Hall questioned whether niche tourism has led to a diversification of the industry, asking 'is it a healthy sign that the industry should appear to be driven by niche tourism? Or is it actually the case that this is an overhyped, politically correct and convenient delusion?' (2003: 24). The growth and significance of niche tourism evolved quickly. Numerous studies emerged in a relatively short period of time, with Novelli (2005) providing evidence of its validity as an alternative to mainstream forms of mass tourism. Niche tourism has since become widely adopted in tourism studies, with growing industry application. A broad range of academic studies on specific niches has since emerged – from medical (Bookman and Bookman, 2007), to diaspora heritage (Newland and Taylor, 2010) and sport tourism (Higham and Hinch, 2018), among others, as well as elaborations into *Long Tail Tourism* and new geographies for marketing niche tourism (Lew, 2008), niche tourism attributes (Wilhelm Stanis and Barbieri, 2013) and niche tourism as a means of fostering sustainable economic development in global peripheries (Ursache, 2015; Novelli, 2016). Accordingly, this strengthens Novelli's (2005) standpoint that niche tourism is a viable way for destinations to develop, diversify and/or reposition themselves.

Novelli's (2005) general definitional approaches of niche tourism remain appropriate to date. The first one is a *geographical and demographic approach* based on the location where the tourism consumption process takes place and the population involved in delivering a service and/or experience. These may include urban, rural, coastal and/or mountainous environments, or a combination of these, within a developed or a developing context, but what matters most is the specific experience and/or activity that the tourists wish to engage in. Secondly, a *product approach* is based on the presence and inclusion of activities, attractions, settlements, food and other amenities contributing to the consumer's unique experience. These constitute the key elements of the niche tourism destination mix, which is shaped in accordance with specific tourists' expectations. Thirdly, a *customer approach* reflecting tourist requirements and expectations is the focus of the niche tourism marketing approach. Attention is placed on the relationship between the demand and the supply sides. This approach looks at what kind of specific activities tourists seek in order to have a satisfactory holiday experience, whether that is a simple observation of nature or direct participation in the unique lifestyle or practice of the host community.

Niche tourism products are tailored to meet the needs of specific market segments, whose size and nature can vary considerably depending upon the demographic characteristics and the social status of the tourists, as well as the geography of the destinations involved. Examples of macro-niche tourism products include outdoor and indoor activities, ranging from sport and adventure to nature-, culture- and heritage-based activities. These can be further segmented into an extensive list of micro-niches including extreme sports; walking safaris, wildlife watching, eco-tourism and turtle conservation holidays; indigenous/ethnic and slum tours; and art, food and wine festivals. These are associated with a whole variety of niche tourism and hospitality services, among others (Figure 0.1).

Although niche tourism does not come without criticism as a concept (Hall, 2004), if developed and managed appropriately, it may lead to more sustainable outcomes (Novelli, 2005). The impact of globalisation, with tourists increasingly searching for authentic experiences and

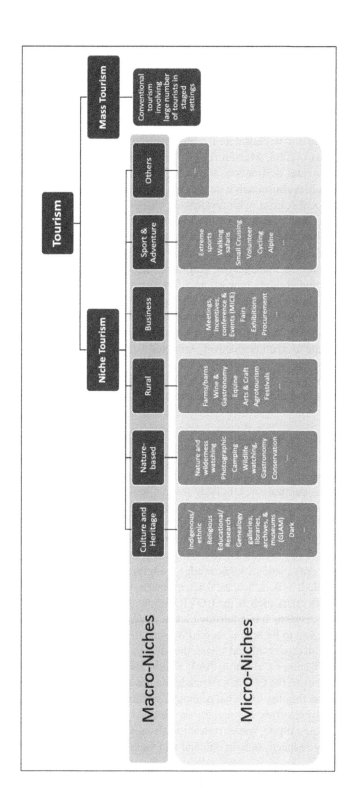

Figure 0.1   Macro vs. micro tourism niches

new forms of tourism (Azarya, 2007; Salazar, 2005), often occurring in fragile and remote settings, may have, however, led to several micro-level positive and negative implications.

After almost two decades of research, the impacts of niche and special interest travellers and how their impacts compare to generalist travellers (mass tourists) remain an under-explored area of research (Weiler and Firth, 2021). While mass tourism is often seen as a potential threat to environments and affecting socio-cultural aspects of the host communities (Dinis and Krakover, 2015), niche tourism is considered a more sustainable alternative by some scholars (Novelli, 2005; Yeoman, 2008; Marson, 2011), providing opportunities for small, resource-constrained, remote or rural destinations (Ursache, 2015). Small-scale tourism programmes can potentially help achieve sustainable rural development and foster local participation. Niche tourism can mean local control, with residents in charge of small-scale nature and culture-related tourism products and utilisation of local knowledge, traditions and networks. Small-scale niche tourism can be particularly beneficial for remote and rural communities to generate and diversify income sources (Dinis and Krakover, 2015).

Over the past 15 years, destination management and marketing organisations' (DMMOs) strategic interventions have included niche tourism as a fundamental component of tourism decision and policymaking. Rightly or wrongly, both special interest and niche tourism are generally viewed as playing a key role in market diversification, inclusive growth and sustainable tourism development. More recently, a blurring of the lines between what was once clearly defined as mass and niche tourism respectively emerged – the latter increasingly used as a strategy to rejuvenate destinations, enhance destination authenticity, diversify tourism products, and respond to changing customer demands and the need for proximity travel caused by travel restrictions imposed during the COVID-19 pandemic.

NICHE TOURISM IN THE COVID-19 ERA

When people think about travel and tourism, it often evokes imagery of holiday locations, sandy beaches, natural reserves, cultural sites, holiday resorts, iconic sceneries, airports and luxury hotels, among others. As tourists, we tend not to think about space politics, social justice, gender equality, poverty alleviation, environmental management or the impact that epidemics and conflict may have on destinations. As consumers, we tend to ignore mobility rights and the privileged freedom of mobilities across the globe granted by holding the 'right passport'. If this is the case, we only come to acknowledge the relevance of this when our own right to travel is suddenly curtailed, as was the case when measures were introduced to contain the spread and impact of a health crisis such as the COVID-19 pandemic.

The diffusion of infectious diseases has been invariably associated with the travel and tourism industry, which has proved to be both a vector (Wilson, 1995; Baker, 2015; Rosselló et al., 2017) and a victim of health crisis outbreaks, with the severe acute respiratory syndrome (SARS) in Southeast Asia (McKercher and Chon, 2004; Smith, 2006) being among the most studied to date. Now, more than ever, the COVID-19 pandemic has outlined the paradox of the global mobility paradigm and the fragility of global economic systems, with travel and tourism being among the most affected industries, particularly as necessary measures to contain the spread of the disease through quarantine, travel restrictions, temporary border closures and lockdown of cities significantly reduced tourism demand and supply, with some of the most dramatic repercussions ever for the supply chains of the aviation, hospitality, tourism and events industries (Craven et al., 2020).

Declining visitor numbers, increasing unemployment, declining profits, reduced investment and considerably reduced government revenue usually aggravate prevailing socioeconomic conditions (Ritchie, 2004), and cause countries to veer into economically depressed conditions (Novelli et al., 2018). However, as the full socioeconomic implications of the COVID-19 pandemic become more apparent, with lockdown measures leading to immobility on an unprecedented scale, any quantification of the impact of the crisis will be approximated. Evidently, the crisis most dramatically impacts the less visible components of the tourism value chain, such as informal sector workers, those on casual contracts and in the gig economy, renters, small-scale farmers and craft traders, and domestic workers, many of which are women.

Rapidly changing consumer behaviours are having an increasing influence on the future of tourism. Current immobility patterns caused by COVID-19 containment measures and volatility associated with the epidemic's patterns have hindered consumers' ability to travel freely.

DMMOs face significant challenges to address an increasingly complex tourism system. Indeed, shifts in consumers' travel attitudes associated with government-imposed COVID-19 containment measures, as well as changes in choices and behaviours in terms of experiences sought and responses to marketing messages, will ultimately impact travel product and destination choices. Evidently, there is a growing commitment to understanding and responding to changes in consumer behaviour, with new products, tools and messages and usage of new digitalised distribution channels. However, the variable level of resources available to do this has meant that some are more successful than others.

In a highly competitive market, tourism DMMOs have historically focused their development interventions on the identification of new tourism and hospitality products spanning the macro- and micro-niche tourism spectrum. In recent years, 'niche tourism has occupied an ambiguous position in regional development discourse and practice. In many developing and emerging economies, while mainstream tourism has often been side-lined to give priority to manufacturing or knowledge-intensive activities, niche tourism has been increasingly positioned as the great development hope for peripheral regions' (Novelli, 2018: 347). The growth of low-cost carriers such as Easyjet, Ryanair and AirAsia, among others, facilitated air access to secondary airports and the entry of lesser-known destinations onto the global tourism map. They have also played a role in boosting the niche tourism value chain and markets in smaller regions and remote destinations (Novelli, 2005). These developments have enabled travellers to engage in activities such as spa and yoga weekends, adventure sport and gastronomic experiences in unusual or exclusive locations (Novelli, 2018). However, with the COVID-19 crisis, all these activities have been placed on hold and it remains to be seen whether and when they will return.

Niche tourism has recently come to be regarded as a potential driver in the development of a new experience economy, particularly linked to the new wave of *proximity tourism* – engaging in tourism and travelling close to home (Diaz-Soria, 2017; Jeuring & Haartsen, 2017). Proximity tourism has been previously studied as a phenomenon, primarily related to the increase of environmental awareness (Dubois et al., 2011) and more recently as a mechanism of adaptation in times of crisis, such as COVID-19 (Romagosa, 2020). The reasons for this lie in a combination of factors: travelling far and freely may not be as widely accessible as before, not only due to travel restrictions, but also because of travellers' reduced spending power compared to the pre-pandemic period.

The digital transformation of tourism allowed niche tourism experiences to maintain some level of competitiveness at the peak of the COVID-19 crisis by turning to digital spaces, as the only means for global connectivity. Concurrently, while the collaborative or sharing economy (such as Airbnb, Uber) had grown exponentially prior to COVID-19 and was forecast to reach USD335 billion by 2025, considerable policy and planning challenges emerged during COVID-19, as they found themselves to operate in a state of crisis. As a result, through the diversification of their offers of online experiences and services, such as cooking classes and food delivery services, they became part of the 'new normal'. Much of this diversification (and growth in some cases) in tourism and hospitality, clearly linked to niche product development strategies, had already changed the industry dramatically, providing new product and service options.

Tourism services have traditionally been provided by businesses such as hotels, taxis, tour guides and tour operators. Before COVID-19, a growing number of people were offering to share – temporarily, and possibly for a charge – what they own (such as their house or car) or what they enjoyed doing (such as having a cooked meal at home or in an off-the-beaten-track restaurant, going on an excursion or visiting a museum) with tourists. Sharing goods and/or services between individuals was not a new concept, but the opportunity provided by Web 2.0, through the growth of internet accessibility, social media and the creation of online platforms, made the 'act of sharing' easier. Since the mid-2000s, several companies managing these types of platforms emerged and further growth post-COVID-19 is expected (Mauguin, 2020a, 2020b).

Without sounding naïve, we believe that niche tourism has provided the opportunity to engage in more meaningful and responsible experiences while travelling. Niche tourism has the potential to stimulate inclusive growth and employment that requires specialised skills (i.e. sport and extreme adventure instructors, gourmet chefs, yoga teachers), as opposed to low- or semi-skilled jobs generally associated with mass tourism. However, akin to mass tourism, the growth of niche tourism may have translated into unsustainable practices, and this volume reflects on existing practices and as a means to query how to restart tourism for the better. While social and spatial inequalities in tourism are generally associated with marginalised communities, other factors – such as environmental damage and pollution linked to overcrowding in environmentally sensitive areas, socio-cultural commodification of culture, loss of authenticity and loss of traditional values – are often a consequence of insensitive and damaging tourist practices. Through furthering our understandings of the evolution of contemporary niche tourism, we explore ways to avoid such predicaments.

Furthermore, although recognising the benefits of certain economies of scale generated through larger mass tourism operations, we maintain that activities, undertaken as part of a niche tourism experience, have the possibility to benefit communities to a larger extent, and generate a better geographic spread of tourism benefits, resulting in more even economic growth and widespread support for planning and development. For managers and planners, niche tourism offers greater opportunities for more sustainable tourism post-COVID-19 (Brandon, 2020; Kampel, 2020). In support of this, Ioannides and Gyimothy (2020: 626) argue for 'the potential decline of mainstream tourism practices, which are currently severely disrupted by COVID-19, with emergent niche activities, for which opportunities might arise from the very same disruptions'. Tourwriter (2020) highlights that whether defined by price, demographics (age, gender, ethnicity, religion), or psychographics (motivation, behavioural characteristics), geographical tourist-generating zones, socio-economic status and/or education, travel and tourism niches are predicted to boom in 2021. As the Tourwriter (2020) website states, 'Tourists will be on the hunt for niche experiences crafted by travel experts; and there will be a great amount of enthusiasm surrounding personalisation, the foundation for niche tourism'.

The COVID-19-induced crisis has altered mobility patterns, causing the neoliberal market mechanisms of global tourism to be severely disrupted. In turn, this situation is leading to the decline of certain mainstream mass tourism business formats and, simultaneously, the emergence of others – such as novel niche tourism trends.

> The crisis has, therefore, brought us to a fork in the road – giving us the perfect opportunity to select a new direction and move forward by adopting a more sustainable path. Specifically, COVID-19 offers public, private, and academic actors a unique opportunity to design and consolidate the transition towards a greener and more balanced tourism. (Ioannides and Gyimothy, 2020: 624)

Niche tourism may offer fertile ground for further sustainable innovations toward a more responsible tourism future.

THE *HANDBOOK OF NICHE TOURISM*: PURPOSE AND CONTENT

The primary purpose of the *Handbook of Niche Tourism* is to provide a critical elaboration of the evolution of the contemporary niche tourism phenomenon. By framing the discussion around sustainable development thinking, concepts and practical applications, authors were invited to critically reflect on niche tourism trends and were particularly encouraged to highlight niche tourism successes and/or failures, as well as discuss the challenges and opportunities faced by countries around the world that pursue tourism as a vehicle for sustainable development.

We were intent on advancing the study of contemporary (niche) tourism by providing a good balance of geographical perspectives and representations of both academics and practitioners. This is reflected in the mix of theoretical, conceptual and empirical elaborations, across diverse geographical locations, as evidenced in the chapters that follow. The *Handbook* includes 28 full chapters and eight short chapters clustered into seven thematic sections. The first section, on nature-based tourism, includes chapters on astro-tourism in the Czech–Polish Izera Dark Sky Park, glacier tourism and climate change in Switzerland, architourism in natural areas, conservation tourism in the Palawan UNESCO Biosphere Reserve, urban eco-tourism in Denmark, as well as a short chapter on geocaching tourism. The second section, on rural tourism, includes chapters on tea tourism in Asia, agritourism and the Prosecco Route in Italy, culinary tourism based on artichoke production in Spain, astro-tourism in Portugal and rural festivals in Albania, as well as a short chapter on Koh Phi Phi, Thailand as victim of film tourism devastated by crisis. The third section focuses on heritage and culture-based tourism, with chapters on personal heritage tourism, Communism heritage tourism in Poland, railway tourism in Brazil, industrial and ceramics-led tourism in the UK, 'Escape Rooms' and cultural tourism in Poland and language tourism, as well as a short chapter on contemporary arts tourism in Ghana. The fourth section, on dark tourism, provides contributions on battlefield tourism in Malaysian Borneo, the Cold War Museum in Lithuania and cemetery tourism in Slovenia, as well as a short chapter on fine dining in a prison: a case study of The Clink restaurants. The fifth section, on spiritual, religious and wellness tourism, includes chapters on faith, New Age spirituality and religious tourism, Babymoon travel in India and pilgrimage tourism in Japan, along with a short chapter on religious tourism in the urban setting of Varanasi in India. The sixth section concentrates on social and inclusive tourism, with chapters on social tourism in Brazil, developmentourism in Zimbabwe, gay tourism and sustainable rainbow tourist destinations, and the 'albergo diffuso' model in Southern Italy, as well as a short chapter on the Wasteland – Graced Land project in South Africa. The seventh and last section provides some reflections on the latest developments in niche tourism, with chapters on COVID-19-induced niches such as South Korean 'one-month stay' travellers and Unseen Tours' virtual pub quizzes as a symbol of social inclusion and empowerment in times of COVID-19, as well as two short chapters on hot air ballooning in the Czech Republic and the flights to nowhere experience born out of the ban on international travel during the COVID-19 pandemic.

REFERENCES

Azarya, V. (2007) Globalization and international tourism in developing countries: Marginality as a commercial commodity, *Current Sociology*, 52(6), 949–67.

Baker, D.M. (2015) Tourism and the health effects of infectious diseases: Are there potential risks for tourists? *International Journal of Safety and Security in Tourism/Hospitality*, 1(12), 1–7. Available at: https://pdfs.semanticscholar.org/3ef1/4e89e7734886af12e51aeb5a48727f9ba1ae.pdf (Accessed: 24 March 2021).

Bookman M. and Bookman, K. (2007) *Medical Tourism in Developing Countries*. New York: Palgrave Macmillan.

Brandon, A. (2020) Emergence of niche travel post COVID-19. Available at: https://hub.wtm.com/emergence-of-niche-travel-post-covid-19/ (Accessed: 24 March 2021).

Claycamp, H.J. and Massy, W.F. (1968) A theory of market segmentation. *Journal of Marketing Research*, 5, 388–94.

Craven, M., Liu, L., Mysore, M., Singhal, S., Smith, S. and Wilson, M. (2020) *COVID-19: Implications for Business – Briefing Materials*. McKinsey & Company. Available at: https://www.mckinsey.com/~/media/McKinsey/Business%20Functions/Risk/Our%20Insights/COVID%2019%20Implications%20for%20business/COVID%2019%20March%2030/COVID-19-Facts-and-Insights-April-3-v2.ashx (Accessed: 24 March 2021).

Diaz-Soria, I. (2017) Being a tourist as a chosen experience in a proximity destination, *Tourism Geographies*, 19(1), 96–117.

Dinis, A. and Krakover, S. (2015) Niche tourism in small peripheral towns: The case of Jewish heritage in Belmonte, Portugal, *Tourism Planning & Development*, 13(3), 310–32.

Dubois, G. and Ceron, J.-P. (2006) Tourism/leisure greenhouse gas emissions forecasts for 2050: Factors for change in France, *Journal of Sustainable Tourism*, 14(2), 172–91.

Dubois, G., Peeters, P., Ceron, J.-P. and Gössling, S. (2011) The future tourism mobility of the world population: Emission growth versus climate policy, *Transportation Research Part A: Policy and Practice*, 45(10), 1031–42.

Galton, F. (1872) *Art of Travel*. London: John Murrey.

Getz, D. (2000a) *Explore Wine Tourism: Management, Development and Destinations*. New York: Cognizant Communication Corporation.

Getz, D. (2000b) 'Festivals and special events: Life cycle and saturation issues', in W. Garter and D. Lime (eds) *Trends in Outdoor Recreation, Leisure and Tourism*. Wallingford, UK: CAB International.

Hall, C.M. (2003) 'Spa and health tourism', in S. Hudson (ed.) *Sport and Adventure Tourism*. London: Haworth Hospitality Press.

Hall, C.M. (2004) *Wine, Food and Tourism Marketing*. New York: Haworth Hospitality Press.

Hannan, M.T. and Freeman, J. (1977) The population ecology of organisations, *American Journal of Sociology*, 82(5), 929–64.

Higham, J. and Hinch, T. (2018) *Sport Tourism Development*. Bristol: Channel View Publications.

Hutchinson, G.E. (1957) Concluding remarks, *Cold Spring Harbour Symposium on Quantitative Biology*, 22, 415–27.

Ioannides, D. and Gyimothy, S. (2020) The COVID-19 crisis as an opportunity for escaping the unsustainable global tourism path, *Tourism Geographies*, 22(3), 624–32.

Jeuring, J.H.G. and Haartsen, T. (2017) The challenge of proximity: The (un)attractiveness of near-home tourism destinations, *Tourism Geographies*, 19(1), 118–41.

Johnson, R.M. (1971) Market segmentation: A strategic management tool, *Journal of Marketing Research*, 8, 13–18.

Kampel, K. (2020) COVID-19 and tourism: Charting a sustainable, resilient recovery for small states. Available at: https://thecommonwealth.org/sites/default/files/inline/THT%20163%20FINAL.pdf (Accessed: 24 March 2021).

Kotler, P. (1994) *Marketing Management* (8th ed.). Englewood Cliffs, NJ: Prentice Hall.

Lambkin, M. and Day, G.S. (1989) Evolutionary processes in competitive markets: Beyond the product life cycle, *Journal of Marketing*, 53(3), 4–20.

Lew, A.A. (2008) Long tail tourism: New geographies for marketing niche tourism products, *Journal of Travel & Tourism Marketing*, 25(3–4), 409–19.

Macleod, D.V.L. (ed.) (2003) *Niche Tourism in Question: Interdisciplinary Perspectives on Problems and Possibilities*. Glasgow, UK: University of Glasgow, Crichton Publications.

Marson, D. (2011) 'From mass tourism to niche tourism', in P. Robinson, S. Heitmann and P. Dieke (eds) *Research Themes for Tourism*. Wallingford: CABI.

Mauguin, M. (2020a) What hotels can learn from Airbnb's response to the COVID-19 crisis. Available at: https://www.hospitalitynet.org/opinion/4100678.html (Accessed: 24 March 2021).

Mauguin, M. (2020b) The great hospitality reset. Available at: https://www.hospitalitynet.org/opinion/4100351.html (Accessed: 24 March 2021).

McKercher, B. and Chon, K. (2004) The over-reaction to SARS and the collapse of Asian tourism, *Annals of Tourism Research*, 31(3), 716–19.

Newland, K. and Taylor, C. (2010) *Heritage Tourism and Nostalgia Trade: A Diaspora Niche in the Development Landscape*. Washington, DC: Migration Policy Institute.

Novelli, M. (2005) *Niche Tourism: Contemporary Issues, Trends and Cases*. Oxford: Elsevier.

Novelli, M. (2016) *Tourism and Development in Sub-Saharan Africa*. Oxford: Routledge.

Novelli, M. (2018) 'Niche tourism: Past present and future', in C. Cooper et al. (eds) *The Sage Handbook of Tourism Management*. London: Sage, 344–59.

Novelli, M., Burgess, L.G., Jones, A. and Ritchie, B.W. (2018) 'No Ebola… still doomed' – The Ebola-induced tourism crisis, *Annals of Tourism Research*, 70, 76–87.

Ohridska-Olson, R. and Ivanov, S. (2010) 'Creative tourism business model and its application in Bulgaria', in *Proceedings of the Black Sea Tourism Forum 'Cultural Tourism – the Future of Bulgaria'*. Varna, Bulgaria, 24.

Porter, M.E. (1980) *Competitive strategy*. New York: The Free Press & Macmillan.

Read, S.E. (1980) 'A prime force in the expansion of tourism in the next decade: Special interest travel', in D.E. Hawkins, E.L. Shafer and J.M. Rovelstad (eds) *Tourism Marketing and Management Issues*. Washington, DC: George Washington Press, 193–202.

Richards, G. and Raymond, C. (2000) Creative tourism, *ATLAS News*, 23, 16–20.

Richards, G. and Wilson J. (2007) 'The creative turn in regeneration: Creative spaces, spectacles and tourism in cities', in M.K. Smith (ed.) *Tourism, Culture and Regeneration*. Wallingford: CABI.

Ritchie, B. (2004) Chaos, crisis and disasters: A strategic approach to crisis management in the tourism industry, *Tourism Management*, 25, 669–83.

Romagosa, F. (2020) The COVID-19 crisis: Opportunities for sustainable and proximity tourism, *Tourism Geographies*, 22(3), 690–94.

Rosselló, J., Santana-Gallego, M. and Awan, W. (2017) Infectious disease risk and international tourism demand, *Health Policy and Planning*, 32(4), 538–48.

Salazar, N.B. (2005) Tourism and glocalization: 'Local' tour guiding, *Annals of Tourism Research*, 32(3), 628–46.

Smith, W.R. (1956) Product differentiation and market segmentation as alternative marketing strategies, *Journal of Marketing*, 21, 3–8.

Smith, R. (2006) Responding to global infectious disease outbreaks: Lessons from SARS on the role of risk perception, *Communication and Management, Social Science & Medicine*, 63, 3113–23.

Tourwriter (2020) Travel niches predicted to boom in 2021. Available at: https://www.tourwriter.com/travel-software-blog/travel-niches-2021/ (Accessed: 24 March 2021).

Ursache, M. (2015) Niche tourism markets – means of enhancing sustainable economic development the in EU's eastern periphery, CES Working Papers, Alexandru Ioan Cuza University of Iasi, Centre for European Studies, Iasi, 7:2a, pp. 648–61.

Weiler, B. and Firth, T. (2021) 'Special interest travel: Reflections, rejections and reassertions', in C. Pforr, Dowling, R. and Volgger, M. (eds) *Consumer Tribes in Tourism*. Singapore: Springer Nature, 11–26.

Wilhelm Stanis, S.A. and Barbieri, C. (2013) Niche tourism attributes scale: A case of storm chasing, *Current Issues in Tourism*, 16(5), 495–500.

Wilson, M. E. (1995) Travel and the emergence of infectious diseases, *Emerging Infectious Diseases*, 1(2), 39–46.

Yeoman, I. (2008) *Tomorrow's Tourist: Scenarios and Trends*. Butterworth-Heinemann.

PART I

NATURE-BASED TOURISM

1. Astro-tourism in the Czech–Polish Izera Dark Sky Park

Grzegorz Iwanicki

INTRODUCTION TO ASTRO-TOURISM

The northern lights, meteor showers and solar eclipses attract hundreds and thousands of participants to shows organised by various entities. These events, together with the offer targeted at tourists visiting astronomical observatories, well-known planetariums or astronomy-related museums have provided the basis for astro-tourism (also called astrotourism or astronomical tourism). The term astro-tourism is sometimes used interchangeably with other terms, such as celestial tourism, star tourism (Weaver, 2011; Sánchez et al., 2019), astronomy tourism (Wen, 2017) or even astrological tourism (Farajirad and Beiki, 2015). Astro-tourism excludes visits to places such as planetariums and includes only those activities which are related to the observation of the sky in a natural way (Weaver, 2011), or referring to experiences beyond the Earth's orbit (Cater et al., 2015), and together with the multitude of names referring to astro-tourism, may cause some confusion (Wen, 2017).

A new niche of astro-tourism has emerged in recent years in response to the negative aspect of light pollution (LP) which adversely affects fauna and flora ecosystems, as well as human health, causing problems with sleep and disrupting hormonal balances (Gaston et al., 2013). LP is also one of the causes of electricity wastage, indirectly contributing to increased CO_2 production (Hölker et al., 2010). The most evident effect of LP is the brightening of the night sky, which is often hundreds of times brighter over urbanised areas then over areas that are not subjected to LP (Falchi et al., 2016). Such a sky is dominated by a yellow-orange glow, and the Milky Way ceases to be visible. As a result of an approximately 2% annual increase in the brightness of the night sky (Hölker et al., 2010), some countries reinforce legal regulations regarding artificial light emission at night (Peña-García and Sędziwy, 2020), and have established dark sky protection areas, known as dark sky parks and reserves, or, informally, starry-sky parks (Mrozek et al., 2012; Collison and Poe, 2013; Rodrigues et al., 2015).

Such parks have become the primary elements of dark sky tourism, an emerging niche highlighted by publisher Lonely Planet as one of the travel trends for 2019 (Eaves, 2019). Dark sky tourism strongly emphasises environmental protection, propagating a rational lighting policy, and corresponding with many of the Sustainable Development Goals (SDGs) (UNGA, 2015). Moreover, this niche develops in depopulated peripheral areas, far from crowds of tourists, minimising the risk of dissemination of infectious diseases such as COVID-19. The benefit of dark sky tourism in peripheral areas, which are often devoid of other significant development options, may allow for the generation of new enterprises and income for the local communities (Morgan-Taylor, 2018; Mitchell and Gallaway, 2019; Blundell et al., 2020; IAU, 2020).

Astro-tourism, particularly that practised in dark sky parks, should be widely promoted due to the aforementioned environmental and socio-economic effects. More than 150 such parks have been established thus far on six continents, according to the Dark Skies Advisory Group

(DSAG, 2020), but knowledge about their existence, or the problem of artificial LP itself, is negligible (Lyytimäki and Rinne, 2013; Iwanicki et al., 2018). One of the objectives of astro-tourism and the established dark sky parks is therefore expanding knowledge about LP among tourists, potentially leading to increases in future awareness regarding the rational use of artificial light at night (ALAN) and minimisation of the negative effects of LP.

Are activities implemented in dark sky parks accompanied by the involvement of local governments, authorities and municipalities in the promotion of astro-tourism and counteracting LP? Do local and regional tourist organisations effectively promote the benefits and scope of dark sky tourism? These questions have not been thoroughly investigated to date. Similarly, issues concerning the division of astro-tourism products and its place in educational and sustainable tourism have also been sparsely addressed.

This chapter attempts to at least partially answer the above questions. It is composed of two parts: theoretical and empirical. The theoretical aspects begin with an analysis of extant astro-tourism literature, followed by a discussion regarding the links between astro-tourism and SDGs. The empirical focus presents results of a study aimed at assessing the level of involvement of local authorities, municipalities and local tourist organisations in the promotion of dark sky tourism in the Izera Dark Sky Park (IDSP), the world's first cross-border dark sky park, established on the Czech–Polish border. In order to answer the question, a survey using the 'mystery tourist' method was conducted in 2019 among: (1) the staff of 12 tourist information centres in the vicinity of the IDSP; (2) residents of the municipalities where the IDSP is located (n = 286); and (3) tourists encountered on the trails in the IDSP (n = 441). The article ends with the discussion and conclusions.

BACKGROUND OF THE IZERA DARK SKY PARK

The beginnings of astro-tourism in the Izera Mountains date back to 2006, when a group of Polish and Czech astronomers organised a hiking trip on both the Czech and the Polish sides of the mountains. The First Edition of School Workshops on Astronomy (SWA) for Polish high school students was organised the next year. An initial concept of the astro-tourism project Astro Izery was created during that event. At one of the working meetings, Sylwester Kołomański, a professional astronomer from Wroclaw, came up with the idea of creating a dark sky park in the Izera Mountains, and later encouraged his Czech colleagues to join the project. The park was officially announced in 2009, thanks to the involvement of a group of Polish and Czech astronomers in cooperation with the staff from local forest districts, and was the first cross-border dark sky park in the world (Kołomański et al., 2014; Mrozek and Kołomański, 2014).

The IDSP covers an area of 75 square kilometres of almost uninhabited land on the Czech–Polish border. The park is like a lonely island almost free of LP (21.3 mag/arcsec^2 at zenith), surrounded by a light-polluted populated region, famous for its mountain tourism products and recreation activities (http://www.izera-darksky.eu/). The park borders two tourist towns inhabited by several thousand people, Świeradów-Zdrój and Szklarska Poręba, located to the north and east, respectively. Spring, summer and autumn tourism activities in the IDSP are based on cycling and hiking trails, which in winter turn into popular trails for cross-country skiers.

As part of the Astro Izera project, some astro-tourist attractions have been created. The most important of them is the Planetary Path, which is a model of the Solar System on a scale of one to one billion. It consists of 14 stones located along the main trial, symbolising the Sun, the eight planets and the six dwarf planets. The whole route is 11.5 km long, starting from the Sun (in the Tourist Station Orle) and ending on the dwarf planet Eris (in the Stóg Izerski) (Mrozek et al., 2012). Three other attractions are the gnomon, the sundial and the Ecological Education Centre Izerska Meadow Natura 2000 (EEC), established in Świeradów-Zdrój near the border with the IDSP. The building of the EEC, which is open all year round, hosts various workshops, presentations and lectures, including those related to astronomy and LP, with simulations of the night sky displayed on the ceiling similar to those in planetariums. The EEC is also equipped with Dobson telescopes, which are used during night sky shows.

In addition to the attractions listed above, the park has organised various astronomical events, including stargazing parties, with the most important of these being the biannual Astronomical Day (last held in 2017 according to the official website of the IDSP). Information about the activities of the IDSP is widely announced by a range of local and national media outlets (Iwanicki, 2019). However, it seems that the creation of the EEC resulted in the termination of earlier grassroots initiatives related to the promotion of the park, including astronomical events organised directly by a handful of park founders. Only annual SWA and commercial astrophotography workshops for a limited number of people (Izera Long Expositions in the centre of Orle) are still organised in the IDSP. Other cyclical events were discontinued in 2016–2017, along with any activity on the official websites of the IDSP (Iwanicki, 2019).

LITERATURE REVIEW

From Solar Eclipses to Stargazing in the Wilderness

Astro-tourism developed many derivations, including various tourism products, during the latter half of the 20th century and in the early decades of the 21st century (Wen, 2017). The definition of astro-tourism can be referred to all travel related to astronomy or astronomical objects, or using Fayos-Solà's (2014) definition of travelling for astronomy-related purposes. Such travel is often divided into three main forms according to the motive of the trip: celestial tourism, astronomical sightseeing and space tourism. The last of these forms includes travel whose primary purpose is to experience events and activities related to astronautics: observing space rocket launches and manned space flights; commercial zero-gravity flights; and, in the near future, orbital and suborbital commercial flights (Friel, 2019). As such, it should be treated almost as a distinct niche of tourism.

Celestial tourism includes all activities consisting of observing the objects of the sky, both during the day (e.g., solar eclipses) and at night (e.g., aurora borealis, meteor showers or general admiration of the night sky from places with dark sky), as well as related products or tourist attractions such as observations of eclipses from aircraft or cruise ships, dark sky parks or hotels designed to allow enjoyment of the aurora borealis from rooms in the form of a glass igloo. Astronomical sightseeing is closely related to celestial tourism and includes tours to places and objects related in various ways to astronomy. Such places feature trips to big meteorites, such as the 60 tonne Hoba in Namibia, or tours to impact craters, including the famous Barringer Crater in Arizona, as well as visits to places fulfilling educational and scientific functions, such as all kinds of astronomic observatories, planetariums, museums and exhibitions related to the history of astronomy.

Other than the presented division, a significant aspect is the discussion on the place of astro-tourism in the face of contemporary challenges. Tourist products related to space tourism and eclipse trips attract tourists who want to satisfy their curiosity and experience something unique and, at the same time, spectacular (e.g., the experience of weightlessness aboard special aircraft). These things are addressed not only to people interested in astronomy, but to anyone seeking new experiences. For example, the next total solar eclipse in Europe will not occur until 2026 (but will be visible only from Iceland and Spain) (NASA, 2020). The uniqueness of such phenomena, despite the fact that they last only for a few minutes, places such journeys on many people's bucket lists, and they generate substantial income, attracting thousands of tourists from all over the world (Levy, 2017; Wyoming Office of Tourism, 2017). Both eclipse tourism and space tourism, and even trips to see the aurora borealis, are considered a type of special interest tourism (SIT) (Soleimani et al., 2019). Therefore, the educational role of these types of astro-tourism is quite limited.

Space tourism products and activities are based on stationary facilities and can be a source of constant income for individual regions (Friel, 2019), but their environmental impact, due to the large amounts of fuel burned during rocket launches, will be rather negative. According to calculations, massively organised orbital and suborbital flights will significantly contribute to the increase in global warming, which makes it difficult to call space tourism sustainable (Duval and Hall, 2015). In addition, due to the high ticket prices it will be reserved for wealthy tourists only. The business of organising aurora borealis trips also has the potential to generate a steady income where there is potential to do so (mainly Scandinavia, Alaska and Canada). To see the northern lights, as well as meteor showers, it is necessary to go to places away from city lights, which may somehow draw tourists' attention to sustainable lighting policy issues. Tourists who have been on trips to popular stargazing areas in the wilderness, such as the astro-tourism destinations of Uluru in Australia or Wadi Rum in Jordan, may have similar impressions, drawing their attention to the issue of LP (Stimac, 2019).

Almost all types of astro-tourism, from a show in planetarium to standing on the edge of an enormous impact crater, can provide a unique experience. In addition, participation in various astronomical events or a visit to an astronomy-related place has a specific, more-or-less educational value. However, only the activities of dark sky parks are so varied and balanced that they can be placed in the middle between sustainability, uniqueness and educational values. Such parks offer a view of a starry sky, unattainable in most inhabited areas, especially for people living in big cities. They also conduct the permanent and active dark sky protection, therefore they are not only focused towards exploiting the qualities of the dark sky, but also contribute to preserving these qualities for future generations. This is not only the case for tourists, but also for considering the ecosystems that inhabit them.

Workshops, public lectures, star parties and other activities organised in darks sky parks are closely connected with educational activities, as they popularise the knowledge of astronomy and the problems of LP. Such parks function not only for rich SIT tourists who can afford to travel to the famous observatories or watch the stars under the pyramids in Egypt or in the desert in Chile, but their offer is addressed mainly to the local community living in the nearest region or country, including school trips to see the beauty of the starry sky. It is estimated that 99% of the population of the United States, the European Union, Japan and many other developed countries live under skies polluted with ALAN (Falchi et al., 2016), so the market is enormous.

The first world's guide to astro-tourism, *Dark Skies: A Practical Guide to Astrotourism*, which was published in 2019 (Stimac, 2019), together with an earlier attempt to put the issue of astro-tourism into practice, *Finding a Million-Star Hotel* (Mizon, 2016), and the growing interest among stakeholders wishing to take advantage of the trend for tourists seeking places far from civilisation (Tapada et al., 2020), proves that the dark sky tourism market is gaining more recognition. Paradoxically, the popularity of admiring the night sky may have been increased by the lockdowns imposed as a result of the COVID-19 pandemic. For people locked in their homes, even in large cities such as London, stargazing became the new meditation and a way to seek solace in the skies. Watching the stars and the very bright comet NEOWISE, which arrived in that period, became a way to fight the feeling of claustrophobia, and represented a form of escapism for many. People had an opportunity, due to lockdown and less light in public spaces, to stop and take a break from normal life and just appreciate astronomy and the view of the night sky (Hampson, 2020).

Astro-Tourism vs SDGs

Occasional astronomical events such as solar eclipses can generate enormous incomes at a local scale (Levy, 2017; Wyoming Office of Tourism, 2017). Dark sky parks designed for year-round tourism offer contributions to the economic development of peripheral areas (Collison and Poe, 2013; Rodrigues et al., 2015). Their revenue-generating activity is in line with the postulates of sustainable and responsible tourism. Out of the 17 primary SDGs stipulated in the 2030 Agenda, as many as nine are met by astro-tourism, particularly by dark sky tourism. Promotion and implementation of the rules of sustainable and responsible lighting policies by dark sky parks enhances awareness of the negative effects of LP among visiting tourists, and contributes to building and promoting sustainable tourism, thereby corresponding with the following aims (UNGA, 2015):

1. ensure healthy lives and promote well-being for all at all ages by substantially reducing the number of illnesses from atmosphere polluted with ALAN (goal 3, target 3.9);
2. ensure quality education and promote lifelong learning opportunities by acquiring the knowledge and skills needed to promote sustainable development through education for sustainable development, including dark sky tourism, and sustainable lifestyles, including responsible lighting consumption (goal 4, target 4.7);
3. ensure access to sustainable energy by increasing energy efficiency (goal 7, target 7.3) through modernisation of the external lighting network and private lighting under IDA guidelines, not only in areas of dark sky protection but also in the neighbouring municipalities;
4. promote sustainable economic growth by implementing policies to promote sustainable tourism, including dark sky tourism, that promote local culture and products (e.g. astronomical sightseeing places and local dark sky values) (goal 8, target 8.9);
5. make cities and human settlements sustainable by enhancing sustainable urbanisation and human settlement planning, considering the possible preservation of the values of the dark sky (goal 11, target 11.3); by strengthening efforts to protect and safeguard cultural and natural heritage related with astronomy and the night skies (target 11.4); and by supporting positive economic, social and environmental links between urban, peri-urban and rural

areas by strengthening national and regional development planning regarding dark sky friendly lighting and dark sky tourism promotion (target 11.a);

6. ensure sustainable consumption by achieving the sustainable and efficient use of dark skies and artificial light at night, which can reduce the waste of electricity by adopting dark sky friendly practices, and promoting them especially in developing countries (goal 12, almost all targets);

7. take urgent action to combat climate change and its impacts by promoting practical solutions for limiting the waste of electricity (goal 13, targets 13.2 and 13.3);

8. conserve and sustainably use marine resources by promoting the protection of night time landscape and astro-tourism, which can support effective protection of sea turtles and other marine animals particularly endangered by the spread of LP (goal 14, target 14.2); and

9. protect, restore and promote sustainable use of terrestrial ecosystems and halt biodiversity loss by establishing dark sky parks and reserves in areas containing ecosystems that are particularly vulnerable to LP (goal 15, targets 15.1 and 15.5).

All the aforementioned goals can be implemented based on recommendations stipulated in SDG no. 17, particularly through:

1. promoting the development, popularisation and propagation of dark sky-friendly lighting technologies in developing countries (target 17.7);

2. enhancing policy coherence for sustainable tourism development, e.g., by establishing dark sky parks and reserves in regions with naturally dark skies (target 17.14); and

3. encouraging the establishment and promotion of efficient public and public–private partnerships, and the application of best practices that led to the creation and operation of the most successful dark sky parks and sustainable astro-tourism products (target 17.17).

RESULTS OF THE PROMOTION OF IZERA DARK SKY PARK

Material and Methodology

In order to answer the question concerning the level of involvement of the local authorities, municipalities and local/regional tourist organisations in the promotion of dark sky tourism, a three-stage study was conducted in 2019 involving:

1. a survey among the staff of 12 tourist information centres (TICs) located in the vicinity of the IDSP (six in Poland – TICs in Gryfów Śląski, Leśna, Mirsk, Stara Kamienica, Świeradów-Zdrój and Szklarska Poręba; and six in Czech Republic – TICs in Frydlant, Harrachov, Korenov, Lazne Libverda, Smrzovka and Tanvald);

2. a survey among 286 residents of the municipalities where the IDSP is located (Mirsk, Szklarska Poręba and Świeradów-Zdrój in Poland; and Frydlant and Tanvald in Czech Republic);

3. a survey among 441 tourists encountered on the trails in the IDSP, conducted in the summer (August) and winter (December) seasons in order to capture possible seasonal differences.

Source: Own elaboration.

Figure 1.1   *Location of the IDSP and visited TICs*

The main method of research was semi-structured interviews based on the mystery tourist interview scenario, a method often used in tourism research (Richards and Munsters, 2012). The first question to each of the respondents was 'How can I get to the Izera Dark Sky Park?' If the respondent had never heard of the IDSP, then additional information was given: 'I have heard that this park was established in 2009 somewhere in the Izera Mountains, but I don't have it on my map, and I don't know how to get there – some astronomical events are organised there'. If the respondent knew about the existence of the IDSP, questions were then asked about the exact location of the park and its astronomy-related attractions and events (with a request to point the IDSP out on the tourist map of the Izera Mountains).

The method and preliminary results of the summer season survey with tourists and residents on the Polish side of the IDSP only were presented by the author at the 1st International Conference on Environmental and Astronomical Light Pollution EALPO, held on 20–21 September 2019 in Cracow.

Survey Results

Tourist information centres
In eight of the 12 TICs visited the staff had some knowledge about the IDSP, and in four centres the staff had never heard of such a tourist attraction. Those four TICs were located in Leśna, Stara Kamienica, Lazne Libverda and Tanvaldof, and in the last one, after receiving a hint about the organised astronomical events, employees stated that 'some night sky shows are held in Jizerka, so maybe the IDSP is located there'. The staff in those TICs were kind and eventually managed to help by providing basic information on the questions asked after finding the

official website of the park. In the eight other TICs, the scope of information provided varied. The most detailed information was given in Szklarska Poreba, Harrachov, Gryfów Śląski, Mirsk and Frydlant. The staff of these TICs had information that was fairly precise about the territorial range of the IDSP, its characteristics and the tourist attractions located there. In other TICs, the employees provided basic information about the park, focusing on the Polish part (TIC in Świeradów-Zdrój) or the Czech part (TICs in Korenov and Smrzovka).

The biggest problem for tourists wishing to get information about the park was the almost complete lack of dedicated promotional materials. Only the TIC in Korenov had such promotional material, which was a type of leaflet providing basic information on the IDSP (also available in digital form: ČAS, 2017). A eight-page folder concerning the surrounding tourist attractions was provided in Szklarska Poręba, but with only one sentence concerning the IDSP and the Planetary Path. A tourist's Vademecum of almost 45 pages which contained some basic information about the IDSP and the EEC was provided in Świeradów-Zdrój. A tourist map of the Izera Mountains with the Planetary Path and the area of the IDSP marked was also provided. The mystery tourists/researchers who visited the EEC in Świeradów-Zdrój received an 11-page booklet on LP and the IDSP.

Tourists
The majority of the respondents encountered on the trails in the IDSP (86.8%) did not even know that they were walking inside one of the dark sky parks. Only 58 of 441 tourists (13.2%) knew about the existence of the IDSP, and 14 of them (3.2%) knew that the park stretches on both sides of the border covering several dozen square kilometres. The same 3.2% could also describe all the astro-tourist attractions: the Planetary Path, sundial, gnomon, occasional night sky shows and the value of the dark skies. The remainder of the tourists who knew about the existence of the IDSP indicated its area incorrectly. Many pointed out a small area around Orle or Hala Izerska. Similar answers were given to places such as Stóg Izerski, Jizerka, Chatka Górzystów or the area around the EEC. A small number answered that the park only covers the Czech side, or only the Polish side of the Izera Mountains.

The gender and age of the respondents had little influence on the answers given, but the survey showed that among the tourists surveyed in the summer (n = 234), more than twice as many people knew about the park (17.5%) than among the tourists surveyed in winter (8.2%, n = 207). There were also some differences in terms of nationality. Polish tourists (n = 267) were a little more likely to know about the park (14.6%) than Czech tourists (11.7%, n = 162), and not a single visitor from other countries (n = 12) had heard of the IDSP.

Residents
Only 11.5% of respondents living in the communities near the park knew about the IDSP, but there were significant differences regarding the location of the surveys. The highest percentage of knowledgeable residents was recorded in Świeradów Zdrój (21.4%, n = 70), with far fewer in Szklarska Poręba (13.6%, n = 66), the municipality of Tanvald (8.6%, n = 58) and the municipality of Frydlant (8.0%, n = 50). None of the 60 respondents asked in Mirsk had heard of the IDSP. Only 6 people (2.1%) from the total number of residents interviewed across the surrounding region could correctly describe the area and attractions of the IDSP. The rest identified the park with particular places such as Jizerka (the most frequent answer among the inhabitants of Czech municipalities), Orle, Hala Izerska, Stóg Izerski, Jakuszyce or the EEC.

Despite this, nearly half of all respondents (48.6%) knew that night sky shows and observations were sometimes organised in various locations in the Izera Mountains.

DISCUSSION AND CONCLUSION

Astro-tourism is quite a new phenomenon, hence there are some problems with the proper naming of its types (Wen, 2017), as shown in the theoretical part of the article. The terms astro-tourism, astrotourism, astronomical tourism or astronomy tourism mean basically the same and should be used in relation to all travels that are motivated by observations of celestial objects and the night sky, or visiting places related to astronomy (e.g., observatories, museums, planetariums, impact craters, meteorites). Space tourism, although it is closely related to astronomy, should be terminologically excluded from astro-tourism because of the main motives of travel, namely, orbital and suborbital flights. Such an approach may help to organise the existing definitions in travel related to astronomy and astronautics, but it should be treated as a proposal.

One of the growing varieties of astro-tourism is dark sky tourism, which develops in dark sky parks and other places where one can observe a starry sky away from urban lights and civilisation (Mrozek et al., 2012; Collison and Poe, 2013; Rodrigues et al., 2015, Blundell et al., 2020). Such parks are at the crossroads of tourism, recreation, education and environmental protection, and they realise almost 20 targets related to as many as 9 of the 17 SDGs. They are therefore unique among the tourism products connected with micro-niches, which have gained popularity in recent times. Tourists simply need to know that dark sky parks exist and function (McMahon, 2006), because only then does the subject of LP and sustainable tourism in such places have a chance of being promoted effectively. Local authorities, municipalities and regional tourist organisations should develop a well-thought-out strategy for promoting their local 'starry-sky parks', and commercial initiatives, such as the publication of the world's first guide to astro-tourism (Stimac, 2019), should only be an additional option.

Results of this study show that the IDSP is an example of unexploited potential as a result of poor promotion by local municipalities. Situated in an attractive area on the Polish and Czech border, and very close to Germany, it is a unique tourist product offering all the value of its dark skies. Despite being the oldest such park in Europe and the oldest cross-border park in the world, members of staff in a third of the TICs visited for this study were unaware of its existence. Moreover, the almost complete lack of promotional materials in most TICs hinders promotion of the IDSP. In conclusion, it is difficult for the IDSP to promote the value of sustainable lighting policy and sustainable tourism when nearly 87% tourists visiting it have no idea about existence of the park, and the local community is mostly unaware that a tourist attraction, unique on both a national scale and that of the entire continent, is right there in front of them.

Greater emphasis on promoting astro-tourism products in the IDSP could translate into a wider development of this tourism niche in the Jizera Mountains on both sides of the Czech–Polish border, especially as examples from other places indicate that the development of astro-tourism in dark sky parks can go hand-in-hand with the success of combining a strong promotion of educational values, and at the same time being part of activities in the field of sustainable tourism (e.g., Collison and Poe, 2013; Rodrigues et al., 2015, Blundell et al., 2020). The development of astro-tourism, not only in the IDSP but also throughout Poland, could additionally contribute to increasing public awareness of and knowledge about LP. This is an important issue, because the research conducted so far shows that only 5% of people have ever heard about the phenomenon of LP (Iwanicki, 2014; TNS 2015).

Greater awareness of the adverse effects of LP, resulting from the educational offer of the IDSP, could in turn translate into more thoughtful lighting investments in public spaces, which in Poland often do not meet criteria related to the protection of the night landscape. This results in a further increase in the brightness of the night sky, not only in cities but also in rural areas (Falchi et al., 2016). Another factor contributing to this is the lack of national legislation regulating the issue of lighting at night, as LP is still not considered a serious problem.

ACKNOWLEDGEMENT

This work was financially supported by the Polish Ministry of Science and Higher Education.

REFERENCES

ČAS (2017) *Jizerska Oblast Tmave Oblohy*. Available at: https://www.astro.cz/userfiles/files/Rady/svetelne-znecisteni/letak_2017_web.pdf (21 August 2020).

Cater, C., Garrod, B. and Low, T. (2015) *The encyclopaedia of sustainable tourism*. Wallingford: CAB International.

Collison, F. M. and Poe K. (2013) Astronomical tourism: The Astronomy and Dark Sky Program at Bryce Canyon National Park. *Tourism Management Perspectives*, 7, 1–4.

DSAG (2020) *World list of dark sky places*. Available at: http://darkskyparks.org/dsag/2020-08-30_DSAG_word_list.htm (10 August 2020).

Duval, T. and Hall, C. M. (2015) 'Sustainable space tourism: New destinations, new challenges'. In C.M. Hall, and S. Gössling (eds) *Routledge handbook of tourism and sustainability*. New York: Routledge, 450–60.

Eaves, M. (2019) *Travel trends for 2019: Dark skies*. Available at: https://www.lonelyplanet.com/articles/travel-trends-for-2019-dark-skies (15 August 2020).

Falchi, F., Cinzano, P., Duriscoe, D., Kyba, C.C.M., Elvidge, C.D., Baugh, K., Portnov, B.A., Rybnikova, N.A. and Furgoni, R. (2016) The new world atlas of artificial night sky brightness. *Science Advances*, 2(6), 1–25.

Farajirad A. and Beiki, P. (2015) Codification of appropriate strategies to astronomical tourism development (Seghaleh, South of Khorasan). *Applied Mathematics in Engineering, Management and Technology*, 3(1), 303–12.

Fayos-Solá, E., Marin, C. and Jafari, J. (2014) Astrotourism: No requiem for meaningful travel. *PASOS. Revista de Turismo y Patrimonio Cultural*, 12(4), 663–71.

Friel, M. (2019) Tourism as a driver in the space economy: New products for intrepid travellers. *Current Issues in Tourism*, 23(13), 1581–6.

Gaston, K.J., Bennie, J., Davies, T.W. and Hopkins J. (2013) The ecological impacts of nighttime light pollution: A mechanistic appraisal. *Biological Reviews*, 88(4), 912–27.

Hampson, L. (2020) Reach for the stars: Why stargazing is London's newest obsession. *Evening Standard*, 18 August 2020. Available at: https://www.standard.co.uk/lifestyle/travel/how-to-stargaze-in-london-best-stargazing-spotsa4527411.html (24 August 2020).

Hölker, F., Moss, T., Griefahn, B., Kloas, W., Voigt, C., Henckel, D., Hänel, A., Kappeler, P.M., Völker, S., Schwope, A., Franke, S., Uhrlandt, D., Fischer, J., Klenke, R., Wolter, C. and Tockner, K. (2010) The dark side of light: A transdisciplinary research agenda for light pollution policy. *Ecology and Society*, 15(4), 1–11.

IAU (2020) *Sustainable local socio-economic development through astronomy.* Available at: http://www.astro4dev.org/sustainable-local-socio-economic-development-through-astronomy-guidelines/ (11 August 2020).

Iwanicki, G. (2014) Lighting policy in the aspect of night time landscape preservation on the example of selected communities of Lublin County. *The Problems of Landscape Ecology*, 37, 15–21.

Iwanicki, G. (2019) The impact of dark sky parks on regional socio-economic development: Are dark sky parks recognizable in the society? Example of Izera Dark Sky Park. *1st International Conference on Environmental and Astronomical Light Pollution EALPO* 2019. Cracow University of Technology, 20–21 September 2019.

Iwanicki, G., Dłużewska, A., Wertag, A. and Kozłowska-Adamczak, M. (2018) Light pollution in the context of accommodation in Zagreb. In *Proceedings of international conference on hospitality, tourism, and sport management.* Tokyo: Waseda Univeristy, 316–29.

Kołomański, S., Mrozek, T. and Żakowicz, G. (2014) Projekt Astro Izery, *Delta.* Available at: http://www.deltami.edu.pl/temat/roznosci/2013/12/30/Projekt_Astro_Izery/ (15 August 2020).

Levy, G. (2017) States brace for solar eclipse tourist. *US.News*, 4 August 2017. Available at: https://www.usnews.com/news/best-states/articles/2017-08-04/great-american-eclipse-is-a-dream-come-true-for-some-businesses (14 August 2020).

Lyytimäki, J. and Rinne, J. (2013) Voices for the darkness: Online survey on public perceptions on light pollution as an environmental problem. *Journal of Integrative Environmental Sciences*, 10(2), 127–39.

McMahon, P. (2006) Wilderness stargazing. *Journal of the Royal Astronomical Society of Canada*, 100(2), 75.

Mitchell, D. and Gallaway, T. (2019) Dark sky tourism: Economic impacts on the Colorado Plateau Economy, USA. *Tourism Review*, 74(4), 930–42.

Mizon, B. (2016) *Finding a million-star hotel. An Astro-tourist guide to dark sky places.* 1st edition. Cham: Springer.

Morgan-Taylor M. (2018) The Island of Saint Helena as an example of metrics based legislation to address artificial light at night problems and to promote dark-sky tourism. *5th International Conference on Artificial Light at Night ALAN 2018.* Snowbird, Utah, Consortium for Dark Sky Studies, 11–14 November 2018.

Mrozek, T. and Kołomański, S. (2014) Izera Dark Sky Park and other initiatives. *Prace i Studia Geograficzne*, 53, 171–85.

Mrozek, T., Kołomański, S., Żakowicz, G., Kornafel, S., Czarnecki, T.L., Suchan, P. and Kamiński, Z. (2012) 'Astro tourism: Astro Izery project'. In Montmerle T. (ed.) *Highlights of astronomy, vol. 16, XXVIIIth IAU General Assembly.* Cambridge: Cambridge University Press, 737.

NASA (2020) *Solar eclipses: Past and future.* Available at: https://eclipse.gsfc.nasa.gov/solar.html (20 August 2020).

Peña-García, A. and Sędziwy, A. (2020) optimizing lighting of rural roads and protected areas with white light: A compromise among light pollution, energy savings, and visibility, *LEUKOS*, 16(2), 147–56.

Richards, G. and Munsters, W. (eds) (2012) *Cultural tourism research methods.* Wallingford: CABI Publishing.

Rodrigues, A.L.O., Rodrigues, A. and Peroff, D.M. (2015) The sky and sustainable tourism development: A case study of a dark sky reserve implementation in Alqueva. *International Journal of Tourism Research*, 17, 292–302.

Sánchez-C., E., Sánchez-Medina, A.J., Alonso-Hernández, J.B. and Voltes-Dorta, A. (2019) Astrotourism and night sky brightness forecast: First probabilistic model approach. *Sensors*, 19, 1–16. doi: 10.3390/s19132840

Soleimani, S., Bruwer, J., Gross and M.J., Lee, R. (2019) Astro-tourism conceptualisation as special-interest tourism (SIT) field: A phenomonological approach. *Current Issues in Tourism*, 22(18), 2299–314.

Stimac, V. (2019) *Dark skies: A practical guide to astrotourism.* Lonely Planet Global Ltd.

Tapada, A., Marques, C., Marques, C.P. and Costa, C. (2020) Astrotourism: Stakeholders' views about a special interest tourism proposal in Tua Valley. *Revista Turismo & Desenvolvimento*, 33, 41–59.

TNS (2015) *The problem of noise, odor and light pollution in the eyes of Poles. TNS Poland report for the Polish Ministry of Environment, November 2015.* Available at: https://blogs.sweco.pl/wp-content/uploads/2018/11/Raport-TNS.pdf (17 May 2021).

UNGA (2015) *Transforming our world: The 2030 Agenda for Sustainable Development.* A/RES/70/1. Available at: https://www.refworld.org/docid/57b6e3e44.html (12 August 2020).

Weaver, D. (2011) Celestial ecotourism: New horizons in nature-based tourism. *Journal of Ecotourism,* 10(1), 38–45. doi: 10.1080/14724040903576116

Wen, J. (2017) Astronomy tourism: Exploring an emerging and market: Group culture, individual experience, and industry future. PhD thesis, James Cook University, Townsville.

Wyoming Office of Tourism (2017) 2017 Eclipse economic impact study. Summary of findings. Dean Runyan Associates and Destination Analysts, Inc.

2. Glacier tourism and climate change in Switzerland

Emmanuel Salim

1. INTRODUCTION

Nature has long been an important element of recreation and tourism. The first studies regarding outdoor recreation in the early 1950s focused on different leisure activities and did not study 'tourism' as defined by the World Tourism Organisation (UNWTO) (Manning, 2011). Since then, some scholars have shifted their focus to study nature-based tourism, or tourism activities primarily related to undisturbed nature (Valentine, 1992). This so-called mega-niche has developed globally and includes activities in the midst of nature, such as hiking or mountaineering (Pomfret, 2011), as their main purpose or attraction (Elmahdy, Haukeland and Fredman, 2017).

Because outdoor recreation is dependent on the natural environment, it is also affected by climate change. A study conducted in the Canadian Rockies suggested that warmer temperatures could have negative impacts on tourism in the region (Scott, Jones and Konopek, 2007). Another study in the Nepalese Himalayas, showed that nature-based tourism faces the threat of increased risk of flooding, rock falls, and avalanches due to climate change (Nyaupane and Chhetri, 2009). The same applies to Arctic communities that are dependent on tourism (Sisneros-Kidd et al., 2019). Among the different forms of nature-based tourism, glacier tourism is perhaps one of the most vulnerable to climate change (Welling, Árnason and Ólafsdottír, 2015). A recent study suggested that up to 90% of the total ice volume of glaciers located in World Heritage areas may disappear by the year 2100 (Bosson, Huss and Osipova, 2019). Climate change has already been impacting outdoor recreation and tourism activities such as hiking (Watson and King, 2018). Glacial retreat and deglaciation that create new lakes (Cathala et al., 2021) and increasing rock falls due to permafrost warming (Purdie, Gomez and Espiner, 2015) have also been noted. However, the threat to glaciers and glacier tourism posed by climate change has given birth to another form of nature-based tourism known as 'last chance tourism' (LCT), defined as 'a niche tourism market where tourists explicitly seek vanishing landscapes or seascapes, and/or disappearing natural and/or social heritage' (Lemelin et al., 2010; p. 478).

This chapter describes and asserts the emergence of LCT as a new niche of nature-based tourism through a case study of the Rhone Glacier in Switzerland. It also broaches ethical questions on the emergence of LCT, given that last chance tourists, especially those who travel internationally to visit LCT sites, increase the risk to, and accelerate the pace of, the destruction of these sites from climate change.

2.   LITERATURE REVIEW

2.1   Touching Ice for Tourism's Sake – the Origins of Present-Day Glacier Tourism

Glacier tourism was first developed in the 1740s in France, with guided visits to the Mer de Glace ('Sea of Ice') (Grove, 1966). Today, glacier tourism includes close-up and experience-driven guided walking tours in Norway and New Zealand (Furunes and Mykletun, 2012; Purdie, 2013), bus tours in Canada (Groulx et al., 2016), and other, more distant and scenery-driven tourist activities at glaciers in France, Italy, and China (Garavaglia et al., 2012; Salim and Ravanel, 2020; Wang, He and Song, 2010). Moreover, more than 73 glacier tourist places have been inventoried in the Alps (Salim, Gauchon and Ravanel, 2021). Despite the relatively small number of mountain glaciers in the world (Zemp et al., 2014), glacier tourism sites attract a significant number of visitors. For example, Baishui glacier no. 1 in China attracts more than three million visitors a year (Wang, He and Song, 2010), Glacier Country in New Zealand attracts 800,000 visitors a year (Purdie, 2013), and Montenvers-Mer-de-Glace, France, attracts almost 400,000 visitors a year (Salim and Ravanel, 2020). Glacier tourism can be considered as a tourism niche, produced by a discourse constructed by tourism operators which places the glacier as the main attraction. Thus, this kind of tourism has been generated by the supply-side (Robinson and Novelli, 2005).

However, glaciers and glacier tourism are already under extensive threat due to climate change. For example, glaciers in New Zealand are increasingly difficult to access due to increased rock falls (Purdie, 2013; Purdie, Gomez and Espiner, 2015; Purdie et al., 2020). Bolivia has already seen the complete disappearance of the Chacaltaya glaciers (Kaenzig, Rebetez and Serquet, 2016), and several other glacier tourism destinations have experienced landscape degradation (Diolaiuti and Smiraglia, 2010; Garavaglia et al., 2012). These are only a few examples of a broad and accelerating worldwide phenomenon (Welling, Árnason and Ólafsdottír, 2015; Salim et al., 2021). In response to these threats, glacier tourism operators have implemented several adaptation strategies, including altering access to glaciers, making spatial and temporal substitutions, attenuating glacier shrinkage, and engaging in educating tourists (Salim, Ravanel, Deline, et al., 2021). However, the sense that these magnificent monuments of nature will soon be gone has sparked the establishment of a new form of tourism: LCT.

2.2   Touching the Ice Before It is Gone – the Emergence of LCT

The concept of LCT emerged in 2010 from the work of several different scholars (Eijgelaar, Thaper and Peeters, 2010; Hall and Saarinen, 2010; Lemelin et al., 2010). These scholars first identified LCT in the context of polar bear-viewing and Antarctic cruises. Today, the concept encompasses a variety of environmental contexts, including the Great Barrier Reef (Piggott-McKellar and McNamara, 2017), endangered birdwatching (Hvenegaard, 2013), and safaris to see large and endangered fauna (Newsome and Rodger, 2012). LCT is a tourism niche that is sometimes used as a marketing argument by tourism operators (Dawson et al., 2011). However, LCT can sometimes be observed as a tourism niche that can emerge from the demand-side (Salim and Ravanel, 2020).

Some scholars have suggested that LCT entails tourism operators taking advantage of ecocide and ecological devastation (Dawson and Lemelin, 2015). This argument has raised questions about its ethics. Dawson et al. (2011) suggest that LCT is something of a paradox, because tourists produce high amounts of greenhouse gas emissions to observe a natural feature which is threatened by climate change. Other scholars have shown that, paradoxically, the more tourists are aware of the human causes of climate change, the more they are motivated to come to LCT destinations (Dawson et al., 2010; Groulx et al., 2016; Salim and Ravanel, 2020). Salim and Ravanel (2020) suggest that this paradox is related to cognitive dissonance. However, although LCT could be a threat to these destinations, it also increases visitors' environmental knowledge and brings about more sustainable consumer behaviour (Lemelin and Whipp, 2019; Salim and Ravanel, 2020). This study hopes to contribute to the literature and to practical understanding and strategies to support tourism-based educational initiatives within the context of LCT.

3.   RESEARCH SETTING AND METHODOLOGY

The Rhone Glacier in the eastern part of Wallis, Switzerland, and is one of the only glacier tourism sites situated less than a 10-minute flat walk from a carpark in the Alps (Figure 2.1).

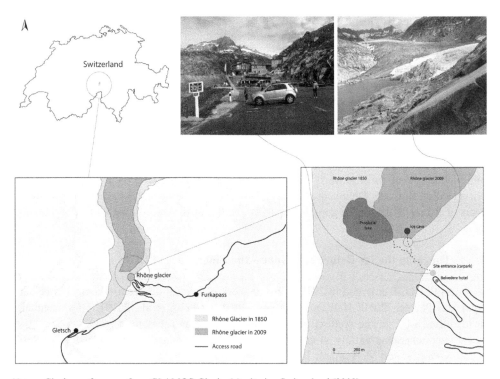

Note: Glacier surfaces are from GLAMOS-Glacier Monitoring Switzerland (2019).

Figure 2.1   Location of the Rhone Glacier

The site includes the Hotel Belvédère (established in 1882), a restaurant, a gift shop, and a path to the ice cave in the front of the glacier. The road to the glacier was built in 1866 and leads to the Furkapass, which affords a famous view of the Goms Mountains. The trail through the ice cave has been maintained every year since 1870 and is 100 m long.

However, the Rhone Glacier is experiencing rapid retreat. Between 1874 and 2007, its ice tongue lost about 1.3 km of length (Jouvet et al., 2009). This led to the development of a proglacial lake which is expected to triple in size as the glacier retreats (Church et al., 2018). Research models show that the glacier could completely disappear by 2100 (Zekollari, Huss and Farinotti, 2019).

This study hypothesises that the Rhone Glacier is experiencing LCT visitation. To test this hypothesis, a quantitative survey of tourists' motivations for visiting the glacier was conducted. The analysis was based on the push and pull theory – namely, the idea that tourists are both 'pushed' to visit certain destinations by internal factors related to their everyday life and 'pulled' in specific ways by the specific attributes of certain destinations (Dann, 1977). Different psychometric scales have been developed to understand tourists' preferences in the context of nature-based tourism (e.g., Manning, 2011). For this study, the recreation experience preference (REP) scale developed by Manfredo et al. (1996) was used. Fifteen items were selected from the original scale related to tourists' experiences of the environment and tourism as an educational experience. To test the link between motivation and LCT, four additional items derived from similar studies (Lemieux et al., 2018; Stewart et al., 2016) were added and four more items related to the specific attractions of the site were included. To test the relationship between tourists' LCT motivations and their perceptions of climate change, some additional items derived from the nature relatedness (NR) scale developed by Nisbet, Zelenski and Murphy (2009) were also included. A five-point Likert-scale was used with questions on socio-demographics and general questions regarding the tourists' trip.

Surveys were conducted over four days in August 2019. The participants answered questions on-site after they had visited the glacier. The purpose of the study was briefly explained to each participant, and their consent was collected with the assurance of data anonymity. The data was collected using tablet computers (c.f. Galaxy Tab Active) and SphinxOnline software. A pre-test was conducted for one day (n = 25) to test the reliability of the survey.

4.   RESULTS

4.1   Respondents' Characteristics and Motivations

In total 227 participants, with an average age of 37, took part in the survey. They originated from Switzerland (31%), France (22%), Germany (9%), and Italy (8%). Most of them planned to spend less than three nights in the area (66.5%) without any tour operator (94%). Of all the participants, 79% were first-time visitors, and 64% had seen another glacier elsewhere.

Figure 2.2 shows that respondents' motivations were mainly related to environmental concerns, and that LCT motivations were secondary. The mean scores for each category (Environment, 4.19; LCT, 4.14; Learning, 3.97; Attraction, 3.52; Relation to others, 2.94; 1 = Not important at all; 5 = Very important) showed the same results, suggesting that LCT motivations existed among visitors to this site. To further test the results an exploratory factor analysis (EFA) with all motivational items was conducted. After removing the cross-load items, the final 16-item EFA was found to be reliable with a Kaiser-Meyer-Olkin (KMO) of 0.776 (Williams, Onsman and Brown, 2010). The EFA revealed five major motivational factors: LCT, resourcing, environment, learning, and storytelling (Table 2.1). The mean score of each factor was similar to the motivational category's mean score, thus further confirming the prominence of LCT motivations.

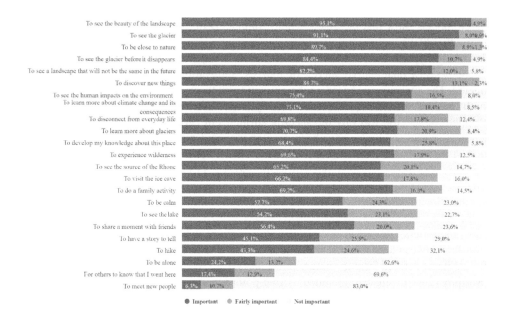

Figure 2.2   Scores for each motivation item included in the survey

4.2   Respondents' Environmental Awareness and Its Correlation with Their Tourism Motivations

Most respondents agreed that climate change is real (89%), human-induced (80%), and that it will lead to the disappearance of the Rhone Glacier (80%). Most of them also indicated that they thought regularly about how their actions impact the environment (73%) and how their everyday actions can have negative impacts even on the other side of the planet (76%). A large segment of respondents indicated that they were aware of and concerned about environmental issues.

The Pearson correlations between constructs in this study showed that the more respondents believed that the Rhone Glacier will disappear because of climate change, the higher their LCT motivations (r = 0.409; n = 218; p < .01). Also, the more respondents were aware of the environmental impact of their actions, the higher their LCT motivations (r = 0.225; n = 217; p < .01 and r = 0.403; n = 214; p < .01, respectively). However, 73% of respondents stated that they would have come to this site even if there was no glacier to visit, indicating that the scenic landscape, and not just the glacier itself, was the main draw for many of them. In addition,

Table 2.1   *EFA on motivations from visitors to Rhone Glacier*

	LCT	Resourcing	Environment	Learning	Story Telling
To see the human impact on the environment	0.769				
To learn more about climate change and its consequences	0.717				
To see the glacier before it disappears	0.699				
To see a landscape that will not be the same in the future	0.668				
To be calm		0.695			
To disconnect from everyday life		0.641			
To experience the wilderness		0.556			
To go on a hike		0.497			
To be alone		0.407			
To see the beauty of the landscape			-0.838		
To see the glacier			-0.661		
To be close to nature			-0.453		
To develop my knowledge about this place				0.805	
To learn more about glaciers				0.695	
For others to know that I went there					0.844
To have a story to tell					0.578
Means score	4.12	3.33	4.55	3.86	2.72

Extraction method: Main axis factoring

Rotation method: Oblimin with Kaiser normalization

a. Rotation convergence in 9 iterations

83% of respondents said they would have visited even if there was no ice cave to see, and 98% reported that they felt that the beauty of the landscape met their expectations.

5.   DISCUSSION

The results indicated that both nature-based tourism and LCT motivations were important to tourists visiting the Rhone Glacier. These results are corroborated by other studies which show that LCT is becoming an increasingly important and significant motivation for glacier tourists around the world (Lemieux et al., 2018; Salim and Ravanel, 2020; Stewart et al., 2016). As mentioned by Johnston, Viken and Dawson (2013) concerning Arctic tourism, LCT could be related to 'first chance tourism', because the disappearance of the glacier has led to the development of a new tourism niche.

Scholars have acknowledged that visitors' LCT motivation can be both conscious or unconscious (Tucker and Shelton, 2014), and that tourism operators have already begun to develop LCT marketing strategies (Newsome and Rodger, 2012). This raises the question of whether LCT in the Rhone Glacier is an actual, or a marketing phenomenon. To answer this question, popular tourism-based social media sites such as TripAdvisor were analysed. The site's users have described the Rhone Glacier as a 'must do' attraction which travellers should see while they still can. Users on other social media and traditional media outlets alike use the example of the Rhone Glacier to talk about climate change and the disappearance of glaciers. However, there is no mention of the shrinking glacier or climate change in the location's branding; information concerning glacier retreat is only available after purchasing the ticket and entering the site. As a result, because LCT motivation is high, we suggest that LCT has emerged here primarily because of media coverage and exchanges on social media.

However, increased LCT and its motivation raise ethical questions (cf. Dawson et al., 2011; Stewart et al., 2016). Newsome and Rodger (2012) state that tourism stakeholders face a dilemma between continuing to earn money and maintaining environmental quality. Hindley and Font (2017) suggest that this dilemma is shared by tourists. These insights are especially applicable to this case study, in which tourists travelled a mean of 1,000 km to see the Rhone Glacier, knowing that human activities are responsible for its retreat. Considering the short length of stay of the respondents, visiting the glacier can be an opportunity trip, but climate issues are definitely part of their motivation to engage. Here, the relationship between tourists' learning and LCT motivations ($r = 0.538$; $n = 220$; $p < .01$) suggests that LCT can be an opportunity to increase tourists' environmental knowledge, which can be an occasion for stakeholders to increase environmental education elements in the location. Recent studies from France suggest that glacier visitation can raise tourists' climate change awareness and concerns, and could aid their acceptance of carbon-reduction policies (Salim and Ravanel, 2020). Other studies (Welling, Árnason and Ólafsdóttir, 2020) have suggested that glacier tourism can provide tourists with environmental education. This study suggests that LCT motivations can, in the context of glacier tourism, contribute to the attainment of UN Sustainable Development Goals 8 and 12 by providing environmental education and increasing environmental awareness. To be effective, the knowledge transmitted must include information on the functioning of ecosystems, resources, and the economic system in addition to aspects related to climate change (Gössling, 2018).

It is proposed that the Rhone Glacier and other LCT destinations have the responsibility to inform their visitors about the climate crisis and the human contribution to it, including tourism activities. Furthermore, the effectiveness of continuing to maintain the ice cave and efforts to reduce melt by covering the glacier with blankets are debatable with regards to sustainability (Salim, Ravanel, Deline, et al., 2021). It is proposed that tourism operators and decision-makers engage in tourism planning to transform the destination while making it more sustainable, to avoid unemployment and the end of a tradition, for example by enhancing the heritage value of glaciers. The future disappearance of glaciers (Bosson, Huss and Osipova, 2019) can be halted with ex-situ experiences such as the 'Experience 2° C' exhibition, which allowed visitors to see the evolution of the Aletsch Glacier (Switzerland) through virtual reality headsets (Salim, Gauchon and Ravanel, 2021), or the physical replica of Chauvet Cave (France), which allows visitors to experience a cave that is no longer accessible to the public (Duval et al., 2020).

Although some scholars have suggested that niche tourism is often driven by tourism operators, not tourists (Robinson and Novelli, 2005), this case study indicates that tourists' LCT motivations appear without any marketing from the site, showing that this tourism niche can emerge from the demand-side. Although this does not apply to all LCT destinations (e.g., Lemelin et al., 2010), this research suggests that tourists have a significant amount of agency in the emergence of the LCT niche. As LCT is a tourism niche based on endangered natural features, it could have an influence on visitor environmental awareness. This hypothesis is debated in the literature, as it shows that visiting LCT destinations can improve visitor pro-environmental behaviour (Miller et al., 2020) yet, contrastingly, visitors to LCT destinations are not inclined to pay for carbon offsetting, despite their high level of environmental awareness (Groulx et al., 2019). Future research could explore how LCT as a niche tourism phenomenon could be a potential vector of sustainability through the examination of stakeholder planning and the relationships between LCT places, awareness, and pro-environmental behaviour.

6.   CONCLUSION

Climate change is causing the rapid retreat and disappearance of glaciers around the world. This study, conducted via a survey of tourists at the Rhone Glacier in Switzerland, showed that tourists are increasingly driven to visit the site to see it before it disappears, in an example of so-called last chance tourism, or LCT. This result is corroborated by other similar studies (Lemieux et al., 2018; Lemelin and Whipp, 2019) and confirms that LCT is emerging as a new tourism niche.

This study also suggests that although some LCT destinations are marketed as such, the character of the Rhone Glacier as a LCT opportunity arises from local media and tourists' exchanges on social media. The development of this tourism niche raises various questions about its paradoxical nature; however, this research suggests that LCT can increase tourists' environmental awareness and that tourism stakeholders could use the opportunity to increase visitors' pro-environmental behaviour by promoting educational tools. However, there are concerns about the willingness of tourism operators to pursue their activity despite the energy consumption and the real value of it. Assuming that the build-and-promote strategy for the ice cave may be hard to stop due to the social and cultural consequences, future studies should take an interdisciplinary and transdisciplinary approach in order to construct research questions with stakeholders which might lead to the development of more sustainable adaptation strategies. Finally, the apparent increase of interest in nature-based tourism observed in the summer of 2020 following the COVID-19 outbreak (Lebrun, Su and Bouchet, 2021) suggests that tourism niches such as LCT and glacier tourism can be important tools for increasing the environmental awareness of visitors, as well as for promoting domestic tourism. As a recent phenomenon, it requires further research to be supported.

FUNDING

This study was funded by the EU ALCOTRA *AdaPT Mont Blanc* project and ANR Labex ITTEM (ANR-10-LABX-50-01).

REFERENCES

Bosson, J. -B., Huss, M. and Osipova, E. (2019) Disappearing World Heritage glaciers as a keystone of nature conservation in a changing climate. *Earth's Future*, 7, 469–79. doi: 10.1029/2018EF001139.

Cathala, M., Magnin, F., Linsbauer, A. and Haeberli, W. (2021) Modelling and characterizing glacier-bed overdeepenings as sites for potential future lakes in the deglaciating French Alps. *Géomorphologie: relief, processus, environnement*, 27(1), 19–36.

Church, G. J., Bauder, A., Grab, M., Hellmann, S. and Maurer. H. (2018) High-resolution helicopter-borne ground penetrating radar survey to determine glacier base topography and the outlook of a proglacial lake. In *17th International Conference on Ground Penetrating Radar (GPR)*, 1–4. doi: 10.1109/ICGPR.2018.8441598.

Dann, G.M.S. (1977) Anomie, ego-enhancement and tourism. *Annals of Tourism Research*, 4(4), 184–94. doi: 10.1016/0160-7383(77)90037-8.

Dawson, J. and Lemelin, R. H. (2015) Last chance tourism: A race to be last? In M. Hughes, D. Weaver, C. Pforr (eds) *The Practice of Sustainable Tourism*. Abingdon: Routledge, pp. 155–67.

Dawson, J., Stewart, E. J., Lemelin, H. and Scott, D. (2010) The carbon cost of polar bear viewing tourism in Churchill, Canada. *Journal of Sustainable Tourism*, 18(3), 319–36. doi: 10.1080/09669580903215147.

Dawson, J., Johnston, M.J., Stewart, E. J., Lemieux, C.J., Lemelin, R. H. and Maher, P.T. (2011) Ethical considerations of last chance tourism. *Journal of Ecotourism*, 10(3), 250–65. doi: 10.1080/14724049.2011.617449.

Diolaiuti, G. and Smiraglia, C. (2010) Changing glaciers in a changing climate: How vanishing geomorphosites have been driving deep changes in mountain landscapes and environments. *Géomorphologie: relief, processus, environnement*, 16(2), 131–52. doi: 10.4000/geomorphologie.7882.

Duval, M., Smith, B., Gauchon, C., Mayer, L. and Malgat, C. (2020) 'I have visited the Chauvet Cave': The heritage experience of a rock art replica. *International Journal of Heritage Studies*, 26, 142–62. https://doi.org/10.1080/13527258.2019.1620832

Eijgelaar, E., Thaper, C. and Peeters, P. (2010) Antarctic cruise tourism: The paradoxes of ambassadorship, 'last chance tourism' and greenhouse gas emissions. *Journal of Sustainable Tourism*, 18(3), 337–54. doi: 10.1080/09669581003653534.

Elmahdy, Y. M., Haukeland, J.V. and Fredman, P. (2017) *Tourism megatrends: A literature review focused on nature-based tourism, 74*. Report. Norwegian University of Life Sciences, Ås. Available at: https://nmbu.brage.unit.no/nmbu-xmlui/handle/11250/2648159 (Accessed: 12 June 2020).

Furunes, T. and Mykletun, R.J. (2012) Frozen adventure at risk? A seven-year follow-up study of Norwegian glacier tourism. *Scandinavian Journal of Hospitality and Tourism*, 12(4), 324–48. doi: 10.1080/15022250.2012.748507.

Garavaglia, V., Diolaiuti, G., Smiraglia, C., Pasquale, V. and Pelfini, M. (2012) Evaluating tourist perceptions of environmental changes as a contribution to managing natural resources in glacierized areas: A case study of the Forni Glacier (Stelvio National Park, Italian Alps). *Environmental Management*, 50(6), 1125–38. doi: 10.1007/s00267-012-9948-9.

GLAMOS-Glacier Monitoring Switzerland (2019) Swiss glacier length change (release 2019). GLAMOS - Glacier Monitoring Switzerland; Laboratory of Hydraulics, Hydrology and Glaciology (VAW) ETH Zürich, Switzerland; Department of Geosciences, University of Fribourg, Switzerland; Department of Geography, University of Zürich, Switzerland. doi: 10.18750/LENGTHCHANGE.2019.R2019.

Gössling, S. (2018). Tourism, tourist learning and sustainability: An exploratory discussion of complexities, problems and opportunities. *Journal of Sustainable Tourism*, 26(2), 292–306. https://doi.org/10.1080/09669582.2017.1349772.

Groulx, M., Boluk, K., Lemieux, C.J. and Dawson, J., (2019) Place stewardship among last chance tourists. *Annals of Tourism Research*, 75, 202–12. https://doi.org/10.1016/j.annals.2019.01.008.

Groulx, M., Lemieux C.J., Lewis, J. and Brown, S. (2016) Understanding consumer behaviour and adaptation planning responses to climate-driven environmental change in Canada's parks and protected areas: A climate futurescapes approach. *Journal of Environmental Planning and Management*, 60(6), 1016–35. doi: 10.1080/09640568.2016.1192024.

Grove, J. M. (1966) The little Ice Age in the massif of Mont Blanc. *Transactions of the Institute of British Geographers*, 40, 129–43. doi: 10.2307/621573.

Hall, C. M. and Saarinen, J. (2010) Last chance to see? Future issues for polar tourism and changes. In C. M. Hall and J. Saarinen (eds.) *Tourism and change in polar regions: Climate, environments and experiences*. Abingdon: Routledge, pp. 415–25.

Hindley, A. and Font, X. (2017) Ethics and influences in tourist perceptions of climate change. *Current Issues in Tourism*, 20(16), 1684–700. doi: 10.1080/13683500.2014.946477.

Hvenegaard, G. T. (2013) Last chance birding: Twitching to see it first or last. In H. Lemelin, J. Dawson, E. J. Stewart, P. Maher and M. Lueck (eds) *Last chance tourism: Adapting tourism opportunities in a changing world*. Abingdon: Routledge, pp. 89–106.

Johnston, M., Viken, A. and Dawson, J. (2013) Firsts and lasts in Arctic tourism: Last chance tourism and the dialectic of change. In H. Lemelin, J. Dawson, E. J. Stewart, P. Maher and M. Lueck (eds) *Last chance tourism: Adapting tourism opportunities in a changing world*. Abingdon: Routledge, pp. 10–24.

Jouvet, G., Huss, M., Blatter, H., Picasso, M. and Rappaz, J. (2009) Numerical simulation of Rhonegletscher from 1874 to 2100. *Journal of Computational Physics*, 228(17), 6426–39. doi: 10.1016/j.jcp.2009.05.033.

Kaenzig, R., Rebetez, M. and Serquet, G. (2016) Climate change adaptation of the tourism sector in the Bolivian Andes. *Tourism Geographies*, 18(2), 111–28. doi: 10.1080/14616688.2016.1144642.

Lebrun, A. -M., Su, C. -J. and Bouchet, P. (2021) Domestic tourists'experience in protected natural parks: A new trend in pandemic crisis? *Journal of Outdoor Recreation and Tourism*, 35, 100398. https://doi.org/10.1016/j.jort.2021.100398.

Lemelin, H. and Whipp, P. (2019) Last chance tourism: A decade in review. In D. Timothy (ed.) *Handbook of globalisation and tourism*. Cheltenham: Edward Elgar Publishing, pp. 316–22. doi: 10.4337/9781786431295.00039.

Lemelin, H., Dawson, J., Stewart, E. J., Maher, P. and Lueck, M. (2010) Last-chance tourism: The boom, doom, and gloom of visiting vanishing destinations. *Current Issues in Tourism*, 13(5), 477–93. doi: 10.1080/13683500903406367.

Lemieux, C. J., Groulx, M., Halpenny, E., Stager, H., Dawson, J., Stewart, E. J. and Hvenegaard, G.T. (2018) 'The end of the Ice Age?': Disappearing World Heritage and the climate change communication imperative. *Environmental Communication*, 12(5), 653–71. doi: 10.1080/17524032.2017.1400454.

Manfredo, M. J., Driver, B.L. and Tarrant, M.A. (1996) Measuring leisure motivation: A meta-analysis of the recreation experience preference scales. *Journal of Leisure Research*, 28(3), 188–213. doi: 10.1080/00222216.1996.11949770.

Manning, R. E. (2011) *Studies in outdoor recreation: Search and research for satisfaction*. Oregon State University Press. Available at: https://muse.jhu.edu/chapter/238438 (Accessed: 11 June 2020).

Miller, L. B., Hallo, J. C., Dvorak, R. G., Fefer, J. P., Peterson, B. A. and Brownlee, M. T. J. (2020) On the edge of the world: Examining pro-environmental outcomes of last chance tourism in Kaktovik, Alaska. *Journal of Sustainable Tourism*, 28(11), 1703–22. https://doi.org/10.1080/09669582.2020.1720696.

Newsome, D. and Rodger, K. (2012) Vanishing fauna of touristic interest. In H. Lemelin, J. Dawson and E.J. Stewart (eds.) *Last chance tourism: Adapting tourism opportunities in a changing world*. London: Routledge, pp. 55–70. Available at: https://researchrepository.murdoch.edu.au/id/eprint/9263/ (Accessed: 25 June 2020).

Nisbet, E. K., Zelenski, J.M. and Murphy, S. A. (2009) The nature relatedness scale: Linking individuals' connection with nature to environmental concern and behavior. *Environment and Behavior*, 41(5), 715–40. doi: 10.1177/0013916508318748.

Nyaupane, G. P. and Chhetri, N. (2009) Vulnerability to climate change of nature-based tourism in the Nepalese Himalayas. *Tourism Geographies*, 11(1), 95–119. doi: 10.1080/14616680802643359.

Piggott-McKellar, A. E. and McNamara, K. E. (2017) Last chance tourism and the Great Barrier Reef. *Journal of Sustainable Tourism*, 25(3), 397–415. doi: 10.1080/09669582.2016.1213849.

Pomfret, G. (2011) Package mountaineer tourists holidaying in the French Alps: An evaluation of key influences encouraging their participation. *Tourism Management*, 32(3), 501–10. doi: 10.1016/j.tourman.2010.04.001.

Purdie, H. (2013) Glacier retreat and tourism: Insights from New Zealand. *Mountain Research and Development*, 33(4), 463–72. doi: 10.1659/MRD-JOURNAL-D-12-00073.1.

Purdie, H., Gomez, C. and Espiner, S. (2015) Glacier recession and the changing rockfall hazard: Implications for glacier tourism. *New Zealand Geographer*, 71(3), 189–202. doi: 10.1111/nzg.12091.

Purdie, H. Hutton, J. H., Stewart, E. J. and Espiner, S. (2020) Implications of a changing alpine environment for geotourism: A case study of Aoraki/Mount Cook, New Zealand. *Journal of Outdoor Recreation and Tourism*, 29, 100235. doi: 10.1016/j.jort.2019.100235.

Robinson, M. and Novelli, M. (2005) Niche tourism: An introduction. In M. Novelli (ed.) *Niche Tourism*. Oxford: Butterworth-Heinemann, pp. 1–11. doi: 10.1016/B978-0-7506-6133-1.50007-X.

Salim, E. and Ravanel, L. (2020) Last chance to see the ice: Visitor motivation at Montenvers-Mer-de-Glace, French Alps. *Tourism Geographies*, 1–23. https://doi.org/10.1080/14616688.2020.1833971.

Salim, E., Gauchon, C. and Ravanel, L. (2021) Seeing the ice. An overview of alpine glacier tourism sites, between post- and hyper-modernity. *Journal of Alpine Research | Revue de géographie alpine*. https://journals.openedition.org/rga/8383.

Salim, E., Ravanel, L., Bourdeau, P. and Deline, P. (2021) Glacier tourism and climate change: Effects, adaptations, and perspectives in the Alps. *Regional Environmental Change*, 21(4), 120. https://doi.org/10.1007/s10113-021-01849-0.

Salim, E., Ravanel, L., Deline, P. and Gauchon, C. (2021) A review of melting ice adaptation strategies in the glacier tourism context. *Scandinavian Journal of Hospitality and Tourism*, 21(2), 229–46. https://doi.org/10.1080/15022250.2021.1879670.

Scott, D., Jones, B. and Konopek, J. (2007) Implications of climate and environmental change for nature-based tourism in the Canadian Rocky Mountains: A case study of Waterton Lakes National Park. *Tourism Management*, 28(2), 570–79. doi: 10.1016/j.tourman.2006.04.020.

Sisneros-Kidd, A. M., Monz, C., Hausner, V., Schmidt, J. and Clark, D. (2019) Nature-based tourism, resource dependence, and resilience of Arctic communities: Framing complex issues in a changing environment. *Journal of Sustainable Tourism*, 27(8), 1259–76. doi: 10.1080/09669582.2019.1612905.

Stewart, E. J., Wilson, J., Espiner, S., Purdie, H., Lemieux, C. and Dawson, J. (2016) Implications of climate change for glacier tourism. *Tourism Geographies*, 18(4), 377–98. doi: 10.1080/14616688.2016.1198416.

Tucker, H. and Shelton, E. (2014) Traveling through the end times: The tourist as apocalyptic subject. *Tourism Analysis*, 19(5), 645–54. doi: 10.3727/108354214X14116690098133.

Valentine, P. (1992) Review: Nature-based tourism. In B. Weiler and C. M. Hall (eds.) *Special interest tourism*. London: Belhaven Press, pp. 105–27. Available at: https://researchonline.jcu.edu.au/1632/ (Accessed: 29 May 2020).

Wang, S., He, Y. and Song, X. (2010) Impacts of climate warming on alpine glacier tourism and adaptive measures: A case study of Baishui Glacier No. 1 in Yulong Snow Mountain, Southwestern China. *Journal of Earth Science*, 21(2), 166–78. doi: 10.1007/s12583-010-0015-2.

Watson, C. S. and King, O. (2018) Everest's thinning glaciers: Implications for tourism and mountaineering. *Geology Today*, 34(1), 18–25. doi: 10.1111/gto.12215.

Welling, J.T., Árnason, Þ. and Ólafsdottír R. (2015) Glacier tourism: A scoping review. *Tourism Geographies*, 17(5), 635–62. doi: 10.1080/14616688.2015.1084529.

Welling, J.T., Árnason, Þ. and Ólafsdóttir, R. (2020) Implications of climate change on nature-based tourism demand: A segmentation analysis of glacier site visitors in southeast Iceland. *Sustainability*, 12(13), 5338. doi: 10.3390/su12135338.

Williams, B., Onsman, A. and Brown, T. (2010) Exploratory factor analysis: A five-step guide for novices. *Australasian Journal of Paramedicine*, (Online), 8(3). doi: 10.33151/ajp.8.3.93.

Zekollari, H., Huss, M. and Farinotti, D. (2019) Modelling the future evolution of glaciers in the European Alps under the EURO-CORDEX RCM ensemble. *The Cryosphere*, 13(4), 1125–46. doi: https://doi.org/10.5194/tc-13-1125-2019.

Zemp, M., Armstrong, R., Gärtner-Roer, I., Haeberli, W., Hoelzle, M., Kääb, A., Kargel, J. S. Khalsa, S. J. S., Leonard, G. J., Paul, F. and Raup, B. H. (2014) Introduction: Global glacier monitoring—a long-term task integrating in situ observations and remote sensing. In J. S. Kargel, J.Gregory, M. P. Leonard, A. Bishop, B. Kääb and H. Raup (eds) *Global land ice measurements from space*. New York: Springer Praxis Books, pp. 1–21. doi: 10.1007/978-3-540-79818-7_1.

3. Architourism in nature areas: a 'Bilbao effect' in the bush?

Ben Wielenga, Stefan Hartman and Jasper Hessel Heslinga

1. INTRODUCTION

Nature areas are increasingly being opened up for leisure and tourism purposes. This deviates from the traditional approach, especially in the Netherlands, which is aimed at closing off such areas to the public as much as possible in order to protect and conserve valuable and/or fragile landscapes and ecosystems (Heslinga et al., 2017). This is reflected in the representation, maintenance (Gaston et al., 2006), enhancement (Muñoz Brenes et al., 2018) and/or protection of biodiversity, landscapes, habitats, species and populations (Gaston et al., 2006). Rethinking the management and development of nature areas is a direct result of the growing interest within society for nature and landscapes, increasing possibilities and needs for leisure, recreation and the pursuit of healthy lifestyles (Hartman and De Roo, 2013). Many management organisations of nature areas have loosened the traditional approach, sometimes also triggered by (major) reductions in public governmental funding and changes to subsidy requirements (Heslinga et al., 2017). This causes a shift in focus, with additional tasks and responsibilities alongside protection and conservation, such as capturing the attention of a variety of visitors, raising their awareness of nature and landscapes, (re)connecting them with nature and, as a result, stimulating them to support nature and encourage funding for preservation and/or reinforcement (Heslinga et al., 2018; Wielenga, 2020). A major challenge is to find a balance between adjusting sites for the development of leisure and tourism purposes on the one hand and ensuring the protection and conservation of valuable and/or fragile landscapes and ecosystems on the other hand. Establishing niche tourism in protected areas is seen as a valuable aspect of attaining these objectives (Blackmore, 2020).

This chapter contributes to the concept of niche tourism in protected areas through the design and development of iconic architectural objects in nature areas as a means to encourage architourism. Architectural objects can be a helpful tool for visitor management to attract, as well as steer and guide, visitor flows to particular locations and help prevent uncontrolled situations and their possible negative destructive force. Therefore, architourism in nature areas is introduced as a self-contained micro-niche tourism phenomenon that is increasingly emerging from a confluence of the macro-niches of nature-based and cultural tourism. Niche tourism, as opposed to mass tourism, entails more sustainable practices that are less damaging than those of mass tourism and offers tourists the opportunity to discover (unknown) places, be part of them and obtain meaningful and educational experiences. In niche tourism, a distinction can be made between macro- and micro-niches. Whereas macro-niches have larger consumer interest, micro-niches are covered under the specific macro-niche umbrella, yet are further segmented and developed into, and contain, more defined interests (Novelli, 2005).

The term architourism is not entirely new (cf. Chang, 2010; Ockman and Frausto, 2005). However, the concept's specific application to nature areas is relatively unexplored.

Architourism describes tourism to specific places in which architecture plays a pivotal role (micro-niche). Visitor motivation (mainly) lies in experiencing, marvelling at and learning about the interior and exterior, yet architourism might also be utilised as an icon or catalyst to experience something else (Wielenga, 2020). In the context of this chapter, this 'something else' is nature and landscapes.

One of the most prominent examples is the 'Bilbao effect', related to the opening of the Guggenheim Museum in 1997. Designed by the world famous 'starchitect', Frank Gehry, the building has had major effects on locals and visitors to Bilbao, in both positive and negative ways. Architecture can give a location a so-called 'sense of place', being aesthetically meaningful and valuable, and therefore capable of attracting visitors to a place (Edwards et al., 2008; Maitland and Newman, 2008; Rahman et al., 2018). As a result, architecture is often used as part of a competitive strategy among cities, whether drawing on historical or modern constructions (Siniecki and Evcil, 2020). Plaza (2010) outlines the (potential) utilization of architecture as an image-making device or a tool to promote city destinations (Najafabadi et al., 2019) among a wider public, which could function as a sign of recognition (Vukadinović, 2011) and contribute to stimulating tourism development (Piatkowska, 2012) in urban environments.

Architecture and architourism's roles are primarily applicable to urban environments and, as a result, are also studied in this context in academic contributions. This chapter explores whether architourism also applies in a non-urban setting, namely that of nature areas. In this chapter, we will specifically assess which meanings and values architourism can offer when it comes to the responsible consumption of nature and landscapes in nature-based tourism. The findings are primarily based on an empirical case study that was carried out on the Tij Bird Observatory (Wielenga, 2020), which is situated in the Haringvliet delta area, a nature area in the Netherlands.

The structure of this chapter is as follows. First, a review of literature on architourism, nature-based tourism and cultural tourism is provided, in order to connect the concepts and identify avenues for how architourism can contribute to nature-based tourism. Second, the research setting and methodology are outlined. Third, the findings from the Tij Bird Observatory case study are presented. Finally, the conclusion reveals the contribution of architourism in nature areas to contemporary and future tourism and provides opportunities for future research.

2.   LITERATURE REVIEW

Architourism in Urban Environments

Occasionally, publications about the role of architecture in tourism contexts appear in the literature that use terms such as architecture tourism, tourism architecture, architectural tourism and architourism (e.g., Vukadinović, 2011; Bokhari and Binthabet, 2019; Specht, 2014; Siniecki and Evcil, 2020). Architourism's first noteworthy appearance, however, was during the conference 'Architourism: Architecture as a Destination for Tourism', where this new concept was discussed (Chang, 2010; Specht, 2014). In 2005, Ockman and Frausto (2005) officially coined the term in their book *Architourism: Authentic, Escapist, Exotic, Spectacular*, in response to the opening of the Guggenheim Museum in Bilbao in 1997, which showed that visitors visited the city because of the, for that time, unique building style of the museum and due to the fact that the Guggenheim was utilised as an attraction in all of the city's official marketing strategies and campaigns (Plaza and Haarich, 2015). The titanium-constructed art building was part of a regional and local development plan tackling urban and economic regeneration in response to years of economic decline during the 1980s in the Basque Country.

With the Guggenheim Museum as the city's main eye-catching feature and its symbol to the outside world (Gómez and González, 2001), Bilbao slowly shifted from a politically unstable (Gómez and González, 2001), industrial (Franklin, 2016), iron-producing (Alayo et al., 2016) city symbolised by large polluting steel furnaces, into a tourist hotspot that is now famous for art, design, food, wine, technology (Schieferdecker, 2017) and culture (Vicario and Martínez Monje, 2003). In the first year after the opening of the Guggenheim Museum, Bilbao attracted 1.36 million visitors, enriching the local economy by USD160 million (Vukadinović, 2011). Nowadays, Bilbao still attracts approximately a million visitors a year (Plaza and Haarich, 2015). The transformation of the city and the resultant positive socioeconomic side-effects – such as more jobs (Plaza, 2010), enhancement of the general perception of the city by citizens and tourists, local pride and improved quality-of-life in the inner city – is described by many as the Bilbao or Guggenheim effect (e.g., Plaza and Haarich, 2015).

Nevertheless, the negative effects should not be ignored. Vicario and Martínez Monje (2003) point to increases in sale and rental prices for land, housing and commercial initiatives, as well as regeneration schemes focused on the most centrally located parts of the city, leaving the periphery mainly as it was. Moreover, Gómez and González (2001) state that the role of the Guggenheim Museum as a vehicle for the development of Bilbao's cultural sector was disregarded, giving the museum a sole consumption-oriented nature without creating local links. Last, most of Bilbao's budget for cultural activities was spent on the Guggenheim Museum, leading to unequal distribution of money across its overall cultural sector.

Is Architourism Part of Cultural Tourism?

Some scholars argue that architourism should be seen as an aspect of cultural tourism. UNWTO (2017) defines cultural tourism as 'a type of tourism activity in which the visitor's essential motivation is to learn, discover, experience and consume the tangible and intangible cultural attractions in a tourism destination'. Robinson and Novelli (2005) describe cultural tourism as a macro-niche market to which a broad set of components can be attributed. One of them is architecture, which may function as one component in visitors' overall cultural tourism experience, or can be the most important component. In the latter case, the micro-niche of architourism may come in. With the conceptualisation of architourism – in which architecture is seen as an essential element in the marking and marketing of a destination – a new niche market in the tourism industry was born (Sion, 2015). Chang (2010, p. 963) defines architourism as travel undertaken by 'tourists that are attracted to places because of iconic buildings'. Bokhari and Binthabet (2019) add that architecture is not just a small part of visitors' motivation in architourism, but rather their prime motivation to visit a specific place. Visitors' interests may vary from just seeing a particular construction to obtaining a deeper understanding of it (Vukadinović, 2011).

Architourism specifically focuses on the exterior and interior of the building that is observed, rather than on what it accommodates, such as exhibitions, artefacts and/or paintings. Architourists' motivations lie in the desire to experience all of a building's characteristics/elements, to marvel at it and to learn about what they experience. Moreover, architectural objects may be used as a means to experience something else outside the object (e.g., the surrounding nature and landscape) (Wielenga, 2020). Resources in architourism – that is, the buildings which attract it – tend to be those of exceptional and aesthetical value, albeit spanning different time periods and representing various building styles (Grčić, 2009). Visits are made to historic sites as well as to contemporary constructions (Specht, 2014) in urban environments; these may include religious buildings (e.g., churches and mosques), infrastructure (e.g., airports and train/bus stations), housing (e.g., bungalows, mansions) education (schools and universities), shopping centres, bridges (Siniecki and Evcil, 2020) and other premises that have (some) architectural value. Nevertheless, architecture in nature areas is a concept that is in its infancy and, as a result, not comprehensively described yet in academic contexts.

Developing the Macro-Niche of Nature-Based Tourism

As this chapter discusses architourism in natural environments, it is worth knowing that a multitude of concepts are generally used in order to frame tourism in natural areas. Nature-based tourism is often used synonymously with ecotourism (e.g., Boo, 1990; Hvenegaard, 1994; Dolnicar, 2006; An et al., 2019) and/or sustainable tourism, although these terms have been more frequently distinguished between in the past few years. Nevertheless, these concepts are all seen as niche tourism markets (Saidmamatov et al., 2020) and more specifically as macro-niches.

Nature-based tourism is defined as 'the segment in the tourism market in which people travel with the primary purpose of visiting a nature destination' (Kuenzi and McNeely, 2008, 158), and as a macro-niche market, nature-based tourism is rapidly increasing (Kim et al., 2019; An et al., 2019). Nature-based tourism primarily takes place in destinations in protected areas (Spenceley et al., 2015), where various forms of tourism may take place, ranging from low-impact to mass tourism (Nyaupane, 2007). Balmford et al. (2015) note that protected areas generally receive eight billion visits per year globally, with visitation to protected areas in Europe totalling approximately two billion visits annually (Schägner et al., 2016). Nature-based tourism is generally regarded as an effective tool in the conservation and management of protected areas, raising awareness of important qualities and potentially bringing funds for conservation or alternative livelihoods for local people (Heslinga et al., 2020a; An et al., 2019; Ballantyne et al., 2009) through the offering of meaningful activities that add value to visitors' experiences with nature. As a result, nature organisations increasingly aim to attract visitors to nature areas in order to establish public support, goodwill and revenue for nature protection (Heslinga et al., 2018; Steckenreuter and Wolf, 2013).

Nature-based tourism benefits people with 'spiritual enrichment, cognitive development reflection, recreation, and aesthetic experiences' (Millennium Ecosystem Assessment, 2005, p. 40) by offering 'the opportunity to experience the various benefits of ecosystems by facilitating the human-ecosystem relationship' (Kim et al., 2019, p. 249). Stamation et al. (2007), Wolf et al. (2014), Wolf and Wohlfart (2014) and Wolf et al. (2017) add that enriching transformative experiences in, and long-lasting memories of visitors with regard to, nature areas are a contributing factor in (future) support for nature conservation, return visits and positive word-of-mouth reports to others. Nevertheless, Steven et al. (2011) see the potential negative effects of nature-based tourism and increased visitation on natural resources, reflected, among other things, in the degradation of resources and disturbance of animals in nature areas (Wolf et al., 2019). Potentially, this may weaken the quality of visitors' experiences and their sense of satisfaction. As a result, new ways of balancing tourism and nature conservation are sought in nature-based tourism, in order to offer quality experiences to visitors on the one hand, while helping to conserve nature on the other. Architourism as a micro-niche may facilitate the macro-niche of nature-based tourism by helping it become more sustainable and meaningful through offering purposeful and responsible attractions in nature-based activities and facilities.

The Use of Architecture in Nature-Based Tourism

Few empirical studies have been carried out on the aesthetics of architecture in nature-based tourism. Herein, harmony, design and attractivness play a central role (Hosany and Witham, 2009; Oh et al., 2007). In Norway, the National Tourist Route (NTR) was established in 2015, designating 18 highway routes with a reputation for passing through extraordinary natural areas. The routes are accompanied by attractions based in architecture, art and design, in order to encourage travellers to enjoy nature and the surrounding landscape physically instead of through the glass windows of a car (Breiby, 2014) and to stimulate knock-on effects in rural societies (e.g., tourist spending in local facilities). Herneoja et al. (2014) give examples of architectural cabins, bridges, viewing platforms and cubes in nature that conform with the surroundings and offer visitors spatial, nature and landscape experiences through architecture. However, along with Breiby (2014), they point out the lack of academic studies on evoking nature-based experiences through architecture and/or man-made environments in nature – a concept that is increasingly applied in Nordic countries, but is still niche from a global point of view.

3. RESEARCH SETTING AND METHODOLOGY

The focal point of the study is Tij Bird Observatory, situated at the edges of the Haringvliet delta area in the southwestern part of the Netherlands, close to the Scheelhoek nature reserve and Haringvliet's coastal defence works.

The name Tij, which is pronounced as it is spelled in Dutch, refers to the partly restored tides, as well as to the egg of the sandwich tern (*het ei* in Dutch), a seabird that is common in the area. It was established under the aegis of Droomfondsproject (a Dutch National Lottery scheme to fund 'dream projects'), and involved national, regional and local stakeholders joining forces in order to complete a nature recovery programme aimed at partly restoring the dynamics of the Haringvliet delta. These were severely altered after the construction of the coastal defence works in 1971. Part of this programme is the development of recreational facilities such as waterways, bicycle and walking paths, viewing towers and other facilities aimed at encouraging society to experience this (new) nature (Haringvliet.nu, 2018). Tij Bird Observatory (Figure 3.1) is one of these facilities, commissioned by Vogelbescherming Nederland (Society for the Protection of Birds) and designed and constructed by a multidisciplinary team of experts.

The building is designed to represent a sandwich tern egg and is set in a way that reflects how that bird lays its eggs: on the bare sand, in a nest of reeds. Natural shapes, curves, forms, patterns and colours were applied in its design principles and mostly sustainable and circular

Source: Photo by L. van Galen.

Figure 3.1   *Visitor perspective; tunnel towards Tij including nestling holes*

materials were utilised, aiming at merging nature and architectural object in ways that complement and strengthen each other (Wielenga, 2020).

Access to Tij is made possible by walking a narrow footpath surrounded by dense and
fragile nature that crosses varying biotopes (Figure 3.2). On the way, several touchpoints are
created where visitors are able to observe wildlife from a respectful and non-disturbing distance and view the surrounding nature and landscape. The last part of the journey goes through
a naturally demarcated area and a tunnel construction in which listening holes and opportunities for nesting have been created. Both are meant to stimulate the experiences of visitors while
preventing disturbance to flora and fauna. Tij's wooden structure is visible from the interior
(Figure 3.3) and viewing slots are placed between the connected wooden parts which enable
visitors to view the nearby Scheelhoek nature reserve, the Haringvliet coastal defence works,
and (artificial) islands and shallows that are used as foraging and breeding grounds by dozens
of bird species.

Tij was chosen for the study as an architectural object that stands out from what is normally
done, and considered acceptable, in fragile natural areas. As a result, Tij could be a starting
point for a revolution, representing a new way of thinking when it comes to dealing with nature
areas in nature-based tourism. This makes it an interesting, if not necessary, object for study
purposes. The lessons learned are extrapolated from, and conceptualised and organised on the
basis of, findings that were obtained in a comprehensive case study through semi-structured
interviews with, among others, architects, project leaders, specialist birdwatchers and forest

Source: Photo by L. van Galen.

Figure 3.2 Visitor perspective; approaching Tij

rangers (Wielenga, 2020), and a small case study on three architectural facilities in nature which was published in 2021 (Wielenga, 2021).

4. LESSONS LEARNED

A number of lessons can be learned about the way natural landscapes are given identity and the value of visitors' experiences increased through architecture, and also about the contribution of architourism as a self-contained micro-niche to the macro-niches of cultural and nature-based tourism.

Giving Natural Landscapes Identity and Experience Value through Architecture

At a local level, a nature area might be given identity as a result of physically adding value to the natural surroundings, by means of a symbolic and/or iconic representation of an area's key characteristic(s) in an architectural object. From a philosophical point of view, the object communicates or radiates the key characteristic(s) of its surroundings to the public through how it is designed, its technical construction, how it is embedded in the surrounding nature and landscape and how it interconnects and merges with them. Regarding Tij, one of the iconic features of the area that is merged with or represented by the architectural object in question is the

Source: Photo by L. van Galen.

Figure 3.3   *Interior of Tij*

sandwich tern. The building's design closely followed natural principles, as a result of which it conforms with and respects the local nature and landscape. Moreover, the area's history of living with water (represented by the famous Dutch coastal defence works that protect inland areas from flooding) is brought to life by the Tij Bird Observatory in a way that can be experienced by visitors. In this way, a range of natural, landscape, cultural and historical features are combined and made experienceable through architecture, directly educating visitors about the area's importance. Beyond this, nature and the surrounding landscape are given deeper aesthetic and intellectual meanings and value by means of architecture, forming the basis for enriching visitor experiences in nature-based tourism. This allows visitors to create their own meanings about nature, and evoke feelings and emotions as a result of contemplating the building's place in its environment and their own stance towards nature and landscape (Figure 3.4).

Architourism's Role in Local Nature-Based Tourism

Offering experiences of nature through architecture is the basis for establishing the micro-niche of architourism in nature-based tourism. Compared to architourism in urban environments, whereby the object mainly constitutes the most important reason for attracting visitors, architourism in nature can go a step further, whereby the appealing power of architecture aims

Source: Photo by L. van Galen.

Figure 3.4   Landscape and nature surrounding Tij

at restoring, initiating or strengthening the visitor's bond with the surrounding nature and landscape (Figure 3.4).

In the specific example of Tij, the iconic architecture attracts a varied public, including those who were not originally interested in nature, as a result of its innovative and unique design. Those who come for the architecture alone are effectively brought into contact with nature and the landscape, resulting in a greater understanding of the environment, a sense of wonder and, one hopes, appreciation. Ultimately, visitors may develop a sense of place and a more positive attitude towards nature, as well as establish supportive viewpoints on conservation. Moreover, if visitors have valuable experiences, this increases the potential for return visits and positive word-of-mouth reports to friends and family. This may serve as a catalyst, increasing awareness of the building and its surroundings among the public, with potentially multiplying effects.

As well as helping to establish nature-based tourism experiences and generate knock-on effects in support of conservation among visitors, architourism can also be used from a visitor management perspective to limit or prevent human impact on protected areas. The appealing features (exterior and interior) of the architectural object can contributes to this, although the incorporation of elements of the surrounding nature and landscape are also important. Depending on the location, there are a number of elements that may be used alongside or incorporated into the object to guide visitors and prevent them from disturbing or damaging the local fauna and flora. Examples include the use of dense shrubs, small trees, thorn bushes, prickly flowers and wetland along footpaths; walls made of natural materials; and the construction of tunnels that ensure that visitors are invisible to the local fauna. These elements contribute to nature conservation while allowing visitors to experience that nature. They can also serve to provoke certain feelings, thoughts and behaviours among visitors, generating a sense of curiosity and excitement before they eventually arrive at the architectural object.

Architourism's Role in Regional Nature-Based Tourism

Regionally, architectural objects may act as a first encounter with a natural area and invite and motivate visitors to make use of other facilities and activities (in nature) nearby. As a result, people may lengthen their stay or return again later. Architourism, in the context of nature-based tourism, can bring economic benefits for regional and local SMEs and can be used as a means for establishing further regional investments, which is one of the principles of niche tourism. Architecture can be deployed in nature-based tourism to promote an area in much the same way it is used in urban contexts: by using the architectural object as an iconic image of the place in promotional materials and commercial products, as a recognisable sign of that destination and a means to promote it among the wider public.

Moreover, by establishing architourism as a micro-niche in nature-based tourism, the offering of facilities and activities is extended and the scope of tourism widened. Lastly, the micro-niche of architourism may be used as a tool for strategic storytelling (Hartman et al., 2019), especially in the case of Tij, where two nature parks (Haringvliet and Biesbosch) have become one national park (NLDelta). Whereas visitors initially merely visited the Biesbosch National Park, where the effects of the delta dynamics are recognisable, they are now able to extend their stay in the Haringvliet and experience the complete story of the Dutch delta through, among other things, Tij Bird Observatory.

5.   CONCLUSIONS

Architecture in natural areas has the capability to stimulate the micro-niche of architourism, which is considered a symbiosis between the macro-niches of cultural and nature-based tourism. It benefits local communities and encourages domestic and regional tourism. Architecture in natural areas can draw society close to nature and the surrounding landscape. Especially in times of (rapid) change (e.g., the COVID-19 pandemic), the urge for different modes of tourism becomes apparent and ways of travelling are reshaped, be it swiftly or over the course of time. Here, the micro-niche of architourism feeds into the macro-niche of nature-based and cultural tourism, as we see signs of the rediscovery of domestic tourism and increased numbers seeking to visit nearby sites they may have overlooked. In addition, society needs to (re)consider its excessive consumption and the effects on climate change and other negative and (potentially) destructive events. Herein, tourism has the capacity to develop into a transformational and inclusive power in which responsible, meaningful and/or conscious tourism is central (Heslinga et al., 2020b). Niche tourism in general and the micro-niche of architourism in particular is vital in this, and it links directly with the sustainable management of natural areas and the protection and restoration of ecosystems, two key values in the Sustainable Development Goals established by the United Nations.

The lessons learned from this case study are generalisable to other nature areas, provided that the (potential) impact of the architectural object on, and its value to, the environment and society are carefully considered, and that a range of critical components are deliberated on in the design phase, to ensure that both tourism/leisure and nature conservation in protected areas remain in equilibrium.

This study contributes to the evolving debate on architourism and sheds light on its usefulness for natural areas. The concept is still in its infancy, but deserves more attention in the context of growing interest in diversification by means of developing niches, particularly in locations outside of main tourist hotspots. Moreover, architourism may contribute substantially to the management of nature areas. Future research on architourism in nature-based tourism could focus on casuistry research, comparative studies, research on visitor experiences and customer journeys, and long-term effects, especially in relation to nature and landscape awareness, altered attitudes, behaviour, public support and willingness to financially contribute to nature conservation as a result of visiting architectural objects in nature.

REFERENCES

Alayo, A., Henry, G. and Plaza, B. (2016) Bilbao case study. In Carter, D.K. (ed.) *Remaking Post-Industrial Cities: Lessons from North America and Europe*. New York: Routledge.

An, L.T., Markowski, J., Bartos, M., Rzenca, A. and Namiecinski, P. (2019) An evaluation of destination attractiveness for nature-based tourism: Recommendations for the management of national parks in Vietnam. *Nature Conservation*, 32(6), 51–80. DOI: 10.3897/natureconservation.32.30753.

Ballantyne, R., Packer, J. and Hughes, K. (2009) Tourists' support for conservation messages and sustainable management practices in in wildlife tourism experiences. *Tourism Management*, 30(5), 658–64. DOI: 10.1016/j.tourman.2008.11.003.

Balmford, A., Green, J.M.H., Anderson, M., Beresford, J., Huang, C., Naidoo, R., Walpole, M. and Manica, A. (2015) Walk on the wild side: Estimating the global magnitude of visits to protected areas. *PLoS Biology*, 13(2), 1–6. DOI: 10.1371/journal.pbio.1002074.

Blackmore, A. (2020) Much ado about nothing: A conceptual discussion on novel or niche tourism in protected areas. *Parks*, 26(2), 37–46. DOI: 10.2305/IUCN.CH.2020.PARKS-26-2AB.en.

Bokhari, A.S. and Binthabet, A.A. (2019) Sustainable development of ecotourism and its relation to architecture – Case study: Al-Baha City, The Emirate of Al-Baha. *Journal of Engineering Sciences*, 47(3), 405–25.

Boo, E. (1990) *Ecotourism: The potentials and pitfalls, volume 2*. Washington: World Wildlife Fund.

Breiby, M.A. (2014) Exploring aesthetic dimensions in a nature-based tourism context. *Journal of Vacation Marketing*, 20(2), 163–73. DOI: 10.1177/1356766713514243.

Chang, T.C. (2010) Bungalows, mansions, and shophouses: Encounters in architourism. *Geoforum*, 41(6), 963–71. DOI: 10.1016/j.geoforum.2010.07.003.

Dolnicar, S. (2006) Nature-conserving tourists: The need for a broader perspective. *Anatolia*, 17(2), 1–22. DOI: 10.1080/13032917.2006.9687188.

Edwards, D., Griffin, T. and Hayllar, B. (2008) *Urban tourism precincts: An overview of key themes and issues*. In Hayllar B., Griffin T. and Edwards D. (eds) *City spaces – tourism places: Urban tourism precincts*, 93–105. Oxford: Elsevier.

Franklin, A. (2016) Journeys to the Guggenheim Museum Bilbao: Towards a revised Bilbao effect. *Annals of Tourism Research*, 59, 79–92. DOI: 10.1016/j.annals.2016.04.001.

Gaston, K.J., Charman, K., Jackson, S.F., Armsworth, P.R., Bonn, A., Briers, R.A., Callaghan, C.S.Q., Catchpole, R., Hopkins, J., Kunin, W.E., Latham, J., Opdam, P., Stoneman, R., Stroud, D.A. and Tratt, R. (2006) The ecological effectiveness of protected areas: The United Kingdom. *Biological conservation*, 132(1), 76–87. DOI: 10.1016/j.biocon.2006.03.013.

Gómez, M.V. and González, S. (2001) A reply to Beatriz Plaza's 'The Guggenheim-Bilbao Museum effect'. *International Journal of Urban and Regional Research*, 25(4), 897–900.

Grčić, L. (2009) Tourist valorization of architectural cultural heritage of Sabac. *Bulletin of the Serbian Geographical Society*, 89(1), 65–94.

Haringvliet.nu. (2018) *Naar een dynamische delta waar natuur en recreatie beleving wordt*. Available at: https://haringvliet.nu/#/info (Accessed 10 August 2022).

Hartman, S. and De Roo, G. (2013) Towards managing nonlinear regional development trajectories. *Environment and Planning C: Government and Policy*, 31(3), 556–70.

Hartman, S., Parra, C. and De Roo, G. (2019) Framing strategic storytelling in the context of transition management to stimulate tourism destination development. *Tourism Management*, 75, 90–98. DOI: 10.1016/j.tourman.2019.04.014.

Herneoja, A., Mäkinen, M., Rantala, O. and Hakkarainen, M. (2014) *Inscrutable nature-based spatial experience*. Proceedings of the 6th Annual Architectural Research Symposium, Finland 2014.

Heslinga, J.H., Groote, P.D. and Vanclay, F. (2017) Using a social-ecological systems perspective to understand tourism and landscape interactions in coastal areas. *Journal of Tourism Futures*, 3(1), 23–38. DOI: 10.1108/JTF-10-2015-0047.

Heslinga, J.H., Groote, P.D. and F. Vanclay (2018) Understanding the historical institutional context by using content analysis of local policy and planning documents. *Tourism Management*, 66 (2018), 180–90. DOI: 10.1016/j.tourman.2017.12.004.

Heslinga, J.H., Groote, P.D. and F. Vanclay (2020a) Towards resilient regions: Policy recommendations for stimulating synergy between tourism and landscape. *LAND*, 9(44), 1–9. DOI:10.3390/land9020044.

Heslinga, J.H., Postma, A. and S. Hartman (2020b) De bezoekerseconomie na COVID-19? Scenarioplanning biedt lange termijn perspectieven voor de toekomt. *Vrije tijd studies*, 38(3), 11–16.

Hosany, S. and Witham, M. (2009) Dimensions of cruisers' experiences, satisfaction and intension to recommend. *Journal of Travel Research*, 49(3), 351–64. DOI: 10.1177/0047287509346859.

Hvenegaard, G.T. (1994) Ecotourism: A status report and conceptual framework. *Journal of Tourism Studies*, 5(2), 24–35.

Kim, Y., Kim, C.K., Lee, D.K., Lee, H.W. and Andrada, R.T. (2019) Quantifying nature-based tourism in protected areas in developing countries by using social big data. *Tourism Management*, 72, 249–56. DOI: 10.1016/j.tourman.2018.12.005.

Kuenzi, C. and McNeely, J. (2008) Nature-based tourism. In Renn, O. and Walker, K.D. (eds) *Global risk governance: Concept and practice using the IRGC framework*, 1–19. Dordrecht: Springer.

Maitland, R. and Newman, P. (2008) Visitor-host relationships: Conviviality between visitors and host communities. In Hayllar, B., Griffin, T. and Edwards. D (eds) *City spaces – tourist places: Urban tourism precincts*, 223–40. Oxford: Elsevier.

Millennium Ecosystem Assessment. (2005) *Ecosystems and human wellbeing: synthesis*. Washington: Island Press.

Muñoz Brenes, C.L., Jones, K.W., Schlesinger, P., Robalino, J. and Vierling, L. (2018) The impact of protected area governance and management capacity on ecosystem function in Central America. *PLOS ONE*, 13(10), 1–20. DOI: 10.1371/journal.pone.0205964.

Najafabadi, F.I., Farsani, N.T., Saghafi, M.R. and Roudkoli, S.M. (2019) Key components for organizing architectural tours in Isfahan, Iran. *Journal of Quality Assurance in Hospitality and Tourism*, 20(3), 259–72. DOI: 10.1080/1528008X.2018.1524811.

Novelli, M. (2005) *Niche tourism. Contemporary issues, trends and cases*. Oxford: Elsevier Butterworth-Heinemann.

Nyaupane, G.P. (2007) Ecotourism versus nature-based tourism: Do tourists really know the difference? *Anatolia, an International Journal of Tourism and Hospitality Research*, 18(1), 161–5. DOI: 10.1080/13032917.2007.9687044.

Ockman, J. and Frausto, S. (2005) *Architourism: Authentic, Escapist, Exotic, Spectacular*. Munich: Prestel Publishing.

Oh, H., Fiore and A.M., Jeoung, M. (2007) Measuring experience economy concepts: Tourism applications. *Journal of Travel Research*, 46(2), 119–32. DOI: 10.1177/0047287507304039.

Piatkowska, K. K. (2012) Economy and architecture. The role of architecture in process of building the economic potential of space. *Humanities and Social Sciences Review*, 1(2), 549–55.

Plaza, B. (2010) Valuing museums as economic engines: Willingness to pay or discounting of cash-flows? *Journal of Cultural Heritage*, 11(2), 155–62. DOI: 10.1016/j.culher.2009.06.001.

Plaza, B. and Haarich, S.N. (2015) The Guggenheim Museum Bilbao: Between regional embeddedness and global networking. *European Planning Studies*, 23(8), 1456–75. DOI: 10.1080/09654313.2013.817543.

Rahman, N.A., Halim, N. and Zakariya, K. (2018) Architectural value for urban tourism placemaking to rejuvenate the cityscape in Johor Bahru. *IOP Conference Series: Materials Science and Engineering, 401*. 2nd International Conference on Architecture and Civil Engineering (ICACE). DOI: 10.1088/1757-899X/401/1/012010.

Saidmamatov, O., Matyakubov, U., Rudenko, I., Filimonau, V., Day, J. and Luthe, T. (2020) Employing ecotourism opportunities for sustainability in the Aral Sea Region: Prospects and challenges. *Sustainability*, 12(21), 1–19. DOI: 10.3390/su12219249.

Schägner, J.P., Brander, L., Maes, J., Paracchini, M.L. and Hartje, V. (2016) Mapping recreational visits and values of European national parks by combining statistical modelling and unit value transfer. *Journal for Nature Conservation*, 31, 71–84. DOI: 10.1016/j.jnc.2016.03.001.

Schieferdecker, A. (2017) Invincible city: The 'miracle' of Bilbao and lessons for post-industrial cities. *Urban Design + Transportation*, 18 October. Available at: https://www.alex-schieferdecker.com/blog/2017/10/14/bilbao-lessons-for-post-industrial-cities (Accessed 3 August 2020).

Siniecki, A. and Evcil, A.N. (2020) Architecture's role in new tourism trends: Cases from Poland and Turkey. In Coşkun, Î.O., Othman, N., Aktaş, S.G., Lew, A. and Yüksek, G. (eds) *Heritage tourism beyond borders and civilizations*. *Proceedings of the Tourism Outlook Conference 2018*, 163–83. Singapore: Springer Nature Singapore Pte Ltd.

Sion, B. (2015) *Memorials in Berlin and Buenos Aires. Balancing memory, architecture, and tourism*. Lanham: Lexington Books.

Specht, J. (2014) *Architectural tourism. Building for urban travel destinations*. Wiesbaden: Springer Gabler Fachmedien Wiesbaden.

Spenceley, A., Kohl, J., McArthur, S., Myles, P., Notarianni, M., Paleczny, D., Pickering, C. and Worboys, G.L. (2015) Visitor management. In Worboys, G.L., Lockwood, M., Kothari, A., Feary, S. and Pulsford, I. (eds) *Protected area governance and management*, 717–49. Canberra: ANU Press.

Stamation, K., Croft, D.B., Shaughnessy, P.D., Waples, K.A. and Briggs, S.V. (2007) Educational and conservational value of whale watching. *Tourism Marine Environments*, 4(1), 41–55. DOI: 10.3727/154427307784835660.

Steckenreuter, A. and Wolf, I.D. (2013) How to use persuasive communication to encourage visitors to pay park user fees. *Tourism Management*, 37, 58–70. DOI: 10.1016/j.tourman.2013.01.010.

Steven, R., Pickering, C. and Castley, J.G. (2011) A review of the impacts of nature based recreation on birds. *Journal of Environmental Management*, 92(10), 2287–94. DOI: 10.1016/j.jenvman.2011.05.005.

UNWTO (2017) *Tourism and culture*. Available at: https://www.unwto.org/tourism-and-culture (Accessed 11 August 2020).

Vicario, L., Martínez Monje, P.M. (2003) Another Guggenheim effect?: The generation of a potentially gentrifiable neighbourhood in Bilbao. *Urban Studies*, 40(12), 2383–400.

Vukadinović, I. (2011) *Architecture in tourism. Case of Copenhagen – Visitors' perspective*. Master thesis. Helsingborg: Lunds Universitet Campus Helsingborg, Sweden.

Wielenga, B. (2020) *The bird hide redesigned. Merging architecture and nature into build objects in natural environments. A case study towards Bird Observatory Tij in Stellendam, Goeree-Overflakkee, and its potential for tourism destination development and management*. MSc thesis, University of Groningen, the Netherlands.

Wielenga, B. (2021) New experiences in nature areas: Architecture as a tool to stimulate transformative experiences among visitors in nature areas? *Journal of Tourism Futures*, in press. DOI: 10.1108/JTF-09-2020-0155.

Wolf, I.D. and Wohlfart, T. (2014) Walking, hiking and running in parks: A multidisciplinary assessment of health and well-being benefits. *Landscape and Urban Planning*, 130(1), 89–103. DOI: 10.1016/j.landurbplan.2014.06.006.

Wolf, I.D., Ainsworth, G.B. and Crowley, J. (2017) Transformative travel as a sustainable market niche for protected areas: A new development, marketing and conservation model. *Journal of Sustainable Tourism*, 25(11), 1650–73. DOI: 10.1080/09669582.2017.1302454.

Wolf, I.D., Croft, D.B. and Green, R.J. (2019) Nature conservation and nature-based tourism: A paradox? *Environments*, 6(9), 1–22. DOI: 10.3390/environments6090104.

Wolf, I.D., Stricker, H.K. and Hagenloh, G. (2014) Outcome-focused national park experience management: Transforming participants, promoting social well-being, and fostering place attachment. *Journal of Sustainable Tourism*, 23(3), 358–81. DOI: 10.1080/09669582.2014.959968.

4. Conservation tourism in Pangatalan island, Palawan UNESCO Biosphere Reserve

Cristina Abreu, Frédéric Tardieu and António D. Abreu

INTRODUCTION

UNESCO Biosphere Reserves (within the UNESCO Man and Biosphere Programme – MAB) are sites aiming to promote biodiversity conservation and sustainable development in communities living in or around these designated areas. The World Network of Biosphere Reserves (WNBR) works to 'foster the harmonious integration of people and nature for sustainable development through participatory dialogue, knowledge sharing, poverty reduction, human wellbeing, respect for cultural values and efforts to improve social ability to cope with climate change' (UNESCO, n.d.b)

As of July 2019, the WNBR includes 701 Biosphere Reserves in 124 countries, including 21 transboundary sites (UNESCO, n.d.a). In area and diversity, the WNBR corresponds to the largest network of legally protected areas. UNESCO Biosphere Reserves' core zones correspond to established protected areas at the national level having as their primary function conservation of biodiversity (UNESCO, n.d.a). Combined with UNESCO World Heritage sites and UNESCO Global Geoparks, Biosphere Reserves account for more than 10 million km^2, and correspond to an area equivalent to China (UNESCO, n.d.a). UNESCO estimates that 250 million people live in Biosphere Reserves worldwide (UNESCO, n.d.a).

The Statutory Framework and related MAB Strategy and Action Plan propose several functional roles to the Biosphere Reserves, including biodiversity conservation, enhancement of local communities' socioeconomic wellbeing, learning and knowledge-building on sustainable development practices, and cooperation between the different geographic and thematic UNESCO Biosphere Reserves Networks. On the socioeconomic side, tourism is a relevant sector for the Biosphere Reserves, where natural assets (biodiversity, landscapes) combined with cultural and historical heritage offer unique touristic experiences. Therefore, tourism is an important economic activity for many Biosphere Reserves which seek to explore its potential under a dual vision: economic benefits to the local communities and environmental conservation (Gebhard et al., 2007).

Sustainable tourism in general, and ecotourism in particular, are closely related to Biosphere Reserves, due to the direct association with natural values such as biodiversity, habitats and landscapes, but also to exclusivity in the form of unique environments offered as part of the singular aspects of each Biosphere Reserve. The need to ensure conservation and a sustainable use of nature and natural resources in Biosphere Reserves helps to differentiate the type and the size of touristic activities that are limited and shaped by existing regulations in Biosphere Reserves, mentioned in the UNESCO MAB Strategy 2015–2025 and Lima Action Plan 2016–2025 (UNESCO, 2017). Consequently, tourism in Biosphere Reserves usually results in small-scale, thematic and specific activities, linking closely to the concept of niche tourism. This chapter intends to explore a case study of environmental niche tourism involving nature and wildlife, as proposed by Robinson and Novelli (2005). Specifically, it focuses on Pangatalan island, a small island in Palawan, Republic of the Philippines, where thorough work is being developed based on management practices and nature conservation strategies in line with sustainable tourism. Here, the idea of the 'niche' corresponds to the dimension, number, type of activities and tourists, organized accordingly with experience content and specific situations and conditions.

Tourism in Biosphere Reserves means proximity with nature and people, combining living experiences with the natural elements and the local communities, culture, identity and life-style, and their concerns, problems, limitations and aspirations. Tourists need to understand and take part in sustainable development at the local level, and this conscience and under-standing is part of the experience offered by the Biosphere Reserves. A similarity with the concept of ecotourism can be mentioned as 'responsible travel to natural areas that conserves the environment, sustains locals' wellbeing, and involves interpretation and education for staff and guests' (TIES, 2015).

Palawan Biosphere Reserve is a cluster of islands composed of one long main island, Palawan, and smaller groups of islands of around 1,150,800 hectares in total (UNESCO, n.d.a). Palawan's main economic activities include agriculture, fisheries and tourism. Other important sectors are on-shore and off-shore mining and pearl farming (UNESCO, n.d.a). Palawan's coastal and marine ecosystems include mangrove swamps, seagrass, coral reefs and marine meadows. In addition to being a UNESCO Biosphere Reserve, Palawan has two UNESCO World Heritage Sites: Puerto Princesa Underground River National Park and Tubbataha Reefs Natural Park (UNESCO, n.d.a).

As in any island in general, human actions in Palawan generate several challenges relating to the sustainable use of natural resources, some of which can induce direct consequences on landscapes and ecosystems. Mass tourism, seashore construction, overexploitation of beaches and natural events are some of the main reasons that have motivated Palawan's decision-makers to implement strategies to improve tourism quality, welfare and nature conservation. The main research objective is: to understand how niche tourism contributes to nature conservation and to the sustainable development of Pangatalan island.

LITERATURE REVIEW

Nature-Based Tourism and Niche Tourism Destinations

Nature provides a great variety of touristic practices (Olafsdottir and Olafsdottir, 2013), with nature-based tourism being one of the sectors that has expanded particularly rapidly in Northern Europe, but also, more broadly speaking, around the world (Bell et al., 2007; Fredman and Tyrväinen, 2010; UNEP, 2011, as cited in Elmahdy et al., 2017: 15). Valentine (1992) presented a simple definition of nature-based tourism as primarily concerned with the immediate enjoyment of some relatively undisturbed phenomenon of nature. Fennell (2000) defined nature-based tourism as responsible travel to natural areas that conserves the environment and improves the welfare of local people. Nature-based tourism enables the carrying out of outdoor activities and accommodation in pristine scenarios, providing unique experiences for tourists, profits for tour operators, environmental conservation funds and local communities' increased wellbeing (Honey, 2008; Ardoin et al., 2015). Fredman et al. (2009: 23) defined nature-based tourism as 'people's activities when they visit natural areas outside of their usual surroundings', stressing the relevance of community management of natural resources and nature protection in the supply of nature-based tourism. Environmental, economic and sociocultural impacts are directly related to tourism activities. In the present case study, we draw particular attention to the first of these, the natural environment, as a basis for niche tourism, demonstrating how nature-based tourism should be managed to ensure enjoyable tourist experiences with minimum impacts on nature and local communities (Cloesen, 2003). Certain other risks are also associated with nature-based tourism, especially when tourism is the only source of income (Kuenzi and McNeely, 2006). Yet, as Nybakk and Hansen (2008) mentioned, entrepreneur attitudes, followed by introducing innovative initiatives in tourism, contribute to improving tourism performance. From a personal perspective, nature-based tourism must reflect the interdisciplinary complexity of the tourism industry and express the need to implement environmental management strategies, as expressed in Cohen-Shacham et al. (2016) and Maes and Jacobs (2017).

Setting the Stage: Niche Tourism and Small Island Tourism

Novelli pioneered the introduction of the concept of 'niche tourism' in 2005, advocating the relationship between niche marketing and the concept of niche in ecology. Robinson and Novelli (2005) presented niche tourism as a sustainable and less damaging form of tourism. Niche tourism is frequently considered the opposite of mass tourism, intrinsically related to moral legitimacy and places where tourists are attracted to spend a lot of money (Robinson and Novelli, 2005). Niche tourism offers, and marketing approaches are based on, tourists' requirements and expectations (Robinson and Novelli, 2005). Assuming the attractiveness and benefits promoted by tourism growth, tourism in small islands can severely strain local capacity and resources (Keane, Brophy and Cuddy, 1992).

Nevertheless, small island destinations are attractive for tourists (Butler, 1993). Notwithstanding, tourists who are more demanding and concerned with sociocultural, economic and environmental impacts participate in and seek out products and live cultural experiences that satisfy these concerns (Donaire Benito et al., 1997). Accordingly, Butler (2002: 88) stated that 'small islands, for a variety of reasons, have long been viewed as attractive destinations for both recreational and touristic purposes'. Consequently, the scarcity of pristine environments in densely populated areas is one reason to travel and reach high-quality sites (Cloesen, 2003). Small islands' unique geographical situation and rich natural and cultural heritage are relevant assets in niche tourism destinations (Robinson and Novelli, 2005). When it comes to expanding tourism in small islands, Goeldner and Ritchie (2006) mentioned niche tourism as unique. It provides a wide range of benefits, such as job creation, local income, natural areas protection and environmental heritage conservation (Tyrväinen et al., 2014). However, some small island destinations can no longer offer sustainable tourism due to overuse and resource damage driven by tourism growth (Oreja-Rodríguez, Lopez and Yanes-Estévez, 2008). The increasing number of more sophisticated tourists has led to niche tourism's development (Ali-Knight, 2011).

Additionally, different factors have favoured the expansion of niche tourism, such as technological advances, new marketing techniques, the diffusion of new and more specialized tour operators and demanding consumers looking for high-level experiences. Products available on the market have been able to spread thanks to the internet, increasing the desire of people to live new experiences in a tourist destination. Thus, communicating the environmental impacts of touristic activities to tourists, as well as intensifying compliance with legislation, is essential to retain competitiveness, as well as to avoid social conflict (Catibog-Sinha, 2013). Catibog-Sinha (2015) adds that besides the economic impact of tourism, small island tourism generates positive externalities in funding, nature conservation and environmental improvement. Moreover, Catibog-Sinha (2015) discusses the role of niche tourism in expanding parks, forest reserves, biosphere reserves, recreational areas, beaches, waterfronts and underwater trails, providing environmental education to visitors and locals. On the other hand, tourism in small islands is confronted with several challenges and vulnerabilities (UNWTO, n.d.a). In addition to the aforementioned points, improvements in the resilience of small islands can contribute to overcoming the effects of resource extraction caused by tourism (Booth et al., 2020); such actions are directly linked with sustainable tourism.

The adoption of sustainability principles in tourism was decisive for the consolidation of the United Nations actions concerning sustainable development, where an approach to sustainability was proposed through a multidimensional, economic, social and environmental perspective, with Agenda 21 for the Travel and Tourism Industry for Sustainable Development, in 1997. Butler (1999: 12) defined sustainable tourism as that which 'is developed and maintained in an area and at a scale that guarantees its viability during a period of indefinite time, without damaging or changing the environment (human or physical) and without compromising the development and wellbeing of other activities and processes'. Moreover, the World Charter for Sustainable Tourism +20 (2015) sets forth the relevance of tourism in obtaining economic benefits for local communities and destinations from an ethical, environmental and social perspective. The Sustainable Development Goals (UN SDGs) and Agenda 2030 (short for 'Transforming our World: The 2030 Sustainable Development Agenda') can be used to address these challenges in small islands. The 17 SDGs and their five pillars (People, Planet, Prosperity, Peace, Partnership), along with the 169 goals of its action plan, seek to eradicate poverty in its various forms, mitigate the effects of climate change, reduce conflicts and encourage sustainable consumption and innovation, integrating the dimensions of sustainability – economic, social and environmental – around the world. Accordingly, the UN SDGs encompass tourism on three of the seventeen goals: Goal (8.9) 'Promote sustained, inclusive and sustainable economic growth, full and productive employment and decent work for all'; Goal (12b) 'Ensure sustainable consumption and production patterns'; and Goal (14.7) 'Conserve and sustainably use the oceans, seas and marine resources for sustainable development' (UNWTO, 2020). Thus, the implementation of the SDGs in tourism is a relevant contribution to sustainable development in small islands.

Sustainable tourism in Biosphere Reserves contributes to generating employment and income for the local population, generates genuine motivation, and encourages conservation in vulnerable ecosystems and protected areas through careful and comprehensive tourism planning and the engagement of key stakeholders in tourism, conservation, economy and territorial policies. It also introduces participatory processes, particularly for the local population (Gebhard et al., 2007). Moreover, sustainable tourism is often linked with the transference of professional working skills to the tourism business (Cunha et al., 2020), providing positive business results as well as entrepreneurial and personal fulfilment (Boluk and Mottiar, 2014). Therefore, sustainable tourism is used in developing countries – including nations with several small islands – as a development strategy, despite practical limitations and challenges (Carter et al., 2015).

METHODOLOGY

This article implements a case-study research design. Case-study research involves the examination of a contemporary phenomenon in its natural setting (Yin, 2003). According to Beeton (2005), case studies are widely used in tourism studies and education (as cited in Rodrigues et al., 2014: 295). Through an inductive approach and direct observations (Bryman, 2012), a qualitative methodology was employed, with the application of one semi-structured interview with the owner of Pangatalan island. Complementarily, the authors' personal experience and knowledge of the island, as implementers of the requirements to achieve Biosphere Responsible Tourism and Etico for Sustainability certifications, and due to our cooperation with the Palawan Council for Sustainable Development and Palawan UNESCO Biosphere Reserve within the World Network of Island and Coastal Biosphere Reserves, is reflected in the current chapter. Relevant documents were consulted and complemented with direct observation during field visits. Data collection and field visits occurred over the period between July 2018 and July 2019.

The semi-structured interview, lasting around 90 minutes, was audio-recorded with the interviewee's consent. Two field visits provided an overview of the island and the nearest communities to collect general information.

Relevant literature was consulted on niche tourism and nature-based tourism, alongside a case description using narratives with qualitative information (Yin, 2003). The data collected helps to show how niche tourism contributes to nature conservation and sustainable development in Pangatalan island.

CASE STUDY OF SMALL ISLAND TOURISM ON PANGATALAN ISLAND

Pangatalan is a small island located on Shark Fin Bay in the North West side of Palawan, Philippines (Figure 4.1). Pangatalan island brings together special conditions concerning the adoption of specific actions in ecosystem recovery, such as forestation, coral restoration and the implementation of a sustainable tourism development model, which can be extended to larger regions. Following the segmentation of niche tourism proposed by Robinson and Novelli (2005), Pangatalan island is considered an environmental micro-niche destination, focusing on nature and wildlife tourism in a small island context. Therefore, benefiting from the small dimension of the island (4.5 hectares), a comprehensive and integrated intervention started in 2011 to restore terrestrial and marine ecosystems and promote sustainable livelihoods for the neighbouring communities, as well as to develop sustainable tourism. In 2011, an inland and marine coastal habitats restoration plan was designed, based on which a deep intervention was performed to recover from timber exploitation and intensive fishing using explosives. The ongoing re-vegetation process brought to the island a total of 68,000 native plants of 52 species which helped with soil restructuring, creating a green stable patch. Simultaneously, a marine protected area covering 46 hectares (Sulubaaï Environmental Foundation, n.d.) was designed and implemented to restore coastal and marine habitats. This marine protected area, which includes mangroves and coral reefs, combined environmental awareness activities, vessel navigation restrictions and the prevention of fishing with explosives.

Source: Photo from Sulubaaï Foundation.

Figure 4.1   *Photo of Pangatalan island, facing the organic farm*

The coral restoration project has produced remarkable results by combining innovative methods for coral settlement and expansion with post-larvae fish aquaculture, supporting food production and the resettlement of natural habitats with selected fish species. Additionally, an area of 7 hectares on the island of Palawan was set aside for an organic farm where vegetables, fruits and meat are now being produced for consumption on Pangatalan. On this piece of land, regenerative agriculture is being practised in association with forestation and ecosystem restoration.

Tourism is the main economic activity on Pangatalan island. Therefore, a responsible tourism strategy is at the core of the Pangatalan island development plan. Accordingly, implementing a sustainable development plan, combining the pursuit of environmental recovery (ecological restoration) with social development and benefits to the local populations, improves their quality of life in terms of both wages and professional training, as well as creating fair, equitable and alternative jobs (Figure 4.2).

In Pangatalan island, tourism is grounded in natural assets. Tourists can experience a stay on a small and exclusive island with indigenous vegetation and private beaches, and enjoy the taste of local food produced on the organic farm. Visitors are invited to participate in active environmental and conservation activities such as habitat restoration, marine life censuses and environmental education.

Pangatalan was previously a non-inhabited island with no public infrastructure, managed by a private owner. Now, the island has established a limited accommodation capacity of nine guests, offering a unique hands-on tourism experience in line with the principles established by the World Charter for Sustainable Tourism +20 (2015) and with the Pangatalan Island Marine Protected Area Management Plan 2017–2020: 10 (Figure 4.2). The island has hosted 60 visitors over the last two years. Visits can last a minimum of one week and are only available during a period of three months of the year (from January to March). Shaping the

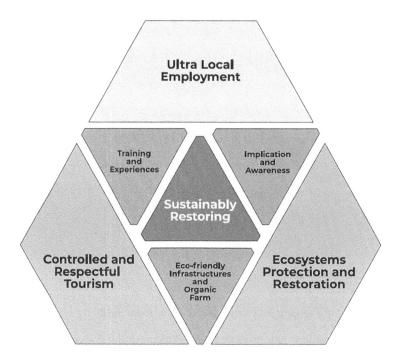

Source: Pangatalan Island Marine Protected Area Management Plan 2017–2020: 10.

Figure 4.2   *Pangatalan sustainable development model*

Pangatalan island product included pre-opening experiences for staff training, facilities and services testing, as well as feedback from selected visitors.

Consequently, Pangatalan island built a coherent tourism story that is visible in all activities and facilities. The island only uses renewable energy. No chemical fertilizers, pesticides, detergent, soaps or any other non-organic, non-biodegradable cleaning or beauty products are allowed in Pangatalan. The food is organic and mainly produced at the property. Any other purchase of goods and products follows local principles and best practice.

Visitors are asked to take part in the environmental and social activities, or are at least informed of their contribution to the SDGs. Examples of activities in which visitors can participate include ongoing initiatives such as coral restoration, biodiversity monitoring and reforestation, as well as educational and awareness activities. Complementing this, scientific tourism is also a segment that Pangatalan wants to target in the future by offering logistics support (laboratory and field facilities) and opportunities for research in ecology, culture, history, heritage and other related scientific fields.

Human activities play an essential role in Biosphere Reserves' dynamics. The development strategy adopted for Pangatalan island combines economic, human and social development and environmental protection in line with the UN SDGs. Ecological restoration is a central element, due to the need to recover devastated marine and terrestrial ecosystems. The island suffered massive deforestation of both its mangrove and the original terrestrial vegetation. The use of explosives and chemicals in illegal fishing has caused structural damaged to the coral reef.

Restoring the marine and terrestrial environment combines visitors' and local communities' awareness through various interventions, including training, capacitation and job creation. Associated with the restoration, support and logistics activities, Pangatalan established cooperation agreements with the Palawan Council for Sustainable Development and the objectives of Palawan UNESCO Biosphere Reserve. These partnerships helped to position conservation and restoration activities as enablers of socioeconomic development, not just conservation based on intrinsic value.

Visiting Pangatalan requires more than a simple process of making a reservation. Reservation includes a communication process during which visitors must acknowledge the above requirements. Pangatalan is also supporting schools (construction, improving existing facilities such as toilets for girls and curriculum development) and university students, as well as providing water harvesting and distribution infrastructure, waste management and other measures to prevent marine and coastal pollution in local communities (Barangay). A total of 1,198 students and 29 teachers from Sandoval National High School, Sandoval Elementary School, Depla Elementary School and Silanga Elementary School are involved in awareness, education and conservation activities promoted by Pangatalan island. The island supports 1,000 households from the local communities of Sandoval, Depla, Silanga and Tay Tay Municipality.

While improving general conditions and promoting better environmental conditions, these activities generate jobs and awareness of conservation and the sustainable use of biodiversity and natural resources.

The tourism experience offered by Pangatalan is based on a significantly reduced number of visitors, as mentioned above, which should contribute to the long-term sustainability of the island and adhere to the principles and practices set forth in the island's Sustainable Development Model.

DISCUSSION AND CONCLUSIONS

The touristic experience offered in Pangatalan island can be classified as niche tourism, as the established carrying capacity and the nature of activities available while on the island targets a specific tourist profile. Apart from assisting and actively contributing to conservation activities directed at natural ecosystems and cultural and heritage features, visitors are asked to understand and experience the possibility of combining nature protection with socioeconomic development while benefiting from high-quality and exclusive hospitality services. Moreover, the opportunity to experience the reality that it is possible to restore damaged landscapes and ecosystems offers a sense of optimism and positivity for visitors, with impacts both during and after their stay on Pangatalan. Ongoing restoration activities in the marine protected area that visitors can participate in include mangrove planting, marine life census surveying, coral monitoring and releasing juvenile fish specimens.

Ecological restoration can be achieved through habitat conservation measures, including access, use restrictions and sustainable initiatives. Nevertheless, in Pangatalan island, it is also necessary to ensure socioeconomic sustainability, such as income and jobs in fisheries, farming, management, maintenance, housekeeping, welfare and other direct and indirect services. An exclusive tourism experience targeting a specific tourist profile implemented in Palawan island is the main economic driver that will continue to support the conservation and sustainable use of natural resources and the socioeconomic development of local communities. Pangatalan island aims to provide enough resources for supporting the conservation activities and socioeconomic development of the communities linked with Pangatalan island. The island seeks to attract tourists looking for exquisite experiences, including an explicit commitment to nature conservation and related social benefits.

The existing natural and human landscape of Pangatalan and the already visible results of ecosystem restoration, particularly with the mangrove swamps and coral reef, provide objective evidence, contributing to a sense of satisfaction and accomplishment from promotors, tourists and locals. Improvements in water and waste management facilities, schools, awareness, training and education, along with increased engagement from local stakeholders and communities, also contribute to demonstrating the decisive and practical contribution of tourism to nature conservation and socioeconomic development in Pangatalan island.

The recent COVID-19 outbreak has had impacts on health and the economy, calling attention to the interlinkages between human and natural systems. Everard et al. (2020) suggest that contemporary livelihood and market patterns tend to degrade ecosystems and their services, driving a cycle of degradation in increasingly tightly linked socioecological systems. This contributes to a reduction in the natural regulating capacities of ecosystem services to limit disease transfer from animals to humans. Risks and crises directly related to tourism and global changes are becoming more frequent and will need to be included in the post-COVID-19 strategy. Pangatalan already proposes a practical experience in line with these concerns, showing how tourism in small islands can accommodate these considerations to construct a resilient and sustainable society supported by healthy natural systems.

To ensure transparency and quality following high-level international standards, Pangatalan island was the first entity to achieve the Biosphere Responsible Tourism certification in the Philippines and the Asia Pacific Region. Pangatalan island evidences a total commitment and alignment with the Sustainable Tourism World Charter +20 (2015), the 2030 Agenda and the UN SDGs, which are fully integrated and visible in the daily life of the island, their employees, suppliers and neighbouring barangays (local communities). Pangatalan is also applying for certification by Etico for Sustainability, a more comprehensive standard including social, cultural, natural and ethical criteria not exclusively oriented towards tourism.

Of course, Pangatalan's model corresponds to a small private island where the decision-making process may benefit from being linear and less complex compared to a more significant tourism destination under public regulatory mechanisms. Notwithstanding, Pangatalan island may provide managerial concepts, tools and inspirational ideas that could be explored by other tourism destinations in the future.

REFERENCES

Ali-Knight, J. The role of niche tourism products in destination development. (Thesis). Edinburgh Napier University. http://researchrepository.napier.ac.uk/id/eprint/5376

Ardoin, N.M., Wheaton, M., Bowers, A. W. and Hunt, C. A. (2015) Nature-based tourism's impact on environmental knowledge, attitudes, and behavior: A review and analysis of the literature and potential future research. *Journal of Sustainable Tourism*, 23(6), 838–858. https://doi.org/http://dx.doi.org/10.1080/09669582.2015.1024258

Beeton, S. (2005) The case study in tourism research: A multi-method case study approach. *Tourism Research Methods: Integrating Theory with Practice*, (March), 37–48. https://doi.org/10.1079/9780851999968.0037

Bell, S., Tyrväinen, L., Sievänen, T., Pröbstl-Haider, U. and Simpson, M. (2007) Outdoor recreation and nature tourism: A European perspective. *Living Reviews in Landscape Research*, 1. Responsible Tourism Institute (RTI). https://doi.org/10.12942/lrlr-2007-2

Boluk, K. and Mottiar, Z. (2014) Motivations of social entrepreneurs: Blurring the social contribution and profits dichotomy. *Social Enterprise Journal*, 10(1), 53–68. https://doi.org/10.1108/SEJ-01-2013-0001

Booth, P., Chaperon, S. A., Kennell, J. S. and Morrison, A. M. (2020) Entrepreneurship in island contexts: A systematic review of the tourism and hospitality literature. *International Journal of Hospitality Management*, 85(November). ISSN 0278–4319. https://doi.org/10.1016/j.ijhm.2019.102438

Bryman, A. (2012) *Social Research Methods* (4th ed.). Oxford, New York: Oxford University Press Inc.

Butler, R.W. (1993) Tourism development in small islands: Past influences and future directions. *The Development Process in Small Island States*. London: Routledge. https://www.cabdirect.org/cabdirect/abstract/19941802429

Butler, R.W. (1999) Sustainable tourism: A state-of-the-art review. *Tourism Geographies*, 1(1), 7–25.

Butler, R.W. (2002) Editorial. *Tourism and Hospitality Research*, 4(2), 101–103. https://doi.org/10.1177/146735840200400201

Carter, R.W.B., Thok, S., Rourke, V.O. and Pearce, T. (2015) Sustainable tourism and its use as a development strategy in Cambodia: A systematic literature review. *Journal of Sustainable Touirsm*, 23(5), 797–818. http://dx.doi.org/10.1080/09669582.2014.978787

Catibog-Sinha, C. (2013) Enabling conditions for sustainability: Community tourism in marine reserves in the Philippines. *Proceedings of the 19th Asia Pacific Tourism Association Annual Conference*, Bangkok, 1–4 July.

Catibog-Sinha, C. (2015) The role of nature-based tourism in the green economy: A broader perspective for conservation and sustainability in the Philippines. In M.V. Reddy and K. Wilkes (eds), *Tourism in the green economy*. London: Routledge, 57–70.

Cloesen, U. (2003) Approaches towards nature based tourism policies in Australia and New Zealand. *Asia Pacific Journal of Tourism Research*, 8, 72–77. https://doi.org/10.1080/10941660308725457

Cohen-Shacham, E., Walters, G., Janzen, C. and Maginnis, S. (2016) *Nature-based solutions to address global societal challenges*. https://doi.org/10.2305/IUCN.CH.2016.13.en

Cunha, C., Kastenholz, E. and Carneiro, M. J. (2020) Entrepreneurs in rural tourism: Do lifestyle motivations contribute to management practices that enhance sustainable entrepreneurial ecosystems? *Journal of Hospitality and Tourism Management*, 44, 215–226. https://doi.org/10.1016/j.jhtm.2020.06.007

Donaire Benito, J., Fraguell i Sansbelló, R. and Mundet i Cerdán, L. (1997) La Costa Brava ante los nuevos retos del turismo. *Estudios Turísticos*, 133, 77–96.

Elmahdy, Y. M., Haukeland, J. V. and Fredman, P. (2017) Tourism megatrends, a literature review focused on nature-based tourism, MINA fagrapport 42, 74. https://doi.org/10.13140/RG.2.2.32481.66402

Everard, M., Johnston, P., Santillo, D. and Staddon, C. (2020) The role of ecosystems in mitigation and management of Covid-19 and other zoonoses. *Environmental Science and Policy*, 111(May), 7–17. https://doi.org/10.1016/j.envsci.2020.05.017

Fennell, D. A. (2000) What's in a name? Conceptualising natural resource-based tourism. *Tourism Recreation Research*, 25, 97–100. https://doi.org/10.1080/02508281.2000.11014903

Fredman, P., Wall-Reinius, S. and Lundberg, C. (2009) Nature tourism in Sweden: Definitions, extent, statistics. *Mid-Sweden University, European Tourism Research Institute ETOUR*, Report no. 2009.

Fredman, P. and Tyrväinen, L. (2010) Frontiers in nature-based tourism. *Scandinavian Journal of Hospitality and Tourism*, 10, 177–189. https://doi.org/10.1080/15022250.2010.502365

Gebhard, K., Meyer, M. and Rot, S. (2007) Sustainable tourism management planning in biosphere reserves. *Ecological Tourism in Europe and UNESCO MaB*, 10.

Goeldner, C. R. and Ritchie, J. B. (2006) *Tourism: Principles, practices, philosophies*. New York: John Wiley & Sons.

Honey, M. (2008) *Ecotourism and sustainable development: Who owns paradise?* Second edition. Washington: Island Press.

Keane, M.J., Brophy, P. and Cuddy, M.P. (1992) Strategic management of island tourism: The Aran Islands. *Tourism Management*, 13(4), 406–414. doi: https://doi:10.1016/0261-5177(92)90008-U

Kuenzi, C. and McNeely, J. (2006) Nature-based tourism. In O. Renn and K. D. Walker (eds) *Global Risk Governance*. International Risk Governance Council Bookseries, 1, 1–19. Dordrecht: Springer. https://doi.org/10.1007/978-1-4020-6799-0

Maes, J. and Jacobs, S. (2017) Nature-based solutions for Europe's sustainable development. *Conservation Letters*, 10(1), 121–124. https://doi.org/10.1111/conl.12216

Nybakk, E. and Hansen, E. (2008) Entrepreneurial attitude, innovation and performance among Norwegian nature-based tourism enterprises. *Forest Policy and Economics*, 10(7–8), 473–479. https://doi.org/10.1016/j.forpol.2008.04.004

Olafsdottir, G. and Olafsdottir, G. (2013) On nature-based tourism. *Tourist Studies*, 13(2), 127–138. https://doi.org/10.1177/1468797613490370

Oreja-Rodríguez, J. R., Lopez, E. and Yanes-Estévez, V. (2008) The sustainability of island destinations: Tourism area life cycle and teleological perspectives. The case of Tenerife. *Tourism Management*, 29, 53–65. https://doi.org/10.1016/j.tourman.2007.04.007

Robinson, M. and Novelli, M. (2005) Niche tourism: an introduction. In M. Novelli (ed.) *Niche tourism: Contemporary issues, trends and cases*, 1–11. Butterworth-Heinemann. https://doi.org/10.4324/9780080492926

Rodrigues, A., Rodrigues, A. and Peroff, D. (2014) The sky and sustainable tourism development: A case study of a dark sky reserve implementation in Alqueva. *International Journal of Tourism Research*, 17, 292–302. https://doi.org/10.1002/jtr.1987

Sulubaai Environmental Foundation (n.d.) Available at: https://sulubaai-foundation.com (accessed 2 June 2020).

TIES (The International Ecotourism Society) (2015) What is ecotourism? Available at: http://www.ecotourism.org/what-is-ecotourism (accessed 11 June 2020).

Tyrväinen, L., Uusitalo, M., Silvennoinen, H. and Hasu, E. (2014) Towards sustainable growth in nature-based tourism destinations: Clients' views of land use options in Finnish Lapland. *Landscape and Urban Planning*, 130, 1–15. https://doi.org/10.1016/j.landurbplan.2014.07.008

UNEP (2011) *Annual report*. United Nations Environment Programme. Available at : https://www.unep.org/resources/annual-report/unep-2011-annual-report (accessed 15 August 2020).

UNESCO (2017) *A new roadmap for the Man and the Biosphere (MAB) Programme and its world network of biosphere reserves*. UNESCO. Director-General, 2009–2017 (Bokova, I.G.). ISBN. 978-92-3-500001-6

UNESCO (n.d.) *Biosphere reserves in Asia and the Pacific*. Available at: http://www.unesco.org/new/en/natural-sciences/environment/ecological-sciences/biosphere-reserves/asia-and-the-pacific/ (accessed 9 June 2020).

UNESCO (n.d.) *Man and the Biosphere Programme*. Available at: https://en.unesco.org/biosphere/wnbr (accessed 9 June 2020).

UNWTO (n.d.a) *Small island destinations in critical need of urgent support as tourism plunges*. Available at: https://www.unwto.org/news/small-island-destinations-in-critical-need-of-urgent-support-as-tourism-plunges (accessed 6 July 2020).

UNWTO (n.d.b) *The sustainable development goals*. Available at: https://sdgs.un.org/goals (accessed 6 July 2020).

Valentine, P. (1992) Review: Nature-based tourism. In B. Weiler and C. M. Hall (eds) *Special Interest Tourism*. London: Belhaven Press, 105–127. https://researchonline.jcu.edu.au/1632/1/Nature-based_tourism.pdf

World Charter for Sustainable Tourism +20 (2015). https://www.biospheretourism.com/en/world-charterfor-sustainable-tourism/25

Yin, R. (2003) *Case Study Research*. Third edition. Beverly Hills, CA: Sage.

5. Urban ecotourism and regime altering in Denmark

Jane Widtfeldt Meged and Jesper Holm

INTRODUCTION

Copenhagen taps into a global trend, with unprecedented high growth rates in tourist overnight stays from 5.5 million in 2008 to 9.9 million in 2018 (VisitDenmark, 2018). The destination management organization (DMO) Wonderful Copenhagen (WoCo) predicts these numbers will double within the next 10 years (Baumgarten, 2018). Until COVID-19 halted the tourism industry, over-tourism was an emergent problem in Copenhagen (Peeters et al., 2018; Husted, 2019), along with the climate crisis, which has been causing uncertainty in the weather and fluctuations in visitor numbers. WoCo adjusted its strategy according to these developments in 2019 to focus on sustainability, with slogans like 'End of Tourism as we know it' and 'people-based growth'. WoCo addresses all 17 Sustainable Development Goals (SDGs) and states that 'The long-term ambition is to make tourism part of the solution, instead of the problem' (WoCo, 2019). This position furthered a long period of deliberation among a small group of SMEs and public authorities on the development of the sustainable tourism niche. WoCo in this regard transcends the Danish government, the environmental and tourism public agencies, and the tourism business trades, as they have all failed to spur any greening of tourism in Denmark (Holm and Kaae, 2017). Thus, alterations in various conditions may spur various forms of innovation and the rise of new niche trends.

A straightforward, but not always easy, way to manage a growing number of tourists is to spread them out in time and space, and for that purpose, a destination may, as WoCo has done, develop new and innovative tourism experiences, which often start out as niche products. Simultaneously with the growth in tourism, Denmark has recently experienced a surge in nature parks and national parks; the first national park was established in 2008, and by 2018, Denmark had 25 new parks (Holm et al., 2020: 10) several of which are situated adjacent to urban centres such as Copenhagen and Roskilde. Accordingly, nature parks may serve as potential tourism destinations to relieve over tourism, as Denmark has no tradition of nature tourism outside coastal areas, especially not in parks (except for one or two very large national parks).

So, on top of the aforementioned problem of over-tourism, the availablility of nature and national parks near cities and the larger cities' blue–greening development efforts (Teknik- og Miljøforvaltningen, 2015), we saw a window of opportunity for an R&D project to start a niche creation in *urban* ecotourism. This could relieve the burden of over-tourism while kickstarting an initial green transition of the tourism industry. This resulted in a major R&D project: Research and Development of Urban Ecotourism (INUT) 2017–2020, with assistance from the Danish Innovation Fund. The project aimed to create a niche from below in Copenhagen city and the adjacent Amager Nature Park, as well as the in the city of Roskilde and Skjoldungernes Land National Park.

This chapter presents and discusses the strategy, methods and results of this R&D project and provides general lessons learned about niche-to-regime development paths. We aspired to establish the niche of urban ecotourism through the formation of a niche arena, as well as destination and product development, to remedy the above-mentioned problems and procure solutions which will we hope will eventually transit into the dominant tourism regime. To be clear, here niche development means encouraging innovation to influence the tourism macro-regime, as sustaining tourism must go beyond niche enclaves, while other niche tourism products, of course are to be maintained as such.

First, we approach nature tourism and ecotourism as niches by briefly reviewing the larger domains or macro-niches of nature-based tourism, sustainable tourism and ecotourism. Then we elaborate on how urban ecotourism will define our area of interest. Thereafter, we present our theory-informed strategic approach to niches and regimes, followed by a methodological section on a Danish R&D project and its results. We conclude by discussing the findings from the R&D project in relation to furthering the niche tourism field and influencing the tourism macro-regime.

ECOTOURISM AND URBAN ECOTOURISM – FROM NICHES TO A REGIME: A TRANSITION THEORY PERSPECTIVE

Fredman and Tyrväinen argue that nature-based tourism is a fairly complex and broad system and that, 'based on a thorough review of literature, no scientifically defined and universally agreed on definition for nature-based tourism was found' (2010: 179). However, it is safe to say that nature-based tourism may encompass all kinds of tourism taking place in nature, whether it is mass tourism applying Fordist production logic or niche tourism addressing a specific market, activity or geographical location (Goodwin, 1996; Robinson and Novelli, 2005). Niche tourism has largely been shaped and understood in opposition to or as a remedy for mass tourism (Dinis and Krakower, 2016; Robinson and Novelli, 2005; Weeden, 2005). According to Robinson and Novelli (2005), we can segment niche tourism into macro-niches from which almost never-ending micro-niches may be encouraged to develop. Robinson and Novelli (2005) propose a typology of macro-niches within cultural, environmental, rural, urban and other types of tourism. Within the macro-niche of environmental (or nature) tourism, they find a number of micro-niches such as adventure tourism (Shepard and Evans, 2005), wildlife tourism (Novelli and Humavindu, 2005) and geotourism with a focus on interpretation and preservation (Hose, 2005). This is also where we find ecotourism.

Ecotourism was first defined in 1965 (Fennell, 2015), and originally seen as a form of micro-niche tourism centred around protected and larger pristine remote habitats that are considered vulnerable. Ecotourism has historically been associated with alternative niche tourism as a marker of distance from mass tourism. However, over time, ecotourism developed in many other sites and is now growing into a macro-niche or a regime that incorporates several of the sustainable tourism principles (UNWTO, 2020a), such as low environmental impact, respect for local culture and maximum earnings for local grassroots, with an experience and learning dimension to it. Ecotourism emerged in the context of an international political agenda which followed the publication of the Brundtland Report (UN General Assembly, 1987) and the Rio Conference in 1992, with Agenda 21 as the central starting point. The International Ecotourism Society (TIES) was founded in 1990 in the US (The International Ecotourism Society, 2017).

In the following year, it made ecotourism a generic effort by delivering a number of guidelines and schemes for destinations to follow.

Ecotourism is marked by its historical origins in pristine natural areas where tourists can seek out the deserted, unmodernized and non-industrialized regions of the world. The original role of ecotourism in protecting natural areas from commercial exploitation lends purpose to its special focus on unpolluted experiences and learning, which thus legitimizes the maintenance of national parks as remote places of experience. However, the climate crisis has unfolded, and the unprecedented growth in tourism has put enormous pressure on the climate and the environment, not only in pristine areas, but in urban destinations as well (Lenzen et al., 2018). Thus, the sustainability and ecotourism agenda cannot be and is no longer reserved for remote natural habitats or exclusive niche tourism businesses. Accordingly, sustainable tourism today is an effort directed towards all kinds of tourism in all places, as illustrated in Figure 5.2, below. This sustainability orientation thus applies to all types of tourism and, combined with ecotourism in protected, rewilded or blue and green natural urban spaces, we find an option for a new niche: urban ecotourism. With an educational/interpretative perspective, this may accelerate ecological awareness among tourists who typically visit cities, and in the tourism sector more widely. It is a window of opportunity for using ecosystems such as urban parks and nature parks near urban areas to become ecotourism destinations. If cities follow the UN's 17 SDGs, the scope is made even more pervasive and comprehensive – particularly Goal 11, which supports efforts to develop sustainable cities and communities. The UNWTO places particular emphasis on SDG 8 – Decent work and economic growth, SGD 12 – Responsible consumption and production and SGD 14 – Life below water, and as a result sustainability comprises all environmental, economic and social aspects of the value chain in tourism productions (UNWTO, 2020a).

There are many obstacles for sustainable tourism in the developed world; however, this is also the case in Denmark, where there is no deep, green purchasing movement among tourists, no legal framework and no regulatory measures or government support schemes. The industry has to find its own solutions, as was the case with the Scandinavian Green Key labelling scheme for sustainable tourism companies, a few front-runners of destinations and guiding bureaus (Holm and Kaae, 2017). Reflecting on the failure over the last three decades to green the tourism industry (Holm and Kaae, 2017), we took a deliberate turn to undertake an R&D project to promote a more sustainable path for tourism by forming a niche arena of actors interested in transforming tourism. It provided an arena in which to undertake experiments on the development of sustainable urban ecotourism, with the aim of making it commercially successful and, eventually, enabling its transition into the larger tourist regime. Such a development path does not just start spontaneously: a multi-layered network of cooperation is required. By using transition theory as a springboard to study the process of change over longer time spans in tourism's socio-technical systems, we took a comprehensive approach to both the study and the practice of the transition process in tourism (Geels and Kemp, 2012). According to this school of thought, transition theory has a focus on market innovations conditioned by local entrepreneurs in networks with corporations, NGOs, government authorities and researchers. These transitions are analysed in the context of multi-level conditions and from a governance perspective. In such an analytical but also generically framed perspective, long-term and radical transitions of markets, product–service areas or trade relate to the dynamics between niches (small entrepreneurial experiments), regimes (the standard way things are done in the trade) and landscapes (the general economic and political conditions). In so-called 'innovation journeys', structural innovations are developed in niches which then need to be scaled up to the regime level to induce a regime shift (Geels and Schot, 2010). This may happen by itself, but more often regulatory or deliberative entrepreneurial efforts are called upon to succeed.

Figure 5.1 gives a dynamic model of structuration from niche to regime development (Geels, 2004). In this school of thought, *socio-technical regimes* dominate the practices, standards, rules, norms and shared assumptions that structure the behaviour of private and public actors. *Niches* are special (local) domains where 'non-standard' solutions, practices and technologies develop (Smith, 2003; Søndergaard et al., 2015).

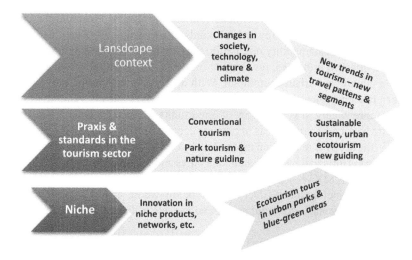

Figure 5.1   Transition theory according to Geels (2004)

Over a period of time, these niches develop accompanying implications as to how social processes shape development, use technology and in turn, open new possibilities for social practices and preferences linked to institutionally structured market incentives and consumer demands (Grin, 2010; Smith et al., 2005). Together, these systems influence the configuration, development and management of, for example, urban green infrastructure and services.

The development of socio-technical regimes is framed under the influence of their societal context, which is termed the *socio-technical landscape*. Thus, the combination of steadily, increasing over-tourism in European cities and climate–political goals have changed the political–economic landscape in Denmark to such a degree that the tourism macro-regime has been put under pressure. Some municipalities, tourism trades and parks have embarked on creating experiments and niche-supporting political initiatives for greening tourism and ecotourism, including in an urban context.

URBAN ECOTOURISM: DEFINITION AND REVIEW

Urban ecotourism is a rather new type of niche, at the intersection of nature-based tourism, sustainable urban tourism and classic ecotourism, but with a distinct urban twist.

   This is illustrated in Figure 5.2.

Urban Ecotourism Niche

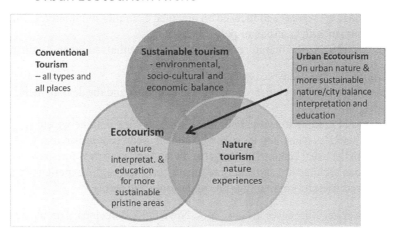

Figure 5.2   *Eco-, nature, common and sustainable tourism*

Urban ecotourism is a relatively new form of ecotourism that takes place in urban settings. The concept first appeared in 1996, when Toronto's Green Tourism Association hired the Blackstone Corporation for consultancy on their efforts to green urban tourism. The concept was defined as 'travel and exploration within and around an urban area that offers visitors enjoyment and appreciation of the city's natural areas and cultural resources, [...] promotes the city's long-term ecological health [...] promotes sustainable local economic and community development and vitality; [...] is accessible and equitable to all' (Gibson et al., 2003: 324). Urban ecotourism shares the same goals for sustainability and community development as traditional ecotourism, but applies them to large cities, industrial wastelands and post-productivist agricultural sites, as opposed to more nature-based venues for traditional ecotourism.

   Higham and Lück (2002) were the first to argue that urban settings may offer superior qualities largely unrecognizable when using ecotourism definitions. Urban ecotourism was originally said to contribute economically to the ecological restoration of previously industrialized areas, a reduction in transport compared to pristine ecotourism, enhanced eco-learning for newcomers and greater stability of the financial potential for tourism in cities (Gibson et al., 2003).

   For ecotourism ventures, a reimagining of the relation between nature and culture opens up new opportunities for tourism in and near cities. Ebbesen and Holm (2018) indicate a recent surge in academic attention on tourism in urban and peri-urban nature, which is accompanied outside of academia with growing interest from cities in sustainable tourism

(Hoang and Pulliat, 2019; Holden, 2015; Maćkiewicz and Konecka-Szydłowska, 2017). While some critics may consider urban ecotourism an oxymoron (Higham Lück, 2002), most of the recent literature posits a positive potential for mutual benefits to the urban environment, population and economy (see Che, 2006; Timur and Getz, 2009; Yanfeng, 2018). However, as an emerging field, urban ecotourism remains under-researched and examples of real-life implementation are relatively scarce. Much of the literature on urban ecotourism is concerned with greening the environmental impact of existing urban tourism rather than the implementation of novel nature-based urban tourism. In our review of ecotourism (Ebbesen and Holm, 2018), we excluded such areas and focused on practical examples of initiatives which combine nature-based tourism with an urban or peri-urban setting.

The cases described in the literature contain various potentials in urban destinations for:

- eco-learning on nature–city ecosystems services;
- ecotourism to encourage blue–green urban development and the development of healthier, safer cities;
- several ways of guiding to learn about local flora, cooking with herbs, etc.;
- broader outreach, as many city tourists who add an urban ecotourism tour to their itinerary will not be in the usual ecotourism 'target audience' and may therefore have more to learn;
- merging urban architecture and nature to create new meaningful experiences; and
- a focus on eco-friendly commuting (bikes), housing and eating.

Except for a few interesting cases in New York, Novo Said, Barcelona, Toronto and Trang An, the literature reveals no macro-niche development in this area, so we were to start almost from scratch, in developing urban ecotourism in Denmark (Ebbesen and Holm, 2018).

THE DANISH INUT R&D PROJECT: METHODOLOGY, STRATEGY AND OUTCOMES

As described in the introduction, the Innovation and Development of Urban Ecotourism (INUT) R&D project ran from 2017 to 2020 and aimed to create a niche form of urban ecotourism to realize the commercial potential of two adjacent cities and parks: Copenhagen city and the adjacent Amager Nature Park, and the city of Roskilde and the nearby Skjoldungernes Land National Park.

The project revolves around the 35 km^2 Amager Nature Park, bordering the capital of Copenhagen, and the 130 km^2 Skjoldungernes Land National Park, which includes parts of Roskilde city, as illustrated in Figure 5.3. Both parks were established in 2015. The project partners were Norrøn Architects, previously specialized in the experience economy, researchers from the University of Copenhagen and Roskilde University, the Tourist Guide Diploma Programme (TGDP) at Roskilde University, and their extensive tour guide/entrepreneur network.

The project builds on three distinct tiers, as illustrated in Figure 5.4, taking transition theory as its starting point on the strategic level, and applying process methodology informed by iterative participatory design (IPD) (Simonsen and Hertzom, 2010) of destinations and services, and the experience economy. Norrøn Architects led the first-tier destination development, which aimed to trace and develop local identities and narratives on top of the identified social, material and ecological resources, followed by concrete infrastructure proposals. The results

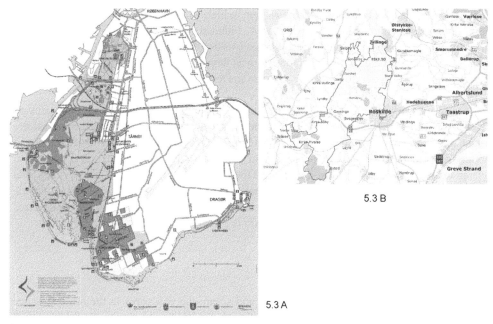

5.3 B

5.3 A

Source: Author.

Figures 5.3 A and B   *Amager Nature Park, Copenhagen and Skjoldungernes Land National Park, Roskilde*

Destination Development	Product development	A scalable model
Establish a common frame and definition of urban ecotourism	Educate urban ecotourist guides: students & entrepreneurs	Recollect, evaluate and reflect on process and results
Explore and develop the parks' narrative, identity and tourism infrastructure in co-operation with local actors and stakeholders	Guide entrepreneurs to develop, market and sell innovative urban ecotourism products as well as guided urban ecotours	A model for development of urban ecotourism
		A toolbox for development of urban ecotourism
	Educate the traveller	

Figure 5.4   *The three tiers of INUT: destination development, product development and a scalable model*

of tier 1 were to feed into tier 2, product development, which was led by the TGDP at Roskilde University. Within this programme, certified tour guide entrepreneurs, tour guide students and a host of stakeholders developed concrete urban ecotourism tours and experiences, tried and tested on the market during the project period. Researchers from the University of Copenhagen and Roskilde University headed the third tier, which provided the embedded conceptual definitions, design framework and evaluations. Induced by transition theory, an analytical–experimental platform of sustainable ecotourism was established and, building on the project's results, a scalable model of urban ecotourism was developed and presented in a blueprint on strategies and tools to develop urban ecotourism in Denmark, with parks close to urban centres as points of departure (Holm et al., 2020).

As described, we build on the part of transition theory that points to the transition pathway of developing innovative sustainable practices from niche formation, which successfully might trigger a regime development. Here we explore the notion of transition as it developed within the formation of a niche arena, not just in terms of products and social practices but also related to actors in the project that transcended their more narrowly defined roles as architects and tour guides to more holistic roles as destination developers, entrepreneurs and innovators. We will present the main results – and shortcomings – and explore how the niche stabilizes along an opening up of the predominant tourism regime towards a more sustainable path.

DESTINATION DEVELOPMENT

The Danish park system is relatively young, and so are the two parks in the project; hence there is no set tradition on how to precisely define their identity and purpose. Unlike national parks in, for example, the US, parks in Denmark may contain cities, villages, conventional farming and even small-scale industries amid the natural landscape, and it may even be difficult to know whether you are inside or outside the park. This is the case with Skjoldungernes Land National Park, which contains parts of Roskilde city close to Roskilde Fjord. Denmark consists mostly of cultural landscape and contains very little pristine nature. In Amager Nature Park, large parts of the area are reclaimed land previously used as either landfill or for military exercises. As such, both parks are in the process of establishing themselves and their main goals have been to address local and domestic needs rather than tourism, which is why the tourism infrastructure is weak.

Norrøn architects developed a model for destination development in the two parks. They worked in collaboration with the management of each park and sought information from park users by applying a P.GIS (Personal Geographical Information System) tool developed by the researchers for the specific task of combining information on visitors' preferences with regard to nature and place with geographical locations. From here, Norrøn took their DREAM method and moved on with interviews, literature, photos and in-depth studies to establish an overall unique narrative and identity in each of the parks to work as a strong brand and give direction to further development. For Amager Nature Park the identity marker became 'The manmade land', referring to the fact that a large part of the park is engineered and kept under control by a symmetric system of canals keeping it dry 1.5 metres below sea level. This narrated identity plays well against the newly established and futuristic neighbourhood of Ørestad that dramatically borders the park, thus highlighting the interrelation between man and nature.

The final step was to suggest physical infrastructure that advances the identity and supports urban ecotourism while adhering to the principles of environmental, social and economic sustainability. Norrøn Architects proposed an attraction, an overnight facility and a transport system in each park. While nature parks are often associated with pristine and natural beauty, Norrøn advocated that Amager Nature Park must cultivate its unique industrial manmade

Source: Norrøn (2018a).

Figure 5.5   *Rail biking in Amager Nature Park: a proposal from Norrøn Architects*

image and suggested the re-establishment of rails once used to transport soil from the reclamation, but now for rail biking in order to get to and from the remote areas of the park.

In Skjoldungernes Land National Park the narrated identity became 'A living legend', referring to the park as a historic seat of one of Denmark's strongest Viking communities close to Roskilde Fjord, with ample evidence of its glorious past. To follow that lead while still adhering to the principles of urban ecotourism, Norrøn Architects suggested a coastal protection for the Viking Ship Museum as a new attraction. The Viking Ship Museum is situated at the edge of Roskilde Fjord and is increasingly threatened by floods due to climate change, so Norrøn proposed a solution that would save the museum by building a circular coastal protection, illustrated in Figure 5.6, named 'the blue ring fortress'. This would protect the museum and the city behind from flooding due to climate change, but also give Roskilde a new multi-functional attraction with maritime activities and a spot for excursions by tourists as well as locals.

Source: Norrøn (2018b).

Figure 5.6   *The blue ring fortress: coastal protection of the Viking Ship Museum in Roskilde, by Norrøn Architects*

The proposals, narratives and physical infrastructure, such as a path and overnight facilities, were received positively by the park management and local stakeholders in Skjoldungernes Land National Park, and have now been incorporated into the national park's plan, where parts of the proposals are being realized. In Amager Nature Park, the proposals have been acknowledged as interesting, but neither the political nor the economic climate favour them.

The proposals are not just concrete suggestions; they are also a source of inspiration and aspiration for sustainable horizons which can be appropriated immediately by small-scale entrepreneurs, tour guides and local stakeholders in and around the two parks. In particular, the original and surprising slogan 'The manmade land' made sense to the actors involved in product development in INUT.

PRODUCT DEVELOPMENT

The next tier was to innovate concrete guided niche tourism experiences and products in and around the two parks. The TGDP orchestrated this part. The TGDP has trained certified diploma tour guides in Copenhagen since 1988 and has strong links with the Association of Authorised Tourist Guides and the tourism industry. Certified guides are independent professionals tailoring their own working life (Meged, 2017), and a small but growing number of guides develop their own niche and become entrepreneurs, registering for VAT (Meged, 2020). These guides may be identified as knowledge entrepreneurs (Meged, 2020) who are in a favourable position for innovation close to the market and consumers (Johannessen, 2019).

Twenty-one tour guide entrepreneurs, most of them certified guides, but also a few nature guides and artists, were handpicked. Together with them, 10 workshops were developed. The workshops alternated between lectures, excursions and actual product development sessions involving a host of other actors, such as students on the TGDP, Nature and Culture Interpreter Education (NACU) students at Copenhagen University, special interest groups, the municipality and, of course, the project partners Norrøn Architects and the researchers. Finally, social and lifestyle entrepreneurs inside and outside the parks were involved along with other actors from the tourism industry, such as attractions and the DMO WoCo. Altogether, more than 100 actors were mobilized in the formation of this transition arena experimenting with the niche of urban ecotourism.

The specific outcome of the 10 workshops was the design of 11 new guided urban eco-tours or experiences. The tours span the blue–green corridors and practices of the city within and outside of the parks, while entertaining the ideal of trans-modern tourism by educating the traveller. Gelter (2018) explains that trans-modern tourism goes beyond co-production, demanding a normative tourism that is transformative and with clear learning goals to protect the planet. Individual responsibility is the centrepiece, for tourists as well as guides, and the reason why the trans-modern guide must comprehend that all tourism experiences have learning elements, hence they must move from interpretation to transformation for sustainability. This is achieved by applying the principles of green pedagogics, relating to the 17 SDGs (Gelter, 2018). The trick is to put the tourists and their immediate interaction with the environment first without jeopardizing the enjoyable ethos of a holiday experience.

By the end of the project in February 2020, nine of the new urban eco-tours, with titles such as 'Meet my urban cow' and 'Green is the new black', were tested commercially on the market, most of them successfully. There has been a considerable spin-off from the 10

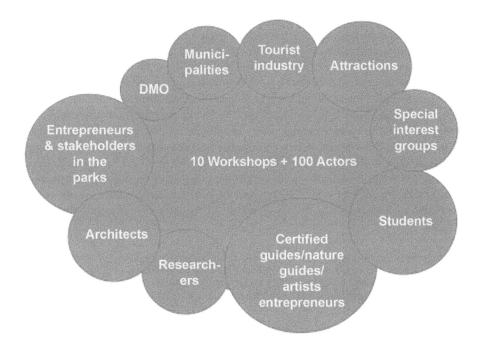

Figure 5.7   Transition arena for product development in urban ecotourism

workshops held in 2018. First, the principles of urban ecotourism have been implemented into the curriculum of the TGDP and all students now work with product development and sustainability, through new modules on entrepreneurship and innovation in tour design and experiences. Second, the network of tour and experience designers has migrated into other public/private projects such as INVIO (Innovation network for the experience economy) (INVIO, 2020). Both actions have resulted in the development of second and third generations of urban eco-tours and experiences.

Another important spin-off was tour guides' ability to adapt the principles of urban ecotourism to classic guided tours (Kaae, 2019), such as the standard three-hour city sightseeing tour, e.g., for cruise tourists. The guide entrepreneurs in the project also take on standard assignments to make ends meet (Meged, 2020), thereby entering the current tourism regime and meeting the expectations of the INUT project.

DISCUSSION: A SCALABLE MODEL

INUT is a supply-driven experimental project, and not all the experiments were tested or transferred into the tourism regime, which lies within the 'nature' of experimentation of niches in transition theory (Smith, 2003). However, to maximize the outcome for others who will work with the INUT model, we recommend a strong link and commitment from park management bodies and, even more importantly, from the political level and citizens, if the larger structural aspects of the projects are to be implemented. In our case, the management of Amager Nature Park turned out to be not truly concerned with tourism, while in Skjoldungernes Land National Park they at least saw tourism as a development strategy. Following the end of our R&D project, WoCo has, as mentioned in the introduction, taken up this area of concern in developing sustainable tourism in Copenhagen. In Skjoldungernes Land National Park it was the other way around; here the proposals from Norrøn Architects enjoyed the most success, but the park still struggles to attract international tourists, despite their fine attractions and excellent guides.

Each park and city follows its own trajectory, and while the tourism industry is in dire need of finding solutions to climate change, over- and under-tourism, profitability and so on, the parks are publicly run entities with very different agendas that may or may not align with the tourism industry. With the outbreak of COVID-19, we found an unexpected window of opportunity for urban ecotourism to enter into the established regimes of both tourism and the urban parks. Professor Burini (2020), from the hard-hit Bergamo, area explains that 'the pandemic affects both the social agency on tourists' sites and on the perception of landscape'. She argues:

> One important effect at the spatial level is the increasing importance of open public spaces or open-air activities, where it is easier to develop strategies to assure the fruition in safer conditions: public gardens and parks, public urban spaces like squares and pedestrian roads will be the new backdrop of future of cultural and artistic initiatives also for tourism. (2020: 85–86)

The need for urban recreational green space, not just to enjoy the nature but also to frame human encounters and activities, has exploded during the pandemic. From 15 March to 1 May 2020, the Danish Nature Agency registered an increase in visitors from 70% to 160% in Amager Nature Park, a trend seen in all nature areas around the big cities. In a survey, they found that one in four people had visited an area where they had never been before; the largest increase was found among the young generation, aged 18–35 years (Naturstyrelsen, 2020). 'The coronavirus crisis has opened the eyes of many to what outdoor life can do. This year, many of us will have summer holidays in a different way than we usually do, and the Danish nature areas have plenty to offer' (Naturstyrelsen, 2020, our translation).

The UNWTO estimated that international tourism dropped by 74% in 2020 and that domestic tourism picked up first (UNWTO, 2020b, 2021). This was also the case for Denmark (Jensen, 2020), but especially a growth in inland staycation in nature tourism changed the tourism patterns. This provided a unique opportunity to develop urban ecotourism products for a domestic market, with the possibility of customizing them for an international market later. The guide entrepreneurs were in fact very innovative in the spring and summer of 2020 and in 2021, offering an array of live virtual tours, walking tours with limited numbers of participants and bicycle rides to underexplored areas of greater Copenhagen. They have also collaborated with hotels in organizing short, themed city breaks for a domestic audience.

When looking into the crystal ball, tourism researchers predict that nature, safety and exclusive niche tourism are among the trends that will accelerate tourism now and post-COVID-19 (Milano, 2020; Novelli, 2020), but whether they will accelerate sustainable development on a grander scale remains to be seen, as it will take concerted efforts with a strong political impetus (Novelli, 2020). On 6 December 2019, Danish politicians passed a national Climate Act with a legally binding target to reduce greenhouse gas emissions by 70% by 2030 (State of Green, 2019), and time will show precisely how this will affect tourism policies. Meanwhile, we have ascertained that concrete initiatives have so far mainly been left to the market (Holm and Kaae, 2017), such as small-scale entrepreneurs, or to isolated initiatives such as the eco-labelling scheme the tourism industry, known as the Green Key, which has pushed sustainable tourism from below. The INUT project builds on these foundations, but we have also shown that it is possible to transcend and enter the tourism regime through small movements and, it now seems, established a group of actors ready for tomorrow's green politics.

The question of scaling the INUT model to other settings geographically lies very much in the willingness to let somewhat unusual actors – such as tour guides, architects and researchers – be drivers of development. In both the developed and developing world, SMEs make up a large central part of the tourism industry, and while small-scale tourism entrepreneurs are vulnerable, they are also flexible and able to customize and innovate in proximity with the tourists (Johannessen, 2019; Meged, 2020). Small-scale projects, along with a hopefully growing demand for sustainable tourism, make the INUT model transferable and adaptable to most parts of the world.

CONCLUSION

Novelli and Benson (2005) ask, in a headline of their book chapter, whether niche tourism is 'A way forward to sustainability?', and to this question, we may reply 'yes'. The Danish INUT project on innovation and development of urban ecotourism 2017–2020 has contributed to the field of niche tourism both in practice and academically. The INUT project has shown that it is possible to create an experimental niche and transition arena of urban ecotourism centred on guide entrepreneurs and architects, with the researchers and guide training as backdrop and sounding board. It is easy and quick to register the impact of the guide entrepreneurs, given that they were in charge of the product development for urban eco-tours, which they successfully took to market, and subsequently adapted their practices in the current tourism regime when organizing ordinary tours. The INUT ethos continues through a new curriculum at the TGDP at Roskilde University, adding sustainability, entrepreneurship and innovation to the traditional subjects. The impact of the architects has a longer timeframe, and more is lost in translation to political and economic realities; however, it is productive for niche formation to work with the visions and infrastructural imagination generated when architects transcend their professional borders and become destination developers.

Urban ecotourism is a small but emergent niche, which may have a promising future in entering the tourism regime as the climate crisis and COVID-19 demand new solutions. Transition theory offers the tools and insight on how to span the gap from niche to regime and may be applied to other areas of tourism at a time in which the socio-technical regime, and hence politicians, are not ready, ambitious or fast enough to act on the sustainability agenda.

REFERENCES

Baumgarten, H. (2018) København forudser fordobling i antallet af turister. *Standby Danmark.* 14 October. https://standb,by.dk/koebenhavn-forudser-fordobling-af-antal-turister (accessed 27 May 2019).

Burini, F. (2020) Spatial effects of a pandemic on tourism. Discovering territorial pathologies and resilience. In F. Burini (ed.) *Tourism facing a pandemic: From crisis to recovery.* Università degli studi di Bergamo: Bergamo, 79–98. DOI: 10.6092/978-88-97253-04-4

Che, D. (2006) Developing ecotourism in First World resource-dependent areas. *Geoforum*, 37(2), 212–26.

Dinis, A. and Krakover, S. (2016) Niche tourism in small peripheral towns: The case of Jewish Heritage in Belmonte, Portugal. *Tourism Planning and Development*, 13(3), 310–32. DOI: 10.1080/21568316.2015.1114014

Ebbesen, E. Ro and Holm J. (2018) *INUT literature review on the role of guiding in sustainable tourism and ecotourism*. Roskilde University.

Fennell, D.A. (2015) *Ecotourism*, 4th edition. Routledge.

Fredman, P. and Tyrväinen, L. (2010) Frontiers in nature-based tourism. *Scandinavian Journal of Hospitality and Tourism*, 10(3), 177–89. DOI: 10.1080/15022250.2010.502365

Geels, F. (2004) From sectoral systems of innovation to socio-technical systems. Insights about dynamics and change from sociology and institutional theory. *Research Policy*, 33(6–7), 897–920.

Geels, F.W. and Kemp, R. (2012) The multi-level perspective as a pew perspective for studying socio-technical transitions. In F.W. Geels, K. Rene, G. Dudley and G. Lyons (eds) *Automobility in transition: A socio-technical analysis of sustainable transports*. New York: Routledge, 49–65.

Geels, F.W. and Schot, J. (2010) The dynamics of transitions. A socio-technical perspective. In J. Grin, J. Rotmans and J. Schot (eds) *Transition to sustainable development. New directions in the study of long term transformative change*. New York/Oxon: Routledge, 11–104.

Gelter, H. (2018) *The transmodern guide – Beyond co-production and traditional sustainability*. Lecture. https://video.ruc.dk/media/t/0_bzas2rg4 (accessed 31 August 2020).

Gibson, A., Dodds, R., Joppe, M. and Jamieson, B. (2003) Ecotourism in the city. Toronto's Green Tourism Association. *International Journal of Contemporary Hospitality Management*, 15(6), 324–7.

Goodwin, H. (1996) In pursuit of ecotourism. *Biodiversity and Conservation*, 5, 277–91.

Grin, J. (2010) Understanding transition from a governance perspective. In J. Grin, J. Rotmans and J. Schot (eds) *Transition to sustainable development. New directions in the study of long term transformative change*. New York/Oxon: Routledge, 223–37.

Higham, J. and Lück, M. (2002) Urban ecotourism: A contradiction in terms? *Journal of Ecotourism*, 1(1), 36–51. DOI: 10.1080/14724040208668111

Hoang, T. and Pulliat, G. (2019) Green for whom? Exploring ecotourism as a climate-adaptation strategy in Trang An, Vietnam. In A. Daniere and M. Garschagen (eds) *Urban climate resilience in Southeast Asia*. Springer, Cham: The Urban Book Series. https://doi.org/10.1007/978-3-319-98968-6_9

Holden, A. (2015) Evolving perspectives on tourism interaction with nature during the last 40 years. *Tourism Recreation Research*, 40(2), 133–43.

Holm, J. and Kaae, B.C. (2017) *Definitionsramme for bæredygtig bynær økoturisme*. Roskilde: Roskilde University.

Holm, J., Kaae, B.C., Meged, J.W. and Caspersen, O.H. (2020) *Strategi og værktøj til udvikling af økoturisme i Danmark - med afsæt i bynære parker*. Aarhus: Innovationsfonden.

Hose, A. T. (2005) Geotourism. Appreciating the deep time of landscape. In M. Novelli (ed.) *Niche tourism: Contemporary issues, trends and cases*. Oxford: Routledge, 26–37.

Husted, P. (2019) Alt for mange turister: Lonely Planet advarer mod at besøge København. *Politiken*, 10 September. https://politiken.dk/rejser/art7378392/Lonely-Planet-advarer-mod-at-bes%C3%B8ge-K%C3%B8benhavn (accessed 5 August 2020).

INVIO (2020) Innovationsnetværk for oplevelseserhverv. Aalborg University. https://invio-net.dk/da/indlaeg/netvaerk-tur-og-oplevelsesdesignere (accessed 26 August 2020).

Jensen, S. (2020) *Turismens udfordringer og muligheder i og efter coronakrisen*. INVIO Webinar. 6 June 2020. https://invio-net.dk/da/event/webinar-turismens-udfordringer-og-muligheder-i-og-efter-corona-krisen (accessed 31 August 2020).

Johannessen, J.-A. (2019) *The workplace of the future. The Fourth Industrial Revolution, the precariat, and the death of hierarchies*. London and New York: Routledge.

Kaae, B.C. (2019) *Evaluering af INUT-projektets guideaktiviteter år 2 (2019)*, Report. Aarhus: Innovationsfonden.

Lenzen, M., et al. (2018) The carbon footprint of global tourism. *Nature Climate Change*, 8, 522–8. https://doi.org/10.1038/s41558-018-0141-x (accessed 17 November 2021).

Maćkiewicz, B. and Konecka-Szydłowska, B. (2017) Green tourism: Attractions and initiatives of Polish *Cittaslow* cities. In N. Bellini and C. Pasquinelli (eds) *Tourism in the city*. Springer, Cham, 287–311. doi.org/10.1007/978-3-319-26877-4_21

Meged, J.W. (2017) Guides crafting meaning in a flexible working life. *Scandinavian Journal of Hospitality and Tourism*, 17(4), 374–87.

Meged, J.W. (2020) Guides on a crossroad between deregulation and entrepreneurship. In A. Walmsley et al. (eds) *Tourism employment in Nordic countries*. Palgrave Macmillan, 19–35. https://doi.org/10 .1007/978-3-030-47813-1

Milano, C. (2020) From overtourism to a COVID-19 immobile world. Webinar 24 April 2020. *OTS Webinar series: After the virus*. http://www.ontourism.online/index.php/jots/webinars (accessed 6 August 2020).

Naturstyrelsen (2020) *Vi bruger naturen mere under coronakrisen*. https://naturstyrelsen.dk/nyheder/ 2020/maj/vi-bruger-naturen-mere-under-coronakrisen/ (accessed 10 July 2020).

Norrøn (2018a) *Naturpark amager – Det menneskeskabte land: Identitetsudvikling af naturpark amager.* Innovationsfonden, Aarhus. https://typo3.ruc.dk/fileadmin/assets/forskning/forskningsprojekter/ INUT/Identitetsudvikling_Naturpark_Amager_Norr%C3%B8n.pdf

Norrøn (2018b) *Nationalpark skjoldungernes land – Et sagn i liveidentitetsudvikling af nationalpark skjoldungernes land.* Innovationsfonden, Aarhus. https://typo3.ruc.dk/fileadmin/assets/forskning/ forskningsprojekter/INUT/Identitetsudvik-ling_Nationalpark_Skjoldungernes_Land_Norr%C3 %B8n.pdf

Novelli, M. (2020) Overtourism and Covid-19 induced tourism crisis in Africa. Webinar 24 April 2020. *OTS Webinar series: After the virus*. http://www.ontourism.online/index.php/jots/webinars (accessed 6 August 2020).

Novelli, M. and Benson, A. (2005) Niche tourism? A way forward to sustainability. In M. Novelli (ed.) *Niche tourism: Contemporary issues, trends and cases*. Oxford: Routledge, 246–50.

Novelli, M. and Humavindu, M.N. (2005) Wildlife tourism – Wildlife vs trophy hunting Namibia. In M. Novelli (ed.) *Niche tourism: Contemporary issues, trends and cases*. Oxford: Routledge, 171–81.

Peeters, P. et al. (2018) *Research for TRAN Committee – Overtourism: Impact and possible policy responses*. European Parliament, Policy Department for Structural and Cohesion Policies, Brussels.

Robinson, M. and Novelli, M. (2005) Niche tourism: An introduction. In M. Novelli (ed.) *Niche tourism: Contemporary issues, trends and cases*. Oxford: Routledge, 3–11.

Shepard, G. and Evans, S. (2005) Adventure tourism. Hard decisions, soft options and home for tea: Adventure on the hoof. In M. Novelli (ed.) *Niche tourism: Contemporary issues, trends and cases*. Oxford: Routledge, 201–9.

Simonsen, J. and Hertzom, M. (2010) Iterative participatory design. In J. Simonsen et al. (eds) *Design research: Synergies from interdisciplinary perspectives*. London: Routledge.

Smith, A. (2003) Transforming technological regimes for sustainable development: A role for alternative technology niches? *Science and Public Policy*, 30(2), 127–35.

Smith, A., Stirling, A. and Berkhout, F. (2005) The governance of sustainable socio-technical transitions. *Research Policy*, 34, 1491–510.

State of Green, (2019) *During COP25, Denmark passes Climate Act with a 70 per cent reduction target*. State of Green, 9 December 2019. https://stateofgreen.com/en/partners/state-of-green/news/during -cop25-denmark-passes-climate-act-with-a-70-per-cent-reduction-target/

Søndergaard, B, Holm, J. and Stauning, I. (2015) Transition theory – sustainable transition of socio-technical systems. In J. Holm, J. et al. (eds) *Sustainable transition of housing and construction*. Frederiksberg: Frydenlund Academic, 37–68.

Teknik- og Miljøforvaltningen (2015) *Bynatur I København – Strategi 2015–2025*. Københavns Kommune.

The International Ecotourism Society (TIES) (2017). *What is eco-tourism?* http://www.ecotourism.org/ what-is-ecotourism (accessed 31 August 2020).

Timur, S. and Getz, D. (2009) Sustainable tourism development: How do destination stakeholders perceive sustainable urban tourism? *Sustainable Development*, 17(4), 220–32.

UN General Assembly (1987) Development and international economic co-operation: Environment Report of the World Commission on Environment and Development. A_42_427-EN.pdf (accessed 17 November 2021).

UNWTO (2020a) *Sustainable eevelopment.* https://www.unwto.org/sustainable-development (accessed 10 June 2020).

UNWTO (2020b). *UNWTO world tourism barometer May 2020. Special focus on the impact of COVID-19.* https://www.e-unwto.org/doi/pdf/10.18111/9789284421930 (accessed 10 July 2020).

UNWTO (2021) *Covid-19 and tourism.* https://www.unwto.org/covid-19-and-tourism-2020.

VisitDenmark (2018) *Destinationsmonitor Januar–december 2018, Status.* https://www.visitdenmark .dk/api/drupal/sites/visitdenmark.com/files/2019-04/Destinationsmonitor%20status%202018.pdf (accessed 15 April 2019).

Weeden, (2005) Ethical tourism: Is its future in niche tourism? In M. Novelli (ed.) *Niche tourism: Contemporary issues, trends and cases.* Oxford: Routledge, 233–45.

WoCo (2019) *Tourism for good. An invitation to a journey towards sustainable tourism by 2030.* https:// api.www.wonderfulcopenhagen.com/sites/wonderfulcopenhagen.com/files/2019-09/tourismforgood .pdf (accessed 1 June 2020).

Yanfeng, Yang (2018) Urban ecotourism: A powerful way to resolve the disputes on traditional ecotourism theory. BT – 4th International Conference on Economics, Management, Law and Education (EMLE 2018), *Advances in economics, business and management research*, 1, Atlantis Press https:// doi.org/10.2991/emle-18.2018.113 (accessed 31 August 2020).

6. In focus 1 – geocaching tourism in Poland

Joanna Kosmaczewska

Geocaching is an outdoor game where players seek special caches based on descriptions and geographic coordinates. Upon finding a cache, the player makes an entry in the paper log located in it and posts the corresponding information on a dedicated webpage. As this activity makes people move around, it could be a form of leisure for local residents and contain potential for niche tourism development.

To analyse motives and behaviour of Polish geocaching players (GPs), a questionnaire-based survey was carried out through Google's platform. The survey link was shared with Geopyra, a closed Facebook group of GPs from Greater Poland, and through the Geocaching Polska Facebook page. The survey (n = 389) included a personal data section (gender, age, working situation, education level, income) and 26 motivation items (push and pull factors) measured on a five-point Likert rating scale. Other questions were also asked to determine whether the territorial scope of this game defines it as recreational or tourist activity. Push and pull factors were adapted from Schneider et al. (2011) and Falcão et al. (2015). The Principal Component Analysis (PCA), based on a varimax rotation, was used to reduce a group of 26 geocaching motivation factors.

The majority of respondents (63.8%) were male, which is consistent with Falcão et al.'s results (2015); 81.2% had been engaging in geocaching activities for more than two years. A major proportion (42.4%) were aged 31–43, unlike in Falcão et al.'s surveyed group (2015), where the most populous group was younger (aged 18–30). The respondents usually had higher (61.7%) or secondary education (32.4%) and assessed their financial situation as good (47.8%) or very good (32.1%). Half of the respondents (50.4%) learned about geocaching from their friends, 21.3% declared that they encouraged others to such activity and 11% shared their opinions about caches on the Internet (e-WOM effect). It was also found that geocaching determines, to some extent, the choice of a tourist destination, as 62% declared they spent the night away from home at least once a year just to play. Furthermore, 19.2% of respondents played that game during each tourist trip. According to 55.9%, 20–40% of geocaching expeditions were carried out outside their home, with booked accommodation. Only 8.9% declared that 100% of their geocaching expeditions took place in the vicinity of their residence. The survey showed that in the initial stage geocaching was treated by participants as recreation, and after about a year they started to take up expeditions further and further, booking accommodation and travel (Figure 6.1).

Major motivations observed include 'to experience new and different things' (M = 4.54; SD = 0.70), 'to get exercise' (M = 4.50; SD = 0.78) and 'to relax physically' (M = 4.50; SD = 0.82). PCA analysis enabled the reduction of 26 items in 5 dimensions: Sociability & Self-expression (explained variation = 35.3%; Cronbach's α = 0.88); Desire of Nature (explained variation = 11.0%; Cronbach's α = 0.87); Solitude Seeking (explained variation = 8.4%; Cronbach's α = 0.85); Challenge (explained variation = 5.2%; Cronbach's α = 0.78); and Routine-breaker (explained variation = 5.0%; Cronbach's α = 0.74).

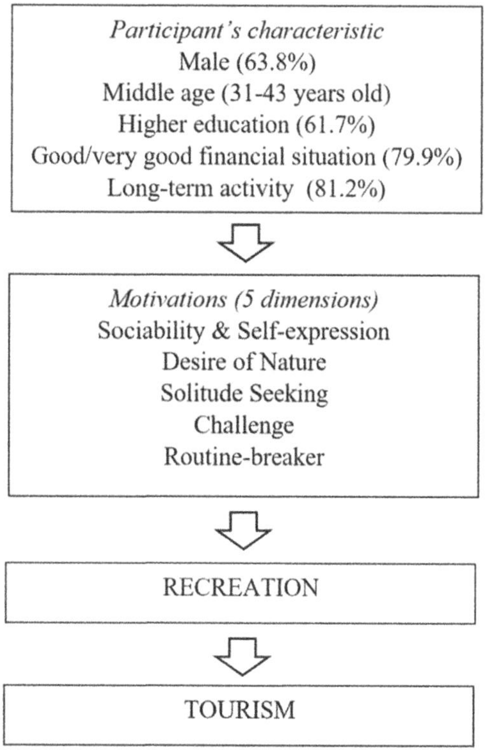

```
┌─────────────────────────────────────┐
│     Participant's characteristic     │
│           Male (63.8%)               │
│    Middle age (31-43 years old)      │
│      Higher education (61.7%)        │
│ Good/very good financial situation (79.9%) │
│     Long-term activity  (81.2%)      │
└─────────────────────────────────────┘
                  ⇩
┌─────────────────────────────────────┐
│      Motivations (5 dimensions)      │
│     Sociability & Self-expression    │
│           Desire of Nature           │
│          Solitude Seeking            │
│             Challenge                │
│          Routine-breaker             │
└─────────────────────────────────────┘
                  ⇩
┌─────────────────────────────────────┐
│             RECREATION               │
└─────────────────────────────────────┘
                  ⇩
┌─────────────────────────────────────┐
│              TOURISM                 │
└─────────────────────────────────────┘
```

Figure 6.1   Research framework

Geocaching, due to the small size of the phenomenon itself and participants' motivations, can be considered in a micro-niche context (Novelli, 2005). It provides opportunities for experiential travel (such as volunteer tourism), where motivations could be defined in four dimensions (physical, mental, social, spiritual) as proposed by Frankl's *Man's Search for Ultimate Meaning* (1997). Moreover, recreational or tourist activities undertaken as part of geocaching fulfil assumptions of the 'sustainability trinity – economy, culture and environment' (Farrell, 1999, p. 189). In the economic context, geocaching, owing to its low participation cost, does not exclude less well-off social groups. Moreover, given the fact that caches are often hidden outside city centres (in parks, forests, etc.), they generate tourist traffic from the city to outside. Even if they are hidden in the city centre, their search is not of a mass character – they are hidden in unusual places, usually far from main tourist attractions, which also increases the level of safety during the journey in times such as the recent COVID-19 pandemic. A strong social engagement can be also noted – the vast majority of participants not only find caches, but also create them, share their opinions and tips on social media, and encourage others to engage in such activity (prosumers). In geocaching, due to the different types of caches and their location in the field, references to the cultural heritage of the region are also quite frequent. Respect for the natural environment is also particularly important, as is reflected in

'Cache In Trash Out' events which consist mainly of cleaning up litter, combating invasive plant species and planting flora.

REFERENCES

Falcão, A.L., Damásio, A.S. and Melo, R. (2015) Motivations for participating in geocaching activities in Portugal. *Sport Tourism Conference 2014 – STC'14, Proceeding E-book*, 176–184.

Farrell, B.H. (1999) Conventional or sustainable tourism? No room for choice. *Tourism Management*, 20(2), 189–191.

Frankl, V.E. (1997) *Man's search for ultimate meaning*. New York: Perseus Book Publishing.

Novelli, M. (ed.) (2005) *Niche tourism: Contemporary issues, trends and cases*. UK: Routledge.

Schneider, I.E., Silverberg, K.E. and Chavez, D. (2011) Geocachers: Benefits sought and environmental attitudes. *LARNet, The Cyber Journal of Applied Leisure and Recreation Research*, 14(1), 1–11.

PART II

RURAL TOURISM

7. Experiential tea tourism in Asia

Lee Jolliffe

1. INTRODUCTION

Tea, the most widely consumed beverage in the world after water, has a long and rich production heritage in global locations where the growing conditions are suitable. Tea-related tourism exists on a global basis, including all experiences related to tea (Jolliffe, 2007). Within the larger scope of tea-related tea tourism at both producing and consuming locales, this chapter examines the micro-niche of experiential tea tourism at producing locations. In rural areas where tea is produced in Asia, such tourism is also related to or forms part of other types of tourism including ecotourism, culinary, food and beverage, nature and cultural heritage tourism.

The rural locations where tea (*camellia sinensis*) is grown, with their tourism resources of tea traditions, landscapes, gardens, production facilities and small-scale lodging, provide the setting for visitors to have small-scale sensory experiences. These areas appeal in particular to domestic tourists who value the tea landscapes and beverage traditions, as well as to international tourists interested in learning about tea and experiencing it where it is grown and processed.

Tourism in tea-growing areas is relevant to local communities in augmenting income from tea production and thus potentially reducing poverty while improving livelihoods. The role of tea tourism in achieving the UN's Sustainable Development Goals (SDGs) is relevant to the aims of ending poverty and improving the planet by 2030, in particular by achieving sustainable development.

In producing areas tea tourism is a micro-form of niche tourism only possible for small groups, in part due to remote geographic locations and limitations in available lodging facilities and the carrying capacity of tea fields, factories, tasting rooms and other rural tea production facilities. Tea-related tourism here provides a sensory form of experiential tourism while spreading knowledge about the tea to buyers and consumers and developing new markets.

Growing tea is not without its challenges and producers face a mix of social, political, economic, social and environmental threats. At rural locations where tea is grown, these threats can limit market access or even prevent the tea from being harvested and are challenging for the development of experiential tea tourism as a micro-niche. For example, COVID-19 restrictions in early 2000, including lockdowns, led to production losses; reduction of the workforce; disappearance of buyers, domestic and international tourists; and restrictions on tea delivery to domestic and overseas markets.

This chapter contributes to the niche tourism literature on experiential tourism in the realm of beverage-related tourism, more specifically within the micro-niche of tea tourism. By examining the nature of the tea tourism experience from the visitor perspective it provides new insights into the niche.

2.   LITERATURE REVIEW

Experiential Niche Tourism

As contemporary tourists desire to experience local cultures, niche forms of tourism have emerged to fulfil visitor demand. This meets the experience economy needs and desires of consumers whereby visitors value experience and authenticity (Gilmore and Pine, 2007). It is suggested that an experience begins as an event, where a tourist experiences an attraction within a particular context or situation, which upon reflection creates a memory and new meaning for the visitor (Pine and Gilmore, 1999). This includes the tourist moment in which a serendipitous experience results in a rewarding and insightful situation for the participant (Cary, 2004). The visitor experience is thus created by tourist interaction with the physical setting and activities and their mental process transforming the occurrence into memories, resulting in a memorable tourism experience (Horváth, 2013).

Niche tourism, as opposed to mass tourism, caters to smaller specialized interests with highly specific offers (Marson, 2011). Visitor experiences are key to the development of niche tourism (Novelli, 2005), offering a more meaningful set of experiences than traditional mass tourism. According to Robinson and Novelli (2005) within niche tourism a variety of micro-niches evolve from the most appealing and vibrant characteristics of the niche, destination locations and the specific interests of tourists. Niche tourism is thought to exist as a product in its own right and also as a supplementary feature to modern mass tourism (Marson, 2011).

Tea Tourism

Tea tourism has been defined as being motivated by an interest in the history, traditions and consumption of tea (Jolliffe, 2007). Tea-related tourism inc.ludes visits to tea museums, exhibits and festivals at consuming locations, and moreover where tea is grown it encompasses visits to tea landscapes, gardens, plantations and factories (Jolliffe and Aslam, 2009). It has become evident that there are a range of motivations and experiences for tea-related tourism in terms of the intent of tourists and the scale of the tourism.

Such tourism in tea regions has been noted as a niche or specialized form of heritage tourism with experiential value (Koththagoda and Dissanayake, 2017). Some niche tea-related tourism products can meet the five standards suggested for experiential tourism (Smith, 2005). These include people creating meaning through direct experience; the experience including the people met, the places visited, the activities participated in and the memories created; and the experience including pre-departure trip planning and post-trip follow-up. In addition, experiential tourism should draw people into local nature, culture and history; and it should be low impact, low volume and high yield.

Tea destination experiences may also fulfil the criteria for creating sensory tourism, whereby the tourist is employing a range of senses during their experience. Countryside destinations, for example tea landscapes, are acknowledged to be full of multisensory aspects that can be employed for experience development (Agapito et al., 2014). Within rural forms of tourism, it is acknowledged that sensory analysis can assist in enhancing tourism product development (Santini et al., 2011).

While few researchers have directly examined experiential tea tourism, Huang and Hall (2007) examined a tea appreciation festival in Hunan Province, China, from the marketing and economic social development perspectives as a model for contributing to gastronomically related tourism in a rural tea-producing area. Cheng et al. (2012) surveyed views regarding the development, management and marketing of tea tourism in Xinyang, a tea-growing area in Central China, finding tea-related tourism here needed better planning, marketing and development through increased stakeholder collaboration and local population involvement.

Studies of tea tourism in Sri Lanka acknowledged potential for developing such tourism through community collaboration (Fernando et al., 2017) and for using production areas as a tool for destination development (Jolliffe and Aslam, 2009). Tea tourism in Sri Lanka has been noted as experiential tourism (Koththagoda and Dissanayake, 2017). In some cases, the low demand for niche tea tourism here is attributed to a lack of relevant activities and marketing.

A study in China identified the potential for tea tourism to benefit tea farmers and tea merchants (Chee-Beng and Yuling, 2010). A leisure agriculture study (Huang et al., 2014) applied the ASEB (Activities, Settings, Experiences and Benefits) grid analysis (Beeho and Prentice, 1997) to the tea gardens of Lonjing, China as a tourism attraction. The authors noted innovation and packaging of tea-related activities was needed for visitor access, as well as preservation of the natural tea landscapes and production areas (Huang et al., 2014).

Tea tourism could thus be considered to be a form of experiential tourism as it involves experiencing and consuming the beverage and coming into contact with its culture. Every tea consumed tells a story of its history and traditions, origins and production. Tea-related tourism in producing contexts is also closely connected to local tea communities and landscapes.

Tea Tourism and Sustainable Development

Producing regions of Asia with their tea communities and landscapes, small tea farms, homestays and tea shops are potential locations where tea-related tourism as a micro-niche form of tourism could be employed for sustainable development. It is acknowledged that tourism has the potential to contribute directly or indirectly to attaining the UN's SDGs, although there is often a gap between theoretical demands and achievements (Ceron and Dubois, 2003). In particular, tourism relates to Goals 5, 8 and 12, corresponding to gender equality, decent work and economic growth, and responsible consumption and production. Key to the development of tea tourism as a micro-niche is the sustainable management and preservation of the resource, achieving a balance between economic development and environmental conservation.

In terms of gender equality in areas such as Darjeeling where women work picking tea, projects such as homestays in tea gardens can help to improve gender equality (Besky, 2014). Relating to decent work and economic growth, tourism can be employed in sustainable livelihood strategies linked to rural poverty reduction (Tao and Wall, 2009). In Nepal the tea value chain is predominately made up of small-holders, although it is acknowledged that such tourism-related endeavours do not always result in increased income, poverty reduction, enhanced livelihoods and the encouragement of gender equality (Mohan, 2016).

Relevant to responsible consumption and production, small-scale niche tea tourism has the potential to play a key role in responsible tourism efforts within tea communities, through diversification positively improving the livelihoods of tea workers and their families. In China it has been observed that through innovative programming for leisure in the tea garden setting, farmers' employment and forms of agriculture in the countryside might be improved (Huang et al., 2014). Such micro-niche tourism is of particular relevance where tea farms and gardens may diversify their operations through tourism (Cheng et al., 2010). In Japan tourism in a rural tea village with a declining population is contributing to rejuvenating the local community (Jolliffe and Nakashima, 2020). In Thailand a case study established that small-scale tea tourism could be used to diversify and reinvent an existing community-based tourism product, making the impact of the meetings and events market more connected to and beneficial to local communities (Jolliffe and Piboonrungroj, 2020). In India rural tea tourism is also acknowledged to have a role in gastronomic experiences (Dixit, 2020). Despite research from the niche tourism supply perspective, little research has been accomplished on tea tourism experiences from the perspective of the participant, a gap in the literature addressed in this chapter.

3.   METHODOLOGY AND SETTING

The study locations for researching experiential tea tourism were a convenient choice, as the author was able to participate in the World Tea Tours (WTT) Intensive Darjeeling Tour in 2018 (Case 1) and the Japanese Tea Master Course in 2019 (Case 2). These locales provide a form of experiential tea tourism with connections to the livelihoods of local communities. A study limitation was that the tour/course participants were not surveyed. This allowed the author to undertake observations while embedded within the milieu of the tourist experience being gained by the participants.

The main research method for this study was participant observation, grounded in the experiential tourism literature. The case study method in tourism research (Beeton, 2005) was adopted as a means of organizing observations at the research locations. Within the cases, the ASEB analysis categories developed for the assessment of experiences and benefits gained by visitors to tourist attractions were used (Beeho and Prentice, 1996). This method assumes elements of experiential consumption combined with the settings are facilitated by interpretive or educational provision, so each visitor with their individual agenda develops their own experience. The criteria for experiential tourism were added into the evaluation (Smith, 2005). This adds elements of pre-trip planning and preparation into the experience evaluation.

Tea-related tourism is applicable to tea-producing destinations in which tea farms and gardens diversify offerings through tourism, while educating visitors about their tea, and thus potentially positively impacting local livelihoods. This is the context for case studies of offerings in the tea production areas of Darjeeling (India) and Kyoto/Uji (Japan). Both areas have long traditions of producing high-quality teas, while their rich tea culture and landscapes are a resource for tourism.

4.   FINDINGS

Case 1: World Tea Tour – Darjeeling Immersion, India

The seven-day Darjeeling Immersion Tour/Workshop is organized periodically by the US-based WTT. This tour is led by Dan Robertson, an experienced tea broker/taster, assisted locally by Rajev Lochan of Lochan Tea, who has been a tea planter and merchant in West Bengal for many years. Darjeeling is a partially autonomous district of the Indian state of West Bengal, located in the foothills of the Lesser Himalayas bordering Nepal, Bhutan and Sikkim. It is known for its views of Kangchenjunga, the world's third highest mountain, and the Darjeeling Himalayan Railway UNESCO World Heritage Site. Tourism and the tea industry are significant contributors to the Darjeeling economy. Some tea estates communities in Darjeeling have added tourism accommodation and tea-associated activities. Darjeeling tea, known as the 'champagne of teas', ranks globally amongst the most popular of black teas.

Activities

The WTT focused on Darjeeling tea, produced in 87 recognized tea gardens and a number of small-holdings. Participants observed the unique agro-climatic conditions in Darjeeling that result in the tea having a distinctive natural flavour recognized by a geographical indicator (GI) (Das, 2006). While there are four seasons of tea, the first flush (spring), the second flush (early summer), the monsoon flush in the (rainy season) and autumnal teas (fall), the tour/ workshop took place during the production of the second flush (2018).

The Glenburn Tea Estate, where participants stayed on site for five nights, dates back to the British Colonial era. Since the road to Glenburn is difficult, drivers pick up guests and bring them to Glenburn from Bagdogra Airport. Visitors to Glenburn are known to appreciate the peaceful rural setting and tea landscape. At the estate experiences took place within the tea gardens (fields), tea nursery, tea factory and main planter's bungalow, with participants interacting directly with the estate managers and innkeepers while at a distance from the host community.

Tour participants were involved (in some cases actively, in others observing) in all aspects of the tea production, from picking and weighing the leaves, through the various subsequent processes as they were transferred to the withering trough, then to the rolling machines, then oxidized, then transferred to the oven, before sorting the final leaf into different sizes and grades (Figures 7.1 and 7.2). There was opportunity to taste Darjeeling teas, in the tasting room of the tea factory and in hospitality settings on site.

Settings

This privately owned tea estate operates as a community, housing workers and providing medical facilities and schooling. Workers are paid for the tasks associated with tea production, receiving housing and rations of food and supplies. The tea industry here faces competition from other areas of India and from neighbouring Nepal. It has been affected by absenteeism of workers on tea estates, worker demands for higher wages and the 2017 Gorkhaland movement workers' strike (seeking an independent Gorkha state) that closed the tea gardens for the season. Glenburn is one of the Darjeeling estates that has diversified into tourism, offering guests accommodation, meals, tea-related tours (of the gardens and factory) and nature activities (nature tours, hiking and camping).

A range of meals featured fresh produce and tea produced on the estate. Meals were provided in the dining room of the original manager's bungalow and adjacent to a newly constructed building that mirrors the style of the original tea planter's bungalow. Food menus used local estate produce prepared by the chef/innkeeper. Meal traditions were adapted to reflect both colonial (Western) and local (Indian) tastes; bed tea (tea brought by a servant at an early

*Figure 7.1   World Tea Tour – Darjeeling Immersion – view of the tea garden during
          field visit at the Glenburn Estate*

hour) is a typical colonial-era service (Skinner, 2019). Guests were seated together for dinner
to encourage dialogue.

Benefits

The small group of four participants and the tour leader (May 2018) were accompanied for
on-site tastings and tours by the estate manager (who had long been employed in the industry)
and at times by one of the owners, with a high level of interaction in terms of asking questions,
observing and discussing. The tasting rooms had attendants who helped to prepare the tea, so
at some points the ratio of instructors to participants was one-to-one.

Participants observed life on the tea estate, such as the ringing of the bell for the start and
end of the work day for the tea and factory workers, and being with the tea pickers adjacent to
the fields as they ate their lunch (carried in the bottom of their tea baskets) while their picked
tea leaves were being weighed. Being present during the season of tea production (second
flush), and being so close to the process, provided a sense of authenticity even though as
participants we were guests.

Experiences

Participants experienced the full range of activities available to guests, including tea garden
and tea factory tours, visits to the local school, hiking and picnicking in the tea gardens.

Figure 7.2   *World Tea Tour – Darjeeling Immersion – silver needle (one bud, one leaf)*
at the Glenburn Estate tea fields, picked by the author

A small shop sold Glenburn teas and a range of tea-related textiles unique to the site, allowing for on-site souvenir shopping.

Other guests staying during the visit period participated in brief tea-related activities, such as a short tour and factory tasting and taking both bed and afternoon tea versus the more intensive and tea-focused activities of the tour group. Most guests were there for leisure, as observed during dinner conversations. Reviewing the guest book for an annual period revealed few dedicated tea tourists, with only a few international tea buyers reporting visiting specifically for the tea.

Standards
The tour included detailed pre-departure trip information provided to the participants, encompassing travel advice and logistical information on what to expect on arrival. Post-trip follow-up was informal, through Facebook postings and comments. In terms of standards, the tour met the requirements for creating a meaningful and memorable experience (Smith, 2005), drawing participants into the local nature, culture and history. The small group size guaranteed that the tour as a form of experiential tourism was low impact, and the price paid by each participant of USD3,995 (inclusive of accommodation, meals and local transport) ensured that it was a high-yield product. As some of the tour participants were also buyers, there was an

added economic impact to the local tea industry that could continue over time. Glenburn also has a programme whereby participants can sponsor one of the children from the estate school.

The tea experience concluded with an examination in written form and a blind tasting of teas for the identification of cultivars, flush and garden. This was a validation for the participants of the knowledge gained and was followed by the presentation of a certificate of participation on the last evening.

Case 2: Japanese Tea Master Course, Japan

This two-week course was implemented by the Global Japanese Tea Association, partnering with Kyoto Obobu Tea Farms. Held in the tea-producing community of Wazuka in Kyoto Prefecture's Uji tea region, it was supported by local stakeholders including the town of Wazuka and local tea farmers and business operators. This is Japan's oldest tea-growing area, portrayed by Kyoto Tourism as the cradle of Japanese tea. Wazuka was designated as 'one of the most beautiful villages of Japan' under a programme founded in 2005 to identify villages that wanted to protect their natural and social capital as intangible resources. The total area of the village is under 65 km². With a declining population (less than 4,000) and just over 300 families, tea tourism has been introduced as a means to encourage appreciation of Japanese tea and to diversify production, with offerings including interpretive signs, a festival, internships, tours and courses.

Activities
During the research period (September 2019) there were 12 participants from nine countries.

The Japanese Tea Master Course included 31 sessions held over 10 days (two five-day sessions with a two-day break in between) focusing on a range of topics including the history of tea, brewing Japanese tea, the tea business, tea packaging, tea science and rare teas. Sessions held in a classroom setting were complemented by tastings of different kinds of tea. Unique field trips were held to the local tea auction and tea research institute, as well as to the fields and factories of a number of tea farmers in the region.

Settings
The base for the course was the municipally owned Wazuka-cho Guest House and adjacent community centre. The guest house, set in the community adjacent to tea fields, was initially built to host school groups and later renovated to receive guests and to have a focus on tea. For example, the cuisine is tea themed, local teas and related merchandise are sold in the lobby for purchase as souvenirs, and the *onsen* (public bath) at the facility is scented with tea.

The course was integrated with businesses in this tea farming community. Catering for the tea-themed meals was from a number of different community sources (Figure 7.3). Over the duration of the course a number of cafes, tea farms and factories, and several tea ceremony instructors were visited, distributing the economic benefits of the course throughout the community. For example, the Wazukcha Café provides information and sold local teas, tea-related food, tea-ware and tea-dyed products as souvenirs, as well as providing bicycle rentals and so on. D-Matcha Café has a focus on *matcha* (green tea) and Wazuka's green tea history, and is situated with a view of the rice and tea fields of the village. Kyoto Obobu Tea Farms (Obobu), a key participating entity, is a social enterprise, aiming to bring Japanese tea to the world.

Figure 7.3   *Japanese Tea Master Course – menu from bento box tea-themed lunch*

Experiences

Many of the participants worked or had worked in the tea industry at their locations, so in an interactive learning situation it was possible to learn from each other. Local instructors (from the tea industry and related associations) were patient with the participants, providing ample opportunity for questions and discussion. Every lecture was accompanied with tastings of various Japanese teas, explained and referred to in the lectures. As special tasting was held of rare teas from various regions of Japan.

The tea-growing and -processing season is typically from May to October. The course was not held during the tea production period of the season, although there was opportunity to pick and process tea, on one day picked by hand and steamed/hand rolled, and on another machine picked and pan fired (Figure 7.4). A combination of classroom sessions with tastings and field trips to tea fields and tea businesses, as well as time in the factory processing and at the Tea Research Centre in Uji provided a rich palette of experiences related to Japanese tea.

Benefits

Scheduling the course during a non-producing time for tea was both a benefit and a drawback. Local stakeholders, including tea farmers, had more time to spend with participants, explaining (through a translator) their work and providing opportunity to ask questions and to purchase their tea at the source. The event length (10 days with a two-day break in the middle) was

*Figure 7.4   Japanese Tea Master Course – author points to the typically picked one bud
and two leaves in a tea field in Wazuka*

a benefit. There were no evening sessions, so participants had a chance to have dinner together
(always with tea cuisine elements) and to relax, rest and reflect on the day's proceedings.

Standards
The course included detailed pre-departure trip information provided to participants in the
form of a handbook. An orientation session was held, supported by information handed out
to participants. Post-experience follow-up was supported through the recently established
Global Japanese Tea Association, who, with the advent of COVID-19, established virtual tea
parties. The course met the parameters for creating a meaningful and memorable experience,
in particular drawing participants into the local nature, culture and history of the tea community of Wazuka. The small group size ensured that the course as a form of experiential tourism
was low impact, and the price paid by each course member of JPY350,000 (approximately
USD3,300), inclusive of lodging and local field trips, ensured that it was a high-yield product
for the sponsors and participating suppliers.

The Japanese Tea Masters Course provided an opportunity to learn about and experience
a wide range of teas, and to practise skills of producing tea including picking, processing,
assessing and tasting. Participants were presented with a certificate of completion on the last
evening of the course. Taking the course gave valuable authentic perspectives on life in a tea

Table 7.1   *ASEB grid analysis*

Factors	Case 1 Darjeeling	Case 2 Japan
Activities	Tea lectures (introductory)	Tea lectures (extensive)
	Tea tastings (factory tasting room)	Tea tastings (classroom, factory)
	Tea factory tours, observation,	Tea factory tours (observation)
	Tea factory work (limited)	Tea factory work (complete)
	Cultural performance (workers)	Tea ceremony (different schools)
Settings	Tea region (Darjeeling) and estate	Tea region (Uji/Kyoto)
	Estate accommodation	Tea gardens, factories
	Tea gardens, factories	Wazuka-cho Guest House
	Tea Estate School (tour)	Tea ceremonies (instructors' homes)
	Road (car from regional airport)	Public transport (train/bus from airport)
Experiences	Picking tea	Picking tea
	Tea tastings	Tea tastings
	Assisting tea production	Hands-on tea production
	Experiencing local tea cuisine	Experiencing local tea cuisine
Benefits	New knowledge of Darjeeling tea	New knowledge of Japanese tea
	Tea main focus on one estate	Overview of different tea farms
	Part of Glenburn Tea Estate life	Participating in Wazuka community life
	Insights into production issues	Insights into production issues
	Tasting different Darjeeling tea types	Tasting different Japanese tea types
	Experiencing tea meals	Experiencing tea cuisine
	Joining an international network	Joining an international network
	Contributing to local livelihoods	Contributing to local livelihoods
Standards	Direct, meaningful tea estate experiences	Direct, meaningful tea community experiences
	Met variety of people, visited estate places, created memories	Met variety of people, visited tea garden, created memories
	Drawn into tea estate nature, culture, history	Drawn into tea community nature, culture, history
	Experienced variation to low-impact, low-volume, high-yield tea tourism	Experienced community-based low-impact, low-volume, high-yield tea tourism

farming community, contributing to responsible tea tourism in a Japanese tea village (Jolliffe & Nakashima, 2020).

5.   DISCUSSION

The ASEB method developed for the assessment of visitor attractions (Light & Prentice, 1994) was used to organize participant observations from the cases into a format for discussion (Table 7.1). Standards of Experiential Tourism proposed by (Smith, 2005) were added as a framework for examining the standards of the experiential micro-niche tea tourism products offered by both cases (Table 7.2).

The *activities* of both cases had common aspects. Both focused in an intense manner on all aspects of tea production, from the field to the factory to the cup, reflecting the focused experiences that are characteristic of micro-niche tourism (the type of tea produced at each place differs). Multiple classroom sessions in Japan provided more in-depth knowledge on topics such as tea science and packaging than the Darjeeling tour/workshop. In both cases, through the use of different learning techniques, participants received an intensive introduction to tea making with rich experiential aspects. What participants did not expect to experience was an intense view of tea community life, lending authenticity to the experience.

The *settings* were alike in both being tea-producing locations. As previously noted by Robinson and Novelli (2005), geography plays a key role in the development of micro-niche tourism. The physical settings for the residential components of both programmes were diverse: the one in Darjeeling was historic (a tea estate with the original tea planter's bungalow) and the other in Japan was contemporary but with traditional elements (a community guest house built in a traditional style). This reflects, in the case of Darjeeling, the incorporation of colonial tea heritage into contemporary tourism, as discussed by Jolliffe and Aslam (2009).

Both locations share the scenic tea landscapes characteristic of tea-producing areas. Such locales are mountainous and reflect the geography of tea, with tea plantings being squeezed into any available space. The means of picking and production differs from Darjeeling, where tea is hand-picked and the landscape appears to be more natural and less manicured than that of Wazuka, where tea is for the most part machine picked. In Japan some of the tea bushes are shaded, a practice that does not exist in Darjeeling.

The *experiences* are both tea-focused and definitely part of the move towards tea tourism as a micro-niche. Participants in both locales had similar experiences with different levels of intensity. The production experience was observational and participatory in Darjeeling, taking place in the tea production season, while it was more intensive and hands-on in Japan, taking place outside of the main production season. The depth of experience was influenced by the environment and demands of tea season production at both locations. The levels of experience were characteristic of both niche (Marson, 2011) and experiential (Smith, 2005) tourism.

The type of tea produced at each place differed. There was extensive tasting at both locations; in Darjeeling it was mostly in factory tasting rooms closely linked to production, whereas the tasting in Japan took place at factories but primarily in the classroom. The factory experience in Darjeeling was a more intense observation of the machinery at work, whereas the small factories visited in Wazuka were not in production. A difference in terms of Japanese tea is that there are factories that sort and process raw finished tea called aracha (crude or unrefined tea) from the farmers (steamed, rolled and dried) and participants visited one of these factories.

The *benefits* of both experiences were for participants and, to some extent, for the tea communities where they were held. In Darjeeling participants gained first-hand experience of tea production on a historic tea estate and insights into daily life there. Participants made contact with tea producers, interacting to a limited extent with the local tea estate community. In Wazuka, those taking the course gained unique insights into Japanese tea and its culture and for a short time became part of the local tea farming community. For this local community there were economic benefits through employment diversification and social results conveying the message of the benefits of Japanese tea to the world. Involvement of local stakeholders, seen as key to the development of tea tourism (Cheng et al., 2012), was limited in the case of Darjeeling but quite strong in the case of Wazuka.

The *standards* of these experiences could be evaluated using the criteria for experiential tourism suggested by Smith (2005). Using these factors, both cases – the Darjeeling Tea Tour and the Japanese Tea Master Course – meet and exceed the criteria (Table 7.2).

It is evident through this evaluation that tea tourism is a high-end micro-niche type of activity, attracting small groups of dedicated tea tourists with high levels of pre-planning, as opposed to the more casual experience of tourists visiting such areas for sightseeing and

Table 7.2   *Standards for experiential tourism analysis*

Standard	Examples from Tour and Course
1	Meaning created through on-site experience in tea-producing areas.
2	Experiential contact with participants, tour guides, instructors, local communities in tea areas creating memories.
3	Experience included pre-departure trip planning, post-trip follow-up, encouraging on-going participant networks.
4	Experience linked to local nature surrounding tea gardens, included cultural heritage components.
5	Experiential tourism in small groups, low impact, high price end.

Source: After Smith, 2005.

general leisure purposes. The types of experiences offered by both the Darjeeling and Japanese cases could only be offered to small groups, as there are local limitations on available lodging and numbers who could be accommodated in estate accommodation and on visits to tea fields and factories (in Darjeeling), and in community lodging and field trips to farmers' tea fields and factories (in Japan).

However, a limitation to the participant observation focus of these case studies has been the limited insights into how the micro-niche of tea tourism could contribute to achieving the UN's SDGs in host communities, a possible focus for future research on the niche.

6.   CONCLUSIONS

This chapter examined tea tourism as a micro-niche form of experiential tourism with potential relevance to addressing the UN SDGs. Through investigative case studies at tea-producing locations with rich resources (tea landscapes, gardens, factories and traditions) for the creation of tea tourism experiences, insights have been gained into the process of creating tea encounters. This is from the perspective of the dedicated tea tourist embedded through participant observation in several related experiences. These insights contribute to the existing literature on tea tourism that, to a large extent, has focused on defining such tourism, examining destination and stakeholder viewpoints, and exploring development and marketing aspects. The discussion of tea tourism has been extended to look in more depth at the visitor experience of this micro-niche in terms of its impact on local communities and the SDGs, in particular at tea-producing locations.

In the cases examined, participants, through interaction with tea-producing locations, gained an in-depth experience of tea culture and production that led to the creation of long-lasting memories. Being immersed in these places, participants were able to construct their own experiences, making connections with local tea industry members, and in some ways taking part in the life of these historic agricultural communities, potentially having an impact on improving livelihoods. A rich experiential form of niche tea tourism for a small market segment is thus demonstrated by the cases of Darjeeling, India, and Wazuka, Japan, where visitors interact with tea farmers, producers and communities. This may offer lessons for developing responsible and sustainable experiential tea-related tourism activities for domestic tourism, especially during the post-COVID-19 recovery stage, at other tea-producing locales. These lessons could include types of offerings, as well as required activities, settings, standards and benefits to local communities. Online tea experiences, pioneered in 2020 during the COVID-19 pandemic by tea associations and producers, have also contributed to making these types of tea tourism experiences more accessible to all.

REFERENCES

Agapito, D., Valle, P. and Mendes, J. (2014) The sensory dimension of tourist experiences: Capturing meaningful sensory-informed themes in Southwest Portugal. *Tourism Management*, 42, 224–37.

Beeho, A. and Prentice, R. (1996) ASEB grid analysis and the Black Country Museum in the West Midlands of England: Understanding visitor experiences as a basis for product development. In L.C. Harrison, and W. Husbands (eds) *Practicing responsible tourism: International case studies in tourism planning, policy, and development*. Wiley, 472–94.

Beeho, A.J. and Prentice, R.C. (1997) Conceptualizing the experiences of heritage tourists: A case study of New Lanark World Heritage Village. *Tourism Management*, 18, 75–87.

Beeton, S. (2005) The case study in tourism research: A multi-method case study approach. In B.W. Ritchie, P. Burns and C. Palmer (eds) *Tourism research methods: Integrating theory with practice*. Cabi, 37–48.

Besky, S. (2014) *The Darjeeling distinction: Labor and justice on fair-trade tea plantations in India*. University of California Press.

Cary, S.H. (2004) The tourist moment. *Annals of Tourism Research*, 31, 61–77.

Ceron, J.-P. and Dubois, G. (2003) Tourism and sustainable development indicators: The gap between theoretical demands and practical achievements. *Current Issues in Tourism*, 6, 54–75.

Chee-Beng, T. and Yuling, D. (2010) The promotion of tea in South China: Re-inventing tradition in an old industry. *Food and Foodways*, 18, 121–44.

Cheng, S., Hu, J., Fox D. and Zhang, Y. (2012) Tea tourism development in Xinyang, China: Stakeholders' view. *Tourism Management Perspectives*, 2, 28–34.

Cheng, S., Xu, F., Zhang, J. and Zhang, Y. (2010) Tourists' attitudes toward tea tourism: A Case study in Xinyang, China. *Journal of Travel & Tourism Marketing*, 27, 211–20.

Das, K. (2006) International protection of India's geographical indications with special reference to 'Darjeeling' tea. *The Journal of World Intellectual Property*, 9(5), 459–95.

Dixit, S.K. (2020) Marketing gastronomic tourism experiences. In S.K. Dixit (ed.) *The Routledge handbook of gastronomic tourism*. Routledge, 323–36.

Fernando, P.I.N., Rajapaksha, R.M.P.D.K. and Kumari, K.W.S.N. (2017) Tea tourism as a marketing tool: A strategy to develop the image of Sri Lanka as an attractive tourism destination. *Kelaniya Journal of Management*, 5(2), 64–79.

Gilmore, J.H. and Pine, B.J. (2007) *Authenticity: What consumers really want*. Harvard Business Press.

Horváth, Z. (2013) Memorable tourism experience. In M.K. Smith and G. Richards (eds) *The Routledge handbook of cultural tourism*. Routledge, 375–82.

Huang, C.-M., Tuan, C.-L. and Wongchai, A. (2014) Development analysis of leisure agriculture: A case study of Longjing Tea Garden, Hangzhou, China. *APCBEE Procedia*, 8, 210–15.

Huang, R. and Hall, D. (2007) The New Tea appreciation festival: Marketing and socio-economic development in Hunan Province, China. In L. Jolliffe (ed.) *Tea and tourism: Tourists, traditions and transformations*. Channel View Publications, 98–114.

Jolliffe, L. (2007) *Tea and tourism: Tourists, traditions and transformations*. Channel View Publications.

Jolliffe, L. and Aslam, M.S. (2009) Tea heritage tourism: Evidence from Sri Lanka. *Journal of Heritage Tourism*, 4, 331–44.

Jolliffe, L. and Nakashima, M. (2020) Responsible rural tourism in Japan's tea villages. In V. Nair et al. (eds) *Responsible rural tourism in Asia*. Channel View Publications, 61–74.

Jolliffe, L. and Piboonrungroj, P. (2020) The role of themes and stories in tourism experiences. In S.K. Dixit (ed.) *The Routledge handbook of tourism experience management and marketing*. Routledge.

Koththagoda, K. and Dissanayake, D. (2017) Potential of tea tourism in Sri Lanka: A review on managerial implications and research directions. *Equality and Management*, University of Szczecin, Poland, 51–68.

Light, D., and Prentice, R. (1994). Market-based product development in heritage tourism. *Tourism Management*, 15(1), 27–36.

Marson, D. (2011) From mass tourism to niche tourism. In P. Robinson et al. (eds) *Research themes for tourism*. CABI, 1–15.

Mohan, S. (2016) Institutional change in value chains: Evidence from tea in Nepal. *World Development*, 78, 52–65.

Novelli, M. (ed.) (2005) *Niche tourism: Contemporary issues, trends and cases*. Routledge.

Pine, B.J. and Gilmore, J.H. (1999) *The experience economy: Work is theatre and every business a stage*. Harvard Business Press.

Robinson, M. and Novelli, M. (2005) Niche tourism: An introduction. In Novelli, M. (ed.) *Niche tourism: Contemporary issues, trends and cases*. Routledge, 1–11.

Santini, C., Cavicchi, A. and Canavari, M. (2011) The Risk™ strategic game of rural tourism: How sensory analysis can help in achieving a sustainable competitive advantage. In K.L. Sidali, A. Spiller and B. Schulze (eds) *Food, Agri-Culture and Tourism: Linking Local Gastronoy and Rural Tourism: Interdisciplinary Perspectives*. Springer, 161–79.

Skinner, J. (2019) *Afternoon tea: A history*. Rowman & Littlefield.

Smith, W.L. (2005) Experiential tourism around the world and at home: Definitions and standards. *International journal of services and standards*, 2, 1–14.

Tao, T.C. and Wall, G. (2009) Tourism as a sustainable livelihood strategy. *Tourism Management*, 30, 90–98.

8. Agritourism and the Prosecco Route of Italy

Marta Soligo

1. INTRODUCTION

In the past decades, niche tourism studies have extensively focused on rural tourism as a successful form of travel based on local agricultural and sustainable practices. Scholars such as Farrell and Russell (2011) and Sharpley and Jepson (2011) argue that contemporary fast-paced lifestyles, often characterised by a detachment from nature, have created a nostalgia for the pre-industrial rural life, especially within Western societies. Therefore, an increasing number of tourists decide to spend their holidays at rural attractions, such as farmhouses and vineyards. This form of tourism does not only offer an opportunity to escape the hurried city life, but also to get in contact with nature and its resources. While experiencing a close relationship with rural life, rural tourism provides the chance to learn about how local cultural practices are linked to the surrounding landscape.

This research focuses on the Italian form of agriturismo[1] (agritourism), where tourists stay in traditional farmhouses, actively participating in agricultural practices and tasting local products. I analyse agriturismo as a micro-niche of the rural tourism macro-niche, trying to understand how this model fits within the main features of niche tourism, such as the focus on sustainable practices and product diversification. More precisely, this study analyses agriturismo in the Prosecco area, famous for the production of prosecco wine. In 2019, the United Nations Educational Scientific and Cultural Organization (UNESCO) included this area in the World Heritage List as a cultural landscape, recognising the region's centuries-old relationship between nature and cultural practices. This chapter represents a contribution to the literature on niche tourism since it looks at the niche itself as part of a system, which is the cultural landscape.

Defining niche tourism, Robinson and Novelli (2005) mention the geographical dimension of the phenomenon, 'by which locations with highly specific offers are able to establish themselves as niche destinations' (p. 6). With this study, I aim at uncovering how the Italian Strada del Prosecco (Prosecco Route) affirmed itself as a niche destination, focusing on the official websites of 21 agriturismo venues located along it. Agriturismo (agritourism) is a kind of bed-and-breakfast with restaurant located on a farm. I divided my findings between the micro-level, investigating the farms and their activities, and the macro-level, which is the relationship between agriturismo and the broader geographic and cultural area.

As my findings show, it is not possible to separate winemaking and farming practices from the cultural processes that built the identity of the Prosecco region. Given their potential in terms of transmitting to tourists first-hand knowledge of the natural and cultural heritage of the region, agriturismo represent optimal means for the promotion of a sustainable development rooted in the host communities' traditions.

Finally, this study aims at working as a starting point for future scholarship on the changes that the COVID-19 pandemic brought to the tourism industry. One aspect to consider are the worldwide travel bans that put international travel on hold (Linka et al., 2020). With people not being able to travel internationally, it became important to centre on domestic tourism and the role of next-door attractions. On the one hand, agriturismo might represent a successful model for domestic tourism, with guests coming from the surrounding areas to discover and learn more about the traditions and resources of the territories where they live.

On the other hand, As Gössling, Scott and Hall (2020) point out, the tourism and hospitality industries should use the COVID-19 crisis to critically reconsider the sectors' growth, and sustainable development is key in this sense. Describing tourism in the Prosecco area, Boatto et al. (2013) explain that 'This is a quality tourism that differs from mass tourism because it is not supported by any appropriate network of facilities required by the latter, also because of the landscape, consisting of a hilly area in which narrow roads wind, often tortuously, between hamlets and villages' (p. 99).

Therefore, the Prosecco area might take advantage of these responsible forms of tourism while planning a sustainable recovery. The case study of this chapter can serve as a baseline for comparison among niche tourism destinations, which could base their post-pandemic recovery strategies on domestic tourism and sustainability.

2. LITERATURE REVIEW

Rural Tourism and Agritourism

This chapter analyses agritourism and wine tourism as micro-niches of the rural tourism macro-niche (Robinson and Novelli, 2005). According to the World Tourism Organization (UNWTO) (2017), rural tourism is 'related to a wide range of products generally linked to nature-based activities, agriculture, rural lifestyle/culture, angling and sightseeing' and takes place in 'non-urban (rural) areas with the following characteristics: i) low population density, ii) landscape and land use dominated by agriculture and forestry and iii) traditional social structure and lifestyle' (p. 15). As Sorea and Csesznek (2020) point out, rural tourism today is becoming one of the most prominent forms of niche tourism, being based on sustainability, small and homogeneous groups of tourists, and product differentiation.

Cawley and Gillmor (2008) argue that the transition from Fordist to post-Fordist production in the 1990s pushed peripheral rural areas in many countries to seek alternatives to traditional activities, and tourism played an important role in this process. Farrell and Russell (2011), for example, centre on the role of rural tourism as a way to escape the mundane, while Sharpley and Jepson (2011) investigate the emotional dimension and spiritual fulfilment related to it. Sociological studies on rural tourism, moreover, often include critical perspectives. An example is the concept of nostalgia, since '(r)ural places are particularly equipped with unique features, cues, and objects that may trigger nostalgic encounters among their visitors' (Christou et al., 2018: 44). As experts highlight, tourists often visit rural settings in order to live an experience that they perceive as authentic (Sims, 2009), frequently dreaming of an idealised past (MacCannell, 1976; Urry and Larsen, 2011) marked by a direct and genuine relationship with nature.

In the past few decades, in the realm of rural tourism, the trend of agritourism has undergone unprecedented growth. The term, which comes from the words agriculture and tourism, 'involves any agriculturally based operation or activity that brings visitors to a farm or ranch' (Jiang and Wang, 2018: 1). Agritourism literature often centres on tourists' contact with agriculture (Phillip et al., 2010) and how it produces benefits not only for the farms but also for local communities and society overall (Tew and Barbieri, 2012). Analysing the phenomenon of agritourism, scholars focus on the concept of sustainable development, explaining how this model can promote environmental sustainability (Garau, 2015; Castellani and Sala, 2012; Giaccio et al., 2018). A large number of empirical analyses 'show positive performances related to tourism farms, such as soil conservation, ecosystem services conservation with the main attention to landscapes and biodiversity' (Giaccio et al., 2018: 2). An important role in this sense is played by 'the predominance of farm-made foods over externally sourced food products' (Sidali, 2011: 10), which enables sustainable practices. This trend in rural tourism mirrors a recent interest in rural studies towards the social role of farms, which are increasingly working to fight marginalization in rural areas and to protect the natural environment (Galluzzo, 2015a).

Gil Arroyo et al. (2013) argue that although agritourism is an established trend worldwide, the meaning of it is still surrounded by ambiguity. As Phillip et al.'s (2010) study shows, there is a need for clarification on what agritourism is or is not, distinguishing it from definitions such as farm tourism or vacation farms. An answer in this sense comes from public institutions, which, in some countries, create ad hoc definitions both for hospitality and agricultural businesses. As this study shows, the Italian government establishes a strict definition of agritourism, which rigorously differs from any other kinds of rural and farm-based tourism.

Agriturismo in Italy

The Italian concept of agriturismo was born in the 1980s 'as a way to keep Italian farmers on the land, allowing them to use their buildings to tap into Italy's rich tourism market' (Johnson, 2012). The 23,407 agriturismo businesses spread all around Italy (ISTAT, 2017) are regulated by a national law issued in 2006 – Legge Nazionale 20 febbraio 2006, n. 96 – that defines the aspects, the typologies and the goals these activities have in enhancing the rural and natural heritage on a national level. Although one might think that agriturismo falls under traditional business categories such as lodging and dining, the law declares that the agriturismo itself has to be an agricultural site rather than a hospitality-related one.

Only people who have the legal status of imprenditore agricolo (small-scale/local agricultural entrepreneur), in fact, can own an agriturismo. According to the Italian National Law 96/2006, to be defined as *imprenditore agricolo*, individuals should have as their main occupation one of the following activities: cultivation, silviculture, livestock breeding and/or other related activities (Gazzetta Ufficiale della Repubblica Italiana, 2001). Moreover, agriturismo businesses have to be located on farmland, and the agricultural activities, such as farming, have to prevail over tourism-related ones, such as lodging and dining.

Another fundamental requisite is related to the origin of the food that is served on an agriturismo, which has to come from the farm where the venue is located. Agriturismo owners, therefore, have to cook and serve locally grown products for the most part. The percentages in this sense are established by the individual Italian regions, since the Italian National Law 96/2006 only sets up a framework of guidelines on a national level. The Italian state delegates regions and provinces for more specific regulations in matters of agriturismo. The region that I analyse in this chapter – the Veneto region – for example, requires that 65% of the food and drinks served in an agriturismo come from the farmland where they are situated (Regione Veneto, 2019). According to Galluzzo's (2018) investigation, tourists mention authentic rural food as one of the main motivations behind their choice of staying in an agriturismo, usually deciding to spend more than one week on the farm to enjoy both the countryside and the local products.

Investigating food production within the rural tourism niche, scholars such as Meneley (2004) and Cavanaugh (2007) often mention the connection between agriturismo and the Slow Food movement. Slow Food was founded in Italy in 1989 by Carlo Petrini and a group of activists, and quickly became a global phenomenon, involving more than 160 countries today. The movement's goal is 'to prevent the disappearance of local food cultures and traditions, counteract the rise of fast life and combat people's dwindling interest in the food they eat, where it comes from and how our food choices affect the world around us' (Slow Food International, 2021). Every year, Slow Food organises events and festivals in Italy and all over the world, with the objectives of raising awareness on topics such as organic food and battles against food waste, with an increasing focus on environmental sustainability (Yepsen, 2010).

Among the numerous initiatives promoted by Slow Food, one of the most successful is Chilometro 0 (0 kilometres), which promotes the idea of serving locally grown food that has, therefore, travelled zero kilometres. Chilometro 0 'refers to non-industrial fruits, vegetables, cheese, meat, honey etc., which [do] not go through global trade chains, therefore [they] does not have big price margins and quality [loss] during long storage in international supermarkets' (Popovic, 2014). One of Chilometro 0's main goals is the reduction of pollution by decreasing food transportation emissions. Restaurants that become part of Chilometro 0 have to offer a number of dishes prepared with local products, and for this reason, several agriturismo have joined the movement. In this sense, it is important to mention that a number of scholars, such as Hall (2006) and Heitmann et al., (2011), have analysed the relationship between Slow Food and the less institutionalised movement of slow tourism. The latter movement lies in the respect for 'local cultures, history and environment and values social responsibility while celebrating diversity and connecting people' (Heitmann et al., 2011: 117). When examined through the lens of the rural tourism niche, it is easy to understand how aspects such as attention towards environmental sustainability and local communities reveal a connection between Slow Food and slow tourism.

Finally, the Italian National Law 96/2006 mentions agriturismo as an integral part of the cultural and historic fabric (Milligan, 2007) surrounding it, listing elements such as heritage, nutrition and the built environment (Tommasini, 2007). This happens also in the case of leisure activities that, according to the law, have to be 'connected "to the agricultural activity and resources of the farm", and to other activities to encouraging exploration of the local historical, environmental and cultural heritage of the territory' (Bianchi, 2011: 64). As Galluzzo (2015b) states, the success of agriturismo businesses lies in their ability to diversify their products within the rural spaces where they are located, offering a wide range of recreational activities such as sports. I will elaborate the notion of agriturismo in its cultural context in the findings and conclusion sections.

Wine Tourism

One of the fastest-growing sectors in rural tourism is wine tourism. Novelli (2012) defines wine tourism as a relatively new form of rural tourism based on locations such as wineries and vineyards and wine-related events. According to Getz and Brown (2006), research in wine tourism started in the 1990s, with an emphasis on comparative and descriptive studies 'aimed at justifying and exploring the dimensions of this new sub-field of tourism' (p. 147).

An analysis of the existing literature in wine tourism shows that, although the topic has been widely investigated, it is not easy to establish a unilateral profile and definition of wine tourists (Charters and Ali-Knight, 2002).

Trying to fill this gap, in the past two decades, scholarship analysing wine tourism has focused on travel motivations. Alant and Bruwer (2004) explain that wine tourism motivations can be divided into 'primary motivations of wine tourists [such] as sampling and buying wine' and 'secondary or peripheral motivations like socialising, learning about wine, entertainment, etc.' (p. 28). Conducting research on Canada's wine travel market, Carmichael (2005) mentions the work of Lang Research (2001), which shows that tourists interested in wine and cuisine are more likely to seek out vacation experiences based on romance, relaxation, exploration and personal indulgence. Finally, as Carlsen (2007) points out, 'wine production and tourism are essentially at opposite ends of the industrial spectrum' (p. 8), the former being supply-led and price-taking and the latter supply-driven and price-making. Therefore, Carlsen suggests that successful wine tourism models are those that are able to integrate the characteristics of both activities in their approach. This can be achieved, for example, by thoroughly analysing the shift from wine production to tourism in a given region and by monitoring how wineries and wine regions diversify and customise their products.

One of the fastest-growing areas in terms of wine tourism is the Mediterranean, whose regions use wine as one of the main products to brand and promote their rural attractions (Hall and Mitchell, 2000). Among Mediterranean countries, Italy plays a key role, with scholars analysing the country's potential as a wine tourism major destination (Romano and Natilli, 2009). According to the XV Report on Wine Tourism in Italy (Associazione Nazionale Città del Vino, 2019), the revenue of wine tourism in Italy today is worth a total of EUR2.5 billion, for a total of about 14 million wine tourists per year. On the wineries side, wine tourists are an increasingly important source of income and today they account for an average of 26.9% of wineries' revenue.

3.   THE FIELD: THE PROSECCO ROUTE

The Prosecco Route (Figure 8.1) is located between the towns of Conegliano and Valdobbiadene, Italy, just one hour's drive from Venice. This area is famous for the production of the world-renowned wine Prosecco Conegliano Valdobbiadene DOCG. The route connects the town of Valdobbiadene to the town of Conegliano and is about 21 miles long. Along the route, visitors can enjoy the hilly landscape with its endless rows of prosecco grapes, while visiting local wineries.

In 2019 the Prosecco area of Conegliano and Valdobbiadene became part of the UNESCO World Heritage List, with the following motivation:

> The Colline [hills] del Prosecco di Conegliano e Valdobbiadene is a viticulture landscape resulting from the interaction of nature and people over several centuries. The adaptation and transformation of the challenging terrain of the hogback geomorphology has required the development of specific land use practices […]. As a result, the vineyards contribute to a distinctive 'chequerboard' appearance with perpendicular rows of high vines, interspersed with rural settlements, forests and small woods. Despite many changes, the history of sharecropping in this area is also reflected in the landscape patterns. (UNESCO, 2019)

One of the main goals of this chapter is to investigate how the rural tourism niche is rooted in the inextricable connection between natural and cultural resources. According to UNESCO (2019), the Prosecco area constitutes a landscape 'where nature and human history have shaped and been shaped by an adapted and specific system for viticulture and land use' (para. 2). Therefore, relevant for this study is the role of cultural heritage in rural tourism, with guests becoming familiar with the natural resources by learning about centuries of historical traditions and practices based on humans' interactions with the surrounding environment.

As Boatto et al. (2013) argue, in the past few years, the Prosecco region has affirmed itself as a 'territory and cultural landscape' (p. 99). UNESCO specifies that the Prosecco area is part of a list of cultural landscapes which was created to 'reveal and sustain the great diversity of the interactions between humans and their environment, to protect living traditional cultures and preserve the traces of those which have disappeared' (UNESCO, 2019). Although some other academic works focus on sustainability in the Prosecco area (Boatto et al., 2013; Boatto et al., 2017) as well as on the preservation of Italian cultural landscapes (Bottazzi and Mondini, 2006; Konaxis, 2018), I noticed a lack of research on the role of agriturismo in the Prosecco cultural landscape. With this chapter I aim at uncovering how agriturismo, which is increasingly becoming one of the most important hospitality models in Italy, transfers to tourists the values of its cultural landscape, especially in terms of interactions between humans and their environment.

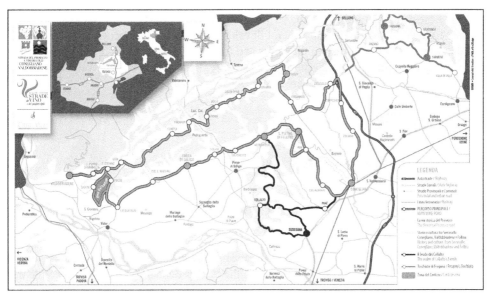

Source: https://www.coneglianovaldobbiadene.it

Figure 8.1   *The Prosecco Route*

4.   METHODS

For this research, I conducted a textual analysis of the official websites of the 21 agriturismo venues located along the Prosecco Route, listed on the route's official website, coneglianoval-dobbiadene.it (Strada del Prosecco e Vini dei Colli Conegliano Valdobbiadene, n.d.). My goal was to understand how agriturismo businesses express the relationship between the natural environment and cultural practices, centring on the concept of rural and wine tourism. I have chosen the Prosecco area for the density of agriturismo sites and the fact it recently joined the UNESCO World Heritage List as a cultural landscape.

Moreover, investigating how the 21 agriturismo promote themselves helped me comprehend which elements they use to market their venues. I also took into consideration the Prosecco Route's official website to understand which natural elements and locally grown products they mention to describe their landscape. In terms of data analysis, I started with an open coding process, condensing and organising the data into categories, followed by focused coding, reviewing my codes and evaluating which ones occurred the most, until I reached a saturation point (Lofland et al., 2006), generating core categories. I analysed websites both in English and Italian. In the case of the Italian quotes, I translated them personally – Italian being my first language – trying to maintain as closely as possible the meaning that agriturismo owners seemed to want to convey.

I focused especially on descriptions of agriturismo, their menus and pictures that highlighted the role of the natural environment and its products within the local culture. My analysis of the material followed a two-fold path, which I develop in the following section. Firstly, I examined the micro-level, investigating the farms and their activities, highlighting aspects such as the role of nature and labour in agriturismo. Secondly, I centred on the macro-level, which is the broader geographic and cultural area where agriturismo are located.

5.   FINDINGS

The Micro-Level: Experiencing the Farm

As previously mentioned, in the agriturismo tourists can be in direct contact with nature and its products – and, therefore the farm's practices – with a deep level of learning about cultural practices playing a key role. We find this aspect especially when it comes to the food and wine served in agriturismo. Guests have the opportunity to spend time on the farm and observe first-hand the labour and practices behind the meals they consume. This represents a unique opportunity for tourists to become familiar with the local products. Several websites state that the agriturismo cannot produce written menus since they follow nature's seasonality:

> Our dishes follow the rhythms of nature, season after season, as they did in the past. For this reason we do not offer you a printed menu from which to choose; but every day, we prepare the fresh ingredients from our garden and the woods around us to give you the best, freshest menu possible. (Ca' Piadera, 2019)

The focus on short-distance sustainable practices goes hand-in-hand with the above-mentioned concept of slow tourism and the Slow Food movement. Thus, food proximity is a central element when it comes to the micro-level analysis. This is particularly interesting if we compare the above quote with today's fast-food models, whose menus are based on repetitive and predictable lists and items (Ritzer, 1993). Reading the descriptions on the agriturismo websites, we also understand the centrality of the origin of the food and its geographic location.

On the one hand, this happens with the main product of the area, which is prosecco wine which, as this agriturismo describes, is:

> produced only in the foothills between Valdobbiadene and Conegliano and it is made in many varie-ties: Still or sparkling, 'frizzante' or Superior of Cartizze. Its light fruity taste and versatility allows it to accompany many dishes exceptionally well, satisfying even the most demanding of palates. (Due Carpini, 2019)

On the other hand, agriturismo along the Prosecco Route also focus on the other products from the farm:

> Enjoy the traditional cuisine of the Veneto region and taste our delicious home-made fresh pasta and our second courses based on meats from the farm. These are seasonal dishes and are rich in typical products of the area [such] as asparagus, pumpkin, radicchio rosso di Treviso (red-leafed chicory) and mushroom. All are prepared in the traditional manner. (Althea, 2019)

Agriturismo cuisine follows local traditions, rather than more mechanised and industrialised techniques. I will focus on this aspect later while analysing the Prosecco cultural landscape. Additionally, one agriturismo declares that every day 'the chef prepares several specialties, such as fresh meats and cheeses, homemade pasta, soups, risotto with seasonal herbs that come from (the) farm' (Le Mesine, n.d.).[2] I noticed that agriturismo venues often describe their menus by using adjectives such as 'fresh', 'homemade' or 'seasonal'. This strategy reveals, once again, that food-related activities in agriturismo depend on the relationship between nature and human labour, such as the labour of the farmer or the chef, which require a deep knowledge of nature and its seasonality.

The websites, moreover, suggest tourists consume the products of the farm while enjoying the surrounding wine landscape. Agriturismo hosts invite guests to sit for a long time inside and outside the country house, in order to relax while experiencing contact with the surround-ing environment, as this example shows:

> At the foot of the Belluno Pre-Alps, between the hills of blond Prosecco we offer you the opportunity to spend days in tranquillity, immersed in the green of chestnut woods, enjoying the genuine tradi-tional products of this generous Veneto land. (AlCol, 2019)

Oftentimes, being immersed in the landscape also means actively becoming part of it. Some agriturismo providers offer workshops, also called teaching farms, which include first-hand experiences. During these workshops, tourists can work on the farm and be involved in activ-ities that range from picking fruit to making jellies.

One agriturismo presents tourists the opportunity to adopt a row, and learn about how to take care of it:

> The farm La Casa Vecchia offers the opportunity to take a row, give [...] name to a set of screws, precious charged clusters that in late summer will become an excellent sparkling wine. The adoption of row [lasts] a year and can be renewed in time. (La Casa Vecchia, n.d.)

Through the workshops, tourists acquire first-hand knowledge of nature, becoming familiar with the garden, the vineyard and the farm's other products. Getting physically in touch with nature can be a particularly meaningful experience, especially for those tourists who live in urban areas. Additionally, these classes allow participants to acquire deep knowledge on the products they eat and drink, since they have a chance to have a direct experience with the natural ingredients. Finally, differently from today's hurried fast-food models, these workshops can last for days, and the agriturismo websites examined did not mention a time limit for them, permitting tourists to enjoy the contact with nature for an extended period of time.

In my analysis, I found that the transmission of cultural practices happens through interactions, based on the relationship between the owners – usually the farmers and their families – and the tourists, who are described as friends or even as a part of the family itself. One agriturismo centres on the family environment and hospitality:

> Every detail of the restaurant has been rigorously overseen. The result is a very tasteful, comfortable and relaxed country house, where family environment, warmth and hospitality prevail and make our restaurant perfect to have dinner with friends or parents on any occasion. (Althea, 2019)

Differently from other kinds of mainstream restaurants, agriturismo offer a chance to be in contact with the families who own the farms, spending time with them, and often learning from them about nature and its products. This last aspect is fundamental to introducing the second finding, which focuses on agriturismo and its natural resources through the lens of the broader cultural context.

The Macro-Level: Experiencing Agriturismo Within the Cultural Landscape

The majority of the websites I analysed pay particular attention to the description of their agriturismo through the lens of the Prosecco area and its traditions. Agriturismo activities, and especially the local products these venues serve, have strong ties with the area where the farms are located, especially when it comes to wine. Agriturismo websites go beyond the mere fact that they serve the local prosecco, since they also explain the importance of this product for their geographic area in terms of history and culture:

> The 'Follo' is an agricultural village in the area of Valdobbiadene, on the famous foothill of Cartizze. Our winery is situated there and also our fine vineyards, as Villa Luigia, are cultivated there. This village of ancient winemaking tradition expresses also the history and the culture of these lands, and it has become our company's brand since 2002. (Il Follo, n.d.)

I found a similar trend with recipes, since the majority of the websites point out that their food follows the rules of tradition and pairs well with prosecco. While depicting the wines and dishes they serve, agriturismo link the seasonality of nature to local traditions. This idea recalls what I described in the previous section, especially how everything in agriturismo depends on a thorough knowledge of nature and its cycles, which is transmitted across generations. Moreover, the websites mention nature and its products as part of the local culture and its winemaking practices. As I will explain in the conclusion, this aspect might be fundamental in terms of raising awareness among tourists on the importance of seeing natural resources as part of the cultural heritage of a destination.

Agriturismo businesses often also refer to the broader cultural context when describing the farmhouse's architectural features and location, as this website depicts:

> Your home away from home, Maso di Villa has been created in accordance with typical, local traditions, in a familiar environment to completely satisfy all the requirements for a comfortable and relaxing break. (Maso di Villa, n.d.)

My analysis of the websites shows an attention also to the architectural features of each agriturismo, which are all different from one another. For example, this agriturismo explains that:

> The Relais Duca di Dolle in the sixteenth century was the seat of a monastery of medieval origin of which remains today the main entrance and the arches of the cloister partly occluded. (Duca di Dolle, 2019)

Another describes that:

> The house dates back to the late 1800s and, after accurate research, has been imaginatively restored using the original materials, preserving the building's architectural features, and adding only pieces in keeping with the relaxed, fresh feel of the place. (Maso di Villa, n.d.)

As these quotes show, although located in the same area, every agriturismo has different features in terms of the natural landscape that surrounds it. The structure of farms, in fact, has to follow the hilly landscape and its characteristics, and this is an element that not only gives uniqueness to every agriturismo, but shows its relationship with the local culture.

6.   CONCLUDING DISCUSSION

As explained at the beginning of the chapter, this study looks at the niche itself as part of a system, which is the cultural landscape. I therefore investigated how the agriturismo model fits within the core characteristics of niche tourism, such as the rejection of mass-oriented operations and the promotion of diversification strategies. Instrumental in this sense is the understanding that, in order to exist, the agriturismo (the micro-level) needs to be situated in its cultural landscape (the macro-level). In the case of this study, for example, it is easy to understand how it is impossible to separate winemaking and farming practices from the cultural processes that built the identity of the Prosecco wine region.

Writing about cultural landscapes, UNESCO (2019) describes how they 'reveal and sustain the great diversity of the interactions between humans and their environment, to protect living traditional cultures and preserve the traces of those which have disappeared'. As my analysis shows, agriturismo businesses largely focus on the importance of transferring traditional knowledge about the relationship between humans and nature to tourists. Moreover, this study's findings show that, although the relationship between nature and local practices plays a key role in the agriturismo experience, food proximity represents one of the most valuable resources of this form of niche tourism. As mentioned above, the connection between the Slow Food movement and slow tourism reveals tourists' increasing interest in consuming local products. During their stay, guests can learn about traditional farming, harvesting and the cultural heritage of the area where they are located. UNESCO's cultural landscape concept goes hand-in-hand with the idea of locating natural resources in the broader cultural context. From my findings, it seems that agriturismo venues are successful in achieving this task, seeing and promoting themselves as part of a cultural heritage consisting of natural products.

The websites I analysed invite tourists to look at what the agriturismo offers as part of the old tradition of the Prosecco area. It is easy to understand the importance of this last aspect in terms of the relationship between hosts and guests, with the latter living in contact with the farmers' families and other members of the local community. This factor is fundamental if we reflect on the fact that the UNESCO's World Heritage List has three categories: natural, cultural and mixed (both natural and cultural). As I explained above, what is meaningful for this study is the fact that, although the area I studied is famous for its natural features, UNESCO included the Prosecco region in the list of cultural – and not natural – heritage sites. This factor is key given the increasingly important role of sustainable development in today's travel industry. Being part of the farming activities, agriturismo businesses are enhanced by the Italian state with the goal of preserving the natural resources, and therefore the natural products, of a given area. Public authorities regularly conduct inspections in agriturismo, making sure they respect the prevalence of the farming activities over hospitality aspects, and that those activities take place in a way that is sustainable for the natural environment.

This direct and close relationship between hosts and guests may lead to more responsible behaviour by tourists, who should be able to better understand how natural resources are fundamentally meaningful for the local community's identity and cultural heritage. Agriturismo hosts invite their guests to take part in winemaking and farming-related workshops, to be in contact with the farmers' families, and to enjoy the natural landscape that surrounds them. In other words, guests are invited to become part of the Prosecco area cultural landscape, just as locals are. In such a context, tourists may be more likely to behave in a more responsible way than might be observed with other forms of tourism where the contact between hosts and guests is reduced to the minimum.

It is important to look at agriturismo as part of a broader system, especially when it comes to the local economy. Agriturismo in fact represents an income-earning opportunity for the locals without falling into the conflicts brought by less responsible forms of tourism. Thus, agriturismo invites tourists to visit the area and come into contact with other local businesses that sell local products, generating additional revenue in the region. This aspect is particularly meaningful in today's tourism studies, given the increasing interest by the sector in the relationship between the travel industry and the UN 2030 Agenda for Sustainable Development and the Sustainable Development Goals (SDGs), which range from climate action to poverty reduction (Boluk et al., 2017; Jones et al., 2017). In line with the SDGs, agriturismo represents a responsible form of hospitality that centres around the main characteristics of niche tourism in general, such as limited numbers of tourists and a focus on sustainability. As my findings reveal, both agriturismo owners and guests show a strong interest towards the protection of natural resources and the respect for the local community. This mirrors some of the Agenda for Sustainable Development's core principles, such as the promotion of sustainable patterns of consumption and production.

If we aim at understanding the role of sustainability in Prosecco Route tourism, it is key to analyse it through the lens of niche tourism. Robinson and Novelli (2005) explain that niche tourism is often referred to in opposition to mass tourism and centres around tailored and individualised services. The main attraction of the region is the prosecco wine, and this makes it possible to target a precise group of visitors – mainly wine lovers – and cater to their needs while ensuring respect for the community and the environment. In particular, this is noteworthy if we think of the proximity of the Prosecco Route to the city of Venice, which in recent years has been at the centre of heated criticisms regarding the so-called overtourism phenomenon.

Moreover, the Italian National Law 96/2006 declares itself to be just a framework law, which leaves to the 20 Italian regions the task of enacting more specific rules for agriturismo, based on the territorial peculiarities of each area. For example, tourists will not find the same forms of agriturismo in Sicily as they will in Tuscany because every region has different rules that are shaped by the landscape and its products. We saw earlier how behind rural tourism there are motivations such as escaping everyday urban life and spiritual fulfilment. In the case of agriturismo businesses, we could also add that these attractions offer tourists the unique opportunity to become familiar with the peculiarity of each region's landscape and cultural heritage.

Today, tourism scholarship is dedicating attention to the post-COVID-19 recovery, and it is important to reflect on niche tourism as a strategy for diversification and sustainable development. At times when tourists are unable to travel internationally, as was the case after the worldwide travel bans in early 2020, agriturismo might represent optimal options for domestic tourism, attracting visitors who are interested in discovering the natural and cultural resources of their home regions. In doing so, locals might learn about aspects of their own cultural landscapes that they had previously ignored, such as traditional farming and winemaking practices.

In terms of how strong the relationship between agriturismo and traditions might be, however, it needs to be said that, especially in terms of future research, it might be worth investigating how agriturismo are starting to follow certain mainstream trends in hospitality. In fact, they are beginning to offer services such as free wi-fi, spas and rooms for business meetings. In this case, agriturismo is following certain globalised trends, meeting the needs of those guests who want some specific services that they can also access in mainstream hospitality-related venues. Similarly, online booking allows agriturismo venues to process rooms reservations faster, helping them reach new tourist markets. To support these kinds of activities, there is also the international online promotion of prosecco wine, which is becoming increasingly well known worldwide. However, even if it is important for agriturismo businesses to show that they are able to innovate and renew themselves by following mainstream strategies in hospitality, their main focus is still the attention towards tradition. As this research shows, at least along the Prosecco Route, agriturismo's main goal is to promote and transmit those practices that have, century after century, built the identity of the surrounding cultural landscape.

NOTES

1. Throughout the chapter, the term agriturismo will be used for both the singular and plural form.
2. Translated by the author.

REFERENCES

Alant, K. and Bruwer, J. (2004) Wine tourism behaviour in the context of a motivational framework for wine regions and cellar doors. *Journal of Wine Research*, 15(1), 27–37.

AlCol (2019) Alcol – Agriturismo, Ospitalità E Degustazione Prodotti Tipici. Available at: http://www.alcol.tv/BorgoCol_agriturismo.html (accessed 5 July 2019).

Althea (2019) Agriturismo Althea. Available at: http://www.agriturismoalthea.it (accessed 4 July 2019).

Associazione Nazionale Città del Vino (2019) XV Rapporto Sul Turismo Del Vino In Italia. https://www.cittadelvino.it/download.php?file=15-rapporto-turismo-vino-anteprima-bit-milano-2019-presentazione_38.pdf

Bianchi, R. (2011) From agricultural to rural: agritourism as a productive option. In: K.L. Sidali, S. A. Spiller and B. Schulze, eds, *Food, Agri-Culture and Tourism*, 56–71. Berlin: Springer.

Boatto, V., Barisan, L. and Teo, G. (2017) Valutazione della risorsa irrigua di soccorso nella produzione del Conegliano Valdobbiadene Prosecco DOCG. *Aestimum*, 70, 31–49.

Boatto, V., Galletto, L., Barisan, L. and Bianchin, F. (2013) The development of wine tourism in the Conegliano Valdobbiadene area. *Wine Economics and Policy*, 2(2), 93–101.

Boluk, K., Cavaliere, C. and Higgins-Desbiolles, F. (2017) Critical thinking to realize sustainability in tourism systems: reflecting on the 2030 sustainable development goals. *Journal of Sustainable Tourism*, 25(9), 1201–1204.

Bottazzi, C. and Mondini, G. (2006) L'analisi Della Domanda Turistica Nei Processi Di Gestione Dei Paesaggi Culturali. *Aestimum*, 49, 15–29.

Ca' Piadera (n.d.) Agriturismo Ca' Piadera – Nogarolo Di Tarzo – Treviso. (online). Available at: https://www.capiadera.com/it/agriturismo/ (accessed 7 May 2019).

Carlsen, J. (2007) A review of global wine tourism research. *Journal of Wine Research*, 15(1), 5–13.

Carmichael, B. (2005) Understanding the wine tourism experience for winery visitors in the Niagara Region, Ontario, Canada. *Tourism Geographies*, 7(2), 185–204.

Castellani, V. and Sala, S. (2012) Ecological Footprint and Life Cycle Assessment in the sustainability assessment of tourism activities. *Ecological Indicators*, 16, 135–147.

Cavanaugh, J. (2007) Making salami, producing Bergamo: the transformation of value. *Ethnos*, 72(2), 149–172.

Cawley, M. and Gillmor, D. (2008) Integrated rural tourism: concepts and practice. *Annals of Tourism Research*, 35(2), 316–337.

Charters, S. and Ali-Knight, J. (2002) Who is the wine tourist? *Tourism Management*, 23(3), 311–319.

Christou, P., Farmaki, A. and Evangelou, G. (2018) Nurturing nostalgia? A response from rural tourism stakeholders. *Tourism Management*, 69, 42–51.

Duca di Dolle (2019) Duca Di Dolle Relais. (online). Available at: http://ducadidolle.it (accessed 5 July 2019).

Due Carpini Agriturismo (2019) Agriturismo Due Carpini. Available at: https://www.duecarpini.it/ (accessed 5 July 2019).

Farrell, H. and Russell, S. (2011) Rural tourism. In: P. Robinson, S. Heitmann and P. Dieke, eds, *Research Themes for Tourism*, 100–113. Oxfordshire, UK: CABI.

Galluzzo, N. (2015a) Relationships between agritourism and certified quality food in Italian rural areas. *Romanian Review of Regional Studies*, 11(1), 77–88.

Galluzzo, N. (2015b) Relation between typologies of agritourism in Italy and agritourists aspirations. *Bulgarian Journal of Agricultural Science*, 21(6), 1162–1171.

Galluzzo, N. (2018) Analysis of staying time in Italian agritourism using a quantitative methodology: the case of Latium region. *Journal of Rural Social Sciences*, 33(1), 56–76.

Garau, C. (2015) Perspectives on cultural and sustainable rural tourism in a smart region: the case study of Marmilla in Sardinia (Italy). *Sustainability*, 7(6), 6412–6434.

Gazzetta Ufficiale della Repubblica Italiana (2001) Decreto Legislativo 18 Maggio 2001, N. 228. (online) Gazzettaufficiale.it. Available at: https://www.gazzettaufficiale.it/eli/id/2001/06/15/001G0272/sg (accessed 11 May 2019).

Getz, D. and Brown, G. (2006) Critical success factors for wine tourism regions: a demand analysis. *Tourism Management*, 27(1), 146–158.

Giaccio, V., Mastronardi, L., Marino, D., Giannelli, A. and Scardera, A. (2018) Do rural policies impact on tourism development in Italy? A case study of Agritourism. *Sustainability*, 10(8), 2938.

Gil Arroyo, C., Barbieri, C. and Rozier Rich, S. (2013) Defining agritourism: a comparative study of stakeholders' perceptions in Missouri and North Carolina. *Tourism Management*, 37, 39–47.

Gössling, S., Scott, D. and Hall, C. (2020) Pandemics, tourism and global change: a rapid assessment of COVID-19. *Journal of Sustainable Tourism*, 29(1), 1–20.

Hall, C. (2006) Introduction: culinary tourism and regional development: from slow food to slow tourism? *Tourism Review International*, 9(4), 303–305.

Hall, C. and Mitchell, R. (2000) Wine tourism in the Mediterranean: a tool for restructuring and development. *Thunderbird International Business Review*, 42(4), 445–465.

Heitmann, S., Robinson, P. and Povey, G. (2011) Slow food, slow cities and slow tourism. In: P. Robinson, S. Heitmann and P. Dieke, eds, *Research Themes for Tourism*. Oxford, MA: CABI, 114–127.

Il Follo Agriturismo. (n.d.) Available at: http://www.ilfollo.it/en/agriturismo/ (accessed 8 January 2021).

ISTAT (2017) Le Aziende Agrituristiche. Available at: https://www.istat.it/it/archivio/221471 (accessed 5 July 2019).

Jiang, Y. and Wang, S. (2018) Spatial distribution characteristics of agritourism consumption. *Sustainability*, 10(4), 992–1006.

Johnson, M. (2012) Land of wine and money. *The Financial Times*. Available at: https://www.ft.com/content/2774a2ee-192b-11e2-af4e-00144feabdc0 (accessed 5 July 2019).

Jones, P., Hillier, D. and Comfort, D. (2017) The sustainable development goals and the tourism and hospitality industry. *Athens Journal of Tourism*, 4(1), 7–18.

Konaxis, I. (2018) *Paesaggi Culturali Ed Ecoturismo: Cultural Landscapes and Ecotourism* (Italian Edition). Milan: Franco Angeli.

La Casa Vecchia (n.d.) La Casa Vecchia – Cantina in Valdobbiadene Dal 1896. Available at: https://www.lacasavecchia.it (accessed 5 July 2019).

Lang Research (2001) Travel Activities and Motivations Survey Wine and Cuisine Report. Toronto: Queenspark Press.

Le Mesine Agriturismo (n.d.) Le Mesine Agriturismo. Available at: https://www.agriturismolemesine.it (accessed 5 July 2019).

Linka, K., Rahman, P., Goriely, A. and Kuhl, E. (2020) Is it safe to lift COVID-19 travel bans? The Newfoundland story. *Computational Mechanics*, 66(5), 1081–1092.

Lofland, J., Snow, D., Anderson, L. and Lofland, L. (2006) *Analyzing Social Settings: A Guide to Qualitative Observation and Analysis*. Belmont, California: Wadsworth/Thomson Learning.

MacCannell, D. (1976) *The Tourist: A New Theory of The Leisure Class*. New York: Schocken Books.

Maso di Villa (n.d.) Maso Di Villa Relais Di Campagna. Available at: http://www.masodivilla.it/it (accessed 6 July 2019).

Meneley, A. (2004) Extra virgin olive oil and slow food. *Anthropologica*, 46(2), 165–176.

Milligan, M. (2007) Buildings as history: the place of collective memory in the study of historic preservation. *Symbolic Interaction*, 30(1), 105–123.

Novelli, M. (2012) Wine tourism events: Apulia, Italy. In: I. Yeoman, M. Robertson, J. Ali-Knight, S. Drummond and U. McMahon-Beattie, eds, *Festival and Events Management*. London: Routledge, 329–345.

Phillip, S., Hunter, C. and Blackstock, K. (2010) A typology for defining agritourism. *Tourism Management*, 31(6), 754–758.

Popovic, A. (2014) Zero km food. *Sustainability Network*. Available at: https://sustainetwork.wordpress.com/2014/01/15/zero-km-food/ (accessed 7 January 2021).

Regione Veneto. 2019. Agriturismo – Regione Del Veneto. Available at: https://www.regione.veneto.it/web/agricoltura-e-foreste/agriturismo (accessed 9 June 2019).

Ritzer, G. (1993) *The Mcdonaldization of Society*. Newbury Park, CA: Pine Forge Press.

Robinson, M. and Novelli, M. (2005) Niche tourism: an introduction. In: M. Novelli, ed., *Niche Tourism: Contemporary Issues, Trends and Cases*, 1–14. Oxford, UK: Elsevier Butterworth-Heinemann.

Romano, M. and Natilli, M. (2009) Wine tourism in Italy: new profiles, styles of consumption, ways of touring. *Turizam: međunarodni znanstveno-stručni časopis*, 57(4), 463–475.

Sharpley, R. and Jepson, D. (2011) Rural tourism: a spiritual experience? *Annals of Tourism Research*, 38(11), 52–71.

Sidali, K.L. (2011) A sideways look at farm tourism in Germany and in Italy. In: K.L. Sidali, S. A. Spiller and B. Schulze, eds, *Food, Agri-Culture and Tourism*, 2–24. Berlin: Springer.

Sims, R. (2009) Food, place and authenticity: local food and the sustainable tourism experience. *Journal of Sustainable Tourism*, 17(3), 321–336.

Slow Food International (2021) *Slow Food International*. Available at: https://www.slowfood.com/ (accessed 7 January 2021).

Sorea, D. and Csesznek, C. (2020) The groups of caroling lads from Făgăraș Land (Romania) as niche tourism resource. *Sustainability*, 12(11), 4577–4598.

Strada del Prosecco e Vini dei Colli Conegliano Valdobbiadene (n.d.) Home – Strada Del Prosecco E Vini Dei Colli Conegliano Valdobbiadene. Available at: https://www.coneglianovaldobbiadene.it/ (accessed 9 June 2019).

Tew, C. and Barbieri, C. (2012) The perceived benefits of agritourism: the provider's perspective. *Tourism Management*, 33(1), 215–224.

Tommasini, A. (2007) L'Agriturismo E La Promozione Di Attività Compatibili Con Lo Speciale Regime Di Tutela Delle Aree Protette. *XXXVI Incontro Di Studio Ce.S.E.T.* 141–150.

UNESCO (2019) Le Colline Del Prosecco Di Conegliano e Valdobbiadene. Available at: https://whc.unesco.org/en/list/1571/ (accessed 4 October 2019).

UNWTO (2017) Report of the Secretary-General Part I: Programme of Work for 2016–2017. Madrid, 11.

Urry, J. and Larsen, J. (2011) *The Tourist Gaze 3.0*. London: SAGE Publications.

Yepsen, R. (2010) Sustainability at slow food cheese event. *Biocycle*, 51(2), 33–34.

9.   Culinary tourism: artichoke from land to table in Spain

Francesc Fusté-Forné

1.   INTRODUCTION

Culinary tourism is a macro-niche form of tourism which has rapidly evolved during the last couple of decades (see Ellis et al., 2018; Hall, 2020). Aligned to its development, a series of special interest typologies of tourism based on foods and drinks have not only appeared but also been consolidated, and they have led to a growing tourist motivation towards gastronomy destinations (Rousta and Jamshidi, 2020). This is largely observed in wine tourism (see, for example, Carlsen, 2004), but also in beer (Plummer et al., 2005), cheese (Fusté-Forné, 2015; 2020) and tea tourism (Cheng et al., 2012), to cite some examples. Following the notion of niche tourism elaborated by Novelli (2005), a specialist food tourism niche is linked to the appreciation and discovery of a vernacular product. In other words, a food tourism niche is an avenue for local, small and rural producers to award tourism value to unique foods and dishes – and to the land, the people and the regional traditions where a specific food heritage comes from.

Tourists can experience the sense of a place by tasting its foods and dishes (see Smith, 2015). This also includes the symbolical meanings attached to culinary heritage (Bessière, 1998; Everett, 2019), which reveal what a society is like and provide a picture of its cultural and natural idiosyncrasies (Fusté-Forné, 2015). This chapter analyses the food tourism micro-niche of *artichoke tourism* in Spain from a conceptual perspective. Artichoke tourism involves visiting destinations where agricultural production is rooted and valorised, and human and environmental values are communicated, through foods. Such a novel micro-niche could be located within a broader critical review of existing published research, linked to a number of macro-niches such as, to name just a few, rural and agrotourism, cultural and heritage, health and well-being and slow tourism, or even at the intersection between these. However, this chapter provides an overview of artichoke tourism within the specific context of food tourism. By drawing on previous experiences, it highlights how festivals or restaurants may contribute to the creation of tourism value through a niche food product such as artichokes. Results discuss the potential of artichoke tourism for food tourism development, and its contribution to the understanding of a handmade, genuine and sustainable niche tourism, both academically and practically.

2.   THE SIGNIFICANCE OF CUISINE AND FOOD IN TOURISM

According to Lew, 'specialty and individualized travel experiences have always been part of the travel and tourism phenomenon' (2008: 417). The progressive rise of tourism during the second half of the 20th century led to the diversification of the tourism offer, as a result of the heterogeneity of demand. As a consequence, 'the niche tourism industry became the "new tourism" in the 1980s and 1990s. Combined with the second boom in Internet growth, the new tourism economy has become the Long Tail tourism economy in the first decade of the 2000s' (ibid.). This approach fits well with the emergence of food tourism. The study of the significance of food in tourism dates back to 1983, when Belisle published his investigation on the relationships between local produce and tourism in *Annals of Tourism Research*. More research followed to further scrutinise the role of food in tourism, and in 1998, Lucy Long defined culinary tourism as the process aimed towards the discovery of other cultures through food.

Later, Richards and Hjalager (2002) further explored the relationships between gastronomy and tourism, and Hall and Sharples (2003) provided the most widely accepted definition of food tourism, understood as the journey to a region which includes visits to food producers and facilities, food fairs and festivals, farmers markets, restaurants or other food-based tourist activities. Nowadays, a surge of academics and practitioners have focused on the development of 'food' in tourism, and culinary tourism is completely established as a type of niche tourism based on 'eating and drinking' (Yayla and Yayla, 2020) which can 'offer greater opportunities and a tourism that is more sustainable, less damaging and, importantly, more capable of delivering high-spending tourists' (Robinson and Novelli, 2005: 1). This is because food tourism as a niche form of tourism provides memorable experiences (Pine and Gilmore, 1998; Stone et al., 2019) which are based on the process of awarding tourism value to food – and *terroir* (see Fusté-Forné and Mundet, 2020). Food tourists are specifically motivated by experiencing a place in an authentic and sustainable manner (Jolliffe, 2019). In other words, 'culinary travellers are looking for a genuine and memorable experience that is enhanced by the role that food plays in it' (Balderas-Cejudo et al., 2019: 3).

Niche tourism refers to specialist forms of tourism that promote local authenticity – for example, food tourism – and were further developed in recent years because of a rising demand towards creative tourism (see, for example, Farsani et al., 2019). In this context, niche tourism 'has become a fundamental component of tourism decision and policy making' (Novelli, 2018: 345). A niche tourism form not only contributes to a greater economic development of territories, but also to the creation of a different and diverse destination's portfolio, and the subsequent building of competitive advantage. As highlighted in other chapters of this *Handbook*, niche tourism is expected to target

> very precise small markets that would be difficult to split further. But as well as niche tourism based around what tourists do, there is also a geographical dimension by which locations with highly specific offers are able to establish themselves as niche destinations. Thus, for instance, a wine growing region can position itself as a niche destination offering tours of its specific wines. (Robinson and Novelli, 2005: 6)

Food tourism represents an opportunity for local growers and producers to promote local heritages and landscapes. By combining agriculture and tourism (Berno, 2011; Telfer and Wall, 1996), the growing impact of food-based activities has created a range of food-based attractions which engage tourists with regional lifestyles in contemporary tourism.

If the focus is narrowed down, 'food tourism also encompasses such categories as beer, cheese or wine tourism, and overall seeks to contribute to a general understanding regarding what tourists consume, and the infrastructure and experience surrounding it' (Duarte Alonso and Kiat Kok, 2020: 3). This may be also transferred to other types of special interest food tourism such as artichoke tourism, as is discussed in this chapter. While culinary tourism is a respected macro-niche, artichoke tourism is an emerging micro-niche. A local product is a driver for food tourism, and 'food' is regarded as a non-human actor which contributes to the construction of a tourist destination (Ren, 2011).

In this sense, the impact of a specific niche food tourism on a destination is extensive: for example, a cheese tourist will not only travel to 'taste cheese', but also to discover both tangible and intangible heritage embedded in cheese – namely, the landscape where animals are grazing and feeding (see Fusté-Forné, 2015), involving the rural context of where such activities would take place, hence potential links to the macro-niche of rural tourism as indicated previously. In a similar vein, recent publications have identified food-based tourism practices which are leading towards the development of micro-niche forms of food tourism focused on hot spring cuisine (Jolliffe, 2019) or temple food (Lee and Wall, 2020).

Food and drink are the cornerstone of gastronomy tourism (see Björk and Kauppinen-Räisänen, 2016), and they are also largely used for marketing purposes (see Getz and Robinson, 2014). The increasing relationship between food and tourism also provides new forms of cuisine commodification (Laeis et al., 2019) which is attached to a vernacular product and its cultural meanings – in a particular territory where local communities protect and communicate them. This is because

> the connotations of a more tailored and individualized service carries its own cachet relating to features like the small scale of operations, implied care and selectivity regarding discerning markets, and a suggested sensitivity of tourists. Such features provide a more apt fit with planning and development policies relating to environmentally sustainable and socially caring tourism. (Robinson and Novelli, 2005: 6)

Food tourism is not only a travel experience where tourist satisfaction remains a main objective of its implementation, it also emerges as an avenue towards the gathering of knowledge about local foods, culinary techniques and gastronomy history (Balderas-Cejudo et al., 2019). In particular, this chapter discusses how destinations can create a tourism attraction with a focus on artichokes.

To end this section, it is important to acknowledge the role of culinary tourism in fulfilling UNESCO's Sustainable Development Goals (SDGs) (2020). The notions around culinary tourism as a niche tourism are aligned with the pursuit of four of these goals. First, food tourism activities and experiences contribute to sustainable community development (SDG 11), given its potential economic impact, but also its implications for local ecological and social well-being (Fusté-Forné and Jamal, 2021). Second, in the framework of Slow Food and slow tourism, culinary niche markets encourage responsible production and consumption (SDG 12). These first two goals both inform and urge permanent action to preserve the climate (SDG 13) and the environment (SDG 15) as the source of our food.

3.   CASE STUDY CONTEXT

Departing from the concept of 'food tourism' and the analysis of existing literature and secondary sources that showcase examples of artichoke tourism activities and practices in Spain, this chapter discusses the valorisation of artichokes and their potential transition from a local product to a tourism attraction. Spain is one of the largest artichoke-producing countries in the world (FAO, 2020). Also, it ranks second globally in terms of international tourism arrivals and income (UNWTO, 2019), as data showed prior to the spread of the coronavirus crisis. In terms of food, previous studies have revealed that 15% of tourists who visit Spain are motivated by food and gastronomy, with a budget 20% higher than average tourists (KPMG, 2019). These figures justify the potential of the relationship between artichokes and tourism, and the chapter critically describes artichoke tourism as a form of niche tourism that attributes tourism value to this product.

While cultural tourism is a form of niche tourism and cultural tourists represent its niche market, this research is built on the framework of food tourism as the macro-niche tourism and food tourists as its macro-niche market. However, it goes beyond in order to focus on a micro-niche tourism in which artichoke tourism and artichoke tourists become the micro-niche segment. No one would hesitate to define beer tourists, cheese tourists or tea tourists. Here, the development of artichoke tourism as a niche is a pathway to communicate an 'expression of identity through specific activities that also overlap with other consumer preferences' (Robinson and Novelli, 2005: 7). Artichoke tourism is a tourism micro-niche, which may contribute to the differentiation and diversification of a destination portfolio of tourism experiences.

4.   ARTICHOKE TOURISM IN SPAIN

The artichoke is an important asset of Spanish agriculture and while we can anticipate its use in restaurant menus, especially as a winter and spring vegetable, there is no specific research that has dealt with the offer of an artichoke-based tourism. The artichoke (*Cynara scolymus*) is 'a plant with a round mass of pointed parts like leaves surrounding its flower that are eaten as a vegetable' (Cambridge Dictionary, 2020). Its most prolific production areas, and its origin, are located on the Mediterranean shores. Artichokes form part of the Mediterranean diet, which was acknowledged by UNESCO as an Intangible Cultural Heritage of Humanity in 2013 (UNESCO, 2013). They can be largely found at local markets and supermarkets (Figure 9.1). From a historical perspective, their

> consumption dates back more than two thousand years. These plants were already considered by ancient civilisations as an appreciable food, and they were especially combined with coriander, wine, olive oil and *garum*, the name of a famous fish sauce used in antiquity. It is a large thistle, as indicated by the Arabic origin of its name, *thorn of land*. (Ajuntament de Benicarló, 2020)

This latter concept reveals a strong attachment to the territory where artichokes grow.

Attributing tourism value to artichokes may rely on a wide range of activities and practices. As previous research has defined with regards to cheese (Fusté-Forné, 2015), chocolate (Prinz and Prinz, 2013) and coffee (Candelo et al., 2019), agri-food producers are engaged with tourism via production and consumption. On one side, tourists may visit the landscape where animals are grazing and feeding, the farms or handcraft workshops where cheese is made, and local fairs and festivals where cheese is sold. On the other, tourists may taste cheese at cheese facilities, buy it at shops or markets or order a cheese-based dish at a local restaurant. In the long term, it becomes an exported product in the global food value chain. Artichoke tourism may be developed following similar pathways.

Source: Author.

Figure 9.1   *Artichokes in a municipal market*

4.1   Valorising the Artichoke with Quality Labels

A quality label is a significant aspect to give visibility to a local product. The most recognised quality acknowledgements are the Protected Designation of Origin (PDO) and the Protected Geographical Indication (PGI). Spain has two artichokes which are certified. First, the PGI *Alcachofa de Tudela* (Tudela artichoke), in the region of Navarra, northern Spain. Second, the PDO *Alcachofa de Benicarló* (Benicarló artichoke), in the province of Castellón, Valencia, eastern Spain. The PDO 'Artichoke of Benicarló' is the highest distinction of an artichoke in Spain; it was approved in 1998 and recognised by the European Union in 2003. A quality label refers not only to the designated product, but the territory where it grows and the people who take care of it. As highlighted on the PDO 'Artichoke of Benicarló' website

> much of this recognition is due to the good traditional work of farmers in the area, who generation after generation have been able to work with commitment and care these lands that always stood out for the quality of their products. This good work is joined by strict regulations that control the entire process of making the Benicarló Artichoke – from its collection in the fields, to its selection, packaging, labeling and shipping – to ensure that, only, the best fruits of these excellent lands arrive to your table. (Alcachofa de Benicarló, 2020)

This process shows the rural production context of the artichoke leading to the enhancement of the product through a 'from field to plate' experience for tourists.

   Tudela is the other great artichoke in Spain. In this context

> The Tudela artichoke is one of the most praised vegetables by local gourmets. Named the flower of the orchard for its characteristic shape, in Navarre only the variety *Blanca de Tudela* is grown and is distinguished from others by its more rounded shape and by having a circular hole at the top. (Verduras de Tudela, 2020)

Artichokes are harvested manually, which means that a direct contact with nature is maintained. This contributes to the preservation of rural entrepreneurs' know-how, which transfers the power of tradition and the proximity of the territory to the final product. In recent years, this artisanal process has resulted in increasing difficulty recruiting people to collect the produce, especially in Tudela, which has led to a decrease in the production area. However, 'consumers are increasingly demanding the differentiated product with the PGI label *Alcachofa de Tudela*, which means that little-by-little we get to be known in the market' (Agronews, 2019). The quality label is, precisely, a firm step towards the visibility of the product, and a key element for the construction of its image as a tourist attraction.

4.2   The Land as a Source of Taste

It is obvious to say that landscapes are crucial for the production of a particular food and any experience associated with it. Specifically, artichokes are heavily dependent upon climate. The production area of Benicarló artichokes is 'located in the gentle coastal plains of the Baix Maestrat (Castellón). Specifically, its growing area is divided between the towns of Benicarló, Càlig, Peñíscola and Vinaròs' (Alcachofa de Benicarló, 2020). These are characterised by a coastal climate, where the Mediterranean

> has a beneficial effect on these rich lands, allowing the artichoke to develop with an excellent, round, consistent and compact quality. These special micro-climatic characteristics naturally confer an extraordinary resistance to the artichoke which, under optimal conservation conditions, offers a long life without compromising its high quality. (ibid.)

From the second half of the 20th century the cultivation of artichokes in this region started to increase thanks to the development of transport infrastructure that allowed it to reach national markets, and little-by-little, popularise the autochthonous production of artichokes.

The inland production area of Tudela artichokes includes 33 towns in the Ribera de Navarra. In this case, the territory is characterised by

> medium-textured soils, free from stones, rich in lime, fresh and well drained. The climate of the area is also very favourable to obtain the excellence of this vegetable. With cold winters and mild springs, it allows a much slower production than in other areas, thus obtaining a more careful quality product. (Verduras de Tudela, 2020)

In addition, it must be considered that both production and harvesting rely on a clearly marked seasonality, which means that *unique* artichokes can only be marketed between late autumn and late spring, in the northern hemisphere, also providing an opportunity for de-seasonalising the tourism experience in the area. This seasonality is expressed through the genuine taste of artichokes, which are impregnated with 'land'. Both the landscapes and processes embedded in artichoke production are a tourism attraction, which may foster the development of sustainable relationships between 'artichokes' and 'tourism'.

4.3   Artichoke-Based Events and Gastronomy

Events are generally seen as a way to protect and promote local heritage and traditions. The most important artichoke-based event in Spain is the Festa de la Carxofa (Artichoke Festival) celebrated in Benicarló during the month of January. People can explore tastings and restaurant menus where artichokes are the main ingredient. The festival also includes a series of social and cultural events that ends with a big toast of artichokes. As discussed above, the relationship between Benicarló and the artichoke is reflected in its agricultural landscapes, and a large thistle even appears on the coat of arms of the city as a manifestation of the historic importance of the product in the region. In this sense, the presence of an 'artichoke' in the city's coat of arms goes back a long way, possibly 'to the final moments of the thirteenth century, when the castle of Peñíscola and its territory, which included the farmhouse of Benigazlún or Binigazló [...], belonged to the *Mestre del Temple*' (Ajuntament de Benicarló, 2020).

There are examples of other artichoke festivals in Spain, predominantly located on the Mediterranean coastline where there is major artichoke production (Gobierno de España, 2020). For example, a fair and gastronomic days celebrating artichokes and rice in Amposta (Ajuntament d'Amposta, 2020; La Vanguardia, 2018) in the southeastern part of Catalonia, take place in February. Local and regional restaurants offer menus where both artichokes and rice are included as remarkable rural products of Delta de l'Ebre, part of their culinary identity given by the Mediterranean climate. Moreover, Carxofada is celebrated every year in March in Sant Boi de Llobregat (Ajuntament de Sant Boi de Llobregat, 2020; El Periódico, 2019), near Barcelona. Llobregat region is a significant area in Catalonia for the production of vegetables, producing distinctive foods that represent both its agriculture and its gastronomy (Leal, 2013). The artichoke of Sant Boi de Llobregat has recently become a symbol of the village and an avenue towards a healthy and sustainable lifestyle. These events invite residents and tourists to celebrate artichoke heritage.

Benicarló is the place that best integrates the artichoke as part of its cultural and social fabric as a destination, through activities such as 'artichoke days', gastronomic events encouraging the participation of local people to support the production and commercialisation of a local product, via restaurants which prepare artichoke-based cuisine. In a similar way, Tudela incorporates artichokes within restaurant menus in the month of May, which is when artichoke season is celebrated. While these events include different activities, the preparation of artichoke-based dishes is critical. The artichoke is a very versatile food which combines well with meat or fish, and it can be cooked with both salty and sweet ingredients. Artichokes are therefore paired with other local products in order to reflect a more robust regional cuisine, which attracts more tourists to local restaurants – understood as spaces of communication of forms of production and consumption which also include the adoption of products and recipes from international cuisines such as Japanese (see, for example, Assmann and Rath, 2010).

The Artichoke Festival's menu and other events mentioned above are added to gastronomic tours proposed by restaurant guides and websites, which mainly focus on artichoke-based cuisine in restaurants in Barcelona and Madrid, where several establishments offer dishes made with artichokes. Examples of original and unique dishes that can be cooked with organic artichokes are included in Figure 9.2, which proposes a selection of dishes gathered from various restaurant menus available during the Artichoke Festival (Festa de la Carxofa, 2020). The implications of this menu are discussed further in the next section.

Starters

Skewer of artichokes and prawns on a bed of artichoke hummus
Hedgehog stuffed with artichoke, red prawn and its bud
Artichoke *nigonyaki* with a touch of wasabi and fresh ginger

Main courses

Cuttlefish rice and galleys with artichokes
Market rockfish *suquet* with artichokes
Ingot of artichoke and lamb's milk with its juice and fried artichoke

Desserts

Sweet artichoke cubes and Manchego cheese with ginger
Artichoke flan
White chocolate soup with artichoke brownie and coffee ice cream

---

Source: Author.

Figure 9.2   *A proposal of an artichoke tasting menu*

5.   DISCUSSION AND CONCLUSIONS

This chapter has approached artichoke tourism as a micro-niche segment of culinary tourism. Previous research has analysed the role of food in tourism to confirm that culinary tourism is a well-established macro-niche tourism (see Ellis et al., 2018). Culinary tourism celebrates food heritage and traditions, conveys both physical and symbolic attributes of foods and drinks, and makes food available to tourists. This work contributes to furthering the niche food tourism by highlighting the case of artichoke-based tourism. Focused on the case of Spain, results reveal that a quality certification may be a proper departing point to the planning and development of a micro-niche tourism. While wine tourism may be used as a reference example to the advancement of specific forms of culinary tourism, food producers and destination managers can also take advantage of simple linkages built between 'food' and 'tourism' through a pint of beer, a piece of cheese or a cup of tea.

In this sense, Ren (2011) says that 'food' is a non-human actor which also contributes to the construction of a destination. Food informs the food tourism landscape of a place (or a nation) and it also influences people's perceptions, which are the foundation for the strategic use of culinary heritage as the driver of people-to-people cultural interactions – gastrodiplomacy (Suntikul, 2019). With regards to Spanish artichokes, there are two examples of certified products: Benicarló and Tudela artichokes. In addition, other regional geographical contexts also produce excellent artichokes, such as the aforementioned Llobregat, in Catalonia, and those from other Mediterranean regions. These places of production become the primary places of consumption. From a theoretical perspective, artichoke-based tourism practices are focused on three issues: the territory, the events and the restaurants. Based on the features of the territory (for example, its climate) and the curated work of growers, artichokes travel from land to table in a sustainable manner. Cultivation fields retain the essence of artichoke heritage in rural settings. Despite its wide availability in markets and supermarkets, especially during winter and spring months, there are also a lot of seasonal annual events which rely on artichokes. Fairs and festivals valorise artichokes and bring them to a shared environment. Production and consumption of certain types of foods are not only a way of nurturing or living, they are also a vital part of leisure and tourist experiences (Hjalager and Johansen, 2013). Furthermore, a focus on the 2030 Agenda for Sustainable Development reveals how food tourism is critically engaged with UNESCO's goals (see, for example, Saarinen, 2020) and, especially, how the relationships between food and tourism improve sustainable directions for *slow* production and consumption (Fusté-Forné and Jamal, 2021).

Also, this chapter states that artichokes are a driver for food tourism. In particular, fairs and festivals exemplify the relationship between artichokes and tourism, and show the potential of artichoke tourism. Events are not only a pathway to experience artichoke heritage, they represent an opportunity for the development of a micro-niche segment of food tourism

> Festivals and events have been created to celebrate arts and culture, encourage visitors to become more actively involved in experiencing local practices (i.e. preparing food, playing music, making crafts), and raise awareness about good causes. Such activities and development expand a destination's reach beyond mainstream tourism markets and into peripheral ones. They may also contribute to inclusive growth through the extension of the tourism season. (Novelli, 2018: 355)

Recent research on other micro-niche forms of culinary tourism confirms that a 'food' can be developed as an ingredient of sustainable tourism (see, for example, Hall and Gössling, 2016). From a practical perspective, this research shows that both landscapes and processes embedded in artichoke production have the potential to become tourism attractions which foster the development of a sustainable relationship between 'food' and 'tourism'. Following the definition of beer tourism (Plummer et al., 2005), this study defines artichoke tourism as a form of travel motivated by the desire to experience the artichoke-growing and harvesting processes, to visit an artichoke fair or festival and to taste artichokes. While it would be difficult to quantify travellers pursuing a specific artichoke-based journey, artichokes can certainly represent a specific market to target within the context of culinary tourism. Further research is required to scrutinise the perspectives of local stakeholders and culinary tourists on the promotion of artichoke tourism. A comparison between local actors, such as producers, restaurants owners and destination management organisations, will also provide useful insights to an adequate design and marketing of artichoke as a micro-niche type of food tourism.

According to Lew

> never before in the history of humankind have more consumers had more choices and more opportunities than today. Because of the many businesses that are vying for consumer attention in a crowded global marketplace, market differentiation and specialization are increasing. There are more market segments today than there were yesterday, and there will be more tomorrow than there are today. (2008: 412)

This urges academics and practitioners to further investigate the connections between different micro-niche examples of culinary tourism. It is evident that artichoke tourism can also be combined with other micro-niche segments. This is observed in the menu presented in the previous section and the wide range of gastronomic applications of artichokes. The incorporation of regional foods, such as seafood, is a primary example. However, menus also promote a national identity by using products such as Manchego cheese. Furthermore, the current cosmopolitan world requires the fusion of culinary traditions, which is manifested in the Japanese savours. The relationship between ingredients is not limited to tasting menus. It is also observed in the cultural applications of a product: the artichoke flower serves to produce rennet, which is used in cheesemaking. Cheese heritage also relies on artichoke (see, for example, Gostin and Waisundara, 2019), thus cheese tourism can also promote artichoke tourism. There are even some national and international examples which showcase the elaboration of artichoke-flavoured beer. Is this the time of artichokes?

While seasonality provides the product with a genuine taste of the land in a certain moment, the pairing with other foods and drinks will accentuate the connection between 'land' and 'table' and increase the collaboration and cooperation between local farmers and growers. Agriculture is also a creative tourism attraction (Farsani et al., 2019) which enhances the preservation and promotion of culinary heritage and traditions, and the creation of meaningful food experiences in unique cultural and natural environments. Also, the potential of artichokes for food tourism development, and their contribution to the understanding of a handmade, genuine and sustainable niche tourism, needs to be developed from a multi-destination perspective in order to provide a worldwide approach and further contribute to the advancement of niche markets in tourism. In this sense, the current context derived from the COVID-19 crisis and its early stages of recovery bring huge uncertainty as to how macro-niche culinary tourism and its micro-niche examples will adapt to the new situation. Food tourism experiences are planned and promoted as differentiation and diversification strategies to attract regional tourists. Artichoke tourism can work in this direction and engage with domestic tourists in order to improve the recovery of post-pandemic tourism (Brouder, 2020; Nepal, 2020). While this chapter discussed the role of artichoke tourism as a vehicle to sustainable development and tourism, upcoming research must focus on the future relationships between food and tourism, and, ultimately, on how residents and tourists will negotiate post-pandemic culinary tourist experiences.

REFERENCES

Agronews (2019) *Arranca la campaña de otoño de alcachofa de Tudela con buenas previsiones.* Available at: https://www.agronewscastillayleon.com/arranca-la-campana-de-otono-de-alcachofa-de-tudela-con-buenas-previsiones

Ajuntament d'Amposta (2020) *Festa de la Carxofa.* Available at: https://www.turismeamposta.cat/festa-de-la-carxofa

Ajuntament de Benicarló (2020) *Festa de la Carxofa.* Available at: https://www.ajuntamentdebenicarlo.org/fes/pfes-carxofa.php3

Ajuntament de Sant Boi de Llobregat (2020) *21a Carxofada de Sant Boi.* Available at: http://www.santboi.cat/carxofada

Alcachofa de Benicarló (2020) *Denominación de origen.* Available at: http://www.alcachofabenicarlo.com

Assmann, S. and Rath, E. C. (2010) *Japanese foodways, past and present.* Chicago: University of Illinois Press.

Balderas-Cejudo, A., Patterson, I. and Leeson, G. W. (2019) Senior foodies: a developing niche market in gastronomic tourism. *International Journal of Gastronomy and Food Science*, 16, 100152.

Belisle, F. J. (1983) Tourism and food production in the Caribbean. *Annals of Tourism Research*, 10(4), 497–513.

Berno, T. (2011) Sustainability on a plate: linking agriculture and food in the Fiji Islands tourism industry. In R. M. Torres and J. H. Momsen (eds), *Tourism and agriculture: new geographies of consumption, production and rural restructuring*. London: Routledge, 87–103.

Bessière, J. (1998) Local development and heritage: traditional food and cuisine as tourist attractions in rural areas. *Sociologia ruralis*, 38(1), 21–34.

Björk, P. and Kauppinen-Räisänen, H. (2016) Local food: a source for destination attraction. *International Journal of Contemporary Hospitality Management*, 28(1), 177–94.

Brouder, P. (2020) Reset redux: possible evolutionary pathways towards the transformation of tourism in a COVID-19 world. *Tourism Geographies*, 22(3), 484–90.

Cambridge Dictionary (2020) *Artichoke*. Available at: https://dictionary.cambridge.org/es/diccionario/ingles/artichoke.

Candelo, E., Casalegno, C., Civera, C. and Büchi, G. (2019) A ticket to coffee: stakeholder view and theoretical framework of coffee tourism benefits. *Tourism Analysis*, 24(3), 329–40.

Carlsen, P. J. (2004) A review of global wine tourism research. *Journal of Wine Research*, 15(1), 5–13.

Cheng, S., Hu, J., Fox, D. and Zhang, Y. (2012) Tea tourism development in Xinyang, China: stakeholders' view. *Tourism Management Perspectives*, 2, 28–34.

Duarte Alonso, A. and Kiat Kok, S. (2020) Sense of place and certainty in uncertain socioeconomic conditions: Contributions of local cuisine to culinary tourism. *Journal of Heritage Tourism*, 16(3), 247–62.

El Periódico (2019) *Sant Boi presenta un paté y una cerveza de alcachofa para su 20a Carxofada*, March 12.

Ellis, A., Park, E., Kim, S. and Yeoman, I. (2018) What is food tourism? *Tourism Management*, 68, 250–63.

Everett, S. (2019) Theoretical turns through tourism taste-scapes: the evolution of food tourism research. *Research in Hospitality Management*, 9(1), 3–12.

FAO (2020) *Production quantities of artichokes by country*. Available at: http://www.fao.org/faostat/en/#data/QC/visualize

Farsani, N. T., Ghotbabadi, S. S. and Altafi, M. (2019) Agricultural heritage as a creative tourism attraction. *Asia Pacific Journal of Tourism Research*, 24(6), 541–49.

Festa de la Carxofa [program] (2020) *XVII Festa de la Carxofa Benicarló 2020*. Benicarló: Ajuntament de Benicarló.

Fusté Forné, F. (2015) Cheese tourism in a world heritage site: Vall de Boí (Catalan Pyrenees). *European Journal of Tourism Research*, 11, 87–101.

Fusté-Forné, F. (2020) Savouring place: cheese as a food tourism destination landmark. *Journal of Place Management and Development*, 13(2), 177–94.

Fusté-Forné, F. and Jamal, T. (2021) Slow food tourism: an ethical microtrend for the Anthropocene. *Journal of Tourism Futures*, 6(3), 227–32.

Fusté-Forné, F. and Mundet i Cerdan, L. (2021) A land of cheese: from food innovation to tourism development in rural Catalonia. *Journal of Tourism and Cultural Change*, 19(2), 166–83.

Getz, D. and Robinson, R. N. (2014) Foodies and food events. *Scandinavian Journal of Hospitality and Tourism*, 14(3), 315–30.

Gobierno de España (2020) *Alcachofa*. Available at: https://www.mapa.gob.es/app/MaterialVegetal/fichaMaterialVegetal.aspx?idFicha=3889

Gostin, A. I. and Waisundara, V. Y. (2019) Edible flowers as functional food: A review on artichoke (Cynara cardunculus L.). *Trends in Food Science and Technology*, 86, 381–91.

Hall, C. M. (2020) Improving the recipe for culinary and food tourism? The need for a new menu. *Tourism Recreation Research*, 45(2), 284–87.

Hall, C. M. and Gössling, S. (2016) *Food tourism and regional development: networks, products and trajectories*. Abingdon: Routledge.

Hall, C. M. and Sharples, L. (2003) The consumption of experiences or the experience of consumption? An introduction to the tourism of taste. In C. M. Hall, L. Sharples, R. Mitchell, N. Macionis and B. Cambourne (eds), *Food tourism around the world. Development, Management and Markets*. Oxford: Butterworth Heinemann, 13–36.

Hjalager, A. M. and Johansen, P. H. (2013) Food tourism in protected areas–sustainability for producers, the environment and tourism? *Journal of Sustainable Tourism*, 21(3), 417–33.

Jolliffe, L. (2019) Cooking with locals: a food tourism trend in Asia? In E. Park, S. Kim and I. Yeoman (eds), *Food tourism in Asia*. Singapore: Springer, 59–70.

KPMG (2019) *La Gastronomía en la Economía Española*. Madrid: KPMG International.

La Vanguardia (2018) *Amposta promociona els productes de proximitat amb la carxofa com a protagonista*. Available at: https://www.lavanguardia.com/vida/20180225/441076986054/amposta-promociona-els-productes-de-proximitat-amb-la-carxofa-com-a-protagonista.html

Laeis, G. C., Scheyvens, R. A. and Morris, C. (2019) Cuisine: a new concept for analysing tourism-agriculture linkages? *Journal of Tourism and Cultural Change*, 18(6), 643–58.

Leal Londoño, M. del P. (2013) *Turismo gastronómico y desarrollo local en Cataluña: el abastecimiento y comercialización de los productos alimenticios*. Barcelona: Universitat de Barcelona.

Lee, A. H. and Wall, G. (2020) Temple food as a sustainable tourism attraction: eco-gastronomic Buddhist Heritage and regional development in South Korea. *Journal of Gastronomy and Tourism*, 4(4), 209–22.

Lew, A. A. (2008) Long tail tourism: new geographies for marketing niche tourism products. *Journal of Travel & Tourism Marketing*, 25(3–4), 409–19.

Long, L. M. (1998) Culinary tourism: a folkloristic perspective on eating and otherness. *Southern Folklore*, 55(3), 181–204.

Nepal, S. K. (2020) Travel and tourism after COVID-19–business as usual or opportunity to reset? *Tourism Geographies*, 22(3), 646–50.

Novelli, M. (2005) *Niche tourism: contemporary issues, trends and cases*. Oxford: Elsevier.

Novelli, M. (2018) Niche tourism: past present and future. In C. Cooper, S. Volo, W. C. Gartner and N. Scott (eds) *The Sage Handbook of Tourism Management*. London: Sage, 344–59.

Pine, B. J. and Gilmore, J. H. (1998) Welcome to the experience economy. *Harvard Business Review*, 76, 97–105.

Plummer, R., Telfer, D., Hashimoto, A. and Summers, R. (2005) Beer tourism in Canada along the Waterloo–Wellington ale trail. *Tourism Management*, 26(3), 447–58.

Prinz, D. R. and Prinz, D. (2013) *On the chocolate trail: a delicious adventure connecting Jews, religions, history, travel, rituals and recipes to the magic of cacao*. Woodstock: Jewish Lights Publishing.

Ren, C. (2011) Non-human agency, radical ontology and tourism realities. *Annals of Tourism Research*, 38(3), 858–81.

Richards, G. and Hjalager, A. M. (2002) *Tourism and gastronomy*. London: Routledge.

Robinson, M. and Novelli, M. (2005) Niche tourism: an introduction. In M. Novelli (ed.) *Niche tourism: contemporary issues, trends and cases*. Oxford: Elsevier, 1–11.

Rousta, A. and Jamshidi, D. (2020) Food tourism value: investigating the factors that influence tourists to revisit. *Journal of Vacation Marketing*, 26(1), 73–95.

Saarinen, J. (2020) *Tourism and sustainable development goals: research on sustainable tourism geographies*. Abingdon: Routledge.

Smith, S. (2015) A sense of place: place, culture and tourism. *Tourism Recreation Research*, 40(2), 220–33.

Stone, M. J., Migacz, S. and Wolf, E. (2019) Beyond the journey: the lasting impact of culinary tourism activities. *Current Issues in Tourism*, 22(2), 147–52.

Suntikul, W. (2019) Gastrodiplomacy in tourism. *Current Issues in Tourism*, 22(9), 1076–94.

Telfer, D. J. and Wall, G. (1996) Linkages between tourism and food production. *Annals of Tourism Research*, 23(3), 635–53.

UNESCO (2013) *Mediterranean diet*. Available at: https://ich.unesco.org/en/RL/mediterranean-diet-00884

UNESCO (2020) *UNESCO and sustainable development goals*. Available at: https://en.unesco.org/sustainabledevelopmentgoals

UNWTO (2019) *International tourism highlights*. Madrid: World Tourism Organization.

Verduras de Tudela (2020) *Alcachofa*. Available at: https://verdurasdetudela.com/alcachofa

Yayla, Ö. and Yayla, Ş. (2020) The Potential of Amasya Cuisine for Gastronomy Tourism. In İ.O. Coşkun, A. Lew, N. Othman, G. Yüksek and S. G. Aktaş (eds) *Heritage tourism beyond borders and civilizations*. Singapore: Springer, 115–24.

10. Astro-tourism in Portugal's rural areas

Áurea Rodrigues and Helena Reis

1. INTRODUCTION

The importance of niche products for the tourism industry is unquestionable and gains relevance in times when, due to the COVID-19 pandemic, the whole industry must be rethought and reassessed, considering the directives of the Sustainable Development Agenda 2030 and the UN's Sustainable Development Goals (SDGs). Niche tourism is a product diversification strategy which aims to attract proximity, domestic and regional tourism, answering the requests of specific markets by offering more diverse and distinguishable tourism activities and experiences (Soleimani et al., 2018). A series of studies has elaborated on the notion of niche tourism related to rural areas and nature and suggested that, through brand image, niche tourism helps destinations to differentiate their products and compete in a more cluttered environment (Hjalager et al., 2018; Huang et al., 2010; Novelli and Benson, 2005).

Robinson and Novelli (2005) posit that the niche tourism development is associated with high levels of innovation and entrepreneurship at the locations, while Boekstein and Tevera (2012) claim the development of this type of tourism is beneficial for rural destinations. These two concepts provide the grounds for the present chapter, which expounds on the processes involved in the implementation, development and establishment of a niche product, astro-tourism, in rural areas in the interior of Portugal. According to Najafabadi (2012), this is a unique form of ecotourism that offers a magnificent way to draw tourists closer to nature. Its main assets – night-skies, celestial domes and a plethora of cosmic happenings – never end, do not need any maintenance and are always available. It is entirely unique in its features, and considered one of the ultimate sustainable attractions.

Although still understudied, the subject of astro-tourism is not new. In 2014, seminal researchers Fayos-Solá et al. (2014) prepared a crucial document meant to set in motion actions to be taken to acknowledge, regulate and create conditions for developing astro-tourism. More recently, Soleimani et al. (2018) asserted that this activity emerges from the special interest of tourists in sky-related activities such as astrophotography and sky observation being also classified within the nature-based tourism (Cater, 2010; Weaver, 2011).

Not many locations in the world can offer the ideal conditions for developing astro-tourism and implementing the necessary features such activity requires. This type of tourism heavily depends on the physical attributes of the locations, combining earthly features with the universally shared sky (Collison and Poe, 2013; Keller, 2010; Soleimani et al., 2018).

The Dark Sky® Alqueva, in Alentejo, Portugal, was created in 2007, aiming at the preservation of the night sky in order to develop tourist activities around astro-tourism. Later on, through a collaborative network, this association helped expand the astro-tourism exigencies to other areas in the country: Dark Sky® Aldeias do Xisto and Dark Sky® Vale do Tua.

This chapter will present evidence of the exquisite conditions found in these Portuguese regions, already internationally acknowledged, showing how an interior rural area can develop into a highly attractive tourism product.

The next section addresses astro-tourism in Portugal, followed by considerations around the relevance of light pollution mitigation for enhancing this activity and its contribution to sustainable development in rural areas. The methodology applied in this study is then explained. The subsequent section covers the case study of the Dark Sky® Network Portugal, stressing how crucial collaboration and networking among locations is when implementing this niche tourism product. Finally, evidence of the success of this project is presented and discussed, along with recommendations for destinations and entrepreneurs who intend to invest in astro-tourism in rural areas. Limitations, which can be converted into avenues for further research, will be shown. This study makes definite practical contributions by disclosing a clearer understanding of the process of implementation and establishment of this specialized segment of niche tourism, underlining the profound value of establishing networks and involving the local communities.

2. ASTRO-TOURISM, A NICHE TOURISM PRODUCT IN PORTUGAL

Our research aligns with the framework provided by Soleimani et al. (2018: 2301) to position astro-tourism within the niche segment. According to the authors:

> Niche implies that there is a place in the market for the product, and that there is a consumer for the product. It is based on the premise that the market should not be seen as a simplistic, homogenous whole with general needs, but rather as sets of individuals with specific needs relating to the qualities and features of particular products.

Moreover, the authors clarify that 'niche tourism can be divided into macro-niches (such as cultural tourism or rural tourism), and these can be further sub-divided into micro-niches such as gastronomy, sport, volunteer, and adventure (Robinson and Novelli, 2005), and in the instance of the present study, astro-tourism' (Soleimani et al., 2018: 2301).

In his study, Steps to Space, Cater (2010) suggests a wide approach to astro-tourism. He theorizes three typologies of space tourism founded within aeronautic terminology, contemplating the Terrestrial Space Tourism category, in which he inscribes a type classified as 'Edu-tainment [...] Popular Culture', under which we find 'Meteorite collecting. Eclipse tours. Stargazing tours', among others. Furthermore, Cater (2010: 844) argues that niche tours such as eclipse tours have been created because human beings are always curious to know 'what it is really like out there'. This type of tourism is where stargazing, meteor shower-loving and eclipse-chasing travellers search for places such as clearings or remote areas, where the sky is the darkest and clearest, to connect with the cosmos. It has been established as a sustainable form of small-scale tourism which provides a genuine experience by combining immersion in the local culture and community engagement with active learning through a creative self-expression process (Edensor, 2015; Rodrigues et al., 2015).

In a precise register, Fayos-Solá et al. (2014: 664) define astro-tourism as 'tourism using the natural resource of unpolluted night-skies, and appropriate scientific knowledge for astronomical, cultural and environmental activities'. Collison and Poe (2013) describe astro-tourism as a sustainable tourism segment that considers dark night sky as its main resource, while Caballero Sánchez et al. (2019) convey that astro-tourism happens when those who are interested in the sky (be they amateurs, professional astronomers or anyone interested in the field) travel from their residence to another place to observe and examine 'the wonders of the sky'.

The astro-tourism market is slowly emerging around the world, seeking to provide tangible socio-economic benefits to communities. Location is a key factor when it comes to observing and absorbing the sky, which requires a clear dark night in an area free from artificial light (Hölke et al., 2010; Najafabadi, 2012). Given that half of the world's population can no longer see the stars due to light pollution (Hamacher et al., 2020; Mizon, 2012), isolated places with their visible emptiness have become major attractions (Ingle, 2010). Niche market-based or alternative forms of tourism such as astro-tourism allow renovation, as well as inclusive empowerment across the industry, since they are characterized by 'small-scale, community-driven, local owned tourism products with low levels of negative impacts and low leakage' (Marschall and Schumacher, 2012: 726). Many astronomical sites have specific features related to agriculture and traditional practices, increasing the potential of wider product development (Collison, 2011). In order to succeed when implementing such a process, host communities must be involved, since they need to understand the potential side-effects of this form of tourism. On the one hand, they have to accept circadian alterations to working patterns, activities and services unfolding during the night, the diminishing of public light in the city, and so on. On the other hand, they may experience new business options, new experiences, new customers and more opportunities for providing varied services, including local gastronomy and fresh products, among others.

In 2011, Dark Sky® Alqueva became the First Starlight Tourism Destination, with the purpose of promoting tourist activities related to the protection of the night-skies. A clear and stable atmosphere is crucial for stargazing, while light pollution is one of its worse enemies. It is also important that the destination provides organized tourist facilities, such as lodging, tourist information, specialized equipment, trained astro-tourism guides and specialized travel activities.

The Dark Sky® Network Portugal (Figure 10.1) started with six municipalities around the Alqueva Lake, and was later extended to 10 municipalities in Portugal and 13 in Spain. It is the first cross-border starlight destination in the world, evidencing that the sky has no boundaries or limits. Due to their responsible tourism principles and international recognition, in 2019, the network integrated two more Portuguese regions: Dark Sky® Aldeias do Xisto and Dark Sky® Vale do Tua.

The major innovative element of the Dark Sky® Network was its original conception of turning difficulties into benefits and creating new tourist destinations engrained on an outstanding preserved night sky. All participating municipalities benefit from the same exceptional conditions, providing a wide range of activities that unfold mostly during the night so that visitors can enjoy these special locations. The network contributes to minimizing negative social, economic and environmental impacts and, at the same time, generates economic benefits for residents by diversifying the tourist offer in these rural areas, further enhancing the well-being of host communities with the mitigation of light pollution.

However, these are not distant remote areas and they display various additional features – landscape, scenery, prehistoric monuments and tourism facilities – and have the potential to attract people with specialized knowledge and skills. They can be considered double-fold destinations, offering daytime and night-time experiences to their visitors, which allows for a rich variety of activities on a single trip. In their anthropological study across different cultures, Galinier et al. share the opinion that 'the spatiotemporal domains of the night have their own

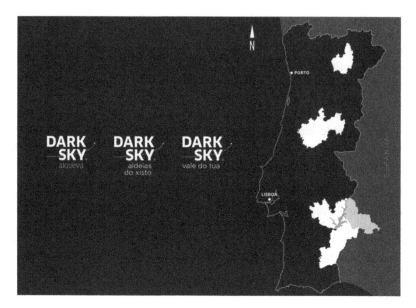

Source: Dark Sky® Portugal.

Figure 10.1   Dark Sky® Network Portugal

specific properties distinct from daytime spaces' (2010: 20), conferring to Edensor's (2015) statement that darkness reconfigures the visual sensing of landscape, offering an expansive spatial scale.

This double perception of the same reality, a reality that discloses in various sceneries, is quite enriching for the tourist offer, since the same destination can provide different sceneries and function as a double target: 'arguably, two sights, at daytime versus night-time, of the same site are two different tourism products. While seasonal differences may be more obvious for some geographic regions than others, day and night differences can be observed in all destinations and can be experienced by tourists in a single trip' (Huang and Wang, 2018: 275).

To understand the starlight as it exists at night, it is necessary to look at its key adversary: the light pollution that spreads across the world.

3.   THE RELEVANCE OF LIGHT POLLUTION

For decades, politicians, engineers, astronomers and many other interested individuals have studied and discussed light pollution and 'the gradual disappearance, since the 1950s, of the night sky' (Mizon, 2012). This author addresses the meeting of the UK Parliament's Science and Technology Select Committee in 2003, and their concerns that it is impractical for students to observe the night sky in their towns. The sky is important for education, for agricultural planting and harvesting, for navigation, telling time, measuring the seasons and health (Edensor, 2015; Fayos-Solá et al., 2014; Galinier et al., 2010; Pauley, 2004). As Gallaway elucidates:

The night sky is a unique and exquisitely valuable cultural asset that is being lost to humanity. Light pollution obscures the heavens, interferes with wildlife, and wastes billions of dollars in energy annually. Light pollution can be easily mitigated, but unfortunately, it has gone largely unnoticed as a preventable environmental problem. (2010: 71)

It is argued that well-lit cities are safer or not so prone to crime; however, there is evidence that criminality arises more from societal and economic problems (Steinbach et al., 2015). The solution is not to eradicate night lighting, although much can be done in this area:

> Often, the compulsion for more lights reflects habits of thought rather than facts. While this propensity is a good fit with the 'more is better' convention of industrial society, little thought is given to what is lost or to verifying supposed gains. For example, constant lighting often does little to deter crime. (Gallaway, 2010: 78)

Individuals living in towns who decide to take a holiday or a break in the countryside are not indifferent to two main differences (among others) they immediately sense: the overall silence of quiet, wide-open air spaces, and the darkness that allows them to look at the skies and enjoy the celestial dome above. While noisy environments can be controlled and regulated, the scarcity of public lightening implies other levels of perceptions, as indicated above. Reactions to these two experiences of silence and darkness can diverge, since not everybody is ready to indulge in the atmosphere they offer, so the stakeholders and Destination Management Organizations (DMOs) involved in the implementation and development of astro-tourism locations in Portugal found themselves faced with a new set of stages to be considered. Moreover, in order to consolidate the successful accomplishments of the first site (Alqueva), it was important to launch a relevant network for this type of niche tourism, so as to share knowledge and cooperate instead of compete. According to UNWTO (2020) after the COVID-19 crisis, destinations will be more resilient if they cooperate at a national and international level. The COVID-19 crisis has also shown that the challenge of tourism is no longer to work only for its growth but also to develop it as an activity with positive impacts on the environment and conservation (Cherkaoui et al., 2020). This may present opportunities for niche tourism options, and niche forms that are already walking this track might have their break. Astro-tourism is an established and acknowledged form in Portugal, so stakeholders, DMOs and local communities should understand their product can represent a serious contribution towards changing tourism from the 'new normal' to a 'new future'.

4.   METHODOLOGY

A holistic single case study approach (DePoy and Gitlin, 2010) was adopted for this chapter. According to Yin (2003: 13), a case study is 'an empirical inquiry that investigates a contemporary phenomenon within its real-life context, especially when the boundaries between phenomenon and context are not clearly evident'. In tourism research, case studies are frequently used to address themes or topics such as alternative forms of tourist experiences (Xiao and Smith, 2006). Moreover, Beeton (2005) posits that a case study is an appropriate method to explain why a tourism innovation worked or failed to work. Bryman (2008: 52) identifies single case in-depth analysis as 'the basic case study' and provides numerous examples of single case research, for example, of a single community, single organization or single event.

According to Benur and Bramwell (2015), most of the niche tourism products developed separately at destinations attract discrete tourist market segments, with the producers of the different niche products potentially failing to cooperate for mutual commercial benefit. These authors argue that the destination's niche products may be used in more integrative ways, with tourists interested in several of the niche offers, and with their producers potentially cooperating (Benur and Bramwell, 2015: 215). The case study presented in this chapter seeks to analyse the implementation and growth of astro-tourism in Portugal through the history of Dark Sky® Network Portugal. It also seeks to explain the importance of destinations functioning in a networking system, working in cooperation to build innovative and sustainable tourism products which are based on the endogenous resources and synergies of the destination. The following data sources were used: i) Documents collected from different sources such as the internet, Portuguese regional bodies and Dark Sky® Network Portugal; ii) Semi-structured interviews (Galletta, 2013; Olson, 2016) conducted with members of the Dark Sky® Network to collect information about the history and organization of the network and the benefits of working in cooperation at the level of learning, exchange and community; and iii) Participant observation (Jorgensen, 2020) undertaken by one of the co-authors, who participated in tourist activities and work meetings as an observer, in order to understand the process of using a network.

5.   DARK SKY NETWORK: HISTORY AND BACKGROUND

In Portugal, migrations have plagued the interior of the country since the 1930s as individuals leave to seek better employment conditions in coastal locations or abroad. This has created the conditions for the progressive demographic decline of these regions and a consequent lack of businesses, a situation which is especially pronounced in the border territories of Portugal and Spain (Natário et al., 2017). The interior of the Alentejo region is one of the most depopulated regions and includes of a large area that has undergone a programme of rural and cultural tourism development. In 2002, the largest artificial lake in Europe, Alqueva Lake, was created. The lake resulted from the construction of a dam; it is 83 km long, distributed along the Portuguese municipalities of Moura, Mourão, Portel, Barrancos, Reguengos de Monsaraz and Alandroal, and extends further to Spain, occupying an area of 250 km^2 (Rodrigues et al., 2015). The Alqueva region experienced a significant landscape change as a result of this lake, drawing the attention of investors who wanted to develop tourism here – especially involving nautical activities – and create 2,500 hotel beds. But in 2008 that plan was abandoned, due to a severe economic crisis in Portugal.

Meanwhile, Dark Sky® Alqueva was created as part of a sustainable tourism strategy that uses endogenous resources and, at the same time, offers a highly innovative and distinct tourism product that helps differentiate this rural destination from others in the country. The project acknowledged that the development of sustainable tourism is complex and that the interaction between society, the environment and the various local actors is crucial. Dark Sky® Alqueva had two main objectives: (i) to implement a sustainable use of light strategy; and (ii) to maximize the tourism opportunities of the region by creating new tourism products linked to the night sky, and to develop area-based marketing involving local and regional stakeholders, residents and the scientific community. Furthermore, the Dark Sky® concept promotes growth by means of integrated management of sustainable locations using the protected night-sky resource as the differentiating and unifying element of all its features: natural, heritage and cultural resources, community and tourists. There is a great commitment to territorial identity and sensory tourism as a means to connect people to the destination, the product and a tourist experience that stimulates personal growth and appreciation. It implies the creation of specific and complementary night activities, especially based upon the vocation of each territory, such as night canoeing, archeoastronomy, blind wine tasting and so on. Thus, these sites provide for unique sensory experiences, from observing the planets to looking at the craters on the moon, moving on to the deeper sky with a cosmic journey among the nebulae, the galaxies and stars which rise above in one of the finest skies in the world. The Official Dark Sky® Observatory in Cumeada is equipped with cutting-edge telescopes for solar and astronomical observations. The vast open spaces around Alqueva also offer a choice of activities, sensations and tastes to supplement the pleasures of stargazing, such as relaxing at sunset while enjoying a cocktail, or taking part in a blind wine tasting by starlight. Outdoor activities include walking, horseback excursions by moonlight or participating in astrophotography workshops, among others.

The certification of a starlight tourist destination aims at fostering worldwide improvement in the quality of tourist experiences and the protection of night-skies in starlight destinations. The criteria were established in December 2010, at the UNWTO Centre in Madrid, with repre-sentatives from UNESCO, UNESCO-Mab and the Instituto de Astrofísica de Canarias (IAC) (Starlight Foundation, 2020).

The requisites for certifying a destination are strict: the ideal conditions for observing the stars must be guaranteed for at least 50% of the year (at Alqueva, this percentage is around 80%); light pollution must be under control; and the site must have appropriate tourism infrastructure: accommodation, means of observation available to visitors, trained staff for astronomical interpretation and so on. Services provided to this type of tourist must bear in mind that these visitors sleep during the day and stay awake all night, inverting the circadian rhythm. To obtain certification, local communities, stakeholders and DMOs must play a vital role in the integration process through the creation of a partner network that includes compa-nies which are available to work with and adapt to this new offer. Integration is preceded by rigorous awareness and training. The Dark Sky® Alqueva was the first region to successfully implement the astro-tourism offer in Portugal; it was recognized and awarded by several inter-national entities, including UNWTO, the European Commission, China Outbound Tourism Research Institute (COTRI), Starlight Foundation, World Travel Awards, World Corporate Awards, World Confederation of Businesses (WORLDCOB), International Travel Awards and the Travel and Hospitality Awards (through its European Travel Awards programme), among others.

This type of tourism is extraordinarily complex to implement since it requires both spe-cialized knowledge on light pollution mitigation and astronomy, and knowledge on how to develop the tourism product in an integrated way, involving the stakeholders at the destination and working with different segments of tourists. After the success of Alqueva, Dark Sky® grew as a result of regional cooperation partnerships and, in 2018, it incorporated two other territories: 14 municipalities centred around Pampilhosa da Serra (Central Portugal), land of the 'Schist Villages', certified in June 2019 and the territory of Tua (North Portugal) which was certified in August 2020.

The three territories work in partnership, and the astro-tourism product developed in each location highlights that although each has different assets, they all nevertheless conform to the same rigorous quality of offer, centred on the certification criteria and mandatory rules of operation for the local stakeholders. They come with the safeguard of using the brand, centred around the principles of high-quality skies and the protection of integrated astro-tourism entrepreneurs, since, in Portugal, the term 'astro-tourism' is also registered and licensed exclusively for the use of members of the Dark Sky Network Portugal.

6. THE IMPORTANCE OF NETWORKING, FOR THE SUCCESS OF THE ASTRO-TOURISM IMPLEMENTATION

Portugal has a great tradition of offering mass tourism sustained by sun and sea along its coastline; yet this country has a rural inland with lots of potential for the development of tourism niches, whose supply bases are nature and rural assets. There are many potential locations in the world for the development of astro-tourism; however, Portugal's competitive advantage is its location and good weather. The facts that many European countries do not present favourable atmospheric conditions for observing the sky, that most people live in urban areas with strong light pollution, and that the three Portuguese destinations are close to airports, with good accessibility and not remote, making them safe for all types of tourist, especially families, are advantages for Portugal.

Even the most adventurous market segment in this niche, amateur astronomers, who display greater willingness to travel to most remote areas to observe the sky, prefer closer and safer destinations when travelling with their families. Furthermore, the equipment for stargazing is expensive and it is difficult to travel by plane with this sort of equipment. To have good telescopes at the destination implies a huge investment from local entrepreneurs; working collaboratively makes it possible for small-scale businesses, as well as specialized tour guides, to share equipment, but above all, to share knowledge in order to innovate and diversify the tourism offer supported by the same theme – the unpolluted sky.

A tourism network can be defined as 'an arrangement of inter-organization cooperation and collaboration' (Hall, 2005: 179). These networks allow the valuable exchange of knowledge, ideas and practices, as well as mistakes and errors that should be avoided. According to March and Wilkinson (2009), the performance of tourist destinations depends heavily on the connections formed by the stakeholders involved, and not only their individual characteristics. Due to the complexity of the tourism product (Zee and Vanneste, 2015) most service companies in a destination depend on each other to provide a holistic product to the customer (Zehrer and Raich, 2010), namely, the tourism offer in rural destinations, which is often based on micro-niches and small, family-centred enterprises that join efforts for promotion and development. Consistent with Saxena et al. (2007), these have a low capital basis and function with limited skills and experience. Concerning the destination, there is an amalgam of various stakeholders from private, public and hybrid parties who deliver and manage services and are involved in the tourism offer, including infrastructure, services, marketing and information. Aiming at mitigating the inherent difficulties in managing and developing innovation products in a rural destination, the concept of networks has been applied in certain areas in the last decades (Campón-Cerro et al., 2017). Departing from previous studies, Gibson et al. (2005) compile the benefits of network cooperation regarding exchange and learning, business activity and community. Table 10.1 summarizes the identified main advantages that occurred with this cooperation.

Due to the network, it was possible for the new destinations to learn from the past experiences of the pioneer location and gain time and resources to focus on the innovation of the

Table 10.1   *Identified benefits of the development of astro-tourism based in a network in Portugal*

Benefit category	Identified in the literature	Dark Sky® Network Portugal
Learning and exchange	Knowledge transfer	Although these are three different regions, the knowledge applied at the *Dark Sky Alqueva* facilitates its application/adaptation in the *Dark Sky Tua Valley* and *Dark Sky Schist Villages*.
	Tourism education process	The concept reinstated the urge to look at the night sky.
	Communication	The existence of three destinations functioning in a network under the same concept and destination brand, facilitates the exchange of experiences.
	Facilitation of the development stage of small enterprises	Networking helps spread knowledge to small businesses.
Business activity	Cooperative activities, e.g., marketing, purchasing, production	The existence of three destinations working in network, under the same concept and under the same destination brand, allows creation of a complete offer with different visiting purposes: water (Alqueva), typical villages (Schist Villages) and archeoastronomy (Tua Valley).
	Enhanced cross-referral	Creation of a quality product offer based on a concept and the main resource – the protected night sky.
	Encouraging needs-based approaches, e.g., staff development, policies	Opportunity to raise awareness of need to reduce light pollution, among companies.
	Increased visitor numbers	Creation of new tourist products, reinforcing and increasing attractiveness of the destination.
	Best use of small enterprise and support agency resources	Network promotion to reach more markets with fewer costs.
	Extension to visitor season	Networking strengthens every destination.
	Increased entrepreneurial activity	Networking strengthens businesses in each destination and increases their reputation.
	Enhanced product quality and visitor experience	However, being networked implies that there is greater accountability of each company in the provision of its services. A poor performance affects everyone.
Community	Fostering common purpose and focus	The Dark Sky concept helps the release of funds to the community by drastically reducing light pollution.
	More repeat business	This helps to generate greater community accountability.
	More income remains locally	The Dark Sky concept favours and increases length of stay and the use of local accommodation units. Being a night-time product, it almost always implies staying overnight in the area, so that astro-tourists are closer to the preserved sky. This also helps to increase consumption of local products and services.

Source: Adapted from Gibson, Lynch and Morrison (2005).

offer. In terms of business activity, all destinations work in cooperation, levelling the product offer to the same quality, maximizing marketing efforts but, at the same time, showing product differentiation emerging from the different landscape and regional characteristics. In this regard, the astro-tourism offer at Alqueva Lake is based on water versus sky, the experiences in the Schist Villages are based on charming typical rural villages, and the Tua Valley offer is focused on nature tourism (since it is a nature reserve) and archeoastronomy. The night sky changes constantly, allowing viewers to observe various celestial phenomena all year round;

at the same time, tourists can gather different experiences in each of those destinations, being assured of the same principles of quality on offer.

Since Portugal created and developed the Dark Sky® Alqueva in 2007, it has achieved international recognition and a strong reputation through several international awards. Moreover, the Dark Sky Network Portugal registered and licensed the term astro-tourism, for its exclusive use in the country.

Recommendations

The implementation and development of astro-tourism at a destination is a rigorous process, obeying strict criteria, and it implies the involvement of stakeholders, DMOs, scientific communities and residents of the destination.

To develop leisure and tourism activities based on the observation of the sky, it is not enough just to have an unpolluted night sky: the atmospheric conditions for sky observation are also relevant. For astro-tourism to be a sustainable tourism product, the following conditions are necessary:

a) The quality of the sky for astronomy activities should remain stable for at least 50% of the year, otherwise this activity will be highly seasonal, and the investment made by the destination will not be sustainable. In addition, the quality of the tourism offer must be certified at the same time as the quality of the sky, because it must be guaranteed that there are enough days throughout the year with the right conditions for night-sky activities.

b) There must be commitment and involvement of all stakeholders from all sectors, including a high level of involvement of the community (residents) and tourists.

c) The development of integrated tourism is key: the offer at the destination must rely on quality instead of quantity, respecting the carrying capacity of the territory.

d) Sharing knowledge and working in cooperation with other astro-tourism destinations is vital.

e) The project should contribute to a positive impact in the destination on the social, economic and environmental levels; businesses should be local; investment should be made into training the local population to cater to the specific needs of astro-tourists (this has the additional benefit of retaining the local young population); and instead of constructing new buildings, advantage should be taken of the existing resources (such as old schools or forest rangers' houses) as observatories and interpretation facilities, fostering investment and support among local entrepreneurs.

7.   CONCLUSIONS

For centuries, the night sky has been a major resource in human life, used for measuring time, marking the seasons, guiding planting and harvesting and navigating the seas. This natural resource has kept its cultural connection with people, and nowadays an increasing number of amateur astro-tourists who enjoy travelling to reach their goals are making astro-tourism a new opportunity in the niche segment of special interest and nature-based tourism (Soleimani et al., 2018).

This chapter's goal has been to demonstrate how the implementation of the astro-tourism process has unfolded in Portugal and how far its consolidation has been established, focusing jointly on Alqueva Lake, the Schist Villages and the Tua Valley.

The implications of this chapter for the tourism industry in Portugal are manifest, not only in relation to the emergence of a truly new product but due to the innovative method of connecting several locations. Instead of competing, these territories established a network partnership, aiming at cooperatively evolving the tourism offer linked to astro-tourism. This allowed them to maximize resources at various levels and to mitigate some of the difficulties of implementing this product, which is extremely complex to establish.

The chapter compiles a growing body of academic literature that recognizes that this phenomenon is worthy of future research. Future research should focus on a better knowledge about the characteristics of the astro-tourism market, especially with regard to the differences between astro-tourism and stargazing as a leisure activity. Understanding the astro-tourists' behaviour and expectations will provide stakeholders and DMOs with valuable knowledge to improve their tourist offer at the destinations.

As Cater (2010: 845) puts it, 'we should not see astro-tourism as completely "out there" and treat it more as the natural progression of a human practice that continually seeks new frontiers'.

REFERENCES

Beeton, S. (2005) The case study in tourism research: A multi-method case study approach. In B.W. Ritchie, P. Burns and C. Palmer (eds) *Tourism research methods, integrating theory with practice*. Wallingford: CABI Publishing, 47–9.

Benur, A. and Bramwell, B. (2015) Tourism product development and product diversification in destinations. *Tourism Management*, 50, 213–24.

Boekstein, M. and Tevera, D. (2012) *Prospects for niche tourism development in South Africa*. Department of Geography and Environmental Studies, University of the Western Cape, Cape Town.

Bryman, A. (2008) *Social research methods* (3rd ed.). Oxford: Oxford University Press.

Campón-Cerro, A., Hérnandez-Mollogon, J.M. and Alves, H. (2017) Sustainable improvement of competitiveness in rural tourism destinations: The quest for tourism loyalty in Spain. *Journal of Destination Marketing and Management*, 6, 252–66.

Cater, C. I. (2010) Steps to Space; opportunities for astro-tourism. *Tourism Management*, 31, 838–45.

Cherkaoui, S., Boukherouk, M., Lakhal, T., Aghzar, A. and Youssfi, L.E. (2020) Conservation amid COVID-19 pandemic: Ecotourism collapse threatens communities and wildlife in Morocco. *E3S Web of Conferences 183*, 01003, 1–8.

Collison, F.M. (2011). Astronomical tourism: An often overlooked sustainable tourism segment, 1–6. Available at https://scholarworks.gvsu.edu/cgi/viewcontent.cgi

Collison, F. and Poe, K. (2013) Astronomical tourism: The astronomy and dark sky program at Bryce Canyon National Park. *Tourism Management Perspectives*, 7, 1–15.

C-Sánchez, E., Sánchez-Medina, A.J., Alonso-Hernández, J.B. and Voltes-Dorta, A. (2019) Astrotourism and night sky brightness forecast: First probabilistic model approach. *Sensors*, 19(13), 2840. https://doi.org/10.3390/s19132840.

DePoy, E. and Gitlin, L. (2010) *Introduction to research, understanding and applying multiple strategies* (5th ed). USA: Elsevier.

Edensor, T. (2015) Introduction to geographies of darkness. *Cultural Geographies*, 22(4), 559–65.

Fayos-Solá, E., Marín, C. and Jafari, J. (2014). Astro-tourism: No requiem for Meaningful Travel. *Revista de Turismo y Patrimonio Cultural*, 12(4), 663–71.

Galinier, B., Bordin, F., Fourmaux, P., Salzarulo, S. and Zilli, T. (2010) Anthropology of the night cross-disciplinary investigations. *Current Anthropology*, 51(6), 819–47.

Gallaway, T. (2010) On light pollution, passive pleasures, and the instrumental value of beauty. *Journal of Economic Issues*, 44(1), 71–88.

Galletta, A. (2013) *Mastering semi-structured interview and beyond: From research design to analysis and publication*. New York: NYU Press.

Gibson, B., Gregory, J. and Robinson, P.G. (2005) The intersection between systems theory and grounded theory: The emergence of the grounded systems observer. *Qualitative Sociology Review*, 1(2), 1–24.

Gibson, L., Lynch, P.A. and Morrison, A. (2005) The local destination tourism network: Development issues. *Tourism and Hospitality Planning & Development*, 2(2), 87–99.

Hall, C.M. (2005) *Tourism: Rethinking the social science of mobility*. Harlow: Prentice-Hall.

Hamacher, D.W., De Napoli, K. and Mott, B. (2020) Whitening the sky: Light pollution as a form of cultural genocide. *Journal of Dark Sky Studies*, 1.

Hjalager, A.-M., Kwiatkowski, G. and Larsen, M. (2018) Innovation gaps in Scandinavian rural tourism. *Scandinavian Journal of Hospitality and Tourism*, 18(1), 1–17.

Huang, J. and Wang (2018) All that's best of dark and bright: Day and night perceptions of Hong Kong cityscape. *Tourism Management*, 66, 274–86.

Huang, J., Li, M. and Cai, L. (2010) A model of community-based festival image. *International Journal of Hospitality Management*, 29(2), 254–60.

Ingle, M. (2010) Making the most of 'nothing': Astro Tourism, the Sublime, and the Karoo as a 'space destination'. *Transformation*, 74(1), 87–111.

Jorgensen, D. (2020) *Principles, approaches and issues in participant observation*. London: Routledge.

Keller, W. (2010) Amateur astronomy's southwestern frontier. *Sky and Telescope*, 120(2), 36–9.

March, R. and Wilkinson, I. (2009) Conceptual tools for evaluating tourism partnerships. *Tourism Management*, 30, 455–62.

Marschall, H. and Schumacher, J. (2012) Arc magmas sourced from mélange diapirs in subduction zones. *Nature Geosci*, 5, 862–7.

Mizon, B. (2012) *Light Pollution*. New York: Springer.

Najafabadi, S.S. (2012). Astronomical tourism (astro tourism) in Cebu, Philippines: Essential features in selected destinations and its complementing visitor attractions. *International Conference on Trade, Tourism and Management*, 21–22, Bangkok, Thailand.

Natário, M.F., Fernando, G., Braga, A. and Daniel, A. (2017) Municípios Portugueses em declínio e fortemente em declínio. In Proceedings of 24th APDR Congress, Intellectual Capital and Regional Development: New Landscapes and Challenges for Planning and Space, UBI Covilhã Portugal.

Novelli, M. and Benson, A. (2005) Niche tourism: A way forward to sustainability? In M. Novelli (ed.) *Niche tourism: Contemporary issues, trends and cases*. Oxford, UK: Elsevier Butterworth-Heinemann, 247–51.

Olson, M. (2016) *Essentials of qualitative interviewing*. New York: Routledge.

Pauley S.M. (2004) Lighting for the human circadian clock: Recent research indicates that lighting has become a public health issue. *Med Hypotheses*, 63(4), 588–96.

Robinson, M. and Novelli, M. (2005) Niche tourism: An introduction. In M. Novelli (ed) *Niche Tourism, Contemporary issues, trends and cases*. Oxford, UK: Elsevier Butterworth-Heinemann, 1–14.

Rodrigues, A., Rodrigues, A. and Peroff, D.M. (2015) The sky and sustainable tourism development: A case study of a dark sky reserve implementation in Alqueva. *International Journal of Tourism Research*, 17(3), 292–302.

Saxena, G., Clark, G., Oliver, T. and Ilbery, B. (2007) Conceptualizing integrated rural tourism. *Tourism Geographies*, 9(4), 347–70.

Soleimani, S., Bruwer, J., Gross, M.J. and Lee, L. (2018) Astro-tourism conceptualisation as special-interest tourism (SIT) field: A phenomenological approach. *Current Issues in Tourism*, 22(18), 2299–314.

Starlight Foundation (2020) *Certifications*. Available at: https://fundacionstarlight.org/en/section/starlight-tourist-destinations-definition/291.html.

Steinbach, R., Perkins, C., Tompson, L., Johnson, S., Armstrong, B., Green, J., Grundy, C., Wilkinson, P. and Edwards, P. (2015) The effect of reduced street lighting on road casualties and crime in England and Wales: Controlled interrupted time series analysis. *Journal of Epidemiology and Community Health*, 69(11), 1118–24.

Weaver, D. (2011) Celestial ecotourism: New horizons in nature-based tourism. *Journal of Ecotourism*, 10(1), 38–45.

Xiao, H. and Smith, S.L.J. (2006) Case Studies in Tourism Research: A state-of-the-art analysis. *Tourism Management*, 27, 738–49.

Yin, R.K. (2003) *Case study research – design and methods*. London: SAGE Publications.

Zee, E. and Vanneste, D. (2015) Tourism networks unraveled: A review of the literature on networks in tourism management studies. *Tourism Management Perspective*, 15, 46–56.

Zehrer, A. and Raich, F. (2010) Applying a lifecycle perspective to explain tourism network development. *The Service Industries Journal*, 30(10), 1683–705.

11. Rural festival and event tourism in Albania

Enrico Porfido

1.   INTRODUCTION

The main aim of this chapter is to examine niche tourism initiatives as an alternative sustainable tourism model in developing countries. Festival and event tourism represents a precious tool for sustainable development, especially when the festival or event takes place in a rural context and with the involvement of the local community (O'Sullivan and Jackson, 2002; Pickernell et al., 2007; Wood and Thomas, 2008; Van Aalst and van Melik, 2011; Mxunyelwa and Tshetu, 2018).

Indeed, events and festivals – considered as belonging to the rural micro-niche of tourism (Robinson and Novelli, 2005) – provide opportunities to reveal the interest and potential of new territories, increase local communities' awareness of their value and generate feelings of belonging (Black, 2015; Jaeger, 2019). The involvement of local communities in the organization and management of tourism activities has many positive impacts in addition to economic ones (Gursoy et al., 2004; Gibson et al., 2010; Chiciudean et al., 2021). The feeling of belonging to a place, and that a local has a stronger connection than a foreigner investor, definitely has a positive influence when dealing with the conservation and protection of local, natural and cultural heritage (Jaeger and Mykletun, 2013; Van Winkle et al., 2013; Duffy and Mair, 2017). At the same time, festivals can create an alternative tourism model based on sustainability, respect and conservation (Mair, 2015). They might also help in reducing the strong tourism pressure on touristic areas, activating the most remote spots and acting as economic and social trigger for local communities.

The Albanian case studies presented in this chapter aim to prove that rural festivals can go beyond simple event organization and generate new economic activities and development, consolidating the socioeconomic structure of a local community. Several festivals have recently taken place in Albania – namely, the UNUM Festival, the International Human Rights Film Festival, the Hemingway Jazz Festival and the South Outdoor Festival, among others, consolidating year by year this tourism niche in the national market.

The chapter presents a literature review of festival and event tourism, focusing on three main aspects: the scale, the beneficiaries and the context, later focusing on the definition of the micro-niche of rural festivals and its characteristics. The case study of Albanian festivals is presented with a map highlighting the most important festivals and events organized in the country so as to provide context to the discussion, which is especially focused on two rural festivals – Natyra Fest in the central mountain area and the South Outdoor Festival in the south – as examples of best practice.

By taking stock of what the chapter presents, the final reflection focuses on the opportunities for adopting festivals as boosters for sustainable tourism development and alternatives to mass tourism.

2. LITERATURE REVIEW: THE MICRO-NICHE OF RURAL FESTIVALS

The term 'festival' is intended here as 'an organized set of special events, usually happening in one place, or a special day or period' (Cambridge International Dictionary of English, 2020). Therefore, while it may be deprived of religious or folkloristic connotations, it may embrace other types of activities besides music.

Defining the niche of festival and event tourism is itself a complex task. Many scholars over the last four decades have been debating – and continue to do so – its features and variations (Getz and Frisby, 1988; O'Sullivan and Jackson, 2002; Robinson and Novelli, 2005; Lyck, 2010; Ali-Knight, 2011; Mxunyelwa and Tshetu, 2018; Dychkovskyy and Ivanov, 2020).

A first point of discussion is the relationship between festivals and events. Most scholars refer to festivals as a subgroup of a more generic 'events' category (Getz, 2008; Lyck, 2010; Ali-Knight, 2011; Getz, 2015; O'Sullivan and Jackson, 2002). As Cudny (2014: 132) observes, 'festivals are often treated as a type of event and their analysis as a part of event studies', but this treatment depends principally on the type and particularly the dimension, context and beneficiaries of the festival discussed.

The scale of a festival plays a fundamental role in defining its impact on regions and local communities, which are the main beneficiaries. However, context is also an important reflection point because it determines the main objective of the festival: (*re*)*generation* in urban areas (Van Aalst and van Melik, 2011) and *generation* in rural ones (Wood and Thomas, 2008).

Niche or Mass Tourism? An Issue of Beneficiaries

The main discussion concerning scale focuses on whether festival and event tourism represents a niche in the market (Robinson and Novelli, 2005; Getz, 2008; Mxunyelwa and Tshetu, 2018) or is another aspect of the mass tourism model (O'Sullivan and Jackson, 2002; Yancheva, 2014; Dychkovskyy and Ivanov, 2020). This is because the term 'festival tourism' is often used 'to include special events tourism and festivals of any size and organizational persuasion' (O'Sullivan and Jackson, 2002: 326).

As early as 1988, festival and event tourism was defined as an 'emerging giant in the tourism industry' (Getz and Frisby, 1988: 22), and its importance grew constantly in the following decades (Quinn, 2009; Getz and Page, 2015). In the broadest framework, festivals and events can be used to extend the tourist season, encourage public and private investment, generate revenue and boost the local economy (Ritchie and Beliveau, 1974; Mitchell and Wall, 1986; Ali-Knight, 2011; Dychkovskyy and Ivanov, 2020), especially in countries undergoing a process of development (Yancheva, 2014; Stipanović et al., 2015; Mxunyelwa and Tshetu, 2018).

In relation to scale and beneficiaries, O'Sullivan and Jackson (2002) distinguished the following three categories of festival and events: *home-grown* – smallest scale and run entirely by local residents; *tourist-tempter* – aimed at attracting visitors to boost the economy; and *big-bang* – intended to be promoted over a broader territory. Almost two decades before O'Sullivan and Jackson's (2002) study, Mitchell and Wall (1986) argued that small-scale festivals produce more benefits for local communities than more established ones, which result in a less significant impact on the local economy. Indeed, as external investment and the festival's scale adjust to reflect a mass tourism event, the benefits no longer fall exclusively under the local community umbrella.

The idea of home-grown festivals – those organized and managed entirely by the local communities (O'Sullivan and Jackson, 2002) – is strictly related to the concept of a community-centred approach. Gursoy et al. (2004) found that festival organizers perceived four 'dimensions' of socioeconomic impact: local community cohesiveness, economic benefits, social costs and social incentives. Indeed, in rural festivals, where the leading entrepreneur is the local community itself, the figure of stakeholder and beneficiary often coincide. Mahon and Hyyryläinen (2019) compared two rural festivals in Ireland and Finland in their study. In the first case, the festival organization was led by external actors and the impact on the local community was partially affected by the presence of entrepreneurs that acted as intermediaries. On the other hand, the second case was entirely run by residents, and 'the value of the festival as a contributor to quality of life in the community [was] recognized and highly regarded' (Mahon and Hyyryläinen, 2019: 631). It is essential to highlight that the scale of the second festival was smaller than the first, and that this allowed an entirely community-focused festival, both in terms of organization and benefits.

In conclusion, the benefits to and involvement of local communities are inversely proportional to the scale of the festival or event (Black, 2015; Mahon and Hyyryläinen, 2019). The smaller the festival, the higher the benefits that the local community receives in the absence of further intermediaries and actors. Indeed, as previously stated by Wood and Thomas (2008) and further discussed in the following paragraphs, the main objective of such festivals is to 'generate' new attractions in developing territories and to boost new economic opportunities for their local communities.

Urban and Rural? An Issue of Context

Many scholars have argued that festivals and events strongly contribute to local economic development through various impacts, both in rural (Wood and Thomas, 2008) and urban areas (Johansson and Kociatkiewicz, 2011).

On the one hand, in a rural context, festivals and small events can be used as tools for sustainable local development (Wood and Thomas, 2008; Alves et al., 2010), particularly given that 'creating a programme of festivals and events is often seen by local policy makers as an imaginative response to creating distinctiveness' (Wood and Thomas, 2008: 149). Festivals can 'generate leadership, local accountability, heightened public-private sector cooperation, and reinvestments of profits in the community' (Getz and Frisby, 1988: 22). Tourism, in a more general vision, is strictly related to the concept of local economic development (LED) and poverty reduction (Goodwin, 2008), and this is why it assumes a fundamental role in the development of rural local communities.

On the other hand, in an urban context, festivals assume the role of regeneration practices, aiming at renovating areas of already consolidated settlements. Indeed, the objective is different: 'decision-makers feel they need to mount a festival to be able to compete with other cities – preferably an international festival that attracts media attention and a wide audience' (Van Aalst and van Melik, 2011: 195–6). Studying small-scale sport events in urban areas, Ritchie stated that 'they can be a useful tool to help towns and cities attract visitors and create economic development in times of urban restructuring' (2005: 157).

Therefore, while in rural contexts festivals provide an opportunity to 'generate' a new stimulus for the local economy and society, in urban contexts, they are used to 'regenerate': to place a destination on the market, attract visitors and media attention, and foster a positive image of a destination (Quinn, 2009).

Small-Scale Rural Festivals: A Micro-Niche of Festival and Event Tourism

Narrowing the analysis to small-scale festivals in rural areas, which are here assumed to be micro-niche tourism initiatives, the following section aims to investigate their main characteristics.

These festivals are mainly representative of an activity-based typology of tourism; many local policymakers have built festivals around local products and sporting activities. As Wood and Thomas comment, 'it seems that festivals have become the elixir of rural economy regeneration' (2008: 149). The type of festivals that O'Sullivan and Jackson (2002) describe as 'home-grown' not only have a positive economic impact on local communities but also provide a showcase for local products, identities and talents.

Based on an extensive literature review (Carlsen, 2004; Daniels et al., 2004; De Bres and Davis, 2001; Dwyer et al., 2001; Hall, 2001; Jones, 2001), Wood and Thomas (2008) list the tangible and intangible benefits and costs of hosting festivals for a local community. These include increased revenue to the local economy and job creation (tangible) as well as the enhancement of community cohesion, investment in the destination location and the development of social and human capital (intangible).

As these studies show, the benefits of micro-niche tourism festivals and events organization range from the economic and social engagement of local communities to the development of hospitality infrastructure. The main characteristics of such festivals are their small-to-medium scale, their rural context and the presence of an active local community that is involved in the entire process and represents the social and human capital.

3. RESEARCH SETTING AND METHODOLOGY

This chapter answers the question: *Can the micro-niche of rural festivals represents a sustainable alternative to mass tourism for local development in emerging touristic destinations?*

To address this, the study is divided in two main parts. The first part is focused on the definition of the rural festival micro-niche, which results from the literature review, and the second presents practical study cases. Qualitative research methods are used in this study. For the first part, this study primarily involved desk research and a literature review of publications about festival and event tourism, with special attention paid to rural experiences. The second section shifts focus to the Albanian case studies, reviewing official documents, statistics and the small quantity of scientific output concerning this context.

A main limitation of the study is the lack of publicly available official data. In the second phase, which involved the collection of empirical data to inform the case studies, these were obtained from the organization teams of the two festivals under examination: through the web content analysis of the South Outdoor Festival's official website (South Outdoor Festival, 2020) and directly with one semi-structured e-mail interview with a representative of Natyra Fest (Ciro, 2020).

The Albanian Study Setting

Recently, tourism in Albania has developed rapidly, seeing a boom over the last 20 years, following the collapse of the Communist regime (Nientied, Porfido and Ciro, 2018; Porfido, 2019). Although small touristic influxes have occurred since the beginning of the last century, tourism has never held a major role in the national economy. Currently, however, it represents one of the greatest challenges and opportunities for the country (Ciro and Toska, 2018). Albania passed from welcoming approximately 40,000 international tourists in 1999 (World Tourism Organization (UNWTO), 2000) to 6.4 million in 2019 (INSTAT Albania, 2020).

The case of Albania is adopted as the focus of this chapter because of its potential for developing an alternative tourism model to the well-known 'sea, sun and sand' one. Indeed, based on its geographical location, Albania is prone to following the coastal tourism example of its neighbouring countries, such as Italy, Montenegro and Greece, but its slow development caused by a long period of political isolation might result in an opportunity to take a different path.

The Geography of Albanian Tourism: A Fragmented Territory

In the last 20 years, a tourism invasion has taken place in a country that was far from ready to receive it. Tourism 'colonized' the coast, which represents the main stage of tourism development in Albania due mainly to the existing distribution of infrastructure, in irregular ways. According to Simeoni et al. (1997), at the beginning of the 21st century, coastal occupation was still low. Today, however, most of the coastline is covered with tourist developments of low environmental quality that significantly impact the landscape and ecology (Porfido, 2020a).

The heart of this tourism network is represented by the counties of Tirana – the capital – and Durrës, which hosts the only Albanian airport, Rinas 'Nënë Tereza', and the main sea port.[1] Soon after tourism emerged in this coastal area, it also arrived on the coast of Vlorë, which hosts the second most important port, and Sarandë, which benefits from the tourist influxes from the Greek island of Corfu immediately in front of it. In the north, the city of Shënjin is the only coastal tourist destination and is especially appreciated by domestic tourists. The last coastal area to start its transformation lies between Vlorë and Sarandë, known as the Albanian Riviera. This piece of coastline has become very well known in recent years, thanks to its dramatic landscapes. The coastline can, therefore, be divided into five main segments according to different stages of development (Figure 11.1).

In recent years, in order to contrast this high concentration on coastal areas, numerous initiatives and programmes dedicated to rural tourism have been undertaken, mainly promoted by international cooperation offices and international organizations (e.g., European Union (EU), United States Agency for International Development (USAID), the World Bank and German and Italian cooperation offices in Albania). These have started to change the territorial assets of tourism, encouraging the development of inland clusters, such as the areas surrounding lakes Ohrid and Prespa, the UNESCO heritage cities of Berat and Gjirokastër, and the Albanian Alps.

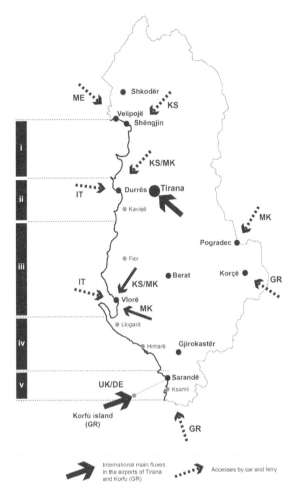

Source: Porfido (2020a).

Figure 11.1   *Tourism segmentation of the Albanian coast with incoming tourists' origin*

Albanian Political Context

Although tourism has developed extremely quickly in the country, governmental and policy responses have been slow. As Kapllani-Proda (2017) and Ciro (2019) describe, the Albanian government promoted several tourism policies and strategies after the collapse of Communism; these occurred in 1993, 2002 and 2007, as well as a 2014 strategy that remained in draft (Porfido, 2020b). However, almost all the previous tourism strategies were discontinued for different reasons. Only the recent 'National Strategy for Sustainable Tourism Development 2019–2023' (Ministry of Tourism and Environment, 2019) is being implemented.

'Strategy 2019–2023' sets specific strategic goals dedicated to the consolidation and development of new tourism products, implemented in the policy sector. The document shows that the Albanian government is focusing on three main categories of tourism product: *marine*, which 'has been the main product for years' (Ministry of Tourism and Environment, 2019: 6); *natural*, intended as rural and sport tourism; and *cultural*.

The government's intention is, therefore, to shift the attention to areas of the country other than the coast and to reduce the pressure on it. The strategy forecasts the creation of six touristic clusters, two of which are located in rural areas. Also worthy of mention is the 'Integrated Rural Development Program', also known as the '100 Villages Programme' (Ministry of Agriculture and Rural Development, 2018), which aims at discovering, collecting information on, mapping and promoting 100 villages in the most remote areas of Albania. This project affirms the government's intentions to invest in new tourism activities. For the purposes of this study, it is necessary to highlight that none of the strategy documents refer to festivals and events as opportunities for tourism development, with the exception of business events.

4. DISCUSSION – FESTIVAL AND EVENT TOURISM IN ALBANIA

As previously mentioned, numerous festivals and events have taken place in Albania over the last few years which have helped to generate an alternative tourist market to the traditional sun, sea and sand mass tourism model (Figure 11.2). Table 11.1 outlines a selection of the most important festivals and events held in Albania, including brief descriptions. It is worth mentioning that due to the the COVID-19 pandemic, all 2020 iterations were either postponed or, in some cases, implemented online.

As Table 11.2 indicates, all festivals and events organized in Albania are of small or medium scale, which means that they attract less than 5,000 participants. Out of the 11 listed, only three are organized in rural contexts, while the other eight take place in urban areas. Excluding the International Human Rights Film Festival, the Hemingway Jazz Fest and the Turtle Fest, the average number of iterations organized for each festival is three, with most festivals first being held in 2016–2017. Concerning activity type, it is worth noting that most urban festivals are dedicated primarily to music (seven out of eight), while the rural ones are activity-based events, related to sport, nature and landscape.

In the following sections, two rural festivals are presented with special attention given to organization, objectives, impact and outcomes. The two festivals selected belong to different geographical regions, taking place respectively in the inland mountain region (Natyra Fest) and on the coast (South Outdoor Festival), providing two experiences developed in completely different contexts and conditions. These case studies will help examine the research question regarding drawing tourism from the coasts and reducing economic inequality, generating an alternative sustainable tourism model.

The Natyra Fest: An Exploratory Festival[2]

The Natyra Fest is a nature- and adventure-themed event, introduced in the Municipality of Gramsh in 2017. The aim of this rural festival is to promote the mid-sized municipality as a tourist destination, primarily focused on nature and adventure tourism. The town is located in the central part of the country and it used to be an industrial settlement throughout the Communist period (Ciro et al., 2019). The surrounding area is rich in natural and cultural

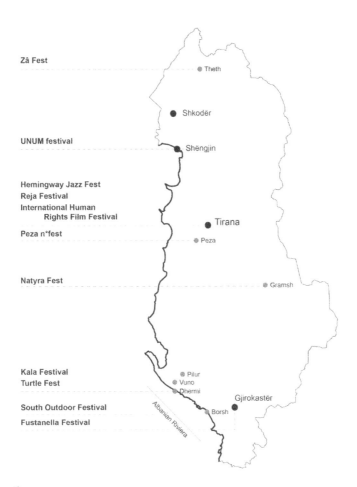

Zâ Fest

UNUM festival

Hemingway Jazz Fest
Reja Festival
International Human
    Rights Film Festival

Peza n'fest

Natyra Fest

Kala Festival
Turtle Fest

South Outdoor Festival

Fustanella Festival

Theth

Shkodër

Shëngjin

Tirana

Peza

Gramsh

Pilur
Vuno
Dhermi

Gjirokastër

Borsh

Albanian Riviera

Source: The author.

Figure 11.2   *Map of the main festivals and events from north to south Albania*

resources, with around 150 documented monuments, and it also contains the remains of the Via Ignatia (Porfido et al., 2016).

From the beginning, the festival was conceptualized as a trigger for touristic activity that would take place all year long. The 2017 and 2018 iterations of the festival were funded by the Italian–Albanian Debt for Development Swap Agreement (IADSA), in partnership with Co-PLAN – Institute for Habitat Development, in the framework of the project 'Planning and Catalytic Investments for Social Cohesion and Sustainable Tourism Development in Gramsh'. The project's overall objective was to promote social cohesion on a territorial basis and to support balanced regional development. In the following iterations of the festival, the leadership was taken directly by the Gramsh Municipality.

During the three iterations of the festival, approximately 750 participants attended the activities, which included hiking, canyoning, climbing, biking and visits to the waterfalls and castle (Ciro, 2020). At least six tour operators joined the festival, managing different activities.

Table 11.1   *The main festivals taking place in Albania, presented following the order of Figure 11.2*

Name	Location	Year established	Short description
Zâ Fest	Theth	2017	An art and sports festival, with activities ranging from movie projections, music sessions and acting performances to hiking and yoga. Located in the Albanian Alps, it aims to promote local culture, heritage and landscapes.
UNUM Festival	Shengjin	2019	An open-air music festival held on the beaches of Rana and Hedhun. Organized by private parties, in 2019, it hosted more than 50 events with international and local artists, drawing 1,000 participants.
Hemingway Jazz Fest	Shkodër-Tirana	2011	A well-established jazz music street festival organized by the Hemingway Fan Club. Aiming to promote jazz culture, it attracts more and more international visitors each year.
Reja Festival	Tirana	2017	Named after Soho Fujimoto's installation in front of the Modern Art Museum of Tirana, this urban art festival includes art, music, dance and theatre performances. The main objective is to raise public awareness of art in all its expressions.
International Human Rights Film Festival (IHRFF)	Tirana	2006	A film festival in its fifteenth year, making it the oldest festival in the country. Organized by the Academy of Film and Multimedia Marubi based in Tirana and sponsored by various institutions and organizations, it is entirely dedicated to human rights issues.
Peza n*fest	Peza	2016	An urban music festival organized in the village of Peza, 20 km from the capital. Its goal is to attract visitors to one of the least visited areas of the country and to promote local products.
Natyra Fest	Gramsh	2018	A two-day sports festival dedicated entirely to the exploration and discovery of rural landscapes, aimed at promoting tourism in remote areas of the country.
Kala Festival	Dhermi	2019	A music, wellness and sports festival at its first year, organized in the small bay of Kala. The organizers define it as a 'boutique festival', where participants can enjoy a variety of activities, from excursions to food tasting to concerts.
Turtle Fest	Dhermi	2011	A techno music festival that has reached its eighth year and is an established appointment of the summer. An example of public–private cooperation, it drew approximately 4,000 people in 2019.

Name	Location	Year established	Short description
South Outdoor Festival	Albanian Riviera	2017	An itinerant festival dedicated to sport, music and gastronomy. Organized by the German Development Cooperation, the festival takes place in a different inland village every year, promoting diverse experiences and involving local communities.
Fustanella Festival	Gjirokastër	2017	A traditional music festival, named after the traditional dress worn by men in the 13th century, that aims to promote a local experience. Visitors have the opportunity to listen to traditional isopolyphonic music, which recently entered the UNESCO Intangible Cultural Heritage list.

Source: The author.

Table 11.2   *Comparative table of Albanian festivals by context, scale, number of iterations, location and activity type*

Name	Context	Scale	Iterations	Location	Activities
Zâ Fest	Rural	S	3	Theth	Art, sport
UNUM Festival	Urban/Coastal	S	1	Shëngjin	Music
Hemingway Jazz Fest	Urban	M	9	Tirana	Music
Reja Festival	Urban	M	3	Tirana	Art, music, dance, theatre
International Human Rights Film Festival (IHRFF)	Urban	M	15	Tirana	Cinema
Peza n*fest	Urban	S	4	Peza	Music
Natyra Fest	Rural	S	2	Gramsh	Sport
Turtle Fest	Urban/Coastal	M	8	Dhermi	Music
Kala Festival	Urban/Coastal	S	1	Dhermi	Music, sport
Fustanella Festival	Urban	S	3	Gjirokastër	Music
South Outdoor Festival	Rural	S/M	3	(itinerant)	Sport, music, gastronomy

Note: Scale: (S) < 2,000 participants, (M) < 5,000, (L) < 10,000, (XL) > 10,000.
Sources: The author, based on the official webpages or social networks profiles of the festivals' organizational teams. Zâ Fest: www.facebook.com/zafestival2017; UNUM Festival: www.unumfestival.com; Hemingway Jazz Fest: www.facebook.com/hemingwayfan; Reja Festival: www.reja.al; International Human Rights Film Festival (IHRFF): www.ihrffa.net; Peza n*fest: www.facebook.com/Pezanfest; Natyra Fest: www.facebook.com/ejanegramsh; Turtle Fest: www.facebook.com/turtlefest; Kala Festival: www.kala.al; Fustanella Festival: www.facebook.com/fustanellafestival; South Outdoor Festival: www.festival.south.al.

The organization team comprised six people fully supported by the municipal authority and the local community, including businesses and young entrepreneurs operating in the fields of hospitality, apiculture and so forth.

The festival was thought of as a 'tangible business card', offered to tour operators who could integrate Gramsh into their tourism marketing. The project aimed not only to boost territorial knowledge and promotion but also to provide support to local community tourism operators to increase their expertise and leadership capabilities. Following annual increases in the number of participants and operators, as well as a growing organization team, the positive impact of the festival also lies in the fact that the municipality and local community are now able to implement it autonomously.

Table 11.3   *The SOF iterations data*

Iteration	Location	Participants	Activities	Operators	Families
2017	Pilur	600	28	18	35
2018	Vuno	900	35	18	30
2019	Borsh	1,300	60	18	-

Source: The author, based on South Outdoor Festival (2020).

Observing the results, the Natyra Fest can be considered an example of best practice in community-centred projects due to the leading role that local community plays today in both the festival organization and management, before and after the event itself. In this way, the festival organization addresses many fundamental issues, such as job creation, local community empowerment, social inclusion and the improvement of local services and resources. Indeed, the festival sets the basis for further development of tourism activities by expanding the seasons over which the festival operates, providing new opportunities for locals and positively affecting the area's emerging economy.

The South Outdoor Festival: An Itinerant Festival

Organized by the German International Cooperation Agency (GIZ) since 2017, the South Outdoor Festival (SOF) takes place every year in a different village of the Albania Riviera. The SOF is 'a celebration of everything that can be enjoyed outdoor. It celebrates sports, culture, tradition, music, nature and culinary' [sic] (South Outdoor Festival, 2020).

Since its first iteration, this festival has taken place in the Albanian Riviera, the portion of coast from Vlorë to Sarandë, famous for its dramatic landscapes. This region is considered one of the richest natural and cultural areas in the country, an agglomeration of protected areas, old churches, archaeological sites and small traditional villages (Rossi et al., 2017). Its numerous resources make it a highly attractive region for potential tourism development (Porfido et al., 2016).

The SOF is funded by the GIZ programme 'Sustainable Rural Development' under the sub-project 'Promotion of the Rural Areas in Albania as Regions to Live and Do Business' (GIZ, 2019). The programme's main objective is to support political decision-makers and relevant expert organizations with modern rural development strategies (GIZ, 2018).

The three iterations of the SOF have been organized as three-day festivals, offering the opportunity to attend specific sport activities or buy packages that include accommodation in tents or hotels, transportation, food and selected activities. The SOF organization acts as an interface and coordinator between participants and associations or local community representatives who offer to lead an activity. In all the iterations so far, 18 tour operators have supported the organized activities.

The first iteration took place in 2017 in the small village of Pilur, with around 600 participants and 35 local families involved in the organization of accommodation, food and activities. The second iteration was held in 2018 in the village of Vuno, during which 30 local families offered accommodation and organic food to promote local products, starting new activities that eventually resulted in established businesses. The last iteration was organized differently. Due to the increasing number of participants, the festival's hub was established in Borsh village, which served as the main location for music and other events, while other places were chosen to host adventure activities, sports and air games. This last manifestation drew a record 1,300 attendants, doubling the numbers of the first one. This fact does not necessarily mean sustainability, but it proves the increasing touristic potential of this region, and that its development should be accompanied by tourism infrastructure investment.

The SOF has successfully promoted a sustainable alternative tourism model in terms of LED and impact on local communities, boosting the change in national tourism geography. As mentioned above, the Albanian Riviera is suffering from pressure caused by the traditional sun, sand and sea model. The introduction of inland activities and the development of rural clusters that are well connected to the coast helps decrease the pressure on the coastal area, shifting the attention to other natural and cultural resources.

The two festivals achieved the main challenges of rural festival organization discussed above, generating new opportunities for territories and communities. At the centre of this, the fact that both festivals involved local communities in organization and management activities led to an equitable distribution of benefits from the tourism sector. Indeed, both projects were designed based on the community-centred model, putting local communities back at the centre of discussion and avoiding a situation in which only a small group of investors benefits from such activities. In this way, local communities are empowered and socioeconomic inequalities are eliminated, or at least reduced.

In a broader sense, the two festivals represent an alternative to the traditional sun, sand and sea tourism model, providing an answer to promoting rural areas and depressurizing touristic impact on coastal areas. The resulting sustainable alternative model works on the three main aspects presented above when discussing the tourism niche of festivals and events: beneficiaries, context and scale. The type of festival embodied by Natyra and South Outdoor defines the main characteristic of this model that aims to empower local communities, ensuring equitable distribution of wealth and depressurization of touristified areas in favour of more remote ones.

5.   CONCLUSIONS: THE RURAL FESTIVAL MICRO-NICHE AS A SUSTAINABLE ALTERNATIVE MODEL?

Understanding the potential impact of rural festivals and events on local communities requires, in a broader sense, an understanding of the effect of this type of tourism on a specific territory. The literature review allowed us to define the main characteristics of rural festivals and their opportunities in terms of LED, based on the scale, the beneficiaries and the context. The rural festival model presented is based on an entirely community-centred approach. The two case studies presented in this chapter touched upon some of the economic and social benefits of these micro-niche tourism initiatives, leading to some broader conclusions.

Natyra Fest, which was initially organized with the support of a non-governmental organization, has since 2019 been run autonomously by the local municipality community. This indicates that the festival itself was well structured from the outset, such that it could become more independent and community-centred year by year. For any local activity to be successful, the local community must be involved, with sufficient time given to explaining and mobilizing their interests before the event takes place. Regardless of the time and resources invested in a local event, if the local community lacks a desire for it and does not understand its benefits, the event will be unsustainable (Ciro, 2020).

The SOF generates small tourism clusters along the rural villages of the Albanian Riviera. Year after year, the number of tourist facilities run by local families in the region is increasing.

For example, the 2018 festival that took place in Vuno left a legacy of four small hotels and two hostels to the town. Most are located in existing, though renovated, buildings, which also initiated a process of heritage protection and valorization. This village has always been considered a passage area, but today is a proper tourist station. Indeed, this development is, to a large extent, a direct result of the festival, which worked in tandem with the local community.

Another positive aspect of this specific micro-niche is the temporary character of festivals. This provides an appropriate timeframe within which to evaluate the effects of a festival between iterations, allowing organizers to take any necessary measures to protect the socioeconomic stability of the community and to avoid the overconsumption of natural and cultural resources. The community impacts of these two festivals also align with the United Nation's Sustainable Development Goals (e.g., achieving gender equality through investments in local businesses managed by women; creating new jobs for youth by generating new activities; reducing inequalities; and making settlements and communities sustainable). Indeed, festivals and events organized in rural areas, especially in emerging economies like Albania's, represent tools for poverty reduction. As previously mentioned, festivals and events are essential devices for LED (Goodwin, 2008). This argument might lead to the conclusion that festivals organized in rural areas and run entirely by local communities strongly contribute to local poverty reduction and territorial development at the same time, generating a more sustainable alternative tourism model.

Learning from the Albanian experience, the rural festival micro-niche provides a sustainable alternative answer to tourism's development in rural contexts, allowing local communities to directly benefit from it and manage it. Of course, external input by an entity or organization is often much needed for starting this process. As observed in both cases presented in this chapter, the role of an external entity is to recognize the potential of a territory, to identify local actors to involve and to train, and to provide the financial support for activating the projects. This micro-niche of tourism can represent a major economic resource for isolated areas, activating regeneration, initiating economic and social processes, and valorizing the local cultural and natural heritage.

Finally, in a historical moment when movements are limited and the tourism sector is in crisis, as during the COVID-19 pandemic, new tourism solutions are greatly needed (Gössling et al., 2020). If health-focused tourism is planned as an alternative for the coming times, destinations must offer services consistent with this. Small-scale rural festivals may represent a good alternative, particularly in terms of health and security. Indeed, the limited number of participants, the remote rural context far away from crowds and open-air activities – which are relatively less dangerous in a pandemic – of these festivals can provide a safer tourism environment. In addition, the economic and social benefits generated by the festival would not only depend on international tourists but also on local ones, strengthening a tourism model which can more easily resist unexpected changes and, in this way, be more resilient to any future crises.

NOTES

1. Due to the fact that Rinas 'Nënë Tereza' is the only airport in the country, it is commonly assumed that it is located in the capital, but it actually lies on Dürres county's territory.
2. This paragraph is based on a semi-structured e-mail interview with the festival's initiative manager, Aida Ciro (Ciro, 2020). More information is available in the book chapter 'Social Innovation and

Sustainable Economic Development: Participatory Tourism Destination Management' (Ciro et al., 2019), which presents in detail the participatory processes adopted during the organization of Natyra Fest.

REFERENCES

Ali-Knight, J. (2011) The role of niche tourism products in destination development. Doctoral dissertation. Edinburgh: Napier University.

Alves, H., Campón-Cerro, A. and Ferreira-Martins, A. (2010) Impacts of small tourism events on rural places. *Journal of Place Management and Development*, 3(1), 22–37.

Black, N. H. (2015) The contribution of small-scale, rural festivals to the social sustainability of their host communities in Northumberland. Doctoral dissertation. Newcastle: Newcastle University.

Cambridge International Dictionary of English (2020) 'Festival'. Cambridge: Cambridge University Press.

Carlsen, J. (2004) The economics and evaluation of festivals and events. In I. Yeoman, M. Robertson, J. Ali-Knight and S. Drummond (eds) *Festival and Events Management: An International Arts and Culture Perspective*, 246–59. Oxford: Elsevier.

Chiciudean, D. I., Harun, R., Muresan, I. C., Arion, F. H. and Chiciudean, G. O. (2021) Rural community-perceived benefits of a music festival. *Societies*, 11(2), 59, 1–13. https://doi.org/10.3390/soc11020059.

Ciro, A. (2019) Tourism governance in Albania: an assessment of the policy framework for the tourism sector in Albania. *Annual Review of Territorial Governance in the Western Balkans, Volume I*, 69–85.

Ciro, A. (2020) Rural festivals in Albania. Interview with Aida Ciro – Initiative Manager and Founder of the Natyra Fest (August).

Ciro, A. and Toska, M. (2018) Sustainable tourism development in Albania. *Annual Review of Territorial Governance in Albania, Volume I*, 84–93.

Ciro, A., Toska, M. and Nientied, P. (2019) Social innovation and sustainable economic development: participatory tourism destination management. In M. Finka, M. Jaššo and M. Husár (eds) *The Role of Public Sector in Local Economic and Territorial Development: Innovation in Central, Eastern and South Eastern Europe*. Cham: Springer, 173–92. doi.org/10.1007/978-3-319-93575-1_10.

Cudny, W. (2014) Festivals as a subject for geographical research. *Geografisk Tidsskrift-Danish Journal of Geography*, 114(2), 132–42.

Daniels, M., Norman, W. and Henry, M. (2004) Estimating income effects of a sport tourism event. *Annuals of Tourism Research*, 31(1), 180–99.

De Bres, K. and Davis, J. (2001) Celebrating group and place identity: a case study of a new regional festival. *Tourism Geographies*, 3(3), 326–37.

Duffy, M. and Mair, J. (2017) Engaging the senses to explore community events. *Event Management*, 22, 49–63.

Dwyer, L., Mellor, R., Mistilis, N. and Mules, T. (2001) A framework for assessing tangile and intangible impacts of events and conventions. *Event Management*, 6, 175–89.

Dychkovskyy, S. and Ivanov, S. (2020) Festival tourism as part of international tourism and a factor in the development of cultural tourism. *Informacijos mokslai*, 89, 73–82.

Getz, D. (2008) Event tourism: definition, evolution, and research. *Tourism Management*, 29, 403–28.

Getz, D. (2015) Festival and event, tourism. In J. Jafari and H. Xiao (eds) *Encyclopedia of Tourism*. Amsterdam: Springer, 352–5.

Getz, D. and Frisby, W. (1988) Evaluating management effectiveness in community-run festivals. *Journal of Travel Research*, 27(1), 22–7.

Getz, D. and Page, S. (2015) Progress and prospects for event tourism research. *Tourism Management*, 52, 593–631.

Gibson, C., Connell, J. and Walmsley, J. (2010) The extent and significance of rural festivals. In C. Gibson, J. Connell and J. Walmsley (eds) *Festival Places: Revitalising Rural Australia*. Bristol: Channel View Publications, 3–24.

GIZ (2018) Sustainable rural development sector project. Available at: https://www.giz.de/en/worldwide/ 77745.html (accessed 10 July 2020).

GIZ (2019) Promotion of the rural areas in Albania as regions to live and do business. Available at: https://www.giz.de/en/worldwide/82937.html (accessed 1 July 2020).

Goodwin, H. (2008) Tourism, local economy development and poverty reduction. *Applied Research in Economic Development*, 5(3), 55–64.

Gössling, S., Scott, D. and Hall, C. (2020) Pandemics, tourism and global change: a rapid assessment of COVID-19. *Journal of Sustainable Tourism*, 29(1), 1–20. https://doi.org/10.1080/09669582.2020 .1758708

Gursoy, D., Kyungmi, K. and Muzaffer, U. (2004) Perceived impacts of festivals and special events by organizers: an extension and validation. *Tourism Management*, 25(2), 171–81.

Hall, C. (2001) *Hallmark Tourism Events: Impacts, Management, and Planning*. London: Belhaven Press.

INSTAT Albania (2020) Lëvizjet e shtetasve në Shqipëri – Dhjetor 2019. Tiranë: INSTAT Albania.

Jaeger, K. (2019) Tourists and Communities in Rural Festival Encounters. A mutually beneficial relationship? Doctoral dissertation. Stavanger: University of Stavanger.

Jaeger, K. and Mykletun, R. J. (2013) Festivals, identities, and belonging. *Event Management*, 17(3), 213–26.

Johansson, M. and Kociatkiewicz, J. (2011) City festivals: creativity and control in staged urban experiences. *European Urban and Regional Studies*, 18(4), 392–405.

Jones, C. (2001) Mega-events and host region impacts: determining the true worth of the 1999 Rugby World Cup. *International Journal of Tourism Research*, 3(3), 241–51.

Kapllani Proda, O. (2017) Tourism development strategy and its impact in number of tourists and Albania economy. *International Journal of Economics and Business Administration*, 3(5), 38–44.

Lyck, L. (2010) Festival management in times of recession. In L. Lyck, P. Long and A. X. Grige (eds) *Tourism, Festivals and Cultural Events in Times of Crisis*. Copenhagen: Copenhagen Business School Publications, 9–22.

Mahon, M. and Hyyryläinen, T. (2019) Rural arts festivals as contributors to rural development and resilience. *Sociologia Ruralis*, 59(4), 612–35.

Mair, J. (2015) The role of events in creating sustainable destinations. In M. Hughes, D. Weaver and C. Pforr (eds) *The Practice of Sustainable Tourism: Resolving the Paradox*. London: Routledge, 247–62.

Ministry of Agriculture and Rural Development (2018) *Programi i Integruar për Zhvillimin Rural – Programi i 100 fshatrave*. Tirana: Ministry of Agriculture and Rural Development.

Ministry of Tourism and Environment (2019) *Strategjia Kombëtare për Zhvillimin e Qëndrueshëm të Turizmit 2019–2023* [National Strategy for Sustainable Tourism Development 2019–2023]. Tiranë: Government of Albania.

Mitchell, C. and Wall, G. (1986) Impacts of cultural festivals on Ontario communities. *Recreation Research Review*, 13(1), 28–37.

Mxunyelwa, S. and Tshetu, L. (2018) Festivals as a niche for Local Economic Development (LED): a case study of the East London Port Festival (ELPF), Eastern Cape, South Africa. *African Journal of Hospitality, Tourism and Leisure*, 7(3), 1–14.

Nientied, P., Porfido, E. and Ciro, A. (2018) Sustainable tourism development in Albania in times of liquid modernity. In F. Adornato, S. Betti, A. Caligiuri, A. Cavicchi, M. Cerquetti, F. Coltrinari, L. Lacchè, R. Perna and F. Spigarelli (eds) *Enhancing Sustainable Tourism in Adriatic-Ionian Region through Co-creation: The Role of Universities and Public-Private Partnerships*. Macerata: eum edizioni università di macerata, 73–91.

O'Sullivan, D. and Jackson, M. (2002) Festival tourism: a contributor to sustainable local economic development? *Journal of Sustainable Tourism*, 10(4), 325–42.

Pickernell, D., O'Sullivan, D., Senyard, J. and Keast, R. (2007) Social capital and network building for enterprise in rural areas: can festivals and special events contribute? In W. Keogh (ed.) *30th Institute for Small Business and Entrepreneurship Conference: International Entrepreneurship – Stimulating Smarter Successful Small Business World-wide*. Harrogate: Perlex Associates, 1–18.

Porfido, E. (2019) From the grand tour to social media: the metamorphosis of touristic landscapes representation in the case of Albania. In R.e.a. Pié (ed.) *Turismo y Paisaje*. Valencia: Tirant humanidades, 96–109.

Porfido, E. (2020a) *From Isolation to 'Pleasure Periphery': The Riviera Perspective. A Tourism Model for South Albania's Coastal Landscapes*. Tirana: POLIS Press.

Porfido, E. (2020b) Tourism development in Western Balkans: towards a common policy. *Annual Review of Territorial Governance in the Western Balkans, Volume II*, 24–45.

Porfido, E., Ciro, A. and Nientied, P. (2016) *Regional Tourism Comparative Analysis in Albania*. Tirana: RisiAlbania.

Quinn, B. (2009) Festivals, events, and tourism. In T. Jamal and M. Robinson (eds) *The SAGE Handbook of Tourism Studies*. Newbury Park: SAGE Publications, 483–504.

Ritchie, B. (2005) Sport tourism. Small-scale sport event tourism: the changing dynamics of the New Zealand Masters Games. In M. Novelli (ed.) *Niche Tourism: Contemporary Issues, Trends nd Cases*. Amsterdam: Elsevier, 157–70.

Ritchie, J. and Beliveau, D. (1974) Hallmark events: an evaluation of a strategic response to seasonality in the travel market. *Journal of Travel Research*, 13(2), 14–20.

Robinson, M. and Novelli, M. (2005) Niche tourism: an introduction. In M. Novelli (ed.) *Niche Tourism: Contemporary Issues, Trends and Cases*. Amsterdam: Elsevier, 1–11.

Rossi, L., Pedata, L., Porfido, E. and Resta, G. (2017) Fragile edges and floating strategies along the Albanian coastline. *The Plan Journal*, 2(2), 685–705.

Simeoni, U., Pano, N. and Ciavola, P. (1997) The coastline of Albania: morphology, evolution and coastal management issues. *Bulletin de l'Institut oceanographique*, 18, 151–68.

South Outdoor Festival (2020) South Outdoor Festival. (Online). Available at: https://southoutdoor.al/en (accessed 18 August 2020).

Stipanović, C., Rudan, E. and Persin, P. (2015) Festival tourism in the repositioning of Croatian tourism destination. *Tourism in Southern and Eastern Europe*, 3, 355–67.

UNWTO (2000) *Datos esenciales 2000*. Madrid: UNWTO.

Van Aalst, I. and van Melik, R. (2011) City festivals and urban development: does place matter? *European Urban and Regional Studies*, 19(2), 195–206.

Van Winkle, C. M., Woosnam, K. M. and Mohammed, A. M. (2013) Sense of community and festival attendance. *Event Management*, 17(2), 155–63.

Wood, E. and Thomas, R. (2008) Festivals and tourism in rural economies. In M. Robertson, A. Ladkin and J. Ali-Knight (eds) *International Perspectives of Festivals and Events*. Amsterdam: Elsevier, 149–58.

Yancheva, K. (2014) Aspects of improving festival tourism in Bulgaria. *IZVESTIA – Journal of University of Economics*, 4, 52–66.

12. In focus 2 – Koh Phi Phi Thailand: an icon of backpacker culture, victim of film tourism and devastated by crisis

Faye Taylor

Increasingly, research has explored the phenomenon of film tourism as a form of niche tourism. There is a consensus that selecting a destination as a filming location for a television programme or movie will bring about an increase in volume of tourists on account of a desire to see the filming location (Hudson and Ritchie, 2006; Beeton, 2010; Riley et al., 1998), and that this will in turn generate positive economic consequences for the destination's stakeholders (Hudson and Ritchie, 2006; Beeton, 2010; Croy, 2011; Yoon et al., 2015) and in some cases positive sociocultural consequences (Dyer et al., 2003).

One such destination is that of Maya Bay, location for the motion picture *The Beach*, starring Leonardo DiCaprio and based upon the novel by Alex Garland. It is located on the island of Koh Phi Phi Leh in Krabi Province on the Thai Andaman coast (Taylor, 2012; Law et al., 2007; Cohen, 2005). *The Beach* follows the story of Richard on his quest to find a backpacker utopia in Thailand. Richard's quest is eased when he meets Daffy, a suicidal drifter who shares knowledge of a secret beach on a paradise island that is free from the parasites and destruction of civilisation. Ironically, the novel was not intended to celebrate backpacker culture and youth tourism but to criticise it. The story tracks the development of the community on *The Beach* to the point at which members' fierce desire for secrecy and isolation erodes the values that drove its establishment. The book and the subsequent film opened the floodgates to millions more backpackers wishing to join the multitude already making their way along the well-trodden tourist trail as a youthful rite of passage.

It is clear that the (permissible) development of tourism on the neighbouring island of Phi Phi Don was catalysed by the recognition afforded to Maya Bay through the filming of *The Beach*, as it represented an important element of the tourist gaze for the Phi Phi islands (Law et al., 2007). This can be seen in the surge in visitor numbers from 150,000 annual visitors in 2000 (at the point of the film's release) to 1.2 million annual visitors pre-tsunami in 2004. However, this growth did not come without controversy, and it is debatable whether the long-standing legacy of *The Beach* is positive. The marked impact upon destination image, flow of visitors and subsequent economic prosperity and infrastructure development needs to be balanced, on both islands, against the accession of carrying capacity, environmental degradation and negative societal impacts on Phi Phi Don. In fact, some studies (Cohen, 2005) have noted parallels between the message of *The Beach* and the effect it catalysed on the Phi Phi islands.

The mass unplanned tourism development in the central 'apple core' area of Phi Phi Don was checked in 2004 when, on 26 December, an underwater earthquake measuring 9.3 on the Richter scale was triggered from an epicentre off the coast of Banda Aceh, Northern Indonesia (Ghobarah et al., 2006). An initial harbour wave 3 metres in height approached Phi Phi Don via Tonsai Bay and a second, more deadly wave of 5.5 metres approached via Ao Lo Dalaam

Bay. This second wave devastated the flat, low-lying apple core area where the two bays meet. Some say that the tsunami offered a 'clean slate' opportunity to replan and rezone the islands along more sustainable lines (Figure 12.1).

Source: Author, photo taken 11 December 2005.

Figure 12.1   *The so called 'clean slate'*

Would the destination rely on the tried and tested forms of niche tourism that had brought about its popularity, or consider alternative forms of tourism? Along with many disaster-affected locations globally came the mantra of 'build back better', with a new interest in the pursuit of high-end tourism, perceived by the regional government to be more aligned with principles of sustainability. In reality, any prospect of sustainability on Phi Phi continues to be undermined by a range of barriers and conflicts connected to land scarcity. Conflicts arise from powerful stakeholders pursuing their own interests and desired outcomes, rather than the needs of the community as a whole, representing a 'Tragedy of the Commons' (Hardin, 1968).

Phi Phi remains a valuable case of analysis, as, within this small geographical location, it showcases a range of contemporary concerns associated with the development of tourism. The environmental impact of film tourists and corresponding overtourism (Milano et al., 2019) is nowhere more evident than on the Phi Phi islands, most specifically Maya Bay, which after over two decades of degradation and mismanagement has finally been closed for environmental regeneration (Taylor, 2018) as global attention is directed to the quality of life below water (UN SDG 14). Combined with this, we have a destination that is arguably still in a state of redevelopment post-crisis. Initial indicators today point to a recreation of the pre-crisis development trajectory, presenting a destination that is socially and environmentally unviable for residents and tourists alike.

REFERENCES

Beeton, S. (2010). The advance of film tourism. *Tourism and Hospitality Planning & Development*, 7(1), 1–6.

Cohen, E. (2005). The beach of 'The Beach'—The politics of environmental damage in Thailand. *Tourism Recreation Research*, 30(1), 1–17.

Croy, G. (2011). Film tourism: Sustained economic contributions to destinations. *Worldwide Hospitality and Tourism Themes*, 3(2), 159–164.

Dyer, P., Aberdeen, L. and Schuler, S. (2003). Tourism impacts on an Australian indigenous community: A Djabugay case study. *Tourism Management*, 24(1), 83–95.

Ghobarah, A., Saatcioglu, M. and Nistor, I. (2006). The impact of the 26 December 2004 earthquake and tsunami on structures and infrastructure. *Engineering structures*, 28(2), 312–326.

Hardin, G. (1968). The tragedy of the commons: The population problem has no technical solution; it requires a fundamental extension in morality. *Science*, 162(3859), 1243–1248.

Hudson, S. and Ritchie, J. B. (2006). Film tourism and destination marketing: The case of captain Corelli's mandolin. *Journal of Vacation Marketing*, 12(3), 256–268.

Law, L., Bunnell, T. and Ong, C. E. (2007). The beach, the gaze and film tourism. *Tourist Studies*, 7(2), 141–164.

Milano, C., Novelli, M. and Cheer, J. M. (2019). Overtourism and tourismphobia: A journey through four decades of tourism development, planning and local concerns. *Tourism Planning & Development*, 16(4), 353–357.

Riley, R., Baker, D. and Van Doren, C. S. (1998). Movie induced tourism. *Annals of Tourism Research*, 25(4), 919–935.

Taylor, F. (2012). Post disaster tourism development of Phi Phi Island: Political economy and interpretations of sustainability.

Taylor, F. (2018). The beach goes full circle: The case of Koh Phi Phi, Thailand. In K. Sangkyun and S. Reijnders (eds) *Film tourism in Asia* (pp. 87–106). Springer, Singapore.

Yoon, Y., Kim, S. and Kim, S. S. (2015). Successful and unsuccessful film tourism destinations: From the perspective of Korean local residents' perceptions of film tourism impacts. *Tourism Analysis*, 20(3), 297–311.

PART III

HERITAGE AND CULTURE-BASED TOURISM

13. Personal heritage tourism

Heather Kennedy-Eden and Ulrike Gretzel

INTRODUCTION

Heritage is 'what we inherit from the past and use in present day' (Timothy, 2011: 3), and heritage tourism encompasses travellers who visit local communities and attractions that feature folkloric traditions, cultural celebrations, arts and crafts, and ethnic history (Hollinshead, 1988). Nostalgia for the past is a motivation for heritage tourists, as is experiencing diverse cultural landscapes and forms (Zeppel and Hall, 1991). Experiencing heritage tourism can restore a sense of times past and trigger nostalgia for times that seem simpler and values less complex (Timothy, 1997). Lowenthal (1975) suggests that to cope with the present, we need this nostalgia as it gives us perspective and increases our present understanding. Heritage tourism is also an opportunity to experience cultural landscapes, both current and past, along with food, performances and handicrafts (Chhabra et al., 2003). Heritage tourism locations symbolize shared recollections of a group of people (Timothy, 1997) but these sites may not have a personal connection to the tourists that visit. However, while some heritage sites are mass tourism sites to some, to others they could carry very personal connections and meanings because of their personal heritage connection to the site.

Ancestry plays a crucial role in heritage tourism (Murdy et al., 2018) and the phenomenon of seeking out one's personal family history and travelling to homelands has captured the interest of a growing number of tourists. The popularity of television shows such as *Finding Your Roots* and *Who Do You Think You Are?* have added to this area of interest (Morehart, 2019; Murdy et al., 2018), with genealogy being one of the most popular hobbies worldwide (Rodriguez, 2014) and people travelling to connect with their discovered heritages creating a new sub-niche of personal heritage tourism within the heritage tourism niche. Personal heritage tourism is an umbrella term for several different types of niche tourism through which tourists try to connect with their own individual heritage, for example, by connecting to their ancestral roots or living relatives in distant homelands. Personal heritage tourism can be defined as a form of special interest tourism, as heritage-related activities constitute the central motivation for travel (Novelli, 2005). While heritage tourism is the broad term for these activities, personal heritage tourism implies that there is a direct connection to the individual who is travelling and seeking out experiences related to their heritage. These personal heritage experiences may span across many other niches in tourism, such as cultural, culinary, rural, and religious tourism, as well as visiting friends and relatives, which makes personal heritage travel a very complex type of niche tourism. Importantly, personal heritage tourism has a well founded link to sustainable tourism, in that connecting to one's roots changes perspective and broadens worldviews by contributing to the social and economic development of these ancestral lands (Dillette, 2021; Marschall, 2017). These strong connections to the destination also result in repeat visits, which further assist in the development of these areas (Poria et al., 2006) as tourists continue to research and seek out personal ancestral connections at the destination.

Niche tourists are generally a more sophisticated type of tourist with a higher spending power who offer sustainable economic opportunities (Ali-Knight, 2011, Robinson and Novelli, 2005). This is particularly true for personal heritage tourists, who generally seek out smaller destinations and stay longer. They are also likely repeat visitors, as family connections and links to their heritage are essentially inexhaustible, with maintenance of family ties requiring regular visits or family trees needing constant additions and refinement (Otterstrom and Bunker, 2013). Furthermore, heritage tourism provides a unique and authentic experience, which tourists are increasingly demanding (Lacher et al., 2013; Agarwal, 2002; Sedmak and Mihalič, 2008). In addition, with the emergence of DNA testing and the growing interest in ancestral visits to distant homelands, the desire for these types of tourism experiences continues to grow (Alexander et al., 2017; McCain and Ray, 2003; Kramer, 2011). Consequently, personal heritage tourism is a niche that is interesting from a theoretical point of view and is extremely attractive from an industry perspective.

Understanding the category of personal heritage tourists can be confusing when looking at all the designations used in the literature and in practice. Sometimes called roots tourists, while other times referred to as ancestral tourists, genealogy tourists, family history tourists, legacy tourists or diaspora tourists, there is no clarity as to what the personal heritage tourist niche encompasses. There is also overlap with other areas of tourism, such as visiting friends and relatives, which can be part of diaspora tourism (Coles and Timothy, 2004b; Mehtiyeva and Prince, 2020; Li et al., 2020). Additionally, some links to dark tourism exist, as participants visit personal heritage areas connected to slavery and the Holocaust (Mehtiyeva and Prince, 2020). Cheer and Reeves (2013) acknowledge the complexity of diaspora tourism and recognize its 'dark' elements arising from feelings of melancholy and trepidation. Thus, it is the goal of this chapter to provide definitional clarity by building a typology of personal heritage tourists and drawing boundaries between sub-niches based on specific motivations and behaviours discussed in the literature.

To achieve this goal, this chapter will present the results of a systematic literature review. Specifically, it will classify personal heritage tourists into different categories based on motivations and behaviours. Understanding motivations of tourists is of substantial interest within the study of tourism, as these motivations drive destination choice and activities during travel (McCain and Ray, 2003). Typology-building is beneficial for future research, as the classification of terms provides a useful tool for understanding relations and differences (Kennedy-Eden and Gretzel, 2012) and offers a foundational common language, which can aid in definition and exploration (Nickerson et al., 2009). This research takes a hermeneutic approach to data collection and analysis, such that a constant re-exploration of the data occurs as new motivations and behaviours are found in the literature. Relevant articles were identified through a Google Scholar search using terms such as roots tourism, diaspora tourism and so on, and any subsequent terms discovered. The resulting typology contributes to theory by consolidating very fragmented streams of literature and guiding future research efforts in this growing research area. From a practical perspective, the typology highlights characteristics that can be translated into targeted tourism experiences and marketing strategies.

LITERATURE REVIEW

Both in academic literature and in practice, heritage tourism takes on many names, all with overlapping but distinct themes and nuances that have created a confusion of terms. Heritage tourism, as defined by Yale (2004: 21), is 'tourism centred on what we have inherited, which can mean anything from historic buildings, to artwork, to beautiful scenery', while the National Trust for Heritage Preservation designates heritage tourism as 'traveling to experience the places, artifacts, and activities that authentically represent the stories and people of the past and present' (Gibson, 2015: 1). Heritage travel continues to receive attention from tourism researchers and practitioners (McCain and Ray, 2003) but there is growing recognition that it is based on a wide variety of motivations (Halewood and Hannam, 2001). What has been widely conceptualized as pertaining to the visitation of spaces that allow one to experience the heritage of a destination (Weaver, 2011), such as castles and battlefields (Yale, 2004), which appeal to the masses, has now become an individual quest as travellers seek out heritage of a more personal nature (Timothy, 1997). These tourists enjoy visits to personal heritage sites and attractions, organized ancestral tours, visiting festivals, ceremonies and family reunions while travelling (Higginbotham, 2012). Acknowledging this trend, this research will focus specifically on personal heritage tourism, meaning tourism that involves heritage that has a personal connection to the individual, such as roots tourism, legacy tourism, diaspora tourism, family history tourism, DNA tourism, genealogy tourism and ancestral tourism.

Roots tourism focuses on journeys of discovery as people participate in a return migration to the lands of their predecessors to reclaim a lost heritage (Basu, 2004). Roots tourism includes a longing for one's distant past and a sense of nostalgia (Mehtiyeva and Prince, 2020; Basu, 2004). Pilgrimage, homecoming and quest are words associated with roots tourists (Basu, 2004) but they are not necessarily homogenous in what they seek at destinations; some seek their actual ancestral home while others just want to enjoy a foreign country where their ancestors lived (Maruyama, 2016). The latter of these are recreational roots tourists who have a general curiosity about ancestral lands but are not looking for self-realization (Maruyama, 2016).

Roots and diaspora tourism both touch on the notion of travellers seeking to recover a lost cultural heritage (Cheer and Reeves, 2013), but diaspora tourism involves people who have left their homeland more recently, for reasons of forced ejection or to seek a better life for their children, usually because of political or economic strife (Benson and O'Reilly, 2009; Safran, 2011). Often, during diaspora tourism, visitors experience strong emotional and spiritual moments (Mehtiyeva and Prince, 2020; Alexander et al., 2017; Basu, 2004). There can be a dark legacy associated with this travel because it involves such things as slavery and the Holocaust (Mehtiyeva and Prince, 2020). Diaspora communities are people that are drawn together by their common bonds of ethnicity, national identity, religion, culture or race but are spread across the world (Coles and Timothy, 2004a). Diasporic communities are connected through the common disconnection of the people from their homeland. Diaspora tourists visit homelands to (re)acquaint themselves with friends and relatives, but also (re)experience their national identity and connect with their emotional home (Mehtiyeva and Prince, 2020; Coles and Timothy, 2004b).

While roots and diaspora tourists have an existing understanding of their personal heritage, ancestral, genealogical and legacy tourism all involve discovering family history and researching an individual's family tree prior to travel. However, family history enthusiasts who travel cannot be homogenized because they all have different goals (Timothy and Guelke, 2008). Ancestral tourism involves travel that is motivated by the individual's need to bond with their ancestral past (Alexander et al., 2017; Murdy et al., 2018; Murdy et al., 2016) and includes significant family history study and research prior to travel (Mehtiyeva and Prince, 2020). In contrast, genealogical travel, one of the fastest growing subsets of heritage tourism, involves amateur genealogists travelling in an effort to do research on their family tree at the destination by gathering dates and records of their ancestors to accumulate knowledge (Santos and Yan, 2010). Genealogy is the building of family trees with names, places and important dates such as births, marriages and deaths (Timothy and Guelke, 2008). One way to differentiate genealogists and ancestral family historians is by saying that genealogists seek out dates and statistical information, whereas family historians seek out information on what happened between the birth date and death date, that is, the life stories and histories of the people they are researching. This helps to explain why a genealogical traveller may not go to their ancestral homeland to do this research; rather, they travel to family history repositories such as the Family History Center of the Church of Jesus Christ of Latter-day Saints in Salt Lake City, Utah, or genealogy sections of libraries, such as the Genealogy Center at Allen County Public Library, Indiana, to do their research and find vital records. Ancestral tourists, also known as family history tourists, record oral histories from relatives, look up newspaper articles, and seek public histories or places where their ancestor lived to create a richer story (Timothy and Guelke, 2008). Legacy tourists have a personal connection to their heritage and they travel to engage in genealogical research (McCain and Ray, 2003) but they go beyond general ancestry by looking for specific connections to their ancestry and roots, as they want to feel a tangible connection to their homeland (Ray and McCain, 2012). Legacy tourists travel to their homelands in an effort to seek out the links and information that connect them to their direct ancestors (Ray and McCain, 2012).

One other kind of heritage traveller is the DNA tourist. DNA tourism is a field that has been subject to very little research due to its relatively new existence. DNA tourists will start by submitting a saliva or cheek swab sample to a DNA testing company, such as Ancestry.com or 23andMe, and within 6–8 weeks they will receive information providing a geographically based percentage of genealogy, possible genetic links to other individuals who have tested, and links to ancestors and family members through autosomal DNA genetic variants (Angelo et al., 2020). Angelo et al. (2020) found anecdotal evidence that older adults who have their DNA tested are looking for genealogy results that spur 'bucket list' travel and younger adults are looking to discover more about their identity without having to do extensive research. They seek to immerse themselves in the areas where their ancestral kin lived and participate in cultural activities (Angelo et al., 2020; Dickinson, 2018). DNA tourists also may seek geographical information about their DNA due to lost records or unknown information, as, for example, in the instance of adoption or slavery. DNA tourism can also involve meeting up with living kin identified through DNA databases.

While this overview of the literature on personal heritage tourism has tried to clarify the different kinds of heritage tourism within this niche, it is very clear that there is significant overlap among these terms and definitional clarity is currently lacking. Building on the coarse outline of groupings provided in this section, the chapter now delves into building a more refined typology to further map different areas of personal heritage tourism.

METHODOLOGY

Tourism researchers explore different meanings of travel in an effort to understand the relationship between the society that a person lives in every day and locations they visit (Cohen, 1979). This research analysed the various terms associated with personal heritage tourism, their meanings and connections with specific motivations and behaviours, to provide a coherent typology of personal heritage tourists. Specifically, searches of relevant articles through Google Scholar were undertaken using terms related to personal heritage tourism, namely, roots tourism, diaspora tourism, legacy tourism, ancestral tourism, genealogy tourism and DNA tourism. The top five articles or book sections for each search were analysed for definitions as well as descriptions of motivations and behaviours, in order to identify differences in the terms. In cases where a book or article could not be located, the next citation would be used. When other articles were referenced in relation to the definition, motivations or behaviours of such tourists, these were sought out to see if they could help delineate the phenomenon. This was accomplished with all terms except for DNA tourism. Since there is very limited research in this area, genetic tourism was also searched for, turning up very few relevant results. Consequently, this specific search involved general Google queries to find relevant articles and information and turned up fewer citations. The articles that were found were usually less academic and more of the public press type. Table 13.1 lists the search results that formed the basis of analysis.

Following a hermeneutic approach to data collection and analysis, the research involved constant re-exploration of the data as new information was found. For each category, the definition was established and motivations and behaviours of that type of tourist were noted. Once each term had a comprehensive list, they were analysed against the other terms to see similarities and differences. This was achieved with the help of a visual chart that facilitated direct comparisons across all categories. In the process of the analysis, it became apparent that legacy tourists and ancestral tourists are basically the same; their motivations and behaviours are so similar that they should be combined into one category. Thus, they will be called ancestral tourists from here on out, as ancestral tourism is the more common term found in the literature.

The resulting list of motivations and behaviours was further classified into sub-themes. Based on all the information, a typology was created to demonstrate similarities and differences among the groupings. In the social sciences, typologies are established analytic tools used to help organize categories for better understanding (Collier et al., 2012). In a typology, groups that act in a homogenous way or who have similar motivations and behaviours are displayed in closer proximity. During the analysis, it was noted that the way these tourists receive their heritage information is also different, so this was added to the typology.

FINDINGS AND DISCUSSION

Table 13.2 presents the combined typology that illustrates similarities and differences among the various groups of personal heritage tourists. The top row after the title shows the five subgroups within the personal heritage niche: DNA tourists, roots tourists, diaspora tourists, ancestral tourists and genealogical tourists. As noted above, legacy and ancestral tourists are combined into a single category of ancestral tourists. The next row designates how the tourists primarily learn about their personal heritage. DNA tourists usually only have their DNA

Table 13.1   *List of articles used for analysis*

Search term	Top five sources listed
Roots Tourism	Route metaphors of 'roots tourism' in the Scottish Highland diaspora (Basu, 2004)
	African American roots tourism in Brazil (De Santana Pinho, 2008)
	Roots tourists' internal experiences and relations with the ancestral land: Case of second-generation Chinese Americans (Maruyama, 2016)
	Seeking roots and tracing lineages: Constructing a framework of reference for roots and genealogical tourism (Higginbotham, 2012)
	'Find their level'. African American roots tourism in Sierra Leone and Ghana (Benton and Shabazz, 2009)
Ancestral Tourism	Delivering the past (Alexander et al., 2017)
	Nostalgic tourism (Russell, 2008)
	What pulls ancestral tourists 'home'? An analysis of ancestral tourist motivations (Murdy et al., 2018)
	Role conflict and changing heritage practice: Ancestral tourism in Scotland (Murdy et al., 2016)
	Guiding tourists to their ancestral homes (Ray and McCain, 2009)
Legacy Tourism	Legacy tourism: The search for personal meaning in heritage travel (McCain and Ray, 2003)
	Personal identity and nostalgia for the distant land of past: legacy tourism (Ray and McCain, 2012)
	Legacy and tourism: Collocating and deviating of tradition and modern (Zhaorong and Xiangchun, 2008)
	Travel constraints and nostalgia as determinants of cross-Atlantic legacy tourism (Rodrigues et al., 2012)
	'It was the Trip of a Lifetime': Viking Ancestors, their Descendants and their Legacy Tourism Motivations and Behavior (Ray and McCain, 2015)
DNA/Genetic Tourism	Is 'DNA tourism' the next travel trend for millennials? (Dickinson, 2018)
	Heritage and genealogy travel health concerns in the era of in-home DNA testing (Angelo et al., 2020)
Genealogy/Genealogical Tourism	Genealogical tourism: A phenomenological examination (Santos and Yan, 2010)
	Seeking roots and tracing lineages: Constructing a framework of reference for roots and genealogical tourism (Higginbotham, 2012)
	Geography and genealogy: Locating personal pasts (Timothy and Guelke, 2008)
	Genealogy Tourism (Birtwistle, 2005)
	Highland homecomings: Genealogy and heritage tourism in the Scottish diaspora (Basu, 2007)
Diaspora Tourism	Poor cousins no more: Valuing the development potential of domestic and diaspora tourism (Scheyvens, 2007)
	Tourism, diasporas and space (Coles and Timothy, 2004a)
	Homecoming or tourism? Diaspora tourism experience of second-generation immigrants (Huang et al., 2016)
	Diaspora tourism and homeland attachment: An exploratory analysis (Huang et al., 2013)
	Towards a conceptual framework for diaspora tourism (Li et al., 2020)

results as their guide, which sets them apart from the other categories. Roots and diaspora tourists mainly receive information from lived experiences and oral history passed down from generation to generation; their personal heritage is largely known to them. The ancestral and genealogy tourists also use some oral history, but since they both undertake extensive research prior to and during travel, their research is their predominant way to learn.

Table 13.2   *Typology of personal heritage tourists*

Personal Heritage Tourist Categories					
Type	DNA	Roots	Diaspora	Ancestral	Genealogical
Information about personal heritage	Genetic test only	Oral and lived history		Oral history and archival research	
Main driver	Sense of self	Sense of belonging	Sense of home	Sense of origin	Sense of lineage
Motivations and Behaviours					
Reclamation		• Reclaim lost heritage/culture • Experience ethnic and cultural sameness • Maintain culture • Establish 2nd home • Homecoming, quest, pilgrimage • Return migration	• Reclaim lost heritage/culture • Experience ethnic and cultural sameness • Maintain culture • Establish 2nd home • Homecoming, quest, pilgrimage • Return migration • Strengthen national identity • Relive personal memories		
Longing	• Connection with genetic heritage • Connection with genetic relatives	• Nostalgia • Emotional connection with ancestral place to overcome alienation • Overcome identity dissonance	• Nostalgia • Emotional connection with ancestral place to overcome alienation • Overcome identity dissonance • Connection with friends and relatives	• Nostalgia • Connection with their family's past	• Connecting the dots
Immersion	• Exploration of dark legacy	• Experience culture (history, art, science, lifestyles, architecture, community) of their ancestral kin • Eating and living as locals	• Exploration of dark legacy • Experience culture (history, art, science, lifestyles, architecture, community) of their ancestral kin • Eating and living as locals	• Experience culture (history, art, science, lifestyles, architecture, community) of their ancestral kin • Eating and living as locals	• Immersion in data

Personal Heritage Tourist Categories					
Type	DNA	Roots	Diaspora	Ancestral	Genealogical
Sense of Place		• Understanding places associated with ancestors	• Understanding places associated with ancestors • Exploring places encompassing part of their specific family heritage or personal past	• Understanding places associated with ancestors • Exploring places encompassing part of their specific family heritage	
Research	• Seek information because of lost or non-existing records		• Seek myths and personal stories	• Seek information because of lost or non-existing records • Extensive research before and during trip • Gather names, places and vital records • Build family tree • Seek myths and personal stories	• Seek information because of lost or non-existing records • Extensive research before and during trip • Gather names, places and vital records • Build family tree
Destinations	• Ancestral areas, places of past or current cultural significance, and places to meet genetic relatives	• Ancestral areas and places of past and current cultural significance	• Ancestral areas, places of past or present significance to family or self, places to meet friends and relatives	• Ancestral areas and places to meet relatives	• Libraries, genealogy centres and repositories

The typology then lists the main drivers of the various forms of personal heritage tourism. DNA tourists travel to establish a 'sense of self' – they want to understand who they are. Roots tourists engage in tourism to create a 'sense of belonging' to the culture of their ancestors. Diaspora tourists seek to re-establish the 'sense of home' that they or their ancestors had given up, either voluntarily or by force. Ancestral tourists want to know where they came from, thus they are driven by a need to discover a 'sense of origin'. Last, genealogy tourists travel mainly to build family trees and establish a 'sense of lineage'.

The next section of the typology has the motivations and behaviours broken down into themes of reclamation, longing, immersion, sense of place and research. Reclamation refers to reclaiming something that a person has a strong emotional connection with, but which was lost to them. Roots and diaspora tourists are keenly aware of their personal heritage and want to re-establish ties with their or their ancestors' homeland. Reclamation is not a motive for the other categories of personal heritage tourists. The longing theme demonstrates the connections these tourists are hoping to establish. For several of the groups (roots, diaspora and ancestral), this involves sentimental longing for an idealized past, that is, nostalgia. DNA tourists and ancestral tourists also long to establish connections with living kin and diaspora tourists often want to reconnect with family and friends. Roots tourists and diaspora tourists seek out strong emotional connections to compensate for alienation and to overcome identity dissonance. Genealogy tourists long to close the informational gaps in their family trees. The immersion subcategory elaborates on the experiences the different types of personal heritage tourists seek while at their destination. DNA and diaspora tourists often immerse themselves in dark tourism experiences to explore the dark legacy connected with their heritage. Roots, diaspora and ancestral tourists immerse themselves in the local culture and ways of life at the destination, while genealogy tourists immerse themselves in the genealogy data they derive from local records.

The sense of place section explains how the various personal heritage tourists seek to connect with the land, buildings and places of their ancestors. For DNA and genealogy tourists, place is irrelevant. Roots, diaspora and ancestral tourists all want to understand places connected with their ancestors. Diaspora and ancestral tourists have a strong interest in exploring places connected with their specific family heritage, such as homesteads. For diaspora tourists, these places sometimes relate to their personal past. The research theme explains what kind of information about their personal heritage these tourists seek before or during their trips and how/when they obtain this information. Roots tourists do not conduct any research and diaspora tourists usually only seek out family myths and personal stories. The other three groups engage in systematic research to uncover lost or create previously non-existing records. Ancestral and genealogy tourists are most similar with respect to research, as their trips are mainly motivated by research and they conduct extensive research before and during travel to inform their family tree-building efforts. Both collect data about names, places and vital records but ancestral tourists also search for myths and personal stories to paint a comprehensive picture of their ancestors' lives.

The final area at the bottom of the typology shows predominant destinations for these tourists. For all sub-niches except genealogy, their travel takes them to their ancestral homeland. DNA tourism could also take tourists to wherever their blood relatives are living, which may not be in their homeland. Genealogy tourists travel to visit the places where genealogical information is stored so that they can do their research. While roots tourists seek out places of general cultural significance, diaspora and ancestral tourists visit places connected to their immediate family. Diaspora tourists might also frequent destinations where they can visit with their family and friends.

Something interesting to note is that one individual can at times fall into one or more categories while they travel or change the type of personal heritage tourism from one trip to the next. Someone may start out as a roots tourist but while travelling come across specific information regarding their family that intrigues them enough to become an ancestral tourist, recording information to further build their family tree and document stories. Another tourist may be travelling to do research as a genealogy tourist for one trip, spending time at a family history centre, for example, and then on their next trip act as an ancestral tourist, documenting stories and experiencing the culture of their ancestors in their homeland.

Roots tourism and diaspora tourism emerge as very similar sub-niches and many articles consider diaspora to be a subcategory of roots tourism. The main differences relate to visiting friends and relatives; diaspora tourists go to visit those they or their ancestors left behind, as they typically left their homeland more recently and still have loved ones there. Diaspora tourism can also have an aspect of dark tourism due to the dislocation of individuals from their homelands, often involuntarily.

Research is a unifying characteristic of genealogical tourism and ancestral tourism. These tourists have spent substantial amounts of time researching their family history prior to travel and continue researching while travelling. The differences between them lie in the location of the research being done and the information they seek. Both groups seek out logistical data, but ancestral tourists also seek out traditions, histories and stories of their ancestors to provide a more complete life story.

DNA tourists have some overlaps with other groups – they may engage in aspects of dark tourism and visit family, in common with diaspora tourists, and some might act like roots tourists if they seek out connections with their genetic heritage. However, in general, they clearly emerged as a distinct group that merits attention.

CONCLUSIONS

This research provides clarification on different types of personal heritage tourists, their motivations and behaviours, where travellers receive their heritage information from and where they go while travelling. As such, the chapter makes an important contribution to understanding this sub-niche within the broader context of heritage tourism. The diversity it uncovered in terms of motivations and behaviours underlines the need to treat personal heritage tourists as a distinct grouping that warrants further exploration. It also helps to disentangle the definitional confusion that currently plagues the literature.

Understanding personal heritage tourists enables tourism providers to better cater to their guests' needs but also provides insights into marketing avenues that can be explored. Genealogical tourists, for instance, will likely visit libraries or other genealogy centres in search of vital records such as birth and marriage certificates. They will probably want areas with a good internet service so they can upload information to family trees. They want hotels close by so that research time is not wasted travelling back and forth. They want restaurants and services nearby so they can remain focused on their research. Learning about the destination and experiencing its authenticity is not of importance. It is not uncommon for these tourists to stay in the library throughout their entire stay and only leave to eat and sleep. Marketing opportunities aimed at these tourists would include webpages for genealogy centres or Facebook pages for genealogy enthusiasts specific to that area. Local tourism agencies could partner with genealogy centres and libraries to offer packages with housing and eateries close by the location. Hosting special speakers who are experts in local genealogy and hosting genealogy-related seminars and conferences are ways to entice genealogists to visit. Many areas have local or regional genealogy organizations that could partner with visitors' bureaus to advertise and provide speakers for these events. National organizations such as the Daughters of the American Revolution also have regional representatives that specialize in genealogy and would appeal to this group of tourists.

Ancestral tourists travel across broader areas as they look for ancestral sites and visit locals to seek out distant relatives in the area. They may be more prone to stay in vacation rentals or bed-and-breakfasts, since they will be travelling to specific ancestral lands that could be outside city limits. They seek immersion in the culture and heritage of the area, so local festivals and traditions are important. Tourism experiences that include immersive activities such as cooking the local cuisine with local products are appealing to this group, as are tours of the community and important historic places. Consequently, personal heritage tourists might participate in local activities that span many types of tourism niches while they travel, including cultural, culinary, rural and religious tourism, as well as visiting friends and relatives. This makes this sub-niche easy to cater to, as no specific infrastructure or services are required. Further, their desire to experience the destination like a local opens up tremendous sustainable small-scale development opportunities that benefit tourists and locals alike. Marketing for these tourists could be linked to genealogy programmes, such as like Ancestry.com, that provide ways to store family history information. Many of these tourists are members of Facebook pages for local heritage and genealogy researchers. Another advantage to these tourists is that the quest for family history knowledge is never-ending, so they are more likely to be return visitors than roots tourists.

Diaspora tourists may stay with friends and relatives as they visit the areas of their personal past or ancestry and participate in family and local traditions. First-generation migrants often stay with those they know, but those from second and third generations are more likely to stay in a hotel because of the distance in time since their family lived there. These tourists may follow local activities online and through social media and look for special opportunities for travelling during festivals and celebrations. They might also be members of social media groups involving people from one area that live in a different area, such as the Facebook group for Texans who live in Australia. They are most similar to tourists who are visiting friends and relatives (VFR tourists) and marketing strategies designed for this niche would also translate to diaspora tourists.

General DNA tourists tend not to have researched the background of their family, so they may participate in tourism via genealogical tours that are prearranged or by hiring specialized tour operators to show them the area. Their tourism experiences are more generic in that they may only know the country or region of their ancestors and not have specific information, so they seek out general cultural heritage tourism sites. Since DNA tourists still want to feel connected to their genetic heritage, they also may enjoy a cooking experience so they can take some new traditions and recipes home as they seek to construct their newfound personal heritage. Souvenirs will also be important for this group as they document their travels and check off their 'bucket list' travel destinations. Advertising to this group could be done through DNA sites and memberships but since this type of tourism also appeals to millennials, avenues such as social media, blogs and podcasts geared to younger travellers are also good options. For DNA tourists, advertising coordinated trips to meet their relatives could be an incentive for them to travel; for example, meetings of sperm donor siblings are growing in popularity.

Roots tourists are seeking to engage in their heritage, so cultural events and festivals would appeal to them. Those who are further removed generationally may lack local connections, so packages that combine these experiences could be sought after by those who want immersive experiences. Museum and historical tours in their ancestral area could shed light on their heritage and the challenges and opportunities of their ancestors, which may help with any sense of identity dissonance. Cooking classes for local cuisine could help such tourists learn skills they can take home and share with others as a way to reclaim some of their lost heritage. Visiting cemeteries, memorials or monuments may also help such travellers feel more connected to their past. Because they want to reclaim their lost heritage, purchasing local art, handicrafts and souvenirs to remind them of their homeland could be a priority.

This niche also provides a resilience that other tourism niches may not enjoy. Since researching family history is often a never-ending journey, personal heritage tourists often return to visited locations repeatedly. Personal ancestry tourists are linked to sustainability because they often stay and eat locally, and use local resources as they research and discover the different aspects of their personal history. This research, along with people's sense of connection to the destination, also makes them more likely to participate in the social and economic development of the visited areas because of their desire to preserve locations connected to their personal history. These tourists also bring certain advantages from the perspective of travelling during a pandemic, such as COVID-19. They typically stay longer at their destinations, so quarantining and testing may not be as much of an issue as for other tourists, and they travel in small groups to less common areas, not participating in typical commercial tourism activities. Their activities tend to be specialized and personal to their heritage discovery. Also, many people turned their focus to family during the recent COVID-19 pandemic because they were staying home, which gives family historians more time to research and plot out future trips as part of their personal heritage journey and be ready to travel when restrictions are lifted. Consequently, interest in personal heritage tourism is likely to increase as a direct result of the pandemic.

Further research opportunities are numerous in this area. The DNA tourism type has received very little attention from researchers; understanding these tourists would provide better opportunities for connecting with them and creating personalized offerings, especially as there seems to be two distinct subgroups. While we know of the motivations and behaviours of some of these types of personal heritage tourists, we do not have sufficient research on the struggles they encounter while travelling. Understanding these struggles and the research needs of genealogical and ancestral tourists, for example, could provide opportunities for visitors' bureaus and local genealogical resources to work together to overcome some of the issues these travellers face while looking for clues to their heritage. Most importantly, while the typology hints at overlaps with established tourism niches such as VFR and cultural tourists, the parallels and differences in terms of motivations, behaviours, destinations and information needs should be empirically explored.

REFERENCES

Agarwal, S. (2002) Restructuring seaside tourism: the resort lifecyle. *Annals of Tourism Research*, 29, 25–55.

Alexander, M., Bryce, D. and Murdy, S. (2017) Delivering the past: providing personalized ancestral tourism experiences. *Journal of Travel Research*, 56(4), 543–55.

Ali-Knight, J. (2011) *The Role of Niche Tourism Products in Destination Development*. Doctoral dissertation, Edinburgh Napier University.

Angelo, K.M., Breiman, J., Wu, H.M., Nemhauser, J. and Walker, A.T. (2020) Heritage and genealogy travel health concerns in the era of in-home DNA testing. *Journal of Travel Medicine*, 27(4).

Basu, P. (2004) Route metaphors of 'roots tourism' in the Scottish Highland diaspora. In S. Coleman and J. Eade (eds) *Reframing Pilgrimage: Cultures in Motion*. London: Routledge.

Basu, P. (2007) Highland homecomings: genealogy and heritage tourism in the Scottish diaspora. London: Routledge.

Benson, M. and O'Reilly, K. (2009) Migration and the search for a better way of life: a critical exploration of lifestyle migration. *The Sociological Review*, 57(4), 608–25.

Benton, A. and Shabazz, K.Z. (2009) 'Find their level'. African American roots tourism in Sierra Leone and Ghana. *Cahiers d'Études Africaines*, 49(193–194), 477–511.

Birtwistle, M. (2005) Genealogy tourism. In M. Novelli (ed.) *Niche Tourism*, 59–72. Oxford, UK: Elsevier.

Cheer, J. and Reeves, K. (2013) Roots tourism: blackbirding and the South Sea islander diaspora. *Tourism Analysis*, 18, 245–57.

Chhabra, D., Healy, R. and Sills, E. (2003) Staged authenticity and heritage tourism. *Annals of Tourism Research*, 30(3), 702–19.

Cohen, E. (1979) A phenomenology of tourist experiences. *Sociology*, 13(2), 179–201.

Coles, T. and Timothy, D.J. (2004a) *Tourism, Diasporas and Space*. London: Routledge.

Coles, T. and Timothy, D.J. (2004b) 'My field is the world': conceptualizing diasporas, travel and tourism. In T. Coles, T. and D.J. Timothy (eds) *Tourism, Diasporas and Space*, 1–30. London: Routledge.

Collier, D., LaPorte, J. and Seawright, J. (2012) Putting typologies to work: concept formation, measurement, and analytic rigor. *Political Research Quarterly*, 65(1), 217–232.

de Santana Pinho, P. (2008) African-American roots tourism in Brazil. *Latin American Perspectives*, 35(3), 70–86.

Dickinson, G. (2018) Is 'DNA tourism' the next travel trend for millennials? *The Telegraph*. https://www.telegraph.co.uk/travel/comment/dna-heritage-ancestral-tourism/ (accessed 8 October 2020).

Dillette, A. (2021). Roots tourism: a second wave of double consciousness for African Americans. *Journal of Sustainable Tourism*, 29(2–3), 412–27.

Gibson, J. (2015) *Preservation Glossary: Heritage Tourism*. Available at: https://savingplaces.org/stories/preservation-glossary-todays-word-heritage-tourism#.XzF2aShKiUk (accessed 8 October 2020).

Halewood, C. and Hannam, K. (2001) Viking heritage tourism. *Annals of Tourism Research*, 28, 565–80.

Higginbotham, G. (2012) Seeking roots and tracing lineages: constructing a framework of reference for roots and genealogical tourism. *Journal of Heritage Tourism*, 7(3), 189–203.

Hollinshead, K. (1988) First-blush of the longtime: the market development of Australia's living Aboriginal heritage. A paper composed of recognition of Australia's Bicentenary: 1988. In *Tourism Research: Expanding Boundaries*. Travel and Tourism Research Association Nineteenth Annual Conference, Montreal, Quebec, Canada, June 19–23. (pp. 183–198). Salt Lake City, UT: Bureau of Economic and Business Research, University of Utah.

Huang, W.-J.; Haller, W.J. and Ramshaw, G.P. (2013) Diaspora tourism and homeland attachment: An exploratory analysis. *Tourism Analysis*, 18, 285–96.

Huang, W.-J., Ramshaw, G. and Norman, W.C. 2016. Homecoming or tourism? Diaspora tourism experience of second-generation immigrants. *Tourism Geographies*, 18, 59–79.

Kennedy-Eden, H. and Gretzel, U. (2012) A taxonomy of mobile applications in tourism. *E-review of Tourism Research*, 10, 47–50.

Kramer, A.M. (2011) Mediatizing memory: history, affect and identity in who do you think you are? *European Journal of Cultural Studies*, 14(4), 428–45.

Lacher, R.G., Oh, C.O., Jodice, L.W. and Norman, W.C. (2013) The role of heritage and cultural elements in coastal tourism destination preferences: a choice modeling–based analysis. *Journal of Travel Research*, 52(4), 534–46.

Li, T.E., Mckercher, B. and Chan, E.T.H. (2020) Towards a conceptual framework for diaspora tourism. *Current Issues in Tourism*, 23, 2109–26.

Lowenthal, D. (1975) Past time, present place: landscape and memory. *Geographical Review*, 65, 1–36.

Marschall, S. (2017). Transnational migrant home visits as identity practice: the case of African migrants in South Africa. *Annals of Tourism Research*, 63, 140–50. doi:https://doi.org/10.1016/j.annals.2017.01.011

Maruyama, N.U. (2016) Roots tourists' internal experiences and relations with the ancestral land: case of second-generation Chinese Americans. *International Journal of Tourism Research*, 18, 469–76.

McCain, G. and Ray, N. M. (2003) Legacy tourism: the search for personal meaning in heritage travel. *Tourism Management*, 24(6), 713–17.

Mehtiyeva, A. and Prince, S. (2020) Journeys of research, emotions and belonging: an exploratory analysis of the motivations and experience of ancestral tourists. *Scandinavian Journal of Hospitality and Tourism*, 20, 85–103.

Morehart, P. (2019) Newsmaker: Kenyatta D. Berry, author and attorney uses genealogy to help create personal stories. *American Libraries Magazine*. https://americanlibrariesmagazine.org/2019/04/26/newsmaker-kenyatta-d-berry/ (accessed 8 October 2020).

Murdy, S., Alexander, M. and Bryce, D. (2016) Role conflict and changing heritage practice: ancestral tourism in Scotland. *Journal of Marketing Management*, 32, 1494–512.

Murdy, S., Alexander, M. and Bryce, D. (2018) What pulls ancestral tourists 'home'? An analysis of ancestral tourist motivations. *Tourism Management*, 64, 13–19.

Nickerson, R., Muntermann, J., Varshney, U. and Isaac, H. (2009) Taxonomy development in information systems: eveloping a taxonomy of mobile applications. *European Conference on Information Systems*, 388–99. Verona, Italy: Association for Information Systems.

Novelli, M. (2005) *Niche Tourism*. Oxford, UK: Elsevier.

Otterstrom, S.M. and Bunker, B.E. (2013) Genealogy, migration, and the intertwined geographies of personal pasts. *Annals of the Association of American Geographers*, 103, 544–69.

Poria, Y., Reichel, A. and Biran, A. (2006) Heritage site perceptions and motivations to visit. *Journal of Travel Research*, 44(3), 318–26. Doi:10.1177/0047287505279004

Ray, N.M. and McCain, G. (2009) Guiding tourists to their ancestral homes. *International Journal of Culture, Tourism and Hospitality Research*, 3(4), 296–305.

Ray, N.M. and McCain, G. (2012) Personal identity and nostalgia for the distant land of past: legacy tourism. *International Business and Economics Research Journal*, 11, 977–89.

Ray, N.M. and McCain, G. (2015) "It was the trip of a lifetime": Viking ancestors, their descendants and their legacy tourism motivations and behavior. In C. Campbell (ed.) *Marketing in Transition: Scarcity, Globalism, & Sustainability*. Developments in Marketing Science: Proceedings of the Academy of Marketing Science. Springer, Cham. https://doi.org/10.1007/978-3-319-18687-0_72.

Robinson, M. and Novelli, M. (2005) Niche tourism: an introduction. In M. Novelli (ed.) *Niche Tourism*, 1–11. Oxford, UK: Elsevier.

Rodrigues, A., Kastenholz, E. and Morais, D. (2012) Travel constraints and nostalgia as determinants of cross-Atlantic legacy tourism. In H. Pechlaner, T.J. Lee and G. Dal Bò (eds) *New Minorities and Tourism–Proceedings of the International Scientific Workshop on New Minorities and Tourism*, 75–92. Bolzano, Italy: Accademia Europea Bolzano.

Rodriguez, G. (2014) How genealogy became almost as popular as porn. *Time*. https://time.com/133811/how-genealogy-became-almost-as-popular-as-porn/ (accessed 8 October 2020).

Russell, D.W. (2008) Nostalgic tourism. *Journal of Travel & Tourism Marketing*, 25(2), 103–16.

Safran, W. (2011) Diasporas in modern societies: myths of homeland and return. *Diaspora: A Journal of Transnational Studies*, 1, 83–99.

Santos, C.A. and Yan, G. (2010) Genealogical tourism: a phenomenological examination. *Journal of Travel Research*, 49(1), 56–67.

Scheyvens, R. (2007) Poor cousins no more: valuing the development potential of domestic and diaspora tourism. *Progress in Development Studies*, 7, 307–25.

Sedmak, G. and Mihalič, T. (2008) Authenticity in mature seaside resorts. *Annals of Tourism Research*, 35, 1007–31.

Timothy, D. J. (1997) Tourism and the personal heritage experience. *Annals of Tourism Research*, 24, 751–3.

Timothy, D. J. (2011) *Cultural Heritage and Tourism: An Introduction*. Bristol, UK: Channel View Publications.

Timothy, D.J. and Guelke, J.K. (2008) *Geography and Genealogy: Locating Personal Pasts*. Farnham, UK: Ashgate Publishing.

Weaver, D.B. (2011) Contemporary tourism heritage as heritage tourism: evidence from Las Vegas and Gold Coast. *Annals of Tourism Research*, 38, 249–67.

Yale, P. (2004) *From Tourist Attractions to Heritage Tourism*. Huntingdon, UK: Elm Publications.

Zeppel, H. and Hall, C.M. (1991) Selling art and history: cultural heritage and tourism. *Journal of Tourism Studies*, 2, 29–45.

Zhaorong, P. and Xiangchun, Z. (2008) Legacy and tourism: collocating and deviating of tradition and modern. *Study in Ethics in Guangxi*, 3, 33–39.

14. Communist heritage tourism in Poland

Robert Pawlusiński, Joanna Kowalczyk-Anioł and Magdalena Kubal-Czerwińska

INTRODUCTION

Communist heritage tourism can be considered special interest tourism based on the politics and history of former communist countries (Light 2000a, 2000b; Ivanov, 2009; Ivanova and Buda, 2020). This phenomenon arose in Central and Eastern European countries after the collapse of the Socialist Bloc in the last decade of the 20th century. Nowadays, the term is also used in other geopolitical contexts, such as China, although there is no agreement on it (Sima, 2017). According to Novelli's (2005) niche tourism classification, communist heritage tourism can be seen as a kind of micro-niche within the framework of macro-niche cultural tourism.

After the fall of communism in the Eastern Bloc in the early 1990s, countries of Central and Eastern Europe opened to international tourists (Hall, 1991; Baláž and Williams, 2005). Although in some destinations – such as Berlin – the communist heritage has become a significant element of the tourist destination's image, it has never become a truly mass tourism product (Hughes and Allen, 2005). Communist heritage has been presented in various ways, from the preservation of socialist urbanism and architecture, through museum exhibitions, to the organization of humorous events and cultural activities relating to this period (Ivanov, 2009; Knudsen, 2010). For many (especially local communities), the material communist heritage has never been worthy of preservation for future generations (Light, 2000b). In fact, it was perceived as something embarrassing, unwanted, preferably to be replaced with something new (Light, 2000b). It is only due to the visible interest of Western tourists in the communist past that a discussion concerning the preservation of these elements and their availability for tourists has begun (Ivanova and Buda, 2020; Light 2000b; Young and Kaczmarek, 2008).

Thirty years after the political transition, researchers began to question whether communist heritage can still be categorized as a tourist product in Central and Eastern European countries. The theoretical framework for this research is a product-related approach to niche tourism (Robinson and Novelli, 2005; Ali-Knight, 2010). As Robinson and Novelli (2005) write, this approach requires an emphasis on presenting and curating the elements that create a niche tourism destination product mix, one subordinated to specific tourists' needs and wants. As Ivanova and Buda (2020) emphasize, communist heritage tourism is related to the political and economic transition of the Central and Eastern European region. However, there are some differences between countries which result to a large extent from the model of communism (socialism) that was in force in a given country and the course of the transformation process itself (Ivanova and Buda, 2020).

Previous research on communist heritage tourism, conducted mainly by English-speaking researchers (including Light, 2000a, 2000b), has focused on selected aspects of this phenomenon (e.g., nostalgia, difficult legacy) and has not taken into account its evolution, tourism practices or what constitutes a tourist product. Moreover, as Richards (2021a) points out relatively little attention is paid to how niches are identified, develop and are consolidated. Using Poland as a case study, we demonstrate its changing nature over time and indicate its significance to the creation of tourist products. Two research questions are posed: (1) How has the model of communist heritage tourism in Poland evolved over the last 30 years? (2) What types of tourist product and related tourism practices constitute communist heritage tourism in Poland today?

Due to the widely defined time horizon and scope of the research, a variety of available sources of information are used in the case study. In addition to the data collected during a critical analysis of the literature and from the content of promotional materials and press reports (along with observation in situ), the study also used interviews with key informants, for instance, representatives of the main destination marketing organizations in Poland. Such a triangulation of sources and methods is often used in a case study approach (Stake, 1995; Yin, 2009). At the same time, as Stake (1995) points out, the advantage of a case study as a method is that it enables a deeper understanding of a wider phenomenon as manifested by a given case. For this chapter, the example discussed will serve to show the trajectory of communist heritage tourism development in Poland, as this has not been specifically studied so far. Moreover, the case discussed will introduce to research an analysis of a tourism niche stimulated by a geopolitical context.

LITERATURE REVIEW

Communist heritage tourism is a part of heritage tourism (Garrod and Fyall, 2001; Light, 2000a; Timothy and Boyd, 2008), also known as cultural tourism (Jovicic, 2016; Richards, 2018; 2021b). According to Li and Hu (2008) there are two models of communism-based tourism development: European (communist heritage tourism) and Asian (red tourism). Although both approaches refer to communist ideology and its material manifestations, fundamental differences between these forms can be identified. In red tourism, the government is the main actor, and it subordinates it to its political strategy to 'stimulate a collective nostalgia for the communist past [...] and ultimately, to justify the legitimacy of the communist reign' (Li and Hu, 2008, p. 159).

In Central and Eastern Europe, the phenomenon of communist heritage tourism is part of the still ongoing process of transition from a centrally planned to a market-oriented economy (Ivanova and Buda, 2020). In Europe, it is private entities that mostly participate in communist heritage tourism development, and this form of tourism is perceived as an 'economic engine to promote the process of transformation and privatization in [the] tourism industry' (Li and Hu, 2008, p. 159). The product is also targeted at different markets. In the case of red tourism, these are mainly Chinese citizens (especially as part of the patriotic education of young people – Hung, 2018) while for countries of Central and Eastern Europe, they are foreign tourists mainly from Western Europe and the USA (Li and Hu, 2008; Sima, 2017).

Other concepts of communism-based tourism development also deserve attention, such as socialism-based tourism in North Korea, where tourism is an element of propaganda and is subject to strict control by the regime (Ouellette, 2020). Tourism in North Korea relies on the influx of foreign tourists who are needed to ensure the financial stability of the regime (Ouellette, 2020). Geopolitical changes in recent years in Cuba encourage the extension of the typology by Li and Hu (2008) and the communist state treats Western tourists as an important source of income (Scarpaci, 2013). Here, communism and its traces are in the form of a living exhibition in an 'open-air museum'. Similar solutions are characteristic of Vietnam, but there the remnants of the war with the USA are exhibited as part of an armed conflict between the communist world and the West (Henderson, 2000).

This cursory look at the literature shows that a contextual view is essential to understand communist heritage tourism (and communism-based tourism) development trajectories. Several contexts should be taken into account: the political (the strength of the regime, its duration, adaptation to the present day), the geographical (links with place), the social and cultural (origin of tourists) and the organizational (producers of communist heritage tourism). In the holistic perspective of communist heritage tourism, these four categories frame the tourist use of communism. Its basis is still communist heritage, both material (tangible) and non-material (intangible). Relationships between the communist heritage and communist heritage tourism are increasingly often referred to as 'reciprocal coproduction' (Gravari-Barbas, 2020).

Ivanov (2009) identifies five characteristics of communist heritage tourism in the countries of Central and Eastern Europe. These are: (1) an ideologically overburdened and (2) controversial type of tourism, (3) representative of a limited time period, (4) focused around a personality cult and (5) related to the conservation of resources in places related to it. The most important distinguishing feature of communist heritage tourism in Europe is the description of the communist heritage using the categories of an unwanted past (Light, 2000a) and an unwanted or dissonant heritage (Banaszkiewicz et al., 2017; Murzyn 2008). Light et al., (2009) state that many people think that this period should be forgotten, and its material relicts should be destroyed. However, the process of rejecting the communist past in individual countries of Central and Eastern Europe proceeded differently and has taken various forms (Light, 2000a, 2000b; Sima, 2017).

Following Poria and Ashworth (2009), communist heritage served in the heritagization process, leading to a change in the perception of the period of 'real' socialism by Polish society. Interestingly, after the first stage of the political transformation in the 1990s, some parts of society refused to accept or even rejected the process of systemic transformation and, at the same time, nostalgia for communism appeared (Light, 2000a; Ziółkowski, 2002). This phenomenon, called 'ostalgia', a portmanteau of nostalgia and *ost*, the German word for east, was especially visible in Eastern Germany, the essence of which is reflected in the film entitled *Goodbye Lenin* (2003) (Light and Young, 2015). Ostalgia has been temporarily reflected in consumer behaviour and in domestic tourism in Germany in the form of holiday vacations at resorts in the style of the former East Germany, the German Democratic Republic (Deutsche Demokratische Republik) (Coles, 2003; Bach, 2002). Although ostalgia was also visible in other countries, including Hungary and Poland, it did not meaningfully motivate its inhabitants toward tourism.

The current literature rarely refers to the potential of communist sites from the point of view of shaping their offering for tourists. Discussion on the commodification of communist heritage is conducted mainly by anthropologists and they point to its negative side (Banaszkiewicz et al., 2017). On the other hand, there are only a few geographic and economic analyses related to issues connected with tourist products (Light, 2000a, 2000b; Derek, 2020), and this chapter attempts to fill this gap. Moreover, although current research identifies heritage as one of the main drivers of tourism, it rarely explores the inverse relationship in which tourism is the driver of heritage (Gravari-Barbas, 2018). Our analysis of communist heritage tourism develops from the thesis of Gravari-Barbas (2018), who describes tourism as a 'heritage producing machine'.

FINDINGS

As previously mentioned, the chapter adopts a product-related approach to niche tourism. Its empirical part (relating to communist heritage tourism in Poland) consists of two sections: the first is chronological and the second is typological. The first section presents (on a timeline) the most important (iconic) characters, places and events that make up the core of communist heritage tourism products at a given stage. The key actors (organizers) and the main processes shaping the development of this micro-niche in Poland are also indicated. The second section presents types of communist heritage tourists, and above all identifies the types of niche products and practices of communist heritage tourism in Poland.

The Evolution of Communist Heritage Tourism in Poland

The first narratives in Poland about the communist past in the early 1990s were associated with the fight against the regime and its leaders (Ziębińska-Witek, 2018). Lech Wałęsa, the leader of the Independent Self-Governing Trade Union 'Solidarity' (Solidarność) and John Paul II, the first Catholic pope originally from Poland, were the most recognizable Poles in the fight against communism on the world stage (Kubik, 2010; Shearer, 2021). Their highly emotional stories were connected to places which the public began to treat in a similar way to temples or pilgrimage sites. Of course, Poles mainly visited these places in combination with other tourist attractions. Today, their importance for communist heritage tourism is much less than just after the fall of the regime. We term this stage in Poland 'pre-communist heritage tourism'.

The first 'must-see' locations for communist heritage tourism were Częstochowa, Gdańsk and Warsaw. Visitors journeyed to the Jasna Góra Sanctuary in Częstochowa – considered the spiritual capital of Poland – to understand Polish aspirations for freedom. This place has been a traditional destination for Polish pilgrimages since Medieval times, including during the communist period when the regime prohibited the pilgrimage (Shearer, 2021). The rank of Jasna Góra was sealed by the fact that in 1983 Lech Wałęsa deposited his Nobel Prize there and also the pen with the image of the Polish Pope with which Wałęsa signed the famous August Agreements between Solidarity and the communist government in 1980. These items, especially at the beginning of the post-communist period, were treated as national relics. In Gdańsk, the best-known sites were the monument to the Fallen Shipyard Workers of 1970, built in December 1980 next to the Lenin Shipyard entrance in Gdańsk, and the St Brygida Basilica, recognized as the official church of Solidarity. In Warsaw, tourists flocked to St Stanisław Kostka Church where the thumb of the priest Jerzy Popiełuszko, an activist brutally murdered by the communist regime, rests. Significantly, this way of presenting the communist past by connecting it to religion and the church is specific to Poland (Shearer, 2021).

Throughout the 1990s, the significance of material traces of the communist past, including buildings, squares or entire urban layouts, were marginalized (Beiersdorf, 1997). The difficult early years of transformation and the fascination with modern architectural ideas typical of the Western world, common in Poland and other countries, meant that these places were not looked after and many fell into disrepair. During the 1990s, the entire material legacy of communism was subordinated to the brutal rules of the free market without any attempt at conservation. Only at the end of the decade did Western tourists, who first expressed interest in learning about communist heritage, initiate discussions on the preservation of communist-era edifices (Beiersdorf, 1997; Pawlusiński, 2006). This resulted in the first decisions on the legal protection of Socialist Realist buildings (Myczkowski and Siwek, 2017).

As a consequence, only in the last 20 years can the emergence of classic niche tourism based on communist heritage be spoken of in Poland. Such tourism was directed mainly at foreign tourists and its transformation has proceeded in two ways. The first involved excessive commercialization of part of the communist heritage at the hands of private enterprises. This excessive commercialization and compliance with consumer (tourist) expectations has contributed to its Disneyfication. As a result, this still-complicated heritage began to be presented in a way that prevented the community from accepting it. Summing up, the first development trend raised several issues, especially in relation to the method and scope of presenting the communist heritage to foreigners. Since humorous and entertaining elements were often included, it grew in popularity (Adie et al., 2017).

The second way encompassed the public sphere, including local authorities who protected and made communist heritage available through museum exhibitions (Ziębińska-Witek 2020). This approach did not directly target tourists. Rather, it was driven by an educational prerogative, or even aimed at achieving wider social effects in the local community (acceptance, respect, etc.). These activities were aimed at revitalizing city centres and other problem areas, as well as supporting various undertakings related to tourism development.

The two-pronged communist heritage tourism transformation process discussed above resulted in the preservation and conservation of communist material heritage. By 2020, more than 200 buildings and structures built between 1945 and 1990 were covered by legal protection as monuments (National Institute of Cultural Heritage, n.d.). The list includes symbolic buildings: the Palace of Culture and Science in Warsaw, the shipyard buildings in Gdańsk and the office buildings of the steelworks at Nowa Huta in Kraków. Steps were taken to enter the Nowa Huta district and the Gdańsk Shipyard onto the UNESCO list, while they gained national rank by appearing on the List of Monuments of History in Poland (National Institute of Cultural Heritage, n.d.).

Secondly, the same process precipitated the musealization of communism (Ziębińska-Witek 2018; Main, 2013). As early as the 1990s, discussion began in Poland on the creation of a high-ranking museum of communism, envisioned as a flagship tourist attraction. From the very beginning, the way museums present communism has caused disputes and this is best illustrated by the example of the Socland Foundation, established by outstanding Polish filmmakers, including Andrzej Wajda (Main, 2013), whose goal was to create a modern museum exhibition devoted to the period of communism which would take a caricaturist and grotesque look at the past.

The original idea is best reflected in the words of one of the founders of Socland, Adam Bielecki, in 1998: 'Others have Legoland and Disneyland. And we, severely hurt by socialism, will recreate the land of *Realsoc – Socland*, to educate and warn future generations'. Initially, the foundation considered the buildings which once housed the steelworks in Nowa Huta as a possible location (Pawlusiński, 2006); however, the exhibition 'One Day in the Polish People's Republic', presented in Nowa Huta in 2001, failed to gain universal acceptance in the city. Visitors pointed out that the complex history of communism cannot be presented solely through mockery, caricature and trivialization. The Foundation moved the project to Warsaw (the capital of Poland), seeking to establish a museum in the Palace of Culture and Science where, with the support of the city, the foundation planned to create a modern exhibition engaging all the senses in a place typically associated with the past regime. Unfortunately, this project was rejected for financial and political reasons (Main, 2013).

Interestingly, the presentation of the communist past follows a similar trajectory in both Warsaw and Kraków. Although various groups, including artists and political leaders, strongly emphasized the need to create museums of communism of a national rank using modern forms of exhibition, public authorities prioritized projects related to the Second World War (Guichard-Marneur, 2018). In Warsaw, the Uprising Museum, opened in 2004. In Kraków, Schindler's Factory Museum was established in 2010 with an exhibition presenting the fate of Kraków's Jews. Both locations gained the rank of 'must-see' museums in these cities. As a result, a reputable museum presenting Polish communism in a multidimensional way has not been established in either of the largest cities in Poland whose urban identities have clearly been shaped by communism (Young and Kaczmarek, 2008).

Although noticeable measures on a national scale contribute to the revival of communist heritage tourism, the Polish past is still omitted in official tourism promotion. None of the communist facilities are recognized as a tourist brand. The Palace of Culture and Science in Warsaw is treated, especially by younger generations, as a symbol of change, rather than a communist creation (Naumov and Weidenfeld, 2019). Practically the entire burden related to the promotion and marketing communication of communist heritage tourism has been taken over by small tourist businesses. Using communication via the internet and social media, they can reach the market with their products. Even in Kraków, Nowa Huta is barely noticeable in the city's tourist offering (Matoga, 2015). These transformations of communist heritage tourism in Poland indicate that it can be identified as mainly urban and multidimensional, leading to a rise in various types of tourist products and different groups of recipients. Interviews with destination marketing organizations demonstrate that in the case of any Polish city, communist heritage tourism is not considered an important tourism product. Only in Kraków, Warsaw and Gdańsk is communist heritage tourism indicated in city development plans as a potential emerging market.

Types of Niche Products and Practices

There are three distinguishable tourism practices which use communist heritage in Poland. Succinctly, they can be termed: a) entertainment, b) reflection tours and c) classical sightseeing. The first practice – still the most common – shows communism in a humorous way, ridiculing elements of social behaviour and living conditions supposedly inferior to their Western equivalents. This approach to the product results from two aspects. Firstly, it responds to the expectations expressed by visitors, especially Western tourists, who want to learn about communism in the style shown in *Goodbye Lenin*. On the other hand, it is a reaction by a part of society to the regime's propaganda, which treated all aspects of contemporary social life very seriously. Mocking communism and its everyday life experience is a response to the difficulties and restrictions that it wrought. Importantly, this trend includes not only private businesses, but also some museums from small ones, established by private individuals, to cultural state institutions.

One of the first instances of communist heritage tourism, the famous 'Bar u Wołodzi' (named after Włodzimierz Lenin) invited visitors to take communist heritage with a grain of salt (Zaborowska, 2001). Located in Hajnówka by the Białowieża Forest, right on the border with Belarus, the small restaurant reminiscent of the communist era attracted guests from all over the world. Communism was treated cheerfully there; guests could dress in a Soviet-era uniforms, portraits and busts of the leaders of the Russian Revolution decorated the interior, and revolutionary communist songs were played. The most attractive part of the restaurant's offering was a staged narrow-gauge railway ride through the Białowieża Forest, during which the staff acted as if the train had illegally crossed the state border. The sudden appearance of soldiers in Belarusian uniforms added to the story's fidelity. The further course of events varied: it could have been a chilling, naturalistic scene of the crew being shot, or a milder one, which involved drinking vodka with actors portraying the Belarusian soldiers, singing and dancing. This quickly gained worldwide reputation and popularity. Unfortunately, in 2014 the place was closed (*Gazeta Wyborcza*, 2013). Although contested by some groups for its extreme approach to the heritage of communism, the model was copied by many businesses.

In 2004, the Crazy Guides began to operate in Kraków, focusing on communism tours of Nowa Huta (Banaszkiewicz, 2017; Knudsen, 2010). The programme of a fictionalized tour via vehicles from the period, such as the East German Trabant or the Polish Nysa van, included, for example, a walk around Nowa Huta, a visit to an apartment furnished with objects for everyday use from the period, and refreshments at a former communist-period restaurant, 'Stylowa'. At the restaurant, tourists drank pure vodka from 100 ml glasses, which was symbolic of communism and Eastern Europe. The Crazy Guide's tourism offering quickly became a magnet (Knudsen, 2010), although it usually did not constitute a tourist's entire visit to Kraków (Pawlusiński and Kubal, 2018) but was rather an element of a multi-day city break there. Communist heritage tours were usually taken individually or in small groups. These offerings were promoted through sales and travel companies, such as TripAdvisor and local travel agencies. Unfortunately, even Kraków's Crazy Guides did not resist the need to adapt their product to the needs of tourists. Currently, the classic plot is supplemented with various, often extreme elements. One British tourist's stay in Kraków turned out to be a real 'bullseye'; Crazy Guides arranged for the Briton to shoot an AK-47 (Kalashnikov) at a military shooting range. A relatively little known but popular product is the Communist Welcome, where guides welcome guests at the airport with vodka and pickled cucumbers and take them to communist-period discos. Admittedly, however, the company also participates in the promotion of other types of heritage; it offers visits to fallout shelters which have been made available to visitors in the building of the former Światowid cinema in Nowa Huta, where the new communism museum in Nowa Huta is also located (Banaszkiewicz, 2017).

Similar heritage tours have appeared in other Polish cities, such as Gdańsk, Warsaw, Wrocław and Poznań. These projects also take an international dimension; crazystag.com offers communist heritage tours in Poland, Prague and Budapest, offering an uncritical approach to tourism combining information about the communist past with the stag parties typical for British tourists.

Martyrology refers to the second practice, representing communism as a time of bloody social revolts against authoritarian regimes (Ziębińska-Witek, 2020). The European Solidarity Centre (ESC) in Gdańsk, the Museum of the Poznań Uprising of June 1956, the Silesian Freedom and Solidarity Centre in Katowice and the History Centre '*Zajezdnia*' in Wrocław represent this practice. A distinguishing feature of these institutions is their location, as these so-called witnesses to history are places where important events related to the fight against the communist regime took place. These institutions not only present the past in the form of an exhibition but are open to various types of activity, including the organization of events, meetings and debates, as well as educational activities (Ziębińska-Witek, 2018). In these institutions, communism is shown not only as the past, but as a background for reflection on the future.

Among them, the ESC in Gdańsk is an institution committed to the promotion and interpretation of the complex heritage of the communist period. It is responsible for the heritagization postulates put forward by Poria and Ashworth (2009). As Ziębińska-Witek (2018) notes, an element of its mission is to establish Solidarity as a Polish national brand. Located in the former Gdańsk Shipyard – the birthplace of the Solidarity movement – the ESC is supported by both government and EU funds (about EUR29 million each) and is focused mainly on Solidarity (ESC, n.d.). The ESC is not a traditional museum exhibition, but a modern multifunctional complex. The permanent exhibition is devoted to the history of Solidarity and the changes that have taken place under its influence in Central and Eastern Europe. Between 2014 and 2017 about 2.3 million people visited the Centre (ESC, n.d.).

In Poznań, the exhibition commemorates the first mass protest against the communist regime, which took place in June 1956. The museum is headquartered in the former seat of the communist municipal authorities in the immediate vicinity of where the protests took place. As Ziębińska-Witek (2018) notes, similarly to the ESC, it presents a story about a foreign enemy, communism, oppressing a captive society and maintaining its power at the cost of many victims. The Silesian Freedom and Solidarity Centre in Katowice heads in a similar direction as well. It is located in the former Wujek coal mine where the state bloodily suppressed protests in 1981, killing nine miners. The exhibition is devoted mainly to this event. The History Centre 'Zajezdnia' in Wrocław is located in the former bus depot where the Wrocław Solidarity Protest of 1980 began. The Centre presents the complicated history of the city from its takeover from the Germans in 1945 to 2016. Visitors can listen to eyewitness accounts (oral histories), play the role of an opposition printer (prepare an illegal anti-communist paper) or sign the message from Polish to German bishops.

The activity of these institutions extends into the field of education on a regional and national level (Ziębińska-Witek, 2018). Communist facilities and museums are sometimes included in school trips. The lessons related to communism are presented from different perspectives, from martyrdom to the humorous, and adapted for different age groups. In recent years, there has also been a noticeable increase in interest in this past among foreign students, including participants of the Erasmus programme, who express a desire to learn the complex histories of their host country. Given the increased interest, this micro-niche has growth potential for the future. The form and content, however, must be adapted to the requirements and expectations of a younger generation as a condition for its development.

The third practice is limited to the exhibition of the material culture of communism, the architecture of cities and art, without any commentary to assign a value to this heritage. Still, it is noticeable that the heritage is perceived as something unwanted. Also, only a few cities designate and promote official communist buildings as tourist attractions in their tourist offering although routes around facilities and places related to the communist past are found in Kraków, Warsaw and Gdańsk. In Kraków, the first museum devoted to communism has operated since 2004 in the form of an open-air museum; it shows the past not through a museum exhibition but through walks around the Nowa Huta district to showcase places in situ (Pawlusiński, 2006). These routes refer to the idea of directing a tourist's gaze (Urry, 2002) by assigning symbols (markings, labels, descriptions) to selected places in a city space.

However, contrary to the basic tourism paradigm from MacCannell (2013) of the desire to visit extraordinary, beautiful places, famous for their magnificent monuments, these routes provide an opportunity to direct tourists to typical places evocative of the period. The grey and rough buildings are treated not as an exotic element, but as a reflection of the reality of those times.

The potential for these tourism practices lies in the general character of the urban fabric, formed according to different assumptions than those in Western Europe. The architecture of housing estates composed of multi-storey tower blocks, public utility buildings, and post-industrial spaces closely related to the socialist industrialization of cities are therefore special attractions for urban sightseeing in a post-communist urban landscape. Guides draw attention to the accompanying mosaics, neon signs and murals. This all creates a visible background as well as an opportunity to learn about the urban design of communist Europe.

A thematic analysis of websites shows that the use of architecture for tourist purposes in Central and Eastern European cities is rare. Information about single sites dominates, while virtual routes (such as the 'Nowa Huta Route' or the 'Modernism Route in Kraków'), thematic publications and guided walking tours are less common. The growing interest in the architectural heritage of Europe that may be termed 'dissonant' or 'uncomfortable' is evidenced by the establishment of the Council of Europe's European Cultural Routes – 'ATRIUM' (Architecture of Totalitarian Regimes in Europe's Urban Memory; http://www. atriumroute. eu). The urban communist heritage is an important part of this, but most Central and Eastern European countries, including Poland, do not participate in the project.

Two types of tourists interested in communist heritage tourism have developed in Poland. The first are the so-called 'communism grippers': these are people who are deeply interested in the communist period and are willing to visit places in Poland and abroad. They are interested in monuments related to communism, retro-style events and the staging of important moments, for example, attacks by the Motorized Reserve of the Citizens' Militia (ZOMO). They form a narrow group composed of both domestic and foreign tourists who are quite knowledgeable about communist heritage and object to its commercialization.

The second group consists of tourists 'en passant' who suddenly learn about communist heritage in passing while spending time in a particular place. These are mainly foreigners on so-called city breaks. Generally, they respond when prompted by travel agents or posts on social media (e.g., TripAdvisor) and buy readymade (comprehensive) packages. A classic product addressed to them is the communism tour, a way of visiting communist buildings and sites via vehicles from the period, but learning about communist heritage is much less valuable for them than having fun. Sometimes, communism tours become a part of another event, often accompanying business meetings or conferences.

CONCLUSIONS

Communist heritage tourism is another example of a niche. Due to its ambiguous nature and reference to an unwanted past, it has not gained, and will probably never gain, a more mass character. It is a self-determined, and self-limiting, kind micro-niche tourism – a conclusion which is relevant to the ongoing debate around this tourism form.

While Novelli (2018) suggests that niche tourism is becoming an important element of destination diversification strategy, our example lags behind in this regard. It is also difficult to clearly refer to this micro-niche's contribution to sustainable development in the destination

(Novelli 2018). Communist heritage tourism's potential for strengthening social sustainability in local communities seems significant, although not as obvious as our case has shown. At the same time, three decades of development of this tourism form confirm the assumptions of Sert (2017) that niche tourism is based mainly on small tourist entrepreneurs. We also largely support McKercher and Chan (2005), in that special interest tourism, such as communist heritage tourism, does not have to be the main reason for choosing a destination, as evidenced by the tourists themselves. At the same time, as we have shown, the products of this micro-niche are often based on co-creation of the tourist experience, which is suggested by both niche tourism researchers (Novelli, 2018) and those of cultural tourism (Jovicic, 2016; Richards, 2021b). Only in these dimensions does our paper show that niche tourism is still an ambiguous and attractive area for academic exploration.

Responding to the question, 'is it still alive?', this chapter shows that communist heritage tourism is an evolving and constantly differentiating micro-niche. Its transformation mechanisms reflect general trends of change in the cultural tourism macro-niche, and tensions in the commercialization of heritage are particularly visible. Communist heritage tourism also follows changing tourism demand, which is increasingly diversifying. The functioning of this micro-niche fits well with the Gravari-Barbas thesis (2018, p. 5) which states: 'contemporary tourism creates a new heritage system that works according to its own needs and expectations'.

The Polish phenomenon of communist heritage tourism presented here, as well as recent research by Light et al. (2020), clearly shows that in Central and Eastern European countries communist heritage is undervalued by local populations. However, as an attractive distinguishing feature for Western visitors, it is constantly commodified and sold in a form which is easily accessible to foreign tourists (Matoga and Pawłowska, 2018). As noted earlier, communism-based tourism is culturally and geographically determined. For this reason, the European model of communist heritage tourism is unlikely to find full application in Asian countries or other geopolitical contexts. As is shown in the Polish example, the tourismification of communism heritage is stretched across the sacred to profane (martyrology to entertainment) spectrum. This is an issue that has been rarely presented in the literature so far. A consequence of the diversification of the communist heritage tourism niche is its overlap with other niche tourisms such as dark, heritage and historical tourisms, as well as an entertainment niche.

The COVID-19 pandemic, coupled with global and local reflections termed the 'post-pandemic new normal', has revived discussion on the conditions and socioeconomic functions of tourism (Lew et al., 2020). Niche tourism may again become an important alternative to mass tourism in the (post-)pandemic new normal. Moreover, referring to Sustainable Development Goals, Trupp and Dolezal (2020) indicate that tourism has immense potential during a health crisis such as COVID-19.

When considering strategies of recovery and post-COVID tourism, revaluing tourism destinations for the domestic traveller (Trupp and Dolezal, 2020) and readapting infrastructure for local needs (Lapointe, 2020), are suggested. For communist heritage tourism in Europe, both scenarios are likely and both are an opportunity and a threat. On the one hand, a new fashion for 'being a tourist in your own city' had appeared among the middle class before COVID-19. Richards (2021b) sees this as a new form of cultural practice. This trend is also noticeable among a younger generation for whom communism is not part of their personal experience but is understood only as history and ideology.

On the other hand, the current geopolitical focus on Belarus and Ukraine may stimulate interest in communism in both. In the above contexts, practices in communist heritage tourism identified in this chapter may surprisingly gain new local and national recipients. However, a hurdle to the development of communist heritage tourism, especially in Poland, is the emotional discussion in society surrounding the interpretation of the communist past and with a probable lower foreign demand. Tourist use of this difficult heritage may become more limited in the near future.

In the perspective of future research, it seems interesting to analyse the nature of communist heritage tourism and generational determinants for shaping this niche tourism in countries further east in Europe: Ukraine, Belarus and Russia. It is also worth asking, after Novelli (2018), whether this type of micro-niche favours sustainable or unsustainable practices. Another direction of research, so far practically absent in relation to communist heritage tourism, is the impact of communication technology and social networking in marketing niche tourism products. According to Lew (2008), the internet-based marketing approach enables small and medium-sized niche tourism companies to compete (successfully) on the global market. The growing importance of (new) technological and social media innovations, especially for stimulating tourist demand, is revealing a new (post-)pandemic normal.

REFERENCES

Adie B., Amore A. and Hall C. (2017) Urban tourism and urban socialist and communist heritage: Beyond tragedy and farce? *International Journal of Tourism Cities*, 3(3), 291–304. https://doi.org/10.1108/IJTC-02-2017-0011

Ali-Knight, J. (2010) *The Role of Niche Tourism Products in Destination Development*. Edinburgh: Napier University.

Bach, J. (2002) 'The taste remains': Consumption, (n)ostalgia, and the production of East Germany. *Public Culture*, 14(3), 545–56. https://doi.org/10.1215/08992363-14-3-545

Baláž, V. and Williams, A. M. (2005) International tourism as bricolage: An analysis of Central Europe on the brink of European Union membership. *International Journal of Tourism Research*, 7(2), 79–93. https://doi.org/10.1002/jtr.514

Banaszkiewicz, M. (2017) A dissonant heritage site revisited – the case of Nowa Huta in Krakow. *Journal of Tourism and Cultural Change*, 15(2), 185–97, https://doi.org/10.1080/14766825.2016.1260137

Banaszkiewicz, M., Owsianowska, S. and Graburn. N. (2017) Tourism in (post-)socialist Eastern Europe. *Journal of Tourism and Cultural Change*, 15(2), 109–21. https://doi.org/10.1080/14766825.2016.1260089

Beiersdorf, Z. (1997) Wartości kulturowe Nowej Huty. Historia i współczesność. In M. Kaczanowska (ed.) *Dziedzictwo Nowej Huty w kontekście rozwoju Obszaru Strategicznego Kraków Wschód*, 81–9. Kraków: Krakowskie Forum Demokracji.

Coles, T. (2003) The emergent tourism industry in Eastern Germany a decade after Unification. *Tourism Management*, 22(4), 217–26. https://doi.org/10.1016/S0261-5177(02)00060-2

Derek, M. (2020) An unwanted past in a contemporary city. Post-communist heritage and tourism in Warsaw. In M. Gravari-Barbas (ed.) *A Research Agenda for Heritage Tourism*. Cheltenham: Edward Elgar Publishing, 135–50.

ESC (European Solidarity Centre in Gdańsk) (n.d.) https://www.ecs.gda.pl/ (accessed 4 April 2020).

Garrod, B. and Fyall, A. (2001) Heritage tourism: A question of definition. *Annals of Tourism Research*, 28(4), 1049–52. https://doi.org/10.1016/S0160-7383(00)00068-2

Gazeta Wyborcza (2013) Kultowy bar 'U Wołodzi' do historii odchodzi. Nikt nie ma pomysłu. https://bialystok.wyborcza.pl/bialystok/7,35241,14535847,kultowy-bar-u-wolodzi-do-historii-odchodzi-nikt-nie-ma-pomyslu.html (accessed 4 April 2020).

Gravari-Barbas, M. (2018) Tourism as a heritage producing machine. *Tourism Management Perspectives,* 25, 173–6. https://doi.org/10.1016/j.tmp.2017.12.002

Gravari-Barbas, M. (2020) Heritage and tourism: From opposition to coproduction. In M. Gravari-Barbas (ed.) *A Research Agenda for Heritage Tourism.* Cheltenham: Edward Elgar Publishing, 1–14.

Guichard-Marneur, M. (2018) Forgetting communism, remembering World War II? The case of the permanent exhibition of the Schindler Factory Museum, Krakow, Poland. *International Journal of Heritage Studies,* 24(8), 811–27. https://doi.org/10.1080/13527258.2018.1428661

Hall D. (1991) *Tourism and Economic Development in Eastern Europe and the Soviet Union.* London: Belhaven Press.

Henderson, J. C. (2000) War as a tourist attraction: The case of Vietnam. *International Journal of Tourism Research,* 2, 269–80.

Hughes, H. and Allen, D. (2005) Cultural tourism in Central and Eastern Europe: The views of 'induced image formation agents'. *Tourism Management,* 26(2), 173–83. https://doi.org/10.1016/j.tourman.2003.08.021

Hung, Ch. (2018) Communist tradition and market forces: Red tourism and politics in contemporary China. *Journal of Contemporary China,* 27(114), 902–23. https://doi.org/10.1080/10670564.2018.1488105

Ivanov, S. (2009) Opportunities for developing communist heritage tourism in Bulgaria. *Tourism,* 57(2), 177–92. https://ssrn.com/abstract=1339564

Ivanova, M. and Buda, D. (2020) Thinking rhizomatically about communist heritage tourism. *Annals of Tourism Research,* 84, 103000. https://doi.org/10.1016/j.annals.2020.103000

Jovicic, D. (2016) Cultural tourism in the context of relations between mass and alternative tourism. *Current Issues in Tourism,* 19(6), 605–12. https://doi.org/10.1080/13683500.2014.932759

Knudsen, B. T. (2010) The past as staged-real environment: Communism revisited in The Crazy Guides Communism Tours, Krakow, Poland. *Journal of Tourism and Cultural Change,* 8(3), 139–53. https://doi.org/10.1080/14766825.2010.510195

Kubik, J. (2010) *Power of Symbols against the Symbols of Power: The Rise of Solidarity and the Fall of State Socialism in Poland.* Pennsylvania: The Pennsylvania State University Press.

Lapointe, D. (2020) Reconnecting tourism after COVID-19: The paradox of alterity in tourism areas. *Tourism Geographies,* 22(3), 633–8. https://doi.org/10.1080/14616688.2020.1762115

Lew, A.A. (2008) Long tail tourism: New geographies for marketing niche tourism products. *Journal of Travel and Tourism Marketing,* 25(3–4), 409–19. https://doi.org/10.1080/10548400802508515

Lew, A.A., Cheer, J.M., Haywood, M., Brouder, P. and Salazar, N.B. (2020) Visions of travel and tourism after the global COVID-19 transformation of 2020. *Tourism Geographies,* 22(3), 455–66. https://doi.org/10.1080/14616688.2020.1770326

Li, Y. and Hu, Z. (2008) Red tourism in China. *Journal of China Tourism Research,* 4(2), 156–71. https://doi.org/10.1080/19388160802313696

Light, D. (2000a) An unwanted past: Contemporary tourism and the heritage of communism in Romania. *International Journal of Heritage Studies,* 6(2), 145–60. https://doi.org/10.1080/135272500404197

Light, D. (2000b) Gazing on communism: Heritage tourism and post-communist identities in Germany, Hungary and Romania. *Tourism Geographies,* 2(2), 157–76. https://doi.org/10.1080/14616680050027879

Light, D. and Young, C. (2015) *Local and Counter-Memories of Socialism in Post-Socialist Romania. In Local Memories in a Nationalizing and Globalizing World.* London: Palgrave Macmillan.

Light, D., Young, C. and Czepczyński, M. (2009) Heritage tourism in Central and Eastern Europe. In D.J. Timothy and G.P. Nyaupane (eds) *Cultural Heritage and Tourism in the Developing World. A Regional Perspective.* London and New York: Routledge, 224–45.

Light, D., Crețan, R., Voiculescu, S. and Jucu, I.S. (2020) Introduction: Changing tourism in the cities of post-communist Central and Eastern Europe. *Journal of Balkan and Near Eastern Studies,* 22(4), 465–77. https://doi.org/10.1080/19448953.2020.1775405

MacCannell, D. (2013) *The Tourist. A New Theory of the Leisure Class.* Berkeley; Los Angeles; London: University of California Press.

Main, I. (2013) How is communism displayed? In O. Sarikova and P. Apor (eds) *Past for the Eyes.* Budapest: Central European University Press, 371–400.

Matoga, Ł. (2015) Exploring the history and heritage of communism in Nowa Huta District in Krakow, Poland: Potential or a problem in managing tourism in a city? *Journal of Hospitality Management and Tourism*, 6(7), 90–103. https://doi.org/10.5897/JHMT2015.0160

Matoga, Ł. and Pawłowska, A. (2018) Off-the-beaten-track tourism: A new trend in the tourism development in historical European cities. A case study of the city of Krakow, Poland. *Current Issues in Tourism*, 21(14), 1644–69, https://doi.org/10.1080/13683500.2016.1212822

McKercher, B. and Chan, A. (2005) How special is special interest tourism? *Journal of Travel Research*, 44(1), 21–31. https://doi.org/10.1177/0047287505276588

Murzyn, M. (2008) Heritage transformation in Central and Eastern Europe. In B. Graham and P. Howard (eds), *The Ashgate Research Companion to Heritage and Identity*. Aldershot: Ashgate, 315–46.

Myczkowski Z. and Siwek A. (2017) Cultural Park Nowa Huta – a new formula for the protection of urban planning and architecture of the second half of the 20th century. *Wiadomosci Konserwatorskie – Journal of Heritage Conservation*, 49, 113–24.

National Institute of Cultural Heritage (n.d.), *Monuments in Poland*. https://www.nid.pl/pl/ (accessed 1 April 2020).

Naumov, N. and Weidenfeld A. (2019) From socialist icons to post-socialist attractions: Iconicity of social heritage in Central and Eastern Europe. *Geographia Polonica*, 92(4), 379–93. https://doi.org/10.7613/GPol.0147

Novelli, M. (2005) *Niche Tourism: Contemporary Issues, Trends and Cases*. London: Routledge.

Novelli, M. (2018) Niche tourism: Past present and future. In C. Cooper, S. Volo, W. Gartner and N. Scott (eds) *The Sage Handbook of Tourism Management: Applications of Theories and Concepts of Tourism*. London: Sage, 344–59.

Ouellette, D. (2020) Understanding the 'socialist tourism' of North Korea under Kim Jong Un: An analysis of North Korean discourse. *North Korean Review*, 16(1), 55–81.

Pawlusiński, R. (2006) Tourism – a new function of post-socialistic city. Case study of Nowa Huta (Cracow). *Folia Geographica*, 10, 412–18.

Pawlusiński, R. and Kubal M. (2018) A new take on an old structure? Creative and slow tourism in Krakow (Poland). *Journal of Tourism and Cultural Change*, 16(3), 265–85. https://doi.org/10.1080/14766825.2017.1330338

Poria, Y. and Ashworth, G. (2009) Heritage tourism – Current resource for conflict. *Annals of Tourism Research*, 36(3), 522–5. https://doi.org/10.1016/j.annals.2009.03.003

Richards, G. (2018) Cultural tourism: A review of recent research and trends. *Journal of Hospitality and Tourism Management*, 36, 12–21. https://doi.org/10.1016/j.jhtm.2018.03.005

Richards, G. (2021a) Rethinking niche tourism: The example of backpacking. *Croatian Regional Development Journal*, 2(1), 1–12.

Richards, G. (2021b) *Rethinking Cultural Tourism*. Cheltenham: Edward Elgar Publishing.

Robinson, M. and Novelli, M. (2005) Niche tourism: An introduction. In M. Novelli (ed.) *Niche Tourism: Contemporary Issues, Trends and Cases*, 1st ed. Amsterdam: Elsevier, 1–11.

Scarpaci, J. L. (2013) Reshaping Habana Vieja: Revitalization, historic preservation, and restructuring in the socialist city. *Urban Geography*, 21(8), 724–44. https://doi.org/10.2747/0272-3638.21.8.724

Sert, A. N. (2017) Niche marketing and tourism. *Journal of Business Management and Economic Research*, 1(1), 14–25. https://doi.org/10.20491/isarder.2020.1010

Shearer, T. M. (2021) *Religion and Social Protest Movements*. Abingdon, Oxford; New York, NY: Routledge.

Sima, C. (2017) Communist heritage representation gaps and disputes. *International Journal of Tourism Cities*, 3(3), 210–26. https://doi.org/10.1108/IJTC-03-2017-0015

Stake, R.E. (1995), *The Art of Case Study Research*. Thousand Oaks, CA, USA: Sage Publications.

Timothy, D. and Boyd, S. (2008) Heritage tourism in the 21st century: Valued traditions and new perspectives. *Journal of Heritage Tourism*, 1(1), 1–16. https://doi.org/10.1080/17438730608668462

Trupp, A. and Dolezal, C. (2020) Tourism and the sustainable development goals in Southeast Asia. *Austrian Journal of South-East Asian Studies*, 13(1), 1–16. https://doi.org/10.14764/10.ASEAS-0026

Urry, J. (2002) *The Tourist Gaze*, 2nd ed. London: Sage Publications.

Yin, R. K. (2009) *Case Study Research, Design and Method*, 4th ed. London: Sage Publications.

Young, C. and Kaczmarek, S. (2008) The socialist past and postsocialist urban identity in Central and Eastern Europe: The case of Łódź. *European Urban and Regional Studies*, 15(1), 53–70. https://doi .org/10.1177/0969776407081275

Zaborowska, M. J. (2001) The height of (architectural) seduction: Reading the 'changes' through Stalin's palace in Warsaw, Poland. *Journal of Architectural Education*, 54(4), 205–17.

Ziębińska-Witek A. (2018) *Muzealizacja komunizmu w Polsce i Europie Środkowo-Wschodniej*, 1st ed. Lublin: Wydawnictwo UMCS.

Ziębińska-Witek A. (2020) Musealisation of communism, or how to create national identity in historical museums. *Muzeológia a Kultúrne Dedičstvo*, 8(4), 59–72. https://doi.org10.46284/mkd.2020.8.4.5

Ziółkowski, M. (2002) Remembering and forgetting after Communism. The Polish case. *Polish Sociological Review*, 1, 7–24.

15. Railways and niche tourism developments in Brazil

Carla Fraga

1. INTRODUCTION

Understanding the differences between mass tourism and niche tourism is an important thematic to sustainable tourism development. In this sense, niche tourism includes micro-components, such as special interest experiences associated with the cultural, environment, rural or urban settings of a destination (Robinson and Novelli, 2005). Thus, transport as a tourism experience provides both macro- and micro-niches. Globally, the sustainable development of certain segments of the tourism market (such as cultural tourism) depends on their synergies with other segments, as well as how those interactions allow for the establishment of new niches. The effective balance between existing tensions and priorities leads to successful initiatives promoting better engagement of local residents, tourists and other tourism stakeholders, which is pivotal to support communities that rely on tourism for their development (Fraga and Borges, 2018). It is part of modern governance practices to aim for sustainable tourism. The relationship between railways and tourism delivers railway tourism as a niche of cultural tourism. This is because cultural railway heritage experiences are the high point of railway tourism.

Conlin and Bird (2014) share global perspectives on railway heritage and tourism. Railway tourism mainly focuses on providing tourists with cultural train journeys, museums, railway stations and so on. This relationship contributes to the development of other tourism micro-niches, such as steam locomotive trips, connected to the concept of 'slow rail travel' (Fraga and Botelho, 2016); railbike tourism, that is, travelling along railway tracks by railbike; and draisine tourism, the use of hand-operated or motorized light rail vehicles (Brauckmann, 2012) – or, indeed, where these various modes of transport are combined to create mixed transport/tourism experiences.

On the other hand, new niches can emerge from the marriage between segments. Fraga, Borges and Almeida (2019) explain that there is a connection between gastronomy, railways and tourism, as exemplified by the historical connections observed between Brazil and Portugal. The wine train in the South of Brazil is another example of a great idea for a micro-niche that can emerge from coupling different segments.

A critical analysis on the role of the relationship between railway and tourism in the development of niches, however, is a point that should be further explored in the literature. This chapter, therefore, offers new clues regarding Brazil's scenery. Brazil is the largest country in South America and has 30,576 km of rail (ANTT, 2015). Although passenger trains are scarce, according to Fraga, Santos and Castro Ribeiro (2014) and the Tourist Guide and Cultural Trains of Brazil (SEBRAE and ABOTTC, 2015a), they are an important resource. Some niches are emerging, such as the Cataguases Biciclotrem (G1, 2017) railbike, together with most of the Brazilian railway tourism system offering recreational rides, or slow rail travel, on steam locomotives, showing potential for rail travel to become an important niche tourism product.

The next section briefly reviews the relevant literature on the macro-niche of transportation as a tourism experience (Page, 2008), before presenting the literature on the specific micro-niche based on the relationship between railway and tourism.

2.   TRANSPORTATION AND TOURISM

Tourism can be viewed as a round trip. Thus, the offer of infrastructure and transport services from tourists' places of origins to their destinations, as well as between and within tourist destinations, is essential (Palhares, 2002; Page, 2008). The various patterns of tourism travel can be demonstrated through a complete model of the tourist transport system developed by Palhares (2005). Lohmann and Castro (2013) explored the role of intermodality – that is, interconnection between modes of transport, transport networks and nodal functions – explaining the meaning of hubs, entrance gates and stopovers, as well as their multiple nodal functions for tourism. From their perspective, transport is not a macro-niche of tourism in principle, but one of its functionalizing elements, along with accommodation and tourist characteristics, among others, in line with Hall's (2005a: 95) view that '[t]ransport as both a tourism facilitator and tourism object performs a number of roles which continue to change and evolve as markets segment or fuse'.

Thus, when the transport experience is the tourist experience itself, as in the case of tourist cruises, bicycle tourism, tourist trains and so on, this individual-centric event can cause the formation of segments and niches focused on transport. Therefore, macro- and micro-niche tourism products can arise from transport. The technological evolution of transport itself can contribute to the emergence and growth of new niches market segments. An example is the popularization of the aerial mode in the second half of the 20th century and the popularization of the tourist cruise market as a segment, in which on-board experience is more important than the trip from origin to destination (Page, 2008; Palhares, 2002). Some of these cruises have even specialized in catering to micro-niches, such as tourist cruises aimed at the LGBTQ+ community or specific leisure-focused themes such as the Disney Cruise Line.

The provision of transportation as a tourist experience itself occurs based on the definition of a series of variables – such as demographics, personal interests and objectives – that assist in tourism segmentation, allowing promoters to reach a specific segment of the tourist market by providing a tourist package tailored for specific individuals or groups. In the tourism market, segmentation variables are defined both on the demand side, based on data – sociodemographic, psychological, motivational, etc. – and on the supply side, based on characteristics and attributes. The objective of defining these variables is that, due to segmentation, there are ideal matches between supply and demand in the product distribution process and in terms of user experience.

Therefore, in cases where the objective is that the transport experience is the tourist experience itself, it is noted that customization is an essential tool to transform the offer of 'transport services' into 'products' and 'tourist experiences' (see Pine II and Gilmore [2011] on the progression of economic value) that stimulate positive emotions and feelings, making them unforgettable to tourists. However, unlike the 'experience economy' (see Pine II and Gilmore,

Table 15.1   Economic distinctions (from experiences to transformation)

Economic offering	Experiences	Transformations
Economy	Experience	Transformation
Economy function	Stage	Guide
Nature of offering	Memorable	Effectual
Key attribute	Personal	Individual
Method of supply	Revealed over a duration	Sustained through time
Seller	Stager	Elicitor
Buyer	Guest	Aspirant
Factors of demand	Sensations	Traits

Source: Adapted from Pine II and Gilmore (2011: 253).

2011), the challenge of the 'transformational economy' is related to what Pine II and Gilmore explain about the customer being the product.

Thus, from the 'economic distinctions' proposed by Pine II and Gilmore (2011), it is possible to observe differences between the experience economy and the transformational economy: (1) when regarding the 'economic function', it becomes a 'guide' rather than a 'stage'; (2) when considering the 'nature of the offering', it becomes 'effectual' instead of 'memorable'; (3) 'key attribute' no longer refers to the 'personal', but the 'individual'; (4) 'method of supply' is no longer based on 'revealed over a duration', but on 'sustained through time'; (5) regarding the 'seller', they become 'elicitor', instead of the 'stager'; (6) the 'buyer' assumes the role of the 'aspirant', rather than the 'guest'; and (7) 'factors of demand' are regarded as 'traits' as opposed to 'sensations' (Pine II and Gilmore, 2011: 253). Thus, more than the transportation experience as the main tourist experience, what is sought is to understand how this experience can be transformational (see Table 15.1).

The feeling of belonging, which integrates everyone who is part of the ecosystem in which the business that originates the transport experience as a tourist experience is inserted, is essential to survival in a highly competitive world. Furthermore, dramatic socioeconomic changes, natural disasters and crises, such as that caused by the COVID-19 pandemic, increase the challenges faced by the sector. Tourism depends on the relationship between hosts and guests (Smith, 1989), with cultural identities (Hall, 2005b) playing an essential role in the sense of belonging, particularly at a time when, for instance, the COVID-19 pandemic has paralyzed attractions and tourist destinations.

In this way, it is possible to observe that strategies involving processes and methodologies that allow agility for the (re)construction of 'products' and 'experiences' as opportunities for 'transformations' have been widely sought. Many of those processes and methodologies derive from other areas, such as the Agile Manifesto statement of principles that underlie agile software development as a relevant milestone (see Agile Manifesto, 2001).

These methodologies allow for fast delivery of answers and solutions that better connect 'seller' and 'buyer' values. It is therefore essential to go beyond the basic definitions of the target audience; it is relevant to understand the importance of building personas, which helps businesses to identify and act in satisfying the needs and desires of customers. As tools for population segmentation, generators of personas assist in the determination of fictional characters created to represent the different types of customers within a target; they serve to humanize the target audience (see Food'n Road, 2020).

Another fundamental aspect is branding and marketing targeted to the 'buyer'. Therefore, stakeholders need to make sure that customized experiences are being effectively communicated to consumers as opportunities for 'transformation'. In brand management, storytelling has been applied to provide a 'transformation', as a compelling story will evoke the empathy of consumers, who are no longer seen as 'customers' or 'guests', but as 'aspirants' to be 'guided'; this has tended to have positive results (Pine II and Gilmore, 2011).

Content gamification (implicit or explicit), with objectives, stages and rewards at the end of each stage of the 'journey', has also been widely used. For example, some digital games allow experiences which mix the real and the virtual. This can help with the transformational aspects in situations such as those created by the COVID-19 pandemic, where the guidance is to 'stay at home'. Virtual tours, including those involving gadgets and increasingly sophisticated technologies, from augmented reality to wearable technology, are also gaining more space recently. For example, the Amantes da Ferrovia (2020) website listed eight virtual tours people could take during the coronavirus lockdowns (Flam Railway, Norway; Geibe Line for the Fukui Line, Japan; Bernina Railway, Switzerland to Italy; North Wales Coast Line, England to Wales; Central Andean Railway, Peru; Sarajevo–Ploče Railway, Bosnia and Herzegovina; South Western Railway, England; Durango and Silverton Narrow Gauge Railway, Colorado, United States).

The next section of this chapter provides an in-depth elaboration of the micro-niche originating from the relationships between transport and tourism, that is, rail tourism. We also discuss the particularities of those relationships.

3.   RAILWAY TOURISM

In 1841, Thomas Cook took the first rail trip in the United Kingdom, organized in a similar fashion to the current practices. The origin of tourism is closely related to the use of rail transport (Palhares, 2002). Frossard and Fraga (2018) studied the construction of senses and meanings through advertising posters between the years 1890 and 1970 in the United Kingdom, allowing us to realize that segmentation, as an idea of macro- and micro-niches of tourism, was already present, even within regular transport. For example, when analysing a 1925 poster about Cheshire Lines Railway, the authors comment that, 'since the beginning of the railway, it has contributed to the structuring of other segments of the tourism market (in this case the segments of business and leisure), in addition to rail tourism itself' (Frossard and Fraga, 2018: 52 – own translation). However, it is worth noting that Allis (2006: 89) observes that 'rail cultural tourism appears as a refinement of the relationship between tourism and cultural heritage' (own translation).

Hall (2005a) focuses on heritage and contemporary recreation and explains the role of transport tourism, citing examples such as the Orient Express and San Francisco's cable cars and discussing their particularities from a tourism point of view. From theses perspectives, cultural tourism would be considered the macro-niche and railroad tourism a micro-niche within it.

While Conlin and Bird (2014) provide an in-depth study on global perspectives on railway heritage and tourism, Camargo, Garza and Morales (2014) focus on the opportunity to diversify tourism in Mexico using its railways, and White (2014) explains the connection between heritage and tourism from the perspective of the regional railway revival in Australia. Studies on Tren Crucero del Ecuador (Monge and Yagüe Perales, 2016) and McCants et al.'s (2016) book on *New uses for old railways* reveal new insights into railway tourism niches. In addition to these, Dinhobl (2016) shares examples of the re-use of railways from a tourism perspective; Cuéllar (2016) focuses on the Spanish context; Fontana (2016: 63) asks if we are entering 'a new age of steam' in his analysis on the Tua Valley Line (Portugal); Cotte (2016) investigates two examples of mountain railways in France; and Maggi (2016) discusses tourism and railways in Italy. All these authors reveal clear links between railway experiences and tourism.

As the relationship between transport and tourism can be functional – that is, transport can act as a geographical distributor of tourist demand (see Page, 2008) – so can the relationship between tourism and the railroad (Fraga et al., 2013). The various railway projects aimed at tourism are very different from each other – from high-speed trains to regional passenger trains, commemorative trains and airport trains, among others. Palhares (2002) classifies railway transport exclusively for tourism as scenic and nostalgic. According to Fraga (2011), however, the attributes that make the experience of rail transport a tourist experience are diverse and also related to other tourism segments, which suggests that the classification established by Palhares (2002) may be overly narrow. Fraga highlights that 'A segment can be defined as grouping of elements based on their similarities, while niche aims at attending particular interests within a segment. For example, cultural tourism is a segment, while the group of tourists interested in railway culture is a niche' (Fraga, 2011: 56, translated from Portuguese).

Thus, it is possible to see that rail tourism micro-niches can be even more specific, with a focus on tailormade tourism experiences. For example, there is luxury rail tourism (e.g., Belmond Hiram Bingham in Peru, operated by Belmond, which operates several other luxury trains around the world – Belmond, 2020) and railway tourism focused on events (e.g., Trem do Forró in Brazil – Trem do Forró, 2020), among others. Although railway tourism is based on tours using tourist trains, it can be observed that railway heritage – such as museums, rolling stock and railway villages – are also part of this segment of tourism (Fraga et al., 2013; Conlin and Bird, 2014).

Therefore, analysing what makes the use of rail transport a tourist experience is crucial to understanding how to better customize this experience such that it becomes transformational, meeting individual expectations of micro-niche tourists interested in trains. Su and Wall (2009) have investigated the perspectives of travellers regarding the link between tourism and rail on the Qinghai–Tibet Railway in Tibet, while Lee and Chen (2017) have explored the determinants of attractiveness for rail tourism in their study on Taiwan. Princz-Jakovics and Vasvári (2019) focused on 'narrow gauge' tracks to study the relationship between railways and tourism in Hungary, demonstrating that technical characteristics of the railway are essential for the emergence of micro-niche products. For example, for railway enthusiasts, this aspect can be a specific attraction within a train-themed trip (see Stefanovic and Koster, 2014).

There are several examples regarding the relationship between railroads and heritage tourism. Henderson (2014) considered the Malaysia–Singapore Line to constitute a 'heritage attraction'. Bird and Conlin (2014) further advance understanding of the relationship between rail transport and heritage tourism, noting that: (1) there is compatibility between the railroad and heritage tourism; (2) that this relationship must be economically sustainable; (3) that heritage railways are repositories of cultural and industrial heritage; and (4) and that the involvement of volunteers is essential. The next section addresses the relationship between rail and tourism in Brazil.

4.   RAILWAY AND TOURISM IN BRAZIL

Brazil is a country of continental dimensions located in South America, with 26 states and one federal district, divided into five regions (South, Southeast, North, Northeast and Midwest). The railway network is more concentrated in the South, Southeast and Northeast regions, as shown in Figure 15.1.

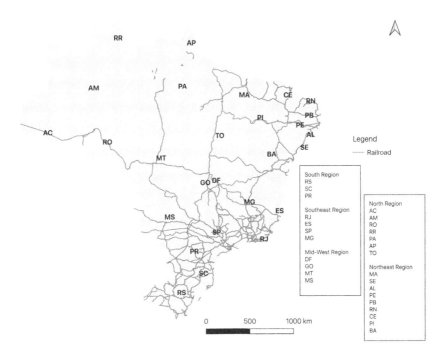

Source: Prepared by author based on Brasil (2020a) and IBGE (2019).

Figure 15.1   Brazil rail network across Brazilian regions

The first railway in Brazil dates from 1854. It was inaugurated by Irineu Evangelista de Souza (better known as the Baron of Mauá) and connected Guanabara Bay to Fragoso Station (14.5 km) in Rio de Janeiro, located in Southeast Brazil (Gerodetti and Cornejo, 2005; IBGE, 2020). After 100 years of rail transport in the country, Brazil had a total of 37,019 km of railway lines, according to Silva (1954). By 2015, the Brazilian railway network existed of 30,576 km, including gauges (metric-gauges, broad-gauges and mixed) (ANTT, 2015). It is worth noting that on 26 November 2003, the provision of non-scheduled passenger rail services was stipulated by Resolution No. 359, which established the procedures, regulations and standards related to the operation of tourist trains to explore cultural and commemorative histories. In short, it can be asserted that 'tourist and historical-cultural trains contribute to the preservation of the historical heritage and memory of the railways and operate throughout the year, while

Table 15.2   *Tourist and cultural trains authorized between 2004 and 2015*

Stretch of the railroad	State	Length	Operator
São João Del Rei/Tiradentes	MG	12km	FCA*
São Lourenço/Soledade de Minas	MG	10km	ABPF**
Passa Quatro/Coronel Fulgêncio	MG	10km	ABPF**
Ouro Preto/Mariana	MG	18km	FCA*
Bento Gonçalves/Carlos Barbosa	RS	48km	Empresa Giordani Ltda.
Tubarão/Imbituba/Urussanga	SC	159km	Sociedade Amigos da Locomotiva a Vapor – Museu Ferroviário de Tubarão
Rio Negrinho/Rio Natal	SC	42km	ABPF**
Piratuba/Marcelino Ramos	SC/RS	26km	ABPF**
Ponta Grossa/Guarapuava/Cascavel	PR	505km	Serra Verde Express Ltda.
Campo Grande/Indubrasil - Corumbá	MS	441km	Serra Verde Express Ltda.
Brás/Mooca	SP	3km	ABPF**
Campinas /Jaguariúna	SP	23.5km	ABPF**
Prolongamento Campinas/Jaguariúna	SP	1.5km	ABPF**
Assis/Paraguaçu Paulista/Quatá	SP	60km	Prefeitura de Paraguaçu
Paranapiacaba	SP	304m	ABPF**
Rio Grande da Serra/Paranapiacaba	SP	12km	CPTM***
Estação de Viana/Estação de Araguaía	ES	46km	Serra Verde Express Ltda.
Morretes/Antonina	PR	17km	ABPF**
São José do Rio Preto/Eng. Schimitt	SP	10.5km	Prefeitura de São José do Rio Preto
Paraíba do Sul/Cavaru	RJ	14km	Prefeitura de Paraíba do Sul
Rio Pardo/Cachoeira do Sul	RS	56km	MCPF****
Campo Grande/Corumbá	MS	459.58km	AGITRAMS*****
Montenegro/Guaporé/Estrela	RS	106km	Ferrotur Passeios Turísticos Ltda.
Guararema/Luiz Carlos	SP	5.5.km	ABPF**

Notes: *Ferrovia Centro Atlântica; **Associação Brasileira de Preservação Ferroviária; ***Companhia Paulista de Trens Metropolitanos; ****Movimento Civil de Preservação Ferroviária; *****Agência de Gestão e Integração de Transportes.
Source: Prepared by author based on ANTT (2013a).

commemorative trains run at specific and isolated events' (ANTT, 2013a) (translated from Portuguese).

Agência Nacional de Transportes Terrestres (the Brazilian National Agency for Terrestrial Transport – ANTT, 2013b) considers the railway sections covering Cosme Velho–Corcovado (Southeast region), Curitiba–Morretes–Paranaguá (South region), Parauapebas–São Luís (North–Northeast regions) and Vitória–Belo Horizonte as those suitable for passenger transport. However, according to the Trem do Corcovado website, this line is considered the first tourism ride in Brazil (Trem do Corcovado, 2020). The same occurs in Paraná with the operation of the Paranaense Train by Serra Verde Express, which demonstrates the complexity of the relationship between tourism and passenger rail transport.

In 2015, the Serviço Brasileiro de Apoio às Micro e Pequenas Empresas (Sebrae) (the Brazilian Micro and Small Business Support Service – SEBRAE and the Associação Brasileira das Operadoras de Trens Turísticos e Culturais (ABOTTC) (the Brazilian Association of Tourist and Cultural Train Operators – ABOTTC) prepared a guide to Brazilian tourist trains (SEBRAE and ABOTTC, 2015a). In this guide it was possible to note the interplay between some authorized sections (Table 15.2) and the trains in operation at that time. Another publication focused on the profiles of train tourists, identifying the perceptions and behaviours of tourists who participated in a focus group. Among these, some elements particularly stood out: homesickness among people over 50; the importance of the internet for young people (Generation Y); the attractiveness of gastronomy; the importance of cultural experiences; the experience at the stopping places (railway stations); the possibility to travel with pets; aspects of the market catering to children; and comparisons of train travel with cruises, among others (SEBRAE and ABOTTC, 2015b).

In 2010, a document was released to regulate how tourist and cultural train projects in Brazil should be undertaken. The guidelines require the provision of information regarding the locations (villages, cities, etc.) that are part of the local history and culture (Brasil, 2010). In this sense, IPHAN's (Instituto do Patrimônio Histórico e Artístico Nacional – the Brazilian National Historical and Artistic Heritage Institute) list of cultural railway heritage (IPHAN, 2019) is essential to understanding the cultural and heritage-based relationships between tourism and railways in Brazil. Furthermore, through culture maps, it is possible to identify entities such as railway-themed museums throughout the country (Brasil, 2020b). Figure 15.2 presents the collected data, organized according to state and region.

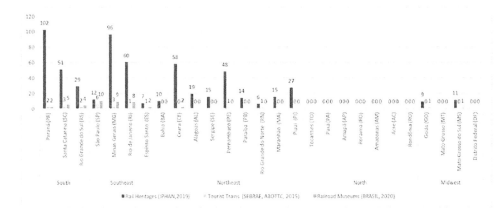

Note: According to SEBRAE and ABOTTC (2015a) some trains were in their implementation phase, for instance, Trem do Vale do Taquari (Rio Grande do Sul), Trem Caipira (São Paulo) and Trem de Guararema (São Paulo).
Source: Prepared by author based on IPHAN (2019); SEBRAE and ABOTTC (2015a); Brasil (2020b).

Figure 15.2   *Rail heritage, tourist trains and railroad museums, organized according to the states within each region of Brazil*

South, Southeast and Northeast Brazil constitute the three regions with more opportunities for the development of rail tourism micro-niches. Considering the role of customization, the following are detailed aspects that elucidate future micro-niches:

a) Train Rides and Trips: The growing number of projects to develop new touristic trains is an indicator that rail tourism has become established as a macro-niche and can deliver micro-niche tailormade experiences, such as Trem do Vinho (a railway experience focused on wine tourism) (Maria Fumaça, 2020) and Trem do Forró (a railway experience linked to the forró, a typical Brazilian dance event) (Trem do Forró, 2020), among others. Fraga,

Borges and Almeida (2019) explain that there is a connection between gastronomy, railways and tourism. In their work, the authors studied nine tourist trains from the South and Southeast regions of Brazil and concluded that:

> It is possible to observe that history and memory play an important role promoting creative gastronomic railway tourism. As history and memory are linked to the past both are representations of what no longer exists, thus establishing an important link in co-creation experiences, notably those that may involve the relationship between visitors and visited. (Fraga, Borges and Almeida, 2019: 33) (translated from Portuguese)

Slow rail travel on the Maria Fumaça (steam locomotive) presents an excellent opportunity to develop a micro-niche within rail tourism. Fraga and Botelho regard the Southeastern region of the country to have the most potential to be explored. They also claim that within slow rail travel tourism, 'The slowness and the value of time are attributes of this nostalgic experience. Another element that adds value to the concept of slow rail travel in Brazil is the use in environmentally protected areas' (2016: 152).

b) Railway Museums: The range of railway museums demonstrates that railway memory and history are essential elements in the relationship between tourism, railways and culture in Brazil. In this sense, these museums are not only part of the railway landscape (because some are located in railway stations); they also play an important role in stimulating tourism and promoting the creation of novel micro-niches. This is the case, for example, with the Railway Museum of Juiz de Fora in Minas Gerais (Southeast region) (Prefeitura de Juiz de Fora, 2020). The existence of a railway museum in a given city represents the beginning of a proposal for a tourist itinerary involving other assets of railway heritage (stations, facilities, land, etc.).

c) Railway Cultural Heritage: Manifestations of railway cultural heritage are quite varied, but they can constitute a railway landscape. One of the most relevant examples in Brazil is the Vila de Paranapiacaba in Santo André district, São Paulo (Southeast region) (see Allis, 2002), as it is an entire village dedicated to rail.

Other, more specific considerations include:

d) Themes and Customization: By means of themes and customization, it is possible to build unusual micro-niches, such as railway cine tourism, since there is an existing demand to know where certain historical dramas were recorded. One example is the Trem das Águas, in the South of Minas Gerais (Southeast region). The railway was inaugurated by Emperor Dom Pedro II, and was a location in many Brazilian soap operas (G1, 2019). Special occasions may also trigger thematic occurrences on metropolitan trains. For instance, the Trem do Samba used to depart on 2 December (National Samba Day) from Central do Brasil station towards the suburbs of Rio de Janeiro. The strength of this cultural manifestation is so strong that in 2019, even though the Trem do Samba was officially running, a group of samba musicians decided to make an 'unofficial' revival of the party (O Globo, 2019).

e) Other Opportunities: There are many opportunities to exploit and develop new uses for railways centred not only around train rides but also on railbikes. An example can be found in Minas Gerais, in the city of Cataguases (Southeast region) (Brasil, 2010; G1, 2017; Fraga and Deutsch, 2020), which will likely create demand for a new micro-niche of railbike tourism from Biciclotrem. Further opportunities can be exploited when opening railway spaces for events, as already occurs at Maria Fumaça Campinas Jaguariúna in São Paulo (Southeast region), where it is possible to hold weddings, sweet-sixteen parties and other celebrations (Maria Fumaça Campinas, 2020). Micro-niches combining railroad, tourism, local gastronomy and events promote the preservation of railways as a public good. This preservation arises from the community's sense of 'being part' of the site's heritage. Another aspect is the use of rail tourism as a tool for education, presenting the history, architecture and geography of a certain location to students during a train journey. Fraga and Santos (2012) discussed the importance of educational games to teaching and learning about railway tourism. Games and school trips can contribute to the development of a sustainable view of railways and heritage.

f) The Role of the Base Community: Moreira and Araújo (2017) draw attention to the importance of abandoned railway branches which now are used exclusively by the community (walkers and cyclists). The authors mention that in the United States there is an entity focused on the preservation of these sites, the Rails to Trails Conservancy, and that in Brazil there is a community focusing its efforts on transforming the old railway branch between Corinto and Diamantina in Minas Gerais (Southeast) into Brazil's first former railway track repurposed for pedestrians and cyclists.

Fraga and Borges (2018) have investigated the connections between rail and community-based tourism in Brazil based on 10 examples of tourist trains. The authors defined the concept of community-based railway tourism as 'one that does not refer to the railway and tourism should be organised and structured based on the social ties between visitors (in the case of tourists) and the community (receiving community), leading to experiences permeated by the feeling of belonging, evoked by the valorization of local culture through elements related to history and memory' (Fraga and Borges, 2018: 37, own translation). They explain that it is essential to investigate the relations between visitors (tourists) and community. It is in this sense that the role of local communities in the development of micro-niches related to rail tourism in Brazil is understood.

Moraes, Passarelli and Oliveira (2019) reinforce the importance of tourism as a means of preserving railway heritage. This heritage is pivotal for the establishment of railway tourism and its interplay with other micro-niches in Brazil. Therefore, governance strategies oriented towards sustainable development of the relationship between tourism and railroads are essential for balancing supply and demand. Since Pine II and Gilmore (2011) point out the importance of transformational economy, it is possible to consider that rail tourism and the various micro-niches that connect to it need to be in constant synergy to promote an experience that is not only than memorable, but also transformative. Ensuring its alignment with the UN's Sustainable Development Goals (UN, 2015) is one of the ways to ensure rail tourism becomes even more important in Brazil. Therefore, creativity and innovation, aligned with preservation and conservation, are important elements in further improving rail tourism in Brazil in the future.

5.   FINAL REMARKS

Exploring specific examples of railway tourism as a form of niche tourism was the main aim of this chapter, with Brazil's railway scene as the focus of the study. Disruptions caused by technological advances, such as the internet, social media and telecommunications, as well as environmental and healthcare crises (including COVID-19) represent challenges faced by humanity that will not only determine our history but also how we shape the future, with railway tourism being affected as much as any other sector globally.

Brazil, as a country that went through a process of concession of its railway network in the 1990s, developing a greater interest in freight transport than passengers (ANTT, n.d.), now seems to need to invent and reinvent its railroad and railway heritage traditions. This includes the development of rail tourism as a niche for cultural tourism, based on the concept of transportation as a tourist experience.

However, the development of tourist trains is not the only way to strengthen the niche of railway tourism in a destination: there are many more micro-niches which derive from or depend on railways and their heritage, from events in railway spaces to the use of railbikes to travel along disused tracks. It is also necessary to consider the challenges of consolidating and/ or developing any new proposition in a sustainable manner. The challenges we will face in the 21st century appear to be many and diverse. For instance, railway tourism can be viewed as a niche tourism diversification strategy to exploit proximity, domestic and regional tourism, and this applies not only in the Brazilian context. Thus the chapter contributes to epistemological advances to the micro- and macro-niches of railway tourism and offers reflections from the perspective of the development of sustainable tourism, making it useful to sector's recovery post-COVID-19, in the Brazilian context and beyond.

Future studies on railway tourism in Brazil and in other destinations are needed to provide an in-depth analysis of regions and their particular features and demands. In the particular context of Brazil, a better understanding of the context in the South, Southeast and Northeast regions was developed in this chapter as a way to explore precisely what the sector has to offer; however, there is potential for further exploration. Furthermore, studying tourists' behaviour and their inclination to engage in railway tourism may provide further understanding of the use of land-based transport as a more sustainable option in the post-COVID era as part of a customer-focused transformational tourism economy.

REFERENCES

Agile Manifesto (2001) *Manifesto para Desenvolvimento Ágil de Software.* Available at: https://agilemanifesto.org/iso/ptbr/manifesto.html (accessed 6 August 2020).
Allis, T. (2002) Ferrovia e turismo cultural – Alternativa para o futuro para a Vila de Paranapiacaba (SP). *Turismo em Análise,* 13(2), 29–33.
Allis, T. (2006) *Turismo, Patrimônio cultural e transporte ferroviário: Um estudo sobre ferrovias turísticas no Brasil e na Argentina.* (Dissertação de Mestrado). Programa de Pós-Graduação em Integração da América Latina. Universidade de São Paulo. São Paulo.
Amantes da Ferrovia (2020) *Tour Virtual: 08 passeios de trem para conhecer* durante a quarentena. Available at: https://amantesdaferrovia.com.br/blog/tour-virtual-08-passeios-de-trem-para-conhecer -durante-a-quarentena (accessed 25 August 2020).
ANTT (2013a). *Trens Turísticos e Culturais autorizados no período de 2004 a 2015.* Available at: http://portal.antt.gov.br/index.php/content/view/43723/Trens_Turisticos_e_Comemorativos.html (accessed 10 May 2020).
ANTT (2013b) *Trens Regulares.* Available at: http://portal.antt.gov.br/index.php/content/view/43717/ Trens_Regulares.html (accessed 10 May 2020).
ANTT (2015) *Ferroviária.* Available at: http://portal.antt.gov.br/index.php/content/view/4751/ Ferroviaria.html (accessed 10 May 2020).
ANTT (n.d.) *Concessões Ferroviárias.* Available at: https://www.antt.gov.br/concessoes-ferroviarias (accessed 10 May 2020).
Belmond (2020) *Hiram-bingham.* Available at: https://www.belmond.com/trains/south-america/peru/ belmond-hiram-bingham (accessed 25 August 2020).

Brasil (2010) Ministério do Turismo. *Cartilha de orientação para a proposição de trens turísticos e culturais.* Brasília, *MTur.* Available at: https://bit.ly/2YN24lf (accessed 25 August 2020).

Brasil (2020a) Ministério da Infraestrutura. *Mapas e bases dos modos de transportes.* Ferroviário. Available at: https://www.gov.br/infraestrutura/pt-br/assuntos/dados-de-transportes/bit/bitmodos mapas (accessed 25 August 2020).

Brasil (2020b) *Mapas Cultura.* Available at: http://mapas.cultura.gov.br/ (accessed 20 August 2020).

Brauckmann, S. (2012) Utilising tourist draisines as a method to conserve railway heritage. *VI Congreso de Historia Ferroviaria.* VI Trenbidea Historia Batzarra.

Camargo, B.A., Garza, G. and Morales, M. (2014) *Railway Tourism: An Opportunity to Diversify Tourism in Mexico.* In M.V. Conlin and G.R. Bird (eds) *Railway Heritage and Tourism: Global Perspectives.* 1st ed. UK: Channel View Publications, 151–65.

Conlin, M.V. and Bird, G.R. (2014) *Railway Heritage and Tourism: Global Perspectives.* 1st ed. UK: Channel View Publications.

Cotte, M. (2016) Two case-studies in heritage and valorization of old montain railways in France. In A. McCants, A. et al. (eds) *New Uses for Old Railways.* Mit Portugal. Projeto Foz tua. Edição: Inovatec, D.L. (Portugal) 83–106.

Cuéllar, D. (2016) From railways to heritage: The closure of railway line in Spain and their valorization as a cultural good. In A. McCants et al. (eds) *New uses for old railways.* Mit Portugal. Projeto Foz tua. Edição: Inovatec, D.L. (Portugal), 35–54.

Dinhobl, G. (2016) Railway heritage: An overview. In A. McCants et al. (eds) *New Uses for Old Railways.* Mit Portugal. Projeto Foz tua. Edição: Inovatec, D.L. (Portugal), 19–34.

Fontana, D. (2016) A new age of steam? The Tua valley line, Portugal: Experience and examples form the technological heritage operations and preserved railways of Britain. In A. McCants et al. (eds) *New Uses for Old Railways.* Mit Portugal. Projeto Foz tua. Edição: Inovatec, D.L. (Portugal), 63–82.

Food'n Road. (2020) *Como criar personas para o seu negócio de turismo.* Available at: https://foodandroad.com/pro/br/criar-personas-turismo/ (accessed 25 August 2020).

Fraga, C.C.L. (2011) Contribuição metodológica para implantação de trens turísticos no Brasil. Rio de Janeiro: Programa de Engenharia de Transportes/COPPE/UFRJ. PhD Thesis, Universidade Federal do Rio de Janeiro.

Fraga, C. and Borges, V.L.B. (2018) Turismo ferroviário e de base comunitária: Algumas conexões para o planejamento e a gestão. *Caderno Virtual de Turismo*, 18, 28–39.

Fraga, C. and Botelho, E. S. (2016) Slow Travel: Uma análise da relação entre ferrovia, meio ambiente e turismo no Brasil. *Dos Algarves*, 1, 137–55.

Fraga, C. and Deutsch, S.F. (2020) Considerações preliminaries sobre Turismo Bici Ferroviário. In P.D.L. Menezes et al. (eds) *Perspectivas da Gestão em Turismo e Hotelaria II.* João Pessoa: Editora CCTA, 434–59.

Fraga, C.C.L. and Santos, M.P.S. (2012) Teaching and learning about railroad tourism through educational games. *Journal of Hospitality & Tourism Education*, 24(2–3), 50–5.

Fraga, C., Borges, V.L.B. and Almeida, C.R. (2019) Turismo Ferroviário Gastronômico no Brasil e em Portugal: Reflexões preliminares a partir da história, memória e criatividade. In J. Lavandoski et al. (eds) *Alimentação e Turismo: Criatividade, Experiência e Patrimônio Cultural* [recurso eletrônico]. 1st ed. João Pessoa: Editora do CCTA, 21–38.

Fraga, C.C.L., Santos, M.P.S. and Castro Ribeiro, S. (2014) Railroad tourism in Brazil. In M.V. Conlin and G.R. Bird (eds) *Railway Railway Heritage and Tourism: Global Perspectives.* 1st ed. Channel View, 137–50.

Fraga, C. et. al. (2013) Destinos turísticos e transportes: Aspectos teóricos e estado da arte. In G. Lohmann et al. (eds) *Transportes e Destinos Turísticos: Planejamento e Gestão.* Rio de Janeiro: Elsevier, Campus.

Frossard, M.S. and Fraga, C. (2018) Turismo, ferrovia e publicidade: A construção de sentidos e significados nos cartazes ferroviários do Reino Unido (1890–1970). *ABET*, 8(2), 43–55.

G1 (2017) '*Biciclotrem' de Cataguases é Calssificado em Premiação de Projetos Sustentáveis.* G1 Zona da Mata, by Fellype Alberto. 29 July. Available at: https://glo.bo/3cXzXn8 (accessed 20 April 2020).

G1 (2019) *Trem das Águas: Conheça a Linha Inaugurada por Dom Pedro II que é Cenário de Novelas em MG.* Lucas Soares. São Lourenço – MG. Available at: https://g1.globo.com/mg/sul-de-minas/

turismo/noticia/2019/12/02/trem-das-aguas-conheca-a-linha-inaugurada-por-dom-pedro-ii-que-e
-cenario-de-novelas-em-mg.ghtml (accessed 10 August 2020).

Gerodetti, J.E. and Cornejo, C. (2005) *Railways of Brazil in Postcards and Souvenir Albums*. São Paulo: Solaris Cultural Publications.

Hall, D. (2005a) Transport tourism – Travelling through heritage and contemporary recreation. In Novelli, M. (ed.) *Niche Tourism: Contemporary Issues, Trends and Cases*. Amsterdam: Elsevier, 89–100.

Hall, S. (2005b). *A identidade cultural na pós-modernidade*. 10th ed. Rio de Janeiro: DP&A.

Henderson, J. (2014) Railways as heritage attractions: The Malasya–Singapore Line. In M.V. Conlin and G.R. Bird (eds) *Railway Heritage and Tourism: Global Perspectives*. 1st ed. UK: Channel View Publications, 190–200.

IBGE (2019) Geociências. Malha Municipal. *Brasil*. 2019. Available at: https://www.ibge.gov.br/geociencias/organizacao-do-territorio/estrutura-territorial/15774-malhas.html?=&t=downloads (accessed 25 August 2020).

IBGE (2020) *Museu Ferroviário [da Estação] Guia de Pacobaíba*. Available at: https://biblioteca.ibge .gov.br/biblioteca-catalogo.html?id=445551&view=detalhes (accessed August 2020).

IPHAN (2019) *Bens do Patrimônio Cultural Ferroviário*. Available at: http://portal.iphan.gov.br/pagina/detalhes/503 (accessed 25 August 2020).

Lee, C.F. and Chen, K.Y. (2017) Exploring factors determining the attractiveness of railway tourism. *Journal of Travel & Tourism Marketing*, 34(4), 461–74.

Lohmann, G. and Castro, R. (2013) Transportes e desenvolvimento de destinos turísticos. In G. Lohmann et al. (2013) *Transportes e Destinos Turísticos: Planejamento e Gestão*. Rio de Janeiro: Elsevier, Campus.

Maggi, S. (2016). Railways and tourism in Italy. In A. McCants et al. (eds) *New Uses for Old Railways*. Mit Portugal. Projeto Foz tua. Edição: Inovatec, D.L. (Portugal) 107–20.

Maria Fumaça (2020) *Passeio de Maria Fumaça*. Available at: https://mariafumaca.tur.br (accessed 25 August 2020).

Maria Fumaça Campinas (2020) *Espaço para eventos*. Available at: https://www.mariafumacacampinas .com.br/descricao-do-passeio/espaco-para-eventos (accessed 25 August 2020).

McCants, A., Beira, E., Cordeiro, J.M.L., Lourenço, P.B. and Pereira, H.S. (eds) *New Uses for Old Railways*. Mit Portugal. Projeto Foz tua. Edição: Inovatec, D.L. (Portugal).

Monge, J.G. and Yagüe Perales, R.M. (2016) Sustainable tourism development: Tren Crucero del Ecuador. *Estudios y Perspectivas en Turismo*, 25(1), 57–72.

Moraes, E.H., Passarelli, S.H.F. and Oliveira, E.R. (2019) Preservação e usos turísticos do patrimônio ferroviário: Panorama dos trens turísticos no estado de São Paulo. *Anais XVIII ENANPUR 2019*. Available at: http://anpur.org.br/xviiienanpur/anais (accessed 25 August 2020).

Moreira, R. A. and Araújo, H. R. (2017) Trilha Verde da Maria Fumaça: Patrimônio ferroviário e turismo no Vale do Jequitinhonha. *Revista Brasileira de Ecoturismo, São Paulo*, 9(6), 751–67.

O Globo (2019) *Trem do Samba não oficial parte da Central do Brasil no Dia Nacional do Samba*. Available at: https://oglobo.globo.com/rio/trem-do-samba-nao-oficial-parte-da-central-do-brasil-no -dia-nacional-do-samba-24114134 (accessed 20 August 2020).

Page, S.J. (2008) *Transportes e Turismo: Global Perspectivas*. Porto Alegre: Bookman.

Palhares, G.L. (2002) *Transportes Turísticos*. São Paulo: Aleph.

Palhares, G.L. (2005) Transportes para turistas: Conceitos, estado da arte e tópicos atuais. In L.G.G. Trigo (ed.) Análises globais e regionais do turismo brasileiro. São Paulo: Rocca, 641–99.

Pine II, B.J. and J.H. Gilmore (2011) *The Experience Economy*, updated ed. Boston, MA: Harvard Business Review Press.

Prefeitura de Juiz de Fora (2020) *Museu Ferroviário*. Available at: https://www.pjf.mg.gov.br/administracao_indireta/funalfa/mf/index.php (accessed 25 August 2020).

Princz-Jakovics, T. and Vasvári, G. (2019) Tourism focused analysis of narrow-gauge railways in Hungary. *Deturope*, 11(3), 80–92.

Robinson, M. and Novelli, M. (2005) Niche tourism: An introduction. In Novelli, M. (ed.) *Niche Tourism: Contemporary Issues, Trends and Cases*. Amsterdam: Elsevier. 1–14.

SEBRAE and ABOTTC (2015a) *Guia de Trens Turísticos e Culturais do Brasil*. Available at: https://bit .ly/2xgasOv (accessed 20 May 2020).

SEBRAE and ABOTTC (2015b). *O Perfil Dos Clientes de Trens Turísticos no Brasil.* Relatório de Pesquisa de Grupos Focais. Abril. Available at: https://bibliotecas.sebrae.com.br/chronus/ARQUIVOS _CHRONUS/bds/bds.nsf/167a1d49c8d75f3b0b717221c3a76e93/$File/5888.pdf (accessed 20 May 2020).

Silva, M.M.F. (1954) *Geografia das Estradas de Ferro Brasileiras em Seu Primeiro Centenário (1854–1954).* In IBGE (1954). Rio de Janeiro: Serviço Gráfico do Instituto Brasileiro de Geografia e Estatística. Available at: https://biblioteca.ibge.gov.br/visualizacao/monografias/GEBIS%20-%20RJ/ centenarioferrovias1954.pdf (accessed 20 August 2020).

Smith, V.L. (ed.) (1989) *Hosts and Guests: The Anthropology of Tourism*, 2nd ed. Philadelphia: University of Pennsylvania Press.

Stefanovic, K. and Koster, R. (2014) Railfans and Railway Heritage Tourism. In M.V. Conlin and G.R. Bird (eds) *Railway Heritage and Tourism: Global Perspectives.* 1st ed. UK: Channel View Publications, 26–41.

Su, M. and Wall, G. (2009) The Qinghai–Tibet Railway and Tibet Tourism: Travelers' Perspectives. *Tourism Management*, 30, 650–57.

Trem do Corcovado (2020) *História.* Available at: https://www.tremdocorcovado.rio/historia.html (accessed 20 May 2020).

Trem do Forró (2020) Available at: https://www.tremdoforro.com.br (accessed 20 May 2020).

UN (2015) *Sustainable Development Goals.* Available at: https://www.un.org/sustainabledevelopment/ sustainable-development-goals (accessed 20 May 2020).

White, L. (2014) *Regional Railway Revival: Connecting Heritage and Tourism in the Spa Centre of Australia.* In M.V. Conlin and G.R. Bird (eds) *Railway Heritage and Tourism: Global Perspectives.* 1st ed. UK: Channel View Publications, 214–26.

WTO (2020) WTO issues new report on how COVID-19-related restrictions on cross-border mobility are affecting global trade. Available at: https://www.wto.org/english/news_e/news20_e/covid _26aug20_e.htm (accessed 30 August 2020).

16. Industrial tourism and ceramics-led tourism in Stoke-on-Trent, UK

Paul Williams

INTRODUCTION

This chapter examines how Stoke-on-Trent, a city renowned as the spiritual home of British ceramics, has positioned itself as a ceramics tourism destination. Often regarded as a less well-known tourist city lacking in conventional attractions, since the formation of a tourism office in the 1980s the city has critically set in motion the necessary processes to purposefully cluster its ceramics heritage and cultural attractions to compete effectively in a continually segmenting tourism market.

> *Out of Victorian buildings, the clay is moulded, shaped and decorated to produce works of art ... cups and saucers and plates and teapots rush like magic out of the clay. May the ovens never grow cold; may Stoke-on-Trent, the pottery town, still continue to be the heart of British craftsmanship.*
> (Adapted from Priestley, 1934: 234)

Following a brief review of the literature on cultural and industrial tourism, using a case study approach, this chapter will analyse how 'the Potteries' evolved and is now the UK's only industrial cluster of scale. This created the foundations which enabled the region to be at the vanguard of developing a ceramics-led cultural movement and for ceramics to be recognised as a relevant niche and an emergent expression of industrial tourism where the motivation to visit is influenced by interest in heritage and curiosity in ceramics.

Described as 'a typological framework' (Stone, 2012: 149), niche tourism refers to the tailoring of a specific tourism product to appeal to a targetable audience or market segment (Novelli, 2005; Ali-Knight, 2011; Agarwal, et al., 2018). Robinson and Novelli (2005: 5) suggest that its status as a contested concept – with no explicit rules for what can be categorised as niche tourism other than a form which, by definition, appeals to a select smaller market – leads to 'considerable variation' in the type of products and markets frequently included under this broad term. Consequently, Robinson and Novelli (2005) argue that contemporary forms of tourism are better located along a spectrum of two extremes with relatively large-scale macro-niches capable of additional segmentation at one end of the spectrum, and smaller, more precise micro-niches at the opposite end.

In this chapter, cultural tourism is identified as the macro-niche and industrial tourism as the micro-niche, with ceramics tourism proposed as a further subset. Whilst it is difficult to further segment types of tourism at the micro-niche end of the spectrum (Novelli, 2005; Stone, 2012), there is sufficient justification for ceramics being proposed as a new form of special interest tourism based on the creative clustering of a critical mass of products and experiences in response to changing tourist needs and motivations.

The environmental landscape and culture in which all ceramics businesses operate has led to serious reflection on the connections between tourism and the 2030 United Nations Sustainable Development Goals (SDGs) (UN General Assembly, 2015). References to sustainability are routinely encountered in emerging niche markets, and it is suggested that ceramics tourism can be closely related to four of the 17 goals: Goal 9 – Industry, Innovation and Infrastructure; Goal 11 – Sustainable Cities and Communities; Goal 12 – Responsible Consumption and Production; and Goal 17 – Partnership for the Goals.

CULTURE AND TOURISM: INEXTRICABLY LINKED BEDFELLOWS

As one of the oldest forms of special interest tourism, cultural tourism is defined by du Cros and McKercher (2015: 6) as 'a form of tourism that relies on a destination's cultural heritage assets and transforms them into products that can be consumed by tourists'. Although regarded initially as a specialist emerging niche activity during the 1980s (Richards, 2018), it is unsurprising that cultural tourism quickly evolved to become a mainstream mass product, with du Cros and McKercher (2015) suggesting cultural tourism comprises four key elements:

- tourism
- use of cultural assets as a building block
- the consumption of experiences
- the tourist.

Smith (2009) suggests all tourism trips can be considered cultural because of the inextricable linkages between culture and tourism. However, in a review of research trends, Richards (2020: 233) questions whether 'the cultural tourist' continues to exist following fragmentation of culture into an eclectic series of niches such as literary tourism, creative tourism and industrial tourism. This clearly differs from the view of du Cros and McKercher (2015: 115) who dispute the notion that the new tourism advocated by Poon (1994) and others has replaced or even fractured the mass tourism market. The crux of their argument is that the core reasons which motivate people to travel and visit destinations have not significantly changed despite the varied and exponentially increased range of tourist activities available in destinations 'clamouring to get onto the proverbial cultural tourism bandwagon' (du Cros and McKercher, 2015: 3).

There is a growing body of evidence (Novelli, 2005; Agarwal et al., 2018) which demonstrates that whilst cultural tourism is considered an umbrella term for a discrete product class, albeit with diverse sub-categories (du Cros and McKercher, 2015), it can equally been seen as a macro-niche capable of being additionally segmented to cater for the needs and interests of specific, constantly growing micro-niche markets by focusing on more diverse and differentiated activities, experiences and products.

THE ALLURE OF INDUSTRIAL TOURISM

Although industrial tourism is regarded as a comparatively unexplored field of academic study (Otgaar, 2012), a number of authors (including Frew, 2000; Otgaar et al., 2010; Pavlakovič and Jereb, 2020) have suggested it emerged in practice over a century ago as organisations started to actively promote visits to companies which subsequently came to be regarded as industrial tourism attractions.

In her empirical study on industrial tourism attractions, Frew (2000: 20) referenced a number of active businesses where tourism is not the organisation's core activity when she defined industrial tourism as: 'visits by tourists to operational industrial sites where the core activity of the site is non-tourism oriented'. As Otgaar et al. (2010) subsequently indicated, this definition views industrial heritage tourism as another type of tourism altogether by excluding visits to non-operational firms. Recognising a lack of clear concepts and definitions, Otgaar et al. (2010: 1) proposed an expanded definition which has been widely referenced within the academic discourse and accepted by industry: 'industrial tourism is a type of tourism which involves visits to operational companies and industrial heritage; it offers visitors an experience with regard to products, production processes, applications, and historical backgrounds'. Importantly, this more comprehensive definition incorporates what Swarbrooke (2002) refers to as a growing trend in 'factory tourism', which he describes as visits to working factories to see industry in action in response to the decline of many traditional manufacturing industries. It should be emphasised that visits to active or redundant sites for industrial tourism purposes enables visitors to learn about socioeconomic activities in the past, present and the future (Otgaar, 2010). This also encompasses 'consumer tourism' (Chen and Morrison, 2004; Mitchell and Orwig, 2002) as well as visits to industrial experience worlds or company museums, as these equally provide opportunities to learn about production processes, as do tours of service providers delivering intangible goods (Frew, 2000).

Referencing Read's (1980: 195) assertion that visitors are motivated to travel because 'they have a particular interest that can be pursued in a particular region or at a particular destination', Frew (2000) was one of the first authors to critically argue that industrial tourism should be regarded as a subset of the growing special interest tourism field. With a focus on post-industrial regions which have lost their former manufacturing base, she also explored how industrial tourism overlaps and has special interest associations with cultural tourism, heritage tourism and education tourism, all of which are underpinned by the significance of cultural learning experiences as a key product component which can be actively and authentically provided by industrial tourism. From a tourist motivation perspective, as people's interests have broadened to include a greater emphasis on nostalgia, the purpose of visiting industrial tourism attractions and sites is often centred around watching and experiencing industrial operational activities for enjoyment and education.

The continuing massification of cultural tourism – to such an extent that it is now considered as no longer a special interest or macro-niche sector, but as 'an umbrella term for a range of tourism typologies and diverse activities which have a cultural focus' (Smith, 2003: 29) – has led to the proliferation of new, diversified micro-niche typologies such as industrial tourism expanding into emerging new markets. Consequently, as an expression of cultural tourism which is being promoted with greater intensity (Vargas-Sánchez, 2015), industrial tourism has developed into a relevant and increasingly important niche of the tourism market (Frew, 2008; Otgaar et al., 2010; Vargas-Sánchez, 2015) that has emerged over the last few decades in response to the trend of individualisation and differentiation as tourists become more experienced, discerning and sophisticated in their needs and preferences (Robinson and Novelli, 2005; Otgaar and Klijs, 2015).

INDUSTRIAL TOURISM BENEFITS

As the demand for tourism continues to expand, it is expected that visits to so-called 'secondary' cities will also grow, with urban destinations offering an alternative portfolio of attractions and experiences, such as industrial tourism, expected to be key beneficiaries. This type of tourism also provides an interesting addition to the existing offer in traditional destinations. Industrial tourism provides opportunities both for individual firms and for towns and cities, particularly those with a considerable industrial base – either at the present time or formerly. To be developed successfully in places once regarded as outside tourism, or even to become a prime force in the expansion of tourism in established destinations, the need for the benefits to outweigh the costs is clearly an important requirement when it comes to encouraging the active participation of companies and tourism organisations. A further pre-requisite for its successful development is the ability of firms to cooperate.

Research conducted by several authors, including Chen and Morrison (2004) and Otgaar (2012), suggests industrial tourism can bring the following tangible benefits and added value to companies:

- improved corporate image and reputation
- promotion of brands and products
- income generation via entrance fees and direct on-site sales
- building a sustainable relationship with local communities and the wider society.

Importantly, as Rudd and Davis (1988) identified, each visitor to an industrial tourism site becomes a potential company ambassador whether they visit for leisure, business or educational purposes – the main motivators of demand. However, it should also be pointed out that even though some firms could potentially 'open their doors' to visitors, they may be reluctant to do so for the following reasons:

- development costs
- safety and security risks
- fear of industrial espionage
- attractiveness of the production or manufacturing processes.

From the destination's perspective, industrial tourism can be an attractive complementary offer, a place marketing tool in the competition between regions, or the core strategy for tourism development. Notably, as Otgaar (2012: 88) identified, it can be seen as 'an instrument to improve the image of individual firms and the image of their home region at the same time'. This co-branding approach presents opportunities for both industries and the regions in which they are located, as the next section will show.

THE SPIRITUAL HOME OF BRITISH CERAMICS

When J.B. Priestley, the novelist and playwright, visited Stoke-on-Trent on his celebrated 'English Journey' in the autumn of 1933, he was charmed by the 'elemental, timeless attraction of ceramics' (Hansard HC Deb., 2016). Founded on traditions dating back to the 12th century and industries born before the first industrial revolution, Stoke-on-Trent's unique ceramics heritage and attractions continue to attract people to be charmed in the spiritual home of British ceramics.

It is widely acknowledged that Josiah Wedgwood was largely responsible for leading ceramics production into the age of mass manufacturing during the 18th century. The particular area of North Staffordshire where Wedgwood set up his ground-breaking factory soon attracted other makers. In his wake came the great houses of Spode, Royal Doulton and Minton, names celebrated around the world for the excellence of their craftsmanship, and the seeds were sown for the development of the necessary infrastructure to underpin the evolution of the pottery industry's industrial beating heart to become the ceramics capital of the world (Hansard HC Deb 2013; Wilhide and Hodge, 2017).

Stoke-on-Trent is a linear city of contiguous towns which came into being in 1910 when the six pottery towns of Tunstall, Burslem, Hanley, Stoke-upon-Trent, Fenton and Longton were united under a single local authority and achieved city status in 1925. With a population of around 255,000, this medium-sized city boasts an unusual convergence of geography and cultural identity, and it may be argued that as a product of the industrial revolution, it is overwhelmingly the formerly dominant ceramics industry that continues to impose an evocative and distinctive landscape and a seemingly indelible identity onto the region (Edensor, 2000). In the same vein, Jayne (2004: 199) makes reference to a myriad of commonly related 'nicknames' such as 'Ceramicopolis, Ceramic City and, more popularly, the Potteries' – as Stoke-on-Trent is still described on Ordnance Survey maps – to conclude that there is little doubt as to what exactly goes on in the city which is still regarded as the UK's foremost industrial and creative ceramics district, and the impact it once had around the world, its name proudly stamped on the bottom of almost every tea cup and saucer produced. This tradition of 'backstamping' ceramic products with the name of the company and 'made in England' goes back to 1772, when Josiah Wedgwood first declared that 'everything made at Wedgwood's pottery, useful or ornamental, caried his name' (Koehn, 2001: 33).

The enduring significance of this city, whose existence owes much to the competitive independent-mindedness of the six pottery towns and a dispersed small-scale structure, is that there is a wide range of historic pottery premises in Stoke-on-Trent (Fernie and Hallsworth, 1998: 440). This means that in an era where culture and heritage tourism is now established as a growing macro-niche segment of the tourism market, the city has many marketable tourism assets, such as the 'V&A Collection at the World of Wedgwood' – recently rebranded because the Victoria and Albert Museum (V&A), the world's leading museum of art, design and performance, owns the collection – and Middleport Pottery, alongside a portfolio of museums, heritage centres, factory tours and pottery shopping outlets. Recognised as the only historic place-based industrial district of significant scale in the UK (Hervas-Oliver et al., 2011), imaginative collaborative work between the city's ceramics industry cluster, policymakers, destination management organisation, key attractions and local residents has enabled the city to develop a diverse set of attractions to reimagine itself and create a new place image around culture and ceramics tourism, despite it, at first sight, appearing to be an 'unlikely tourist destination' (Bramwell and Rawding, 1994: 425).

As DeBres (1991: 14) noted, 'Stoke is one of the smokestack cities hoping to lure tourist money north. It possesses no castles, cathedrals, or stately homes. Its landscape is not prepossessing'. However, it does possess an internationally renowned reputation as the 'world capital of ceramics', an attribute with both tangible and intangible qualities that, through effective and coherent packaging, supports the promotion of ceramics-inspired tourism products, activities and experiences. These act as 'key draw cards' (Benur and Bramwell, 2015: 222) to attract visitors to a destination described by Edensor (2000: 12) as 'a palimpsest, a city in which the old and new mingle and the eye of the discerning tourist can seek out a host of unpredictable pleasures'.

CERAMICS TOURISM: FIRING THE IMAGINATION

Stoke-on-Trent originally began to market itself as a tourist destination to build on the decision to hold a National Garden Festival in 1986. It has been at the vanguard of developing a ceramics-led cultural and tourism movement ever since. Initially, 'an unusual and important objective behind [the city's] tourism marketing [was] to use the increase in visitors to boost sales in the shops attached to the city's ceramics factories, thereby providing direct benefit to this traditional industry' (Bramwell and Rawding, 1994: 430). Swarbrooke (2002: 349) subsequently highlighted how Stoke-on-Trent's tourism office capitalised on its international ceramics' renown and 'turned this into a tourism product, the only real major product the area has to offer tourists'. Swarbrooke also reported how an initiative funded by the European Regional Development Fund Objective 2 scheme encouraged tourists to 'Visit the Potteries for a China Experience'. By promoting a range of attractions linking the history of ceramics production in the area with the contemporary industry, the city attracted visitors 'from all over the world for what can be described as ceramics tourism' (Swarbrooke, ibid.)

As tourism continued to be identified as a potentially important element in the regeneration of industrial urban economies (Ball and Stobart, 1998), there was a critical awareness of the perceived lack of an adequate infrastructural base within the city; for example, the level and quality of accommodation and hospitality facilities lagged behind other comparable destinations. However, the prevailing view amongst policymakers was that the excellent network of factory shops and visitor centres associated with the ceramics industry could help kickstart Stoke-on-Trent's profile as a tourist city by attracting more day visitors and short-stay tourism.

Early successes in terms of increased visitor numbers on the back of a promotion-led strategy were clearly unsustainable. The award-winning 'Do China in a Day' promotion, which began in 1987, was subsequently integrated with a 'China Link' bus service in 1990 and then relaunched in 1992 as 'Visit the Potteries for a China Experience'. However, these campaigns were a victim of their own success, because despite the titles, which were taken too literally by many visitors to the city, it is impossible to visit the Potteries and see all its china or ceramics-associated attractions in one day, not least because of the linear nature of the six pottery towns.

ENGINEERING CERAMICS TOURISM DEVELOPMENT

Aspirations to engineer tourism development (Stobart and Ball, 1998) to create visitor experiences, nurture attractions and ultimately generate jobs and wider economic benefits led to the formation of a number of tourism partnerships and wider public–private sector forums and the publication of policy documents, strategies and action plans. These linked strategic investment to the sustainable development of Stoke-on-Trent as a multi-product destination whilst also capitalising on a competitive advantage in ceramics as a form of special interest tourism. Simultaneously, there was growing recognition of the benefits of using the quality and marketability of attractions to support civic boosterism and identity building by mobilising residents and visitors to help to enhance the image of the city, which was deemed vital to the delivery of wider economic impact and attracting inward investment.

On the back of extensive consultations, a 10-year North Staffordshire Tourism Strategy, launched in 2004, described tourism as a tool and an agent of regeneration, and explicitly stated that with several hundred ceramics companies within the urban core, the world-known ceramic brands and their visitor facilities could be used to draw and disperse visitors to other attractions in the area. Additionally, it stressed that a contemporary take on the ceramics industry, connected through an overarching design theme and a focus on developing 'made in Stoke-on-Trent' as a quality hallmark, should be explored. Notably, the strategy also proposed that partners should work together to develop flagship projects, including a ceramics festival.

Charged with delivering transformational projects to significantly boost the economy, the North Staffordshire Regeneration Partnership (NSRP, 2008) envisaged the area in 2030 as:

- a place at the heart of the UK's creative ceramics businesses and ceramics tourist industry
- a place for growing knowledge businesses and for ambitious knowledge workers
- a place for enjoying the delights of the city, the market towns and the countryside
- a place for working, studying and enjoying attractions
- a place ambitious for growth but concerned always with sustainability.

Based on research findings a new vision for the cluster included a 'quality visitor experience' priority:

> the new renewed dynamism and international profile of the local ceramic industry has driven change in the provision of services associated with the local visitor economy, for both leisure and business visitors, and this has had knock-on effects on leisure services which enhance the quality of life of local residents. (SQW Consulting, 2009)

Unlike other 'smaller urban-industrial authorities which have joined the [proverbial] tourism development bandwagon only relatively recently' (Ball and Stobart, 1998: 348), Stoke-on-Trent responded strategically to growing competition from established destinations by working closely with its ceramics cluster network. This included collaborative engagement between the local destination management organisation and the private sector to promote coherent, interlinked ceramics-themed packages as part of a broader destination offer to meet the competition 'head-on' to attract visitors.

CLUSTERING THE CERAMICS TOURISM OFFER

It is the particular combination or amalgam of ceramics-related products which provides the basis for Stoke-on-Trent's growth and development as a destination. Pottery and ceramics are rightly regarded as visible and widely accessible tourist lodestones, giving the city an authentic sense of place as a destination where the motivation to visit is influenced by interest in industrial heritage, curiosity in ceramics or shopping. As a subset of cultural and industrial tourism niches, ceramics tourism is defined as place-based passive engagement or active participation in ceramics-themed experiences of an educational, creative, entertainment or retail nature.

From the destination marketing mix perspective, the city possesses a mosaic of 'success story' attractions cited as key motivators in choosing to visit Stoke-on-Trent and which frequently create positive television and other media coverage, for example:

- World of Wedgwood, a £34 million attraction promoted as the ultimate destination to experience the Wedgwood story. The attraction's museum houses the 'V&A Collection at the World of Wedgwood', described by UNESCO as one of the most complete ceramic manufacturing archives in existence.
- Following a £9 million restoration, Middleport Pottery, a canal-side, working Victorian pottery in Burslem, the 'Mother Town of the Potteries' is now a living, breathing heritage destination.
- The city council-owned Gladstone Pottery Museum is a fascinating window into a time when British crafts were in huge demand. With its cobbled yard and bottle kilns, it creates an atmospheric time warp which has no equal.
- Since its launch in 2009, the British Ceramics Biennial (BCB) is now regarded as the UK's premier contemporary ceramics festival underpinned by an exciting year-round programme of artists' commissions, education and community engagement projects.

Benur and Bramwell's (2015: 214) assertion that destinations should seek to develop their primary tourism assets 'ensuring there is a sufficient number and diversity of these products, they have coherence, and there are synergies and linkages between them' is reflected in Stoke-on-Trent's current visitor economy strategy which highlights how it 'will lead with cultural tourism and in particular ceramics because that is the city's unique positioning for tourism' (Stoke-on-Trent City Council, 2016a: 3). Crucially, from a tourism development and management perspective the strategy also states:

> Ceramics is synonymous with Stoke-on-Trent; it has shaped the city and is integral to our history. That history is visible in our attractions, our museums, and our canals. Ceramics is also a contemporary story. The industry is alive and experiencing a renaissance, driven by demand for quality design and craftsmanship. Contemporary ceramics is an important driver for repositioning the city as a place to live, work and visit.
> This strategy is about realising Stoke as the World Capital of Ceramics for visitors and using that positioning to inspire our levels of ambition and quality for tourism in the city. This positioning will create a stronger and more competitive framework in which to take to market all our assets and attractions.

Building on its reputation as a centre of ceramics excellence and its deep-rooted heritage with more than 300 ceramics and clay-producing businesses and many globally renowned star brands, Stoke-on-Trent's composite ceramics tourism product is the sum of physical and psychological features together with ancillary services which creates a differentiated, multifaceted offering for the satisfaction of potential visitors, as presented in Table 16.1.

CERAMICS TOURISM TYPOLOGY

The portfolio of ceramics products listed in Table 16.1 forms the essence of the tourism offer for visitors with different interests or visit motivations. Discussions with Visit Stoke confirmed that for destination marketing purposes, the ceramics tourism product is augmented and

Table 16.1   Stoke-on-Trent's composite ceramics tourism product

Tangible Product Features (Physical)	Augmented Product Features (Psychological)
• a ceramics tourist trail providing the 'Complete Ceramics Experience'	• national and international exposure through the *Great Pottery Throw Down* and *Great British Canal Journeys* television
• operational pottery sites with guided factory tours (Wedgwood, Middleport, Emma Bridgewater, Moorcroft), visitor centres and interactive studios	programmes and films
	• centres of excellence in ceramic research, technology and design
• over 20 pottery factory shopping outlets	• established ceramics design courses taught at Staffordshire
• the celebrated Potteries Museum & Art Gallery, home to the finest collection of Staffordshire ceramics in the world	University, and the recently formed Clay College's skills-based diplomas in studio pottery making taught by master
• Gladstone Pottery Museum, recently voted the UK's best small visitor attraction	potters and ceramicists
• museums promoting tangible and intangible ceramics heritage, such as the Wedgwood Museum, Spode Museum Trust Heritage Centre, Dudson Museum and the Etruria Industrial Museum	• close connections with significant ceramics cities and centres in the UK
	• active participation with European destinations including Limoges (France), Delft (Netherlands), Faenza (Italy), Höhr-Grenzhausen (Germany) and museum and industry partners
• independent craft potteries, ceramic art studios, galleries and workshops	in European Union-funded projects to create a competitive and sustainable 'European Route of Ceramics' connecting key
• the British Ceramics Biennial, a hallmark contemporary cultural and ceramics festival	ceramics cities and networks
• Spode China Hall, currently home to the British Ceramics Biennial and adjacent Spode Creative Village which incorporates improved visitor facilities, digital incubator, exhibition and creative workspaces, boutique hotel, restaurant and tea rooms	• exchange links and collaborations with renowned international ceramicists linked to the Korean Ceramic Foundation, Kasama City in Japan, the Indian Ceramics Triennale and other global ceramics festivals
• Love Clay Ceramics Centre located within Valentine Clays, as well as Potclays – companies supplying clay and other raw materials to the ceramics industry with expanded visitor experience, community engagement and education workshop facilities	• civic relationships with great historical Asian ceramic centres including a formalised partnership agreement with the city of Jingdezhen, the Chinese porcelain capital, to cultivate shared historic heritage interests linked to culture, tourism and education
• industrial manufacturers of ceramic hotelware and tiles	• home to the British Ceramics Confederation, the trade body
• Potteries Tile trail celebrating architectural ceramics and the historic built environment.	representing all sectors of ceramics manufacturing in the UK.

engineered as an experience and is best defined as 'an amalgam of different goods and services offered as an activity experience to the tourist' (Gilbert, 1990: 20).

After several years of strong policy, the latest economic impact assessment shows that 5.2 million visitor trips contributed £357 million to the local economy and supported around 6,600 jobs (Stoke-on-Trent City Council, 2018a). Furthermore, a visitor survey (Stoke-on-Trent City Council, 2016b) suggests a significant proportion of visitors were motivated to some extent by the ceramics tourism offer. For example, visiting an attraction (41% of respondents) was the most often noted main primary activity undertaken by visitors, with a further 11% citing shopping as a primary activity. It is worth noting that 11 of the 16 attractions listed in the survey were ceramics attractions or factory shopping outlets, reflecting the prominence of ceramics within the destination's overall offer. Given the demand-generating role of its star ceramics brands in shaping destination appeal, coherently clustering these complementary attractions and activities to form a critical mass of jointly promoted experiences has helped to create 'spin-off benefits in terms of generating increased aggregate visitor numbers' (Weidenfeld et al., 2011: 597) whilst simultaneously enhancing multiplier and externality effects (Michael, 2003).

To support targeted marketing activity, visitors are currently aligned broadly with cultural typologies proposed by Bywater (1993) and McKercher (2002). Visitors are categorised as being 'purposefully ceramics motivated', 'ceramics-inspired sightseers' or 'incidental ceramics participators'. However, it is acknowledged that further research is needed to profile ceramics tourists and better understand the experiences sought to inform marketing planning. As changes in consumer behaviour create more segmented, specialised and sophisticated tourism markets (Robinson and Novelli, 2005), the need for a collaborative and integrative approach to product development and diversification remains clear. Visit Stoke continues to work with partners to create new thematically linked experiences, coherently packaged complementary attractions and products, and develop joint campaigns and events that are environmentally sustainable, and which encourage appreciation of the city's special character as a destination where industrial heritage tourism meets present-day ceramics tourism.

REMOULDING A WORLD CAPITAL REPUTATION

'Making the Creative City', Stoke-on-Trent's 2018–2028 cultural strategy, highlights the creativity, pioneering inventions, iconic brands and extraordinary crafts skills, alongside the city's geography, identity and industrial heritage, as being key to its ongoing cultural renewal and the development of ceramics-led tourism:

> We are Stoke-on-Trent. We make things. We make art from dirt. What we make here reaches the four corners of the globe. There is nowhere like us in the UK. The city is uniquely polycentric – six distinct towns, one city – a radical idea of place.
> We are the place where art, technology and commerce come together to create beauty through craftsmanship. Collective production, once of industry and now of culture, is our hallmark. Innovation is our watchword. (Stoke-on-Trent City Council, 2018b)

The strategy explicitly recognises that ceramics and the story of the city's origins and growth are invaluable to its future as it seeks to build on its proud history as a cradle of the industrial revolution and world centre of ceramics. In order to maximise the tourism value of Stoke-on-Trent's myriad assets, a recent 'Cultural Destinations' project funded by Arts Council England, the national development agency for creativity and culture, brought the city's arts, cultural and ceramics organisations together to work in partnership with Visit Stoke, the local destination management organisation. As well as helping to position the city as a vibrant cultural destination, the partnership contributed to the growth of its visitor economy.

To address a historic lack of embedded cooperation across cultural organisations due to the fragmented geography of the six towns, the Cultural Destinations partnership supported 'Ceramic Cities: Four Sites', a city-wide, innovative exhibition staged simultaneously across four attractions as part of the 2019 BCB. As ceramics tourism continues to gain traction, it is also helping to preserve and safeguard the region's rich, yet fragile ceramics heritage by connecting the past with the present and future. Building upon the cross-cultural work of Neil Brownsword, an artist and professor of ceramics, there is a renewed focus on bringing attention to the value and sustainability of the city's endangered industrial heritage.

SPRINGBOARD TO RELATED TOURISM DEVELOPMENT

Additionally, the ceramics tourism niche is used as a springboard to support Stoke-on-Trent's growing reputation for literary tourism and a film location with a plentiful supply of interesting, filmable cultural resources and heritage assets. Many of the acclaimed literary works of Arnold Bennett, the Chronicler of the Potteries, feature ceramics links located in the industrial district in which he was born. He was featured on the Visit Britain Year of Literary Heroes 2017 map to promote literary tourism. The Stoke-on-Trent Literary Festival also provides a platform for eclectic cultural encounters in the creative surroundings of Emma Bridgewater's pottery factory.

Described in a *Guardian* newspaper editorial as 'the only programme of its particular type rooted in a specific place and culture' (2021), the fourth series of *The Great Pottery Throw Down* was broadcast on primetime television in the UK in 2021, with the previous three series shown on the American TV giant HBO Max's streaming service from September 2020. Originally filmed at Middleport Pottery, the latest series is located at Gladstone Pottery Museum, and will provide further national and international impetus for increased tourism to the city's ceramics attractions and also bring the traditional craft skills of the region's potters back into the public eye.

Similarly, the *Great British Railways Journeys* and *Great Canal Journeys* series, along with other popular TV programmes, regularly provide screen-inspired tourism opportunities linked to ceramics. Embracing the growing fascination for ceramics, Sky Cinema and Creative England have announced that *The Colour Room*, a new film production on the life of the acclaimed Potteries-born ceramicist Clarice Cliff, who become one of the greatest Art Deco designers, will be released in 2021.

Looking to the future, ceramics is increasingly regarded as an area rich in innovation (Portlock, 2019). In the same way Wedgwood was renowned for marrying science and technology with design and creativity, the chief executive of Lucideon, a Potteries-based research company, widely references the importance of the city's advanced ceramics research to the future of technology-based civilisation. The ceramics sector and strategic partners are looking to remould Stoke-on-Trent's reputation as a global centre for ceramics based around design-led production, digital manufacturing, materials and technological innovation. Building on its pioneering heritage, the ambition is to create an international institute for ceramics to underpin a wider economic renaissance. This will also augment Stoke-on-Trent's growing profile as a cultural tourism destination and have a catalytic impact on the city, which prides itself on being an 'aspirational place of living heritage; a place of cultural and creative capital, connected nationally and internationally around the word' (Williams, 2018).

CONCLUDING COMMENTS

Stoke-on-Trent provides a useful case study of how a city can transform cultural heritage and an agglomeration of co-located, marketable industrial assets to develop a form of special interest tourism to be consumed by an emerging niche tourism market. However, the single case study approach, whilst allowing for a series of activities and actions to be examined in the context of tourism development, does have limitations.

As with other developing concepts, applied research around specific visitor motivations, the degree to which visitors engage in ceramics tourism experiences, their level of engagement and wider spillover impacts is needed. Additionally, further work is required to understand how ceramics tourism is being sustainably developed throughout the destination.

The innovative use of ceramics, and ceramics tourism in particular, helps to safeguard, protect and promote the city's culture and heritage, and at the same time contributes directly to many of the SDGs. This is evidenced in the regeneration and restoration of Wedgwood, Emma Bridgewater and Middleport Pottery, alongside the preservation of intangible industrial heritage and the transmission of specialist skills and craftsmanship, as featured at Gladstone Pottery Museum and the BCB festivals. Ceramics tourism's role in accelerating progress in achieving many of the SDGs, particularly goals 9, 11, 12 and 17 (referenced previously), has also been significantly strengthened as sustainable development has become a shared responsibility across the city's ceramics, culture and tourism sector businesses.

REFERENCES

Agarwal, S., Busby, G. and Huang, R. (eds) (2018) *Special Interest Tourism: Concepts, Contexts and Cases*. Oxford, UK: CABI.

Ali-Knight, J. M. (2011) *The Role of Niche Tourism Products in Destination Development*. PhD Thesis, Napier University, Edinburgh, UK.

Ball, R. and Stobart, J. (1998) Local authorities, tourism and competition. *Local Economy*, 12(4), 342–53.

Benur, A. M. and Bramwell, B. (2015) Tourism product development and product diversification in destinations. *Tourism Management*, 50(C), 213–24.

Bramwell, B. and Rawding, L. (1994) Tourism marketing in organisations in industrial cities: Organisations, objectives and urban governance. *Tourism Management*, 15(6), 425–34.

Bywater, M. (1993) The market for cultural tourism in Europe. *Travel and Tourism Analyst*, 6, 30–46.

Chen, Y. and Morrison, A. (2004) Manufacturing a new source of visitors: A pilot study of industrial tourism in the U.S. *Proceedings of Research and Academic Papers*, Vol. 16, International Society of Travel and Tourism Educators.

DeBres, K. (1991) Seaside resorts, working museums and factory shops. *Focus*, 41(2), 10–16.

du Cros, H. and McKercher, B. (2015) *Cultural Tourism* (2nd ed.). Oxford, UK: Routledge.

Edensor, T. (ed) (2000) *Reclaiming Stoke-on-Trent: Leisure, Space & Identity in The Potteries*. Stoke-on-Trent, UK: Staffordshire University Press.

Fernie, J. and Hallsworth, A (1998) England's potteries: Past and present pioneers of factory shopping. *International Journal of Retail & Distribution Management*, 26(11), 439–43.

Frew, E. A. (2000) *Industrial tourism: A Conceptual and Empirical Analysis*. PhD Thesis, Victoria University, Australia.

Frew, E. A. (2008) Industrial tourism theory and implemented strategies. In A. Woodside (ed.) *Advances in Culture, Tourism and Hospitality Research*, 2. Bingley, UK: Emerald Group Publishing, 27–42.

Gilbert, D. C. (1990) Conceptual issues in the meaning of tourism. In C. P. Cooper (ed.) *Progress in Tourism, Recreation and Hospitality Management*, 2. Belhaven, UK: Wiley, 4–27.

Hansard HC Deb. (2013) *Country of Origin Marketing (Manufactured Goods)*. 559, 27 February. https://hansard.parliament.uk/Commons/2013-02-27/debates/130227101000004/CountryOfOrigin Marking(ManufacturedGoods) (accessed 23 August 2020).

Hansard HC Deb. (2016) *Ceramics Industry*. 607, 8 March. https://hansard.parliament.uk/commons/2016-03-08/debates/16030869000001/CeramicsIndustry (accessed 23 August 2020).

Hervas-Oliver, J-L., Jackson, I. and Tomlinson, P. R. (2011) 'May the ovens never grow cold': Regional resilience and industrial policy in the North Staffordshire ceramics industrial district – with lessons from Sassoulo and Castellon. *Policy Studies*, 32(4), 377–95.

Jayne, M. (2004) Culture that works? Creative industries development in a working-class city. *Capital & Class*, 28(3), 199–210.

Koehn, N. F. (2001) *Brand New: How Entrepreneurs Earned Consumers' Trust from Wedgwood to Dell.* Boston, MA: Harvard Business School Press.

McKercher, B. (2002) Towards a classification of cultural tourists. *International Journal of Tourism Research*, 4(1), 29–38.

Michael, E. J. (2003) Tourism micro-clusters. *Tourism Economics*, 9(2), 133–45.

Mitchell, M. A. and Orwig, R. A. (2002) Consumer experience tourism and brand bonding. *Journal of Product and Brand Management*, 11(1), 30–41.

North Staffordshire Regeneration Partnership (2008) One Vision, NSRP Business Plan 2008–11. Stoke-on-Trent, UK. https://webapps.stoke.gov.uk/uploadedfiles/North%20Staffordshire%20Regeneration%20Partnership%20Business%20Plan%202008-11.pdf.

Novelli, M. (ed.) (2005) *Niche Tourism: Contemporary Issues, Trends and Cases*. Oxford, UK: Elsevier.

Otgaar, A. (2012) Towards a common agenda for the development of industrial tourism. *Tourism Management Perspectives*, 4, 86–91.

Otgaar, A. H. J. and Klijs, J. (2010) How to measure the regional impact of tourism? *50th Congress of the European Regional Science Association*, Jönköping.

Otgaar, A. H. J., Van den Berg, L., Berger, C. and Feng, R. X. (2010) *Industrial Tourism: Opportunities for City and Enterprise*. UK: Routledge.

Pavlaković, B. and Jereb, E. (2020) Human resources in industrial tourism. *Academica Turistica*, 13(1), 51–65.

Poon, A. (1994) The 'new tourism' revolution. *Tourism Management*, 15(2), 91–2.

Portlock, S. (2019) We are Stoke-on-Trent: How ceramics power your car and phone. *BBC*, 24 September https://www.bbc.co.uk/news/uk-england-stoke-staffordshire-49641133 (accessed 4 January 2021).

Priestley, J. B. (1934) *English Journey*. London, UK: Heinemann.

Read, S. E. (1980) A prime force in the expansion of tourism in the next decade: Special interest travel. In D. Hawkins, E. Shafor and J. Rovelstad (eds) *Tourism Marketing and Management Issues*. Washington, USA: George Washington Press, 193–202.

Richards, G. (2018) Cultural tourism: A review of recent research and trends. *Journal of Hospitality and Tourism Management*, 36 (September), 12–21.

Richards, G. (2020) Culture and tourism: Natural partners or reluctant bedfellows? A perspective paper. *Tourism Review*, 75(1), 232–4.

Robinson, M. and Novelli, M (2005) Niche tourism: An introduction. In. M. Novelli (ed.) *Niche Tourism: Contemporary Issues, Trends and Cases*. Oxford, UK: Elsevier Butterworth-Heinemann, 1–11.

Rudd, M. and Davis, J. (1988) Industrial heritage tourism at the Bingham Canyon Copper Mine. *Journal of Travel Research*, 36, 85–9.

Smith, M. K. (2003) *Issues in Cultural Tourism Studies*. London, UK: Routledge.

Smith, M. K. (2009) *Issues in Cultural Tourism Studies* (2nd ed.). Oxford, UK: Routledge.

SQW Consulting (2009) The ceramics cluster in North Staffordshire.

Stobart, J. and Ball, R. (1998) Tourism and local economic development: Beyond the conventional view. *Local Economy*, 13(3), 228–38.

Stoke-on-Trent City Council (2016a) Stoke visitor economy strategy and action plan 2016–2019.

Stoke-on-Trent City Council (2016b) Stoke-on-Trent visitor survey 2016.

Stoke-on-Trent City Council (2018a) Economic impact of tourism.

Stoke-on-Trent City Council (2018b) Making the creative city: A cultural strategy for Stoke-on-Trent 2018–2028.

Stone, P. (2012) Niche tourism. In P. Robinson (ed.) *Tourism: The Key Concepts*. Oxford, UK: Routledge, 149–51.

Swarbrooke, J. (2002) *The Development and Management of Visitor Attractions* (2nd ed.). Oxford, UK: Routledge.

The Guardian (2021) The Guardian view *on The Great Pottery Throw Down*: Eccentric and kind. https://www.theguardian.com/commentisfree/2021/jan/15/the-guardian-view-on-the-great-pottery-throw-down-eccentric-and-kind?CMP=gu_com (accessed 17 January 2021).

United Nations General Assembly (2015) Transforming our world: The 2030 Agenda for Sustainable Development, 21 October 2015, A/RES/70/1. https://www.refworld.org/docid/57b6e3e44.html (accessed 3 May 2021).

Vargas-Sánchez, A. (2015) Industrial heritage and tourism: A review of the literature. In E. Waterton et al and S. Watson (eds.) *The Palgrave Handbook of Contemporary Heritage Research*. Palgrave Macmillan, 219–33.

Weidenfeld, A., Butler, R.W. and Williams, A.M. (2011) The role of clustering, cooperation and complementaries in the visitor attraction sector. *Current Issues in Tourism*, 14(7), 595–629.

Wilhide, L. and Hodge, S. (2017) *The Great Pottery Throw Down: A Celebration of the Art and Craft of Ceramics*. London, UK: Pavilion.

Williams, P. (2018) City primed for next industrial revolution. *Sentinel*, 16 June http://www.stoke-sentinel.co.uk/news/stoke-on-trent-news/city-primed-next-industrial-revolution-1682789 (accessed 4 January 2021).

17. 'Escape rooms' and cultural tourism in Poland

Andrzej Stasiak

1.   INTRODUCTION

Currently we are dealing with new-generation cultural tourism, characterized by a multitude of needs and interests. Tourists seek new, original and often not obvious attractions. They are eager to visit places which, until recently, have been regarded as uninteresting, for example, industrial buildings, technological artefacts, sports stadiums, cemeteries and street markets. They want to see ordinary residential, office, industrial, recreation and entertainment districts to see the authentic lives of their inhabitants.

However, merely looking does not satisfy contemporary tourists any longer. On holiday, they wish to experience exciting adventures, take part in something unusual and exceptional, and develop their skills. This is what creative tourism provides. It enables authentic meetings with local people and experiencing living culture in a very personal, emotional and creative manner. It is connected with domains such as art, crafts, design, gastronomy, language, spirituality and sport. Creativity can be applied in tourism in a variety of ways: through creative people, creative processes, creative products and creative places. Creative tourism enables people not only to learn more about the local heritage, but also to become a component of it, if only for a while, to feel the joy of creation, develop one's own personality and skills and, finally, to shape one's own and other people's experience. By becoming co-creators and co-performers, tourists gain unique, authentic, participatory experiences (Gretzel and Jamal, 2009; Richards, 2011; OECD, 2014; Kaczmarek and Paluch, 2015; Al-Ababneh and Masadeh, 2019).

Another interesting phenomenon of 21st-century cultural tourism is 'gamification', using role-playing and computer games to 'manipulate' tourist behaviours in order to increase involvement. The term was first used in 2008. Three years later, gamification was considered to be one of major trends in tourism. Competition tourism offers tourists fun by providing them with new, more satisfying experiences. It involves an activity based on a game with a specific structure, scenario and rules, which a player enters of their own will and which always ends with some kind of outcome. The combination of game components, mechanics and dynamics can be mixed in any possible way to create the spectrum of experiences. Participation in a game is an interactive experience, where the user interacts with the real as well as the fictional world. The elements of key importance are vivid emotions, participant activity and interaction, which together generate the experience of an unforgettable adventure. It presents an attractive alternative to traditional sightseeing (Deterding et al., 2011; Weber, 2014; Xu et al., 2017; Bakhsheshi and Ghaziani, 2019).

Weber (2014) indicates ten different applications of games before, during and after the visit to a destination. Games used in tourism can also be divided into indoor (fictionalized visits) and outdoor (questing, geocaching, Ingress, Pokémon Go) types. Escape rooms belong to both groups; generally, they are situated in buildings, but the game may also take place outdoors.

The introduction of games into tourism raises internal and external motivations (imaginative thinking, entertainment, flow, competing), which result in a stronger interest and involvement in the exploration of the destination.

It is also worth mentioning a new type of post-modernist attraction in which the border between reality and imagination is blurred. Due to modern technologies, constructing alternative worlds is becoming easier and increasingly popular. Hyper-reality satisfies the very particular needs of today's consumers: a continuous pursuit of novelty, originality and uniqueness, a wish for exciting experiences and extreme emotions, the hedonistic imperative of constant fun and the desire to escape (even if only elusively and temporarily) from everyday problems (Stasiak, 2019).

All three phenomena (creativity, gamification and hyper-reality) provide the basis for the escape room experience. As a result, they can be regarded as brand-new attractions within cultural and urban tourism (due to their localization). Escape rooms represent a particular niche, referred to as creative cultural tourism. (Al-Ababneh and Masadeh, 2019). They are also travel destinations for tourists with a special interests in this form of entertainment.

The precursors of escape rooms are, among others, computer games (point-and-click adventures), adventure game shows and movies (Nicholson, 2015). The idea of this game is to solve some puzzle within a set time limit and escape from the room. Transferring the game from the virtual to the real world made it real, the player can enter a mysterious room, experience it with all their senses and 'accomplish the mission'.

The first genuine escape rooms were created in 2007, in Japan. A few years later, they appeared in the USA and Europe, and in subsequent years they have become popular on all continents. In the second decade of the 21st century their numbers soared. Today, the overall number of escape room companies worldwide is estimated at 5,700–6,400 (Villar Lama and García Martín, 2021). Escape rooms have become a trendy form of recreation in large cities and they are also increasingly visited by tourists.

This chapter is a case study presenting the rapid growth of the escape room sector in Poland in 2016–2019. The purpose of the work is to give a general description of supply and demand. Individual objectives include the following: presenting the quantitative development of escape rooms in Poland from 2013 to 2020, identifying the location factors (spatial concentration) in the largest Polish cities and defining the character and themes of escape rooms. With regard to the sphere of demand, the aim was to describe the psychological and social profile of the typical Polish escape room enthusiast (personal traits, motivations, emotions accompanying the game).

2.   LITERATURE REVIEW

Escape rooms have not yet been extensively studied or discussed. So far, only a few articles have been published, but a pioneering work was written by Nicholson (2015) who, on the basis of a global survey among escape room owners, was the first to describe the phenomenon.

Stasiak (2016) and Villar Lama (2018) have written geographical studies, presenting the spatial development of escape rooms in Poland and Spain. In both these countries, a similar diffusion of innovation was observed: escape rooms first appeared in metropolises, followed by their expansion to smaller cities and towns, including tourist destinations. Kubal and Pawlusiński (2016) claimed that escape rooms had enriched the broad cultural offer of Kraków and are used not only by residents, but also by temporary city users, such as students and tourists. Nagy et al. (2018), when exploring creative tourism in Budapest, considered escape rooms to be among the most popular attractions in this sector. The phenomenon is also rapidly growing in many countries beyond Europe, such as Iran (Bakhsheshi, 2019; Bakhsheshi and Ghaziani, 2019).

The dynamically increasing number of escape rooms strengthens competition and forces the owners to look for new solutions and strategies in experience design. Gündüz (2018) showed the possibility of repeatedly using the Blue Ocean Strategy – searching for a way to escape from the intense Red Ocean by creating the Blue Ocean – which does not involve competition. Pakhalov and Rozkova (2020) emphasize the need to spend substantial sums of money on staff training and innovative technological solutions (special effects, virtual reality) in order to effectively build positive consumer impressions. The phenomenon has also been analysed in the wider context of the theory of serious games and serious gamification (Bakhsheshi and Ghaziani, 2019).

Studies on the demand for escape rooms mainly focus on customer experience. Analysis usually focuses on comments posted on the TripAdvisor website (Kolar, 2017; Kolar and Čater, 2018; Dilek and Dilek, 2018), proving that new, peak, unique and fun experiences, gained from solving difficult puzzles on the one hand, and team work (the social component) on the other, are involved. To be ultimately satisfied, the following factors are important to players: the novelty of the attraction, the theme of the room and the storytelling, strong experiences and emotions, being engaged in the task, the feeling of being outside place and time and a group challenge. Pakhalov and Rozkova (2020) also demonstrated that a more authentic experience and deeper immersion can be achieved with advanced technological solutions. At the same time, technical failures and errors may considerably decrease customer satisfaction.

Stasiak's research (2019) had a slightly different character. On the basis of an online survey, he tried to define the profile of a Polish escape room enthusiast and the emotions experienced during a game. Similarly, Qian Pink et al. (2019), with the help of a goal-directed behaviour model, conducted an in-depth analysis of the experiences of twenty Malaysian players immediately after they left an escape room.

3.   RESEARCH SETTING AND METHODOLOGY

This chapter summarizes the research which the author conducted in Poland in 2016–2020. A wide spectrum of research methods was used: investigation and critical review of available academic and popular publications (press, websites, blogs) dedicated to escape rooms; an analysis of the lockme.pl database for 2016–2020; and a survey conducted among escape room fans in 2018.

Lockme.pl is a unique and innovative internet platform enabling users to review, book and express opinions about escape rooms. It presents about 95% of all escape rooms in Poland. The portal dominates the domestic market and has become the main escape room promotion and distribution channel, presenting details of individual escape rooms. Data verification shows that it is reliable and credible as a source. The first comprehensive supply analysis was conducted in 2016 and data was collected at six-monthly intervals over the following years. As a result, escape rooms could be studied across time and with reference to the whole country, individual regions and the ten largest cities.

The survey was carried out online between 12 April and 11 May 2018. A total of 718 respondents were recruited by means of an invitation posted on lockme.pl and the company's profile on Facebook. As a result, the participants were not 'ordinary' Polish escape room visitors but true enthusiasts, actively engaged in the players' community. The relatively large number of respondents allowed the author to provide a credible description of the most common attitudes and opinions expressed by Polish escape room fans.

4.   FINDINGS AND DISCUSSION

4.1   Escape Room Sector Development in Poland

The first escape room in Poland was opened in 2013 in Wrocław and instantly gained popularity, with similar attractions appearing in large numbers all over the country; over 600 rooms offering a variety of themes opened in three years (Stasiak, 2016). For the next two years they continued to develop, though slightly less dynamically, and experts estimate that towards the end of 2018, there were about 1,000 operational escape rooms in Poland (*Rynek EscapeRoom*, 2018). After this the market stabilized; older rooms were replaced with new ones, and the overall number grew less rapidly. Experts even forecast a natural correction down to approximately 800 escape rooms.

Poland became one of the market leaders in escape rooms in Europe, due to:

- the primacy effect – the first escape rooms appeared shortly after their debut in Hungary and Switzerland
- the relatively large number of firms running this kind of business[1]
- certain innovative solutions increasing the attractiveness and efficiency of escape rooms.

The first rooms, arranged in adapted flats using private resources, were based on simple puzzles. They were quickly replaced by places offering an intricate storyline and meticulously designed interiors. Those, in turn, were replaced by third-generation rooms, with multilayer scenography, special effects, modern technological solutions, authentic props or even real actors playing some scenes. Various types of escape room appeared: for children, for adults, mobile (assembled, e.g., during company events), underwater, out in a field or on a bus cruising all over the city. Back then, open-air 'mass escape' events were also organized. In October 2017, in Wrocław, the world's first national championships in this 'discipline' were held. The elimination rounds involved 1,767 competitors, forming 537 teams. The 2nd Poland Escape in 2018 included 2,750 players and 892 teams.

The optimistic forecasts concerning further development of the escape room market in Poland changed on 4 January 2019. On that day, in Koszalin, a tragic accident took place in an escape room. An unsealed gas bottle caused a fire in which five teenage girls died due to carbon monoxide poisoning, while the game master who tried to save them was seriously burnt. The event was widely commented on across the world, and Polish media reported on it for several days. Instructed by the authorities, the fire department and building inspectors conducted detailed inspections of all escape rooms in Poland, revealing serious inadequacies in 90% of them regarding fire prevention (lack of fire extinguishers, poor organization of emergency exits, and lack of regular maintenance of utility installations such as gas, electricity and ventilation). The inspections resulted in hundreds of fines and the immediate closure of

69 rooms. It also emerged that the activity of escape rooms had not been controlled by any regulations. Therefore, a new law was passed very quickly, strictly defining the conditions that had to be met to run this sort of activity. The escape room sector itself implemented a number of safety measures, such as full monitoring, full contact with the game master, permanently open doors, a panic button, emergency lighting, only low voltage appliances within a player's reach and an emergency door-opening system. Staff were trained in first aid and promotional campaigns were run to neutralize the effects of the negative media campaign.

Administrative restrictions forcing room owners to invest huge financial resources in safety improvements, as well as the negative atmosphere created by the media, caused a deep contraction of the escape room sector in Poland. By January 2019, the number of escape rooms had dropped by 24% to 780 (Nawrot, 2019); by July 2019 it had fallen further to 565 (lockme.pl), and by the end of the year, the number decreased by 60% and in some large cities by even 75%. This trend continued until March 2020, when the outbreak of the coronavirus pandemic and the consequent economic lockdowns and later limitations on access to recreational facilities worsened the situation even more.[2]

4.2   The Location of Escape Rooms

In 2016, nearly 600 escape rooms were identified at 67 destinations in Poland. Spatially, they were unevenly distributed from the outset, with the majority in the largest cities: Warsaw, Gdańsk, Poznań, Łódź, Kraków, Wrocław and the Upper-Silesian conurbation. In Polish cities there was an average two or three firms, managing five to six rooms per 100,000 inhabitants. The smallest numbers of escape rooms were found in the less urbanized eastern and northeastern provinces (Stasiak, 2016). Escape rooms soon appeared in medium-sized urban centres and popular tourist destinations. However, the disproportional spread between large and small cities continued until 2018, when escape room development peaked. At that point there were, on average, nearly eleven rooms per 100,000 inhabitants of host cities (from 7.4 in Warsaw to 19.4 in Poznań), which in many cases meant market saturation and led to a small decrease in numbers.

A rapid decrease in the number of escape rooms came in 2019 after the Koszalin tragedy, mostly affecting provinces with the largest agglomerations. The smallest drop was noted in the eastern parts of the country, and in two provinces the number of escape rooms even increased slightly (Figure 17.1).

A more in-depth data analysis shows that the phenomenon was more complex: on the one hand, escape rooms were closed down, but on the other new establishments were opening at the same time. Therefore, in many small urban centres, including popular tourist destinations such as Wisła, Zakopane, Krynica and Zamość, the number of rooms increased (Figure 17.2).

The considerable concentration of escape rooms in cities was easy to notice, given that the ten largest Polish cities hosted ca. 60% of all the escape rooms in the country. The leader had always been Warsaw (132 in 2017), but more than 100 were also found in Poznań. In the remaining centres, the number usually ranged from 30 to 60, with numbers in some cities peaking in 2017 and in others in 2018. The crisis in 2019 led to half the rooms closing down (Figure 17.3). The smallest declines were found in Wrocław (-21.5%) and Gdańsk (-25.6%). In most cities, 40–50% of the rooms were closed and the effect was greatest in non-tourist cities: Katowice (-73.2%), Łódź (-73.6%) and Szczecin (-75%). The 'saturation' index also visibly decreased, with a return to 2016 levels of 5.3 rooms per 100,000 inhabitants.

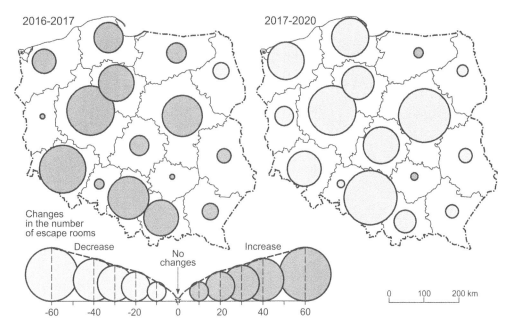

Source: Author.

Figure 17.1   Changes in the number of escape rooms in Poland in 2016–2020, by province

In Poland, from the very outset, a tendency to locate this type of attraction in city centres could be seen. This was due to the constant presence of residents and tourists generating potential demand for all kinds of attractions, the high accessibility of urban central zones, and a large supply of unoccupied flats in historical tenement houses which could be easily adapted to become atmospheric escape rooms.[3] High rent was not a barrier because escape rooms were a profitable business.

Stasiak's research (2016) proved that 80% of escape rooms in Polish cities were situated within a 2.5 km radius from the central point (the Old Town marketplace). The exceptions were in Warsaw (rooms clustered within a 5 km radius), Łódź (rooms clustered along the main street, Piotrkowska) and Gdańsk.

The development of escape rooms in 2017–2018 resulted from:

- further saturation of the historical space in the central district
- locating new establishments further from the centre, sometimes even on the city outskirts (Figures 17.4 and 17.5).

The direct consequences of the fire in Koszalin included administrative decisions regarding the closure of rooms which did not comply with the basic safety standards, and the indirect consequences included the need to invest in proper safety measures and smaller demand due to visitors' fear for their safety. The first to disappear were rooms in central districts, as their modernization would have cost too much or, due to the historical character of the buildings, would have been impossible. The clusters became looser, and the area where they could be

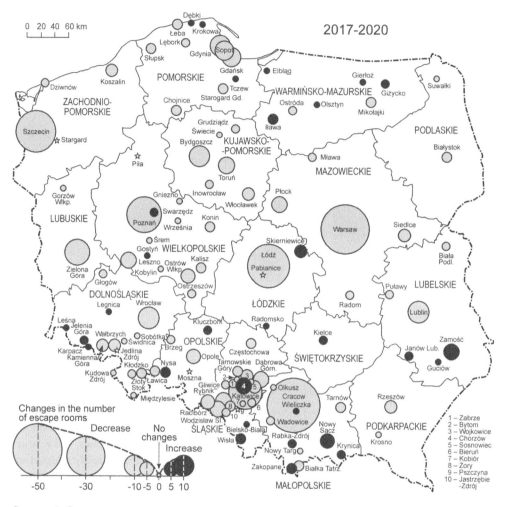

Figure 17.2   Changes in the number of escape rooms in Poland in 2017–2020

found often spread, reaching the city boundaries. In non-tourist urban centres (Łódź), escape rooms completely disappeared from the city centre; in business and tourism cities (Poznań) their number slightly decreased, but some still continued to operate within the city centre and the tourist penetration zone (Figures 17.4 and 17.5).

The model of escape room location described above is typical for Poland, and perhaps for other cities in Central and Eastern Europe (e.g., Budapest). In Western Europe, city centres have already been developed and rents are markedly higher. In Spain, for instance, escape rooms are created on the edges of historical city centres and, albeit much more rarely, on the outskirts. Their location is determined by the following factors: transport accessibility, the price of purchasing or renting the facility and the proximity of a tourist area. At seaside resorts,

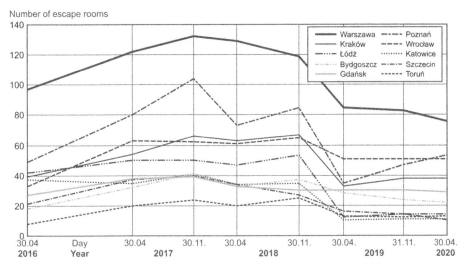

Source: Author.

Figure 17.3   The number of escape rooms in ten largest Polish cities in 2016–2020

small start-up firms located their rooms in side streets, while franchises and larger projects were situated along avenues, popular promenades and in tourist zones (Villar Lama, 2018).

4.3   Escape Rooms – a Description

Over the few years when escape rooms flourished in Poland, certain standards were established, sometimes differing from those in other countries. Here are the main features of an escape room:

- a game in an escape room is a team game, which is usually played by two to five people
- the teams consist of people who know one another, often a family, representing different skills needed for the game
- a typical game lasts 45–60 minutes
- players usually pay per game, regardless of the number of team members.

The prices for escape rooms in Poland are several times lower than in the USA or Western Europe. Initially, it was assumed that the cost of game per person should be more or less equal to the price of a cinema ticket (one game = 4–5 tickets), but due to rapidly growing demand, prices quickly rose.[4]

Escape room adventures are usually based on an original concept, so their themes are highly varied. Naturally, the overall idea of the game is similar in all settings, based on escaping from some unpleasant room: a prison, doctor's surgery, hospital, disaster site and so on. Over time, other motifs have appeared: solving crime puzzles, preventing terrorist attacks, spying, taking part in a robbery, working in a laboratory or staying at a space station. Alongside themes borrowed from computer games, literature or film, original concepts and motifs based on the local heritage (history, art, legends) have appeared in escape rooms as well.

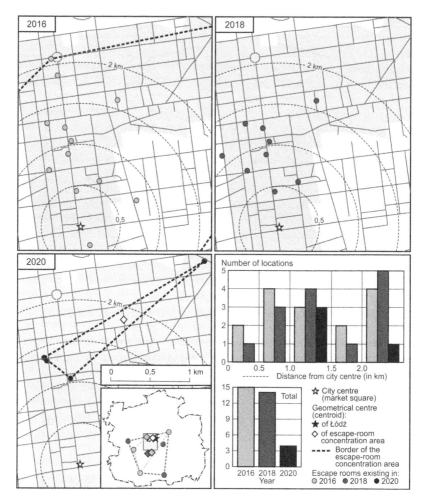

Source: Author.

Figure 17.4   Escape room companies in Łódź in 2016–2020

The global study by Villar Lama and García Martín (2021), encompassing over 1,000 answers, shows that most escape room themes may be allocated to three main thematic families:

- mystery–horror–fantasy (ca. 30%)
- science and science-fiction, including technology, space, nuclear/chemical hazards, terrorist attacks, war, army and military (ca. 22%)
- police and crime topics, including detectives, secret agents, robberies, prisons, the mafia and other similar subjects (ca. 22%).

Other leading themes include history and art (cinema, music, literature, cartoons).

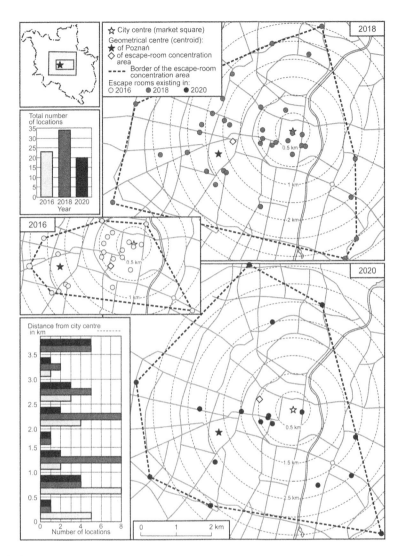

Source: Author.

Figure 17.5   *Escape room companies in Poznań in 2016–2020*

The themes of escape rooms in Poland are not much different from those around the world. The majority are thriller–crime rooms (28.1%),[5] in which the players, as policemen or detectives, have to identify the murderer, find the hidden loot or locate an abducted person, or – as criminals – rob a bank. One popular genre is the horror story (14.2%). Every tenth room refers to literature and film (11%) or history (10.5%). Much less popular are science rooms – 6.3%, adventure – 5.3%, futurist and science-fiction – 4.2%, military and medical – 3.2% each, or logical/abstract rooms – 2.1% (Stasiak, 2016).

Room themes may be looked upon from the point of view of their relation to the place where they operate (Villar Lama, García Martín, 2021). Two groups can be distinguished: rooms unconnected with the heritage of the city (region) and rooms which take advantage of the local heritage. The former group, much more numerous (ca. 75%), includes rooms for which a specific location is irrelevant (abstract puzzles, a desert island, submarine, space station) and which refer to global mass culture or to recognizable but culturally distant places (Egyptian pyramids, ancient Rome, the Wild West, Chernobyl). The latter group is much more interesting, as their themes, plot and interior design have an authentic local character and elements which can be used include local events and historical figures, culture, legends, urban folklore or traditional cuisine. Giving the game unique attributes typical of a given region makes escape rooms an effective, if not obvious, tool for interpreting local heritage and enables the users to discover the *genius loci* of the visited destination. Such solutions enrich the tourist offer of this place and, at the same time, increase its attractiveness in the eyes of tourists, as they offer a unique holiday experience. Regrettably, as it turns out, entrepreneurs very rarely reach out for local themes, believing that well-proven formats, referring to unified, mass culture will guarantee them market success.

Inspirations for escape rooms in Poland are, above all, well-known crime stories (Sherlock Holmes, James Bond), thrillers and horror films (*Jigsaw, The Shining*), science-fiction and fantasy films (*Alice in Wonderland, Star Wars, Lords of the Rings, Matrix, Game of Thrones*) or adventure stories (*Indiana Jones*) (Stasiak, 2016). Rooms which appeared more recently referred to *Jurassic Park, 2001: A Space Odyssey, The Shawshank Redemption, Frankenstein, The Silence of the Lambs, The Chronicles of Narnia, Finding Nemo* and many other titles. As for Polish motifs, only two have been used: *Seksmisja* (*Sexmission*) and *Stawka większa niż życie* (*More Than Life at Stake*).

Escape rooms much more frequently refer to various (real and legendary) events from Polish history. As a result, we can, for instance, fight the Wawel Dragon; search for the treasure of Gdańsk pirates, the Amber Chamber or the Golden Train; try to break the Enigma Code or steal the secrets of the Riese Project; help Warsaw insurgents from 1944; or confront the absurdities of the Polish socialist era (Stasiak, 2016). In 2020, there were also rooms revealing the background of the Wielkopolskie Insurrection of 1918, the mysteries of German Breslau (Wrocław) from before 1939, intelligence activity during the Cold War and the introduction of martial law in 1981. Historical rooms are more popular in smaller towns and attractions than in large cities where the offer is diversified. For example, they might be opened near museums, or in palaces, castles or mines. They have also become interesting for public authorities who want to use them as a modern educational tool, within the framework of the politics of memory. In 2017, the Institute of National Remembrance opened an escape room in Warsaw dedicated to the memory of the Cursed Soldiers.[6]

4.4 Escape Room Customers

In 2017, about 4,133,000 visits to Polish escape rooms were recorded, and the income for the whole sector was estimated at ca. PLN 200 million (*Rynek EscapeRoom*, 2018).[7]

Escape room users can be divided into three main groups:

- residents – usually inhabitants of large cities who visit escape rooms as part of their recreation, students in school groups or company employees on team-building events

- tourists, who usually decide to visit escape rooms incidentally during trips (weekend or longer) as an additional attraction, enabling them to learn something about the culture of the visited destination, or simply relax after a day of sightseeing
- special interest tourists – escape room enthusiasts who travel to other cities in a pre-organized group in order to play in unfamiliar rooms (i.e., escape rooms are the main purpose of the trip).

The most numerous is the first group – escape rooms should be treated first of all as a form of urban recreation, but their role in tourism is growing steadily. Increasingly, escape rooms are seen as urban cultural tourism attractions, separate tourist products at nodal points of traffic routes, or even event tourism destinations attracting fan conventions, escape marathons and national or international championships. The most interesting escape rooms are recommended for tourists on the TripAdvisor portal, in Lonely Planet guides and on the promotional websites of tourism organizations (such as VisitLondon, Parisinfo).

The balance between residents and tourists is difficult to establish. Villar Lama and García Martín (2021) estimate that about two thirds of escape room customers are local inhabitants. Tourists make up 34.8% of the clientele; broken down by origin, this includes 23.2% domestic tourists and 11.6% foreign tourists. However, in some parts of the world, e.g., in Southern Europe, the share of tourists reaches 40% of the clientele, and in tourism 'meccas' such as Dubrovnik, Rome or Corfu, there are more foreign customers than domestic ones.

In Spanish cities, tourists make up 26% of demand. The predominant group of escape room visitors, however, are young people, aged 21 to 35 years old (80%), playing mainly with friends (53%), families, in couples or with co-workers (Villar Lama, 2018). The millennial generation is characteristic of Polish escape room enthusiasts as well: 91% are below 40 years of age. A typical customer is young, 20 years old (57%), female (71.5%), has a higher education qualification (65.1%), is a white-collar worker (60.6%) or a student (18.9%) and lives in a large city (53.2%) (Stasiak, 2019). This profile of a typical player is not surprising except, perhaps, for the disparity between genders; however, other studies (Nawrot, 2019) confirm that women outnumber men among escape room visitors in Poland. What is absolutely clear is that escape rooms attract, above all, young, educated, well-off inhabitants of metropolises.

To most respondents, a visit to an escape room is a form of recreation practised both at weekends (73.7%) and on weekdays (61.3%). A large number of respondents look for rooms away from their place of residence. Nearly 46% said that they visited escape rooms during holidays within Poland, while 26.5% said that they take trips specifically to visit rooms in other cities. This form of entertainment is rarely a part of a business trip or trip abroad (7.8% and 5.6%, respectively).[8]

The studied sample turned out to be strongly engaged in their passion. The respondents visited escape rooms often and regularly (over 80% visited at least once every three months, while 20% went up to several times a month). Their playing companions were most commonly friends (87.7%) who often formed a regular team, and less commonly spouses/partners (57.2%).

The motivations declared by the respondents can be divided into three main groups: the first includes those with a desire to spend free time in an attractive way (79%), experience something new, original and exciting (67.3%) and take break from the boredom of traditional forms of recreation (15.3%). The next group is characterized by a love of puzzles and mind games

(74.5%), as well as computer games (12.3%). The third group are motivated by curiosity (57.8%) and the desire to get away from everyday problems and stress (52.5%).

The most important aspects of escape rooms mentioned by respondents were original, varied and surprising tasks and puzzles, requiring creativity (93.2%), followed by the room theme (81.3%), interior design (75.8%), the atmosphere of the game (64.2%) and the plot (57.4%). For nearly half of the respondents, the strong emotions accompanying the escape from the room were important (the result of full engagement, competition and time pressure). Technical elements such as special effects (45.4%), staff (31.5%) and the recreation of the world of computer games (12.1%) were markedly less appreciated. This is in contrast with the findings of Pakhalova and Rozhkova (2020), who found that employees and modern technologies were deemed essential for creating experiences, though they also noticed that visitors were more focused on the outcome of special effects (atmosphere) than the technical solutions themselves.

The amazing popularity of escape rooms greatly depends on saturating a game with strong emotions. Practically nobody who has tried this kind of entertainment remains indifferent. Respondents were asked to indicate the emotions they felt during games, choosing from among 24 emotional states from the circle of emotions (Plutchik, 1980). In most answers, positive emotions were predominant, such as interest (87.7%), joy (77.4%), surprise (66.6%), vigilance (64.8%), admiration (33.4%) or even ecstasy (30.8%). Negative feelings were also mentioned: fear (13.7%), annoyance (13.2%), apprehension (12.4%), distraction (5.9%), terror (5%) and anger (4.5%). It is symptomatic that the smaller frequency of negative emotions was paralleled by their lower intensity.

Escape room users certainly have highly personalized reactions to games. Their emotions depend both on the course of the game (the theme and arrangement of the room, game scenario, technical problems, final result) and on the player's personal traits. The study revealed more distinct differences as regards the player's gender (Figure 17.6). Women, more often than men, admitted that they felt surprised (68.6% to 61.4%) and also turned out to be more sensitive (joy – 79.3%, ecstasy – 32.8%) while men were more inclined to feel admiration (38.1%).

The respondents defined the intensity of emotions on a scale from 1 (weak) to 10 (extreme). The arithmetical mean was 7.7, and the most commonly chosen ratings were 8 (32%) and 7 (28.1%). Nearly a quarter of the respondents rated the game very highly (9 and 10). Nobody indicated a minimal level of emotions (1 or 2). It is interesting that over half of the respondents said they would be willing to pay more for a more exciting game.

The results obtained by the author are consistent with those obtained by other researchers (Kolar, 2017; Kolar and Čater, 2018; Dilek and Dilek, 2018) who emphasize that to be fully satisfied, escape room players need full immersion and a sense of 'flow' (Csikszentmihályi, 1990) – that is, a feeling of being totally involved in the task, of being beyond time and place, peak experiences and sometimes even ecstasy. However, by and large, the results presented in these works have a strongly aggregated form; they do not consider personal aspects (players' individual character traits, the mood of the moment) or the spatial context (the country, city, cultural circle) and their impact on the experience.

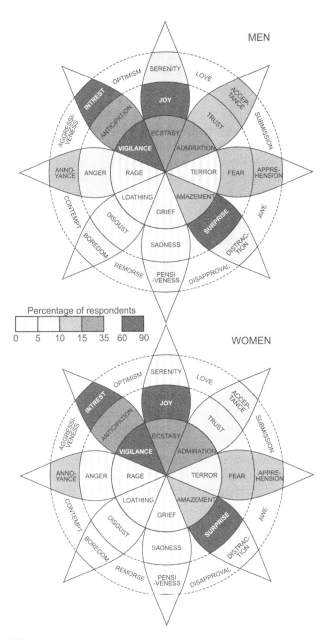

Source: Stasiak (2019).

Figure 17.6   Emotions felt during the game

5.   CONCLUSIONS

Escape rooms are an extremely interesting phenomenon. On the one hand, they are a manifestation of modern, global and computerized culture, and on the other, they may be a way of interpreting local heritage and promoting a given city or region. From the point of view of the tourism sector, they may be seen as:

- a component of the destination's multi-product which tourists use (often by chance or spontaneously) as a recreational activity while on holiday
- new attractions within creative cultural tourism which – because they involve competition, stimulate creativity and create exceptional experiences saturated with strong emotions – are addressed to tourists who seek more significant cultural interactions with local communities
- the main purpose of travel among tourists with special interests in this form, namely, escape room fans looking for new, exciting challenges.

The development of the escape room sector in Poland is proof of the very quick diffusion of innovation on global and national scales. The concept of a new form of entertainment, well-proven in Japan, was adapted to the local character and creatively developed, first in Europe, then in Polish cities, and finally in smaller cities and tourist destinations. All over the world, escape rooms are a form of entertainment created by millennials for millennials (Villar Lama, 2018). Their success on the market was initially driven by small firms run by young entrepreneurs, flexibly adjusting to the demand for original, exciting forms of recreation. The factors stimulating the development of the sector included the simplicity of copying ideas, low starting and running costs and high profitability (Stasiak, 2016). The development of escape rooms followed explosively, spontaneously and uncontrollably, which led indirectly to the tragedy in Koszalin. The lack of legal regulation, strong competition and the pursuit of maximal profits resulted in a lack of respect for safety regulations. The tragic fire brought an immediate and deep contraction of this market. Paradoxically, it also had positive effects: escape rooms gained greater recognizability due to the constant media coverage, and there was an instant improvement in safety standards, with enterprises focused purely on fast profit soon eliminated, leading overall to the sector's integration in order to respond to the crisis. However, hopes for rebuilding the market have been seriously undermined by the coronavirus pandemic.

The course of the phenomenon presented here corresponds to a product lifecycle. The introduction of escape rooms to the Polish market in 2013 was followed by a rapid development stage in 2014–2017. In 2018, there was consolidation and a short stagnation, and in 2019, as a result of the tragic accident, a decline, further worsened by the coronavirus pandemic. Is a new stage of rejuvenation possible?

The year 2020 turned out to be extremely difficult for escape rooms in Poland. Firms had to suspend their activity twice, for the spring and autumn lockdowns. Only a few obtained financial backing from the state, as a part of the so-called 'anti-crisis shield' scheme. Looking for any sources of income during lockdown, escape rooms enlarged their offer with new services, such as selling board games, competitions for puzzle lovers and the possibility of distance gaming (Live Video Escape, Avatar Online Room). In summer, despite the required security measures (gloves, antibacterial gel, room disinfection), the demand for this type of services markedly decreased. As a result, in January 2021, the escape room market in Poland had dwindled to only 305 rooms (lockme.pl). The prospects for this sector are very feeble.

Despite the fact that escape rooms are extremely sensitive to crises, it can be assumed that they will not completely disappear from the market because they are a product of wider processes occurring in the contemporary world and follow directly from experience economy assumptions (Pine and Gilmore, 1999). Escape rooms make it possible to turn an ordinary product into an extraordinary experience which will always be remembered by the buyer:

> They offer sequences of events which engage the players on an emotional, physical, intellectual or even spiritual plane. The product, meticulously prepared, guarantees a departure from everyday routine, moving to a different reality, engaging all the senses, the so-called 'emotional story', dramatization of space, interactivity, active participation and co-creating one's own and others' experiences. (Stasiak, 2016: 45)

The main weakness of escape rooms is their once-only consumption and the need to constantly look for new customers. Tourism may bring customers from outside the city, on the condition that escape rooms are attractive to the visitors. There are two niche segments: escape room enthusiasts looking for challenges in other cities (the less numerous group) and cultural tourists who want to 'discover' the place where they are staying in an original way (the more numerous group). However, escape rooms must enrich and vary the free-time offer at the destination by providing tourists with a unique, memorable experience. Rooms based only on unified and trivialized pop culture are not enough. It is necessary to relate this type of entertainment more strongly to local culture, so that there is a creative discourse between the game master, representing both the inhabitants and the visitors. Escape rooms should help users to interpret local heritage in a more effective and attractive way, as well as understand its exceptionality (*genius loci*).

Escape rooms may also be approached as way to rejuvenate the mature tourist reception area. From the point of view of managing/administering the destination, it is a challenge to include escape rooms in cooperation with tourist companies, to add them to the general tourist offer and to use them to create an attractive brand and image of the region. At the strategic level, escape rooms may become a tool used to implement the latest marketing strategies, based on tourist experience (Stasiak, 2021), by supporting the development of creative tourism at a given destination.

On the local (micro-)scale, escape rooms may be a tool of tourism deglomeration, pulling mass tourists away from the central tourist district and directing them to other, non-touristic parts of the city. In this way, they may contribute to a more balanced urban development and reduce over-tourism in the very centre of a city.

The study presented here is among the first dedicated to escape rooms as recreational tourism facilities and probably the first which is comprehensive, embracing both supply and demand. The lack of similar publications on other countries makes it impossible to conduct a comparative analysis. Thus, it cannot be asserted whether the obtained results are characteristic only of Poland, or whether they will be confirmed in different socioeconomic contexts. Perhaps similar publications will soon appear. It would also be interesting to have access to more detailed analyses of escape rooms in the context of heritage, creative and sustainable tourism or the over-tourism phenomenon in tourist cities.

NOTES

1. Poland belonged to the 'Big 7', that is the group of seven European countries with over 200 such establishments. The others are Spain, Great Britain, the Netherlands, Germany, France and Italy.
2. It is difficult, however, to define the scale of the crisis on the basis of available statistics, which show firms that are currently inactive but still remain formally registered.
3. This was another attempt, after pubs and hostels, to develop higher storeys of buildings in the very centre of Kraków (Kubal and Pawlusiński, 2016).
4. In 2016, the average price for a game in the ten cities was slightly below 94 PLN (highest in Warsaw: 120.61 PLN), while in 2018, it was already necessary to pay over 100 PLN in 32 places, with the highest prices in Warsaw (147.33 PLN), Wrocław (130.13 PLN) and Kraków (119.42 PLN). Prices in Budapest are at a similar level. The cost of one game for 2–6 people is HUF10–12,000 (Nagy et al., 2018).
5. It was possible to indicate several thematic groups.
6. Soldiers fighting against the Communist authorities after 1945.
7. There is no data for 2018, but it can be assumed that the effects were even better.
8. Similarly, Bakhsheshi (2019) reports that half of the 1,100 users of the Escape Room Lover blog in Iran include this activity in their travel plans, sometimes (29%) or always (21%).

REFERENCES

Al-Ababneh, M. and Masadeh, M. (2019) Creative cultural tourism as a new model for cultural tourism, *Journal of Tourism Management Research*, 6(2), 109–18.
Bakhsheshi, F.F. (2019) Escape rooms: A new phenomenon in tourism. In *2019 International Serious Games Symposium* (ISGS). IEEE, 38–41.
Bakhsheshi, F.F. and Ghaziani, G. (2019) Tourism based games: A study of challenges and profits. In *2019 International Serious Games Symposium* (ISGS). IEEE, 1–8.
Csíkszentmihályi, M. (1990) *Flow: The Psychology of Optimal Experience*. New York: Harper and Row.
Deterding, S., Dixon, D., Khaled, R. and Nacke, L.E. (2011) From game design elements to gamefulness: Defining 'gamification', *Mindtrek 2011 Proceedings*. Tampere, Finland: ACM Press.
Dilek, S.E. and Dilek, N.K. (2018) Real-life escape rooms as a new recreational attraction: The case of Turkey, *Anatolia*, 29(4), 1–12.
Gretzel, U. and Jamal, T. (2009) Conceptualizing the creative tourist class: Technology, mobility, and tourism experiences, *Tourism Analysis*, 14(4), 471–81.
Gündüz, Ş. (2018) Preventing Blue Ocean from turning into Red Ocean: A case study of a room escape game, *Journal of Human Sciences*, 15(1), 1–7.
Kaczmarek, J. and Paluch, M. (2015) Kreatywność turystyki vs. turystyka kreatywna – wstęp do dyskusji, *Turystyka Kulturowa*, 7, 54–76.
Kolar, T. (2017) Conceptualising tourist experiences with new attractions: The case of escape rooms, *International Journal of Contemporary Hospitality Management*, 29(5), 1322–39.
Kolar, T. and Čater, B. (2018) Managing group flow experiences in escape rooms, *International Journal of Contemporary Hospitality Management*, 30(7), 2637–61.
Kubal, M. and Pawlusiński, R. (2016) Escape rooms – Nowe zjawisko w przestrzeni turystycznej Krakowa, *Annales Universitatis Paedagogicae Cracoviensis Studia Geographica*, 221, 244–58.
Nagy, A., Petykó, C., Kiss, D.D. and Egedy, T. (2018) Kreatív turizmus Budapesten – Szabadulószobák az innovatív turisztikai piacon, *Turizmus Bulletin*, XVIII (4), 30–40.
Nawrot, A. (2019) *Funkcjonowanie escape rooms w Łodzi*. Masters thesis. Promoter: Andrzej Matczak. Łódź: Uniwersytet Łódzki.
Nicholson, S. (2015) Peeking behind the locked door: A survey of escape room facilities. White paper available at http://scottnicholson.com/pubs/erfacwhite.pdf (Accessed: 30 August 2020).
OECD (2014) *Tourism and the Creative Economy*, OECD Studies on Tourism, OECD Publishing. Available at: https://www.oecd.org/publications/tourism-and-the-creative-economy-9789264207875-en.htm (Accessed: 30 August 2020).

Pakhalov, A. and Rozhkova, N. (2020) Escape rooms as tourist attractions: Enhancing visitors' experience through new technologies. *Journal of Tourism, Heritage & Services Marketing*, 6(2), 55–60.

Pine, B.J. and Gilmore, J.H. (1999) *The Experience Economy: Work Is Theater & Every Business A Stage*. Boston, Massachusetts: Harvard Business School Press.

Plutchik, R. (1980) *Emotion: A Psychoevolutionary Synthesis*. New York: Harper and Row.

Qian Pink, L., Ridzuan Darun, M. and Nawanir, G. (2019) Decrypting the real-life escape room experience, *KnE Social Sciences*, 3(22), 385–407.

Richards, G. (2011) Creativity and tourism: The state of the art, *Annals of Tourism Research*, 38(4), 1225–53.

Rynek EscapeRoom w Polsce. Raport (2018). Available at: https://lockme.pl/userfiles/files/RynekERw Polsce_raport.pdf (Accessed: 30 August 2020).

Stasiak, A. (2016) Escape rooms – A new offer in the recreation sector in Poland, *Turyzm/Tourism*, 26(1), 31–47.

Stasiak, A. (2019) Escape rooms in Poland: A demand-led approach using netnographic research, *Turyzm/Tourism*, 29(1), 71–82.

Stasiak, A. (2021) Experience-centric strategy – Przejściowa moda czy trwały trend? In A. Rapacz (ed.) *Nowe wyzwania i możliwości rozwoju turystyki*. Wrocław: Wydawnictwo Uniwersytetu Ekonomicznego we Wrocławiu, 26–44.

Villar Lama, A. (2018) Ocio y turismo millennial: El fenómeno de las salas de escape, *Cuadernos de Turismo*, 41, 615–36.

Villar Lama, A. and García Martín, M. (2021) Decoding escape rooms from a tourism perspective: A global scale analysis, *Moravian Geographical Reports*, 29(1), 2–14.

Weber, J. (2014) Gaming and gamification in tourism – best practice report, Digital Tourism Think Tank, 1–14.

Xu, F., Buhalis, D. and Weber, J. (2017) Serious games and the gamification of tourism, *Tourism Management*, 60, 244–56.

18. Language tourism

Montserrat Iglesias

INTRODUCTION

The desire to travel has increasingly been coupled with the desire to learn a foreign language. Language trips can be experienced in several ways and contexts by different individuals, as illustrated in the following fictitious case examples. Jane started learning French at home last year. This middle-aged designer plans to leave her hometown in California to spend three months in Paris next spring, where she will take a general French language course in the mornings. In the afternoons, she will find out about the history of dressmaking through specialised French for fashion language classes. Klaus is an Erasmus student from Frankfurt who will take advanced Spanish language classes and continue his Bachelor's Degree in Hispanic Studies at the University of Barcelona for a semester. Luigi is 12 years old and this summer he will travel from Milano to Cork. He will attend English language classes and practise sports activities for four weeks at a summer camp based in Ireland. Camila would also like to learn English, so she will take care of two little children as an au-pair for nine months in Melbourne. Everything will be organised through an Argentinian au-pair agency. All of them have something in common: the purpose of their trips is to acquire a foreign language, and all will be using an array of touristic services, and so they will all become language tourists for some time.

Although the language tourism business has been growing for the past two decades, this phenomenon has so far been under-researched by academicians (Castillo Arredondo et al., 2018; Iglesias, 2015b; Redondo-Carretero et al., 2017). This chapter aims at filling this research gap and analyses language tourism as a micro-niche within the educational tourism market.

Niche tourism as 'a more sophisticated set of practices that distinguish and differentiate tourists' (Robinson and Novelli, 2005: 1) has been compared to mainstream tourism, which has been associated with larger numbers of people in staged settings. From the supply tourism planning and management perspective, such diversity enables more sustainable activities, while from the demand-side it offers more meaningful experiences, since it is tailored to specific market segments. For Robinson and Novelli (2005) tourism niches have not only been seen as a response to growing specific consumers' demands, but also as a competitive strategy in order to attract new markets. This entails extraordinary business opportunities for small companies providing their expertise and personalised services, as well as for some destinations associated with very specific touristic offers (Marson, 2011; Robinson and Novelli, 2005).

This conceptual chapter discusses language tourism's idiosyncrasy with a special focus on its global sustainability potential, and is grounded on research conducted in this field during the last decade. The chapter commences with conceptualising language tourism and the tourism niches it is related with. Next, an account of the main characteristics and impacts of language tourism activities is provided. To conclude, an overview of further research lines and proposals in relation to language tourism after the COVID-19 pandemic are presented.

THE LANGUAGE TOURISM MICRO-NICHE

This section of the chapter examines the position of language trips from a niche tourism perspective in relation to both educational and cultural tourism. As there has been no definitive scholarly systematic analysis of language tourism, this topic will be explored from various angles and alternating perspectives.

The World Tourism Organization (UNWTO) has categorised tourism according to the main purpose of the trip and the main touristic activities linked to it (UNWTO, 2010). When travelling for personal purposes as opposed to business and professional reasons, one of the key segments of tourism demand is driven by education and training, with a specific reference made to formal or informal study programmes and the acquisition of specific competences, including language skills:

> Education tourism covers those types of tourism which have as a primary motivation the tourist's engagement and experience in learning, self-improvement, intellectual growth and skills development. Education Tourism represents a broad range of products and services related to academic studies, skill enhancement holidays, school trips, sports training, career development courses and language courses, among others. (UNWTO, 2019: 52)

More specifically, UNWTO identifies students taking courses for less than one year as tourists, while those enrolled in study abroad programmes for one year or more cannot be considered tourists. UNWTO also states that subcategories can be proposed as an additional level of classification, and that this is precisely the case of those tourists motivated by education and learning (UNWTO, 2010). Thus, the macro-niche of educational tourism encompasses different subsegments. In the *SAGE International Encyclopedia of Travel and Tourism*, three forms of educational travel activity are pinpointed: excursions or field trips in higher education, research tours and expeditions carried out by scientists, and cultural touristic activities undertaken by individuals who have an interest in foreign languages or history (Rundshagen, 2017). This conceptualisation of educational tourism alludes to some elements that share a learning component and are frequently mentioned in the research literature, such as higher education, cultural activities, and foreign languages. Nevertheless, in the past there has been limited consensus on the scope and the interrelations between cultural tourism, educational tourism, language tourism, and academic tourism. The higher education market, referred to by some authors as academic tourism (Martínez-Roget and Rodríguez, 2021), is a micro-segment of educational tourism which can be combined with language tourism (Iglesias, 2021). As for cultural tourism, UNWTO gives the following operational definition:

> It is a type of tourism activity in which the visitor's essential motivation is to learn, discover, experience and consume the tangible and intangible cultural attractions/products in a tourism destination. These attractions/products relate to a set of distinctive material, intellectual, spiritual and emotional features of a society that encompasses arts and architecture, historical and cultural heritage, culinary heritage, literature, music, creative industries and the living cultures with their lifestyles, value systems, beliefs and traditions. (UNWTO, 2019: 30)

Language is a key element of a community's cultural identity and constitutes a vehicle for oral traditions and expressions, which is one of the domains of intangible cultural heritage (UNESCO, 2003). This is why travelling to acquire language skills has also been categorised within cultural tourism (Iglesias, 2017b; Iglesias and Feng, 2017; Piédrola Ortiz, Artacho

Ruiz and Villaseca Molina, 2012; Redondo-Carretero et al., 2017; Taboada Zúñiga Romero, 2012). On the other hand, taking into account that a major motivation for both educational and cultural tourists is learning, as stated by UNWTO (2019), educational tourism and cultural tourism are very closely linked, and boundaries are blurred. Whether educational tourism can be viewed under the umbrella of cultural tourism or not, most authors seem to agree that language tourism is a micro-niche of the educational tourism market, in line with UNWTO's definition of educational tourism (Aliaga et al., 2018; Barra, Marco and Cachero, 2019; Gómez et al., 2018; Iglesias, 2016a; Martínez-Roget and Rodríguez, 2021).

The position of educational tourism is contested, with some authors considering it a micro-niche of cultural tourism (Robinson and Novelli, 2005), while other authors have viewed these two forms of tourism as separate niches (Marson, 2011). For Richards (2011), due to the increased popular consumption of culture, one of the main macro-niches is cultural tourism, which is comprised of a number of different micro-segments. Richards considers language tourism and educational tourism to be separate micro-niches alongside religious tourism, gastronomic tourism, wellness and spa tourism, creative tourism, volunteer tourism, and spiritual and holistic tourism. More specifically, the language tourism micro-niche is considered an important market in those destinations where tuition of key global languages is offered, often in combination with local cultural activities (Richards, 2011).

Menzel and Weldig (2011) offer another micro-segmentation breakdown of the educational tourism niche based on different primary learning objectives complemented with recreation: guided study trips, language learning sojourns, and stays to attend professionally related conferences or seminars. These authors consider that language tourism may be the most significant micro-niche within educational tourism due to the global demand to learn English, Spanish, and Chinese. This underlies the design of study programmes and leisure activities in the countries where these target languages are spoken (Menzel and Weldig, 2011).

Ritchie, a reference author in terms of conceptualising educational tourism, has distinguished between purposeful study trips and trips that include learning elements (Ritchie, 2003). He outlines two main markets: on one hand, adults and seniors engaging in edu-tourism (i.e., education-first) activities, and on the other, school and higher education students who take part in tourism-first activities where recreation and leisure are prioritised over education. His proposal of an educational tourism market system is based on socioeconomic, demographic, psychographic, and geographic segmentation from a systems perspective.

McGladdery and Lubbe (2017) present educational tourism as a transformative experience that is outcomes-based and process-driven. According to these authors, educational tourism experiences can be very varied in nature, from informal self-discovery trips to formal courses. They can be aimed at all age segments as long as a desire to learn exists, the experience is adequately designed and staged, and the process of learning has behavioural, affective, and cognitive outcomes. Furthermore, educational tourism can be conducive to global peace deriving from global learning, and has a considerable hybridisation potential with other touristic and non-touristic segments and sectors (McGladdery and Lubbe, 2017). Since language travel is an educational experience, all these features also characterise it.

In order to reconcile the contested views that have been presented in this section and situate language tourism with respect to educational tourism and cultural tourism, an unambiguous stance has been adopted for the remainder of the chapter. Thus, language tourism is considered a micro-niche of educational tourism, and educational tourism is in turn regarded as part of cultural tourism. More specifically, language tourism can be defined as 'a tourist activity undertaken by those travellers (or educational tourists) taking a trip which includes at least an overnight stay in a destination outside their usual place of residence for less than a year and for whom language learning is a primary or secondary part of their trip' (Iglesias, 2016a: 31). The next section gives a more detailed account of language tourism activities.

CHARACTERISTICS AND IMPACTS OF LANGUAGE TOURISM

Looking at language travel as an idiosyncratic phenomenon, a fundamental question to bear in mind is what distinguishes it from other educational tourist niches. Two major interrelated characteristics can be clearly identified: firstly, the motivation to learn a foreign language, i.e., the target language that is the main purpose of the trip; secondly, the fact that all language tourism experiences require a key element which determines the rest of the components, namely some sort of linguistic input other than the tourists' own language. Unlike language tourists, other educational tourists can take part in study abroad or domestic programmes where learning may or may not be facilitated in their mother tongues. Instead, specialised language tourism products and destinations cater precisely to the linguistic interests of language learners. In all language tourists' stays the main educational input is the target language, which also becomes an indispensable touristic resource. These considerations underlie the typification of language tourism as a distinct micro-niche.

Even though most language tourists receive formal tuition through courses in a wide range of settings as part of their tourist experience (Iglesias, 2017a), foreign language acquisition also takes place in informal learning contexts where the linguistic input is not specifically facilitated by educators, for example, in the case of au-pairs staying with host families (Aliaga et al., 2018). Therefore, language tourism can take place in formal and/or informal educational environments.

There seems to be a consensus among researchers that the language tourism micro-niche is characterised by longer stays and higher expenditure than in mass tourism (Gómez et al., 2018; Piédrola Órtiz, Artacho Ruiz and Villaseca Molina, 2012; Taboada de Zúñiga Romero, 2010). Formal language learning environments include courses that range from intensive periods of a few weeks to academic stays of up to one year, longer stays being more usual for language tourists in secondary or higher education. For instance, an annual survey conducted by Study Travel among inbound language tourists studying Japanese in Japan in 2019 reported that their average length of stay was 26 weeks (Norris, 2021). As language tourism experiences can occur all year round and not just in the summer, seasonality is not a driving force, so the economic impact is significant (Barra, Marco and Cachero, 2019; Redondo-Carretero et al., 2017; Taboada de Zúñiga Romero, 2010).

The characteristics of language tourism are usually related to its benefits. Language tourists who spend a longer period in their destinations use public transport networks and move around by bicycle or on foot (Iglesias, 2017b), so their carbon footprint is often lower than that of traditional tourists. Moreover, unlike mainstream tourists, language tourists tend to stay in student residence halls, shared apartments, or homestay accommodation. These accommodation options, in addition, have more positive sociocultural impacts for the visitors and the residents, as they favour more fruitful interactions (Iglesias, 2017b; Iglesias et al., 2019).

In contrast with traditional mass visitors, long-stay language tourists are keen to integrate through acculturation processes (Iglesias, 2016a) and look for authentic encounters with the local community in the destination (O'Rourke and DePalma, 2017). Language tourism providers, in turn, increasingly try to avoid trivialisation. In order to facilitate meaningful interactions with the host community members and provide opportunities for first-hand knowledge of the local culture and lifestyle, they organise cultural activities and use the services of local suppliers, like language exchanges with local students in bars or language schools (Iglesias, 2017b). This effective experiential approach contributes to reducing the tension between the commodification of linguistic and cultural assets and the authentication of a community's heritage and resources (O'Rourke and DePalma, 2017).

Other considerable sociocultural benefits for both the language tourists and the hosts are linked to strengthening cultural identities, promoting the local culture internationally, and activating cultural services and complementary leisure activities, as well as getting to know and appreciate heritage (Redondo-Carretero et al., 2017). A unique characteristic of language tourism is that, unlike other cultural resources that remain unaltered over time, languages change to meet new communicative needs, so linguistic resources evolve constantly (Gómez et al., 2018). They are intangible heritage assets that can be viewed as a pull factor for visitors. The cities with rich heritage and historic universities are very appealing for language tourists (Taboada de Zúñiga Romero, 2010), together with coastal locations (Campón and Hernández, 2011; Redondo-Carretero et al., 2017). Therefore, language tourism experiences can be connected intimately or tangentially with different cultural and natural attractions.

Language tourists tend to create strong bonds with locals, develop destination loyalty, return frequently, have a multiplying effect as they also attract their friends and relatives to the target destination, and eventually become destinations' cultural ambassadors worldwide (Iglesias, 2017b; Piédrola Órtiz, Artacho Ruiz and Villaseca Molina, 2012; Redondo-Carretero et al., 2017; Taboada de Zúñiga Romero, 2010). After researching language tourists with an interest in learning a minoritised language, O'Rourke and DePalma (2017) have concluded that they can also serve as cultural promoters for their hosts. Tourists' ideological commitment and relationship with the destination can contribute to changing residents' attitudes towards their own local community, providing a positive reorientation. Additionally, language as a vehicle for interaction among individuals from varied cultural backgrounds helps to raise awareness and modify the value system of the participants – that is, tourists, residents, professionals, and administrators – who undergo personal transformation. Such values are related to global citizenship, multiculturalism, tolerance, and inclusiveness (Iglesias, 2017b).

To gain a full understanding of the distinctive nature and scope of this micro-niche, a comprehensive taxonomy of the various aspects that shape language tourism experiences has been produced by Iglesias (2015a, 2015b, 2016a, 2016b, 2016c, 2017a, 2017b; Iglesias and Feng, 2017) grounded on Ritchie's conceptualisation of educational tourism (Ritchie, 2003). Figure 18.1 shows an array of aspects related with language tourists as key components of the language tourism market system.

With respect to the demand, the language tourists' demographics, perceptions, motivations, and travel behaviours must be taken into account. In turn, the supply encompasses elements connected with language destinations' resources, management and marketing, and product configuration, as depicted in Figure 18.2. These are also fundamental components of the language tourism market system that play an important role in designing, planning, and staging memorable experiences.

A fine-grained categorisation and description of the language tourism market system is the first step towards a more detailed analysis of the language tourism micro-niche. In this respect,

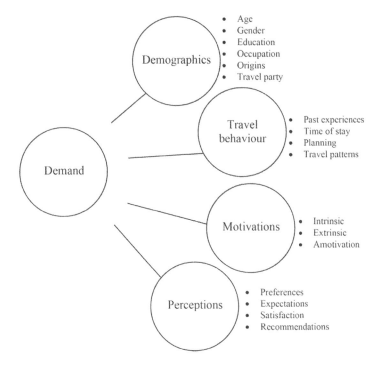

Figure 18.1   *Language tourism demand*

different typologies of tourists, products, and activities can be established depending on which element of the market system is put in the spotlight. Thus, language tourism can be segmented in terms of tourists' age ranges, inner motivations, previous knowledge of the target language, the length and period of their stay, the language education providers, or the type of accommodation used (Iglesias, 2022). Figure 18.3 shows all these typologies and the position of this micro-niche in relation with the other niches described in the previous section.

This segmentation can be useful for experiential design and promotion in order to tailor to specific needs and evaluate the resulting impacts (Ritchie, 2003; UNWTO, 2010). However, the eclecticism of touristic behaviours, activities, and motivations makes categorisation difficult, and setting clear-cut typologies is a challenge for tourism marketing (Robinson and Novelli, 2005). For example, a language tourist may also be a backpacker or an adventure traveller simultaneously. Indeed, gastronomic tourism, beach tourism, agro-tourism, voluntourism, and language tourism can be combined in the same trip (Iglesias, 2017a), so language tourism can interplay with other tourism niches or be an added product. In order to market educational trips, hybridisation and new multi-varied segment approaches are therefore increasingly necessary owing to the blurring of categorisations when it comes to the consumption patterns and value systems of different generations of travellers, including sustainability concerns (Wee, 2019).

In the next section the most relevant aspects of language tourism experiences are related to the United Nation's Sustainable Development Goals (SDGs) in accordance with UNWTO's general guidelines (UNWTO and United Nations Development Programme, 2017).

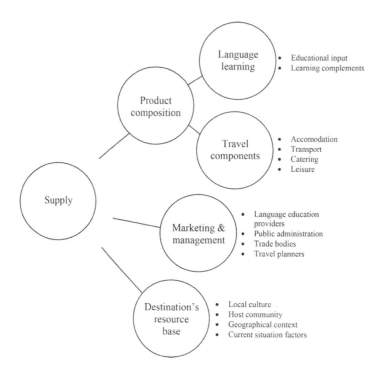

Figure 18.2   Language tourism supply

LANGUAGE TOURISM AND SDGs

A wide range of SDGs can be met through developing and promoting language tourism. The impacts of this micro-niche on sustainability are illustrated next by describing how language tourism can be used to support specific SDGs.

In relation to SDG 8 ('Promote sustained, inclusive and sustainable economic growth, employment and decent work for all') and SDG 10 ('Reduce inequality within and among countries'), language tourism activities can lead to economic growth and development, enabling developing countries like Mexico and Argentina to have greater weight in the global economy. After Spain, these two countries are the most popular language tourism destinations for learners of Spanish (Iglesias, 2021), so all are in the same league in respect of Spanish language tourism. The language tourism micro-niche can also be a source of livelihood in many regions, since it involves opportunities for direct, indirect, and induced jobs in education, tourism, hospitality, and commerce (Taboada de Zúñiga Romero, 2010). The economic impact has a broad scope given the numerous supply components within the language tourism market system with regard to both language learning and tourism services, i.e., accommodation, catering, transport, and leisure (Campón and Hernández, 2011; Iglesias, 2017a; Redondo-Carretero et al., 2017). More specifically, the most significant economic impacts have been reported in terms of employment and income regarding accommodation and the education sector (Barra, Marco and Cachero, 2019). A growing language tourism industry also spurs entrepreneurship (Campón and Hernández, 2011; Taboada de Zúñiga Romero, 2010) not only in larger-scale organisations, but also in micro- and medium-sized enterprises, like language schools. In

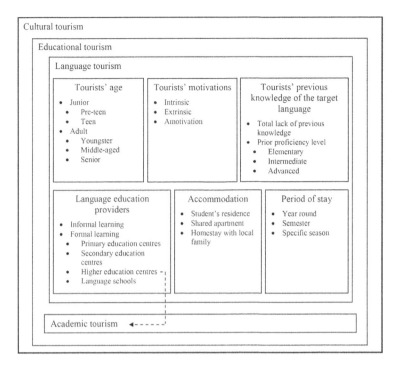

Figure 18.3   *Language tourism typologies*

addition, language tourism also facilitates income provision through jobs with medium or low skills requirements, for example, for support staff at students' residences. Homestays can be an inclusive source of revenue for local families that welcome language students with just a few prior orientation guidelines (Aliaga et al., 2018). This benefits local families and reduces economic leakage, as incomes stay within the local community. Therefore, sustained economic growth and employment is promoted.

With respect to SDG 5 ('Achieve gender equality and empower all women and girls'), the recruitment of a local workforce can serve to empower less advantaged groups by facilitating income-generating opportunities for elderly people and women (OECD, 2020). In their study of the role of accommodation in the language tourism micro-niche, Aliaga et al. (2018) reported that host families were contacted by language tourism agencies via a women's entrepreneurial forum. Most agencies relied on retired hosts who lived alone, and hosting language tourists was an incentive that complemented their pension plan. Alongside economic motivations for hosting international students, cultural and emotional benefits for this specific collective were also perceived (Aliaga et al., 2018).

As for SDG 4 ('Ensure inclusive and equitable quality education and promote lifelong learning for all'), due to the nature of language tourism experiences with core educational and cultural components, they foster lifelong learning, particularly as regards key linguistic competences that incentivise personal and professional growth (Castillo Arredondo et al., 2018; Iglesias, 2017b). This can be applied not only to language travellers, but also to language teachers and tourism services providers. Ongoing staff training allows for the professional development of a skilled workforce, and cross-border agreements encourage international labour mobility, for instance, in the case of language teachers from partner higher education institutions. Language tourists who volunteer to collaborate with local associations can also contribute to host communities' lifelong learning. Iglesias (2017b) gives an account of how American university students learning Spanish in Barcelona cooperate with a Spanish association to help children with hearing impairments. The programme Allies in English (https://t-oigo.com) makes it possible for these language tourists to visit hearing-impaired children and engage them in play while using English, which helps children become more proficient in this language (Iglesias, 2017b). Besides gaining knowledge of foreign languages and cultures, local residents also learn more about their own while they are acting as hosts (Aliaga et al., 2018), and value their local culture more (O'Rourke and DePalma, 2017). Language tourism can thus contribute to inclusive education and lifelong learning.

Concerning SDG 11 ('Make cities and human settlements inclusive, safe, resilient and sustainable') and SDG 13 ('Take urgent action to combat climate change and its impacts'), longer stays by language tourists have been associated with the use of less polluting methods of transport (i.e., public transport, walking, or cycling) and accommodation options that are more environmentally friendly than large hotel chains (i.e., student residence halls, shared apartments, or homestays), especially in coastal areas (Iglesias, 2017b; Iglesias et al., 2019). On the other hand, language tourists are often integrated in formal educational contexts, where sustainability and climate change are regarded as cross-curricular topics for oral discussion and written essays, and eco-friendly measures like recycling are encouraged. This may result in the adoption of more respectful behaviours among local and international students, and facilitate a change in their usual waste disposal routines. Language tourists can also complement language learning with volunteering projects like cleaning beaches and forests or restoring monuments as part of their tourist experience. Since the local culture and the destinations' natural and cultural heritage are a pull factor for language tourists, these visitors respect and value them (Redondo-Carretero et al., 2017). Such appreciation has a mirror effect for the local administrations and communities, who see their own resources with new eyes (O'Rourke and DePalma, 2017), and may take greater care of them. It is through these opportunities that SDG 15 'Protect, restore and promote sustainable use of terrestrial ecosystems and halt biodiversity loss' can be supported.

SDG 16 ('Promote peaceful and inclusive societies, provide access to justice for all and build inclusive institutions') and SDG 11 ('Make cities and human settlements inclusive, safe, resilient and sustainable') can be achieved through sustained contact between local community members and language tourists, united though the target language. Their intercultural relationships foster mutual understanding, respect for diversity, non-discrimination policies, and violence prevention. These values lay the basis for more peaceful societies, particularly in post-conflict contexts, and can be a way to fight negative attitudes, for instance in overcrowded destinations. In those destinations, language tourists show more respectful behaviour and residents tend to modify their rejection towards them and value their efforts to learn the target language (Iglesias et al., 2019).

Finally, with regard to SDG 12 ('Ensure sustainable consumption and production patterns'), language tourists seek integration and authentic interactions with the host community (Iglesias, 2016a; O'Rourke and DePalma, 2017). They try to practise the target language, adopt the local lifestyle, and are more prone to engage in sustainable consumption practices, for example, when buying items in a shop next door, having fun at local nightclubs, or working out at a neighbouring gym (Iglesias, 2017b). In this vein, the language tourism activities that are carried out in rural areas deserve a special mention. They can be combined with agro-tourism and generate extra revenue for the local communities, while fostering fair trade of local produce and offering a valuable experience for language tourists. Farm stays and language summer camps in the countryside are increasingly popular, since a language learning sojourn in a rural area can be a significantly sustainable alternative, offers remarkable immersion opportunities, and is more personalised and authentic (Campón and Hernández, 2011). All in all, the sustainable benefits associated with the language tourism micro-niche by itself or in combination with other touristic niches must highlighted and promoted.

CONCLUDING REMARKS

This chapter has contributed to further understanding the niche tourism field by presenting an argued view of language tourism as a micro-niche of educational tourism. Despite its growth, language travel has scarcely been studied (Barra, Marco and Cachero, 2019; Gómez et al., 2018; Iglesias, 2021). This is surprising given the extraordinary prospects for specific educational products aimed at different demographic segments (McGladdery and Lubbe, 2017) and the entailed diversification opportunities (Barra, Marco and Cachero, 2019; Campón and Hernández, 2011). Consequently, exploring its suitability as an alternative to other traditionally prevailing tourism models such as mass tourism is highly relevant. It must be born in mind that due to the COVID-19 pandemic many destinations have realised that having a narrow approach and relying on the same touristic resources have made them overdependent and more vulnerable (Brouder et al., 2020), hence the interest in investigating diverse tourism niches and developing them. The global crisis caused by the COVID-19 pandemic and its impact on tourism in the short- and long-term can be regarded as both a challenge and an opportunity to rethink the tourism ecosystem. The disruptive effects can spearhead new approaches towards problems like the need for more responsible behaviour from a more sustainable perspective (Koh, 2020). The last part of this chapter offers some final considerations and recommendations concerning the role of the language tourism micro-niche in a post-pandemic scenario.

The dramatic reduction of international tourism flows due to the COVID-19 pandemic was particularly critical for language travel, since it is predominantly an overseas activity. Domestic tourism was encouraged to enhance the local value chain (UNWTO, 2020) and rebounded faster, so it was specially promoted in those geographical areas that were more dependent on tourism (OECD, 2020). The opportunities for immersive foreign language learning experiences within the same country or in nearby countries go beyond that critical period. A domestic language sojourn like a summer camp for children or youngsters, where they can learn a foreign language in combination with adventure sports or farming, broadens business prospects for local language tourism providers. For language tourists it is more affordable than transcontinental trips, aligns with SDGs, as already mentioned, and meets safety concerns (Tonda and Iglesias, 2021). Fostering special interest experiences targeted at individual travellers and small groups is one of the guidelines proposed by UNWTO, together with developing segmented products focusing on culture, nature, and rural settings and promoting new destinations with local inspiration and added value (UNWTO, 2020).

As for long-haul travel, longer stays abroad should be encouraged, since they are more potentially transformational (Brouder et al., 2020) and they support year-round activity, two features associated with the language tourism micro-niche. This allows for a redistribution of the benefits among recipients other than large multinational organisations, for example, among local language learning institutions, host families, or student residence halls. In addition, long-term language learning sojourns produce a reduced carbon footprint caused by transport with respect to shorter frequent journeys, so the positive effects on climate change are also a contribution towards the SDGs. Taking into account that visa restrictions are a major obstacle for some international language students (Iglesias, 2016a), the facilitation of visa policies recommended by UNWTO must be born in mind (UNWTO, 2020).

FINAL RECOMMENDATIONS

The 'new normal' scenario involves a new notion of hospitality, where trust and mutual respect between visitors and residents are key (Brouder et al., 2020). The challenge for host communities is to avoid new tourismphobic attitudes, and the opportunity for previously overcrowded destinations is to adopt more sustainable measures than in the past (OECD, 2020). In this respect, language tourism has a valid role to play, and effective local policies and marketing campaigns should be carried out to highlight the benefits of language tourism activities among visitors and local populations, for example, in terms of encouraging meaningful integration through volunteering and language exchange projects. Furthermore, language tourism destinations can attract repeat loyal visitors who wish to continue improving their linguistic skills in familiar environments perceived as safe, by underscoring attributes like the local language and offering a wide range of hybrid language acquisition experiences, such as language learning and creative tourism.

The rapid proliferation of online language learning initiatives and resources may be seen as a threat to language tourism. However, virtual learning or augmented reality should rather be considered a complement to than a competitor of immersive language tourism activities, since the linguistic acquisition and the holistic touristic experiences facilitated through immersion have a wider range of long-lasting transformational impacts. Another challenge for the language tourism industry is to manage unknowns and uncertainty, and also to meet digitalisation requirements. Being digitally updated can be fundamental to obtaining and offering personalised information on the demand, the destination, travel services, and language learning support before, during, and after the stay. For instance, it is best practice to find out well in advance if language tourists prefer to stay with local families and enjoy more personalised care, stay in student residence halls where safety protocols are applied and monitored, or share apartments where contact can be restricted more easily, since increased hygiene and risk assessment are important matters for travellers.

The above-mentioned threats and challenges can be the focus of further research. For this purpose, the creation of an international observatory of language tourism is highly recommended in order to collect data and foster research and knowledge on several aspects (Iglesias et al., 2019), such as new consumer patterns or successful governance policies. Thus, academia would be able to contribute with research and look for solutions to the industry's problems, while the industry would provide professional expertise and up-to-date first-hand data. An international observatory of language tourism could also be a catalyst to establish partnerships and collaboration agreements across sectors and domains to share information and facilitate sustainable strategic planning and implementation worldwide. This initiative would be in line with SDG 17, which involves 'strengthening the means of implementation and revitalising the global partnership for sustainable development' (UNWTO and United Nations Development Programme, 2017: 16–17).

The cooperation between tourism principals, educational institutions, and providers of complementary services must be strategically planned and monitored. Moreover, the involvement of all stakeholders – including the governments, related industries, host communities, and visitors – must be strengthened at local, regional, national, and international levels (Campón and Hernández, 2011; Gómez et al., 2018; Piédrola Órtiz, Artacho Ruiz and Villaseca Molina, 2012; Redondo-Carretero et al., 2017; Taboada de Zúñiga Romero, 2010). For the language tourism micro-niche to flourish sustainably, public and private partnership agreements must be reached and maintained in the long term, so there is still a long way to go.

REFERENCES

Aliaga, B., Corno, V., Iglesias, M., Luengo, C. and Puigneró, J. (2018) Trips of the tongue: Language tourism in Barcelona. *Ara Journal of Tourism Research*, 8(1), 7–20. Available at: http://revistes.ub .edu/index.php/ara/article/view/20092 (accessed 12 December 2020).

Barra, P., Marco, B. and Cachero, C. (2019) Economic impact of language tourism on mature sun and sand destinations: The case of Alicante (Spain). *Tourism Economics*, 25(6), 923–41. doi: 10.1177/1354816618811556.

Brouder, P., Teoh, S., Salazar, N.B., Mostafanezhad, M., Pung, J.M., Lapointe, D., Higgins Desbiolles, F., Haywood, M., Hall, C.M. and Balslev Clausen, H. (2020) Reflections and discussions: Tourism matters in the new normal post COVID-19. *Tourism Geographies*, 22(3), 735–46. doi: 10.1080/14616688.2020.1770325.

Campón, A.M. and Hernández, J.M. (2011) Turismo idiomático en el medio rural: Una propuesta para su desarrollo y comercialización. *TURyDES. Revista de Investigación y desarrollo local*, 4(10). Available at: http://www.eumed.net/rev/turydes/10/cchm.htm (accessed 29 July 2020).

Castillo Arredondo, M.I., Rodríguez Zapatero, M.I., Pérez Naranjo, L.M. and López-Guzmán, T. (2018) Motivations of educational tourists in non-English-speaking countries: The role of languages. *Journal of Travel and Tourism Marketing*, 35(4), 437–48. doi: 10.1080/10548408.2017.1358238.

Gómez, M., Imhoff, B., Martín-Consuegra, D., Molina, A. and Santos-Vijande, M.L. (2018) Language tourism: The drivers that determine destination choice intention among U.S. students. *Tourism Management Perspectives*, 27, 125–35. doi: 10.1016/j.tmp.2018.06.001.

Iglesias, M. (2015a) Second language acquisition and the language tourism experience. *Procedia. Social and Behavioral Sciences*, 178, 139–45. doi: 10.1016/j.sbspro.2015.03.170.

Iglesias, M. (2015b) Language travel demand: New insights into language tourists' perceptions. *Procedia. Social and Behavioral Sciences*, 199, 149–56. doi: 10.1016/j.sbspro.2015.07.499.

Iglesias, M. (2016a) The language tourism market system: Conceptualising language tourism. *International Journal of Scientific Management and Tourism*, 2(1), 25–40. Available at: http://www .ijosmt.com/index.php/ijosmt/article/view/69/79 (accessed 5 August 2020).

Iglesias, M. (2016b) Language travel supply: The language learning programme. *Procedia. Social and Behavioral Sciences*, 232, 242–49. doi: 10.1016/j.sbspro.2016.10.010.

Iglesias, M. (2016c) Language travel supply: Marketing and management structures. *International Conference on Tourism (ICOT 2016)*. Naples, Università degli Studi di Napoli Federico II, International Association for Tourism Policy (IATOUR), 29 June – 2 July.

Iglesias, M. (2017a) Language travel supply: Language tourism product composition. *International Online Journal of Education and Teaching (IOJET)*, 4(1), 1–17. Available at: http://iojet.org/index .php/IOJET/article/view/135/145 (accessed 3 August 2020).

Iglesias, M. (2017b) The role of travel-related aspects in the language tourism experience. *Enlightening Tourism. A Pathmaking Journal*, 7(2), 125–53. doi: 10.33776/et.v7i2.3153.

Iglesias, M. (2021) Language tourism in higher education: An overview. In J.P. Cerdeira Bento, F. Martínez-Roget, E.T. Pereira and X.A. Rodríguez (eds) *Academic Tourism*. Cham: Springer, 85–100. doi: 10.1007/978-3-030-57288-4_6.

Iglesias, M. (2022) Language tourism. In D. Buhalis (ed.) *Encyclopedia of Tourism Management and Marketing*. Cheltenham, UK and Northampton, MA, USA: Edward Elgar Publishing. doi: 10.4337/9781800377486.language.tourism.

Iglesias, M. and Feng, Y. (2017) Language travel supply: The case of Idealog. *International Journal of Scientific Management and Tourism*, 3(3), 91–110. Available at: http://www.ijosmt.com/index.php/ijosmt/article/view/249/237 (accessed 3 August 2020).

Iglesias, M., Aliaga, B., Corno, V., Luengo, C. and Puigneró, J. (2019) The sociocultural impacts of language tourism in Barcelona. *Ottoman: Journal of Tourism and Management Research*, 4(1), 348–64. doi: 10.26465/ojtmr.2018339519.

Koh, E. (2020) The end of over-tourism? Opportunities in a post-Covid-19 world. *International Journal of Tourism Cities*, 6(4), 1015–23. doi: 10.1108/IJTC-04-2020-0080.

McGladdery, C.A. and Lubbe, B.A. (2017) Rethinking educational tourism: Proposing a new model and future directions. *Tourism Review*, 72(3), 319–29. doi: 10.1108/TR-03-2017-0055.

Marson, D. (2011) From mass tourism to niche tourism. In P. Robinson, S. Heitmann and P. Dieke (eds) *Research Themes for Tourism*. Wallingford: CABI, 1–15.

Martínez-Roget F. and Rodríguez X.A. (2021) Academic tourism: conceptual and theoretical issues. In J.P. Cerdeira Bento, F. Martínez-Roget, E.T. Pereira and X.A. Rodríguez (eds) *Academic Tourism*. Cham: Springer, 7–20. doi: 10.1007/978-3-030-57288-4_2.

Menzel N. and Weldig A. (2011) Educational tourism. In A. Papathanassis (ed.) *The Long Tail of Tourism*. Wiesbaden: Gabler, 201–11. doi: 10.1007/978-3-8349-6231-7_21.

Norris B. (2021) Direction: Global languages market report. *Study Travel Magazine*, 311(January/February), 31. Available at: http://studytravel-magazine-pdfs.azurewebsites.net/janfeb21web/ (accessed 28 August 2021).

OECD. (2020) *Tourism Policy Responses to the Coronavirus (COVID-19)*. Available at: https://read.oecd-ilibrary.org/view/?ref=124_124984-7uf8nm95se&title=Covid-19_Tourism_Policy_Responses (accessed 20 August 2020).

O'Rourke, B. and DePalma, R. (2017) Language-learning holidays: What motivates people to learn a minority language? *International Journal of Multilingualism*, 14(4), 332–49. doi: 10.1080/14790718.2016.1184667.

Piédrola Órtiz I., Artacho Ruiz C. and Villaseca Molina E.J. (2012) Tourism and learn spanish in historic cities: A case study in Córdoba. In A. Gil-Lafuente, J. Gil-Lafuente and J. Merigó-Lindahl (eds) *Soft Computing in Management and Business Economics*. Berlin, Heidelberg: Springer, 305–18. doi: 10.1007/978-3-642-30451-4_21.

Redondo-Carretero, M., Camarero-Izquierdo, C., Gutiérrez-Arranz, A. and Rodríguez-Pinto, J. (2017) Language tourism destinations: A case study of motivations, perceived value and tourists' expenditure. *Journal of Cultural Economics*, 41(2), 155–72. doi: 10.1007/s10824-017-9296-y.

Richards, G. (2011) Cultural tourism trends in Europe: A context for the development of cultural routes. In K. Khovanova-Rubicondo (ed.) *Impact of European Cultural Routes on SMEs' Innovation and Competitiveness*. Strasbourg: Council of Europe Publishing, 21–39. Available at: http://www.coe.int/t/dg4/cultureheritage/culture/routes/StudyCR_en.pdf (accessed 10 December 2020).

Ritchie, B.W. (2003) An introduction to educational tourism. In B.W. Ritchie, N. Carr and C. Cooper (eds) *Managing Educational Tourism*. Clevedon: Channel View Publications, 1–24.

Robinson, M. and Novelli, M. (2005) Niche tourism: An introduction. In M. Novelli (ed.) *Niche Tourism: Contemporary Issues*. Oxford: Elsevier, 1–11.

Rundshagen, V. (2017) Educational tourism. In L.L. Lowry (ed.) *The SAGE International Encyclopedia of Travel and Tourism*. Thousand Oaks, CA: Sage, 405–8.

Taboada de Zúñiga Romero, P. (2012) The teaching of Spanish as a sustainable resource for tourism. In J. Mondejar-Jimenez, G. Ferrari and M. Vargas-Vargas (eds) *Research Studies on Tourism and Environment*. New York: Nova Science Publishers, 289–312.

Tonda, L. and Iglesias, M. (2021) Analysis of domestic language tourism in Spain. *Studia Periegetica*, 35(3), 109–28. doi: 10.5604/01.3001.0015.6393.

UNESCO (2003) *Convention for the Safeguarding of the Intangible Cultural Heritage*. Available at: http://www.unesco.org/culture/ich/en/convention (accessed 10 August 2020).

UNWTO (2010) *International Recommendations for Tourism Statistics 2008*. Available at: http://unstats.un.org/unsd/publication/Seriesm/SeriesM_83rev1e.pdf (accessed 10 August 2020).

UNWTO (2019) *UNWTO Tourism Definitions*. Madrid: UNWTO. doi: 10.18111/9789284420858.

UNWTO (2020) *Global Guidelines to Restart Tourism*. Available at: https://webunwto.s3.eu-west -1.amazonaws.com/s3fs-public/2020-05/UNWTO-Global-Guidelines-to-Restart-Tourism.pdf (accessed 20 August 2020).

UNWTO and United Nations Development Programme (2017) *Tourism and the Sustainable Development Goals. Journey to 2030*. Madrid: UNWTO. doi: 10.18111/9789284419401.

Wee, D. (2019) Generation Z talking: Transformative experience in educational travel. *Journal of Tourism Futures*, 5(2), 157–67. doi: 10.1108/JTF-02-2019-0019.

19. In focus 3 – contemporary arts tourism in West Africa

Marina Novelli, Maria Pia Bernardoni and Clive Allanso

The contemporary arts period is generally associated with arts produced since the 1960s. If we fast forward to the last 20 years, a process of 'cultural diplomacy' involving both leading cultural institutions such as the Venice Biennale, and international museums like the British Museum, the Berlin Stiftung Preußischer Kulturbesitz, the London Victoria & Albert Museum, the Shanghai M50 and the Hong Kong M+ has aimed at stimulating internationalized virtuous dialogues (Guerzoni, 2019). Linking Global North and Global South artists and institutions has been the focus of a number of their initiatives, supporting a flow of arts, artists, curators, researchers, arts experts and enthusiasts travelling across borders and shaping a new niche tourism segment.

Art tourism has been a growing field of enquiry in tourism studies and is broadly defined 'as any activity that involves travel to see art and would include those people who travel very specifically to see art somewhere else as well as those who often or occasionally include visits to see art among other activities during tours, holidays or other trips away from home' (Franklin, 2018: 399–400). Some view art tourism as part of the broader macro-niche of cultural tourism (Origet du Cluzeau, 2017), others claim art tourism to be 'obscured under cultural tourism's voluminous bounds' (Franklin, 2018: 399). Artists, critics, galleries and a multitude of exhibition events and platforms have been stimulating a desire for people to engage with art, in ways which very often involve travel to see a plethora of arts productions that cannot or rarely move (Jagodzińska, 2018).

Art has been identified as an important self-standing form of thinking, representation and expression since classical times (Franklin, 2018), with Rakic and Lester (2013) elaborating on the fascinating relationships between travel, tourism and art, encompassing a wide range of phenomena from historical 'Grand Tours', during which a number of travellers experienced or produced artwork, to present-day travel inspired by art, artworks produced by contemporary travellers or artworks produced by locals for tourist consumption. New discoveries and developments in art practices and techniques have drawn people to visit places in proximity to their residence (particularly in times of COVID-19), neighbouring locations and even very distant destinations, whether for reasons linked to their profession as artists, architects, designers and/or exhibitors or their personal interests as collectors and/or as people seeking self-improvement. Franklin's (2018) insights into the relationships between art, mobility and place-making evidence the clear connection between the travelling cultures of artists and their arts; the aestheticization of landscapes, places and cultures; the creation of touristic desire; and the subsequent creation of 'places' as tourist destinations.

In Africa, we have witnessed the emergence of a fast-evolving contemporary arts sector based on biennials, festivals, fairs and residencies that offer opportunities for networking, research, new collaborations and projects. These events have been providing alternative spaces for interactions, some of a commercial type, others of a more cultural exchange nature,

Table 19.1   *A segmentation of contemporary arts tourists*

Type	Description
Good amateurs, collectors	Good amateurs and collectors may travel from one art fair to another around the world, as well as go to auctions, galleries and visit artists privately in their studio. Among them are those who will bet on new artists, not so much as speculators, but because they like to bring promising artists to light and thus participate in a new trend. For this group, contemporary arts are a strong motivating factor and can even be a unique reason to travel. As travellers, they are few in number (compared to cultural tourism flows in general) but high-spending and their numbers are on the rise: there were about 500,000 great collectors in the world in the 1950s; they now amount to 70 million.
Fair amateurs of contemporary arts	Fair amateurs will occasionally buy a lithography or a small piece of art, often during short breaks in large cities, where visiting exhibitions and fairs are their major, but not only, purpose. They also participate in guided tours organized by highly specialized incoming agencies such as Go Art in Berlin or Art Process in Paris.
Eclectics	Eclectics are the most common visitors of museums, fond of every kind of art, including contemporary arts. These travellers may be just adding contemporary arts to their many objects of curiosity, though some may feel a deep attraction to artistic creations that express their time and synchronize with it. In Western Europe, they are part of the c. 33% of the population that regularly go to museums and are city-break addicts. This could be by far the largest segment in the flows of contemporary arts visitors. It is therefore not surprising that they are the main targets of tourism communication and advertisement (Prentice, 2001).
Onlookers	Onlookers are interested in anything they can discover during their holidays, and are most likely to encounter contemporary arts via exposure through outdoor events (such as the White Nights in Rome and Paris), in outdoor exhibitions or in a permanent display. Many contemporary artists are fond of this particular audience, which tends to be fresher and less prejudiced than the three mentioned above, and less cultivated. They may sometimes be accompanied by young children (an even fresher audience!). They may like, or dislike, what they see, but, displayed as it is, they cannot avoid it. Some of them, apparently very few, will join one of the three other segments.

Source: Adapted from Origet du Cluzeau (2017: 33).

providing the opportunity to appreciate different representations of the African continent, overcoming conventional and limited images and narratives of the continent and possibly offering a more truthful and multifaceted representation of reality. While events such as the Africa-based biennales have experienced a considerable growth since early 1990s, with the Dakar Biennale being undoubtedly the most famous of all these, more recently commercial fairs, such as ArtX have positioned cities such as Lagos (Nigeria) on the international contemporary arts fair circuit, providing additional West Africa-based spaces for contemporary arts knowledge exchanges and mobility, supporting a growing form of arts-induced tourism to the city. Furthermore, festivals such as the LagosPhoto Festival, hosted annually in Lagos, and 360La in Accra have played a key role in facilitating knowledge exchanges that look beyond the prejudiced and sensationalist imagery of the continent and its communities. This has been achieved through the engagement with issues of contemporary relevance, such as those at the centre of the 10th edition of the LagosPhoto Festival (2019), called 'Passports', which reflected on the paradoxical aspects of contemporary life, where goods experience a much vaster and freer mobility than human beings, particularly those originating from the Global South; or the 1st edition of 360La (2018), which was built on principles of community empowerment through contemporary arts and responded to the need to make the arts more inclusive and accessible. In such contexts, cultural operators such as Azu Nwagbogu (director of the African Artists' Foundation), Ghanaian contemporary artist Serge Attukwei Clottey, or Marwan Zakem (founder of Gallery 1957) may be considered as cultural ambassadors of their respective countries and/or the region in which they operate, for facilitating access to spaces which are traditionally deemed exclusive.What is happening in West Africa reflects Origet du Cluzeau's (2017) description of places where the public can be confronted and experience contemporary arts, from performances at festival and events, to installation at traditional cultural sites, outdoor urban and rural spaces and artists studios' visits, evidencing the potential of this kind of fast-evolving cultural tourism micro-niche.

For instance, the merit of the African Artists' Foundation, and specifically the LagosPhoto Festival, is that in just over a decade, they have proven to offer a space where artists can meet on neutral ground to share ideas, innovation and capacities. The festival itself can be considered an example of a transnational community, built on shared values and cross-cultural dialogues, beyond barriers evidently imposed by different languages, cultures or national borders. Participants gather in Lagos to appreciate artistic expressions, exchange knowledge and engage in a number of additional organized and spontaneous activities around the city involving the local culture, the food, the atmosphere – and very often challenging misconceptions about the city and its people.

Equally, Gallery 1957's work expands beyond the gallery walls through a public programme that includes fairs, talks, residencies, off-site projects, studio visits and site-specific installation commissions, continuously supporting cultural initiatives in Ghana and beyond, and shaping a more inclusive and authentic appreciation of grassroots contemporary arts.

Finally, 360La has been providing an open space using the arts as a vehicle to inspire public interaction, firstly between La's community members themselves and then between La's community and those who visit their neighbourhood, where Clottey's studio is located. Workshops, art talks and research collaborations with local and international organizations with an interest in exploring the role of grassroots contemporary arts as a vehicle to stimulate community development are among the key features of 360La.

Exhibitions spaces, mentoring schemes for emerging artists, residencies and studio visits facilitated by the African Artists' Foundation (Lagos, Nigeria) and by Gallery 1957 (Accra, Ghana), as much as grassroots festivals like 360La and LagosPhoto Festival, are behind new patterns of mobility towards 'off-the-beaten-track' locations where artistic practices are performed, facilitating a plurality of narratives, cultural exchanges and dialogues that also challenge ignorance, racism and stereotyped views about certain niche tourism destinations.

REFERENCES

Franklin, A. (2018) Art tourism: A new field for tourist studies. *Tourist Studies*, 18(4), 399–416.
Guerzoni, G. (2019) La Biennale e il rilancio della cultural diplomacy. Available at: https://www.artribune.com/arti-visive/2019/05/biennale-musei-cultural-diplomacy/ (accessed 14 November 2020).
Jagodzińska, K. (2018) *Australian Art Museums*. Warsaw: Jagiellonian University Press.
Origet du Cluzeau, C. (2017) Tourism and contemporary arts: A particular case in Cultural Tourism. *Methaodos.revista de Ciencias Sociales*, 5(1), 21–37.
Prentice, R. (2001) *Experiential Cultural Tourism*. Edinburgh: Queen Margaret College.
Rakic, T. and Lester, J. (2013) *Travel, Tourism and Art*. Farnham: Ashgate.

PART IV

DARK TOURISM

20. Battlefield tourism: the legacy of Sandakan in Malaysian Borneo

Balvinder Kaur Kler and Cassie Perpetua Forsythe

1. INTRODUCTION

Battlefield tourism in Sabah, Malaysian Borneo, is a niche market facilitated by the strategic decision of local government to support the development of historical tourism. Fifty years earlier, the tragic events of World War Two (WWII) set into motion the following heritage attractions: a memorial park at the site of a former prisoner of war (POW) camp, an adventure trek along the death march route walked by prisoners of war (POWs), two annual commemorative events and a range of WWII memorials. This chapter explores how the tragedy of war in Borneo evolved into a niche market five decades later and contributes to the macro-niche of dark tourism, specifically, the micro-niche of battlefield tourism in Asia. Place theory is introduced as a framework to explore stakeholder relationships to battlefield sites. The backstory of the research setting explains how POWs were transferred from Singapore to Sandakan, on Borneo Island during the Japanese occupation of South East Asia. Subsequently, an exploratory qualitative case study approach is utilised to produce the case titled 'Battlefield Tourism in Sabah'. Key factors which supported the evolution of battlefield tourism in Sabah are compared to the literature and a link is drawn to the UN's Agenda 2030 Sustainable Development Goal (SDG) 16. A final note elaborates on how the pandemic created an avenue for the live stream of an annual memorial service.

2. LITERATURE REVIEW

Sites associated with war and conflict attract hundreds of thousands of visitors (Ryan, 2007) and constitute the subject of the highest number of studies within the field of dark or thana tourism research between 1996–2016 (Light, 2017). Defined as the act of visiting sites associated with death and atrocity, dark or thana tourism includes visits to sites of executions, massacres, assassinations, cemeteries, mass graves, memorials, prisons, concentration camps and battlefields (Miles, 2014). Battlefield tourism is a well-studied micro-niche of dark tourism across the demand and supply spectrum, including studies on visitor motivations, experiences, interpretation, site management, marketing, ethical debates, politics and methods (Light, 2017). However, the literature is Eurocentric (Light, 2017) and few studies investigate battlefield tourism in Asia.

Battlefield tourism includes visiting war memorials, war museums, 'war experiences', battle re-enactments, cemeteries and battlefield tours (Dunkley et al., 2011). 'Commemoration is central to any nation's mnemonic community and its representation' (ibid.: 861), and for this reason memorials are integral as sites to remember, mourn and heal. Visits may be undertaken to fulfil an obligation, as an act of remembrance, for educational purposes (Winter, 2011) or, for some, as a secular pilgrimage to sacred ground (Hyde and Harman, 2011). The aftermath of war creates powerful tourist attractions in the form of military, political and physical heritage (Butler and Suntikul, 2013), as is well documented in the literature. Generally, battlefield tourism literature focuses on experiences of the Western Front and D-Day (Bird et al., 2016; MacCarthy, 2017; Miles, 2017; Winter, 2018). Notably, nostalgia travel to battlefields strengthens family bonds (Fallon and Robinson, 2017). Studies of the Australian experience focus on Gallipoli (Hyde and Harman, 2011; Cheal and Griffin, 2013; Packer et al., 2019). In Asia, recent studies from South Korea have explored POW camps as tourist attractions (Kang and Lee, 2013) and the relationship between enduring involvement and visitors' connection to a dark tourism site (Kang et al., 2018). An interesting volume of warscapes covering both world wars includes cases from Sarawak (Malaysia), Vietnam and Singapore (Reeves et al., 2015). Also, Upton et al. (2018) have explored the reflections of battlefield tourists to Vietnam, and Chen and Tsai (2019) have examined visitors' motivations at a battlefield site in Taiwan.

At any site, what connects visitors to the past, present and future are the stories, objects and places of battle (Packer et al., 2019). The paradox of the battlefield 'is the freedom of the tourists to wander [...] where the agony of the combat has given way to the tranquillity of peace' (Prideaux, 2007: 17). Such sites depend on not being overlooked and their stories being kept alive through military history and modern-day tourism. Battlefield accounts must be uncovered, documented and shared, else they are forgotten. Additionally, these sites must be developed and preserved, or they may be lost, as in the case of the WWII Changi prison in Singapore, demolished in 2004 (Beaumont, 2009). Sandakan has a unique military heritage. Poignantly, the events of WWII contributed to war memorials, including Sandakan Memorial Park (SMP), situated at the former POW camp. Although the Japanese occupation of Borneo Island is well documented (Ooi, 2011), bar the studies by Braithwaite and Lee (2006), Masanti (2016) and Polus et al. (2016), battlefield attractions of Sandakan remain under-studied in tourism. Sabah is promoted as a nature, adventure and culture destination, with Sandakan the gateway to rich wildlife (Hutton, 2004). Yet, annually, Australian tourists travel specifically to visit SMP as a site of national heritage, with learning and education, event validation (remembrance) and pilgrimage cited as motivating factors (Polus et al., 2016). This chapter contributes to the literature on battlefield tourism in Asia by exploring how a military tragedy turned into a niche market.

Sense of Place

How does a site of tragedy evolve into a tourism attraction? We propose the emergence of battlefield tourism is best conceptualised through Place theory by addressing 'place as a centre of meaning' which seeks to characterise experience, meaning and relationships to place in experiential terms (Williams, 2014). This phenomenological approach interprets how place meanings advance and how individuals form relationships through lived experience (Seamon, 2014). Deep emotional ties constructed over time turn lived space into a special place depending on the individual, their relationship and effort with place (Williams, 2014). Four layers of meaning range from inherent (aesthetic), instrumental, socio-cultural (symbolic) and expressive which are either 'tangible, common, of interest' or 'intangible, unique and attached', encouraging individuals to form different types of sense of place (SoP) (Williams, 2014). SoP, or place meanings, are the descriptive, symbolic associations people ascribe to place based on emotional connections (Raymond et al., 2017). We apply SoP as a framework to analyse how stakeholders connect to sites of tragedy.

3.   RESEARCH SETTING

The story of Sandakan begins across the South China Sea. On 15 February 1942, Singapore fell under Japanese occupation, causing the Australian 8th Division to surrender alongside British forces in Malaya (Dawson, 1995). Australian and British POWs were relocated to Changi, Singapore, and separated further into work parties around the island. Between 1942 and 1943, the Japanese transferred POWs to new camps overseas: 'A' Force was sent to Burma. In July 1942, a work party of 1,500, called 'B' Force, was recruited and boarded the *Ubi Maru* vessel, headed to Borneo (Wall, 1997). As the Japanese implied that living conditions in the new location were better than the current circumstances the POWs found themselves in, volunteers were easily persuaded to join this work party (Silver, 2007). In March 1943, 'E' Force, consisting of 500 Australian POWs, departed for Sandakan: their mission was to build two military airstrips (Moffitt, 1989; Reid, 2008). In total, an estimated 2,400 Australian and British POWs arrived at the Mile 8 Camp in Sandakan (Wall, 1997).

In January 1945, the Japanese started to lose power in several occupied areas. In Borneo, they moved the POWs westwards, some 260 km inland from Sandakan (Reid, 2008). POWs were grouped in smaller numbers to walk through thick jungle and challenging topography over an average of 12 days. According to Smith (2000), about 789 soldiers set out on the Sandakan–Ranau Death Marches. Of these, only six survived: two escaped on the second march (Bombardier Richard Braithwaite and Gunner Owen Campbell) and four from the Ranau POW Camp (Warrant Officer William Sticpewich, Private Keith Botterill, Private Nelson Short and Lance Bombadier William Moxham) (Commonwealth of Australia, 2005). The death rate in Sandakan for Australian POWs was 99.75% and 100% for the British (Silver, 2007). Several POWs survived either because they were sent to Kuching (Sarawak), 805 km away, or managed to escape from the POW camp and were assisted to freedom by locals and allied forces. On 15 August 1945, the war officially ended in Borneo. Among these survivors were Bunny Glover, Russ Ewin (Glover, 2011) and Keith William ('Billy') Young (Silver and Young, 2016), who subsequently conveyed their accounts of the POW camps.

Knowledge of the atrocities which befell the POWs, the three death marches, the bravery of local civilians who helped these prisoners, the controversies behind the failed rescue mission, and the late acknowledgement of this tragedy are well documented (Wallace, 1958; Dawson, 1995; Wall, 1997; Silver, 1998; Smith, 2000; Reid, 2008; Moffitt, 1989; Glover, 2011; Cunningham, 2013; Braithwaite, 2016; Silver and Young, 2016). By no means an exhaustive list, this highly emotive body of literature is distressing, depicting in detail the worst tragedy in Australian military history. POWs died from sickness, starvation, torture and violence, or were killed by the guards on the forced marches; yet stories of bravery, friendship and survival abound (Cunningham, 2013). Therefore, the legacy of Sandakan to battlefield tourism, and how it facilitated a niche market in Malaysian Borneo decades later, is noteworthy (see Figure 20.1 for a map of present day war memorials in Sabah).

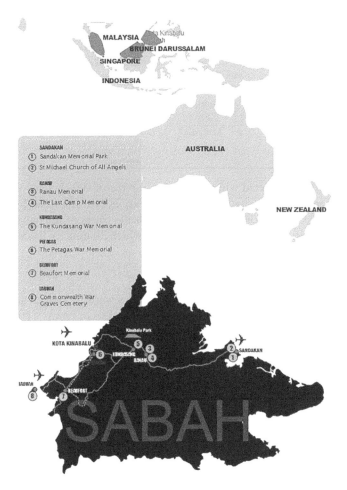

Source: Reproduced with kind permission, Sabah Tourism Board.

Figure 20.1   Map of war memorials in Sabah

4.   METHODOLOGY

One research question guided this study: to understand how battlefield tourism developed as a niche market in Sabah. Both study context and research question were suited to an interpretive inquiry design, which necessitates an exploratory qualitative approach through a value-laden lens and an emic perspective (Silverman, 2018). Specifically, an empirical case study approach was chosen to produce a record of what has occurred by investigating a contemporary phenomenon (the 'case') within a real-world context to illuminate an issue and contribute to an explanation (Yin, 2018). A range of secondary data or material in the public domain (programme booklets, published articles, books, blogs, archival footage on YouTube, and related websites) was scrutinised, as recommended for case study research (Yin, 2018).

Table 20.1   *List of participants*

No.	Name	Age	Nationality	Background
1	Rodney Bramich	75	Australian	Retired military (Royal Australian Engineers)
2	Johnny Lim	40	Malaysian	Director, Sandakan Tropical Wildlife Adventure
3	Ryan Rowland	79	Australian	Travel agent/WWII researcher/Chairperson, Borneo Exhibition Group WA Inc.
4	Lynette Silver	74	Australian	Writer/historian/specialist tour leader
5	Malcolm 'Mick' Smith	82	Australian	Retired military (Royal Australian Air Force)
6	Tham Yau Kong 'TYK'	59	Malaysian	Director, TYK Adventure Tours
7	John Tulloch (Major)	74	British	Retired military (Royal Regiment of Artillery)/amateur historian/author

Interviews were also conducted with a purposive sample of stakeholders to understand their role in facilitating this niche market. This case study is also informed by the late Richard Braithwaite (2016), whose voice is audible through the pages of his biography. Ultimately, the chosen methods in combination produce a case which illuminates the research question.

Timeframe

We assume battlefield tourism advanced from 1995 onwards, although smaller ceremonies attended by visitors were held earlier, as smaller memorials or cairns were set up at various WWII sites. Also, the Petagas War Memorial (Kota Kinabalu), dedicated to the local resistance movement, does not attract tourists, but has held commemorative ceremonies since 21 January 1946 (Wong, 2019). Although war memorials existed in Sabah prior to 1995, these were not tourist attractions.

Purposive Sample

Presently, commemorative ceremonies held at SMP include ANZAC Day and Sandakan Day Memorial. A purposive sample of war historians, military enthusiasts and travel industry professionals who attend either or both ceremonies annually, and have done so for several years, were invited to participate in this study. The selection of a purposive sample contributes to the credibility of findings, as participants are information rich and have lived through the experience (Silverman, 2018). Accessibility to participants was negotiated through the second author, an officer at Sabah Tourism Board (STB) who collaborated on the project, has a personal connection to the participants and a shared appreciation of Borneo's war history. An invitation sheet detailing the purpose of this study and a consent form were emailed to participants. Fourteen invitations were sent out but only seven replies were returned in the given timeframe. A list of participants is presented in Table 20.1, indicating their involvement with SMP for over twenty years.

Email Interviews and Oral History

Two novel adaptations were incorporated into the case study method. The first was the use of asynchronous email interviews, because participants were geographically dispersed and not accessible in person to the researchers (Meho, 2006; Burns, 2010). Written answers to questions may nudge a participant into a reflective attitude if the task of writing is not a constraint for participants (van Manen, 1997). Based on the age and backgrounds of our participants (see Table 20.1), we received detailed responses to the questions. The second novel adaptation was using oral history to approach the interviews; such an approach gives voice to unheard or overlooked persons who collectively fit under the banner of having lived the same experience but share moments from their own unique perspectives (Mackenzie et al., 2020). Here, oral history is used to develop insights about SMP by participants whose testimony might otherwise be lost. Oral history is also the only method within which the identity of participants is imperative to gauge their relationship to the topic (ibid.). Interview questions focused on understanding their experiences of 'place as a centre of meaning' (Williams, 2014). This method, developed by Schroeder (1996), involves asking people who have strong feelings about a place to write about the kinds of experiences that have contributed to those feelings. In this way, the method acknowledges the conceptual elements from an emic perspective. The questions asked were:

1. Please describe your first experience with WWII history in Sandakan/Sabah.
2. Please describe what SMP means to you (what thoughts and feelings connected with SMP stand out for you).

The use of email interviews saved time, as the data was already written and did not require transcription.

Data Analysis

An inductive, thematic analysis of interview data included reading and coding transcripts line-by-line, individually (Braun and Clarke, 2013). Codes were compared across all seven transcripts to produce sub-themes that were amalgamated into two key themes: 'tribute' (people) and 'mindfulness' (place). Themes were cross-checked with material gathered from documents and observations as a form of triangulation to produce the case study (Silverman, 2018; Yin, 2018). At an interrogative level, both themes provided an understanding of the emotional connection between participants and their duty of care towards SMP, which explained their deep commitment to facilitating this niche market. Table 20.2 clarifies the qualitative data structure of the interview analysis.

The value-laden nature of the research design enabled the subjective experiences of our participants to be heard. Interpretation of data necessitates that we reveal our backgrounds as an exercise in reflexivity (Silverman, 2008). The first author is a third-generation Sabahan who has grown up listening to stories of WWII from her grandparents and parents, and has an academic background. The second author is employed with the tourist board and has for several years managed the Australian inbound sector, which connected her to the participants. She assists in organising and attends the annual ceremonies in Sandakan, which intrigued her to study the Sandakan–Ranau Death Marches.

5.   CASE STUDY: BATTLEFIELD TOURISM IN SABAH

Battlefield tourism in Sabah is a small, dynamic niche market that has grown steadily since 1995. Key attractions include SMP (former POW camp), a jungle trek on the route of the death marches, two key events (ANZAC Day and Sandakan Day Memorial) and several other

Table 20.2　　Qualitative data structure

Verbatim extracts	Inductive		Interrogative
	Sub-Themes	Themes	
'tribute to fallen soldiers'	i.　Remembering sacrifices	Tribute (People)	
'significant place of carnage'	ii.　To honour the POWs		
'to be maintained for all			
generations'			
'honour those who paid			
ultimate price'			Duty of Care towards Sandakan
			Memorial Park
'…led to Commemorative	i.　Building awareness	Mindfulness (Place)	*(Place as a centre of meaning)*
area being placed inside the	ii.　Ensuring appreciation		
Australian Camp perimeter'			
'many locals who are not			
aware of the history'			
'to remember WWII'			

unique memorials. Although a range of war memorials exist in Sabah, those related to allied forces in Borneo during WWII attract international visitors mainly from Australia. This case study provides a chronological account of this niche market and identifies key stakeholders who facilitated the process.

The first public memorial to WWII in Sabah commemorates the Kinabalu Guerrillas, a local resistance movement (Wong, 2019). In the early 1960s, in a town at the foothills of Mount Kinabalu, the Kundasang War Memorial Gardens were dedicated to honour all Australian and British servicemen, as well as Sabahans who died during WWII (Silver, 2010). In 1985, survivor Keith Botterill returned to Sabah and shared the story of Gunner Cleary's death in Ranau, thus a cairn was officiated at this site. During the same visit, Botterill and several other survivors found a boiler, an excavator and an alternator while exploring the old camp in Mile 8 (Wall, 2007). With a grant of around AUD100,000, a memorial park was officially opened on 29 October 1985 (Wall, 2007).

Although the war ended in 1945, the story of Sandakan remained in the private possession of the survivors and in classified military documents (Silver, 2007). The commemoration of the 50th anniversary served as an important milestone that brought media attention to this tragedy and opened pathways for its acceptance into the Australian national consciousness (Braithwaite, 2016). As part of the 1995 anniversary marking the end of WWII, a Borneo Pilgrimage tour was organised by the Department of Veterans' Affairs (Australia), which brought across many servicemen involved in the liberation of Borneo in 1945 (Wall, 2007). In conjunction with this tour, STB (then the Sabah Tourism Promotion Corporation), assisted the Australian Government in reaching out to Malaysian WWII veterans and family members who helped in the war relief effort and wanted to participate in the auspicious service (N. Othman, personal communication, 2020). A commemorative booklet was produced about wartime in Borneo, with first-hand accounts of local Sabahans who assisted the POWs (Charuruks, 1995). The sacred legacy of Sandakan was finally being recognised at an international scale.

During this event, the Returned and Services League (Australia) and the Sabah Government discussed the direction of the memorial park and agreed for the area to be upgraded to serve as the premises to honour this history. The Office of Australian War Graves (OAWG) contributed a sum of AUD750,000 towards the upgrade (Silver, 2007). Presently, SMP is located

Table 20.3   *War memorials in Sabah*

	Name/location
1.	Labuan War Memorial, Labuan War Cemetery
2.	Labuan Cremation Memorial (Indian Infantry War Memorial)
3.	Sandakan Municipal Square
4.	Chinese War Memorial, Sandakan Cemetery
5.	Heroes Grave, Kuching (Sarawak)
6.	Petagas War Memorial Garden
7.	Kundasang War Memorial Gardens
8.	Peace Monument, Labuan
9.	Ranau War Memorial
10.	Sandakan Memorial Park
11.	Japanese War Memorial, Japanese Cemetery, Sandakan
12.	Sandakan Memorial Windows, Church of St Michael's and All Angels, Sandakan
13.	Last Camp Memorial, Ranau
14.	Quailey's Hill, Ranau
15.	British Sandakan POW Memorial, Ranau

Source: Braithwaite (2016: pp. 480–81).

adjacent to the site of the original camp under the jurisdiction of the Sandakan Municipal Council, and its upkeep is undertaken by the OAWG. It is well-maintained, and its landscape incorporates tall trees, a designated walkway, a memorial obelisk made of granite and the old boiler, alternator, excavator and concrete water tanks. A commemorative pavilion with stained-glass windows houses educational materials in English and Bahasa (Malay language) and a scale model of the POW camp.

As the 60th anniversary of the Sandakan–Ranau Death March approached, the Sabah Society (a non-governmental organisation) commissioned the foremost trekking specialist in Sabah, Mr Tham Yau Kong (TYK Adventure Tours) to organise a re-enactment trek along the route of the death marches in August 2005 (Lee, 2019). This event led historian Lynette Silver to collaborate with TYK in order to clarify the accurate route and the company has been successfully running regular treks since 2006 (Lee, 2019). These adventure tourism itineraries are customised for participants, with history an integral element of the trek by beginning, making stops en-route and ending at key memorials (https://sandakandeathmarch.com/). Newer memorials along this trek have been discovered, including the Tuaty Akai Pavilion (Bauto Hill) and the Zudin platform (within Taviu Forest Reserve) which overlooks the hardest section of the trek (Kan, 2018). Table 20.3 lists fifteen war memorials, most of which form the itinerary of present-day tours.

Two memorial services held annually at SMP are ANZAC Day (25 April) and Sandakan Day (15 August), attracting up to 500 people. Both events attract special interest groups from Australia, with an influx of tourists in the months of April and August. Sandakan Day Memorial was conceived in 2004 by the then Sandakan Municipal Council President, Adeline Leong (*Datuk*) in collaboration with STB. This service commemorates both soldiers and locals who suffered during WWII. The municipal council had a tourism committee consisting of individuals from the tourism industry, community, state and local government which collectively agreed to complement the successful nature tourism market with this 'newer' historical tourism market (Braithwaite and Lee, 2006). Workshops were held in August 2004, providing the impetus to improve historical tourism products, including the commission to uncover the death march route. The motivation behind this historical tourism strategy was to encourage visitors to learn about the WWII experience and contribute to healing (Braithwaite, 2016). Moreover, the strategy aimed to increase arrivals from the underdeveloped Australian market, an idea supported by Irene Chararuks (*Datuk*), the General Manager of STB (Braithwaite, 2016). Since 2004, STB has successfully engaged with local and Australian travel agents to promote historical tourism. Therefore, it is surmised that public and private stakeholders, both local and international, came together to facilitate this niche market. At a finer level, through the lens of Place theory, we uncovered emotional connections between stakeholders and SMP which provide another insight into the evolution of battlefield tourism.

Place Meanings for SMP: Tribute and Mindfulness

SMP is a special place with deep personal meanings for each participant, in that it is the centre from which all meaning emanates and thrusts a duty of care upon them. Two key themes, 'tribute', and 'mindfulness', captured participants' relationship to SMP. Commemorative activities held at SMP bring benefit to both the dead and the living.

Every step taken by participants at SMP has been to remember the fallen who perished during WWII. The following narratives allow the voices of our participants to elaborate on 'tribute':

> Sandakan Memorial Park is a tranquil and fitting tribute to our fallen soldiers. (Rod Bramich)

> Sandakan 8 mile, always a significant place of carnage, man's inhumanity to man. Ghosts amongst the trees. We believe each visit to this place we release the souls of those tormented men who suffered and died in their camp. Memories and memorials for all war history is symbolic to be maintained for all generations with the hope we do not follow the same path. (Ryan Rowland)

> All Memorials are very significant. Not just for the POWs but for the many local people and imported forced labour. The purpose of these memorials is to honour those who paid the ultimate price. [...] significant places where people can come to remember, honour, pay homage, learn and try to understand the horrors that befell those who suffered. (Mick Smith)

'Mindfulness' expresses the second theme, to understand participants' relationship to place. The word denotes both 'being aware' and 'a form of therapy'. For these participants, their acts of meticulously uncovering facts to ensure accuracy of details creates enhanced awareness for visitors to SMP. Moreover, by doing so, they gain a form of peace, knowing they are doing their part for those who no longer have a voice. The following narratives elaborate the theme 'mindfulness':

> I became involved in 1995, when I visited OAWG Director Alan Heggan in Canberra, and told him that the POW camp was not at the place where the RSL had previously erected a memorial – the camp started, beyond it, at the crest of the hill. He told me that he had sent for aerial photographs, [...] and was coming to that conclusion himself. This led to the commemorative area being placed inside the Australian Camp perimeter. (Lynette Silver)

> SMP is a very special place as it is the actual camp site during the WW2. [...] I feel that schools and local NGO should conduct study trip over there to inform more locals about the history of WW2 and what we have ... gone through. There are still many locals who are not aware of the history and do not even know why we have ANZAC Day celebrated in Sandakan. (Johnny Lim)

SMP is a very important site for us when doing war tourism because these were places where things happened [...] to remember WWII. Later we discovered and established the Allan Quailey Memorial and POWs last camp site which added on more meaningfulness to this war history tour. (TYK)

SMP was the catalyst for battlefield tourism development in Sabah. The discovery of SMP and that of a personal link has motivated one participant to bring awareness about British POWs and Borneo war history to the United Kingdom:

[...] 1999. We arrived at Sandakan [...] Purely by chance I picked up a magazine in the hotel and I saw a small advertisement mentioning the opening of [...] the Sandakan Memorial Park, stating that it was the site of Australian POWs. I had never heard of it, [...] I was appalled at what had happened and equally so when I learnt that none of the UK POWs survived. Over half were from my regiment, the Royal Artillery. [...] And it was mostly Australian and hardly any mention of British POWs. (Major John Tulloch)

These narratives not only provide an insight into the relationship that stakeholders have with SMP but also explain the motivations for their decisive action towards contributions to facilitating the Sandakan legacy.

6.   DISCUSSION

Sandakan is a dark tourism site with a greater level of perceived authenticity (Miles, 2014). As a micro-niche of dark tourism, battlefield tourism in Sabah remains a unique niche market. Travel to sacred grounds (Hyde and Harman, 2011) and acts of commemoration, mourning and healing (Dunkley et al., 2011) occur annually due to the legacy of Sandakan, as does continued education and learning about this tragedy (Winter, 2011; Polus et al., 2016). Australians with or without family ties (Fallon and Robinson, 2017) arrive in Sabah annually to commemorate this military heritage (Butler and Suntikul, 2013). Battlefield tourism's development into a niche tourism market in Sabah was made possible by two factors.

First, it occurred through the combined efforts of multiple stakeholders, including local and overseas governments and public and private actors who collectively ensured the memory of the tragedy of Sandakan was protected and that memorials were developed at significant locations. Stakeholders involved in this endeavour encompassed a diverse range of individuals from different socio-demographic backgrounds: survivors, historians, military enthusiasts, local community and pioneers of the tourism industry, all focused on a common goal: to accord a duty of care and due respect to the legacy of WWII in Sabah. Raymond et al. (2017) apply affordance theory to SoP to suggest it is a property of the relationship between perception–action and social construction processes, both within and across place-based experiences. One reason Sandakan remains an important part of military heritage is because stakeholders reacted with intangible, unique and attached meanings to place. Second, policy decisions supporting historical tourism encouraged both the redevelopment of SMP in 1995 and the search for the death march route in 2005 in time to mark key war anniversaries. Once uncovered, sites were developed and preserved, and niche tourism succeeded in facilitating the preservation of military heritage in Sandakan. Considering SDG 16, we propose that battlefield tourism plays an essential role in ensuring accountable and inclusive institutions remain relevant. The dissemination of the Sandakan story is one way to promote peaceful and inclusive societies for sustainable development.

The use of Place theory to study people–place relationships enhances our understanding of stakeholder participation (Light, 2017) in the facilitation and protection of special places. Battlefield tourism in Sabah supplies sites of remembrance, education and pilgrimage. The tragedy of war left a legacy in Sabah that was uncovered, documented, shared and developed into a niche market. SDG 16 promotes peaceful and inclusive societies, with the understanding that true sustainable development comes when we learn not to repeat the mistakes of the past. The story of WWII in Sandakan reminds us that every effort should be made to encourage nations to refrain from waging war.

7.   CONCLUSION

This chapter presented a case study of battlefield tourism in the Sandakan, a niche market which exemplifies the human spirit of perseverance. In Australia and Britain, the legacy of Sandakan has yet to reach the masses. A new book by Tulloch (2020) focused on the British POW experience at Sandakan should spark interest in the British market. Evidence dictates that this micro-niche market will remain dynamic and an integral part of tourism in Sabah.

Source: Used with kind permission, Tracia Goh/Sabah Tourism Board.

Figure 20.2   Sandakan Day Memorial ceremony, 15 August 2020

On 15 August 2020, to commemorate the 75th anniversary since the end of WWII, amidst the pandemic, STB remained steadfast and organised a live stream of the Sandakan Day Memorial ceremony (http://sandakanday2020.sabahtourism.com/) complete with a catafalque party (see Figure 20.2). Both the British and Australian High Commissioners attended from their base in

Kuala Lumpur (interstate travel was permissible at that time) and laid wreaths alongside other local guests, whose numbers were limited to fifty. National anthems were played, speeches delivered and the Last Post sounded to commemorate the fallen. This livestream has ignited a new line of interest from extended relatives of POWs and military enthusiasts, who would never have been able to attend the service due to distance and cost.

In the classic work *War and Peace*, Tolstoy advises that 'there is nothing stronger than those two: patience and time, they will do it all [...] patience and time are my warriors, my champions' (1993: 637–39). WWII in Sandakan is a story which only came to light from 1995 onwards. Patience, time and the efforts of multiple stakeholders have ensured the continuity and growth of interest in the history of WWII in Borneo. Significantly, niche tourism has acted as a vehicle to carry this legacy forward – *lest we forget*.

REFERENCES

Beaumont, J. (2009) Contested trans-national heritage: The demolition of Changi Prison, Singapore. *International Journal of Heritage Studies*, 15(4), 298–316.

Bird, G., Claxton, S. and Reeves, K. (eds.) (2016) *Managing and Interpreting D-Day's Sites of Memory: Guardians of Remembrance*. London: Routledge.

Braithwaite, D. and Lee, Y.L. (2006) Dark tourism, hate and reconciliation: The Sandakan experience. *International Institute for Peace Through Tourism*, Occasional Paper, 8.

Braithwaite, R.W. (2016) *Fighting Monsters. An Intimate History of the Sandakan Tragedy*. North Melbourne, Victoria: Australia Scholarly Publishing Pty Ltd.

Braun, V. & Clarke, V. (2013) *Successful Qualitative Research: A Practical Guide for Beginners*. London: Sage Publications Ltd.

Burns, E. (2010) Developing email interview practices in qualitative research. *Sociological Research Online*, 15(4), 24–35.

Butler, R. and Suntikul, W. (eds) (2013) *Tourism and War*. London: Routledge.

Charuruks, I.B. (ed.) (1995) *Lest We Forget 1945–1995. Commemorating 50 years since the End of World War II*. Kota Kinabalu: Sabah Tourism Promotion Corporation.

Cheal, F. and Griffin T. (2013) Pilgrims and patriots: Australian tourist experiences at Gallipoli. *International Journal of Culture, Tourism and Hospitality Research*, 7(3), 227–41.

Chen, C.M. and Tsai, T.H. (2019) Tourist motivations in relation to a battlefield: A case study of Kinmen. *Tourism Geographies*, 21(1), 78–101.

Commonwealth of Australia (2005) *Sandakan Memorial Park*. Canberra: Department of Veterans' Affairs, Office of Australian War Graves.

Cunningham, M. (2013) *Hell on Earth. Sandakan – Australia's Greatest War Tragedy*. Sydney, New South Wales: Hachette Australia Pty Ltd.

Dawson, C. (1995) *To Sandakan. The Diaries of Charlie Johnstone: Prisoner of War 1942–45*. Allen and Unwin.

Dunkley, R., Morgan, N. and Westwood, S. (2011) Visiting the trenches: Exploring meanings and motivations in battlefield tourism. *Tourism Management*, 32(4), 860–68.

Fallon, P. and Robinson, P. (2017) 'Lest we forget': A veteran and son share a 'warfare tourism' experience. *Journal of Heritage Tourism*, 12(1), 21–35.

Glover, L.B. (2011) *The Boy from Bowen. Diary of a Sandakan POW*. Robina, Queensland: Kristan Enterprises Pty Ltd.

Hutton, W. (2004) *Sandakan. History, Culture, Wildlife and Resorts of the Sandakan Peninsula*. Kota Kinabalu, Malaysia: Natural History Publications (Borneo).

Hyde, K. and Harman, S. (2011) Motives for a secular pilgrimage to the Gallipoli battlefields. *Tourism Management*, 32(6), 1343–51.

Kan, Y.C (2018) Stunning recognition for 2 Death March witnesses, *Daily Express*, 9 September. Available at: http://www.dailyexpress.com.my/news.cfm?NewsID=127083 (accessed 17 July 2020).

Kang, E.J. and Lee, T.J. (2013) War and ideological conflict: Prisoner of war camps as a tourist experience in South Korea. In L. White and E. Frew (eds) *Dark Tourism and Place Identity: Managing and Interpreting Dark Places*. London: Routledge, 236–47.

Kang, E.J., Lee, T.J. and Han, J.S. (2018) The influence of enduring involvement on tragedy-related tourism experiences. *Journal of Travel Research*, 57(5), 658–70.

Lee, C.T. (2019) Sandakan Ranau Death March – An experience and journey that can never be forgotten. 1 November. Available at: https://hellosabah.my/sandakan-ranau-death-march-an-experience-and-journey-that-can-never-be-forgotten/ (accessed 21 July 2020).

Light, D. (2017) Progress in dark tourism and thanatourism research: An uneasy relationship with heritage tourism. *Tourism Management*, 61, 275–301.

MacCarthy, M. (2017) Consuming symbolism: Marketing D-Day and Normandy. *Journal of Heritage Tourism*, 12(2), 191–203.

MacKenzie, N.G., Pittaki, Z. and Wong, N. (2020) Historical approaches for hospitality and tourism research. *International Journal of Contemporary Hospitality Management*, 32(4), 1469–85.

Masanti, M. (2016) Understanding dark tourism acceptance in Southeast Asia: The case of WWII Sandakan–Ranau Death March, Sabah, Malaysia. In P. Mandal and J. Vong (eds) *Development of Tourism and the Hospitality Industry in Southeast Asia*. Springer: Singapore, 113–25.

Meho, L. (2006) E-Mail interviewing in qualitative research. A methodological discussion. *Journal of the American Society for Information Science and Technology*, 57(10), 1284–95.

Miles, S. (2014) Battlefield sites as dark tourism attractions: An analysis of experience. *Journal of Heritage Tourism*, 9(2), 134–47.

Miles, S. (2017) Remembrance trails of the Great War on the Western Front: Routes of heritage and memory. *Journal of Heritage Tourism*, 12(5), 441–51.

Moffitt, A. (1989) *Project Kingfisher: Untold Story of the Massacres of the Sandakan Prisoners-of-war in Borneo and the Secret Plan for a Rescue That Never Happened*. Sydney: Angus & Robertson.

Ooi, K.G. (2011) *The Japanese Occupation of Borneo, 1941–1945*. London: Routledge.

Packer, J., Ballantyne, R. and Uzzell, D. (2019) Interpreting war heritage: Impacts of Anzac Museum and battlefield visits on Australians' understanding of national identity. *Annals of Tourism Research*, 76, 105–16.

Polus, R.C., Bidder, C. and Jones, T.E. (2016) Understanding tourists' motives and sought experiences at Sandakan Memorial Park Borneo. *Asian Journal of Tourism Research*, 1(1), 154–71.

Prideaux, B. (2007) Echoes of war: Battlefield tourism. In C. Ryan (ed.) *Battlefield Tourism: History, Place and Interpretation*. Oxford: Elsevier, 17–28.

Raymond, C.M., Kyttä, M. and Stedman, R. (2017) Sense of place, fast and slow: The potential contributions of affordance theory to sense of place. *Front Psychol.*, 8, 1674. doi: 10.3389/fpsyg.2017.01674

Reeves, K., Bird, G.R., James, L., Stichelbaut, B. and Bourgeois, J. (eds) (2015) *Battlefield Events: Landscape, Commemoration and Heritage*. London: Routledge.

Reid, R. (2008) *Sandakan 1942–1945*. Expanded edn. Canberra: Dept. of Veterans' Affairs.

Ryan, C. (ed.) (2007) *Battlefield Tourism: History, Place and Interpretation*. Oxford: Elsevier.

Schroeder, H.W. (1996) *Voices from Michigan's Black River: Obtaining Information on Special Places for Natural Resource Planning*. Gen. Tech. rep. NC-184. St. Paul, MN: USDA, Forest Service, 1–25.

Seamon, D. (2014) Place attachment and phenomenology: The synergistic dynamism of place. In L. Manzo and P. Devine-Wright (eds) *Place Attachment: Advances in Theory, Methods and Applications*. London: Routledge, 11–22.

Silver, L.R. (1998) *Sandakan. A Conspiracy of Silence*. Burra Creek, New South Wales: Sally Milner Publishing.

Silver, L.R. (2007) *Sandakan. A Conspiracy of Silence*. 4th revised edn. Kota Kinabalu: Opus Publications.

Silver, L.R. (2010) *Blood Brothers. Sabah and Australia 1942 – 1945*. Kota Kinabalu: Opus Publications.

Silver, L. and Young, B. (2016) *Billy. My Life as a Teenage POW*. Burra Creek, New South Wales: Sally Milner Publishing.

Silverman, D. (2018) *Doing Qualitative Research: A Practical Handbook*. 5th revised edn. London: SAGE Publications.

Smith, K. (2000) *Borneo: Australia's Proud but Tragic Heritage*. Armidale, New South Wales: K.R. Smith.

Tolstoy, L. (1993) *War and Peace*. Hertfordshire: Wordsworth Editions Ltd.

Tulloch, J. (2020) *The Borneo Graveyard*. Kota Kinabalu: Opus Publications.

Upton, A., Schänzel, H. and Lück, M. (2018) Reflections of battlefield tourist experiences associated with Vietnam War sites: An analysis of travel blogs. *Journal of Heritage Tourism*, 13(3), 197–210.

Van Manen, M. (1997) *Researching Lived Experience*. Winnipeg: The Althouse Press.

Wall, D. (1997) *Sandakan Under Nippon: The Last March*. 5th revised edn. Mona Vale, New South Wales: D. Wall Publications.

Wallace, W. (1958) *Escape from Hell. The Sandakan Story*. London: Robert Hale Limited.

Williams, D.R. (2014) Making sense of 'place': Reflections on pluralism and positionality in place research. *Landscape and Urban Planning*, 131, 74–82.

Winter, C. (2011) Battlefield visitor motivations: Explorations in the Great War town of Ieper, Belgium. *International Journal of Tourism Research*, 13(2), 164–76.

Winter, C. (2018) The multiple roles of battlefield war museums: A study at Fromelles and Passchendaele. *Journal of Heritage Tourism*, 13(3), 211–23.

Wong, D.T.K (2019) *One Crowded Moment of Glory. The Kinabalu Guerrillas and the 1943 Jesselton Uprising*. Kuala Lumpur: Universiti of Malaya Press.

Yin, R.K. (2018) *Case Study Research and Applications: Design and Methods*. 6th revised ed. London: SAGE Publications.

21. Cold War Museum in Lithuania

Rasa Pranskūnienė and Viltė Kriščiūnaitė

INTRODUCTION

This chapter presents an empirical study of visitor experiences at the Cold War Museum in Zemaitija National Park, Lithuania. This museum is the only modern exhibition located in a former missile base bunker in Europe. Tourists can visit the underground labyrinthine missile silos and learn about the Cold War period, propaganda strategies, the consequences of nuclear explosions and life in a military base (Zemaitija National Park, 2020).

This chapter explores the experiences of visitors to this dark tourism site as various layers of the niche tourism experience. Dinis and Krakover (2016) argue that the term 'niche tourism' is currently attached to an increasing number of specialized activities, as it includes various forms of special interest tourism, from gastronomy to adventure to heritage tourism, as well as dark tourism.

According to Light (2017), the role of dark tourism itself is significant and the inclusion of the concept has allowed tourism scholars to uncover new issues and to steer research in new directions. In recent years, as Light (ibid.) notes, dark tourism research has become increasingly important when studying visitor experiences. According to Packer and Ballantyne (2016), visitor experiences are multifaceted. Tribe and Liburd (2016) note that various online sources (comments, feedbacks, etc.) are increasingly being used for dark tourism research. Thus, in order to develop the Cold War Museum harmoniously, it is important to understand visitors' experiences of this dark tourism site as a niche tourism object through applying theoretical understandings and conducting an empirical study on the topic.

LITERATURE REVIEW

The concept of 'niche tourism' has emerged as a counterpoint to what is commonly referred to as 'mass tourism' (Novelli, 2005). Ali-Knight (2011) argues that niche tourism offers destinations a valid opportunity to reinvent and reposition themselves and has a key role to play in destination imaging and the development of the tourist experience. Whatever the mechanisms behind niche tourism, whatever its deceptions and contestability, as Robinson and Novelli (2005) note, it provides a connection between tourist dreams, desires, imaginings and experiences – no longer can we understand tourism as a composite and solid whole with its implications of defining markets and mainstream tourists.

According to Biran and Poria (2012), the post-modernist move in tourism research perceives the tourist experience as a subjective and interactive process involving the tourist and the tourismscape. Topsakal and Ekici (2014) notice that it is not easy to define special interest tourism, as niche tourists have special interests related to authenticity, namely existential authenticity (Sorea and Csesznek, 2020). Thus, Stone (2011) suggests that scholars need to transgress traditional disciplinary borders and interests, and to adopt post-disciplinary research approaches that are characterized by increased reasonableness, flexibility and inclusivity. Niche tourism offers researchers an opportunity to utilize innovative research methods, focusing on the complementary use of qualitative and quantitative techniques (Ali-Knight, 2011). Handayani (2018) notices that (re)enactment and active participation of tourists have promoted the framing of niche tourism in post-modernism.

Despite the years of research into dark tourism and the growth of the dark tourism market and growing academic interest, as Kennell and Powell (2020) argue, there has been little interest shown in understanding the relationship between dark tourism and other forms of tourism. As Light (2017: 275) points out: 'two decades of research have not convincingly demonstrated that dark tourism and thanatourism are distinct forms of tourism, and in many ways they appear to be little different from heritage tourism'. When developing dark tourism, as Kennell and Powell (2020) note, it is clear that stakeholder education and familiarization is necessary, to help stakeholders understand the different shades of dark tourism, to make way for a more balanced judgement on their acceptability. Furthermore, as Ivanova and Light (2018) claim, it is apparent that the term 'dark tourism' embraced a wide range of sites offering different sorts of experiences for their visitors.

Sharma and Kumar Nayak (2020) notice that experience quality has been emerging as the dominant construct of interest for the success of the tourism industry. Still, as Collins-Kreiner (2016) argues, those words appear to be inadequate to describe such experiences, and they are often not amenable in the case of both pilgrims and dark tourists. In both phenomena – as in other forms of tourism – the visitor experience is not homogeneous and comprises different subgroups – visitor motivations are also highly diverse, ranging from curiosity to a search for meaning; visitors from differing market segments often visit the same sites and coexist, despite the fact that the reasons for their visits vary considerably, as do the activities in which they engage at the sites. Collins-Kreiner (ibid.) points out that this is also consistent with the recent calls for a fundamental rethinking of the paradigms and norms that shape scholarship on tourism – one that requires a 'new era', and a new generation of researchers capable of stepping out of the analytical and disciplinary 'straightjackets' that have formed in recent decades.

Venter (2017) notes that visitation to museums and attractions that display military heritage have progressively increased; lately, however, there is a growing interest in the stories, lives and experiences of those who fought and lived and those who died during times of war in faraway places, as this kind of heritage tourism helps visitors to immerse themselves in a destination. According to Axelsson et al. (2018), it is obvious that the material culture from the Cold War attracts huge public interest. It is part of a discourse in the processes of narration, remembrance and identity creation in a number of informal forums on the internet; yet states and their formal departments often encounter difficulty in handling this heritage.

However, as Axelsson et al. (ibid.) argue, at the same time, the Cold War is on a general level imminent in the overall identity-creating discourse and remembrance of the period. According to Bechmann and Noack (2019), the Cold War was rooted in ideological antagonism, geographical division and nuclear deterrence. Bechmann and Noack (ibid.) notice that the latter resulted in a stalemate, especially on the European continent, which made the 'cultural front' all the more important as a Cold War battleground. Thus the response, naturally enough, was to study the Cold War competition for hearts and minds around the world.

RESEARCH METHODS

The subject chosen for the research – the Cold War Museum – is the only modern exhibition in Europe located in a missile base bunker (Figure 21.1) (Zemaitija National Park, 2020).

Source: Photo by Zemaitija National Park.

Figure 21.1   Cold War Museum, Lithuania

When the United States started building underground military bases, the Soviet Union felt it had to maintain its military advantage (Zemaitija National Park, 2020). For that reason, in September 1960 in the village of Plokščiai, the Soviets began to rapidly build an underground military base, one of the first in the Soviet Union. The shore of the nearby Lake Plateliai and the Plokštinė forests were ideally suited for the construction of the military base. The location was 170 m above sea level, the soil was easy to excavate and the local population was small. Furthermore, from this location all of Europe would be covered by the missiles, which could reach Turkey and southern European countries.

The former underground missile base – where in the Soviet period, from 1963 to 1978, four medium-range ballistic SS-4 missiles armed with two megaton thermonuclear warheads had been deployed – was newly opened after the reconstruction (Figure 21.1) and hosts the Cold War Museum (Zemaitija National Park, 2020). It was initially opened for visitors in 1996, as an exhibition on militarism. The then modest exhibition received about 11,000 visitors a year. A project to renovate the Cold War Museum started in 2010 and was mostly funded by the European Regional Development Fund, which aims to strengthen economic and social cohesion in the European Union by correcting imbalances between its regions. Europe's only Cold War Museum reopened its doors to visitors in 2012, and subsequently received more than 35,000 visitors in a year, not only from Lithuania, but from all over the world.

The thematic analysis applied to this study should, according to Clarke and Braun (2013), be flexible – not limited to any particular theory or system – so as to reveal the true experiences of visitors to Zemaitija National Park Cold War Museum. Clarke and Braun (ibid.) view thematic analysis as theoretically flexible and suited to a wide range of research interests and theoretical perspectives, and useful as a 'basic' method because it works with a wide range of research questions, from those about people's experiences or understandings to those about the representation and construction of particular phenomena in particular contexts.

To provide data for the thematic analysis, Tripadvisor visitor reviews of two specific sites – Zemaitija National Park and the Cold War Museum – were selected. All visitor reviews written between November 2014 and November 2019 on the Tripadvisor platform were included in the study. In order to preserve confidentiality while analysing the visitor reviews, original names or icons were not listed, only the country of residence was mentioned (for those who did not indicate their country, nicknames such as Anonymous 1, Anonymous 2 and so on, were assigned). Six phases of thematic analysis (as proposed by Clarke and Braun, 2013) were used: familiarization with the data, generating initial codes, searching for themes, reviewing themes, defining and naming themes and writing up. The analysis started from the first phase, 'familiarization with the data' in which the authors began to look for patterns of meaning and issues of potential interest in the data. In the second phase of thematic analysis, 'generating initial codes', the authors built on their notes from the previous stage of familiarization with the data, generating an initial list and ideas outlining what was in the data and what was interesting about it. The third analysis phase, 'searching for themes' (Clarke and Braun, 2013: 76), allowed the authors to re-focus the analysis at the broader level of themes, rather than codes. This involved revisiting all relevant statements that were similar to certain codes to form the initial themes, i.e., trying to combine different codes that were very similar or dealt with the same aspect. In the fourth phase of thematic analysis, 'reviewing themes', the authors cross-checked the chosen themes, trying to cohere the data within themes together meaningfully, while finding clear and identifiable distinctions between themes. In the fifth phase, 'defining and naming themes', the authors clearly defined the themes and named them, trying to give the reader a sense of what the theme was about. For the sixth phase, 'writing up', the authors had a set of fully worked-out themes. In keeping with Clarke and Braun (2013), the analysis was not viewed as a linear but rather a recursive process, and the thematic analysis involved a constant moving back and forth between the entire dataset, the coded extracts of data that were analysed and the analysis that was produced. Thus, writing was an integral part of the analysis, not something that took place at the end.

FINDINGS

The thematic analysis of visitor experiences at Zemaitija National Park's Cold War Museum resulted in the identification of several themes, which were divided into three thematic groups: 'between space and uniqueness', 'between history and experiences' and 'between nature and darkness' (Table 21.1).

The first thematic group, 'between space and uniqueness', connects the following themes: 'experiencing the space of the Cold War Museum', 'experiencing the Cold War Museum's accessibility' and 'experiencing the uniqueness of the exhibition'.

After analysing visitors' reviews on Tripadvisor, a first subtheme emerged within the theme 'experiencing the space of the Cold War Museum': 'the hidden space of the Cold War Museum'. Visitors appeared to be fascinated by the unique space of this museum, describing it as a large complex located underground. In their reviews, they explained that the exhibition

Table 21.1   Thematic analysis results: thematic groups, themes and subthemes

Thematic group	Themes	Subthemes
Between space and uniqueness	Experiencing the space of the Cold War Museum	The hidden space of the Cold War Museum
		Unexpected layout of the visiting spaces
		Rocket shaft – a unique object and unique space
		The uniqueness of the object's spatial layout
	Experiencing the Cold War Museum's accessibility	Adaptation of the object to the visitors
		Innovative solutions for visitors
		Challenging museum location
	Experiencing the uniqueness of the exhibition	The only Soviet missile base that survived so well
		A provocative place
		Authenticity of the exhibition
Between history and experiences	Experiencing historical value	The value of knowledge
		The exhibition – an important part of history
		Madness of nuclear war
	Diversity of experiences	Emotional experience
		Emotional connection
		Involvement in the historical narrative
		Experiencing the Cold War era
		Experiencing dark tourism
Between nature and darkness	Experiencing nature	Arrival path
		Experiencing Plateliai village
	Experiencing darkness	Dark history as an experience
		Fair
		Harshness
	Experiencing (dis)connecting unity	The Cold War Museum's relationship with nature
		Reminder of the possible consequences for humanity

spaces surprised them and that they liked the place for its very interesting infrastructure, because the whole exhibition is located underground, with only a small portion visible above ground. This is supported by the comment of a visitor from Sweden: 'it was so cool to be able to go down in an old Soviet bunker'.

Similar reviews were shared by other visitors. One (Anonymous 3) remarked that 'the missile silos are huge but deep underground, you can only see a small part on the ground'. Another, from Denmark, made the following comment: 'You go beneath the ground to see this new amazing and hidden museum'. The second subtheme, 'unexpected layout of the visiting spaces', opens up the understanding that visitors also enjoyed the fact that the museum was spread out across several rooms that once housed the missile base. The exhibition has a unique and exclusive architecture, allowing the visitor to feel and walk as if in a real bunker. A visitor from Canada indicated that the exhibition space consists of many different rooms: 'we were guided through the various rooms'.

The reviews revealed a third subtheme, the 'rocket shaft – a unique object and unique space': it is noteworthy that the rocket shaft was the most memorable exhibition space for visitors, who appreciated the opportunity to see it up close. They described it as an impressive and breath-taking space. A visitor from Sweden commented that this place surprised her the most: 'being able to go into one of the rooms where one of the missiles used to be – WOW'.

The subtheme 'the uniqueness of the object's spatial layout' covers critical reviews of the layout of the museum space. Visitors noticed that the infrastructure of the exhibition was a concern for certain tourist groups, such as the elderly, young children or those with medical conditions or phobias. A visitor from Alabama wrote that 'there are steep steps and low ceilings, so accessibility in some places is a bit challenging', adding: 'not good for anyone with claustrophobia or difficulty navigating tight spaces'. According to a visitor from Virginia: 'it is a bit challenging as some of the doorways are short and it takes some climbing here and there'. Although visitors considered the layout of this space to be a shortcoming, from the perspective of niche tourism, it is one of the important details that make this museum an authentic niche tourism object.

The theme 'experiencing Cold War Museum accessibility' is also divided into subthemes. The first one, 'adaptation of the object to the visitors', presents how visitors experience the guiding infrastructure. The exhibition was reworked in 2012, and visitors now report being able to orient themselves freely and that it features clear descriptions and English-language signposts, as explained by a visitor from England: 'the site was really easy to navigate as an English family with lots of good clear signage in English'. A visitor from Canada wrote: 'I was given an English audio guide which served me well'. While exploring the exhibition, visitors noted that they were independently monitored by guides via security cameras, thus ensuring their safety and quick assistance should they get lost: 'an attendant can contact you and come to your rescue'.

A second subtheme, 'innovative solutions for visitors', reveals that the updated exhibition provides opportunities to visit more rooms and incorporates more interactive elements, and that the renovated rooms provide safety and comfort while walking. A visitor from Australia remarked that 'it was very interesting to walk around and you can walk nearly everywhere'. A visitor from Lithuania also commented on the museum's improved condition after the restoration: 'I have been there before and after, and although it was amazing before renovation, now it is even better'. However, some visitors felt that the exhibition was sometimes overloaded with information and that some elements were kitschy. A visitor from Minnesota wrote: 'The displays have lots of (sometimes too much) information. [...] The site is a little kitschy (mannequins in uniforms)'.

A final subtheme, 'challenging museum location', showed that the location of the museum was one of the visitors' greatest concerns. Visitors found the place hard to find and affirmed that getting there without their own transportation was impossible. They reported that reaching the site was very difficult, but worth the trouble: 'Missile base is quite difficult to find but worth it'. Visitors admired the exceptional exoticism of the place, which is located in the middle of a forest, away from civilization. They associated this experience with secrecy and integrity, as described by one of the visitors (Anonymous 1): 'it is in a forest down the end of a rough road'.

The second theme, 'experiencing the uniqueness of the exhibition' also consists of several subthemes. 'The only Soviet missile base that survived so well' refers to the uniqueness of the object: only three underground Soviet missile bases were built during the Cold War, and this is the only underground Soviet base in which a modern Cold War exhibition has been installed. A visitor from the UK explained this: 'There were only 3 sites of such type in the Soviet Union and this one was preserved the best'. Visitors from foreign countries expressed the idea that visiting such a missile base is a very rare opportunity. A visitor from Canada thus wondered: 'when or where else will you get to enter a former Soviet nuclear missile base[?]'. For this reason, the Cold War exhibition appeared to be greatly appreciated not only in Lithuania, but also in Europe, with one visitor from Lithuania calling it 'one of the most amazing museums in Lithuania and Europe'.

The second subtheme, 'a provocative place', shows the experiences of visitors who called the object a 'provocative museum', a 'provoking place' or affirmed that it was 'very though[t] provoking being there'. The subtheme 'authenticity of the exhibition' reveals the idea that the exhibition is unique in that it has largely maintained its authenticity. Most of the exhibition equipment, premises and exhibits have survived from Soviet times. Visitors pointed out that the items, radio stations or original documents preserved in the exhibition made their visit particularly special, with one highlighting that it was possible 'to hear the original tapes from the secret radio stations, watch some original documentaries'.

Visitors noticed the original Soviet weapons, equipment and photos ('old pictures, old weapons', Anonymous 10). One aspect of the authenticity comes from the local guides, who have lived all their lives in the area. A visitor from Lithuania was surprised by the guides' stories: 'the guide-woman is very good. She spent all her life in this district and didn't know what's going on underground'. Thus, the shared experiences of visitors show us that the museum is unique, as the only surviving underground Soviet missile base. This exceptional construction was kept secret for many years but can now be accessed by any visitor.

The thematic group 'between history and experiences' combines two themes, 'experiencing historical value' and 'diversity of experiences'.

Within the first theme, the subtheme 'the value of knowledge' points to visitors' experiences of the exhibition as a very important lesson in history, providing a great deal of historical knowledge. Indeed, a visitor from Australia described it as a 'great history lesson', while a visitor from the United States noted: 'You can't get any closer to Cold War History than this'. The visitor claimed that this trip had changed his understanding of Cold War history: 'prior to this visit, my knowledge of the Cold War was minimal and I doubted that this tour would make a difference. How wrong I was, it turned out to be one of the best tours I have had in many years'. According to the reviews, the historical material about the Cold War period is presented in an interesting and informative way, as explained by a visitor: 'exhibits help to understand what was going on and preparing for war'. This exhibition has a strong connection to history, which changed some visitors' perceptions of the Cold War period. A visitor from North Carolina wrote that this exhibition opened up opportunities to look at this era differently: 'this was quite eye opening'.

A second subtheme, 'the exhibition – an important part of history', addresses the fact that this exhibition presents a highly complicated period in history. Very important political events could have taken place in that space, which may have left a painful history. Visitors from many different countries are involved in this historical heritage; therefore, this site is of interest not just to residents of Lithuania, but to foreigners as well. A visitor from Lithuania suggested that this object must be visited by everybody: 'It is a must in Lithuania'. A visitor from Switzerland also noted that 'this place is an important place looking at the history'.

The subtheme 'madness of nuclear war' reveals the consequences of the Cold War and makes it possible to imagine the damage that one missile can do to humanity and nature. A visitor from the UK understood the Cold War exhibition as representing a historical but also a painful event and offering reflection on its consequences: 'it is well worth the visit, wandering around this underground Soviet missile complex is fascinating and brings the reality of the madness of nuclear war'. A visitor from Oregon noticed that this tour allowed them 'to remember the dangers of the Cold War'. Thus, the exhibition has a very strong historical value, as it represents the Cold War period and its consequences. It has become a special place for reflection on what might have happened if different political decisions had been taken, forcing visitors to think of it as a creation that could have destroyed the beauty of humanity and nature.

The first subtheme within the larger theme 'diversity of experiences', 'emotional experience', shows that visitors' experiences were related to emotions such as excitement, fear, surprise and curiosity and triggered painful and serious reflections. A visitor from Canada described the exhibition as a place for emotions and reflections, remarking that 'it's chilling to think what could've happened to the world had the secret base fulfilled a gruesome purpose'. An Israeli visitor's description of the emotional experience is particularly strong: 'This is the story of lives endangered, of mass destruction, of weapon development – it is by no means "fun" or "amazing" (unlike the opinions of other reviewers) but rather a kick to your stomach'.

A second subtheme, 'emotional connection', concerns the strong emotional link between visitors and personal memories. For example, a visitor from Virginia felt a connection with people who lived during the Cold War and remembered their own childhood while participating in the tour: 'having grown up in the Cold War era, and then many years later, finding ourselves in an underground Soviet nuclear weapon site, was just too amazing!'. For others, a strong emotional connection emerged in connection with their country, as a visitor from the UK remarked: 'interesting when you realize that one of the missiles was aimed at UK in the early 60s'.

The subtheme 'involvement in the historical narrative' shows that during the visit, visitors had opportunities to engage with the whole story and were encouraged to go through a variety of experiences. Visitors had the opportunity to try on Soviet clothes and be photographed, to try to put on gas masks, or to press the 'red' button, thus 'causing' an artificial rocket launch. A visitor from Australia mentioned these aspects of the exhibition: 'you can dress up in military uniforms and take a photo behind the wire fence'. Another visitor, from California, enjoyed trying on clothes and hold weapons, noting that 'once you are there they have old Soviet overcoats and guns you can model and pose for some fun photos'. The opportunity to press the red button and watch the events in Hiroshima and Nagasaki unfold by launching a rocket also left an impression: 'you can push the button and see atomic bomb explodes and what happens'.

The subtheme 'experiencing the Cold War era' reveals that the exhibition allowed visitors to feel the atmosphere of the Cold War era. While visiting the site, a visitor from Sweden imagined the soldiers who worked there at the time: 'feels quite surreal to go underground to see the rooms where the people worked and stood on alert if nuclear war was coming'. A visitor from Lithuania also remarked: 'you can feel the Soviet spirit there'.

A final subtheme, 'experiencing dark tourism' presents the impressions of visitors who portrayed the museum as a frightening place revealing Cold War experiences. A visitor from Colombia describes the experience as follows: 'it is an experience, glad we went but as I mentioned very creepy at the same time when you realize its purpose and how you lived through those Cold War years'. Dark tourism experiences were also reflected in the empathy felt by visitors when they realized what the purpose of this site may have been during the Cold War. A visitor from England wrote that looking at the empty missile silos was frightening: 'you can stare down the hole where a nuclear missile was once housed. Chilling'. The emotional experiences created by the exhibition are very important elements of the visit. Visitors experienced different feelings and impressions during the tour: emotional connection, emotional experience, personal experience, the atmosphere of the Cold War and the shadow of a dark tourism object.

The thematic group 'between nature and darkness' combines three themes: 'experiencing nature', 'experiencing darkness' and 'experiencing (dis)connecting unity'.

The theme 'Experiencing nature' comprises several subthemes. Given that the Cold War Museum is located in Zemaitija National Park, the subtheme 'arrival path' highlights the attention paid by visitors to the road leading to the exhibition. Visitors perceived the rugged road as muddy, stretching through the woods, gravelly and difficult to find. However, the road represents sustainability, as it reflects only a low level of infrastructure.

This poses challenges but also introduces visitors to the nature of Zemaitija National Park. Along the way, visitors have the opportunity to visit a wildlife sanctuary and occasionally spot wild animals. A visitor from the UK described how to find this road, as well as its condition: 'This museum is not easy to find, but if you drive about 5 miles southwards from the village of Plateliai with its helpful visitor centre, or turn north off the 164 towards Plateliai you will find it signposted, down a long dirt road into the forest for about another 3 miles'. A visitor from North Carolina was impressed with the road to the Cold War Museum: 'it's a beautiful drive out to the site through the countryside to a national park from our cruise ship dock. That's part of the value in going here'. The road also reminded a visitor from the UK of Soviet times: 'This place [is] tucked in a remote part of the countryside. 5km along a dirt road. It is like stepping back in time, into the underground Soviet nuclear facility'.

The subtheme 'experiencing Plateliai village' describes the nearby area: after the Cold War exhibition, visitors mentioned the nearby village of Plateliai and noted that it is also unique, beautiful and worthy of attention. The village is not only located at the centre of Zemaitija National Park, but also offers the services of local residents (diving academy, accommodation, etc.). A visitor from Norway remarked that Plateliai is a wonderful little-known village, worth exploring for a few days: 'Plateliai in general is quite an unknown gem for Western tourists. I suggest spending at least a couple of days, enjoying the national park, eating at a certain local restaurant, and of course – visiting this museum'.

Visitors suggested stopping by Plateliai village after visiting the Cold War Museum, because it features several interesting places, services offered by locals, authentic homesteads, cafes and one of the largest and cleanest lakes in Lithuania. A visitor from the UK wrote that the area is full of opportunities to engage in interesting activities: 'there is plenty to do in the surrounding area, with little villages, cafes and lakeside stops'. After visiting the Cold War Museum, visitors went on walks around Lake Plateliai and visited the nearby village of Plateliai.

The theme 'experiencing darkness' consists of several subthemes. The first, 'dark history as an experience', reveals that the Cold War Museum connects visitors with historical experiences. The exhibition provides a lot of information about the Cold War period, changing visitors' established opinions on the historical events that took place during this era. Visitors appreciated the fact that this exhibition does not defend either side of the conflict and tries to present the historical events as they really were. A visitor from Israel praised it for 'telling the history of Cold War in the Baltics from both sides of the barricade (US and USSR), with no discounts given'.

The subtheme 'fear' underlines the scary atmosphere of the museum. Some visitors felt intimidated, describing an 'eerie' (Anonymous 4) or 'cold and dark place' (visitor from Lithuania). Visitors wrote that the museum has an exceptional atmosphere that depicts dark times, as expressed by a visitor from Scotland: 'dark times indeed'. A visitor from Sweden noted that it is an interesting place reminiscent of a dark time in history: 'this is a very interesting travel through a dark part of our history'.

A third subtheme, 'harshness', arose from the museum's ability to connect the visitor with harsh experiences, as a painful reminder of the Cold War period. Visitors also reported that this exhibition caused them to reflect deeply on the possible consequences of the conflict. A visitor from New York shared his experience: 'it's a chilling reminder nonetheless'. A visitor from Australia commented that the four empty shafts triggered emotions: 'perish the thought if a single missile had ever been launched'. A visitor from Poland also noted that 'it is very interesting but also kind of scary to be inside a silo where nuclear warheads were directed towards Europe a few decades ago...'. These comments reveal the impact of this dark tourism site on its visitors, which allowed them to understand the consequences of the Cold War on a personal level, as well as changed their thinking. The Cold War Museum, as an object of dark tourism, fosters strong emotions and independent reflections in its visitors. The space and atmosphere of the site evoke difficult and harsh emotions, allowing visitors to understand the possible consequences of the Cold War era more deeply.

The theme 'experiencing (dis)connecting unity' has 'the Cold War Museum's relationship with nature' as its first subtheme. This theme reveals how visitors reflected upon the Cold War Museum and described finding this 'terrible' object in a very beautiful place. They were fascinated by the fact that it was built in the middle of a forest to make it less visible. This implies an emerging connection between the site and nature, as the latter (the forest) plays a very important role here. Visitors were delighted to enjoy not only the interesting exhibition, but also the beautiful surroundings, recalling 'looking round, enjoying the history and the peace and quiet of the forest' (Anonymous 1). Another visitor (Anonymous 4) was surprised by the location of the museum: 'in the middle of a National Park with a small footprint, we discovered this "eerie" place'.

The subtheme 'reminder of the possible consequences for humanity' expresses visitors' understanding of the object as a reminder of the events that might have taken place there and their consequences, with the surrounding nature making it possible to understand what may have been lost and what must now be protected and nurtured. A visitor from Sweden discussed the impact of this exhibition as a reminder for younger generations: 'I think that this museum is very important for the remembrance of those terrible days, especially for our young generation, so that this never will be forgotten'.

The thematic analysis demonstrates that the Cold War Museum in Zemaitija National Park is a unique object. Visitors to the site described different layers of experiences: some admired the site's infrastructure and its preserved authenticity, others reported on the diverse thoughts and emotions that arose there, and some said that the place seemed intimidating and uncomfortable to them. Visitors expressed fascination not only with the site itself, but also with its location, surrounded by the beautiful Plokštinė forest in Zemaitija National Park, and with the nearby village of Plateliai.

CONCLUSION

The analysis has shown that the Cold War Museum closely combines niche tourism and dark tourism. The thematic analysis of the experiences of visitors led to the identification of themes, which were combined into three thematic groups ('between space and uniqueness', 'between history and experiences' and 'between nature and darkness'). These themes between them explained different layers of the visitors' experiences. The analysis revealed the nature of this dark tourism site as a niche tourism object and illustrated various layers of the niche tourism experience. The unique opportunity to experience a former underground missile base located in the middle of a national park not only highlights the connection between nature and history, but also conveys an important message to future generations and gives each visitor the opportunity to immerse themself in personal reflections.

The analysis also underlined the importance of paying attention to the unique experiences of visitors, which could help to foster the development of sustainable niche tourism in Zemaitija National Park in the future. Consequently, the future development of the Cold War Museum should be oriented towards authenticity and future research should also focus on in-depth analysis of visitor experiences.

Cold War studies have witnessed a transformation in the wake of the cultural turn and debates about the distinction between Cold War tourism and tourism in the Cold War (Bechmann and Noack, 2019). Thus, it seems appropriate to call on future tourism researchers and tourism practitioners to debate the definition of Cold War tourism in the context of the future development of niche tourism.

REFERENCES

Ali-Knight, J. (2011) *The Role of Niche Tourism Products in Destination Development*. PhD Thesis. Edinburgh Napier University. Available at: http://researchrepository.napier.ac.uk/id/eprint/5376 (accessed 15 June 2020).

Axelsson, T., Gustafsson, A., Karlsson, H. and Persson, M. (2018) Command Centre Bjorn: The conflict heritage of a Swedish Cold War military installation. *Journal of Conflict Archaeology*, 13(1), 59–76, doi: 10.1080/15740773.2018.1536407.

Bechmann, P. S. and Noack, C. (2019) *Tourism and Travel during the Cold War. Negotiating Tourist Experiences across the Iron Curtain*. London: Routledge.

Biran, A. and Poria, Y. (2012) Re-conceptualising dark tourism. In R. Sharpley and P. Stone (eds) *The Contemporary Tourism Experience: Concepts and Consequences*. London: Routledge, 62–79.

Clarke, V. and Braun, V. (2013) Teaching thematic analysis: Overcoming challenges and developing strategies for effective learning. *The Psychologist*, 26(2), 120–23.

Cold War Museum. Reviews on TripAdvisor Available at: https://www.tripadvisor.com/Attraction _Review-g1185602-d3369210-Reviews-Cold_War_Museum-Plateliai_Zemaitija_National_Park _Telsiai_County.html (accessed 15 May 2020).

Collins-Kreiner, N. (2016) Dark tourism as/is pilgrimage. *Current Issues in Tourism*, 19(12), 1185–9, doi: 10.1080/13683500.2015.1078299.

Dinis, A. and Krakover, S. (2016) Niche tourism in small peripheral towns: The case of Jewish heritage in Belmonte, Portugal. *Tourism Planning & Development*, 13(3), 310–32.

Handayani, B. (2018) Going to the Dark Sites with intention: Construction of niche tourism. In M. Korstanje and G. Babu (eds) *Virtual Traumascapes and Exploring the Roots of Dark Tourism*. Hershey, PA, USA: IGI Global, 50–66.

Ivanova, P. and Light, D. (2018) 'It's not that we like death or anything': Exploring the motivations and experiences of visitors to a lighter dark tourism attraction. *Journal of Heritage Tourism*, 13(4), 356–69. doi: 10.1080/1743873X.2017.1371181

Kennell, J. and Powell, R. (2020) Dark tourism and world heritage sites: A delphi study of stakeholder perceptions of the development of dark tourism products. *Journal of Heritage Tourism*, 16(4), 367–81. doi: https://doi.org/10.1080/1743873X.2020.1782924

Light, D. (2017) Progress in dark tourism and thanatourism research: An uneasy relationship with heritage tourism. *Tourism Management*, 61, 275–301.

Novelli, M. (ed.) (2005) *Niche Tourism: Contemporary Issues, Trends and Cases*. Oxford, UK: Elsevier.

Packer, J. and Ballantyne, R. (2016) Conceptualizing the visitor experience: A review of literature and development of a multifaceted model. *Visitor Studies*, 19(2), 128–43. doi: 10.1080/10645578.2016.1144023.

Robinson, M. and Novelli, M. (2005) Introduction. In M. Novelli (ed.) *Niche Tourism: Contemporary Issues, Trends and Cases*. Oxford, UK: Elsevier Ltd, 1–11.

Sharma, P. and Kumar Nayak, J. (2020) Examining experience quality as the determinant of tourist behavior in niche tourism: An analytical approach. *Journal of Heritage Tourism*, 15(1), 76–92. doi: 10.1080/1743873X.2019.1608212.

Sorea, D. and Csesznek, C. (2020) The Groups of caroling lads from Făgăraş Land (Romania) as niche tourism resource. *Sustainability*, 12(11), 4577.

Stone, P. (2011) Tourism anthropology. Dark tourism: Towards a new post-disciplinary research agenda. *International Journal of Tourism Anthropology*, 1(3/4), 318–32.

Topsakal, Y. and Ekici, R. (2014) *Dark Tourism as a Type of Special Interest Tourism: Dark Tourism Potential of Turkey*. Available at: https://www.researchgate.net/publication/268448602 (accessed 15 May 2020).

Tribe, J. and Liburd, J.J. (2016) The tourism knowledge system. *Annals of Tourism Research*, 57, 44–61.

Venter, D. (2017) Examining military heritage tourism as a niche tourism market in the South African context. *African Journal of Hospitality, Tourism and Leisure*, 6(1), 1–19.

Zemaitija National Park (2020). *Zemaitija National Park Directorate*. Available at: http://zemaitijosnp.lt/en/expositions/ (accessed 22 May 2020).

Zemaitija National Park. *TripAdvisor*. Available at: https://www.tripadvisor.com/Tourism-g10476718-Zemaitija_National_Park_Telsiai_County-Vacations.html (accessed 15 April 2020).

22. Cemetery tourism in Slovenia

Lea Kužnik and Tanja Ostrman Renault

INTRODUCTION

Digital technology enables us to 'visit' the most interesting, remote, dangerous and exotic places on earth from the comfort of our homes. Why should someone want to go anywhere if everything is only two clicks away? In particular, to places which are generally unknown, such as the small town of Ptuj in Slovenia? Ptuj is the oldest town in Slovenia located in the northeast of the country, close to the Austrian and Hungarian borders. First mentioned in 69 AD by the Roman historian Tacit, in relation to the election of Vespasian to emperor, it was one of the most important Roman towns in Pannonia, comprising twice as many inhabitants as it has today.

A strong military and civil presence in Roman Poetovio is attested to by five Mithraea (temples dedicated to god Mithras) that have been discovered so far in Ptuj, while Illyrian customs covered the area from present-day Switzerland to the Black Sea. In the Middle Ages, Ptuj prospered as a result of its strategic position on the Drava River, which brought to town traders, merchants and artisans. From the 10th century to the end of WWI, Ptuj was, with minor interruptions, under German-speaking rule, an influence still detectable in the architecture and culture in general. In the 16th century, Italian traders settled in town.

The town cemetery is not in use any longer; the last funerary service was held there in 1978. For decades it was an ideal venue for drug-dealers, vandals and clandestine meetings, but in 2018 it was converted into a memorial park. The majority of the dilapidated and partially destroyed monuments were repaired, the exuberant vegetation that had covered some of the finest tombstones along the walls was cleaned up, and new trees were planted. At night the park is closed, but during the day many students pass through, or sit and eat their midday snacks on benches, and some even come to jog. The plethora of monuments has finally been made available, and the place is ready for the development of cemetery tourism. The real challenge, however, is how to present the rich history of Ptuj through the life stories of those laid to rest there.

This chapter explores the current situation in relation to cemetery tourism in Ptuj, and aims to identify potential narratives that can contribute to the development of a new tourism product based on the cultural heritage and history of the town. The study applies ethnographic methods with the main goal of developing interpretative content related to the cemetery. Moreover, it spotlights a variety of new opportunities based on storytelling for the development of cemetery tourism in Ptuj, including the design of innovative heritage-based thematic trails.

CEMETERY TOURISM

Cemeteries are sacred and emotional places, but more importantly, they bear witness to local history. They are a common feature of every city and town in Europe, helping residents

Source: Personal archive: Tanja Ostrman Renault.

Figure 22.1   *Slovenia in Europe and Ptuj in Slovenia*

remember events steeped in local history that communities do not wish to or should never forget. According to Tobias, cemeteries are places somewhere in nature where the dead are buried or their ashes are either kept in urns or scattered. Cemeteries can either be functional – that is, burials take place regularly and they contain all the necessary facilities for funerary ceremonies and infrastructure, including organised access to graves – or they can be 'sleeping', as in the case of numerous ancient cemeteries where interments no longer take place, making them memorial parks (Tobias, 1999).

Cemetery tourism is only starting to develop in Slovenia, though some larger cemeteries offer guided tours using either a conventional analogue guide or smart-phone-based applications. The visits revolve around renowned people, mostly of Slovenian origin; however, there are also some internationally well-known personalities, such as doctor Filip Terč, father of the modern apitherapy, Jože Plečnik, a renowned architect from the beginning of the 20th century, and others. Generally, biographies of the deceased are presented during these visits, most of which are attended by Slovenian nationals, unless there are visits planned through the ASCE (Association of Significant Cemeteries of Europe) and the ECR (European Cemeteries Route), of which both of Slovenia's largest cemeteries (Žale in Ljubljana and Pobrežje in Maribor) are members. Both of these cemeteries are also of interest from an architectural point of view, particularly Žale, the entrance of which was designed by the most prominent Slovenian architect, Jože Plečnik (1872–1957), whose unique style is also visible in both Prague and Vienna.

Cemetery tourism is generally considered a branch of dark tourism (Gosar, 2015; Stone, 2006; Seaton, 1996), which, in turn, is often referred to as thanatourism, grief and morbid tourism or even black spot tourism in academia. Nevertheless, Light (2017) draws parallels among these terms only to show the major differences often disregarded by researchers, pointing out that 'dark tourism [is] used as an umbrella term for any form of tourism that is somehow related to death', while thanatourism, as Seaton (2002) termed it, is 'behavioural rather than essentialist' where the 'motivation of tourists to visit places associated with death' is more important than 'the supply dimension of dark tourism'.

One of the major advocates of dark tourism, Stone (2006), includes 'dark resting places' (cemeteries) among dark tourism products, despite the fact that, as he himself states, such places have 'both dark and light elements', are generally well-maintained in order to conserve 'Romantic and Gothic architecture and sculpture' and are sometimes converted into memorial parks and/or green areas of a town or city. The fact is that both cemetery and dark tourism can be defined as niche tourism. Within the context of dark tourism, a question arises as to when and in which cases visiting cemeteries can be defined as dark tourism and why it is different from cemetery tourism.

The main difference lies in the fact that a dark tourist visits mostly places and sites marked by violent death (sites of the Holocaust, mass killings, great battles and other murders in the contemporary world) or death as a consequence of natural disasters (hurricane Katrina in New Orleans, a tsunami in Thailand, etc.). When a tourist is interested in tragic and shocking stories of people who have died violent deaths and visits cemeteries to see their tombstones, this epitomises dark tourism (Kužnik and Veble, 2018). Cemetery tourism can be described as based on individual or guided visits for the purpose of learning about the diverse ethnologic, art-historical, historical or architectural heritage of a specific place or area.

Cemeteries as cultural heritage represent an important element of human history and art, as well as a touristic feature of towns and cities through which visitors learn about the culture and way of life of people in a certain period of time and place. The past of a nation is also narrated through epitaphs, described by Stanonik (1999) as being a part of cultural wealth that must be preserved, as they represent fragments of linguistic tradition, history and culture. Although epitaphs are predominantly meant to express piety, they also show deep reverence for the dead and convey a much wider social dimension (ibid.). According to the ASCE, during a visit to a cemetery, visitors establish a very personal relationship with local people by reading the various epitaphs on tombstones, at the cemetery entrance and on certain sacral objects, because epitaphs strike the emotional chords of individuals and groups. Besides epitaphs, the architectural aspect of tombstones is also an element of the wider cultural heritage.

Cemetery tourism is very popular in many countries, and cemeteries such as Père Lachaise Cemetery in Paris, Wiener Zentralfriedhof in Vienna, Highgate Cemetery in London, Mirogoj Cemetery in Zagreb and several in the United States (Green – Wood Cemetery in New York, Arlington National Cemetery in Virginia, Mount Auburn Cemetery in Massachusetts) are especially well-known (Dancausa Millán et al., 2019). There are also well-developed creators of tourism content, such as Veverka and Associates (http://www.heritageinterp.com), which offers courses on interpretation of gravestones and historic cemeteries, or Dearly Departed Tours (https://dearlydepartedtours.com) offering tours centred around deceased Hollywood celebrities and calling itself the 'authority on the dark side of Hollywood'.

The Merry Cemetery in Romania (Mionel, 2020) can also be considered a staged death scene due to its carved and painted wooden crosses and black-humour epitaphs. It has become one of the 'must see' tourist attractions in Romania. It is an example of Romanian folk culture, and although some epitaphs sound rather ironic and satirical, they nonetheless tell stories of the dead. Marques (2018) designates cemeteries as being 'cities of the dead' that mirror actual cities, as each chapel and each grave represents a house and thus becomes a secondary home. The deceased also have an address (Beyern, 2013; Marques, 2018), as their resting place is either located within a 'division', 'sector' or 'line' marked by a letter or number that people write to, leaving letters on the tombstones of the intended recipients (e.g., Jim Morrison, Princess Diana, Alfred de Musset). In addition, from the way cemeteries are conceived, including the vegetation and architecture, it can be deduced that they are replicas not only of cities per se, but also indicators of the socioeconomic status of the deceased and their living descendants, which is easily determined by the position of the grave, its size and whether it bears an epitaph or just a mere inscription.

This vision is shared by many others, most notably those who are professionally involved in cemetery operations, as well as members of the ASCE. The latter strongly oppose the use of the term 'dark tourism' when talking about non-military cemeteries. They consider cemeteries as sites whose architectural and historical dimensions must be preserved in order to safeguard an important part of cultural heritage. Their mission is to raise awareness about the importance cemeteries represent for each community as they reflect their history, architecture, culture and the people who lived there.

Within the European Institute of Cultural Routes, ASCE members have developed the ECR (https://cemeteriesroute.eu/european-cemeteries-route.aspx) which has been certified as a Cultural Route of the Council of Europe since 2010. The ECR's mission is to open cemeteries so that visitors can take a walk through local history and learn about different religions, customs, nationalities and values. In addition, the ASCE prepares annual Days of European Cemeteries Heritage, temporarily turning cemeteries into venues for various cultural events that attract hundreds of people. The ECR refers to cemeteries as places of life, environments that are linked to the history and cultural history of the community to which they belong.

Cemeteries are in fact full of life and are meant for the living, as Beyern (2013) explains. He coined the term '*nécrosophe*' a word has come to designate his profession as a 'necro-philosopher', which denotes a passion for cemeteries. According to Beyern, cemeteries are places for the living because if they were not, there would not be all these monuments and epitaphs. They evoke memories and emotions, and induce us to travel back in time. As a guide at the Père Lachaise cemetery, Beyern is aware that tourists come to visit the tombs of celebrities and that encountering an epitaph on the tomb of even an unknown individual makes that person metaphorically come alive. In a sense death is disguised and hidden in the theatre-like environment of a cemetery.

INTERPRETATION OF HERITAGE

Storytelling is the oldest and most effective form of interpretation, and the primary environments for this are around an evening bonfire, in front of the stove on a winter evening, by the fireplace or at an inn. Fog et al. (2010) enumerate the key elements of the story that form the essence of storytelling and describe its key components as: the message, the conflict, the characters and the plot or course of the story. In storytelling, the emotional component is exposed and it becomes a means for achieving various goals. In the tourism sector, storytelling serves as an important tool that conveys a message about the destination in question (Kužnik and Veble, 2018).

Interpreting relevant heritage is one of the most important elements in heritage tourism, as it can be argued that nowadays 'everything is and must be a story'. Personal perception of something unknown very much depends on the interpretation of its meanings. A good interpretation incites listeners to reflect, which may lead to a change of heart or even a new way of life. Interpreting cultural heritage is not just a matter of giving information, but is primarily about discovering meaning, influencing attitudes and behaviours, and attracting interest. Interpretation should be informative, raise awareness, enrich knowledge and arouse interest in gaining new insights, and must always be based on facts and authentic stories. American poet and civil rights campaigner Maya Angelou (2005) said that people will forget what they say and do, but they will never forget the feelings that were aroused in them.

Visitors' emotional experiences are likely to be enhanced by nuanced and insightful interpretation, along with the authenticity of the site being visited. Interpretation can be defined as a set of information-focused communication activities designed to facilitate a rewarding visitor experience (Moscardo and Ballantyne, 2008), and has been spoken of as the primary means of communication between a site and its visitors (Sharpley and Stone, 2009; Wight and Lennon, 2007). Importantly, interpretation plays a crucial role in sites or attractions which reflect tragic events, given that without interpretation such sites may be meaningless to visitors (Moscardo and Ballantyne, 2008). In other words, effective interpretation of such sites remains essential to enhance visitor experiences and fulfil the need for understanding and meaning (Sharpley and Stone, 2009).

Interpretation in large cemeteries where famous and well-known people are interred seems to be more rewarding than in smaller cemeteries where local celebrities repose. At least there is usually a choice of topics and thematic trails, as, for example, at the cemetery of Père Lachaise in Paris, where there are tours of the graves of famous writers, poets, painters and musicians, as well as tours dedicated to humour and satire, dark tours and many others dedicated to famous people. The complete opposite is the case at the small cemetery in Skagway, Alaska, the small port town where the Klondike gold-rush path starts. The town has around 1,200 inhabitants, yet it is visited by more than one million tourists every summer. Cruise ships visit and tourists converge on the town, which has preserved its gold-rush appearance through the restoration of significant historical buildings. This little gold-rush cemetery disappoints many visitors – as can be seen from commentaries left on Tripadvisor (https://www.tripadvisor.com/Attraction_Review-g60877-d4937041-Reviews-Gold_Rush_Cemetery-Skagway_Alaska.html) – enchants others, with the rest more or less unmoved. But not one commentor reported travelling to Skagway with the explicit aim of visiting the cemetery. Why is it then that tour operators take tourists there if they do not clearly ask for it? Why are some disappointed while others simply adore it and call it 'the highlight of the tour'? Browsing through different comments it can be said that the majority of those who most appreciated this gold-rush cemetery were part of a guided tour, and some even named the guides whose interpretations made the stop worthwhile. Interestingly enough, those who rated the visit to the cemetery 'terrible' were also part of guided tours, while those that rated it 'poor' went there on their own.

What makes a visit to the Skagway cemetery unforgettable is the guide-interpreter, for the place in itself has neither monumental tombstones nor touching epitaphs, no landscape or vegetation or unique features. It is a very uncomplicated place where many of those who followed the Klondike gold-rush path were laid to rest. One such story is the grave of Soapy Smith, a local con artist and gangster who exploited the confidence of gold miners and was finally shot by the local sheriff. A blunt story heard and seen many times before, but competently interpreted, it provokes visitors' curiosity not only because it depicts the life of gold miners in the 19th century, but because it evokes the history of the entire region. The associated narration about the verbal fight which eventually ended in a shooting makes the whole story worth listening to. Thus, the end comes rather as a surprise when the guide-interpreter explains that Soapy died instantly, while his opponent (the sheriff) died 12 days later of a shot he received in his left leg and groin area.

Efficient, clear and accessible communication in storytelling is essential for cemetery tourism. Incorrect, non-factual or bizarre interpretations can arguably change or degenerate the value of the messages conveyed by stories, for they are strongly connected with visitors' feelings. Misguided interpretation of dark places and events risks conveying too much romanticism or political/ideological bias, while making stories sound more sanitised or adapting them to individual target groups comes at the cost of depriving them of credibility and authenticity. The interpretation of the dark past must be based above all on respect for the participants involved.

RESEARCH METHODS

This chapter presents an exploratory study based on a multi-method approach. Besides the analyses of scientific and professional literature, the main research method is fieldwork with partially structured interviews. The purpose was to find out whether there might be different stories and/or historical places in Ptuj Cemetery – Memorial Park that have the potential to be used in cemetery tourism.

The main research question is: Does Ptuj Cemetery – Memorial Park fit in the category of a niche tourism destination due to its interesting stories, and can it be efficiently incorporated into a new comprehensive tourism product?

Before searching for 'dark' information, we first analysed the literature and existing documentation (old newspapers articles, photographs) in the Ptuj-Ormož Regional Museum and Ptuj Archives. From these sources, the first potential cemetery stories were identified. The main goal was to describe the most interesting stories related to Ptuj Cemetery in as much detail as possible. Furthermore, we also conducted fieldwork by visiting the cemetery to discover related stories and employing the observation with participation method by being part of a guided tour of the park. More detailed information and descriptions of stories were obtained by means of partially structured interviews with two curators of the Ptuj-Ormož Regional Museum and two experts from the Ptuj Archives. All interviews were recorded.

The most important information was recorded in the field notes. We also searched for residents connected with each of the stories, such as those who lived through a certain historical period or who witnessed various events involving those buried in the cemetery. The first three interviewees were proposed by the museum curators, and the other three were found using the snowball sampling technique. The information and descriptions of cemetery stories were gathered in short, unstructured interviews from three male and three female residents ranging in age from 69 to 83 years. All respondents were asked for stories related to Ptuj Cemetery.

With the information gathered through these interviews and observation with participation, we supplemented previously identified stories from the literature and documentation resources with additional details. The interviews also provided us with a few stories that we had not found in the literature before. Detailed information about these was recorded in the field notes. We additionally identified and described 13 stories that have a potential for inclusion in cemetery tourism at Ptuj Cemetery – Memorial Park.

HISTORY OF PTUJ MEMORIAL PARK

Beginning in the Middle Ages and continuing until the 18th century, the town of Ptuj had several cemeteries, while lords and nobility were buried in crypts in churches. During the Josephine reforms in the 18th century, the city had to relocate the cemetery at least one mile outside of its centre. In the mid-18th century, when a new city cemetery was established, a line of tombs was arranged by the wall for richer citizens. The desire for prestige also stimulated the artistic creativity of stonecutters, who created images in monumental shapes and built mausoleums for the tombs.

The cemetery was in use as far back as 1751, when military invalids were being buried there, but it is officially recognised that the old Ptuj Cemetery was in operation from the late 18th century until 1978.

After that, it was abandoned and often vandalised until 2017 when the local authorities decided to do something with it and had it converted into Memorial Park in 2018.

Stories from Ptuj Cemetery – Memorial Park

Some stories that have the potential to be used in cemetery tourism were collected during fieldwork and study of literature.

Archaeologists by chance
The rich past of Ptuj has always invited experts and adventurers to research and study it. Archaeological excavations have unearthed many interesting items that help reconstruct the life of this Roman town and the reason for its existence, which is undoubtedly due to its strategic position along the mighty Drava River, as the only crossing (bridge) was at this particular spot.

One of the finest vaults is dedicated to the Schickelgruber – Wibmer family. One member of the former, Leopold (1772–1843), was a carpenter who was fascinated by the river. One day while he was repairing the bridge, he noticed huge blocks of cut stones. He followed the river upstream and discovered the site where the ancient Roman bridge, built during the time of Hadrian and destroyed by the river in the 14th century, had been (Hernja Masten, 1991).

Another non-conventional archaeologist was Viktor Skrabar (1877–1938), who was a jurist but also attended classes in archaeology and epigraphy. He was present at all major discoveries, among which the excavations of Mithraeum III and the remains of the Roman bridge across the Drava deserve special mention. Thanks to his knowledge of Latin, he was able to trace the origin of the bridge to the time of Emperor Hadrian (Lamut, 1993).

Internationally renowned artists
Two tombstones have unique attributes as they were made by the same artist-painter, Jan Oeltjen (1880–1968), who sculpted a monument for his parents-in-law, Alois and Theresia

Source: Photo from Tanja Ostrman Renault (2020).

Figure 22.2   One of many remarkable monuments saved from ruin

Kasimir, after the drawing made by their daughter, Elsa Kasimir. The entire composition, of which Elsa's father is the central figure and is supported by an angel whose face resembles Elsa's, is reminiscent of the Resurrection. Another tombstone made by Jan Oeltjen that attracts visitors is the one made for his beloved wife, Elsa Kasimir (1887–1944), and himself. Their tombstone displays a figure of Jan in a mourning pose which resembles August Rodin's *Thinker*, holding a painter's palette, while above him hangs one of his favourite motifs, a boat, taking him and Elsa towards the sun.

Jan was from northern Germany but moved with Elsa to Ptuj and the surrounding hills, for, as Jan would often say: 'There are three things I love: Elsa, winegrowing-hills, and Ptuj'. But their relationship was far from calm, and they very often lived separated from each other due to their artistic obligations.

When Elsa was studying at the Vienna School of Arts and Crafts, Oskar Kokoschka was first her classmate (1907), and a year later her drawing teacher. A graphic paper from the Passion series gives evidence of their relationship, which might not have been purely platonic (Ciglenečki, 2017).

Source: Photo from Tanja Ostrman Renault (2020).

Figure 22.3   Too big to be stolen

Wealthy German-speaking wine merchants
There are many tombstones designating well-situated families, and the majority of them bear German names, as the area was mostly under German-speaking rule from the 10th century until 1918. Between the two world wars, Ptuj often witnessed tensions and frictions between German and Slovene nationals, although it has to be said that very many Slovenes proclaimed themselves German in order to access better positions. Many of them were wealthy and, besides their commerce in town, owned vineyards in the neighbouring vine-growing hills of Haloze and Slovenske Gorice. As a matter of fact, the grapevine was brought to the area by the Romans, though viticulture did not truly develop until the arrival of Minorite and Dominican monks in the 13th century.

The oldest vintage in Slovenia
One of the most prominent family vaults at the cemetery is the sepulchre of the Ornig family, dating to the beginning of the 20th century and in the Secession style.
   Joseph Ornig (1859–1925) was a successful businessman and long-time mayor of Ptuj (1894–1918). Although born to Slovenian parents in the nearby hills, he considered himself German and opposed everything that could help the Slovenians in their strivings for national

Source: Photo from Tanja Ostrman Renault (2020).

Figure 22.4   *Alois Kasimir (Elsa's father)*

recognition. Nevertheless, the town prospered during his term of office. After WWI, he fled to Graz, Austria and, having failed to persuade the emperor to reclaim the northern part of Slovenia, remained there until his death. Later his body was transferred to Ptuj, where he is now buried.

While in Graz, he ordered his son, who had remained in Ptuj, to put aside a few bottles of every wine vintage, and it is thanks to him that the Ptuj wine cellar boasts the oldest vintage in Slovenia, the 1917 Golden Vine. He was a very charitable man who helped poor people, and this feature of his personality is represented on the relief on the vault by an angel carrying a dish and a jug, while another one is leaning on a walking stick (Ciglenečki, 2017).

Final justice for the wine merchant?

A massive tombstone leaning on the western wall in the park bears the name of the Fürst family. The first member arrived in Ptuj in the 17th century, and at the beginning of the 19th century the family prospered in the wine trade and built one of the most beautiful bourgeois manors in town. The family had to leave everything behind and flee in 1945 after the war, and they were deprived of everything during the nationalisation process. In 1991, Slovenia became

Source: Photo from Tanja Ostrman Renault (2020).

Figure 22.5   Elsa Kasimir Oeltjen and Jan Oeltjen

independent and the family managed to get the house back in 2009 (Walter Fürst, personal communication).

White roses of innocence
Child mortality was considerably lower at the turn of the 20th century compared to previous eras, as the number of children who were stillborn at home and in hospitals increased. Stillborn children were handed over from the hospital to the gravedigger, who buried them. If the family had their own grave, they found a place in it, if not, they were buried in a designated part of the cemetery. Their tombs are smaller and generally designated by a cast-iron cross, an angel or a small stone with only the first name on it.

In the past, children were baptised almost immediately after birth for fear they would die before baptism and thus could not be buried in sacred ground. According to Christian doctrine, anyone present at a birth, such as a midwife, could baptise the child with water (Ptuj Historical Archives, personal communication).

Before 1960, deaths were determined in the field by coroners, who often relied on the use of various primitive devices for their determinations, such as a mirror placed before the mouth and nose of the supposed deceased which would fog up if they exhaled, thus indicating they were not in fact dead (Pšajd, 2017).

A tragic story of two brothers

Some tombstones contain photographs of the deceased, and among these is the tombstone of the Tomašič family, which depicts a tragic story of two brothers, both pilots, who died on the same day, within two hours of each other, in the same country and at almost the same spot.

They were both from Ptuj, temporarily working in Serbia. On the gloomy morning of Monday 10 October 1967, after spending the weekend together with their families, each accidentally took the other's jacket before saying goodbye and rushing to their respective planes. The extremely bad weather caused both planes to crash within two hours' time.

Their mother received the first telegram about her son Jure's death, and soon another telegram arrived with the same bad news about Jure's death. 'It must be a mistake, they sent the same telegram twice', she thought. But the only mistake was the name. Jure, a military pilot, was on a mission and everyone knew who he was, while Vili was a civil pilot and to identify the corpse they had to search for personal documents; thus, they found in Vili's pocket Jure's identity card, as they had switched jackets.

When the unfortunate mother, waiting for her son Vili to come and carry Jure's coffin, saw two coffins, she asked her third son: 'Who is the second coffin for?' 'Brother Vili', was the answer. It was only then that she realised the horrible truth and started to cry.

Monument-tombstones of public importance commemorate all those fallen in both wars.

These were still heroes...

WWI: The white marble plaque bears 72 carved names showing that the fallen and the deceased came from various parts of the monarchy. There is an inscription reproducing the record of one of the most famous battles of the ancient Greek world, the Battle of Thermopylae in 480 BC ('Stranger, go tell at home that you saw us lying here, since we followed the sacred laws of the fatherland!').

Symbols of local fight for freedom

WWII: Memorials to the National Liberation Struggle (NOB) are the most widely represented group of public monuments in Slovenian history. Most of these monuments were created in the 1950s and 1960s.

The obelisk tomb is dedicated to 45 fallen combatants in the NOB. After the Battle of Mostje on 8 August 1942, the Germans subjected the dead bodies of the fallen combatants to shaming in front of the headquarters of the gestapo in Ptuj for one day, and then buried them behind the cemetery wall.

The tombstone dedicated to Yugoslav soldiers who fell in battles with the Germans in April 1941 is close by. Another monument, erected in 1950, is dedicated to 20 hostages shot by the Nazis on 8 February 1945, behind the cemetery wall.

'My wife, my children...' were Lacko's last words

The statue of national hero Jože Lacko is made of bronze. Lacko was actively engaged in WWI, in which he served as an Austro-Hungarian soldier at the Isonzo Front. He was politically active between both world wars, and during World War II, he joined the Slovenjegoriška troop. Lacko was one of the three combatants who managed to escape from the enemy's ring

Source: Photo from Tanja Ostrman Renault (2020).

Figure 22.6   *WWI Memorial*

on 8 August 1942. Betrayed, he was caught by the Germans, imprisoned and brutally tortured until 12 August 1942, when he succumbed to the consequences of this inhumane treatment. Streets in several Slovenian cities are named after him (Regional Museum Ptuj-Ormož, permanent exhibition).

DISCUSSION

Cemetery tourism in Slovenia is still to be discovered and has the potential for the development of a variety of niche tourism products in the modern tourism supply. The main purpose of this research is to explore and identify the potentially interesting stories in connection to Ptuj to find out if it is possible to include them in niche tourism offers.

The main research question was: Does the Ptuj Cemetery – Memorial Park fit into the category of niche tourism sites due to its interesting stories, and can these be efficiently incorporated into a new comprehensive tourism product?

The field research outlined above shows that the answer to our research question is yes, as 13 interesting stories were identified and described, of which just some are presented in this chapter. Three stories are related to famous citizens, one to children, two to wine merchants and four to wars. According to the content, the identified stories can be ranked in the following typological segments:

- stories of famous citizens (the story of archaeologists, Schickelgruber and Skrabar, and the story of the renowned couple of artists Elsa Kasimir and Jan Oeltjen);
- stories of those who fashioned the local economy (the story of wine merchants Ornig and Fürst);
- stories of children (the story of the stillborn babies and the story of the tragic death of two brothers); and
- traces of war (the story of the WWI and WWII monuments, and the story of national hero Jože Lacko).

Many interesting, tragic, sad and terrifying stories from different historical periods were discovered in the study area which would be of interest to a specific segment of tourists. This leads us to conclude that the potential for the development of cemetery tourism certainly exists. Different thematic sets of stories can serve as a basis for the planning of a new niche tourism product at the cemetery.

Back in the first 15 months of the Memorial Park's existence, four guided tours were proposed and carried out, free of charge, by a local guide who specialises in cemetery tourism: two for the local inhabitants, one for the Society of Ptuj's Inhabitants living in Ljubljana, and one for the Ptuj Society of Blind and Visually Impaired. Altogether, 73 Slovenian nationals took a guided tour of the Memorial Park.

In 2020, professionals from the Ptuj Tourism Public Institute took over this role and have since been offering tours of Ptuj Cemetery – Memorial Park; however, according to the statistics, there has not been much interest. Of course, it is too soon to draw any conclusion as to the interest from visitors, as the global pandemic almost completely stopped tourist activities everywhere. Nevertheless, the tour is still available and can be booked on the internet (https://www.visitptuj.eu/en/see-do/tours/guided-tours/memorial-park-ptuj-old-town-cemetery).

The stories of Ptuj Cemetery – Memorial Park can be considered a tourist product on their own, as they attract a specific segment of tourists, or could be part of an integral tourism product offering an alternative introduction to Ptuj's history. Tours of the cemetery are thus thematic and intended for different segments of visitors, whether locals or tourists from elsewhere in Slovenia or abroad.

The perception of stories depends a lot on their interpretation. A question arises as to whether visitors can get their own, personal experience while listening to somebody else's interpretation. Therefore, interpreters need to be cautious not to cross the line and, in the desire to convince, make the story sound like mere propaganda. On the other hand, there is a danger of excessive generalisation and banalisation of historical facts. Both deviations from good interpretation potentially diminish the visitor's sense of creating a personal relation with the cemetery.

CONCLUSION

Cemetery tourism undoubtedly deserves to be researched and studied from different points of view, such as the artistic, historical, architectural and floral, but cemeteries are also places where one learns to come to terms with death and, especially, with one's own eventual disappearance. Cemetery routes often combine cultural heritage with natural heritage. The spatial contexts where cemeteries are located convert these sites into parks or gardens for public enjoyment (Dancausa Millán et al., 2019). On the other hand, it is also important to know who potential visitors might be and what their motivations are. As sites of peace and piety, recollection and remembrance, meditation and respect, it should be stressed that tourist visits to a cemetery need to be conceived differently from ordinary tours.

Cemetery stories can contain elements of both dark tourism and heritage tourism. In the context of death, and more particularly the cruel stories of individuals in relation to suffering, torture, violence, murder and other perverted acts, this type of tourism can be called dark tourism. However, if we highlight the bright stories and way of life of deceased individuals and their creation in various fields during their lifetime, it is heritage tourism.

Cemetery tourism, when considering the stories of the people interred, thus encompasses elements which define heritage and dark tourism, while genealogical tourism mostly relates to specific and generally individual research into past generations (although this branch of tourism is well developed in Ireland, for instance). It seems impossible to separate heritage and dark tourism when speaking of civil cemeteries. However, the interpretation can vary and be more or less 'dark', 'grief-oriented' or 'heritage-oriented'.

The notions of slow and smart tourism should be incorporated as much as possible to allow all visitors their own unique experience. Cemetery stories educate, awake memories, inform and sometimes try to appeal to people and their decisions. Death is common to all. As with other types of niche or special interest tourism, cemetery tourism provides a different experience for tourists and visitors which is, in general, both educational and emotional, and, at sites such as the ones tied intimately to war, also therapeutic. The reinforcement of visitor experiences through authenticity is very effective.

The creation of an actual cemetery product should be examined more closely from different perspectives. Above all, it is necessary to explore the opinions of potential cemetery tourists and the local community. The local community is an important factor in the design of a new cemetery tourism product, because the topic may sometimes be perceived as too sensitive by locals and therefore inappropriate to connect with the tourism industry.

Cemetery stories of the past reflect different relationships between people, their way of life and their understanding of the world, and have great potential to communicate their viewpoint. Ptuj Cemetery – Memorial Park shows how small cemeteries can contribute to local tourism supply by addressing different audiences through storytelling.

REFERENCES

Angelou, M. (2005) Quotes by Maya Angelou. Avaliable at: http://www.goodreads.com/author/quotes/3503.Maya_Angelou (accessed 19 August 2020).

Beyern, B. (2013) Available at: https://www.youtube.com/watch?v=W_JdiKKqD_8 (accessed 14 August 2020).

Ciglenečki, M. (2017) The Old Ptuj Graveyard: Confronting the past. *Heritage and Society, 4th Heritage Forum of Central Europe*, 1–2 June 2017, Krakow, Poland.

Dancausa Millán, M.G., Peréz Naranjo, L.M., Hernández Rojas, R.D. and Millan Vazquez de la Torre, M.G. (2019) Cemetery tourism in Southern Spain: An analysis of demand. *Tourism and Hospitality Management*, 25(1), 37–52.

Fog, K., Budtz, C., Munch, P. and Blanchette, S. (2010) *Storytelling, Branding in Practice*. Belin Heidelberg: Springer – Verlag.

Gosar, A. (2015) Dark tourism: Post-WWI destination of human tragedies and opportunities for tourism development. *Proceedings of the International Workshop*, University of Primorska.

Hernja Masten, M. (1991) Človek, ki se je v zgodovino zapisal sam - Leopold Schikelgruber. *Kronika*, 39(1/2), 71–5.

Kužnik, L. and Veble, N. (2018) Into the dark – dark stories in the cities of Brežice and Krško in Slovenia as a basis for the future dark tourism products. *International Journal of Tourism Cities*, 4(1), 40–53.

Lamut, B. (ed.) (1993) *Ptujski arheološki zbornik: Ob 100-letnici muzeja in Muzejskega društva*, Pokrajinski muzej Ptuj.

Light, D. (2017) Progress in dark tourism and thanatourism research: An uneasy relationship with heritage tourism. *Tourism Management*, 61, 275–301.

Marques, J.A.M. (2018) Turismo cemeterial – O 'porquê' e o 'onde'. *Revista Turismo & Desenvolvimento*, 29, 47–63.

Mionel, V. (2020) (Not so) Dark tourism: The merry cemetery in Săpânța (Romania) – An expression of folk culture. *Tourism Management Perspectives*, 34, 100656.

Moscardo, G. and Ballantyne, R. (2008) Interpretation and attractions. In B. Garrod and S. Wanhill (eds) *Managing Visitor Attractions*. Oxford: Butterworth-Heinemann, 237–52.

Pšajd, J. (2017) *Čez ta prag me bodo nesli, ko zatisnil bom oči*. Pomurski muzej, Murska Sobota.

Seaton, A.V. (1996) Guided by the dark: From thanatopsis to thanatourism. *International Journal of Heritage Studies*, 2, 234–44.

Seaton, A.V. (2002) Thanatourism's final frontiers? Visits to cemeteries, churchyards and funerary sites as sacred and secular pilgrimage. *Tourism Recreation Research*, 27(2), 73–82.

Sharpley, R. and Stone, P.R. (2009) *The Darker Side of Travel, the Theory and Practice of Dark Tourism*. Bristol: Channel View Publications.

Stanonik, M. (1999) Nagrobni napisi na slovenskih pokopališčih. In N. Brun and M. Remic (eds) *Tihi pomniki minljivega časa: drobci o šegah slovesov in pokopališki kulturi na slovenskem etničnem ozemlju*. Ljubljana, Forma 7, 66–73.

Stone, P. (2006) A dark tourism spectrum: Towards a typology of death and macabre related tourist sites, attractions and exhibitions. *SelectedWorks, Tourism*, 54(2), 145–60.

Tobias, F. (1999) Tipi pokopališč. In N. Brun and M. Remic (eds) *Tihi pomniki minljivega časa: drobci o šegah slovesov in pokopališki kulturi na slovenskem etničnem ozemlju*. Ljubljana, Forma 7, 74–81.

Wight, A.C. and, Lennon, J.J. (2007) Selective interpretation and electic human heritage in Lithuania. *Tourism Management*, 28(2), 519–29.

23. In focus 4 – fine dining in a prison: The Clink restaurants in the UK

Alison McIntosh, Maria Gebbels and Tracy Harkison

Within the Western developed world, statistics showing high incarceration, increasing crime rates and high rates of prisoner reoffending are a cause for concern. To tackle these issues, which relate globally to the United Nation's Sustainable Development Goals (SDGs) – most notably Goal 4: Quality Education, Goal 8: Decent Work and Economic Growth and Goal 16: Peace, Justice and Strong Institutions – a number of initiatives have been pioneered within prisons. Among such initiatives, a trend of responsible, socially conscious hospitality has emerged. While former prisons turned into museums have become popular tourist experiences worldwide (Strange and Kempa, 2003), working prisons are not usually considered places tourists choose to visit. That said, fine dining in working prisons has grown in popularity. Visitors can now receive culinary experiences by dining at restaurants within minimum- or medium-security prisons staffed by inmates who are close to release. Notable examples include The Clink restaurants in the UK, the Gate to Plate festival event in New Zealand, the InGalera restaurant in Italy and the INTERNO in Columbia. Here, we consider the emerging niche tourism and hospitality experience of dining in prisons through the case of the four successful Clink training restaurants in the UK to show how fine dining in these restaurants may see 'tourist dollars' go towards making a positive social change.

In partnership with Her Majesty's Prison Service, The Clink Charity in the UK operates four public restaurants within working prisons in Brixton, Cardiff, High Down and Styal (see Table 23.1), as well as The Clink Café in Manchester, Clink Events and Clink@Home.

Through the operation of the four training restaurants, the charity aims to change attitudes, transform lives and create second chances by focusing on prisoner rehabilitation and social reintegration (The Clink Charity, 2020). The food is prepared and served by prisoners in training. The Clink recruits prisoners with 6 to 18 months left on their sentence and who have completed all other restorative courses. The prisoners volunteer to be trained and are then screened by the prison service to ensure that they fulfil the prison's security criteria and are also safe to work with the public. The charity delivers training and work experience to prisoners via a five-step integrated model. The steps are: recruitment, training, support (while in prison), then employment and mentoring (post-release). The students, as The Clink prefers to call prisoners, also gain formal qualifications in catering, as all four restaurants are registered catering colleges.

As they are dining in a working prison, visitors to The Clink restaurants must undertake initial security clearance, phones and cameras must be left outside, and there is a no alcohol policy. The attraction of paying to dine at a Clink restaurant is associated with the memorable experience it provides, the enjoyment of high-end meals comparable to any conventional fine dining establishment, and the professional and welcoming customer service. Moreover, while from a host perspective, offering dining in one of these restaurants is proving a means to change the deep-set negative social assumptions about prisoners, from a visitor's point-of-view, the

Table 23.1   *The Clink restaurants*

The Clink restaurants	Category of prison**	Men's/ Women's prison	Opened	Seating capacity	TripAdvisor rating ***	Website
HMP* High Down	B	Men	2009	94	5.0 Ranked 1st of 214 restaurants in Sutton	https://theclinkcharity.org/ restaurants/high-down
HMP Cardiff	B	Men	2012	90	5.0 Ranked 17th of 823 restaurant in Cardiff	https://theclinkcharity.org/ restaurants/cardiff
HMP Brixton	C/D	Men	2014	120	5.0 Ranked 27th of 23,790 restaurants in London	https://theclinkcharity.org/ restaurants/brixton
HMP Styal	C	Women	2015	120	5.0 Ranked 2nd of 68 restaurants in Wilmslow	https://theclinkcharity.org/ restaurants/styal

Notes: *HMP: Her Majesty's Prison. **Category B: local or training prisons holding long-term and high-security prisoners; Category C: training and resettlement prisons; Category D: open prisons where eligible prisoners carry out work or education away from the prison. ***As of the 30/11/20. A score of 5.0 = Excellent (the highest score on TripAdvisor).

choice of engaging with this type of niche tourism and hospitality experience resonates with responsible tourism and hospitality principles through the act of doing something that contributes to the social good. Analysis of 3,951 TripAdvisor online customer reviews shows that diners report great meals and service, and come to view their prisoner wait staff more as trainee hospitality employees delivering the same professional service expected at other fine dining establishments (McIntosh, Gebbels and Harkison, 2020). The Clink Charity's ethos was also inspiring for customers who recognise the key drivers of prisoner rehabilitation and second chances, and hence comment that they are happy to support this worthwhile cause.

Due to COVID-19, the charity had to adapt its business model by providing a takeaway service, Clink@Home, from their Brixton restaurant. To use this service, customers place their orders online, meals are prepared by trainee chefs using fresh local produce, and then they are home delivered by ex-prisoners.

Only a few academic studies have considered the potential of specific hospitality training or prison restaurant operations for rehabilitating offenders (Beier, 2015; Harkison and McIntosh, 2019). That said, statistics released by The Clink Charity provide evidence that inmates who have participated in their training programme had a significantly lower rate of recidivism. Less is known, however, about demand-related perspectives, such as customer motives and satisfaction of dining at the prison restaurants, or how customer interactions with prisoner staff may potentially dismantle the existing stigma of an offender. Therefore, we call for a holistic perspective which considers education (SDG #4) as a vehicle able to change societal perceptions of prisoners, and as a means to understanding the benefits of the five-step integrated model championed by The Clink and its value for both the prisoners and the public.

There also remains much to be learned about how this niche form of gastronomy tourism may offer opportunities to differentiate tourist experiences within destinations, especially as niche products are seen to offer a more meaningful and sustainable type of tourism (Novelli, 2005) That said, there is increased public media reporting of gourmet restaurants inside prisons (Thomas-Graham, 2019), which are bound to bring future economic benefits to local communities through providing employment and career opportunities in hospitality (SDG #8). In this way, anecdotal evidence increasingly suggests that the emerging trend for fine dining inside prisons is a compelling niche idea that seems to be spreading and is worthy of further investigation.

REFERENCES

Beier, S. (2015) An analysis of the potential restaurant operations have for rehabilitating offenders: A case study of Her Majesty's Prison, The Verne. In P. Sloan, W. Legrand and C. Hindley (eds) *The Routledge Handbook of Sustainable Food and Gastronomy*. London: Routledge, 219–28.

Harkison, T. and McIntosh, A.J. (2019) Hospitality training for prisoners: A second chance? *Hospitality Insights*, 3(1), 5–6.

McIntosh, A., Gebbels, M. and Harkison, T. (2020) Serving time: How fine dining in jail is helping prisoners and satisfying customers. *The Conversation*, 19 November. https://theconversation.com/serving-time-how-fine-dining-in-jail-is-helping-prisoners-and-satisfying-customers-149161.

Novelli, M. (ed). (2005) *Niche tourism: Contemporary Issues, Trends and Cases*. Oxford, UK: Elsevier.

Strange, C. and Kempa, M. (2003) Shades of dark tourism: Alcatraz and Robben Island. *Annals of Tourism Research*, 30(2), 386–405.

The Clink Charity (2020) *Introduction*. https://theclinkcharity.org/ (accessed 27 November 2020).

Thomas-Graham, P. (2019) The gourmet restaurants in the world inside a prison. *Dandelion Chandelier*, 9 August. https://www.dandelionchandelier.com/2019/08/09/restaurants-inside-prisons/.

PART V

SPIRITUAL, RELIGIOUS AND WELLNESS TOURISM

24. Faith, new age spirituality and religious tourism

Daniel H. Olsen

INTRODUCTION

For centuries, humankind has travelled to sites deemed sacred for both religious and leisure purposes. Rivers, mountains, forests and caves have long been gathering places for people searching for meaning (Timothy, 2012; Olsen, 2020). In addition, people from various faith and cultural traditions have built sacred places either set within these natural settings, such as the Neolithic temples in Malta (Grima and Farrugia, 2019), or have imprinted sacred buildings and complexes onto the natural landscape. These natural and human-built sites serve as an *axis mundi* or a nexus between heaven and earth and humans and their gods. They are not just repositories of faith and meaning (Aulet and Vidal, 2019), but also cultural symbols and sites related to nature conservation that are visited by people for cultural and recreational purposes. Pilgrimage, as travel to these sites is commonly termed, has historically led to both an increased mobility among people of lower socioeconomic classes and an extensive pilgrimage economy in many world regions (Olsen, 2019b). This is more so the case in modern times, where efficiencies in transportation systems and increases in income and discretionary time have led people of all socioeconomic classes to become more mobile, as seen in the rise of the number of people travelling domestically and internationally for leisure purposes (Olsen, 2019b). Parallel to these increasing number of tourists has been the growth in the number of people who travel for religious purposes. As such, academics have a growing interest in the interface between religion and economics (e.g., Iyer, 2016; Barro and McCleary, 2019; Faccarello, 2020), including tourism (e.g., Olsen, 2003; Timothy and Olsen, 2006a; Stausberg, 2011; Fourie et al., 2015). While there are few reliable statistics regarding the religious tourism niche market and precise numbers are not known, the United Nations World Tourism Organization (UNWTO, 2011) estimates that approximately 600 million people a year travel domestically and internationally for religious purposes, with most religious tourism taking place in Europe and Asia. As such, the religious tourism niche market is a multi-billion USD industry.[1]

However, there are questions as to what exactly constitutes the religious tourism market, particularly with the rise of spiritual tourism, which some view as a separate tourism niche market. In addition, at least academically, a pilgrimage or religious journey involves 'any journey undertaken by a person in quest of a place or state that he or she believes to embody a valued ideal' (Morinis, 1992: 4) or some sort of aspirational endeavour that is 'redolent with meaning' (Digance, 2006: 36). This view, however, suggests that any form of travel can be 'religious' in nature and therefore all travel is a pilgrimage. Another issue revolves around differentiating between religiously motivated tourists who visit religious sites and those who visit the same sites but are motivated by educative, cultural or curiosity reasons.

In the past two decades, tourism operators, promoters, marketers and religious organizations have increasingly developed this niche market. Academics have also matched this interest, with the almost exponential growth of publications related to the supply and demand sides of the religious tourism niche market over the past 20 years (see Heidari et al., 2018; Rashid, 2018; Kim et al., 2020; Collins-Kreiner, 2020; Illiev, 2020). However, this market niche is still vastly understudied (Griffin and Raj, 2018; Matema, 2018), in part because this market niche is often subsumed under the broader cultural or heritage tourism niche markets.

The purpose of this chapter is to discuss the scope and nature of the present-day religious tourism market. The chapter first discusses various definitions of the religious tourism market and its fracturing into four sub-markets: the religious tourism market, the pilgrimage or faith tourism market, the spiritual tourism market and the New Age tourism market. The chapter then looks at the supply side of the religious tourism market, examining the various market suppliers that have further fragmented this tourism sector. Then, attention turns to examine the demand side of this market and the mixed motivations behind why people travel to religious sites. The positive and negative economic, sociocultural and environmental impacts of religious tourism are given brief consideration, after which this chapter concludes with suggesting potential futures of religious tourism in a post-COVID-19 world.

DEFINING THE RELIGIOUS TOURISM MARKET

While defining what constitutes religious tourism may seem like a banal way to start this chapter, there has been some confusion regarding what exactly constitutes the boundaries of this market. This seemingly conceptual exercise is an important starting point, particularly for tourism marketers and entrepreneurs in terms of determining who their potential clients are and what types of attractions and experiences they seek. Defining and reflecting upon the nature of the religious tourism market also helps scholars better focus on what constitutes the objects and subjects of study in this field.

Unfortunately, there is presently no universally accepted definition of religious tourism, and a quick look at the academic literature suggests that there seems to be relatively little interest in defining the boundaries of this tourism niche market. This may be due to the postmodern streak that runs through the social sciences – where boundaries around objects and subjects of study are an anathema. This is manifest in this context of the myriad of discussions related to the (de)differentiation or the convergence/divergence (Cohen, 1992) of the boundaries between what constitutes pilgrimage and tourism, which Collins-Kreiner (2020) correctly notes is probably the most discussed aspect of religious tourism in the academic literature. For many scholars, pilgrimage is considered the oldest form of tourism (Timothy and Olsen, 2006a; Butler and Suntikul, 2018) and is seen as being structurally and experientially akin to religious tourism (MacCannell, 1976; Graburn, 1989; Osterrieth, 1997). As noted by Gupta (1999: 91), 'apart from the devotional aspect, looked at from the broader point of view, pilgrimage involves sightseeing, travelling, visiting different places and, in some cases, voyaging by air or sea, etc. and buying the local memorabilia, almost everything a tourist does'. Because of this, it is difficult to distinguish, at least empirically, between who is a 'pilgrim' and who is a 'tourist'. However, some scholars and theologians believe that there is a stark delineation between pilgrimage and tourism (Vukonić, 2002). From this perspective, tourism is considered as a superficial, diversionary activity that lacks the deeper cultural and spiritual significance of pilgrimage. As such, tourism does not lead to a 'substantial' change or a trans-formation in a person's life, unlike pilgrimage travel (Kotler, 1997: 103). In addition, equating pilgrimage to a type of tourism puts it on par with other, more hedonistic, tourist activities such as wine tourism or sex tourism, which offends the sensibilities of many religious leaders and tour organizers (Ostrowski, 2000).

The lack of a definition for religious tourism also stems from difficulties in deciding whether this niche market should be defined based on traveller motivation (demand) or the types of activities in which people engage and the places they visit when they travel (supply). As Timothy and Olsen (2006b: 272) note

> the term [religious tourism] is generally used by tourism promoters and researchers to describe the phenomenon in two different ways: those whose impetus to travel combines both religious (domi-nant) and secular (secondary) motives and people who visit sacred sites during their journeys to other attractions and destinations.

Indeed, many academics and industry marketers divide tourism into niche markets based on the 'activities tourists engage in during their travels' rather than their motivations – where 'a person travelling to participate in a cultural festival would be considered a cultural tourist, while a person wanting to experience the thrill of skydiving may be considered an adventure tourist' (ibid.). As such, from an industry perspective, traditional 'pilgrimage' mobilities and practices are just another tourism niche market, and by extension, 'pilgrims' are 'a type of tourist who travels for religious or spiritual reasons' (ibid.). However, others define religious tourism based the motivations that drive people to travel. Here, religious tourism 'is separate from other forms of tourism because it is characterized by its aims, motivations, and destina-tions' (ibid.; see Liszewski, 2000). Even though there is evidence that historically pilgrims engaged in both religious and recreational activities (Turner and Turner, 1978; Olsen, 2010; Paine, 2020), pilgrimage is considered as a higher form of travel. As such, the term 'religious tourism' is considered oxymoronic – an attempt to combine two seemingly incompatible or contradicting dichotomous terms and activities (pilgrimage/tourism) (Stausberg, 2014; Giumbelli, 2019).

This supply/demand side or push/pull definitional impasse, as well as the growth of tourism offerings related to religious travel (see below), has led to a fragmentation of the religious tourism market into four specific sub-niche markets. The obvious sub-niche market is the 'religious tourism' market itself, which more generically describes travels by those who visit religious sites as a part of broader cultural itineraries. Olsen (2008: 22) defines this sub-niche market as 'travel by tourists to religious destinations, cultures and sites regardless of moti-vation, whether the visits to these sites are of primary or secondary interest'. This definition takes an industry or supply-side approach to religious tourism, highlighting the fact that many people who visit religious sites do so for cultural, historical and educational reasons, as well as for curiosity, rather than the search for religious meaning and participation in religious sites and ceremonies. As such, religious tourists are people who visit religious sites during their sightseeing travels.

The second sub-niche is the 'pilgrimage tourism', 'faith tourism' or 'faith-based tourism' market, which focuses on the 'believer as tourist' (Terzidou et al., 2018) and describes trips undertaken by people who travel because they are motivated by religion (e.g., Lopez, 2013; Sharma, 2013; Isaac, 2016; Izberk-Bilgin and Nakata, 2016). Because religious marketers and operators understand that religiously motivated travellers have specialized dietary and religious needs (Weidenfeld and Ron, 2008), this market sub-niche focuses on 'developing faith-friendly offerings to address consumers' religious sentiments' (Izberk-Bilgin and Nakata, 2016: 286). The development of both of these sub-niche markets is in many cases encouraged by religious authorities for both the economic potential of these markets and to fulfil religious goals, such as proselytization, outreach, pastoral care and the solidification of the religious identities of adherents (Olsen, 2011, 2012; Terzidou et al., 2018).

The third sub-niche is the 'spiritual tourism' market, which is differentiated from these other sub-niche markets by its emphasis on 'tourism characterized by a self-conscious project of spiritual betterment' (Norman, 2012: 20). The spiritual tourism market focuses on helping people who seek answers to transcendent questions through unmediated, institutionally unbound and intensely personal and subjective spiritual manifestations (Beyer, 2007; Norman, 2012; Olsen, 2015). This focus on the unmediated 'self' is due in part to the rise of the modern consumer economy, which has led to 'life and society [being redefined] as arenas of choice rather than transmission of traditions and belonging' (Gauthier et al., 2013: 270). However, spiritual betterment is also a part of religion ritual and experience (Cheer et al., 2017), and thus spirituality is located 'both within and beyond' religion (Stausberg 2011: 355). As such, many spiritual tourists utilize sacred and secular spaces and routes as a part of their search for spiritual experiences and meaning (Margry, 2015; Warkentin, 2018).

Related to spiritual tourism is the fourth sub-niche market – 'New Age tourism'. As a part of the broader umbrella of religious tourism (Pernecky and Poulston, 2015), New Age tourism, like spiritual tourism, involves the search for meaning through self-improvement and spiritual enlightenment. However, New Age tourism is characterized by a greater experimentation with a bricolage of modern and ancient religious and spiritual traditions. This is done through combining beliefs, worldviews, spiritual practices, mystical healing practices, sacred sites and 'beyond the planet' extra-terrestrial sightings to come up with new experiences and interpretations of reality (Zwissler, 2011; Olsen, 2015). As such, New Age tourists draw upon a veritable and sometimes incoherent 'spiritual marketplace' of spiritualties, worldviews, power places and products that are designed to enhance one's quest for meaning (Aupers and Houtman, 2006; Pernecky and Johnson, 2006; Timothy and Pernecky, 2006).

The above discussion highlights the increasingly fractured nature of the religious tourism market, with modern individualism and the decline in religious adherence leading to the move towards finding the spiritual self through seeking experiences and spaces outside of traditional religious institutions. As such, many tourism marketers have begun catering to the spiritual tourism/New Age markets, treating these market segments as separate from religious and faith tourism (Olsen, 2015). Therefore, and due to space constraints, the rest of this chapter focuses on the religious and faith tourism markets.

THE SUPPLY SIDE OF THE RELIGIOUS AND FAITH TOURISM MARKETS

Tarlow (2014) suggests that the religious tourism niche market has a wide appeal to many different cultures and faiths around the world. Indeed, religious culture and affiliation play an important role in the decision-making process regarding how people utilize their leisure time, including where they travel, the activities in which they engage and how they behave while travelling (e.g., Kelly 1982; Mattila et al., 2001; He et al., 2013). This is why approximately

600 million people travel for either religious purposes or visit religious sites (UNWTO, 2011). Even though the religious and faith tourism markets are very elastic (Fang, 2020; Olsen, 2013), tour operators and agencies, travel wholesalers, tourism marketers and promoters, and churches and religions/non-profit organizations (Moore, 2007) are very interested these recession-resistant tourism markets (Singh, 1998; Tarlow, 2014). Growing interest in these markets can be seen in the creation of wider tourism organizations that focus on branding and marketing this tourism sector, including the Faith Travel Association (https://ntaonline .com/markets/faith-travel-association/) and the presently defunct World Religious Travel Association (2007–2011). The UNWTO has held several international conferences related to religious and spiritual tourism. In addition, other organizations, such as the British Pilgrimage Trust (https://britishpilgrimage.org), focus on the redevelopment of pilgrimage trails for recreational and religious purposes, in part to increase domestic and international tourism to the country. Academically, the rise in the number of people travelling for religious reasons has led to several research articles examining the potential of the religious tourism niche market in many world regions (e.g., Horák et al., 2015; Kartal et al., 2015; Okumus et al., 2015; Okonkwo, 2015; Navurz-Zoda and Navurz-Zoda, 2016; Gupta and Kumar, 2017; Giuşcă et al., 2018; Heydari Chianeh et al., 2018; Ozcan et al., 2019; Javed, 2019; Shaikh and Afraz, 2019).

In an era where 'the tourism and hospitality industries are constantly searching for new customer segments' (Weinfield and Ron, 2008: 358), the religious and faith tourism markets have become highly fragmented, with multiple sub-niche markets that cater to a wide variety of faith communities and socioeconomic classes, and travel to a wide variety of sacred sites (Olsen, 2013; Tarlow, 2014). For example, Seyer and Muller (2011) and Fang (2020) suggest that there are several sub-niche markets or segments within the religious tourism market (see Table 24.1).

Because tourism marketers recognize that religion plays an important role in people's travel motivations and activities (Weidenfeld and Ron, 2008), new tourism sub-markets have been developed to cater to specific religious organizations or people from specific backgrounds. For example, the religious and faith tourism markets have been sub-divided into the Buddhist tourism (e.g., Hall, 2006; Agrawal et al., 2010; Bruntz and Schedneck, 2020); Islamic or Muslim tourism (e.g., Wang et al., 2010; Zamani-Farahani and Henderson, 2010; Jafari and Scott, 2014; Nassar et al., 2015; Battour et al., 2017; Luz, 2020); Jewish tourism (e.g., Ioannides and Ioannides, 2002; Collins-Kreiner and Olsen, 2004; Cohen Ioannides and Ioannides, 2006; Collins-Kreiner, 2010; Maoz and Bekerman, 2010); and Christian tourism (e.g., Collins-Kreiner et al., 2006; Ron, 2009; Timothy and Ron, 2018; Ron and Timothy, 2018), among other specialized markets.[2] These markets can further be sub-divided into specialized types of tourism offerings, such as Halal tourism, which caters towards Muslim families who abide by the rules of Islam when they travel (e.g., Battour and Ismail, 2016; Hall and Prayag, 2019), or Ultra-Orthodox Jewish tourism, which is geared to the specified dietary and religious needs of Ultra-Orthodox Jews (Mansfeld and Cahaner, 2013). This has led to the development of hotels in many places in the world that cater to both these specialized religious markets (e.g., Cohen Ioannides and Ioannides, 2006; Henderson, 2010) and the use of religious theming to attract religious customers (e.g., Shoval, 2000; Hung, 2015; Hung et al., 2015). Other specialized religious tourism offerings include church tourism (e.g., Duff, 2009; Sharpley, 2009; Morpeth, 2011; Kiely, 2013) and mosque tourism (Kessler, 2015; Kessler and Raj, 2018; Aminudin and Jamal, 2020).

Table 24.1 *Sub-niche markets within the religious and faith tourism markets*

Sub-niche market	Description
Pilgrimage tourism	This market focuses strictly on explicit religious motivations and travel with little attention paid to leisure activities. Participants in these tours focus strictly on religious sites and the performance of rituals at said sites.
Religious meetings, incentives, conferences and events (MICE)	This sub-niche market focuses on booking and planning religious meetings, conferences and events and their associated accommodations and amenities.
Religiously themed cruises, safaris, adventure travel, weekend getaways, leisure vacations and retreats/guesthouses	These sub-niche markets use existing tourism market segments and religious theming to entice religious and faith tourists to participate in these activities. Participants usually travel in groups of like-minded religious individuals of varying size to engage in recreational activities.
Missionary travel	While not necessarily considered a form of pilgrimage, travel for missionary work is an evangelical activity that sacralizes the areas in which this work is performed (Fife, 2004). Since missionaries also need time to relax and rejuvenate, missionary travel, particularly short-term missionary travels, have become a popular form of faith tourism (Priest and Priest, 2008).
Volunteer vacations	Related to missionary travel, volunteer vacations have also become popular, particularly in Western countries where mainly Christian youth groups travel to lesser developed countries to 'carry out religiously motivated and framed voluntary service' (Priest and Priest, 2008: 55).
Visiting religious attractions	This sub-niche market includes visiting sacred sites where religious events important to a faith's history occurred; sites of worship and ritual; sites related to the history of a faith community; and ceremonies and pilgrimages. These visits can be for religious, educational or cultural reasons. One of the more unique and newer religious attractions is religious theme parks, which combine leisure, recreation and religion together 'to fulfil a "religious" role, to inspire and educate the faithful, and to spread the word among others' (Paine, 2020: 3; see Shinde, 2020).

Source: Own compilation, based on Seyer and Muller (2011) and Fang (2020).

THE MOTIVATIONS OF RELIGIOUS TOURISTS

Religion has long been a strong influence on how people utilize their leisure time (Kelly, 1982; Hall, 2006), as well as 'a strong pull factor for [domestic and international] tourists' travel' (Fourie et al., 2015: 52). Fourie et al. (2015: 52) point out that

> religious belief is a cultural attribute that shapes tourists' perceptions of their destination. Even if religion is not an explicit factor in a tourist's decision-making process, the fact that the dominant religion of a destination is the same as theirs may be a significant (but implicit) determinant of their choice.

Indeed, religious and faith tourists are pushed and pulled by both material or immaterial aspects of religious beliefs, buildings, customs, ceremonies and artefacts. Bremer (2004: 3–7) suggests four ways in which religious and faith tourists share similar interests when travelling. First, both groups demonstrate concern about and attachment to special places. Second, the practices that maintain the special character of religious sites lead to the construction of personal and group identities which can strengthen or shift religious identities (Olsen, 2012). The practice of visiting these sites also reinforces the special nature of these places. Third, religious tourists are generally concerned with primarily authentic aesthetic experiences which frame their experiences of religion as they journey, while faith tourists seek authentic religious experiences which can be enhanced through aesthetics. Fourth, the desire for aesthetically pleasing and authentic experiences by both tourists and religious travellers leads to the commercialization of religious sites.

There is a growing literature on the motivations of religious and non-religious visitors to sacred sites. This research highlights that even when people are motivated to visit these sites for religious purposes, they tend to combine a variety of sacred and secular motivations. This is because travel is a heterogeneous activity involving various forms of transportation, accommodation, activities, destinations and experiences. For example, Andriotis (2009) suggests that the motivations of visitors to an exclusive male sacred shrine in Mount Athos, Greece – which motivations can be extrapolated to men and women who visit other sacred sites – can be segmented into five overlapping elements:

- *Spiritual motivation*: Where visitors are motivated by faith and are not interested in the touristic aspects of travel.
- *Cultural motivation*: Where visitors see sacred sites as 'living museum[s] of history and art' (p. 74), and thereby seek cultural experiences within a religious architectural frame untouched by modernity.
- *Secular motivation*: Where visitors seek a relaxing, socially cohesive experience, treating sacred sites as tourist attractions and expecting that photography and souvenir purchases are a part of the overall experience.
- *Environmental motivation*: Where visitors seek solitude or quiet in a wilderness or aesthetically pleasing natural setting.
- *Educational motivation*: Where visitors seek experiences that invite learning and education.

In the same vein, Drule et al. (2012) suggest that while many visitors to religious sites are motivated by religious purposes, the most important non-religious intrinsic motivations include curiosity, knowledge-based education, escape from the daily routine and leisure/recreation. Other non-religious motivations among participants in their study included interactions with nature and cultural elements, discovering new life experiences and interacting with people. Afferni et al. (2011) suggest that visitors to the Sacred Mount of Varallo in Italy come with a mix of sacred and secular motivations that range from religious to historical/cultural, artistic, environmental, recreational and place attachment. Choe et al. (2015) found that non-Buddhists visiting the Chua Ba Thien Hau Buddhist temple in Los Angeles, California, were motivated to visit because of intellectual of educational pursuits, a desire to engage with diverse cultures and lifestyles and a wish to escape from daily life. Many seniors who visit religious sites do so for spiritual succour and support, to maintain friendships and to experience a sense of accomplishment (Kuo, Chen and Liu, 2019).

Other research suggests that while non-religious visitors to religious sites are not seeking religious or spiritual experiences, they are still 'exposed to religion on their travels' (Stausberg, 2011: 15), with many people reporting what they characterize as having such experiences at these sites. For example, Jackson and Hudman (1994) found that visitors at English cathedrals who labelled themselves secular tourists experienced some sort of emotional or 'peak' moment, as respondents described them, during their visit. Indeed, the sacred architecture, sense of place and the style of site interpretation can all contribute to non-religious visitors deriving some sense of sanctity, divinity, awe or calm at religious sites (Voase, 2007; Williams et al., 2007; Gutic et al., 2010). At the same time, people who participate in religiously motivated travel may not have the religious or spiritual experiences that they were seeking, leading

Kaell (2016) to note that pilgrimage, as well as religious and faith tourism, can fail in its intended experiences. As such, the research presented here suggests that visitors to religious sites visit these sites due to a mix of sacred and secular motivations and can also have a mix of experiences either related or not related to their expectations (see Olsen, 2013).

THE IMPACTS OF THE RELIGIOUS TOURISM MARKET

While tourists are exposed to religion when they travel, religions are also exposed to tourism and tourists (Stausberg, 2011). As Bremer (2005: 9260) notes, tourism and its associated practices 'interact with religious life and the institutions of religion in virtually every corner of the world'. Indeed, tourists are commonplace at most religious sites and ceremonies, and, as noted above, tourism marketers and promoters readily utilize religious culture in their tourism itineraries. While the mix of religion and tourism can be profitable, there are several negative impacts on host destinations and communities that also occur. This section focuses briefly some of the positive and negative impacts of the broader religious tourism market.

Positive Impacts

Pilgrimage and religious tourism, as motivators for travel, have historically led to the development of entire pilgrimage economies revolving around the provision and sale of sacred commodities and basic travel services at religious sites and along pilgrimage routes (Greif, 2006; Sumption, 2003). With the inclusion of religious tourism sites and pilgrimage trails as a part of a destination's larger cultural tourism offer (Olsen and Trono, 2018), several studies have discussed the positive economic impacts of religious heritage development. For example, these studies suggest that investment in the religious tourism market can lead to increased entrepreneurship and bolster regions in economic decline (Vukonić, 2002; Shinde, 2010; Pourtaheri et al., 2012). Religious groups also use visitation to their religious heritage sites to maintain a strong economic base (Reader and Tanabe Jr., 1997; Olsen, 2003) through pay perimeters and gift shops (Shackley, 2001, 2003; Olsen, 2006; Griffiths, 2011).

Socioculturally, religious tourism development can lead to the revitalization of tangible and intangible religious cultural customs, including religious cuisine, rituals, dances, buildings, local crafts and stories, as well as the natural environment within a community (e.g., Jenkins and Catra, 1997; Zhu, 2012; Di Giovine, 2010, 2016; Pourtaheri et al., 2012). For example, catering to the specialized religious and social needs or requirements of religious groups not only makes destinations more appealing to religious heritage tourists, but also helps maintain the religious customs of the host community (e.g., Cohen Ioannides and Ioannides, 2006; Weidenfeld and Ron, 2008; Zamani-Farahani and Henderson, 2010). Religious leaders may also seek to utilize tourism to accomplish specific religious and organizational goals, such as proselytization, outreach and pastoral care (Vukonić, 2000; Cohen, 1998; Olsen, 2011). Religious tourism can also contribute environmentally, such as in cases where religious sites act to protect biological diversity and endemic and endangered species, or when active conservation of wilderness areas takes place specifically to enhance the environmental aesthetics of those visited by religious tourists (Olsen, 2020; Shinde, 2022).

As such, religious tourism can be considered a 'soft' form of tourism (Lusby, 2017) that leads to 'mutual understanding[s] between the local population and their guests' while 'not endanger[ing] the cultural identity of the host region and [...] tak[ing] care of the environment as best as possible' (Broggi, 1985: 286). While many religious heritage sites receive millions of visitors a year, religious and faith tourists are sometimes considered 'gentler' travellers, being more ethical and sensitive towards local cultures, religious traditions and the natural environment and more willing to enter into inter-religious dialogue (Howard, 2012; Vidal-Casellas et al., 2019).

Negative Impacts

However, like other tourism niche markets, religious tourism development can also lead to several negative impacts. These negative impacts are rarely intentional in nature, and only become more noticeable and intense because of overcrowding, heightened political and social instability (Shackley, 2001) and instances where almost an entire tourism industry revolves around pilgrimage and religious tourism (Lasserre, 1974; in Vukonić, 2002).

For instance, economic investment in the religious tourism market can lead to the commodification and re-contextualization of religious icons, symbols and rituals which are subsequently valued for their market value rather than their use-value or utility (Cohen, 1988; Shepherd, 2002; Ornella, 2013). This leads to questions regarding religious authenticity and the ethics of religious commodification (e.g., Ornella, 2013; Swanson and Timothy, 2013). Examples of this commodification include the sale of sacred masks as tourist souvenirs in Bali, the modification of religious rituals in Tibet and Nepal to cater to the compressed itineraries of religious tourists, and the favouring of commercial transactions over hosting visitors at religious sites (Barker et al., 2006; Hung et al., 2017). Religious heritage tourism development may also exacerbate management challenges at religious heritage sites, including an increase in general wear-and-tear, overcrowding, congestion, vandalism, noise pollution and microclimatic change, among others (Shackley, 2001; Woodward, 2004; Olsen, 2006). The use of religious culture and heritage in tourism marketing and promotion can also lead to tensions among communities regarding maintaining religious traditions and progressive socio-economic transformation that may violate religious convictions and societal norms and values (Di Giovine, 2010). This, in turn, may lead to a deterioration of residents' attitudes towards tourism development and religious heritage tourists in general (Pfaffenberger, 1983; Uriley et al., 2003). Religious tourism may also cause damage to fauna, particularly when religious sites are located inside of protected areas (Seshardi and Ganesh, 2011), and overcrowding at religious sites often leads to an increase in air and water pollution and deforestation, especially in developing countries (Shinde, 2007; Shinde and Olsen, 2020). While Uriley et al. (2003) argue that religious heritage tourism development should occur in conjunction with residents to minimize sociocultural degradation, others have noted that residents may tolerate the negative impacts of tourism if it produces substantial economic benefits (Baedcharoen, 2000; Terzidou et al., 2008).

THE FUTURE OF RELIGIOUS TOURISM

With an estimated 600 million people travelling either for religious purposes or to visit religious sites, the religious tourism market is one of the largest tourism niche markets in the world. This has led to the intense development of this niche market, to the point where it has fractured into four sub-niche markets: the religious tourism market, the pilgrimage or faith tourism market, the spiritual tourism market and the New Age tourism market. These sub-niche markets, however, are not mutually exclusive to each other, and there is significant overlap between these markets (although the New Age and faith tourism markets seem to have little in common) that leads to definitional difficulties defining and delineating their edges (see Figure 24.1). However, considering that tourism is a heterogeneous identity-building project, this lack of definitional consistency is fine, as people seek a wide variety of both sacred and secular embodied experience as a part of their travels (Olsen, 2017; Terzidou et al., 2018).

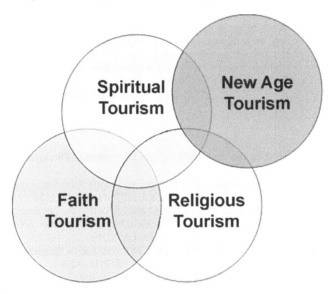

Source: The author.

Figure 24.1   *The author's conception of the overlapping nature of the religious tourism market's four sub-niches markets*

While the present-day COVID-19 pandemic has had dramatic effects on the tourism industry, the religious tourism market may be one of the first tourism niches to flourish in a post-COVID-19 world. This is because of the importance of religion, religious identity and religious travel in a post-secular world, and the need for faith communities to 're-forge sacred community bonds and spiritual *communitas*' after being unable to gather to worship together (Olsen and Timothy, 2020: 176). However, current calls for an environmentally and socially friendly resetting of the tourism industry post-COVID-19, plus the potential increased medicalization of religious travel, may constrain future growth of the religious tourism market, as the sheer number of people in this niche market who travel domestically and internationally means that market is not a form of sustainable travel. Indeed, can religious tourism as it is presently constituted continue unabated in the context of the 2030 Agenda for Sustainable Development? While domestic religious tourism markets will help shore up struggling economies the short term, if future pandemics continue to constrain international travel, it is possible that virtual religious gatherings will become the 'new normal', eventually leading to a post-sacred world where sacred space is recreated to cater to an increasingly immobile religious public (Olsen and Timothy, 2020).

NOTES

1. While the amount of money made from religious tourism is unknown, some scholars and news reporters turn to Wright's (2008) figure of religious tourism being a USD 18 billion industry (e.g., Okumus et al., 2015; Enongene and Griffin, 2019; Ali and Cobanoglu, 2020). But this statistic, however it was derived, is over 12 years old. Taking the UNTWO (2011) number of 330 million religious travellers, this would mean that religious travellers only spend $60 each, making the 18 billion USD figure a very low estimate. In addition, as Olsen (2019a) notes, people spend billions of dollars every year on religious souvenirs, making this $18 billion figure outdated.
2. Even though there is a 'Hindu tourism' market, this term is not utilized in the academic literature. See Singh (2006) and Kanvinde and Tom (2018).

REFERENCES

Afferni, R., Ferrario, C. and Mangano, S. (2011) A place of emotions: The sacred mount of Varallo. *Tourism*, 59(3), 369–86.

Agrawal, M., Choudhary, H. and Tripathi, G. (2010) Enhancing Buddhist tourism in India: An exploratory study. *Worldwide Hospitality and Tourism Themes*, 2(5), 477–93. doi: 10.1108/17554211011090102

Ali, F. and Cobanoglu, C. (2020) Religious tourism has been hit hard in the pandemic as sites close and pilgrimages are put on hold. *The Conversation*. Available at https://news.yahoo.com/religious-tourism -hit-hard-pandemic-122601820.html (accessed 3 September 2020).

Aminudin, N. and Jamal, S.A. (2020) Types of tourism: The travelogue of the greatest traveler. *Journal of Islamic Marketing*, 11(2), 497–506. doi: 10.1108/JIMA-05-2018-0089

Andriotis, K. (2009) Sacred site experience: A phenomenological study. *Annals of Tourism Research*, 36(1), 64–84. doi: 10.1016/j.annals.2008.10.003

Aulet, S. and Vidal, D. (2018) Tourism and religion: Sacred spaces as transmitters of heritage values. *Church, Communication and Culture*, 3(3), 237–59. doi: 10.1080/23753234.2018.1542280

Aupers, S. and Houtman, D. (2006) Beyond the spiritual supermarket: The social and public significance of New Age spirituality. *Journal of Contemporary Religion*, 21(2), 201–22. doi: 10.1080/13537900600655894

Baedcharoen, I. (2000) *Impacts of religious tourism in Thailand*. Masters thesis, University of Otago, Dunedin, New Zealand.

Barker, T., Putra, D. and Wiranatha, A. (2006) Authenticity and commodification of Balinese Dance performances, in Smith, M. and Robinson, M. (eds) *Cultural tourism in a changing world: Politics, participation and (re)presentation*. Clevedon, UK: Channel View Publications, 215–24.

Barro, R.J. and McCleary, R. (2019) *The wealth of religions: The political economy of believing and belonging*. Princeton, NJ: Princeton University Press.

Battour, M. and Ismail, M.N. (2016) Halal tourism: Concepts, practises, challenges and future. *Tourism Management Perspectives*, 19, 150–54. doi: 10.1016/j.tmp.2015.12.008.

Battour, M., Ismail, M. N., Battor, M. and Awais, M. (2017) Islamic tourism: An empirical examination of travel motivation and satisfaction in Malaysia. *Current Issues in Tourism*, 20(1), 50–67. doi: 10.1080/13683500.2014.965665

Beyer, P. (2007) Religion and globalization, in Ritzer, G. (ed.) *The Blackwell companion to globalization*. Malden, MA: Blackwell, 444–60.

Bremer, T.S. (2004) *Blessed with tourists: The borderlands of religion and tourism in San Antonio*. Chapel Hill, NC: The University of North Carolina Press.

Bremer, T.S. (2005) Tourism and religion, in Jones, J. (ed.) *Encyclopedia of religion*. Detroit: Macmillian Reference USA and Thomas Gale, 9260–64.

Broggi, M. (ed.) (1985) *Sanfter tourismus: Schlagwort oder chance fur den alpenraum?* Vaduz: Commission Internationale pour las Protection des Regions Alpines (CIPRA).

Bruntz, C. and Schedneck, B. (2020) *Buddhist tourism in Asia.* Honolulu: University of Hawai'i Press.

Butler, R. and Suntikul, W. (2018) *Tourism and religion: Issues and implications.* Bristol, UK: Channel View Publications.

Cheer, J.M., Belhassen, Y. and Kujawa, J.M. (2017) Spiritual tourism: Entrée to the special issue. *Tourism Management Perspectives*, 24, 186–7. doi: 10.1016/j.tmp.2017.07.019.

Choe, J., Blazey, M. and Mitas, O. (2015) Motivations of non-Buddhists visiting Buddhist temples. *Current Issues in Tourism*, 18(1), 70–82. doi: 10.1080/13683500.2013.771627

Cohen, E. (1988) Authenticity and commoditization in tourism. *Annals of Tourism Research*, 15, 371–86. doi: 10.1016/0160-7383(88)90028-X

Cohen, E. (1992) Pilgrimage and tourism: Convergence and divergence, in Morinis, A. (ed.) *Sacred journeys: The anthropology of pilgrimage.* Westport, CT: Greenwood Press, 18–35.

Cohen, E. (1998) Tourism and religion: A comparative perspective. *Pacific Tourism Review*, 2, 1–10.

Cohen Ioannides, M.W. and Ioannides, D. (2006) Global Jewish tourism: Pilgrimages and remembrance, in Timothy, D.J. and Olsen, D.H. (eds) *Tourism, religion and spiritual journeys.* London and New York: Routledge, 156–71.

Collins-Kreiner, N. (2010) Current Jewish pilgrimage tourism: Modes and models of development. *Tourism*, 58(3), 259–70.

Collins-Kreiner, N. (2020) Religion and tourism: A diverse and fragmented field in need of a holistic agenda. *Annals of Tourism Research*, 82, 102892. doi: 10.1016/j.annals.2020.102892

Collins-Kreiner, N. and Olsen, D.H. (2004) Selling diaspora: Producing and segmenting the Jewish diaspora tourism market, in Coles, T. and Timothy, D.J. (eds) *Tourism, diasporas and space.* London and New York: Routledge, 279–90.

Collins-Kreiner, N., Kliot, N., Mansfeld, Y. and Sagi, K. (eds) (2006) *Christian tourism to the Holy Land: Pilgrimage during security crisis.* Burlington, VT: Ashgate.

Di Giovine, M.A. (2010) Rethinking development: Religious tourism to St. Padre Pio as material and cultural revitalization in Pietrelcina. *Tourism*, 58(3), 271–8.

Di Giovine, M.A. (2016) The everyday as extraordinary: Revitalization, religion, and the elevation of Cucina Casareccia to heritage cuisine in Pietrelcina, Italy, in Brulotte, R.L. and Di Giovine, M.A. (eds) *Edible identities: Food as cultural heritage.* London and New York: Routledge, 77–92.

Digance, J. (2006) Religious and secular pilgrimage: Journeys redolent with meaning, in Timothy, D.J and Olsen, D.H. (eds) *Tourism, religion and spiritual journeys.* London and New York: Routledge, 36–48.

Drule, A.M, Chiş, A., Băcilă, M.F. and Ciornea, R. (2012) A new perspective of non-religious motivations of visitors to sacred sites: Evidence from Romania. *Procedia – Social and Behavioral Sciences*, 62, 431–5. doi: 10.1016/j.sbspro.2012.09.070

Duff, A. (2009) Unlocking the potential of church tourism. *Tourism Insights.* Available at http://cvta.org.uk/wp-content/uploads/2014/11/insights_church_tourism.pdf (accessed 16 September 2020).

Enongene, V. and Griffin, K. (2019) Tackling the problems of deficient data when planning for religious tourism management, in Griffiths, M. and Whiltshire, P. (eds) *Managing religious tourism.* Wallingford, UK: CABI: 79–91.

Faccarello, G. (ed.) (2020) *Political economy and religion: Essays in the history of economic thought.* London and New York: Routledge.

Fang, W-T. (2020) *Tourism in emerging economies: The way we green, sustainable, and healthy.* Singapore: Springer. doi: 10.1007/978-981-15-2463-9

Fife, W. (2004) Extending the metaphor: British missionaries as pilgrims in New Guinea, in Badone, E. and Roseman, S.R. (eds) *Intersecting journeys: The anthropology of pilgrimage and tourism.* Urbana: University of Illinois Press, 140–59.

Fourie, J., Rosselló, J. and Santana-Gallego, M. (2015) Religion, religious diversity and tourism, *Kyklos*, 68, 51–64. doi: 10.1111/kykl.12066

Gauthier, F., Martikainen, T. and Woodhead, L. (2013) Acknowledging a global shift: A primer for thinking about religion in consumer societies. *Implicit Religion*, 16(3), 261–76.

Giumbelli, E. (2019) Religious tourism and religious monuments: The politics of religious diversity in Brazil. *International Journal of Latin American Religions*, 3, 342–55.

Giuşcă, M. C., Gheorghilaş, A. and Dumitrache, L. (2018) Assessment of the religious-tourism potential in Romania. *Human Geographies*, 12(2), 225–37. doi: 10.5719/hgeo.2018.122.6

Graburn, N.H.H. (1989) Tourism: The sacred journey, in Smith, V.L. (ed.) *Hosts and guests: The anthropology of tourism*. Philadelphia: University of Pennsylvania Press, 21–36.

Greif, A. (2006) *Institutions and the path to the modern economy: Lessons from medieval trade*. Cambridge, UK: Cambridge University Press.

Griffin, K. and Raj, R. (2018) The importance of religious tourism and pilgrimage: Reflecting on definitions, motives and data. *International Journal of Religious Tourism and Pilgrimage*, 5(3), 2–9. doi: 10.21427/D7242Z

Griffiths, M. (2011) Those who come to pray and those who come to look: Interactions between visitors and congregations. *Journal of Heritage Tourism*, 6(1), 63–72. doi: 10.1080/1743873X.2010.536234

Grima, R. and Farrugia, S. (2019) Landscapes, landforms and monuments in Neolithic Malta, in Gauci, R. and Schembri, J.A. (eds) *Landscapes and landforms of the Maltese Islands*. Cham, Switzerland: Springer, 79–90.

Gupta, P. and Kumar, S. (2017) The growing business of religion in India. *LiveMint*. Available at https://www.livemint.com/Politics/2Vpsk1a1j4RwcIg9eKMErL/The-growing-business-of-religion-in-India.html (accessed 4 September 2020).

Gupta, V. (1999) Sustainable tourism: Learning from Indian religious traditions. *International Journal of Contemporary Hospitality Management*, 11(2–3), 91–5. doi: 10.1108/09596119910250751

Gutic, J., Caie, E. and Clegg, A. (2010) In search of heterotopia? Motivations of visitors to an English cathedral. *International Journal of Tourism Research*, 12(6), 750–60. doi: 10.1002/jtr.790

Hall, C.M. (2006) Buddhism, tourism and the middle way, in Timothy, D.J and Olsen, D.H. (eds) *Tourism, religion and spiritual journeys*. London and New York: Routledge, 172–85.

Hall, C.M. and Prayag, G. (eds) (2019) *The Routledge handbook of halal hospitality and Islamic tourism*. London and New York: Routledge.

He, L., Park, K. and Roehl, W.S. (2013) Religion and perceived travel risks. *Journal of Travel & Tourism Marketing*, 30(8), 839–57. doi: 10.1080/10548408.2013.835674

Heidari, A., Yazdani, H.R., Saghafi, F. and Jalilvand, M.R. (2018) The perspective of religious and spiritual tourism research: A systematic mapping study. *Journal of Islamic Marketing*, 9(4), 747–98. doi: 10.1108/JIMA-02-2017-0015

Henderson, J.C. (2010) Sharia-compliant hotels. *Tourism and Hospitality Research*, 10(3), 246–54. doi: 10.1057/thr.2010.3

Heydari Chianeh, R., Del Chiappa, G. and Ghasemi, V. (2018) Cultural and religious tourism development in Iran: Prospects and challenges. *Anatolia*, 29(2), 204–14. doi: 10.1080/13032917.2017.1414439

Horák, M., Kozumplíková, A., Somerlíková, K., Lorencová, H. and Lampartová, I. (2015) Religious tourism in the south-Moravian and Zlín regions: Proposal for three new pilgrimage routes. *European Countryside*, 7(3), 167–78. doi: 10.1515/euco-2015-0012

Howard, C. (2012) Speeding up and slowing down: Pilgrimage and slow travel through time, in Fullgar, S., Markwell, K. and Wilson, E. (eds) *Slow tourism: Experiences and mobilities*. Bristol, UK: Channel View Publications, 11–24.

Hung, K. (2015) Experiencing Buddhism in Chinese hotels: Toward the construction of a religious lodging experience. *Journal of Travel & Tourism Marketing*, 32(8), 1081–98. doi: 10.1080/10548408.2014.959632

Hung, K., Wang, S. and Tang, C. (2015) Understanding the normative expectations of customers toward Buddhism-themed hotels. *International Journal of Contemporary Hospitality Management*, 27(7), 1409–41. doi: 10.1108/IJCHM-12-2012-0264

Hung, K., Yang, X., Wassler, P., Wang, D., Lin, P. and Liu, Z. (2017) Contesting the commercialization and sanctity of religious tourism in the Shaolin Monastery, China. *International Journal of Tourism Research*, 19(2), 145–59. doi: 10.1002/jtr.2093

Illiev, D. (2020) The evolution of religious tourism: Concept, segmentation and development of new identities. *Journal of Hospitality and Tourism Management*, 45, 131–40. doi: 1 0.1016/j.jhtm.2020.07.012

Ioannides, D. and Ioannides, M.W.C. (2002) Pilgrimages of nostalgia: Patterns of Jewish travel in the United States. *Tourism Recreation Research*, 27(2), 17–25. doi: 10.1080/02508281.2002.11081216

Isaac, R.K. (2016) Pilgrimage tourism to Palestine, in Isaac, R.K., Hall, C.M. and Higgins-Desbiolles, F. (eds) *The politics and power of tourism in Palestine*. London and New York: Routledge, 124–35.

Iyer, S. (2016) The new economics of religion. *Journal of Economic Literature*, 54(2), 395–441. doi: 10.1257/jel.54.2.395

Izberk-Bilgin, E. and Nakata, C.C. (2016) A new look at faith-based marketing: The global halal market, *Business Horizons*, 59(3), 285–92. doi: /10.1016/j.bushor.2016.01.005

Jackson, R.H. and Hudman, L.E. (1994) Pilgrimage tourism and English cathedrals: The role of religion in travel. *The Tourist Review*, 4, 40–48. doi: 10.1108/eb058206

Jafari, J. and Scott, N. (2014) Muslim world and its tourisms. *Annals of Tourism Research*, 44, 1–19. doi: 10.1016/j.annals.2013.08.011

Javed, A. (2019) Potential and need of promoting tourism in Pakistan. *Daily Times*. Available at https://dailytimes.com.pk/477232/potential-and-need-of-promoting-tourism-in-pakistan/ (accessed 4 September 2020).

Jenkins, R. and Catra, I.N. (1997) Taming the tourists: Balinese temple clowns preserve their village tradition. *Performance Research: A Journal of the Performing Arts*, 2(2), 226. doi: 10.1080/13528165.1997.10871547

Kaell, H. (2016) Can pilgrimage fail? Intent, efficacy, and evangelical trips to the Holy Land. *Journal of Contemporary Religion*, 31(3), 393–408. doi: 10.1080/13537903.2016.1206254

Kanvinde, P. and Tom, B. (2018) Hinduism and tourism, in Butler, R. and Wantabee, S. (eds) *Tourism and religion: Issues and implications*. Bristol, UK: Channel View Publications, 83–98.

Kartal, B., Tepeci, M. and Atlı, H. (2015). Examining the religious tourism potential of Manisa, Turkey with a marketing perspective. *Tourism Review*, 70(3), 214–31. doi: 10.1108/TR-09-2013-0048

Kelly, J.R. (1982) *Leisure*. Englewood Cliffs, NJ: Prentice Hall, Inc.

Kessler, K. (2015) Conceptualizing mosque tourism: A central feature of Islamic and religious tourism. *International Journal of Religious Tourism and Pilgrimage*, 3(2), 11–32. doi: 10.21427/D7RB0G

Kessler, K. and Raj, R. (2018) Religious tourism in the Sultanate of Oman: The potential for mosque tourism to thrive, in Jamal, A., Griffin, K. and Raj, R. (eds) *Islamic tourism: Management of travel destinations*, Wallingford, UK: CABI, 124–40.

Kiely, T. (2013) Tapping into Mammon: Stakeholder perspectives on developing church tourism in Dublins Liberties. *Tourism Review*, 68(2), 31–43. doi: 10.1108/TR-01-2013-0001

Kim, B., Kim, S., and King, B. (2020) Religious tourism studies: Evolution, progress, and future prospects. *Tourism Recreation Research*, 45(2), 185–203. doi: 10.1080/02508281.2019.1664084

Kotler, J.A. (1997) *Travel that can change your life: How to create a transformative experience*. San Francisco: Jossey-Bass Publishers.

Kuo, C-M., Chen, L-H. and Liu, C-H. (2019) Is it all about religious faith? Exploring the value of contemporary pilgrimage among senior travelers. *Asian Pacific Journal of Tourism Research*, 24(5), 379–92. doi: 10.1080/10941665.2019.1572632

Lasserre, P. (1974) *Etude geographique de Lourdes*. Lourdes: Centre Mondial de Pelgrimage.

Liszewski, S. (2000) Pilgrimages or religious tourism? in Jackowski, A. (ed.) *Peregrinus cracoviensis*, Cracow, Poland: Publishing Unit, Institute of Geography, Jagiellonian University, 47–51.

Lopez, L. (2013) How long does the pilgrimage tourism experience to Santiago de Compostela last? *International Journal of Religious Tourism and Pilgrimage*, 1(1), 1–14. doi: 10.21427/D7C133

Lusby, C. (2017) Hard and soft tourism, in Lowry, L.L. (ed.) *The SAGE international encyclopedia of travel and tourism*. Thousand Oaks, CA: SAGE Publications, 565–8.

Luz, N. (2020) Pilgrimage and religious tourism in Islam. *Annals of Tourism Research*, 82, 102915. doi: 10.1016/j.annals.2020.102915

MacCannell, D. (1976) *The tourist: A new theory of the leisure class*. New York: Schocken.

Mansfeld, Y. and Cahaner, L. (2013) Ultra-orthodox Jewish tourism: A differential passage put of a sociocultural bubble to the 'open space', *Tourism Analysis*, 18(1), 15–27. doi: 10.3727/108354213X13613720283566

Maoz, D. and Bekerman, Z. (2010) Searching for Jewish answers in Indian resorts: The postmodern traveler. *Annals of Tourism Research*, 37(2), 423–39. doi: 10.1016/j.annals.2009.10.015

Margry, P.J. (2015) To be or not to be…a pilgrim: Spiritual pluralism along the Camino Finisterre and the urge for the end, in Sánchez-Carretero, C. (ed.) *Heritage, pilgrimage and the Camino to Finisterre*. Springer: Cham, 175–211.

Matema, M. (2018) Religious tourism: An USD$18 billion industry? *Nomad Africa*. Available at https://www.nomadafricamag.com/religious-tourism-an-usd18-billion-industry/ (accessed 4 September 2020).

Mattila, A. S., Apostolopoulos, Y., Sonmez, S., Yu, L. and Sasidharan, V. (2001) The impact of gender and religion on college students spring break behavior. *Journal of Travel Research*, 40(2), 193–200. doi: 10.1177/004728750104000210

Moore, C. (2007) $18 billion religious travel industry gives birth to international association. *Cision PRWeb*. Available at https://www.prweb.com/releases/religious/travel/prweb500224.htm (accessed 14 September 2020).

Morinis, A. (1992) Introduction: The territory of the anthropology of pilgrimage, in Morinis, A. (ed.) *Sacred journeys: The anthropology of pilgrimage*. Westport, CT: Greenwood Press, 1–28.

Morpeth, N.D. (2011) Church tourism and faith tourism initiatives in Northern England: Implications for the management of religious tourism sites. *International Journal of Business and Globalisation*, 7(1), 93–101. doi: 10.1504/IJBG.2011.040848

Nassar, M.A., Mostafa, M.M. and Reisinger, Y. (2015) Factors influencing travel to Islamic destinations: An empirical analysis of Kuwaiti nationals. *International Journal of Culture, Tourism and Hospitality Research*, 9(1), 36–53. doi: 10.1108/IJCTHR-10-2014-0088

Navruz-Zoda, B. and Navruz-Zoda, Z. (2016) The destination marketing development of religious tourism in Uzbekistan. *International Journal of Religious Tourism and Pilgrimage*, 4(7), 9–20. doi: doi.org/10.21427/D7G01X

Norman A. (2012) The varieties of the spiritual tourist experience. *Literature and Aesthetics*, 22(1), 20–37.

Okonkwo, E. (2015) Religious activities and their tourism potential in Sukur Kingdom, Nigeria. *International Journal of Religious Tourism and Pilgrimage*, 3(1), 1–11. doi: doi.org/10.21427/D7QF06

Okumus, F., Kar, M., Bilim, Y., Kartal, B., Tepeci, M. and Atlı, H. (2015) Examining the religious tourism potential of Manisa, Turkey with a marketing perspective. *Tourism Review*, 70(3), 214–31. doi: 10.1108/TR-09-2013-0048

Olsen, D.H. (2003) Heritage, tourism, and the commodification of religion. *Tourism Recreation Research*, 28(3), 99–104. doi: 10.1080/02508281.2003.11081422.

Olsen, D.H. (2006) Management issues for religious heritage attractions, in Timothy, D.J. and Olsen, D.H. (eds) *Tourism, religion and spiritual journeys*. London and New York: Routledge, 104–18.

Olsen, D.H. (2008) *Contesting identity, space and sacred site management at Temple Square in Salt Lake City, Utah*. PhD Dissertation, University of Waterloo, Waterloo, Ontario, Canada.

Olsen, D.H. (2010) Pilgrims, tourists, and Webers 'ideal types'. *Annals of Tourism Research*, 37(3), 848–51. doi: 10.1016/j.annals.2010.02.002

Olsen, D.H. (2011) Towards a religious view of tourism: Negotiating faith perspectives on tourism, *Journal of Tourism, Culture and Communication*, 11(1), 17–30. doi: 10.3727/109830411X1304957 1092633

Olsen, D.H. (2012) Negotiating religious identity at sacred sites: A management perspective. *Journal of Heritage Tourism*, 7(4), 359–66. doi: 10.1080/1743873X.2012.722642.

Olsen, D.H. (2013) A scalar comparison of motivations and expectations of experience within the religious tourism market. *International Journal of Religious Tourism and Pilgrimage*, 1(1), 41–61. doi: 10.21427/D7ZQ51

Olsen, D H. (2015) Definitions, motivations and sustainability: The case of spiritual tourism, in UNWTO (eds) *First UNWTO International Conference on Spiritual Tourism for Sustainable Development*. Madrid, Spain: World Tourism Organization, 35–46.

Olsen, D.H. (2017) Other journeys of creation: Non-representational theory, co-creation, failure, and the soul. *Tourism Recreation Research*, 42(1), 120–24. doi: 10.1080/02508281.2016.1261782

Olsen, D.H. (2019a) Religion, pilgrimage, and tourism in the MENA region, in Timothy, D.J. (ed.) *Routledge handbook on tourism in the Middle East and North Africa*. London and New York: Routledge, 109–24.

Olsen, D.H. (2019b) Religion, spirituality, and pilgrimage in a globalizing world, in Timothy, D.J. (ed.) *Handbook of globalisation and tourism*. Cheltenham: Edward Elgar Publishing, 270–83.

Olsen, D.H. (2020) Pilgrimage, religious tourism, biodiversity, and natural sacred sites, in Shinde, K.A. and Olsen, D.H. (eds) *Religious tourism and the environment*. Wallingford, UK: CABI, 23–41.

Olsen, D.H. and Timothy, D.J. (2020) COVID-19 and religious travel: Present and future directions. *International Journal of Religious Tourism and Pilgrimage*, 8(7), 170–88. doi: 10.21427/D7VC7D

Olsen, D. H. and Trono, A. (eds) (2018) *Religious Pilgrimage routes and trails: Sustainable development and management*. Wallingford, UK: CABI.

Ornella, A.D. (2013) Commodification of religion, in Runehov, A.L.C. and Oviedo, L. (eds) *Encyclopedia of sciences and religions*. Dordrecht, The Netherlands: Springer, 430–31.

Osterrieth, A. (1997) Pilgrimage, travel and existential quest, in Stoddard, R.H. and Morinis, A. (eds) *Sacred places, sacred spaces: The geography of pilgrimages*. Baton Rouge, LA: Department of Geography and Anthropology, Louisiana State University, 25–39.

Ostrowski, M. (2000) Pilgrimages or religious tourism, in Jackowski, A. (eds) *Peregrinus cracoviensis*. Cracow, Poland: Publishing Unit, Institute of Geography, Jagiellonian University, 53–61.

Ozcan, C. C., Bişkin, F. and Şimşek, Ç. (2019) Regional economic effects and marketing of religious tourism: The case of Konya, in de la Cruz del Río Rama, M. and Gómez-Ullate García de León. M. (eds) *Handbook of research on socio-economic impacts of religious tourism and pilgrimage*. Hershey PA: IGI Global, 250–74.

Paine, C. (2020) *Gods and rollercoasters: Religion in theme parks worldwide*. London: Bloomsbury.

Pernecky, T. and Johnston, C. (2006) Voyage through numinous space: Applying the specialization concept to new age tourism. *Tourism Recreation Research*, 31(1), 37–46. doi: 10.1080/02508281.2006.11081245

Pernecky, T. and Poulston, J. (2015) Prospects and challenges in the study of new age tourism: A critical commentary. *Tourism Analysis*, 20(6), 705–17. doi: 10.3727/108354215X14464845878237

Pfaffenberger, B. (1983) Serious pilgrims and frivolous tourists: The chimera of tourism in the pilgrimages of Sri Lanka. *Annals of Tourism Research*, 10(1), 57–74. doi: 10.1016/0160-7383(83)90115-9

Pourtaheri, M., Rahmani, K. and Ahmadi, H. (2012) Impacts of religious and pilgrimage tourism in rural areas: The case of Iran. *Journal of Geography and Geology*, 4(3), 122–9. doi: 10.5539/jgg.v4n3p122

Priest, R.J, and Priest, J.P. (2008) 'They see everything, and understand nothing': Short-term mission and service learning. *Missiology: An International Review*, 36(1), 53–73. doi: 10.1177/009182960803600105

Rashid, A.G. (2018) Religious tourism – A review of the literature. *Journal of Hospitality and Tourism Insights*, 1(2), 150–67. doi: 10.1108/JHTI-10-2017-0007

Reader, I. and Tanabe, Jr, G.J. (1997) *Practically religious: World benefits and the common religion of Japan*. Honolulu, HI: University of Hawai'i Press.

Ron, A.S. (2009) Towards a typological model of contemporary Christian travel. *Journal of Heritage Tourism*, 4(4), 287–97. doi: 10.1080/17438730903045548

Ron, A.S. and Timothy, D.J. (2018) *Contemporary Christian travel: Pilgrimage, practice and place*. Bristol, UK: Channel View Publications.

Seshardi, K.S. and Ganesh, T. (2011) Faunal mortality on roads due to religious tourism across time and space in protected areas: A case study from south India. *Forest Ecology and Management*, 262(9), 1713–21. doi: 10.1016/j.foreco.2011.07.017

Seyer, F. and Muller, D. (2011) Religious tourism: Niche or mainstream? in Papathanassis, A. (ed.) *The long tail of tourism: Holiday niches and their impact on mainstream tourism*. Heidelberg: Springer, 45–56.

Shackley, M. (2001) *Managing sacred sites: Service provision and visitor experience*. London and New York: Continuum.

Shackley, M. (2003) Management challenges for religion-based attractions, in Fyall, A., Garrod, B. and Leask, A. (eds) *Managing visitor attractions: New directions*. Oxford, UK: Butterworth-Heinemann, 159–70.

Shaikh, H. and Afraz, N. (2019) Pakistan is uniquely placed to take advantage of religious tourism. What is stopping us? *Prism*. Available at https://www.dawn.com/news/1479801 (accessed 4 September 2020).

Sharma, V. (2013) Faith tourism: For a healthy environment and a more sensitive world. *International Journal of Religious Tourism and Pilgrimage*, 1(1), 15–23. doi: 10.21427/D7772J

Sharpley, R. (2009) Tourism, religion and spirituality, in Jamal, T. and Robinson, M. (eds) *The SAGE handbook of tourism studies*. Thousand Oaks, CA: SAGE, 237–53.

Shepherd, R. (2002) Commodification, culture and tourism. *Tourist Studies*, 2, 183–201. doi: 10.1177/146879702761936653

Shinde, K.A. (2007) Pilgrimage and the environment: Challenges in a pilgrimage centre. *Current Issues in Tourism*, 10(4), 343–65. doi: doi.org/10.2167/cit259.0

Shinde, K.A. (2010) Entrepreneurship and indigenous entrepreneurs in religious tourism in India. *International Journal of Tourism Research*, 12(5), 523–35. doi: 10.1002/jtr.771

Shinde, K.A. (2020) Religious theme parks as tourist attraction systems. *Journal of Heritage Tourism*, doi: 10.1080/1743873X.2020.1791887

Shinde, K.A. (2022) The environmental impacts of religious and spiritual tourism, in Olsen, D.H. and Timothy, D.J (eds) *Routledge handbook of religious and spiritual tourism*. London and New York: Routledge, 315–31.

Shinde, K.A. and Olsen, D.H. (eds) (2020) *Religious tourism and the environment*. Wallingford, UK: CABI.

Shoval, N. (2000) Commodification and theming of the sacred: Changing patterns of tourist consumption in the 'Holy Land', in Gottdiener, M. (ed.) *New forms of consumption: Consumers, culture, and commodification*. Lanham, MD: Rowman & Littlefield, 251–63.

Singh, R.P.B. (2006) Pilgrimage in Hinduism: Historical context and modern perspectives, in Timothy, D.J. and Olsen, D.H. (eds) *Tourism, religion and spiritual journeys*. London and New York: Routledge, 220–36.

Singh, S. (1998) Probing the product life cycle further. *Tourism Recreation Research*, 23(2), 61–3. doi: 10.1080/02508281.1998.11014839

Stausberg, M. (2011) *Religion and tourism: Crossroads, destinations and encounters*. Abingdon, UK and New York: Routledge.

Stausberg, M. (2014) Religion and spirituality in tourism, in Lew, A.A., Hall, C.M. and Williams, A.M. (eds) *The Wiley Blackwell companion to tourism*. New Jersey: Wiley, 349–60.

Sumption, J. (2003) *The age of pilgrimage: The medieval journey to god*. Mahwah, NJ: Hidden Spring.

Swanson, K.K. and Timothy, D.J. (2012) Souvenirs: Icons of meaning, commercialization and commoditization. *Tourism Management*, 33(3), 489–99. doi: 10.1016/j.tourman.2011.10.007

Tarlow, P. (2014) The importance of the religious tourism market. *Travel Mole*. Available at https://www.travelmole.com/mediakit_pmi/The%20importance%20of%20the%20Religious%20Tourism%20Market.html (accessed 6 September 2020).

Terzidou, M., Scarles, C. and Saunders, M.N. (2018) The complexities of religious tourism motivations: Sacred places, vows and visions. *Annals of Tourism Research*, 70, 54–65. doi: 10.1016/j.annals.2018.02.011

Terzidou, M., Scarles, C. and Saunders, M. (2018) The vow and tourist travel, in Butler, R. and Suntikul, W. (eds) *Tourism and religion: Issues and implications*. Bristol, UK: Channel View, 117–27.

Terzidou, M., Stylidis, D. and Szivas, E.M. (2008) Residents' perceptions of religious tourism and its socio-economic impacts on the island of Tinos. *Tourism and Hospitality Planning & Development*, 5(2), 113–29. doi: 10.1080/14790530802252784

Timothy, D.J. (2012) Religious views of the environment: Sanctification of nature and implications for tourism, in Holden, A. and Fennell, D.A. (eds) *The Routledge handbook of tourism and the environment*. London and New York: Routledge, 53–64.

Timothy, D.J. and Olsen, D.H. (eds) (2006a) *Tourism, religion and spiritual journeys*. London and New York: Routledge.

Timothy, D.J and Olsen, D.H (2006b) Conclusion: wither religious tourism? in Timothy, D.J. and Olsen, D.H. (eds) *Tourism, religion and spiritual journeys*. London and New York: Routledge, 271–8.

Timothy, D.J. and Pernecky, T. (2006) Nature religion, self-spirituality and New Age tourism, in Timothy, D.J. and Olsen, D.H. (eds) *Tourism, religion and spiritual journeys*. London and New York: Routledge, 139–55.

Timothy, D. J. and Ron, A. S. (2018) Christian tourism in the Middle East, in Timothy, D.J. (ed.) *Routledge handbook on tourism in the Middle East and North Africa*. London: Routledge, 147–59.

Turner, V. and Turner, E. (1978) *Image and pilgrimage in Christian culture*. New York: Columbia University Press.

UNWTO (2011) *Religious tourism in Asia and the Pacific*. Madrid: World Tourism Organization.

Uriely, N., Israeli, A. and Reichel, A. (2003) Religious identity and residents' attitudes toward heritage tourism development: The case of Nazareth. *Journal of Hospitality & Tourism Research*, 27(1), 69–84. doi: 10.1177/1096348002238881

Vidal-Casellas, D., Aulet, S. and Crous-Costa, N. (2019) Introduction, in Vidal-Casellas, D., Aulet, S. and Crous-Costa, N. (eds) *Tourism, pilgrimage and intercultural dialogue: Interpreting sacred stories*. Wallingford, UK: CABI, 1–13.

Voase, R. (2007) Visiting a cathedral: The consumer psychology of a 'rich experience'. *International Journal of Heritage Studies*, 13(1), 41–55. doi: 10.1080/13527250601010851

Vukonić, B. (2000) Pastoral care, in Jafari, J. (ed.) *Encyclopedia of tourism*. New York: Routledge, 429.

Vukonić, B. (2002) Religion, tourism and economics: A convenient symbiosis. *Tourism Recreation Research*, 27(2), 59–64. doi: 10.1080/02508281.2002.11081221

Wang, Z., Ding, P., Scott, N. and Fan, Y. (2010) Muslim tourism in China, in Scott, N. and Jafari, J. (eds) *Tourism in the Muslim world*. Bingley, UK: Emerald Group Publishing Limited, 107–20.

Warkentin, B. (2018) Spiritual but not religious: The fine line between the sacred and secular on the Camino de Santiago. *Social Work and Christianity*, 45(1), 109–21.

Weidenfeld, A.D.I. and Ron, A.S. (2008) Religious needs in the tourism industry. *Anatolia*, 19(2), 357–61. doi: 10.1080/13032917.2008.9687080

Williams, E., Francis, L.J., Robbins, M. and Annis, J. (2007) Visitor experiences of St Davids Cathedral: The two worlds of pilgrims and secular tourists. *Rural Theology*, 5(2), 111–23. doi: 10.1179/rut_2007_5_2_004

Woodward, S.C. (2004) Faith and tourism: Planning tourism in relation to places of worship. *Tourism and Hospitality Planning & Development*, 1(2), 173–86. doi: 10.1080/1479053042000251089

Wright (2008) *The Christian travel planner*. Nashville, TN: Thomas Nelson.

Zamani-Farahani, H. and Henderson, J.C. (2010) Islamic tourism and managing tourism development in Islamic societies: The cases of Iran and Saudi Arabia. *International Journal of Tourism Research*, 12(1), 79–89. doi: 10.1002/jtr.741

Zhu, Y. (2012) Performing heritage: Rethinking authenticity in tourism. *Annals of Tourism Research*, 39(3), 1495–513. doi: 10.1016/j.annals.2012.04.003

Zwissler, L. (2011) Pagan pilgrimage: New religious movements research on sacred travel within Pagan and New Age communities. *Religion Compass*, 5(7), 326–42. doi: 10.1111/j.1749-8171.2011.00282.x

25. Babymoon travel in India

Senthilkumaran Piramanayagam and Partho Pratim Seal

INTRODUCTION

Globalization, increased diversity of tourism markets, continuously changing business environments and competition, evolving technology and a diminishing effect of traditional marketing methods have increasingly given birth to niche marketing (Dalgic, 2011). In the marketing context, the word 'niche' refers to both the market for a product and the target customer for the specific product – it defines a market that is markedly small and not served by competing brands (Keegan, Moriarty and Duncan, 1995). The distinctiveness of 'niche' customers lies in their unique need and willingness to pay a premium for a product that maximizes their satisfaction (Kotler and Keller, 2010). In the context of tourism, the term 'niche tourism' is borrowed from the term 'niche marketing', where tourism products are tailored to fulfil the needs of the specific market segment. The efficient management of tourism offers three-fold benefits: generating quality jobs, reducing poverty and generating incentives for conserving the environment, all of which are included in the broader objectives of the UN's Sustainable Development Goals (SDGs) (UNWTO, 2018). Tourism plays a role in these SDGs, with travel niches having gradually become significant contributors to the further growth of tourism (McKersie, 2013) and appearing to be more environmentally sustainable and beneficial to host communities. In addition, destinations' distinctive appeal in the market creates a long-term sustainable competitive advantage (Hsu, Kang and Wolfe, 2002). 'Niche tourism' is thus a new form of special interest tourism where the desires, preferences and wishes of individuals are coordinated, packaged and sold. Niche tourism legitimizes individuals' intimate proclivities (Robinson and Novelli, 2005), making it both an economy of imagination and an economy of experience.

'Babymoon' travel is a form of niche tourism where the preferences of expecting couples are sold as a tourism package. Pregnant mothers are considered a lucrative market segment, as expectant mothers tend to pursue significant changes in lifestyle and are willing to spend more to ensure their comfort and well-being (McKersie, 2013). A shift in parents' intention to give a grand welcome to the new-born child has fuelled the growth of babymoon travel. There are two main definitions for the term 'babymoon', as either a trip or vacation taken by a couple shortly before the birth of a child, or a period of time for parents to spend alone with their new child soon after the child's birth (Merriam-Webster's Learner Dictionary, 1979). In this study, we define a babymoon as a vacation taken by young couples after conception and before the delivery of the child.

Changing lifestyles, guaranteed paid leave for pregnancy and rising disposable income are the key drivers of demand linked to the global parents-in-waiting market for prenatal travel. This new market is characterized as 'cash-rich, time-poor', where consumers would like to spend their leisure time to foster intimacy and consider it a rare chance to reconnect with their loved ones (Amadeus, 2016). Opting for a babymoon is considered a status symbol in modern society. The photographs and the shared experiences of celebrities opting for babymoon vacations in exotic destinations covered in the media, to some extent, contribute to the increased interest towards babymoon vacations (Voigt and Laing, 2010). More than three million people take babymoon vacations worldwide per year, with beach destinations being the most preferred among such vacationers. The babymoon vacation helps couples eliminate stress, gain intimacy and realize other social benefits (Gabor and Oltean, 2019).

An increasing number of nuclear families and dual-career couples characterized by rising affluence, changing lifestyles, increased consciousness of well-being and a firm intention to get away from a stressful urban life propelled the need for babymoon vacations in India. Although this form of travel is not entirely new, it has been a media-led phenomenon driving the demand for babymoon services. It is a market niche for luxury hotels and resorts, generally offered as an all-inclusive package with a hefty price tag (Cox and Kings, 2017).

Although the phenomenon of babymoon travel has been gaining popularity in India, there are very few tourism marketing firms serving this niche market, and very few states in India trying to promote Indian regions as the best destination for babymoon travel. The babymoon, as a niche segment of tourism, is not well acknowledged due to the scarcity of research about consumer behaviour by tourism marketers, hospitality service providers and tourism policymakers. The research published on this type of niche tourism appears to be very limited (Dalgic, 2011). However, it deserves more attention as the number of babymoon travellers is increasing and the economic value it contributes to both the international and Indian tourism economies is substantial.

Considering this research gap, this study aims to identify the demographic profile of babymoon couples, analyse their motives and examine their travel behaviour in India. As there is no existing literature available on the Indian context, and due to the explorative nature of the study, a qualitative research method was adopted to fulfil its objectives. The data was collected from nine young mothers and six pregnant women who opted for a babymoon trip before their delivery. The outcome of the study significantly contributes to the creation of knowledge on Indian babymoon consumers' behaviour, which will assist both Indian and international marketers, researchers and tourism practitioners to better understand and develop strategies to serve this emerging micro-niche tourism market.

LITERATURE REVIEW

Niche Tourism

'Niche tourism' is a new wave of tourism that emerged as an alternative against 'mass tourism', often criticized for its adverse impact on the environment, residents and the sociocultural interaction between tourists and the residents in a destination. Destinations have a desperate need to distinguish and differentiate their offerings in a globalized world, where tourism offers are often perceived as homogeneous. Niche tourism offers an excellent opportunity for destinations to deliver more meaningful experiences to high-spending tourists, which is also more sustainable and less damaging to the environment and the destination's sociocultural space (Robinson and Novelli, 2005).

The level of expertise and experience of tourists as consumers has also increased over time. The more experienced and increasingly sophisticated tourists demand specialized holiday experiences to fulfil their needs. Nowadays, tourists have a thorough recognition of their role and power as consumers. Consumption is increasingly associated with emotional pleasure, distinction and identity, and is seen more as a means for creating social bonding than a functional process. The choice of vacation destination, type of holiday and activities to get involved in at the destination is seen as a part of identity-making (Robinson and Novelli, 2005). This customer behaviour has given a further opportunity to develop the 'niche', based on a more specialized and sophisticated tourism market.

Babymoon Vacation – A Micro-Niche Vacation

Babymoon travel is part of wellness tourism, which can be regarded as the macro-niche. Couples seeking physical, mental and social well-being emphasize the nature of proactive behaviour towards health and well-being (Gabor and Oltean, 2019; Zhang, 2015). However, the babymoon can be classified as a micro-niche, as it is currently a small market that cannot be further divided into sub-categories (Robinson and Novelli, 2005). According to McKersie (2013), the babymoon is also a part of reproductive tourism. Rest, relaxation and preparation for the delivery of a baby are the primary motives for the babymoon. This emerging market segment has opened up scope for a range of products and services varying from skincare products to babymoon holidays. Consumerism and increased adoption of technology have played a crucial role in the growth of this form of niche tourism (McKersie, 2013).

Stage of life, in reference to the different phases of life that an individual passes through, plays a significant role in individuals' lifestyles and choice of activities. Individuals' leisure and tourism behaviour also changes depending on their stage in life (Chang and Chung, 2018). Voigt and Laing (2010) state that babymoon travel is a way to celebrate the experience and commemorate the bride and groom as they transition from being a couple to being parents. Babymoon vacations are therefore travel products that target expectant parents wishing to enjoy a romantic gateway and celebrate the pregnancy before delivering their child.

Voigt and Laing (2010) listed three factors that fuelled the practice of combining pregnancy and tourism. The first reason is that air travel is considered safer for pregnant women and babies in utero than other modes of travel. The second reason is marketers' continued efforts to offer more customized tour packages and services targeting individuals in different life cycles stages. The third reason is that changes in society have led to the commodification of pregnancy and childbirth. The authors further argue that in Western societies, pregnancy and childbirth are not considered physical conditions; they are individual and social experiences that can become a commodified experience that can be marketed. The term 'commodification' thereby denotes the transformation of something which does not possess the nature of saleable goods into one that does. Voigt and Laing (2010) concluded that pregnancy is intrinsically connected with consumerism. Thus, travel associated with childbirth becomes just another increasingly important purchase decision by expectant parents. Voigt and Laing (2010) also caution couples to avoid tropical destinations for pregnancy-related travel, as pregnant women have a high risk of developing medical conditions associated with high temperatures and humidity. Travelling should be avoided during the first trimester, as the risk of miscarriage is high. The second trimester of pregnancy is safest for travel. While opting for a destination, appropriate measures should be taken to check that adequate and appropriate obstetric and neonatal care is available at the destination.

Today, pregnancy is celebrated more than ever. The growing trend in sharing life events on social media is an impetus to growth in pregnancy-related celebrations and pre-baby vacations, a romantic gateway before the delivery of a baby. The idea of the babymoon was introduced by Sheila Kitzinger, an anthropologist, in 1996 (Gabor and Oltean, 2019). She suggested that the babymoon trip aims to strengthen the role and identity of the father, as it helps the father to fill the gap in children's caregiving, as often the father's interaction with a child is less than that of a mother.

Babymoon Vacations in India

India is a distinctive example of diversity and convergence for culture, heritage, topography and language influenced by modernity and Western ideas (Rameshkumar, 2017). Globalization and the liberalization of the economy has considerably impacted society and the lives of individuals in many ways, substantially affecting people's identity, lifestyle, work culture, values, attitudes and eating habits. Globalization also has a significant effect on family structure and the role of women, breaking down the traditional joint family structure and leading to the emergence of the nuclear family and Indians' moving towards a more Western lifestyle. Adopting a more Western lifestyle has impacted the way people in India dress, eat, celebrate and spend (Upadhyay, 2014). Post-liberalization advertising in the media exposed the Indian citizens to consumerism, propounding a cosmopolitan lifestyle (Pathak, 2019). Cosmopolitanism is an ideology of people who are keen to explore, adapt to and assent to different cultures (Arora and Aggarwal, 2018). Various consumption areas such as choice of food, sports and lifestyle are determined by the degree of individuals' cosmopolitan orientation (Cleveland, Papadopoulos and Laroche, 2011). Participation in niche tourism allows tourists to become 'cosmopolitans' to an extent (Hannerz, 1996). Changing lifestyles and the adoption of a cosmopolitan ideology has led to a rise in consumerism and Indians seeking more opportunities to spend money. Conspicuous consumption therefore is no longer considered a sin (Pandey, 2011).

Babymoon tourism is relatively new and at a nascent stage in India. A market study conducted by Cox and Kings (2017) among new mothers and pregnant women in India indicates that about 82% of pregnant women are willing to go for a babymoon vacation and about 72% of new mothers opted to take a babymoon trip during their pregnancy. The study also revealed that about 65% of the women in the survey expressed the desire to take an international babymoon vacation (Cox and Kings, 2017). Babymoon travel has great market potential as many women in urban India have a strong willingness and purchasing power.

Vacation Decision Process

The tourist as a consumer makes multiple decisions in the process of purchasing tourism products and services. These products and services may include the tourist destination, the mode of travel, accommodation, activities and attractions. There are five stages in the decision process a tourist undergoes (Kotler, Bowen and Makens, 2009). The buying process begins as the tourist recognizes the need. In the first stage, the need for travel arises when a potential tourist recognizes the difference between the actual state and the desired state. This is a critical stage in the customer decision process, as it motivates the consumer to action (Hoyer and MacInnis, 2010). Both internal and external stimuli can trigger the need. The needs of men and women as travellers are different. Meng and Uysal's (2008) study found that female travellers assign more importance to natural attributes and recreational activities than men. Women also prioritize security and respect as a traveller as compared to men. Heimtun (2012) described how identities differ for women when travelling along with a companion and the perception of the tourist gaze, with female travellers experiencing the sexual gaze more often.

The primary motive for a babymoon vacation is relaxation, undergoing medical treatments or procedures and a 'last' child-free gateway to experience intimacy by the couple. It helps the would-be parents relax and reconnect (Voigt and Laing, 2010). Zhang (2015) found both pull and push motives motivating Chinese babymoon travellers. The push motives included relaxation, escape from daily routines, well-being, fertility benefits and improving one's relationship with one's spouse. Enjoyment, learning new things, excitement and freedom were all pull motives cited by Chinese babymoon travellers.

Searching for information on requirements related to the trip is the second stage. Information may be obtained from personal, commercial and public sources. An existing study on babymoon travel in China reveals that family and friends, the internet and travel agents are all vital sources of information (Zhang, 2015). Evaluation of alternatives is the third step in the decision-making process. A tourist evaluates each alternative tourism product and service against the stated need. In the fourth step, once the competing tourism products and services are ranked based on the purchase intention, the tourist chooses the most preferred tourism products and services (Gabor and Oltean, 2019; Zhang, 2015).

Zhang (2015) observed that destinations close to water were popular among Chinese babymoon travellers, and that most babymoon travellers preferred domestic locations than foreign ones. Another significant factor in destination choice is a place with a good climate (Zhang, 2015). The most preferred activities in a destination are shopping, sunbathing and walking on the beach, as well as other recreational activities. The most preferred accommodation is a luxury hotel with a spa, and the most common duration opted for by babymoon vacationers is a week or more. Researchers also believe that the second trimester is the most suitable time for a babymoon (Gabor and Oltean, 2019). However, the choice of tourism product, service and activities in the destination is influenced by family members, peers and other factors, such as family income, price and the perceived benefit of products and services.

The final stage is post-purchase behaviour. The purchase and consumption of products will lead to satisfaction or dissatisfaction. The valuation of satisfaction and dissatisfaction depends on the difference between tourists' expectations and the perceived performance of the product and service. If the perceived performance exceeds expected performance it leads to satisfaction, and vice versa. Level of satisfaction has a significant impact on tourists' repurchase and other behavioural intentions (Kotler et al., 2009; Vargas-Sánchez, 2012). Although tourist consumption behaviour has been thoroughly analysed in the existing tourism marketing literature, babymoon tourists' consumption behaviour is not well documented in the Indian context, an emerging babymoon market.

METHODOLOGY

In-depth semi-structured interviews were used to investigate babymoon travellers' motivations and consumer behaviour, guided by a phenomenological research approach. Phenomenological research, a qualitative approach adopted to explore humans' lived experience about a phenomenon, helps to generate rich descriptions of experiences by participants. A qualitative method of study was chosen, as babymoon tourism in an Indian context is relatively new and has not been previously studied. A qualitative methodology provides more flexibility in the research design, which helps obtain more details from the participants, thereby providing a better understanding of the phenomenon (Cresswell, 2009). The researchers envisaged this approach would provide material which enabled in-depth discussion of babymoon tourism and help our understanding of the phenomenon as a whole. The study involved in-depth interviews with eligible participants, using the laddering technique (Veludo-de-Oliveira, Ikeda and Campomar, 2006), according to which a semi-structured one-to-one interview with probing questions is undertaken to establish why a particular factor was important for an individual. The response obtained from the first question is used to formulate the next question. The interviews were conducted until the information was saturated, and no new information was obtained (Guba and Lincoln, 2006).

The respondents for the study were identified through multiple sources. The search for qualifying participants was undertaken via travel agencies and tour operators that had facilitated babymoon trips by couples, as well as on social media networks such as Facebook and Twitter where participants had shared their babymoon experiences. Two online travel agencies that offer babymoon travel packages accepted the researchers' request to approach potential participants. However, these travel agencies asked the researchers to send a formal request to all participants to obtain their consent and willingness to participate in the survey. Other participants who had shared experiences on social media were contacted through a more formal communication explaining the study's objective, and asked for their consent to participate in the study. Some participants later suggested friends who had motivated them to take a babymoon vacation or, conversely, friends whom they had encouraged to do so. In total, data was collected from nine young mothers and six pregnant women who opted for a babymoon trip before the delivery. All nine young mothers had opted for a babymoon abroad. Among the six pregnant women, four had opted for an international destination, while two had opted for domestic destinations.

The interviews were semi-structured, and included both face-to-face interviews and telephone interviews. In an Indian context, discussing a babymoon is a sensitive issue, and participants may be reluctant to discuss the topic with an outsider. However, the participants were assured that their opinions would be valued and not judged, their data would be kept confidential, and the information they provided would be used only for educational purposes and no other. Responses were either written down or recorded with an audio recorder, with the participants' prior permission. Four respondents did not want their conversation recorded, so these were written down as field notes. The questions for the semi-structured interviews were developed based on a literature review. The interviews were held between December 2019 and January 2020.

The data was coded using NVivo and analysed by both authors along with an independent coder. A codebook that included codes and memos was prepared and evolved as the coding proceeded (Patton, 2015). A procedure suggested by Gall, Gall and Borg (2003) was followed, according to which 15% of the content was compared between the two coders to check the interrater reliability. The second author coded the interview transcripts, and the independent coder coded 20% of the textual data. The interrater agreement was found to be 90%, which suggests that there was strong consistency between the two coders. The first author then oversaw the entire data coding process, verified the results and resolved any inconsistency between the two coders.

Table 25.1   *Demographic profile of respondents*

ID	Age	Education	Annual family income (in USD)	Occupation	Place of residence	Destination	Duration of vacation (days)	Amount spent (in USD)	Family structure
1	25	Master's	24,000	Service	Mumbai	Tuscany, Italy	7	4,000	Nuclear
2	28	Bachelor's	21,600	House wife	Pune	Atlantic City, New Jersey, USA	14	10,000	Joint
3	29	Bachelor's	22,800	Business	Bengaluru	Amsterdam, the Netherlands	15	9,200	Nuclear
4	32	Doctorate	-	Service	Ahmedabad	Marbella, Spain	8	10,800	Nuclear
5	33	Master's	24,000	Service	Mumbai	Sicily, Italy	7	4,200	Nuclear
6	24	Master's	18,000	Service	New Delhi	Seychelles	7	6,800	Nuclear
7	26	Bachelor's	16,800	House wife	Mangalore	Maldives	5	1,500	Joint
8	31	Bachelor's	25,200	Business	Hyderabad	Hawaii, USA	21	12,800	Nuclear
9	27	Master's	21,600	Business	Gurgaon	Paris, France	15	6,400	Nuclear
10	32	Master's	20,400	Service	Chennai	Kochi, India	5	560	Joint
11	29	Bachelor's	14,400	Service	Lucknow	Mauritius	7	3,500	Nuclear
12	24	Bachelor's	-	Business	Kolkata	Pondicherry, India	7	715	Joint
13	31	Master's	-	Service	Mangalore	Dubai, UAE	7	1,600	Nuclear
14	28	Master's	18,000	Service	Kasaragod	Maldives	7	1,400	Joint
15	32	Master's	21,600	Business	Mangalore	Bali, Indonesia	7	1,800	Joint

Source: The authors.

DEMOGRAPHIC PROFILE OF THE PARTICIPANTS

The objective of this study was to explore the motives and decision-making processes of babymoon vacationers. The initial question in the interview aimed to identify the demographic profile of the respondents. The demographic information included their age, education level, annual household income, occupation, city of residence and the destination to which they travelled for their babymoon. The annual household income expressed in Indian Rupees was converted to USD. The demographic profile of the participants is presented in Table 25.1.

The age of participants ranged between 24 and 33 years. The results showed that all the participants had some form of higher education. Six participants had a graduate degree, while eight had a postgraduate degree, and one participant has completed her research degree. The range of annual family income of the participants varied between USD14,400 to USD25,200. All participants belonged to higher income groups with an average income of USD20,700 per annum, as compared to the country's average of USD2,100 (World Bank, n.d.). However, three respondents expressed their unwillingness to share the family income. In terms of respondents' occupation, eight were employed in service, five had their own business and two were housewives. Nine participants described themselves as being in a nuclear family, while the other six were members of a joint family. All the participants in the study were residing in different cities and mostly cosmopolitan in nature.

Among the 15 respondents, two respondents selected a domestic destination and the remaining 13 respondents opted for international destinations for their babymoon. The two participants who opted for a domestic destination did so as their parents and relatives opposed them going far away, taking into account the couple's safety. The participants who opted for international destinations spent between USD1,400 and USD12,800 and their trip durations were between 7 and 15 days. The respondents who opted for domestic destinations spent between USD560 and USD715, and the duration of their babymoons was five days to a week. For all the destinations, the participants were accompanied only by their husband.

FINDINGS

Motivations Behind Indian Babymoon Travel

Eight distinct motives for babymoon were revealed in the data. Relaxation, escape from routine, enhancement of their relationship, romance, enjoyment, destination environment, novelty and seeking blessing from spiritual gurus were the major motives among babymoon vacationers.

The most common motive behind a babymoon vacation among respondents was relaxation, followed by escape from routine and enhancement of the relationship. There was a desire to leave the everyday environment behind and opt for something different. Travel is a means for people to get away from the repetitive and stressful daily routine. For instance, one participant said:

> We are both employed in IT services in different multinational companies; the vacation at this time had helped us to escape from our Monday-to-Friday machine-like life. (Age 33, residing in Mumbai, vacationed in Sicily, Italy)

A babymoon vacation has positive outcomes for most people. The participants' responses indicate that taking a babymoon allowed them to disconnect from their daily routine and relax. One couple specifically stated that:

> We were alone after a long time [...]. After our marriage, which was held four years ago, he [the husband] was also happy to be with me alone and away from his continuously ringing mobile phone. (Age 27, residing in Gurgaon, vacationed in Paris, France)

Leisure travel gives the opportunity to build on the relationship between the couple; respondents mentioned that the babymoon vacation helped them to solve issues that were affecting their day-to-day family relationship. One participant stated:

> The babymoon actually helped us to spend more time together as we are in a joint family setup. We sorted out some issues that are continuously hurting our relationship. It also helped us to be private, spend time together and enhance [our] relationship. (Age 26, residing in Mangalore, vacationed in the Maldives)

Another participant stated:

> When we are away from our routine life, it is much easier to feel free and [...] excited [...] forgetting about work, home and office while walking on the beach at an island, [...] I was more excited. (Age 31, residing in Mangalore, vacationed in Bali)

The two respondents who spent their babymoon in India stated that, other than relaxation, they had chosen their destination in order to receive a blessing from their spiritual gurus. One participant stated:

> In our family, it is a tradition to get blessings from our guru. So we went to Vallikavu to get blessings from Amma [Mata Amritanandamayi, a Hindu spiritual leader] before our vacation to Kochi. We were blessed with a female baby, and we named her 'Amrita'. (Age 33, residing in Chennai, vacationed in Kochi, India)

The other respondent visited Sri Aurobindo Ashram, Pondicherry, India.

These varied narratives regarding the motivations for taking a babymoon indicate that relaxation, escape from routine, enhancement of the relationship, enjoyment, novelty and seeking blessing were the most important ones among the respondents.

Babymoon Vacation Decision-Making

The participants mostly obtained information on their babymoon destinations from the travel agency that booked their itinerary. Seven respondents got information from friends who had been on a babymoon and went to the same destination as them. Nine of the respondents found information on various social network sites, while five received information from tourist destinations' websites.

However, some of the respondents used more than one source of information about a destination. One justified the need to obtain all the necessary information about a destination:

> So sometimes, it is necessary to look for information from friends and social media instead of completely relying on a travel agency. For example, friends and relatives with past experience are the best sources about restaurants, local attractions and the best choice of accommodation. (Age 29, residing in Bengaluru, vacationed in Amsterdam, the Netherlands)

This participant indicates that babymoon travellers rely more on social media and personal references from friends and peers as a primary source of information on their destination and choice of tourism product. Although they relied on peers, friends, social media and the internet as a source of information on their chosen vacation, all the participants in the study utilized the services of tour operators and travel agencies for planning their babymoon vacations.

Factors Influencing the Choice of Babymoon Destination

Geographical location is a dominant factor that determines the choice of holiday destination by babymoon couples. Twelve participants opted for beach or riverfront destinations, and three opted for places with strong heritage associations. Another important factor is the climate of the destination. An area with warm weather and known for its food is also considered essential.

Participants stated that, while choosing a destination, they did '*consider destinations that slow down our hectic life like beaches that are more preferred*' (Age 31, residing in Mangalore, vacationed at Bali). One participant also stated that '*choosing a destination where there is a place to relax and go out and explore may be a bit difficult for some with a baby so we prefer a location which would be to just relax for a period*' (Age 29, residing in Bengaluru, vacationed in Amsterdam, the Netherlands). Another participant stated that '*beautiful scenery and tranquil beaches help to connect with one another and remove the stress at home'*. She also said that '*choosing a destination already familiarized and staying at locations nearest to hospitals is also preferred*' (Age 29, residing in Lucknow, vacationed in Mauritius).

The various narratives from participants about their choice of babymoon destination indicate that geographical location and destination image were essential elements in their choice, with less crowded and waterfront destinations most preferred.

Choice of Accommodation and Activities

The study respondents opted for various accommodation choices, including homestays, private villas, luxury hotels and resorts. All the participants preferred locations with a pool attached to the accommodation. One participant also preferred a destination:

> where there is not much walking and climbing of staircases and are near to an eating joint. Room service is a most blessing as I don't want to walk much. The hotel must have option for spa and massage. (Age 31, residing in Hyderabad, vacationed in Hawaii)

All the respondents either visited a spa or went for a massage during their babymoon. One participant stated:

> we preferred to have food in room through room service and then occasionally went to pool, relaxed and enjoyed the time together with my husband. (Age 24, residing in New Delhi, vacationed in the Seychelles)

Another participant said:

> We wanted to relax the whole day in the room or in the pool [...] and in the evening, we walked around the hotel before dinner or for ice cream. So we both opted for a special babymoon spa and massage package in the hotel. (Age 24, residing in Kasaragod, vacationed in the Maldives)

One respondent who opted for Pondicherry, a domestic destination, stated that:

> All most every day we stayed in Pondicherry [we] visited the ashram for meditation. We did a lot of shopping of new clothes and bought handicrafts for our new home, which we would be shifting after a month. We both planned to do different things during our tour while relaxing in a calm and serene environment. (Age 24, residing in Kolkata, vacationed in Pondicherry)

The responses reveal that rest and relaxation were the most common activities undertaken by the couples. Shopping and wellness-related services were the second most common activities. Their narratives also reveal that the couples wanted to spend most of their time together in the hotel or resort, enjoying the spa and massage services. Activities involving strenuous physical activity and extensive travel were avoided by most participants. The most preferred activities within the premises of the accommodation were going around the hotel or resort premises and relaxing in the swimming pool.

Overall Experience of the Babymoon

The data suggests that all the respondents had a very positive and memorable babymoon experience. The following statements illustrate these experiences, which in many cases led to a desire for a repeat visit:

> Our experience, yes […] a memorable story to share with our baby. It was a great time away from our mechanized life. We both decided to visit once again the destination with our baby. (Age 29, residing in Lucknow, opted for Mauritius)

> It was a big and much-needed break. He got time to look after me. We came here to relax, and Bali is really a heaven. People were very polite and respectful. The trip is something special, like a gift. (Age 31, residing in Mangalore, vacationed in Bali)

> I called my friend to thank her for suggesting the ashram. I felt so happy that my baby had been blessed to visit the ashram. (Age 24, residing in Kolkata, vacationed in Pondicherry, India)

The responses highlight that their babymoon vacation helped the couples get away from the mundane and was considered a memorable experience associated with the pregnancy. The comments also narrate the significance of the characteristics of the destination and the activities undertaken while there on couples' overall perception of their experience.

Post-Babymoon Behaviour

Only two of the participants did not recommend the destination; the others had a great experience at the place they visited and were willing to recommend it to others. The statements by the two respondents who hesitated to recommend the destination reflect the causes of their dissatisfaction:

> We had some problems with the transport facility in the city as the cab drivers were found to be overcharging and were quite impolite. (Age 25, residing in Mumbai, vacationed in Tuscany, Italy)

> Bad experience with airport personnel: while we were going through the immigration process, a lady security [guard's] query about [our] travel was quite intimidating. (Age 31, residing in Hyderabad, vacationed in Hawaii).

Although some respondents faced other issues during their babymoon, these did not affect their overall experience. The following statement reflects a problem faced by some of the respondents:

> The travel abroad was a bit tiring, especially in the flight where I had to move out from the aisle seat, walk around and stretch during our flight to the USA. (Age 28, residing in Pune, holidaying in Atlantic City)

Few participants in the study said they had faced multiple obstacles that negatively affected their overall experience or post-consumption behaviour, for example, in terms of their intention and willingness to recommend the babymoon destination to others.

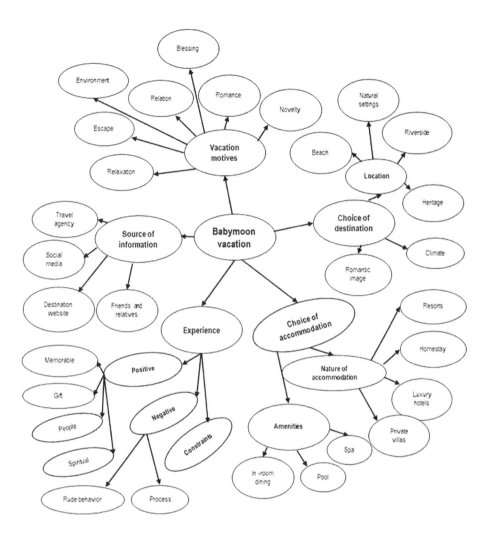

Figure 25.1   *Thematic analysis of babymoon vacation*

DISCUSSION

This study was undertaken to better understand the behaviour of Indian babymoon travellers. The following five dimensions were explored to achieve this: (1) travel motives, (2) source of information, (3) factors that influence the choice of destination, (4) factors that determine the choice of accommodation and activities during the vacation and (5) overall experience and post-vacation behaviour. The key findings are depicted as themes in Figure 25.1.

The data reveals that among the couples who went on a babymoon for relaxation, the significant motives included escape from routine and enhancing their relationship. The push motives had a stronger influence than the pull motives. The motive of going on a babymoon in order to receive a blessing from a spiritual guru and/or visiting a spiritual ashram has not previously been recorded in the literature, but it is an important source of information on babymoon products and services, particularly for tour operators, as well as social network sites.

The study's findings reveal the continued importance of tour operators within tourism services in a world currently dominated by the internet, given that every participant opted to use the services of a travel agency to plan their babymoon vacation. However, the use of multiple sources of information was common among respondents. There was a notable preference for destinations that were located near the sea (beaches, islands, coastal areas) or a lake. This finding reflects those of Gabor and Oltean (2019) and Zhang (2015). The most common accommodation choice was luxury hotels. In-room service; a pool – either in the room or on the premises; and facilities for meditation, yoga as well as spa and massage services were commonly desired features that determined the babymoon vacationers' choice of accommodation. The most common activity, other than relaxation in their room or by the pool, was walking within the premises of the accommodation. Respondents also tended to enjoy shopping, visiting a spa, tasting the local food and visiting nearby tourist attractions and spiritual places. However, the intention to sunbathe was not expressed by respondents, in contrast to other findings in the literature (Zhang, 2015). The study participants' overall experience was of a positive and memorable effect on their lives, and this had a significant influence on their behavioural intention. The findings of this study are similar those of Zhang (2015), who found that the babymoon vacation experience had a significant effect on travellers' satisfaction and behavioural intention.

Marketing Implications and Conclusions

Tourism is the fastest-growing economic sector and recognized as a vital contributor to economic growth, environmental protection, poverty alleviation, and job and wealth creation. The tourism sector seeks to adopt strategies for sustainable consumption and production in order to maximize those benefits (UNWTO, 2018). Sustainable tourism, as an alternative to mass tourism, aims to meet present and future tourists' needs while preserving resources. Like other forms of niche tourism, babymoon tourism is more sustainable and beneficial to the host community than mass tourism. Niche tourism products like babymoon vacations help the destination to achieve multiple benefits (Robinson and Novelli, 2005). First, they can be an effective tool to uniquely brand the country, which ultimately benefits tourist destinations by overcoming seasonality and giving them a competitive advantage. Second, the promotion of babymoon tourism may positively contribute to the health services infrastructure in the destination (Gabor and Oltean, 2019).

The participants' reflections in the present study show that their babymoon vacation provided a meaningful experience and generated a high level of satisfaction. The consumption behaviour of babymoon travellers revealed in this study gives impetus to explore opportunities for local businesses to benefit from this trade, generating decent jobs in the destination community, including jobs for women. It should furthermore encourage linkage between multiple stakeholders – such as hotels, hospitals, airlines, logistics companies and local manufacturers – that reflects the three dimensions of sustainable development. Unlike mass tourism, the benefits obtained by stakeholders through niche tourism are more sustainable (Marson, 2011). Therefore, well-planned niche tourism can help the destination sustain its economy and maximize the benefits through sustainable local economic activity (Alekseeva and Hercegová, 2021).

As island and beach destinations are the most preferred locations for babymoon vacations; these can be promoted as a niche tourist product by Small Island Development States (SIDS) which are small in size, remote and with limited resources. Babymoon tourism offers two benefits to SIDS. As babymoon vacationers tend to have a high spending ability and choose a higher-than-average length of stay, it opens up opportunities for small- and medium-scale local entrepreneurs capable of providing a tailored offering that indirectly benefits the host community. Second, as babymoons are an experience-based tourism product, it can help the destination diversify its tourism portfolio (O'Regan, 2014).

The findings of this study have multiple implications for tourism service providers and policymakers. The results reveal that babymoon travellers in India favour international tourism destinations over domestic ones (Cox and Kings, 2017). Studies in the Indian context report a greater volume of medium- and long-haul travel than regional travel, which is in contrast to the destination choice of other babymoon travellers from other nations (Amadeus, 2016). India is expected to generate over two million outbound tourists annually (Economic Times, 2019), which is twice the current foreign tourist arrivals to India. This offers both opportunities and challenges to domestic tourism marketers. The increased interest in babymoons by Indian couples represents an opportunity to build a new niche market, if managed effectively. The challenge is to motivate Indian babymoon travellers to opt for domestic tourism destinations. Creating a favourable image, developing the right tourism product and communication are all key to converting these challenges into an opportunity. Given that international border crossings were widely prohibited in many countries as a result of the COVID-19 pandemic, this would offer domestic tourism service providers and tourism planners an opportunity to promote various regional tourism destinations as favoured babymoon locations. In the present scenario, promoting domestic babymoon tourism destinations could help to revive the sector, which has been seriously affected by the restrictions on international travel.

A babymoon is a form of niche tourism that creates opportunities for airlines, travel agencies, destination managers and accommodation service providers alike. It encourages service providers to develop the right products and activities that appeal to and satisfy high-spending babymoon travellers' needs. The discomfort faced by women during long journeys could be considered an opportunity for airlines to develop a value-added service by offering better seating, with benefits for both the prospective mother and the service provider. Visitor satisfaction has a critical effect on the post-purchase behaviour of babymoon vacationers. The results of this study reveal that they are more sensitive to issues that hinder their journey or experience, which may result in negative post-purchase behaviour. This may be issues relating to, for example, the immigration process, or misbehaviour by taxi drivers at the desitnation. This implies that tourism planners in the destination need to sensitize service providers and develop policies to facilitate babymoon vacationers if they want to build a promising babymoon destination.

This study contributes to the theoretical foundation for further research on babymoon vacationers' motives and decision-making behaviour. The findings are a starting point for further investigation on babymoon travel. Future empirical studies could explore babymoons as a micro-niche, for example, investigating the impact of memorable experiences on the post-purchase behaviour of babymoon travellers. Furthermore, research related to various opportunities and challenges in tourism-generating regions, transit regions, modes of transport and destinations will enable the marketers to develop comprehensive knowledge of the babymoon market. Lastly, babymoon travellers' desire to visit spiritual places and interact with a spiritual leader could be examined, as this is unique to this study context.

Although this study makes a worthwhile contribution to understanding the Indian babymoon travellers' behaviour, it has some limitations. It adopted a qualitative approach in which data was collected by interviewing a relatively small sample; this limits the possibilities to generalize based on the findings. Some of the respondents were young mothers who may not have been able to recollect all details of their babymoon, considering the passage of time, which introduces memory and recall bias. As the researchers discussed a very sensitive subject, some participants may not have shared all their experiences with the researchers; as such, actual opinions may have varied from those expressed. Despite these limitations, this study is among the first of its kind to provide valuable insights into the motives and travel behaviour of Indian babymoon travellers. The research outcomes imply that extensive market research, developing the right tourism packages, creating a unique image and extensive coordination between different stakeholders by destination marketers are vital for sustaining the benefits of the babymoon vacation micro-niche.

REFERENCES

Alekseeva, N. and Hercegová, K. (2021) Energy and industrial tourism: A specific niche on the tourism market. *E3S Web of Conferences*, 250, 01002. EDP Sciences.

Amadeus (2016) Shaping the Future of Luxury Travel: Future Traveller Tribes 2030. Available at: http://www.amadeus.com/web/amadeus/en_JO-JO/Amadeus-Home/Resources-and-downloads/Research-reports/shaping-the-future-of-luxury-travel/1319550928244-Page-AMAD_DetailPpal?assetid=1319680224868andassettype=AmadeusDocument_Candparent=1319609444141

Arora, G. and Aggarwal, D.J. (2020) Cosmopolitanism and clothing interest determinants amongst college students of Delhi. *Fashion Practice*, 12(2), 288–307. DOI:10.1080/17569370.2020.1769352

Chang, S. and Chung, G.E. (2018) Leisure-tourism connection behaviors by life stage and gender. *International Journal of Culture, Tourism and Hospitality Research*, https://doi.org/10.1108/IJCTHR-03-2018-0036

Cleveland, M. Papadopoulos, N. and Laroche, M. (2011) Identity, demographics, and consumer behaviors: International market segmentation across product categories. *International Marketing Review*, 28(3), 244–66.

Cox & Kings (2017) Babymoon vacation on rise in India: Cox & Kings Survey. Accessed on November 2020.

Cresswell, J. W. (2009) *Research Design: Qualitative, Quantitative and Mixed Methods Approaches*. 3rd edn. New Delhi: SAGE Publications Inc.

Dalgic, T. (2011) *Handbook of Niche Marketing: Principles and Practice*. London: Routledge.

Economic Times (2019) India to generate over 2 million outbound tourists annually by 2020: Report. Available at: https://economictimes.indiatimes.com/industry/services/travel/india-to-generate-over-2-million-outbound-tourists-annually-by-2020/articleshow/69852349.cms?utm_source=contentofinterest&utm_medium=text&utm_campaign=cppst

Gabor, M. R. and Oltean, F. D. (2019) Babymoon tourism between emotional well-being service for medical tourism and niche tourism. Development and awareness on Romanian educated women. *Tourism Management*, 70, 170–75. DOI: 10.1016/j.tourman.2018.08.006

Gall, M., Gall, J. and Borg, W. (2003) *Educational Research: An Introduction*. Boston: Pearson Education.

Guba, E.G. and Lincoln, Y.S. (2006) *Fourth Generation Evaluation*. Thousand Oaks: Sage.

Hannerz, U. (1996) *Transnational Connections: Culture, People, Places*. London: Routledge

Heimtun, B. (2012) The friend, the loner and the independent traveller: Norwegian midlife single women's social identities when on holiday. *Gender, Place & Culture*, 19(1), 83–101.

Hoyer, D.W. and MacInnis, D. (2010) *Consumer Behavior, South-Western*. Mason, OH: South-Western. DOI: 10.1002/cb.84

Hsu, C.H.C. Kang, S.K. and Wolfe, K. (2002) Psychographic and demographic profiles of niche market leisure travellers. *Journal of Hospitality and Tourism Research*, 26(1), 3–22. https://doi.org/10.1177/1096348002026001001

Keegan, Warren J., Moriarty, S.E. and Dungan T.R. (1995) *Marketing*. New Jersey: Prentice-Hall.

Kotler, P. and Keller, K.L. (2010) *Marketing Management*. 13th edition. New Delhi: Pearson Education.

Kotler, P., Bowen, J.T. and Makens, J.C. (2009) *Marketing for Hospitality and Tourism*. 5th edition. New Jersey: Pearson Education.

Marson, D. (2011) *From Mass Tourism to Niche Tourism: Research Themes for Tourism*. Oxfordshire: CABI.

McKersie, T. (2013) Reproduction Tourism. Student research paper on International Tourism Trends. Available at: https://atrium.lib.uoguelph.ca/xmlui/handle/10214/5921?show=full

Meng, F. and Uysal, M. (2008) Effects of gender differences on perceptions of destination attributes, motivations, and travel values: An examination of a nature-based resort destination. *Journal of Sustainable Tourism*, 16(4), 445–66.

Merriam-Webster's Learner Dictionary (1979) Babymoon. Available at: https://www.merriam-webster.com/dictionary/babymoon

O'Regan, M. (2014) Fragmenting tourism: Niche tourists. In S. McCabe (ed.) *The Routledge Handbook of Tourism Marketing*. DOI:10.4324/9781315858265.ch20

Pandey, M.T. (2011) Globalisation and social transformation in India: Theorising the transition. *International Journal of Sociology and Anthropology*, 3(8), 253–60.

Pathak, S. (2019) *Effects of Social Media Advertisement on Buying Behaviour, US*. Amazon Digital Services LLC – KDP Print US. ISBN:9789386897954.

Patton, M.Q. (2015) *Qualitative Research and Evaluation Methods*. London: Sage.

Rameshkumar, S. (2017) *Consumer Behaviour: The Indian Context (Concepts and Cases)*. India: Pearson.

Robinson, M. and Novelli, M. (2005) Niche tourism: An introduction. In M. Novelli (ed.) *Niche Tourism: Contemporary Issues, Trends and Cases*. Oxford: Routledge, 1–11.

UNWTO (2018) Tourism and the Sustainable Development Goals – Journey to 2030. DOI: 10.18111/9789284419401. Available at: https://www.unwto.org/global/publication/tourism-and-sustainable-development-goals-journey-2030

Upadhyay, R.K. (2014) Socio-cultural impact of globalization in India. *The Discussant: Journal of Centre for Reforms, Development and Justice*, 2(3), 65–72.

Vargas-Sánchez, A. (2012) Research themes for tourism. *International Journal of Contemporary Hospitality Management*, 24(6), 958–60. DOI: 10.1108/09596111211247263.

Veludo-de-Oliveira, T.M., Ikeda, A.A. and Campomar, M C. (2006) Laddering in the practice of marketing research: Barriers and solutions. *Qualitative Market Research*, 9(3), 297–306. DOI: 10.1108/13522750610671707

Voigt, C. and Laing, J.H. (2010) Journey into parenthood: Commodification of reproduction as a new tourism niche market. *Journal of Travel and Tourism Marketing*, 27(3), 252–68. DOI: 10.1080/10548401003744685

World Bank (n.d.) GDP per capita (current US$) – India. Available at: https://data.worldbank.org/indicator/NY.GDP.PCAP.CD?locations=IN (accessed 29 August 2020).

Zhang, R. (2015) Exploring the phenomenon of Chinese babymoon tourism. Available at: https://docs.lib.purdue.edu/open_access_dissertations/1478/

26. Pilgrimage tourism and the Shugendō programs in Japan

Ricardo Nicolas Progano

INTRODUCTION

Religion and tourism have developed a close relationship during the 20th century, as religious sites, traditions, buildings and artefacts have become utilized as tourism resources. From the perspective of niche tourism, it can be stated that the micro-niche of religious tourism, part of the cultural tourism macro-niche (Robinson and Novelli, 2005), is populated with a great variety of products and destinations, ranging from wellness-related programs, individual quests for spirituality and heritage to more orthodox travels to traditional sacred sites. Each of these products and destinations aim to engage a wide variety of markets. This diversification in religious tourism is far from unique, and mirrors the general development of the tourism sector as visitors' motivations expand towards specific interests and activities (WTO, 1985; Marson, 2011). The present chapter aims to discuss the variety of the micro-niche of religious tourism through the example of the Shugendō experience program, carried out by Shippōryū-ji temple, Japan. Data was obtained from conducting semi-structured interviews with tourism stake-holders and temple authorities, as well as participant observation, and later discussed in the context of the rise of the experience economy. Considerations about the experience program in the current context of COVID-19 are included as well, as the pandemic has had a considerable impact on overall performance. Finally, from this discussion, conclusions, as well as implications for future research and policy-makers, are drawn, particularly with regard to the Sustainable Development Goals (SDGs), established in 2015 by the United Nations General Assembly and intended to be achieved by 2030. These global goals, included in the UN Resolution called Agenda 2030, have been receiving increasing attention from policy-makers and academics in recent years, showing their importance in future tourism development and research. In particular, this chapter argues that a critical approach is needed to understand their potential impacts on local tourism and culture.

LITERATURE REVIEW

Religious Tourism as a Micro-Niche Subset

A niche market is understood as a narrowly defined group whereby individuals who engage with it can be identified by their specific needs or interests, and share a strong desire for the product offered (Robinson and Novelli, 2005; Marson, 2011; Dinis and Krakover, 2016). It is similar in many aspects to special interest tourism, which is defined as specialized tourism involving people who wish to develop certain interests and/or visit related sites (WTO, 1985). As expected, many niches in the tourism industry exist, addressing different motivations, experiences and behaviours. According to Novelli and Benson (2005), niche tourism can be classified into macro-niches, such as cultural, environmental and urban niches, among others. These macro-niches can be further categorized into micro-niches, such as cultural, environmental, rural and urban tourism (Robinson and Novelli, 2005; Marson, 2011). Following the categorization by Novelli and Benson (2005), religious tourism is considered a subset of the cultural micro-niche. The placement of religious tourism as a sub-category of cultural tourism can be attributed to the 'heritagization' process that religious traditions, places and artefacts undergo for their commodification in the tourism market, which brings many changes to their use and preservation (Di Giovine and Garcia-Fuentes, 2016). However, it is important to point out that religious tourism itself is not a uniform market, but rather contains a wide range of products, behaviours and motivations, showing the further fragmentation of its products as the market develops (Marson, 2011).

Religion is still among the most common motivations for travel, and pilgrimage has emerged as a central tourism phenomenon in our contemporary society, with growing economic importance that remains to be appropriately measured (Collins-Kreiner and Wall, 2015; Griffin and Raj, 2017). Sacred places are deeply interconnected with contemporary tourism (Olsen and Timothy, 2006; Timothy, 2018), attracting many visitors and being promoted by the local authorities. Advances in health care, economic conditions and mass transport systems have made access to pilgrimage locations easier (Mori, 2005). Following this development, the academic study of religious tourism has also grown in recent decades, leading to an increasing amount of published research (Duran-Sanchez et al., 2018; Collins-Kreiner, 2020). Analysing this context through the lens of the experience economy can shed new light on the importance of this micro-niche subset in our contemporary tourism industry. According to Pine and Gilmore (2011), the creation of experiences for consumers (or in this case, visitors) is considered the next step of the progression of economic value and is no longer exclusive to the entertainment industry. Transformative experiences, in particular, are considered to add more value than shopping, sightseeing or commodified cultural products, as they offer visitors the opportunity to gain new perspectives on the world and their own life, leading to long-lasting changes (Richards and Wilson, 2006; Birkhorst and Den Dekker, 2009). Researchers have also emphasized the importance of transformative experiences in different tourism niches, such as adventure tourism (Arnould and Price, 1993), volunteer tourism (Zahra and McIntosh, 2007) or educational tourism (Brown, 2009).

Religious Travel in Japan

In Japan, religious travel is a centuries-old tradition that emerged from ascetic practices in sacred mountains and pilgrimage to sacred sanctuaries. Mountains are traditionally believed to be an 'other world', inhabited by magical beings, gods and the spirits of the dead (Miyake, 1966). Later on, with the arrival of Buddhism in 552 CE, mountains were interpreted as Buddhist pure lands, creating a syncretic view. This sacred geography became the practice ground of religious ascetics, who went to the mountains to perform their esoteric practices.

One of the earliest examples of pilgrimage performed by a lay figure is the travel from the ancient capital of Heian-kyō (present Kyōto) to the faraway mountains of the sacred Kumano region by the retired Emperor Uda in 907 CE. This first lay pilgrimage popularized the practice among laymen in Japan, mixing leisure, faith and politics. After the Edo period, as Japan opened up to Western technology and ideas in the late 19th century, the notion of leisure hiking was popularized. This led to climbing sacred mountains for scientific and sightseeing purposes. In contemporary Japan, sacred locations have become important tourism destinations, promoted by transport companies, media outlets and public organizations.

The post-war development of transport infrastructure facilitated access for large segments of the population to previously remote and even dangerous regions. Present developments should be understood in the wider context of the national government's policies towards the development of Japan as a tourism nation to generate economic revenue and local revitalization of aging communities, through measures including the Visit Japan Campaign in 2003, the Tourism Nation Promotion Basic Law in 2007, the Tourism Nation Promotion Basic Plan in 2007 (renewed in 2012) and the establishment of the Japan Tourism Agency in 2008. Still, it is important to note that the contemporary development of religious tourism is not entirely motivated by faith; instead, individual and non-affiliated notions of spirituality and wellness (Matsui, 2013). Sacred sites have downplayed traditional narratives in favour of contemporary spirituality (Mori, 2005). This is because traditional narratives based on religion are believed to appeal to a smaller market in comparison to broad, non-affiliated spirituality (Nakai, 2011). Also, traditional religions have experienced a decline in contemporary Japan (Reader, 2012), further reducing their appeal for tourism development.

CASE STUDY AND METHODOLOGY

Brief Outline of Shugendō

According to previous studies, the mountain ascetism beliefs that were later systematized as Shugendō (修験道) are believed to antecede Buddhism's arrival to Japan in 552 CE (Gorai, 1991). Based on influences from Buddhism, Daoism and Confucianism, Shugendō emerged as a syncretic religious system by the end of the Heian period (794–1185 CE). The ascetic En no Gyōja (役行者) is traditionally revered as its founder, who is believed to have lived during the Asuka period (538–710 CE) (Miyake, 1966; Swanson, 1981). The main premise of Shugendō is the acquirement of supernatural powers through ascetic practices in sacred mountains and the utilization of such powers for the benefit of society (Miyake, 1966) by its followers, who are called *yamabushi* ('those who dwell/deeply bow or worship the mountain' – 山伏) or *shugensha* ('those who accumulate power' – 修験者) (Swanson, 1981). In contemporary society, Shugendō is perceived as a way to commute with nature and be thankful, in a nostalgic contrast against busy urban lifestyles in metropolitan areas. It is also portrayed as a way of testing oneself because of its ascetic nature. This portrayal also permits religious institutions to reach out to a wider audience (Nakai, 2011; Yamanaka, 2017; Amada, 2019). This broader conception of Shugendō can be attributed to the spread of individualized spirituality, as well as the loss of the relationship between Shugendō and rural villages in modern Japan (Nakai, 2011; Yamanaka, 2017; Amada, 2019). Nowadays, the tourism industry is also interconnected to locations related to Shugendō, such as Kumano Kodō, Mount Fuji and Mount Ōmine, which have become important destinations in Japanese society. In recent years, Shugendō rituals, festivities and sites have been registered as cultural heritage through national and international organizations, and utilized as tourism resources, producing a reinterpretation of Shugendō from a religion to a traditional culture (Suzuki, 2015). This process has not come without conflicts, as some *yamabushi* resist certain aspects of it and believe it meddles with their ascetic practices. Previous studies mention conflicts related to tourism infrastructure and site access (McGuire, 2013; Jimura, 2016). Lastly, several Shugendō temples have formulated experience programs, which offer the opportunity to participate in short programs aimed at providing a sample of Shugendō practices to the general public. Their duration varies according to the season and the temple itself, ranging from half a day to three days of austerities in the mountains. These programs provide a vehicle for Shugendō temples to remain relevant in contemporary society, as well as a means for acquiring donations to support themselves. It shares many characteristics with niche tourism, as it is a tourism activity that caters to visitors in specific settings.

Case Study: Shippōryū-ji Temple

The Shippōryū-ji temple is the eighth station of the Katsuragi pilgrimage, which consists of 28 sacred sites in the Kansai area where copies of the Lotus Sutra are buried. The temple itself, located on Inunaki-yama (Mount Inunaki), occupies a preeminent place in the pilgrimage. According to tradition, Shippōryū-ji was founded in 661 CE by En no Gyōja and is mainly dedicated to Fudōmyō (不動明王), a wrathful Buddhist deity (Anami, 1986). The temple's ascetic practices are centred around its seven sacred waterfalls. Nowadays, Shippōryū-ji and Inunaki-yama are both located within Izumisano city (Osaka Prefecture). Inunaki-yama and its surroundings are an important tourism resource for the city. Apart from the Shippōryū-ji temple and hiking paths, this area contains important historical sites and hot springs, a rarity in Osaka Prefecture. In 2019, 24 tangible, intangible and mixed resources in Izumisano city, including Shippōryū-ji, were designated under the Japan Heritage program, managed by the Agency for Cultural Affairs, as the 'Medieval Hinenosho Landscape'. In 2020, the Inunaki-yama area was designated as another Japan Heritage site, the 'Katsuragi 28 Stations', which contains related resources from Wakayama, Nara and Osaka prefectures. Finally, the chief abbot of Shippōryū-ji temple participates in the Izumisano Tourism Association. To resume, the Shugendō sites and practices related to Shippōryū-ji temple constitute important tourism resources for the local community of Izumisano and the wider area of South Osaka Prefecture.

METHODS

Temple authorities such as the chief abbot and other high-ranking religious figures, as well as administrative staff, were interviewed in Japanese by the researcher to understand the program's contents and significance, as well as the *yamabushi*'s complex hierarchal structure and activities. The Izumisano Tourism Association was also interviewed through a written questionnaire sent by e-mail regarding the role of Inunaki-yama in local tourism development. Finally, the Educational Board of Izumisano provided documents in Japanese to further supplement the study, as written materials on Shippōryū-ji are relatively scarce. The researcher also was invited by the temple authorities to assist to special religious services, which provided an opportunity to interact with the larger *yamabushi* community, as well as to collect graphic and written material. These encounters also helped to identify the temple's 'gatekeepers' and obtain their assistance. The experience program was cancelled from March to September

Source: Author.

Figure 26.1   Waterfall for ascetic practices at Shippōryū-ji temple

2020 due to the COVID-19 pandemic. In October 2020, the researcher carried out participant observation of the experience program.

FINDINGS AND DISCUSSION

The experience program at Shippōryū-ji is carried out once a month, except from December to February, when it is not offered. Its lasts for approximately four-and-a-half hours, starting in the morning and finishing around midday. The program contains a number of ascetic practices which take place as participants are guided by *yamabushi* through one of Inunaki-yama's mountain circuits, called Omote Gyōba (表行場). Access to this area is not allowed to the public without the guidance of the *yamabushi*, due to its dangerous terrain.

While the experience program can be conceptualized as a niche product, it is important to note that the temple authorities fundamentally view it as an ascetic practice, and therefore do not refer to it as 'program' or call the participants 'tourists' or 'visitors'. While they promote the program on the temple's webpage, they do not utilize any kind of 'marketing strategy' to capture 'new markets'; therefore, it is not a 'tailored' experience as seen in other niche tourism suppliers (Robinson and Novelli, 2005; Marson, 2011). The lack of tailored approaches can be attributed to the temple's authorities, who have a traditional approach to religion. In the

Table 26.1   Practices during the experience program

Practice	Description
Kigan (祈願)	Prayers asking for safety before departure.
Kusariba (鎖場)	Climb steep rocks using chains.
Ari no Dowatari (アリの戸渡)	Walk narrow mountain paths.
Nishi no Nozoki (西の覗き)	Confess one's faults while being suspended head-on from a high cliff.
Tainai Kuguri (胎内くぐり)	Go through a tight rock tunnel.
Takigyo (滝行)	Waterfall ascetic practice.

words of the chief abbot, the program was started in the 2000s as a way to reconnect younger generations to the merits of hardship (*kurō* – 苦労), and the temple authorities remarked that the program's structure and practices have a symbolic meaning of death and rebirth. As mentioned before, similar resistance by religious figures to perceived commodification or 'touristification' of their religious traditions is found in other Shugendō sites (McGuire. 2013; Jimura, 2016). Still, the chief abbot supports the idea that visitors should bodily experience the program and find meaning for themselves through the ascetic practices. This point, in the context of the rise of the experience economy, provides Shugendō experience programs with a unique opportunity to develop and reach out to a wider audience, both domestic and international. It is also important for site managers, as unique experiences are complex to reproduce elsewhere and help destinations to differentiate themselves (Richards, 2010). The Shugendō experience program provides exceptional experiences (Japanese ascetism) in specific locations (sacred mountains) and is provided by specially trained staff (the *yamabushi*), making it a unique micro-niche product difficult to replicate elsewhere. Contrary to other micro-niche experiences related to religion such as yoga tourism (Lehto et al., 2006) or temple stays (Kaplan, 2010), which emphasize wellness and slow activities, the Shugendō experience program is physically demanding, as the participants are led by the *yamabushi* across steep mountain paths and guided to perform hazardous ascetic practices. This characteristic differs from other pilgrimage destinations such as Kumano Kodō (Kato and Progano, 2017) and Shikoku Henro (Mori, 2005; Matsui, 2013), which emphasize slowness, low-impact walking and wellness elements. This shows how religious tourism further fragments as it develops, in line with other niche tourism markets (Marson, 2011). It also offers a stark contrast to the 'mass' cultural tourism found in Japan, characterized by heritage sightseeing in urban centres such as Kyōto.

This uniqueness can lead to an increase in the number of visitors to rural and suburban areas, such as Izumisano, where the Shugendō mountains are mostly located, contributing to the sustainability of local culture. This would be particularly relevant for the survival of Shugendō practices in contemporary Japan, as experiences programs have the potential to rebuild and resignify the relationship between society and Shugendō, by providing unique experiences to eager urban visitors.

Given the existing transport infrastructure within Izumisano city, including the Kansai International Airport, it would be possible to bring this micro-niche experience to international markets and thus further diversify the tourism products of Izumisano with an accessible and unique experience that would satisfy visitors looking beyond sightseeing, in line with the general premises of experience economy. However, as the program is only conducted in Japanese, its potential expansion to international markets is currently limited, although the temple does in theory allow foreigners to participate. Given the hazardous nature of the program, effective communication between participants and *yamabushi* is a key requirement for its safe conduction. The temple's disinterest in marketing strategies also hinders its expansion to inbound markets. Therefore, while the program is a unique tourism experience with potential for international markets, its actual promotion in the current conditions is complex. Still, this does not mean that it is impossible, as there are a few examples of organizations in Japan that have effectively marketed Shugendō programs to inbound visitors, such as Dewa Sanzan in Yamagata Prefecture. Regardless, Shippōryū-ji provides an attractive location for these experiences to domestic markets, as it is located relatively close to major urban centres and has good access. In contrast, other locations offering these programs are located in remote rural areas.

Apart from its importance to local tourism, the described Shugendō program is also relevant to global sustainability initiatives, as it can potentially serve a number of SDGs. For example, the program exemplifies a sustainable and low-impact usage of Inunaki-yama's natural environment through local culture, as the Katsuragi pilgrimage has been in use for over a millennium. This shows its relevance for the 'Life on land' and 'Responsible production and consumption' SDGs, despite that fact that the *yamabushi* value nature due to its symbolic meaning and not its environmental relevance. Also, its importance and uniqueness in the local tourism economy of Izumisano city, as well as its promotion of local traditions, supports the 'Decent work and economic growth' SDG. Still, the inclusion of the SDGs program and similar discourses into non-Western communities, especially in traditional religious institutions such as Shippōryū-ji, is a delicate subject that should be critically analysed and reflected upon, as there are cases of frictions due to attempts by global and national technocratic organizations to impose external values and policies on local communities. For example, McGuire (2013) relates how UNESCO's assumptions on shared universal values and access for all came into conflict with the traditional beliefs of Shugendō groups of Mount Ōmine (Nara Prefecture), which traditionally ban women from climbing this mountain. While this prohibition is not legally enforced, the ascetics criticized UNESCO for being an external organization interfering in their centuries-old local traditions. On a similar note, Yasuda (2010) points out that the UNESCO designation of the Kumano Kodō pilgrimage route of Ise-ji created conflicts with the local forestry sector, as communities experienced top-down restrictions on their traditional economic activity. The cause of this issue is that UNESCO designations favour simplified and unified narratives while giving less importance to locals. In this sense, parallelisms to Eurocentric discourses can be observed, as Western-centric paradigms continue to shape and influence the values and usage of the local Other. Therefore, while Shugendō programs, as well as the micro-niche subset of religious tourism in general, can support the achievement of global sustainability programs such as the SDGs in different ways, actual implementation and monitoring in a culturally diverse context is potentially a sensitive subject related to power relationships and Western-centric approaches.

In the current context of the COVID-19 pandemic, carrying out the Shugendō program is challenging. Research points out that religious gatherings can help to spread the novel coronavirus, with examples seen across various countries including South Korea, Israel and Malaysia. Due to this, collective worship has been reduced, while individual and online prayers are on the rise (Dein et al., 2020; Quadri, 2020). Naturally, pilgrimage locations, where mass worship gatherings often take place, have been partially or completely closed for the time being. For example, the government of Saudi Arabia decided to suspend all *umrah* pilgrimage on 4 March 2020, as well as to limit the *hajj* (Quadri, 2020). Going back to the situation at

Shippōryū-ji, as the chief abbot and other authorities explained, while the temple remained open, the program was temporally suspended following a nationwide escalation of reported cases and a subsequent national state of emergency declared by the Japanese government from 16 April to 25 May 2020. Two characteristics of the program pose a risk. Firstly, both participants and *yamabushi* are in close contact with each other, and secondly, the senior age of some of the *yamabushi* and participants poses an additional risk factor. While the researcher observed that the *yamabushi* at times used face masks during their rituals, performing ascetic practices in mountains while keeping social distance and hygiene protocols is a complex issue. Also, while religious institutions can adapt their practices during the pandemic (McLaughlin, 2020; Sulwoski and Ignatowski, 2020), the alteration of central religious practices can be at odds with the temple's preservation of traditional practice. On the other hand, studies show that uncertain times such as the COVID-19 pandemic may spur religiosity among the population as a coping mechanic (Bentzen, 2020). Regarding Shippōryū-ji's case, the program restarted on September 2020, with preventive measures such as social distancing and hand sanitizers. Other temples in Japan switched to virtual and online alternatives as a way to continue the engagement of the population with religious institutions and avoid public criticism (McLaughlin, 2020). However, given the emphasis on bodily practices of asceticism, virtual alternatives to Shugendō programs are complex, if not impossible to satisfactorily implement. The difficulties of carrying out the experience program negatively affect the cultural and economic sustainability of Izumisano. On the other hand, the program takes place in outdoor settings, thus avoiding religious buildings, which often have poor ventilation.

Source: Author.

Figure 26.2   The entrance to Inunaki-yama

CONCLUSIONS

The presented chapter aimed to discuss the micro-niche of religious tourism through the lens of transformative tourism, by presenting a case study on the Shugendō experience program performed at Shippōryū-ji temple, Japan. The program is considered to be a particularly unique experience in its micro-niche, with distinctive characteristics that make it complex to reproduce in other locations, providing Shugendō temples with a distinctive experience to offer. In particular, its emphasis on physical challenge as a means for personal transformation is a differentiating aspect when compared to other experiences in pilgrimage tourism, which often emphasize wellness and slowness. It is also a distinctive experience in comparison to other 'mass' cultural tourism destinations in Japan, which emphasize the passive sightseeing of temples and shrines. As religious tourism grows in Japan, activities beyond sightseeing, such as experience programs, would help to diversify the tourism offer.

In the current context of the experience economy, as described by Pine and Gilmore (2011), micro-niche products such as Shugendō programs acquire a new relevance as visitors seek memorable experiences that may even change their viewpoints in life. Certain differences were found in comparison to other tourism micro-niches in general (Robinson & Novelli, 2005; Marson, 2011), such as the temple's disinterest in conducting marketing strategies and an unwillingness to tailor the program to suit the visitors' tastes. In this sense, it can be stated that marketing strategies may be influenced or even largely ignored due to the operator's religious view on its product and on the tourism industry itself, in contrast to the general 'tailored' approach of niche tourism. Also, the program holds importance for the preservation of Shugendō traditions in today's society and the sustainable development of its surrounding community, as well as the potential for contributing to the SDGs. However, the implementation of global programs in non-Western local communities may be problematic, as previous studies suggest (Yasuda, 2010; McGuire, 2013).

This chapter also raises several topics that future studies may further research. For example, the potential for analysing experiences in religious travel through the framework of transformative tourism is particularly relevant in the current context of the experience economy, where visitors demand valuable experiences instead of goods and services. Shippōryū-ji supports the idea that participants should create their own meanings from the program, further increasing the relevance of this framework. Products of the religious tourism micro-niche may be analysed through this framework, in order to understand their importance in the current experience economy, following previous research on other tourism niches (Arnould and Price, 1993; Zahra and McIntosh, 2007; Brown, 2009). Another important topic is the impact of the COVID-19 pandemic and the subsequent countermeasures on the micro-niche of religious tourism. In the case of the Shugendō program presented in this chapter, it was noted that adopting preventive countermeasures was a complex issue due to the close distance between participants and the physical nature of the activity. The performance and behaviour of participants are expected to change, in line with previous reports from other religious practices (McLaughlin, 2020; Sulwoski and Ignatowski, 2020). The complexity of providing virtual alternatives to Shugendō programs shows that the governmental restrictions imposed due to COVID-19 affect various sections of micro-niches differently, with certain activities potentially being more resilient than others. For example, virtual alternatives to niches such as yoga tourism are likely to be easier to implement. On the positive side, Shugendō programs are commonly carried out in low-density outdoor settings, facilitating air circulation and the avoidance of crowds. Regardless, policy-makers are encouraged to collaborate and assist religious stakeholders in the context of the COVID-19 pandemic, as temple organizers may need guidance in disaster management practices because they are outside the scope of their religious training. Next, the relationship between pilgrimage and the sustainability of both local communities and their environment remains an important topic to explore. Shugendō in particular has a symbolic interpretation of nature, as mountains are revered not strictly because of their ecological importance or socioeconomic value, but because they are part of a sacred space where *yamabushi* perform austerities. Because of this, the *yamabushi* do not provide an interpretation of the environment of Inunaki-yama during the program. However, the alteration or degradation of the environment is a pressing issue for Shugendō, with tourism infrastructure and pollution playing a role here (McGuire, 2013; Jimura, 2016). Novelli and Benson (2005) mention that the sustainability of niche tourism cannot be stated through generalizations. Instead, it depends on a number of factors such as location, activity, scale of operation, community and type of visitors. Further studies on this aspect of religious tourism would be of interest.

The study of religious stakeholders' views, organization and practices in micro-niche tourism settings would be not only important from an academic perspective, but also for public and private stakeholders who aim to revitalize their communities through tourism. Shugendō sacred mountains are commonly located in rural areas that suffer from depopulation and the stagnation of traditional economic activities such as farming and forestry. As religion-related resources are often found in such locations, their utilization for tourism development can provide local communities with new ways to develop. This development can also be beneficial for religious institutions themselves, offering methods to preserve their tangible and intangible heritage, as well as new opportunities to engage with society. However, the introduction of tourism infrastructure and marketing strategies can create misunderstandings and conflicts with religious stakeholders, who are suspicious of the commodification of their traditions. As Robinson and Novelli (2005) mention, niche tourism utilizes terminology from marketing practices, which may further attract misunderstandings. Therefore, effective communication and negotiation are important for the development of the Shugendō tradition as tourism resources while respecting the temples' viewpoints. In this regard, the author suggests that familiarization with the religion and participation in the temple's activities can help build positive relationships, reassure the religious stakeholders that their traditions are respected and obtain cooperation from the location's 'gatekeepers'. This suggestion can be translated to similar case studies, where religious stakeholders play a large role in tourism development and management.

ACKNOWLEDGMENTS

This work was supported by JSPS KAKENHI Grant Number JP20K20078. Any opinions, findings and conclusions or recommendations expressed in this material are those of the author and do not necessarily reflect the views of the author's organization, JSPS or MEXT.

REFERENCES

Amada, A. (2019) *Religious sociology of contemporary Shugendo*. Tokyo: Iwata Shoin (in Japanese).

Anami, T. (1986) Shippōryū-ji. In H. Miyake, (ed.) *Shugendo dictionary*. Tokyo: Tokyodō Shuppan, 165 (in Japanese).

Arnould, E.J. and Price, L.L. (1993) River magic: Extraordinary experience and the extended service encounter. *The Journal of Consumer Research*, 20(1), 24–54.

Bentzen, J.S. (2020) In crisis, we pray: Religiosity and the COVID-19 pandemic. *CEPR Covid Economics*, 20, 52–79.

Birkhorst, E. and Den Dekker, T. (2009) Agenda for co-creation tourism experience research. *Journal of Hospitality Marketing & Management*, 18(2–3), 311–27.

Brown, L. (2009) The transformative power of the international sojourn: An ethnographic study of the international student experience. *Annals of Tourism Research*, 36(3), 502–21.

Collins-Kreiner, N. (2020) A review of research into religion and tourism: Launching the Annals of Tourism Research Curated Collection on religion and tourism. *Annals of Tourism Research*, 82, 1–22.

Collins-Kreiner, N. and Wall, G. (2015) Tourism and religion: Spiritual journeys and their consequences. In S.D. Stanley (ed.) *The changing world religion map: Sacred places, identities, practices and politics*. New York and London: Springer, 689–707.

Dein, S., Loewenthal, K., Lewis, C. A. and Pargament, I. (2020) COVID-19, mental health and religion: An agenda for future research. *Mental Health, Religion and Culture*, 23(1), 1–9.

Di Giovine, M. A. and Garcia-Fuentes, J. M. (2016) Sites of pilgrimage, sites of heritage: An exploratory introduction. *International Journal of Tourism Anthropology*, 5(1/2), 1–23.

Dinis, A. and Krakover, S. (2016) Niche tourism in small peripheral towns: The case of Jewish heritage in Belmonte, Portugal. *Tourism Planning & Development*, 13(3), 310–32.

Duran-Sanchez, A., Alvarez Garcia, J., Del Rio, R. and Oliveira, C. (2018) Religious and pilgrimage tourism: Bibliometric review. *Religions*, 9, 249, doi:10.3390/rel9090249.

Gorai, S. (1991) *Mountain religion*. Tokyo: Kadokawa Bunko (in Japanese).

Griffin, K. and Raj, R. (2017) The importance of religious tourism and pilgrimage: Reflecting on definitions, motives and data. *International Journal of Religious Tourism and Pilgrimage*, 5(3), 2–9.

Jimura, T. (2016) World Heritage Site management: A case study of sacred sites and pilgrimage routes in the Kii mountain range, Japan. *Journal of Heritage Tourism*, 11(4), 1–13.

Kaplan, U. (2010) Images of monasticism: The temple stay program and the re-branding of Korean Buddhist temples. *Korean Studies*, 34, 127–46.

Kato, K. and Progano, R. N. (2017) Spiritual (walking) tourism as a foundation for sustainable destination development: Kumano-kodo pilgrimage, Wakayama, Japan. *Tourism Management Perspectives*, 24, 243–51.

Lehto, X. Y., Brown, S., Chen, Y. and Morrison, A. M. (2006) Yoga tourism as a niche within the wellness tourism market. *Tourism Recreation Research*, 31(1), 25–35.

Marson, D. (2011) From mass tourism to niche tourism. In P. Robinson, S. Heitmann and P. Dieke (eds.) *Research themes for tourism*. Oxfordshire: CABI, 1–15.

Matsui, T. (2013). *Language and marketing: A social consumption history of the iyashi boom*. Tokyo: Sekigakusha (in Japanese).

McGuire, M.P. (2013) What's at stake in designating Japan's sacred mountains as UNESCO World Heritage Sites? Shugendo Practices in the Kii Peninsula. *Japanese Journal of Religious Studies*, 40(2), 323–54.

McLaughlin, L. (2020) Japanese religious responses to COVID-19: A preliminary report. *The Asia-Pacific Journal: Japan Focus*, 18(9), 1–23.

Miyake, H. (1966) Genjutsu in Shugendō: Its mechanism and world view. *Tetsugaku*, 48, 47–70 (in Japanese).

Mori, M. (2005). *The modernization of Shikoku Henro: From a 'modern pilgrimage' to a 'healing journey'*. Tokyo: Sogensha.

Nakai, J. (2011) The nostalgic value of travelling Kumano Kodo. *Bulletin of the Faculty of Sociology, Ryūkoku University*, 39, 43–53 (in Japanese).

Novelli, M. and Benson, A. (2005) Niche tourism: A way forward to sustainability? In M. Novelli (ed.) *Niche tourism: Contemporary issues, trends and cases*. Oxford: Routledge, 247–50.

Olsen, D.H. and Timothy, D.J. (2006) Tourism and religious journeys. In D.J. Timothy and D.H. Olsen (eds.) *Tourism, religion and spiritual journeys*. United States and Canada: Routledge, 1–15.

Pine, B. J. and Gilmore, J.H. (2011) *The experience economy*. Boston: Harvard Business Review Press.

Quadri, S.A. (2020) COVID-19 and religious congregations: Implications for spread of novel pathogens. *International Journal of Infectious Diseases*, 96, 219–21.

Reader, I. (2012) Secularisation, R.I.P.? Nonsense! The 'Rush Hour Away from the Gods' and the decline of religion in contemporary Japan. *Journal of Religion in Japan*, 1, 7–36.

Richards, G. (2010) Tourism development trajectories: From culture to creativity? *Tourism & Management Studies*, 6, 9–15.

Richards, G. and Wilson, J. (2006) Developing creativity in tourist experiences: A solution to the serial reproduction of culture? *Tourism Management*, 27, 1209–23.

Robinson, M. and Novelli, M. (2005) Niche tourism: An introduction. In M. Novelli (ed.) *Niche tourism: Contemporary issues, trends and cases*. Oxford: Routledge, 1–11.

Sulwoski, L. and Ignatowski, G. (2020) Impact of COVID-19 pandemic on organization of religious behavior in different Christian denominations in Poland. *Religions*, 11, 254, https://doi.org/10.3390/rel11050254

Suzuki, M. (2015) *Mountain faith: Exploring the roots of Japanese culture*. Tokyo: Chūō Kōron Shinsha (in Japanese).

Swanson, P.L. (1981) Shugendō and the Yoshino-Kumano pilgrimage: An example of mountain pilgrimage. *Monumenta Nipponica*, 36(1), 55–84.

Timothy, D.J. (2018) Making sense of heritage tourism: Research trends in a maturing field of study. *Tourism Management Perspectives*, 25, 177–80.

WTO (1985) *The role of recreation management in the development of active holidays and special interest tourism and consequent enrichment of the holiday experience*. Madrid: World Tourism Organization.

Yamanaka, H. (2017) Transformation of modern religion in consumer society. *Shūkyō Kenkyū*, 91(2), 255–80 (in Japanese).

Yasuda, H. (2010) World heritage and cultural tourism in Japan. *International Journal of Culture, Tourism and Hospitality Research*, 4(4), 366–75.

Zahra, A. and Mcintosh A.J. (2007) Volunteer tourism: Evidence of cathartic tourist experiences. *Tourism Recreation Research*, 32(1), 115–19.

27. In focus 5 – religious tourism in the urban setting of Varanasi in India

K Thirumaran, Simona Azzali, Zilmiyah Kamble, Yash Prabhugaonkar and Manisha Agarwal

Religious tourism, as one the earliest niche forms of tourism, attracts millions of visitors to destinations. It brings social and economic benefits, shapes the destination and its image, and prompts the need for tourism authorities to understand different needs, motives and behavioural patterns – including those of religious tourists (Gertner, 2019). When it comes to research on religious tourism, there is an inclination to explore the impacts on visitors who come for religious tourism, including traveller experiences and tourist behaviour (Collins-Kreiner, 2010; Bond et al., 2015), as well as the impact on the local communities and the built environment. In particular, the commercial facets of religious tourism are underpinned by indulgence in touristic activities, sacred destinations faced with increased growth, infrastructure needs, pollution, and issues of resilience and sustainability.

This case study explores Varanasi, a holy city in India, also referred to as the spiritual capital for Hindu pilgrims, which has great potential for religious tourism. It receives a huge number of domestic religious tourists, as well international tourists, and therefore constitutes a key religious hub in Asia. Among the international religious tourists, the Balinese have for centuries had a historical connection to Varanasi. Balinese visitors are not only interested in Hindu practices, they also participate in temple prayers. Some even are interested in exploring and understanding the lives of the residents. This desire to explore and experience the daily life of the people of Varanasi is reflective of the ancient bonds between India and countries in Southeast Asia dating back to the 1st century CE. In addition to the religious aspect of their travels, the Balinese also look for more conventional tourist activities, such as shopping and visiting historic sites. The experiences of Balinese visitors on their pilgrimage tours suggest that shopping and sightseeing tours, which are tangential to the religious tours, expand the boundary of niche tourism itself. Varanasi is also quickly transforming, as a result of Prime Minister Modi's focus on development and increasing tourism in the city. Singh (2009: 8) describes the threat of this increasing number of tourists and associated urbanization growth to Varanasi, noting that 'The old city center and other important cultural and religious places (heritagescapes) are today enclosed within the modern city and are seriously threatened by pressures of modernization and development'.

As Singh would agree, the city is far too complex for outsiders to understand. Within this complexity, layers of narratives for religious travel appear to be weaving into and absorbing the subtle changes, reaffirming the diverse nature of religious travellers' desires as depicted in their engagements in Varanasi. Two aspects of Varanasi's progress as a tourism city can be highlighted in this case study. Firstly, a continuing religious bond that attracts tourists can be identified, especially that between Balinese pilgrims and their Indian hosts. There is a sizable population of Hindu believers who 'look up' to India and Varanasi as the motherland of their religion. Varanasi, after all, is a key stop for Hindu pilgrims (Ramstedt, 2008; Thirumaran,

2009). Secondly, the pilgrims' interaction with the city's landscape goes beyond religiosity, with urbanization working in tandem with religious tourism. Politics, urbanization and religious tourism have enabled Varanasi to emerge as an important city for visitors who want to see the *rishis* (sages or saints) and the holy River Ganga, and to seek blessings in the ancient city's numerous temples, as well as to shop at street-side stalls. However, what was once solely a tour of holy sites is no longer so. Modern Balinese travellers are now interested in exploring the shopping and residential sights of the city. It is also interesting to observe that modernization may usurp the lived experiences of the people in the city. However, visitors may not feel the same way, as the view from the outside in is guarded both by temporality and spatial distance. In this sense, cities with religious tourism sites must continuously ensure that urbanization does not destroy the heritage, while still being able to provide modern amenities for visitors (Taheri and Khatibi, 2016; Bogan et al., 2019; Figure 27.1).

Exploring religious tourists' interests can inform urban planners and industry stakeholders on allocating resources for this shift. Travel interests continue between various regions such as Southeast Asia and Indian cities. Knowing the main areas that tourists are coming from helps in drafting the city's tourism development plans, in accordance with UN Sustainable Development Goal 11: 'Make cities and human settlements inclusive, safe, resilient and sustainable' (UN, 2015). The information can be used to create a better tourist profile. From a theoretical viewpoint, religious pilgrimage requires an expansive, multi-focal view given the changing profile of pilgrims. This case study reaffirms the diverse nature of religious travellers' engagements and highlights the need for sustainable and resilient development in Varanasi.

Source: Authors.

Figure 27.1   *Demolished temples and houses for Kashi Vishwanath to Ganga Ghats corridor*

REFERENCES

Bogan, E., Cercleux, A. and Constantin, D.M. (2019) The role of religious and pilgrimage tourism in developing and promoting the urban tourism in Bucharest. *Calitatea*, 20(2), 94–101.

Bond, N., Packer, J. and Ballantyne, R. (2015) Exploring visitor experiences, activities and benefits at three religious tourism sites. *International Journal of Tourism Research*, 17(5), 471–81. doi: 10.1002/jtr.2014

Collins-Kreiner, N. (2010) Researching pilgrimage: Continuity and transformations. *Annals of Tourism Research*, 37(2), 440–56.

Gertner, R.K. (2019) The impact of cultural appropriation on destination image, tourism, and hospitality. *Thunderbird International Business Review*, 61(6), 873–7. doi:10.1002/tie.22068

Ramstedt, M. (2008) Hindu bonds at work: Spiritual and commercial ties between India and Bali. *The Journal of Asian Studies*, 67(4), 1227–50. doi:10.1017/S0021911808001769

Singh, R.P.B. (2009) *Banaras: Making of India's Heritage City*. Newcastle Upon Tyne: Cambridge Scholars Publishing.

Taheri, P. and Khatibi, S.M.R. (2016) Proposing historic-religious tourism development approaches with an emphasis on identity of urban spaces (case study of imam Khomeini Street, Qazvin). *Space Ontology International Journal*, 5(4), 69–80.

Thirumaran, K. (2009) Renewing bonds in an age of Asian travel: Indian tourists in Bali. In T. Winter et al. (eds) *Asia On Tour: Exploring the Rise of Asian Tourism*. Abingdon: Taylor & Francis, 127–37.

United Nations (2015) The 17 Goals. United Nations. Department of Economic and Social Affairs. Sustainable Development. https://sdgs.un.org/goals

PART VI

SOCIAL AND INCLUSIVE TOURISM

28. Social tourism in Brazil

Ernest Cañada

INTRODUCTION

Social tourism was originally characterized by a desire to contribute to greater social access to holidays and tourism, given the barriers that certain groups faced. This vision became progressively more complex, sanctioned by the 1996 Montreal Declaration, which substituted the 1972 Vienna Charter by the International Bureau of Social Tourism (BITS) (currently known as the International Social Tourism Organisation – ISTO). The concept was opened up to include the well-being of tourism workers and the local communities that host social tourism (Schenkel, 2017). At the same time, increasing causes of barriers to tourism were identified. From the initial financial handicaps that were taken as a basic criterion for inclusion in social tourism initiatives, there was a shift toward the development of programmes for groups like senior citizens, youths, people with disabilities or severe illnesses and groups suffering from social exclusion (Minnaert et al., 2013).

This segmentation has boosted the growth of social tourism (Schenkel, 2020), in parallel with the general trend toward segmentation in the tourist sector. To some extent, segmentation in social tourism might also be considered to be a consequence of this general trend, with the progressive consolidation of 'niche tourism' (Novelli, 2005) and segmented markets targeted at meeting certain interests or special needs, based on changes brought about by post-Fordist systems of production and consumption (Ioannides and Debbage, 1997). There is a contradictory element to niche tourism. On the one hand, it is a mechanism for segmenting markets in order to take advantage of potential profits, with differing consequences on destinations. On the other hand, it is also a way of addressing ethical calls for greater inclusion and sustainability in tourism. In this study, the term 'niche tourism' is used to describe a certain trend in the tourism market, as opposed to examining it from a normative perspective. This distinction is necessary in order to avoid potential confusion, because although niche tourism is a term that defines a certain way of organizing tourism today, no ethical associations should automatically be identified with it.

In times of rapid global change in tourism and with the abrupt decline in international mobility due to the COVID-19 pandemic, calls for a change in the tourism model have led to renewed interest in social tourism as a form of proximity tourism with a low environmental impact and a greater capacity for boosting the economy. However, debate on social tourism is split between two contrasting approaches. The prevailing approach seeks to boost its segmentation in response to increasing private interests and profit-making opportunities, which basically makes it another form of niche tourism. Meanwhile, other visions of social tourism stick to the initial goal of seeking to benefit disadvantaged groups, rather than pursuing business opportunities. SESC (Serviço Social do Comércio) Bertioga in Brazil encapsulates this second vision. It shows how the initial goals of social tourism have been maintained over and above possible business interests.

LITERATURE REVIEW

Social tourism is a source of extensive literature, and so attention will be focused on identifying aspects that can offer an insight into its links with the current debate on niche tourism. Social tourism's origins are complex and contradictory and, right from the outset, it varied in form. In the 1930s and 1940s, special attention was paid to the leisure and recreation of the working classes. Worker demands for a reduction in the working day to an initial eight hours and then for weekends off were followed by calls for paid holidays. France was the first country to introduce paid holidays, in 1936, when Léon Blum's Front Populaire alliance government approved mandatory annual paid leave of two weeks. This came after big strikes across the country and the subsequent signature of the Matignon Agreement of 7 and 8 June 1936 by the government, employers and trade unions (Cross, 1989). Shortly after, on 24 June of the same year, the International Labour Organization (ILO) approved its convention on paid annual leave.

This set a precedent in both Europe and Latin America. At the same time, there were ongoing disputes about how to organize this holiday time – i.e., through what kind of infrastructure, bodies and activities. One option was passive consumption through the purchase of leisure goods and services, although several contradictory policy proposals were also made. Religious institutions, trade unions, worker associations, Socialist and Communist parties and other Fascist ones all put forward numerous proposals on how to organize workers' leisure time, given its growing relevance with the introduction of paid holidays. These varying initial approaches to social tourism gave rise to different forms. For example, preventive initiatives were taken to control and integrate the working classes in response to their growing unionization. Another approach was to try and respond to social demands through official bodies in a bid to ensure greater equality and to boost working class well-being. With 1930s Fascism, there were even places where it was used as a way of indoctrinating the working classes; for example, by using sports activities to foster nationalist sentiments (Broder, 2019). Hence from its early days, there was an ambivalence to social tourism, and its development in one country might have little to do with the form it took in others.

The literature on social tourism is particularly broad ranging (McCabe and Qiao, 2020). Despite the abundance of published studies, their geographic coverage is uneven, with greater attention being paid to rich countries, particularly Western Europe (Thomas, 2018). One region with few studies on the subject is Latin America, even though historically sociopolitical initiatives of this kind have featured strongly since the 1940s. There are some notable exceptions, however, such as the work of Érica Schenkel (2017, 2019a) and Marcelo Vilela de Almeida (2011) (Schenkel and Almeida, 2020).

Some of this literature has focused on analysing the broad positive effects of social tourism policies as a way of reducing exclusion and poverty (La Placa and Corlyon, 2014) and improving the well-being and health of certain groups (Sedgley et al., 2018), in addition to boosting inclusive social policies (McCabe, 2020). Other studies look at the long-term social benefits from a broad perspective or the social policies that act as a framework for them (Diekmann et al., 2018). Mention must also be made of research studies that analyse the institutional structures that favour the development of social tourism or that evaluate its performance and impact, particularly from a social or charity-related perspective (Hunter-Jones, 2011; McCabe, 2009; Minnaert, 2020).

As social tourism policies have gradually come to focus on different vulnerable social groups with difficulty in accessing tourism, so the academic literature has concentrated much of its efforts on segmented analyses of social tourism experiences. In the case of social tourism for senior citizens, studies have been made of the various benefits it offers, and research has been conducted into programmes such as IMSERSO in Spain (Ferrer et al., 2016; González et al., 2017; Lopes et al., 2020; Sedgley et al., 2018). In the United Kingdom, analyses of this type of social tourism highlight the key role played by the public authorities and charities (Diekmann et al., 2018; Morgan et al., 2015). Other studies have looked at how low-income families or marginalized people stand to benefit from social tourism (Hazel, 2005; Kakoudakis et al., 2017). In the case of Latin America, Schenkel (2017, 2019b) sheds light on various social tourism models and their results in terms of the effective inclusion of underprivileged groups.

Recent debate on social tourism revolves around the real objectives of different initiatives, comparing those that seek to meet the needs and uphold the rights of broad majorities and those that regard social tourism as a business opportunity (Schenkel, 2019a). SESC Bertioga in Brazil highlights the possibilities of a social tourism model targeted at a wide variety of groups. Although it is mainly focused on workers from the trade, tourism and services sectors and their families, it also encompasses groups with different needs. This model has little to do with the increasing segmentation of the population by characteristics such as age, financial income or disability.

OBJECTIVES AND METHODOLOGY

This chapter analyses SESC Bertioga, a beach resort and one of the units run by SESC São Paulo, a leading reference in social tourism in Brazil and Latin America. The aim is to identify how a social tourism model has been developed that meets varying needs. It also shows that social tourism can be inclusive, both for staff and for the community in which it is located.

This case study is based on a review of documents drawn up by SESC Bertioga and SESC São Paulo (SP São Paulo), secondary documentary sources and fieldwork carried out during a two-week stay in Bertioga and São Paulo in April 2019. A previous visit had been made in September 2017 to identify our case study and build up the necessary contacts. The fieldwork entailed observation at the resort and interviews with 17 people (nine females and eight males), 14 of whom were directly involved with SESC Bertioga and three who were from SESC São Paulo, in order to gain a better understanding of the organization to which the resort belongs and its social tourism strategy. Different departments, responsibilities, job categories and functions at the resort were taken into account in order to complement the analysis.

The 17 interviews were voice recorded, transcribed, coded and manually analysed. The analysed variables included the functioning of the department or service where the interviewees worked, the type of target public, the type of holiday product, the working conditions of SESC Bertioga's staff and the resort's integration into the local community (taking into account the latter's needs). The interviews, held in the offices of SESC Bertioga or SESC São Paulo, were semi-structured lasting for approximately 45 to 90 minutes. During the interviews at SESC Bertioga, the interviewee was asked about his or her job, responsibilities and functions. Then the conversation turned to the functioning and characteristics of the department or service where the person worked. Other interviews, mainly with people from SESC São Paulo and, to

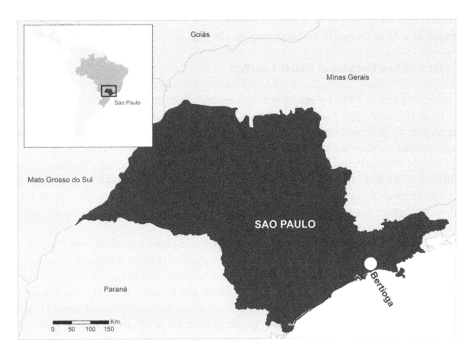

Source: Author.

Figure 28.1   Location of SESC Bertioga, Brazil

some extent, with the manager of SESC Bertioga, focused on their vision of social tourism and how related strategies were put into practice at SESC São Paulo and SESC Bertioga.

During our stay in Bertioga, in addition to the formal interviews, we spoke to other people, including guests, staff, people living in Bertioga, and people with jobs associated with SESC Bertioga but not attached to the staff, such as artisans who sometimes displayed their work at the resort or tourist guides. Details of these informal conversations and the observation work were noted down daily in a field diary. This was especially useful in the analysis and explanation of the case study.

RESULTS

SESC Bertioga was founded as a beach resort in 1948 and it has been in operation ever since. The resort, which can accommodate some 1,000 people, is targeted at members of the Brazilian working classes and is an international reference point in social tourism. It can be regarded as a good example of social tourism for a broad majority of workers for several key reasons: it offers a tourism product to the working classes that incorporates leisure activities and educational ones conceived to cultivate critical awareness; a clear concern is shown for the working conditions of its staff; and harmonious relations are fostered with the local community (Cañada, 2020). SESC Bertioga shows that coastal mass tourism can be organized in accordance with the principle of inclusive tourism as a desirable and feasible alternative, to paraphrase Erik Olin Wright in his 'real utopias' (2010).

SESC: Over Seven Decades of Social Tourism

SESC was founded in 1946 by business entrepreneurs from the trade, services and tourism sectors in Brazil. Its origins can be traced back to the structural changes that the country was undergoing at the time and to the political and ideological debate on social issues. Big socioeconomic changes were taking place in the 1940s as a result of early industrialization in an attempt to move toward a model of accumulation that would lead to the substitution of imports (Schenkel, 2019a). Industry's growing importance went hand-in-hand with a big demographic shift from inland areas to some large cities. São Paulo and Rio de Janeiro grew in an uncontrolled way, without the required infrastructure to take in the new migrants, causing rising inequality and social tensions.

Many of these changes happened during the populist dictatorship of Getulio Vargas, who governed from 1930 to 1945 in successive governments. During this time, he combined repression with social policies. He was subsequently elected and governed again from 1950 to 1954. Among the business and political elites, there was concern about the possible growth of syndicalism, and so some sort of broad agreement with the workers was pursued (Gomes, 2005). At the same time, inspired by the 'Rerum Novarum' by Pope Leo XIII, through the Church's social doctrine, it proposed a way of combating the expansion of Communism through social alternatives. All these factors led to what might be described as preventive social reforms and, through them, many Latin American states attempted to create bodies and to put into practice public policies aimed at meeting the specific needs of the emerging urban proletariat (Schenkel, 2019a).

Within this context, several business employers proposed initiatives in the field of education and vocational training with a view to fostering greater well-being among workers. In 1942, the National Industrial Training Service (SENAI) was created, followed shortly afterwards by the National Commercial Training Service (SENAC), in order to train staff to work in industry and trade. At the same time, in May 1945, the First Conference of Producer Classes was held in Teresópolis, organized by the Associação Comercial do Rio de Janeiro under the auspices of various business associations. As a corollary at the conference, a Social Peace Charter was approved and later formalized in 1946. This charter paved the way for a commitment between workers and entrepreneurs.

Certain initiatives were then taken by the business sector in the fields of culture, sport, leisure, art and formal education. In 1946, the Social Service for Industry (SESI) and Social Service for Trade (SESC) were created. In the case of SESC, it was organized and run by the National Trade Confederation for Goods, Services and Tourism (CNC), as the association representing management bodies in Brazil. In São Paulo, the corresponding business association was the State of São Paulo's Trade Federation for Goods, Services and Tourism (FecomercioSP), founded in 1938.

These bodies (SENAI and SESI for industry and SENAC and SESC for the trade sector) are funded through compulsory contributions by the business community of their respective sectors in the form of a percentage of the wages paid to their workers: 1% in the case of SENAC and 1.5% for SESC. This funding system has ensured a high level of financial stability for over 70 years. Each of the bodies is regulated by a specific law, which establishes that they are privately administrated. Their functioning is therefore governed by a legal framework specific to each one and not by a state body. In turn, this legal setup is described in Article 240 of the 1988 Constitution, which establishes that the revenue collected for each of these bodies cannot be used for other purposes.

In addition to collecting the said funds, the state has supervisory functions over these bodies. By law, their budget and their budgetary implementation reports must be approved by a state court of auditors called the Tribunal de Cuentas de la Unión (TCU). Their governing bodies, at both a regional and national level, include a representative of TCU, as do the Fiscal Committees in charge of approving their accounts (made up, in this last case, of seven members, including four state representatives, two representatives of the business sector and one representative of the workers).

SESC São Paulo's Social Tourism Programme

SESC is divided into 27 regional groups, with one per state, in addition to a national department in Rio de Janeiro. Although joint programmes are run, they vary substantially based on local characteristics, the financial capacity of each state group, and the approach of those in charge. Initially, SESC São Paulo (SP SESC) was predominantly welfare-oriented, seeking immediate solutions to basic needs, mainly in matters related to worker healthcare. Thus, hospitals and kindergartens were created and action was taken to improve hygiene and nutrition. However, from the late 1970s, its focus shifted to non-formal education, tied in with leisure and tourism (Almeida, 2011; Cheibub, 2014).

Over time, the working classes' possibilities of access to tourism changed, calling for urgent reflection on the coherence of the organization's activities. In the 1970s and 1980s, tourism products for low-income consumers were practically non-existent in Brazil. Workers did not have access to tourism, and only people who could afford it were able to travel. However, shortly afterwards, tour operators with holiday products targeted at lower-income sectors of the population started to appear. According to Flávia Costa, the coordinator of SP SESC's Social Tourism Unit, the difference between these products and what SESC offers is the approach that the latter takes: 'It is not only about offering cheap products for people with lower incomes, but about offering products with added value – not just entertainment for the sake of entertainment or leisure for the sake of leisure, but an activity that gives people access to some kind of added benefit'.

The key difference to SP SESC's approach is that social tourism is seen as a tool in education. Although this had always been an underlying part of the ideology of social tourism since its inception, it was not until the 1990s that SP SESC managed to put it into action in all its dimensions. The idea was to democratize access to tourism for lower-income members of the population, adding an educational component to this goal in the form of education in tourism through tourism, with the participants' active involvement. SESC's educational activities are designed to cultivate a critical awareness among citizens. Hence, through the activities held at SP SESC's various units, access to varying forms of culture, in particular the arts, is provided in the understanding that by fostering a capacity for critical thinking, a fuller process of personal development can be achieved.

SP SESC has a very broad target public. In 2018, it had 2,133,848 accredited visitors, approximately half of whom worked in the trade, tourism and services sectors, while the other half were dependents (SESC, 2018). This accredited status has a validity of two years. SESC has 43 units in the State of São Paulo in 21 different cities: 23 of these units are located in the São Paulo metropolitan area and 17 in inland or coastal areas, including SESC Bertioga, plus there are three specialist units. At the units, all kinds of artistic, sports, and socio-educational activities are organized, and they even offer low-cost dental services. The organization also has a television channel, a web portal, a publishing house, a DVD and CD label and a research and training centre. In 2018, SP SESC had a total directly employed workforce of 7,650 people (SESC, 2018).

There are five main cornerstones to its social tourism policy: (1) social accommodation at SESC Bertioga; (2) outbound tourism from the state's various units, which organize trips (more than one day), walks (one day) and tours (half a day); (3) a fostered raised awareness of tourism, through the trips that the organization prepares and broader input; (4) local community development and the promotion of responsible tourism, based on ethical criteria, including support for the consolidation of local initiatives; and (5) reflection on tourism and knowledge-building through the organization's Research and Training Centre.

SESC Bertioga: A Holiday Centre for the Working Classes

In the coastal town of Bertioga, in the State of São Paulo, a holiday resort for workers from the trade, tourism and services sectors has been in operation since 1948. SESC Bertioga currently encompasses five big areas of land, with the resort itself occupying a total of 439,000 m^2. These areas contain the visitor centre's various facilities; that is, its accommodation, bar and restaurant, swimming pools, sports facilities, multi-purpose hall, children's games rooms, library, exhibition rooms, chapel, nature interpretation centre, nursery, nature reserve, car park, dental service, training rooms and office area. Bicycles and buses are available to move around the premises. There is also a medical centre for primary medical care, and an ambulance permanently on hand in case a patient needs to be transferred to a public hospital for more specialist care.

SESC Bertioga can currently accommodate up to 1,000 people in its 12 accommodation units and 50 houses. Its cultural and artistic programme is the same as that of any other unit run by SP SESC; visitors can enjoy various cultural events, such as music, theatre, dance and literature. Sport and leisure pursuits of all kinds are also organized, as well as regular activities for children and healing or well-being activities. Traditionally, food is one of the most important factors in the evaluation of customer satisfaction, with priority being given to its quality and nutritional value. In the hospitality policy of SP SESC, and its Bertioga unit in particular, big efforts have been made to improve accessibility, with the loan of amphibious chairs so that people with a disability can bathe in the sea.

The occupancy rate of SESC Bertioga is remarkably high, with a mean annual figure of 94% showing the very high demand. This has led to major efforts to organize an efficient booking system, with the introduction of packages so that groups of visitors arrive and leave at the same time and timetables and operational aspects can be more easily streamlined.

Bookings for the resort can be made either online through its website or on site at one of SESC's units, since no intermediaries are used. Duly accredited workers from the trade, tourism and services sectors take priority, together with their spouses and children under the age of 24. First-time visitors and people who have not been to the resort for the past three years are also given precedence. Unaccredited members of the public can also use the facilities, but the cost is different, because only visitors from the trade, tourism and services sectors are subsidized.

The overall daily running cost of SESC Bertioga (including food, shows, wages, water and energy) is BRL263 per person (approximately EUR60 in April 2019). Despite this, accredited visitors only have to pay BRL75 a day (approximately EUR17). During the high season (from the second half of December to February), access is solely reserved for accredited visitors, with two permitted guests for every accredited one. During the low season, people without the necessary accreditation can also stay at the resort, but they are charged for the full cost of their stay: that is, BRL263. There is a specific pricing policy for children under the age of 13.

The registration process at SESC Bertioga is as follows. A package must be chosen and a booking made once the registration period opens. There are three registration periods each year, five months before the start of a stay. Stays can range from a minimum of two-and-a-half days to a maximum of eight-and-a-half days. Once the booking period is over, a draw is held and payment must be made by the winners before a certain deadline. Anyone failing to pay in time will be replaced by the next person on the list until all the places have been allocated. If places are still available one month before a given date, they are sold directly though SESC Bertioga's website in order to reduce costs and facilitate access for people with a low purchasing power. In 2010, packages of four-and-a-half days, three-and-a-half days and two-and-a-half days began to be offered. A variety of payment facilities are available; for instance, bank card payments can be made in eight instalments and cash payments in four instalments. Payments must be made prior to arrival.

In addition to the above registration process, group stays with a guide can also be arranged through SP SESC's various units which organize stays at SESC Bertioga and other accommodation centres run by SESC's regional offices in other states. These groups do not enter the general draw system but a draw for their unit. When an exchange agreement exists, groups from other regional SESC units can also stay at SESC Bertioga to give them the opportunity to visit other centres in Brazil. Agreements for group visits are also reached with trade unions.

Lastly, visits can also be made on a one-day basis. The centre can currently host up to 300 day trippers a day, from 8 a.m. to 6 p.m. One-day visits include lunch, access to all the activities and the whole leisure programme and use of the changing rooms. The cost for accredited visitors is BRL25 a day (less than EUR6) including lunch in the restaurant, or BRL19 (EUR4.3) including lunch in the bar. For unaccredited visitors, the cost is BRL89 (just over EUR20) or BRL73 (almost EUR17) respectively. This type of visit is very popular and practically all the available tickets for the year are sold out.

In 2018, SESC Bertioga had a total of 44,612 guests and 75,839 day trippers. By income, the distribution of the visitors was as follows: 87% had an income equivalent to 0 to 5 times the minimum wage, 8% had an income comparable to 6 to 9 times the minimum wage and 5% earned a sum tantamount to over 10 times the minimum wage. The minimum wage in 2019 was BRL950 a month (about EUR220), which means that the equivalent of five times the minimum wages would be around EUR1,100. The vast majority of people who stay at SESC Bertioga would not be able to afford other similar holiday resorts.

Work Conditions

In keeping with the traditions of social tourism, SESC Bertioga not only aspires to offer good-quality tourist facilities to workers from the sector, but it is also committed to guaranteeing decent working conditions for its staff. SP SESC has a labour policy based on the principles of a decent wage (higher than average for each of the employment categories and jobs), strict compliance with labour legislation, broad-ranging social benefits, regular opportunities for dialogue and information exchanges between the staff and management of each of the units, individual training, the possibility of promotion and professional career development within the organization and retirement at 57 on full wages. However, some activities are outsourced, such as security services and the cleaning of communal areas.

In April 2019, SESC Bertioga had a direct workforce of 400 people, employed in the following areas: management, administration, customer information and care, programming, bookings, food and beverage, housekeeping and services, dental treatment and maintenance. Work conditions at Bertioga are the same as at any other unit. Certain initiatives have also been taken to improve the working conditions and atmosphere. For instance, there are five rest areas for the workers in different parts of the unit, and the staff have breakfast and lunch in the same restaurant as the guests, with access to the same food.

As for the housekeeping staff in charge of the cleaning and accommodation – one of the most insecure jobs internationally (Cañada, 2019) – special emphasis is placed on their work conditions. SESC Bertioga has 35 chambermaids, one supervisor and five housekeeping managers, plus a head of department. In 2018, the chambermaids earned BRL1,989 a month (around EUR515), when the minimum wage in the country was BRL937 (around EUR243). With a working week of 44 hours and a timetable from 8 a.m. to 4.20 p.m., they have to clean five apartments a day on check-out dates or eight apartments if the guests are still staying at the centre, spending 40 minutes on each. When they were asked, none of them reported having to do overtime, since the assigned work could be done during their normal shift.

From the comments that were made by these workers, their working day was not considered to be especially hard, with no peaks when they felt pressurized. This is due to the management policy, which seeks to facilitate the cleaning and maintenance process without overloading the staff, despite the high average occupancy rate. Usually, when guests leave, their room is not re-occupied until the following day, allowing the chambermaids and maintenance managers to work without pressure. For instance, if a guest checks out of their room at 2 p.m., cleaning and maintenance can be done until 8 p.m., avoiding possible rushes. Hence, workloads can be better distributed.

Furthermore, when the facilities at SESC Bertioga were last refurbished, the chambermaids were asked what changes could be made to improve their jobs. Based on their comments, all the furniture in the rooms was fitted with wheels to make the beds, wardrobes and fridges easier to move. The rooms are not cluttered with objects, and they are minimalist in design, making them far easier to clean. Each pavilion also has a storeroom where the cleaning supplies, sheets and towels for its rooms are kept so that heavy loads do not have to be moved to the pavilions. Guests are asked to leave dirty laundry at the entrance to each apartment for its collection with a motorized trolley, as opposed to the heavy hand-operated ones found at most beach hotels.

All these factors help to avoid occupational health problems. Neither the departmental head nor the managers identified absenteeism as being a significant problem – another sign of how well this department works.

A Resort in the Community

Ordinarily, tourist resorts do not contribute to the greater well-being or development of the local population. In fact, the opposite tends to occur through dynamics of exclusion and marginalization (Blázquez et al., 2011). Initially, SESC Bertioga mainly focused on the needs of workers from the trade, tourism and services sectors and their families. However, in accordance with new wider visions of social tourism, it gradually broadened its scope to encompass relations with the local community, having discovered that it had failed to take into account the local population in its development as occurs with conventional beach resorts. It was clear to Marcos Roberto Laverti, SESC Bertioga's manager, that the resort should not become just another tourist ghetto: 'We cannot become an island, with high walls that protect those who stay here'. Thus, it was decided that the unit should grow and develop in harmony with the local community, avoiding situations of marginalization.

Hence, a policy began to be designed and implemented aimed at opening up Bertioga to the local community and integrating it in the municipality. The steep growth in the local population and its resulting rising needs also had to be taken into account. The town of Bertioga had grown substantially in recent years, above all its housing estates and condominiums, whose population account for most of the local residents who come to SESC Bertioga. In addition, practically all SESC Bertioga's workers live in the municipality. Initially, with the new plan to open up the resort to the local community, occasional activities were organized and held at SESC. Later they became increasingly regular, with growing attendance by people from the local community. This led to a paradigm shift in the concept of what a resort such as this should be like and, without relinquishing its role as an accommodation centre, it also became actively involved in the social and cultural development of the local community.

Today, this policy of local inclusion has given rise to several well-defined functions:

1. A hub for knowledge-building and debate. If controversial issues arise locally (for instance, in the field of healthcare, urban mobility or sanitation), specialist speakers are brought in or seminars or debates are organized.
2. A municipal convention centre. When activities are organized in the town that might be of interest to the population, SESC Bertioga hosts them free of charge in its facilities.
3. Membership of local municipal committees. Staff from SESC Bertioga are involved in committees such as the Municipal Tourism Board, the Senior Citizens Committee and the Environmental Council.
4. Cultural activities. Like any other of SESC's units, SP SESC's programme of theatre, music, live arts and socio-educational activities are brought to Bertioga to be enjoyed by various groups.

One outcome of this strategy is the population of Bertioga's high level of participation in SESC Bertioga's activities. The town has a population of some 60,000 people, 11,380 of whom registered to take part in activities or programmes run by SESC Bertioga in 2018. Like SESC's other units, accredited visitors must work in the trade, tourism or services sectors, or else must be a dependent of someone working in these fields. In 2018, 360,000 enrolments in SESC Bertioga's different programmes and activities were made by local people (including repeat enrolments by the same person).

CONCLUSION

The expansion of tourism, in a context of worldwide touristification, has triggered repeated examples of dispossession, exploitation and destruction, involving implicit physical, symbolic or structural violence (Devine and Ojeda, 2017). In parallel with this, the tourist supply has become increasingly segmented and specific, in the form of niche tourism products. Segmentation, as a move away from standard mass tourism products, does not in itself imply greater sustainability, equality or inclusion. In fact, it reflects a system of tourism production and consumption more consistent with current post-Fordist capitalism, with multiple consequences. Segmentation also occurs in social tourism, with programmes closely tailored to meet the needs of certain vulnerable groups. This trend seems to be more attributable to market needs and possible private business interests than to greater efficiency in attending to these groups.

Within this framework, it is not easy to come up with alternative systems of tourism production and consumption. However, the COVID-19 health crisis, which brought tourism to a halt and called into question the global tourism model, makes it even more essential to rethink tourism. Any alternative models must be based on emancipatory principles; that is, they must seek to eliminate any form of oppression or domination, while also encouraging human development and the possibility of a decent life in a fair society at peace with the planet (Goulet, 1995; Wright, 2010).

SESC Bertioga illustrates the best traditions of social tourism in Latin America, demonstrating the potential of initiatives targeted at low- and middle-income working-class groups living within a short distance of the holiday resort, thus reducing the environmental impact of travel. Its tourism programme is mainly focused on boosting its visitors' well-being, although it also has a high educational component, aimed at fostering greater personal development and a higher critical awareness. In turn, the unit also strives to guarantee decent working conditions and the resort's integration into the local community. Far from echoing the general trend in segmentation that other examples of social tourism elsewhere have done, SESC Bertioga serves broad-ranging groups of people, demonstrating a capacity to integrate different needs.

ACKNOWLEDGEMENTS

This article was drafted as part of the 'Inclusive tourism, a demand for global justice' project, run by Alba Sud with the support of Barcelona City Council (2020). It was written as part of the Postdoctoral Margarita Salas Fellow at the University of the Balearic Islands. I would like to acknowledge the Ministerio de Ciencia e Innovación (MCI), the Agencia Estatal de Investigación (AEI) and the European Regional Development Fund (ERDF) for their support for project RTI2018-094844-B-C31.

REFERENCES

Almeida, M. V. (2011) The development of social tourism in Brazil. *Current Issues in Tourism*, 14(5), 483–9.

Blázquez, M., Cañada, E. and Murray, I. (2011) Búnker playa-sol. Conflictos derivados de la construcción de enclaves de capital transnacional turístico español en el Caribe y Centroamérica. *Scripta Nova*, 15(368) (online edition).

Broder, D. (2019) Socialists invented summer vacation. *Jacobin*, 8 July. https://jacobin.com/2019/08/socialists-invented-summer-vacation-popular-front-france/.

Cañada, E. (2019) El trabajo de las camareras de piso: un estado de la cuestión. *Papers de Turisme*, 62, 67–84.

Cañada, E. (2020) *SESC Bertioga, donde el turismo social construye esperanza*. Barcelona: Alba Sud Editorial, colección Informes en Contraste, 11.

Cheibub, B.L. (2014) A história das prática turística no serviço social do comercio de Sao Paulo (Sesc-SP). *Rosados Ventos. Turismo e Hospitalidade*, 6(2), 247–62.

Cross, G. (1989) Vacations for all: the leisure question in the era of the popular front. *Journal of Contemporary History*, 24(4), 599–621.

Devine, J. and Ojeda, D. (2017) Violence and dispossession in tourism development: a critical geographical approach. *Journal of Sustainable Tourism*, 25(5), 605–17.

Diekmann, A., McCabe, S. and Ferreira, C.C. (2018) Social tourism: research advances, but stasis in policy. Bridging the divide. *Journal of Policy Research in Tourism, Leisure and Events*, 10(3), 181–8.

Ferrer, J.G., Sanz, M.F., Ferrandis, E.D., McCabe, S. and García, J.S. (2016) Social tourism and healthy ageing. *International Journal of Tourism Research*, 18(4), 297–307.

Gomes, A. (2005[1998]) *A invenção do trabalhismo*. Rio de Janeiro: Editora FVG.

González, E.A., Sánchez, N.L. and Vila, T.D. (2017) Activity of older tourists: understanding their participation in social tourism programs. *Journal of Vacation Marketing*, 23(4), 295–306.

Goulet, D. (1995) *Ética del desarrollo. Guía teórica y práctica*. Madrid: IEPALA.

Hazel, N. (2005) Holidays for children and families in need: an exploration of the research and policy context for social tourism in the UK. *Children & Society*, 19(3), 225–36.

Hunter-Jones, P. (2011) The role of charities in social tourism. *Current Issues in Tourism*, 14(5), 445–58.

Ioannides, D. and Debbage, K. (1997) Post-Fordism and flexibility: the travel industry polyglot. *Tourism Management*, 18(4), 229–41.

Kakoudakis, K. I., McCabe, S. and Story, V. (2017) Social tourism and self-efficacy: exploring links between tourism participation, job-seeking and unemployment. *Annals of Tourism Research*, 65, 108–21.

La Placa, V. and Corlyon, J. (2014) Social tourism and organised capitalism: research, policy and practice. *Journal of Policy Research in Tourism, Leisure and Events*, 6(1), 66–79.

Lopes, M.C., Liberato, D., Alcn, E. and Liberato, P. (2020) Social tourism development and the population ageing: case study in Portugal and Spain. *Smart Innovation, Systems and Technologies*, 171, 527–36.

McCabe, S. (2009) Who needs a holiday? Evaluating social tourism. *Annals of Tourism Research*, 36(4), 667–88.

McCabe, S. (2020) Tourism for all? Considering social tourism: a perspective paper. *Tourism Review*, 75(1), 61–4.

McCabe, S. and Qiao, G. (2020) A review of research into social tourism: launching the Annals of Tourism Research Curated Collection on Social Tourism. *Annals of Tourism Research*, 85, 103103.

Minnaert, L. (2020) Stakeholder stories: exploring social tourism networks. *Annals of Tourism Research*, 83(June), 102979.

Minnaert, L., Maitland, R. and Miller, G. (eds) (2013) *Social tourism. Perspectives and potential*. Abingdon: Routledge.

Morgan, N., Pritchard, A. and Sedgley, D. (2015) Social tourism and well-being in later life. *Annals of Tourism Research*, 52, 1–15.

Novelli, M. (2005) *Niche tourism: Contemporary issues, trends and cases*. Oxford: Butterworth-Heinemann Ltd.

Schenkel, E. (2017) *Política turística y turismo social. Una perspectiva latinoamericana.* Edicciones CICCUS / CLACSO.

Schenkel, E. (2019a) Turismo social en América Latina. Aprendizajes de las experiencias regionales. Barcelona: Alba Sud Editorial, colección Informes en Contraste, núm. 10.

Schenkel, E. (2019b) Turismo social en Brasil: 70 años de historia del Sesc Sao Paulo. *Alba Sud*, 6 October.

Schenkel, E. (2020) Cinco propósitos para repensar la gestión del turismo social. *Alba Sud*, 7 July.

Schenkel, E. and Almeida, M.V. (2020) Social tourism in Latin America: regional initiatives. In A. Diekmann and S. McCabe, *Handbook of Social Tourism* Cheltenham: Edward Elgar Publishing, 33–42.

Sedgley, D., Haven-Tang, C. and Espeso-Molinero, P. (2018) Social tourism and older people: the IMSERSO initiative. *Journal of Policy Research in Tourism, Leisure and Events*, 10(3), 286–304.

SESC (2018) *Realizações 2018*. Sao Paulo: Serviço Social do Comércio.

Thomas, T.K. (2018) Inclusions and exclusions of social tourism. *Asia-Pacific Journal of Innovation in Hospitality and Tourism*, 7(1), 85–99.

Wright, E.O. (2010) *Envisioning real utopias*. London: Verso.

29. Developmentourism and school tours in Zimbabwe

Kathleen Smithers and Joanne Ailwood

INTRODUCTION

For at least the last decade, discussions on mass tourism have focused on the potential impacts of mass tourism on local communities (Mowforth and Munt, 2009). Partly due to this ongoing critical engagement with the impact of mass tourism, a range of alternative forms of tourism have emerged, which are marketed as 'sustainable' or 'ethical' (Baptista, 2011; Lacey et al., 2012; Novelli, 2016; Mowforth and Munt, 2009), including volunteer tourism, community-based tourism and philanthropic tourism. Given that these forms of niche tourism overlap and intersect, Baptista (2011) labelled the macro-niche that incorporates multiple elements of philanthropic, volunteer and community-based tourisms as 'developmentourism'.

Within this relatively new macro-niche of developmentourism sits the micro-niche of school tours. As tourism-orientated organisations are becoming more prevalent in countries in the Global South (Clausen, 2019; Scarth and Novelli, 2019; Wondirad et al., 2020), touring schools as part of a philanthropic tourism is becoming more frequent (Chilufya et al., 2019). School tours usually form part of a larger itinerary for tourists in low- and/or middle-income countries. The application of this kind of tourism as a panacea for development has been previously explored in the tourism literature (Mutana et al., 2013; Novelli, 2016; Spenceley and Meyer, 2012), with education also having a long history of being viewed as a panacea for poverty reduction (UNESCO Institute for Statistics, 2017). The micro-niche of the school tour thus merges these two ideas in one concept.

In this chapter, we reflect on one school community that hosts such tourists in Matabeleland North, Zimbabwe. This study thus addresses an under-researched space in the literature, namely that of the micro-niche of the school tour (Chilufya et al., 2019; Novelli, 2016). This research contributes to an understanding of the impact of tourist groups visiting schools as part of their tour itinerary.

Given the complexity of this kind of tourism, this chapter uses developmentourism as a macro-niche to frame the discussion. The micro-niche of the school tour sits within a broader 'safari-style itinerary', which usually includes visits to famous landmarks, safari parks and places of cultural significance, across multiple Southern African nations. Novelli (2016) describes such school tours as a 'questionable growing phenomenon in niche tourism, aimed at attracting and retaining more tourist spending' (p. 181). In the present study, the companies that visit the school advertise their products as providing alternative experiences to mass tourism. One company aims to provide 'off-the-beaten-track'-style tours for elderly Americans, while the other offers education-focused tours for the same market with comprehensive reading materials suggested prior to each tour. Both companies market themselves as offering unique experiences that allow tourists to engage with communities in an 'authentic' manner. As part of this 'authentic interaction' the companies report the ways they 'give back' to the local communities they visit. The market segment of this niche tourism is, therefore, elderly American tourists who are looking for a 'authentic' experience in a small-group, either 'off the beaten track' or with an educational focus.

Following this introduction, we discuss the discursive foundations of developmentourism and school tours. We then move on to describe the research setting and methodology. Next, the findings section outlines two main points: a) balancing the learning impacts on the school with the main benefits of tourism and b) the professional complexities of being both a school and a tourism destination. The concluding section discusses the residual consequences of living within a long-term economic crisis, as Zimbabwe has since the late 1990s, and how this governs the school founders' and teachers' decision-making. This includes commentary on the importance of community consultation as a tool for minimising the potential harmful impacts of school visits.

THE SCHOOL TOUR AS A MICRO-NICHE

Developmentourism is a term used to acknowledge the 'integration of "development" discourse, knowledge and action into the tourism experience' (Baptista, 2011: 663). Developmentourism reflects the ways in which communities in the Global South 'have become producers, product, and sellers of tourism and "development"' (Baptista, 2011: 656). By naming the intersection of development and tourism, Baptista aims to make explicit what this category discursively represents and the power relations and discourses it camouflages. Although studies have previously explored community-based tourism and volunteer tourism, since Baptista coined the term 'developmentourism' there has been little exploration of the concept, in terms of its use for examining tourism ventures that do not fit into the previously established categories. For example, at the intersection of volunteer tourism, philanthropic tourism and community-based tourism is the act of visiting a school as a wealthy tourist in a low-income country. This chapter therefore contributes new understandings of the macro-niche of developmentourism and the micro-niche of the school tour.

Developmentourism is the blend of development and tourism, so a brief note about 'development' as a concept is needed. Sustainable Development Goal 4 is 'quality education', and education is considered one of the key elements towards 'development'. With education considered a panacea for poverty reduction, there has been a great deal of interest from NGOs in investing in, and improving education systems (see, for example, Novelli, 2016: 168). Dominant discourses of development legitimise institutions that intervene to help African countries progress towards becoming more 'developed' (Baptista, 2011; Scarth and Novelli, 2019). In particular, Southern Africa has endured many interventions in the name of 'development', whether through philanthropic donations or economic interventions by international organisations such as the World Bank (Scarth and Novelli, 2019; Wondirad et al., 2020). In Southern Africa, these NGOs often partner with tourism companies as a method of funding, allowing the tourism companies to display corporate social responsibility (CSR) and the NGOs to receive much-needed funds. Further, tourism is also considered a panacea for development as it provides income and employment opportunities (Clausen, 2019; Spenceley and Meyer, 2012). In the micro-niche of the school tour, these two ideas combine.

There has been limited work to define and delineate in which type of tourism the school tour 'fits'. Scarth and Novelli (2019) define a school tour, as part of a tourism package, to be a type of travel philanthropy that results from the 'compassionate by-products of a wildlife safari' (p. 90). There has been some investigation into school tours as part of CSR by hotels in schools in Southern Africa (Chilufya et al., 2019; Mutana et al., 2013; Snyman, 2019); however, this compassionate by-product remains mostly unexamined in the research literature (Novelli, 2016), as the current niche categories allow the act of visiting a school to remain uninterrogated (one exception is Chilufya et al., 2019).

Chilufya et al. (2019) recently examined tours of schools, as part of CSR, in Zambia and Fiji. They identified that, while CSR practices aim to develop communities, these initiatives prioritise the tourists' wants and needs. Mutana et al. (2013) have noted that tour operators in Matabeleland North, Zimbabwe, are participating in philanthropic or community development programmes focused on 'giving back' to the communities they operate alongside. While Mutana et al. (2013) found that while most tourism operators in their study participated in some form of community contributions – for example, through payment of school fees or building of infrastructure – there was no significant exploration of the impact of these activities on school communities.

Another example of tourism in schools is volunteer tourism, which developed in the early 2000s as a form of 'giveback', through which young, wealthy and predominantly white Westerners pay large fees to visit low-income countries and volunteer their time, while also enjoying tourism and leisure activities (Bandyopadhyay and Patil, 2017). Previous research suggests the exchange between host communities and volunteer tourists to be uneven, with volunteer tourists gaining work-related experiences and the host communities receiving very little benefit (Bandyopadhyay and Patil, 2017; Mostafanezhad, 2013). With a flow of volunteers usually from high-income to low-income countries, it has been argued that volunteer tourism is unsustainable and linked to discourses which normalise wealth inequality (Clausen, 2019; Mostafanezhad, 2013). Volunteer teaching placements are perhaps the most problematic type of volunteer tourism, with volunteers often underqualified and inexperienced (Bargeman et al., 2018). Despite growing concern regarding volunteers in schools, there has been little examination of the impact on schools that are volunteer tourism destinations (Bargeman et al., 2018; Chilufya et al., 2019).

The behaviour of tourists on a school tour may be shaped by the discourses of 'giving back' which are perpetuated in volunteer tourism advertising, thus linking the latter with the micro-niche of the school tour (Nyahunzvi, 2013). However, in this case study, the tourists who visit the school do not pay a fee to volunteer, and do not undertake their trip to Southern Africa for the purpose of volunteering. The tourists are therefore not volunteer tourists, although they may draw on discourses which are prevalent in volunteer tourism, such as the notion of 'giving back'. Further, the tourists who visit the school in this project do not undertake their tour of Southern Africa with a purely philanthropic mindset, although they are encouraged to bring small gifts for the school. As such, the school tour forms its own micro-niche space, wherein it draws on various discourses and practices from other forms of tourism. This adds a layer of complexity and nuance to any examinations of this tourism, as it does not fit neatly within other micro-niches within developmentourism.

RESEARCH SETTING AND METHOD

The Zimbabwean Context

In the last couple of decades, alongside sustained neocolonial interventions, Zimbabwe has experienced a severe economic decline, resulting in a turbulent economy and high unemployment. One victim of the turbulent economy has been the Zimbabwean school system (Chitiyo et al., 2010). There is minimal and inconsistent government funding for schools, and teachers in government schools are often unpaid or paid late, and more recently have regularly been on strike to argue for better and more consistent pay (Mangwaya et al., 2012). Within this economic context, many privately funded schools have been established across Zimbabwe. These schools are reliant on donors, sponsors or on wealthier parents who can pay large fees (Mangwaya et al., 2012). For some schools, such as the one researched here, donors and sponsors are sourced through tourism ventures (Mutana et al., 2013). In 2009, Zimbabwe's economic crisis saw teachers on strike for a year, closing schools and leaving most children without access to any formal education. The COVID-19 pandemic of 2020/21 repeated the break in formal learning, as schools faced long closures during national lockdowns and examinations were postponed or cancelled (ZIMSTAT, 2020). As is often the case in Zimbabwe, rural communities are more vulnerable than urban communities due to limited or a lack of the resources required for online learning such as electricity, internet and computer access (ZIMSTAT, 2020). Schools that depend on the economic support of tourists have been hard hit as they respond to the twin shocks of the long-term and ongoing economic crisis and the sudden loss of international tourists due to the COVID-19 pandemic.

Research Methods and Tour Description

This chapter presents one aspect of a larger ethnographic study undertaken by the first author, prior to the COVID-19 pandemic. This research was conducted over the course of three months (one school term), where the researcher, who is also a qualified Australian teacher, engaged as a participant/observer and classroom teacher. A range of data was generated including field notes, interviews with adults and children, observations and children's art. In this chapter we focus on the 12 adult interviews with two school founders, two tourism operators and eight teachers. Adults in the school community, including teachers, school leaders, school founders and tourism workers who visited the school, were invited to participate in a semi-structured interview. Prior to these interviews, informed consent was given. Each adult interview was 45–90 minutes long and was audio recorded and transcribed. Participants were provided the opportunity to edit their transcript and all names in this chapter are pseudonyms of the participant's choosing.

Data was analysed using thematic analysis and framed through Michel Foucault's notions of power relations and discourse. By tracing the history of institutions over time, Foucault (1975/1991; 1976/2008) interrogated the ways in which individuals are governed and the ways individuals govern themselves in the process of being/becoming a subject. This chapter uses two of his concepts, power relations and discourse, to identify 'whose voices are speaking and whose interests are being served' (Baptista, 2011: 656). In a Foucauldian sense, power is understood as productive and relational; there are a multitude of these networks of power in which 'power is exercised from innumerable points' (Foucault 1976/2008: 94). Foucault

(1976/2008) identifies the relationship between power relations and discourses by asking, 'how did [power relations] make possible these kinds of discourses, and conversely, how were these discourses used to support power relations?' (p. 97). In other words, discourses create and constrain conditions of possibility which enable power relationships.

Matopo School (a pseudonym) was founded and is funded by a tourism operator as part of their 'giveback' to the local community in exchange for tours of the village and school grounds (Chilufya et al., 2019). The tourism company funds infrastructure projects and pays teachers through their charitable organisation, a common practice in Southern Africa (see Chilufya et al., 2019; Mutana et al., 2013; Novelli, 2016; Snyman, 2019). Matopo School hosts three different tour companies: Education Tours, Adventure Company and Shumba Safaris. While each tour company differs slightly in approach and length of time at the school, there is a similar pattern for each visit. Visits are frequent, at least once each week, and sometimes happen on days when the school is closed, for example, on Saturdays. For a weekend visit, teachers who live on-site are expected to greet and guide the visitors, with children who live nearby also attending.

The tours follow an established pattern. First, the tour bus arrives and the tourists are greeted as they step out of the bus; each tourist is greeted by one child who holds the tourist's hand and guides them to the other waiting students. At this point the tourists might hand over small gifts to the children, such as pencils or soccer balls, and the children perform welcome dances. For Education Tours and Shumba Safaris, the dancing is performed by the whole school. For Adventure Company, an 'entertainment group' of about 20 selected children perform. The dance display involves singing, clapping and drumming, with the dances and songs being a mix of Southern African songs and Western songs. At certain points audience participation is encouraged, and many tourists take photographs or videos of the performances.

Following the welcome performance, the tourists are presented with an oral history of the school. This history is delivered by the teacher on duty and is about 30 minutes long. Following the history talk, all tour groups undertake a school tour which includes the school grounds, every classroom, the local health clinic and the school kitchen. For the Adventure Company tour, students act as tour guides for the group with one child paired with each tourist. As the tourists visit each classroom, lessons are stopped and children are expected to greet the visitors and talk to them as they enter the classroom.

FINDINGS/DISCUSSION

Learning Impacts and School Benefits

This section explores the conflicting priorities of the teachers in the school as they navigate disruptions to the school day. It outlines the perceived benefit of the tourism, and the challenges created through the disruptions caused by the tourism.

For each visit, there was one teacher assigned to supervise the tour, with the aim of minimising disruption to the remaining classroom teachers. The teacher on duty was responsible for supervising the child guides and ensuring the tour is conducted correctly; however, this also means they were absent from their own classroom for the duration of the tour. The children in the on-duty teacher's class remained in the classroom and could be unsupervised for up to two hours. When left alone the children might continue their work well, but other times they became distracted or unruly, thus leaving very little opportunity for learning.

Bridget, and other teachers in the study, attempted to mitigate the disruption by planning ahead for the tourists' arrival:

> When I know that the visitors will be coming I just make up a plan – especially when it is my duty. I make sure that from the time I go out to attend to the visitors they [the class] have something to do. I don't just leave them, I utilise the time, I make them occupied at that particular time, so the time doesn't get wasted. (Bridget)

Given the need for the children to be self-directed, the assigned activities were often 'busy work' such as textbook-based exercises, copying from the blackboard or practising individual reading. These circumstances were replicated across the school, from early childhood through to the upper grades, with the children left unattended aged between about 3–12 years.

Bridget's concern was the children's learning, but she acknowledged the need to attend to the tourists as they were considered important guests within the broader school community. It could be argued, then, that for Bridget there was a conflicting need to conform to the dominant discourses about what a 'good teacher' might do when called away from their classroom, while also engaging with discourses of what an 'African school' or an 'African welcome' should look like for the tour groups (Thompson and Taheri, 2020). Despite her professional misgivings and frustrations with the interruption of the tour groups, and her acknowledgement of time wasted, Bridget governed her own behaviours in ways that conform to the dominant, and powerful, discursive expectations (Foucault, 1975/1991). These dominant discourses on what an 'African school' or 'African welcome' should be have enabled and constrained the conditions of possibility for her actions, as well as the actions of the children in her care.

Teachers were not the only group disrupted in the school. Some of the children were expected to guide the tourists, holding their hands to personally show them the school, under the supervision of the on-duty teacher. The child guides were those whose English levels were either the highest or lowest. One teacher explains this:

> What we do is we check those who can hear and understand English. Then we match them with those who are still learning and in pairs they go together. One will be doing the talking and the other one will be learning. (Ayanda)

For these children, the impact on their learning was something the teachers could not ignore. Astrid, a classroom teacher, explains:

> You find most of the times they are the same kids that do that routine, each and every time. They end up losing a lot because we cannot wait for them to finish with the visitors and then proceed. We just carry on whatever is happening in the classroom. When they come later, sometimes you tend to forget that they didn't get the concept that you taught the other kids who were left in the classroom. (Astrid)

Despite the misgivings expressed by all teachers and illustrated here by Bridget and Astrid, the dominant expectations for tours, sitting as they do within the existing power relationships between the teachers and the tour operators, led teachers to comply with the routines for tourist visits.

Many of the teachers participating in this research indicated that they would prefer to work at a school with tourism, as the working conditions were more favourable due to the infrastructure the school has developed from tourism funds and the number of children who receive sponsorship. This reflects the work of Mutana et al. (2013), who interviewed tour operators in Matabeleland North. They found that tourism operators consider tourism an important tool for development, with teachers hoping to work at schools which were visited by tourists due to the increased resources and funding. Precious, a teacher at Matopo School, justified the school tours:

> Even though there will be some interruptions we like their coming. Because they are so helpful. They are so helpful to the community, so helpful to us teachers, they are also helpful to the children. (Precious)

This also illustrates the ways in which the complex web of power relations surrounding the school and the tourist visits governs the ways the teachers can talk about these visits. Precious acknowledges the interruptions the tour causes but immediately counters this by acknowledging the ways in which the tourists help the school. This demonstrates the dominant discourses which govern perceptions of the benefits and disadvantages of having the tour groups visit the school (Bargeman et al., 2018; Mutana et al., 2013). The teachers' professional lives are produced within the dominant discursive framing – that tourism is useful due to its positive economic and material effect on their workplace – and in the process, they also minimise the educational impacts of the regular interruptions to their teaching. Teachers seemed less able or willing to critique or acknowledge the aspects of tourism which are not so helpful. To do so would be risky, pushing back against the dominant discourse that monetary/time interventions by a donor (or NGO) are useful and productive (Bandyopadhyay and Patil, 2017). Such resistance is risky when their work and salaries could be at stake.

At Matopo School, the relationships of power are enmeshed within the perceived interests and needs of the tourists and the tourism companies. For teachers, especially given the school was founded by a tourist company, their professional opinions about the educational needs of the children are marginalised. Instead, the teachers engage in a delicate balancing act of managing the educational needs of the children in their class, alongside the powerful discourse that tourist visits are necessary for the ongoing functioning and growth of the school. In this example, the micro-niche of the school tour presents some complexities that need to be considered. Key amongst these is a consideration of the balance between the business of learning with the business of tourism. Both are important. These complexities are unique to the micro-niche of the school tour, and in the following section we explore the teachers' reflections on their professional experiences of school tours.

Schools as a Tourist Destination

From its inception, Matopo School has been a tourism destination. In their daily routines, the teachers attempt to manage the learning disruptions created by the tourist visits. The regular interruptions created by tourists in teachers' day-to-day professional lives is accepted and managed as routine. As part of their professional duties, all teachers in Zimbabwe are obliged to conform to expectations which are set by the government, such as following the teachers' dress code.

Matopo School is a privately funded school but must also conform to government accreditation requirements, meaning the Ministry of Education in Zimbabwe can conduct spot inspections at any time. For teachers, this tension between maintaining their professional role as the classroom teacher and their supplementary role as tour guide is deeply complex and potentially risky. Nolly, a school teacher, explains:

> Sometimes the Ministry of Education is around and here comes the visitors. You know the interruption will be bad. It will give us a bad picture, particularly to our Ministry. Because they will come here, they will find us dancing over there. I don't know what they would think or how they would judge us as a school. (Nolly)

Ministry inspections and school tour groups place competing and contradictory demands upon the teachers. For the ministry inspection, teachers are assessed through presentation of correct timetables, pedagogy, children's uniforms, compliance with the teachers' dress code and fulfilment of curriculum objectives. For the school tour groups, on the other hand, they are expected to play the part of an 'African' school, arguably a different uniform in itself, and govern the behaviour of both themselves and the students to the perceived expectations of the tourist visits (Thompson and Taheri, 2020).

While teachers were worried about managing the interruptions to children's learning during the tourist visits, they were unsure whether, or how, they could change the routine. Ayanda explains why:

> Because [the school founders] have made agreements with those who arranged the groups. They say when you go to Matopo School you will find this and that. They'll be coming and expecting to see those things. (Ayanda)

Ayanda is one of the senior leaders within the school, but even from her position of relative power she was not sure if she could change the routine of the visits as the tourism companies had standard procedures, particularly when advertising what tourists would see on their tour. If the school tours were part of an ongoing consultation process, Ayanda would be able to better understand the agreements that have been made and she may feel more enabled to speak about the educational disruptions that result from the school tours.

When asked how they would change the tours if they could, the teachers were unanimous in their wish to change the time the tourists visited, preferring visits to occur after lunch or during school break times. They felt that the structure of the school day, in which the afternoons were usually allocated to sports or co-curricular activities, suited an afternoon visit. Some of the teachers also identified that having learning time allocated to the morning allowed them to maximise on the students' attention, which often faltered in the hot afternoons. As one teacher noted:

> It may be that they can give us the morning, when the mind is so fresh. Then they should come later, when the kids are a bit tired. That's the only thing that I think I can change. (Tabitha)

The teachers identified that tourists coming in the afternoon would allow the teachers and students to complete their timetabled subjects and also allow the tourists to play games with the children, rather than disrupting the classes. However, the teachers were not consulted by the school founders, or the tourism companies, on the time that they felt was most appropriate. In developmentourism there are expectations regarding how communities will engage with tourists; as Baptista (2011: 656) terms it, communities must become 'producers, product, and sellers'. The teachers, in their role as 'sellers' of developmentourism, must conform to the dominant expectation that the development of the school will be privileged over their own professional knowledge and needs.

Thompson, as a tour guide and the school founder/director, argues that a trade-off is necessary to ensure continued tourist visits. He says:

> For some people [tourists] it is a lifetime experience. That 10 minutes of dancing, to some people, is all they will remember in their minds when they go away. We have to look at it in the sense that, yes, it is taking time and it is probably asking the kids to do something that they wouldn't usually do when meeting someone. But, you have to look at the guest side of things, and also think, these are the people who are helping us. Potential helpers, some *are* already helping, what are they taking away?

Thompson argues the time taken is necessary to provide the tourists with a beneficial experience, thus providing further funding to the school. Both Thompson and the other school founder are not school teachers. They both own and manage the tourism company which funds the school and serve as directors on the school board. This means they control all decisions, and as Astrid, one of the teachers, pointed out:

> For every major thing that we are doing here, it has to pass through Thompson. (Astrid)

The school founders are also managing a balance between the success of the school as both an educational institution and as a micro-niche tourism destination, although their more powerful position as the owners of the safari company means they are more able to define how and when the tourist visits and the school activities occur.

The school founder responsible for the financial side of the tourism company, Alison, identified how little the school needed the school tours:

> Most of it at the start, and then going forwards, has been from either personal donations or a handful of our guests. (Alison)

Further, as Alison went on to explain in her interview, much of the funding has been from personal donations of individuals who had *not* visited the school. However, as demonstrated in this chapter, the teachers rationalise – and attempt to mitigate – the classroom disruptions by identifying the benefits that tourism has for the school (Bargeman et al., 2018).

School tours have their own complexities that need to be considered outside of discussions of developmentourism itself. Within this micro-niche, the disruption to the teaching staff and students must also be understood. While the 'development' of the school may be advancing, tour operators should consider whether this advancement is to the detriment of student learning and a diminishing of teachers' professional decision-making. This dilemma is a unique challenge for the future of these kinds of school tours, and warrants further investigation.

CONCLUSION

Niche tourisms aim to support communities and inject funds back into the economy (Novelli, 2018). This chapter demonstrates that while the micro-niche of the school tour may provide benefits through funding buildings and teachers, it also creates complex relationships that the school community must navigate throughout the day-to-day functioning of the school. There have been few examinations of the impact of the micro-niche of school tourism on school communities themselves (Bargeman et al., 2018; Chilufya et al., 2019; Novelli, 2016).

The findings presented in this chapter are reflective of the tensions inherent in foreign aid; inevitably one day the funding will finish, and the community must source alternative avenues of income (Thompson and Taheri, 2020). In an exercise of hope, Matopo School continues to welcome tourists who provide very little monetary value in the present, but who may bring some sort of value at a later date (Mutana et al., 2013). This is reflective of the economic situation in Zimbabwe, in which income and cash flows are transient and unpredictable, creating a sense that there can be no forward-planning. One of the school founders reflects on this point:

> I think our success came from there being no planning. If we had sat down and said, 'you know I've got to do a, b, c, d it's going to be complicated' and come up with all these big plans, maybe things would have failed. I have never looked and said I want to achieve everything. I have said, 'let's do what we can now'. Tomorrow will find itself or it will open up, or something will give in. (Thompson)

The teachers and school founders have been constrained by this inability to forward-plan, creating the conditions of possibility in which catering to the perceived interests of the tourists is prioritised.

In the context of the COVID-19 pandemic, the precarious nature of both schooling and niche tourism funding has been amplified. In Zimbabwe schools were closed most of 2020, and into the beginning of 2021, meaning children who were not able to move to online learning were not being formally educated and many teachers were unemployed. With international tourism also at a standstill during this time, the combined repercussions of the loss of the tourist economy are coupled with a loss of education, and the long-term consequences are yet to become apparent. It is in this time that the unsustainability of so called 'sustainable tourism' initiatives, such as volunteer tourism, CBT and CSR, becomes clear – when there are no tourists, the tourism cannot continue and the economic benefits dry up. To work towards a more sustainable tourism outlook, tourism companies working with communities should be working to ensure their support extends beyond economic shocks.

This case study of the micro-niche of school tours has explored aspects of the complex relationship between schools as tour sites and the day-to-day functioning of the school. The teachers and children at Matopo School are engaged in a daily balancing act as they negotiate and engage in their complex roles as both a school community and a tourist destination. In their professional lives, teachers are managing their own professional identities, supporting the ongoing provision of valuable educational resources such as infrastructure received through tourism, while also ensuring disruptions to the school day are somewhat managed (see also Bargeman et al., 2018). This professional and identity labour on the part of teachers is marginalised, when the emphasis is placed upon the value of the tourist visits for the school community. In this sense the school tour is unique to other developmentourism ventures, as the main 'sellers' and 'producers', that is the school teachers, may not receive the benefits of their work. In fact, there is a distinct lack of consideration of the teachers and their professional work.

Conducting developmentourism in schools has particular challenges. This chapter has explored the ways that Matopo School's teachers and the school founders are positioned in unequal relationships of power, highlighting a consideration for those who work with, or in the macro-niche of developmentourism. Further, we have argued that consideration needs to be made for a time when/if communities are no longer tourism destinations.

Developmentourism and school tours should be working to ensure that schools become sustainable in and of themselves, meaning there is no need for tourists to visit. The micro-niche of school tourism presents a difficult balancing act between the business of learning and the business of tourism. Both are valuable and serve to ameliorate poverty, but a school's core business must be the care and education of children and young people.

REFERENCES

Bandyopadhyay, R. and Patil, V. (2017) 'The white woman's burden' – the radicalized gendered politics of volunteer tourism. *Tourism Geographies*, 19(4), 644–57. doi:10.1080/14616688/2017.1298150

Baptista, J.A. (2011) The tourists of developmentourism – representations 'from below'. *Current Issues in Tourism*, 14(7), 651–67. doi:10.1080/13683500.2010.540314

Bargeman, B., Richards, G. and Govers, E. (2018) Volunteer tourism impacts in Ghana: A practice approach. *Current Issues in Tourism*, 21(13), 1486–501. doi:10.1080/13683500.2015.1137277

Chilufya, A., Hughes, E. and Scheyvens, R. (2019) Tourists and community development: Corporate social responsibility or tourist social responsibility? *Journal of Sustainable Tourism*, 27(10), 1513–29.

Chitiyo, G., Chitiyo, M., Rumano, M., Ametepee, L. K. and Chitiyo, J. (2010) Zimbabwe education system: Emerging challenges and the implications for policy and research. *Journal of Global Intelligence and Policy*, 3(3), 35–42.

Clausen, H.B. (2019) NGOs, tourism and development. In R. Sharpley and D. Harrison (eds) *A research agenda for tourism and development*. Cheltenham: Edward Elgar Publishing, 71–87.

Foucault, M. (1975/1991) *Discipline and punish: The birth of the prison* (trans. A. Sheridan). Melbourne: Penguin Books Australia Ltd.

Foucault, M. (1976/2008) *The History of sexuality: Volume 1* (Trans. R. Hurley). Melbourne: Penguin Group.

Lacey, G., Peel, V. and Weiler, B. (2012) Disseminating the voice of the other: A case study of philanthropic tourism. *Annals of Tourism Research*, 39(2), 1199–220.

Mangwaya, E., Jeko, I. and Manyumwa, C. (2012) Availability of print curriculum materials and its consequences for the quality of education in schools located on newly resettled farm areas in Zimbabwe. *Asian Social Science*, 9(1), 249–56.

Mostafanezhad, M. (2013). 'Getting in touch with your inner Angelina': Celebrity humanitarianism and the cultural politics of gendered generosity in volunteer tourism. *Third World Quarterly*, 34(3), 485–99.

Mowforth, M. and Munt, I. (2009). *Tourism and sustainability: Development globalisation and new tourism in the Third World* (3rd edn). London: Routledge.

Mutana, S., Chipfuva, T. and Muchenje, B. (2013) Is tourism in Zimbabwe developing with the poor in mind? Assessing the pro-poor involvement of tourism operators located near rural areas in Zimbabwe. *Asian Social Science*, 9(5), 154–61.

Novelli, M. (2016) *Tourism and development in Sub-Saharan Africa: Current issues and local realities*. London: Routledge.

Novelli, M. (2018) Niche Tourism: Past, present and future. In C. Cooper, S. Volo, W.C. Gartner and N. Scott (eds) *The SAGE handbook of tourism management: Applications of theories and concepts of tourism*. Thousand Oaks: SAGE Publications Ltd, 344–59.

Nyahunzvi, D.K. (2013) Come and make a real difference: Online marketing of the volunteering experience to Zimbabwe. *Tourism Management Perspectives*, 7, 83–8. doi:10.1016/j.tmp.2013.04.004

Scarth, A. and Novelli, M. (2019) Travel philanthropy and development. In Sharpley, R. and Harrison, D. (eds) *A research agenda for tourism and development*. Cheltenham: Edward Elgar Publishing, 88–109.

Snyman, S. (2019) Case study on Wilderness Safaris: Innovations consistent with CSR 2.0. In D. Lund-Durlacher, V. Dinica, D. Reiser and M.S. Fifka (eds) *Corporate sustainability and responsibility in tourism*. Springer Nature: Switzerland, 319–26.

Spenceley, A. and Meyer, D. (2012) Tourism and poverty reduction: Theory and practice in less economically developed countries. *Journal of Sustainable Tourism*, 20(3), 297–317. doi: 10.1080/09669582.2012.668909

Thompson, J. and Taheri, B. (2020) Capital deployment and exchange in volunteer tourism. *Annals of Tourism Research*, 81. doi: 10.1016/j.annals.2019.102848

UNESCO Institute for Statistics (2017) *Reducing global poverty through universal primary and secondary education.* Available at https://unesdoc.unesco.org/ark:/48223/pf0000250392

Wondirad, A., Tolkach, D. and King, B. (2020) NGOs in ecotourism: Patrons of sustainability or neo-colonial agents? Evidence from Africa. *Tourism Recreation Research*, 45(2), 144–60. doi: 10.1080/02508281.2019.1675269

ZIMSTAT (2020) *Poverty and social impacts of COVID-19: Results from the rapid PICES phone survey data.* Available at http://www.zimstat.co.zw/wp-content/uploads/publications/Income/Finance/RAPID_PICES_Wave1.pdf

30. Gay tourism and sustainable rainbow tourist destinations

Fabio Corbisiero and Salvatore Monaco

INTRODUCTION

This chapter offers a critical review of extant literature on tourism practised by gay people and demonstrates why it falls under the category of tourism niches (Novelli, 2005). We employ a sociological approach that provides insights into contemporary socio-territorial transformations and changes in gay destinations, and propose a rethink of the experiences and practices of 'rainbow travel'. This approach, centred on social sustainability, is compatible with the host of local initiatives that aim to promote social inclusion as well as the sustainable transformation of destinations to render them more accessible to gay travellers.

The chapter is grounded in two main currents of work, each with its own distinct theoretical and conceptual literature. The first explores the local socio-geographical dynamics and evolution of cultural and creative tourist districts in various global contexts, alongside correlated processes such as 'gaytrification' (Rothenberg, 1995). The second pursues dialogue and links to recent analyses of rainbow destinations. The analysis relies on a review of the literature on tourism, homosexuality and tourist destination growth. The output is an ideal model of a 'sustainable rainbow tourist destination'. An ideal model is a heuristic prototype that is useful in identifying fields of observation and intervention in order to better analyse and improve certain critical aspects of destinations.

The model proposed does not correspond to a specific place; instead, it accentuates and emphasizes some of the features of a model destination to suggest new questions for further research and to discuss how studying gay tourism informs our understanding of tourism in general.

Various synonyms for 'gay tourism' are used in the literature, such as 'homosexual tourism', 'pink tourism' and, by extension, 'LGBT(IQ+) tourism' or 'queer tourism' (Kotlíková, 2013). Nevertheless, it is worth emphasizing that no single term encompasses the variety of travel attitudes and behaviours among gay people that have existed from antiquity to the present. Existing sociological research suggests that gay people's need for travel – now freed from the outdated cliché of indulging in 'gay activities' such as the sex tourism niche – has always been significantly shaped by a number of factors.

Travel by gay people is not a recent phenomenon: people have been setting out for centuries in search of 'safe Arcadias' (Aldrich, 2004) where homosexuality is not ostracized as much as it is in their home countries. For instance, Robert Aldrich (1993), in his examination of sexually motivated travel to the Mediterranean, found that many gay men in the late nineteenth and early twentieth centuries shared a 'cultural and political creed' which he defines as the 'Mediterranean myth'. The connection between travel and sexuality was first identified by social scientists with regard to European colonialist erotic–exotic journeys. Littlewood (2001) describes such travellers as 'sexual pilgrims' and identifies gay men as a significant contingent among them. Later gay travel has been studied as part of the bourgeois practice of the 'Grand Tour', as well as the 'literary expatriation' to large bohemian cities such as Paris, Berlin or Tangier.

According to the International Gay and Lesbian Travel Association (IGLTA), gay tourism began to be recognizable as a specific tourist segment due to the development and marketing of tourism products and services, such as facilities, accommodation and amenities, specifically designed for people belonging to gender and sexual minorities. In this regard, the creation of publications targeting gay male travellers was probably the earliest recognition of this group as a market segment with specific interests and needs. The first of such examples was the 1960s gay men's travel guide, *The Damron Address Book*, which published an annual directory listing establishments frequented by and friendly towards gay men (Sosa, 2019).

Another important development granting increasing visibility to gay tourism has been broad community participation in global mobility linked, above all, to the civil rights movements and developments in LGBT liberation that took place from the 1960s onwards in major North American and European cities whose liberal climates attracted people of all sexual orientations and gender identities.

Rainbow cities such as San Francisco and New York not only became synonymous with the LGBT rights movement, they also triggered the mobility of large groups of gay travellers, causing a butterfly effect even in large European cities such as Amsterdam, London and Paris (Corbisiero, 2016). Later, beachside communities such as Provincetown or Key West in the USA, and Ibiza, the Gran Canarias and Mykonos in Europe supported the growth of gay tourism, so much so that LGBT travellers are today considered a key target market for destinations across the globe.

The question as to why gay travel has been defined as niche tourism rests on several premises. Hughes (1997) argued that vacations, especially holidays spent abroad, offer gay men the opportunity to experience homosexual cultures, practices and lifestyles that might not be readily available in their homelands. Furthermore, especially regarding Western perspectives on homosexuality, travelling abroad has frequently been understood as a personal journey of self-discovery and self-expression in new spaces: learning about the ways of others was ultimately a means to discover and understand oneself (Hughes et al., 2010).

Over time, travel has taken on different forms and meanings for gay people (Vorobjovas-Pinta, 2021). The ways in which this specific form of mobility takes place is the result of a series of factors that go beyond simple personal inclinations. In fact, while heterosexual people in contemporary society are ideally free to travel following their inclinations and passions, matters are still somewhat different for gay travellers (Stuber, 2002; Moreira and Campos, 2019) in that their reception and treatment varies from one local area to another. Too often, gay people continue to face prejudice and discrimination. Depending on the character of the tourist destination, therefore, these travellers might be more likely to conceal their sexual orientation when travelling or conversely, if in gay-friendly destinations, feel encouraged to come out (Friskopp and Silverstein, 1996). The United Nations World Travel Organization has noted that this tourism niche is closely associated with the development and spread of LGBT rights (UNWTO, 2012). Unsurprisingly, therefore, gay tourism can also be considered a political tool to promote social and economic equality.

On the basis of these considerations, it can be argued that this tourism niche significantly contributes to sustainable development as well. In fact, the recent model of sustainable development defined by the United Nations in its 2030 Agenda (2015) identifies overcoming discrimination and respecting all people's differences as one of the 17 goals of sustainable development. As stated in the World Code of Ethics for Tourism adopted by the UNWTO General Assembly in 1999 and recognized by the UN in 2001, the sustainable development of tourism is capable of guaranteeing the right to mobility and travel for all by dismantling both tangible and intangible obstacles. National and international tourism is universally accessible and sustainable if more and more people around the world can exercise the right to personal discovery and to enjoy the wealth of the planet.

The claim that the full inclusion of gay citizens in general (and their right to mobility in particular) is guaranteed throughout the globe remains questionable. We thus set off from the construction of the ideal model of a 'sustainable rainbow tourist destination' to identify specific directions for future research into the role that gay tourism can play in local development. More specifically, the sustainable rainbow tourist destination perspective offers an original, critical contribution to sociologists' efforts to understand the ongoing transformative processes that foster equal opportunities for all, allowing everyone to take part in and benefit from tourism activity based on the principles of sustainable development.

THE EVOLUTION OF HOMOSEXUAL TOURISM

The mobility of gay people has its roots in the Enlightenment era, a period in which tourism was not yet as formalized and institutionalized as it is today. In that period, the practice of taking a Grand Tour was frequent and widespread. This tour was a long journey practiced mainly by young English, French and German intellectual men and heirs to upper-class families. While its main purposes were cultural and socio-pedagogical, the Grand Tour also represented a recreational opportunity and an affirmation of participants' social status (De Seta, 1993). During this period of travelling to discover Europe, (Grand) tourists came into contact with Mediterranean culture and the vast historical-artistic heritage of classicism found in the Mediterranean area (Hersant, 1988). This experience also represented a means for aristocrats to send children or relatives they considered 'inverts' because of their homosexual orientation away from home.

With the excuse of study and education, the relatives of young gay men were able to send them out of the home country in the hope that the trip would somehow make them 'come to their senses' (Fagiani, 2010). At the same time, however, many young gay men of the time also experienced the Grand Tour with the hidden intention of being able to live their identities more freely away from home (Clift and Wilkins, 1995). These travellers stayed mainly in Italy and Greece, as these, more than other Mediterranean countries, were able to offer young gay men spaces for freedom and self-realization. Unlike many Northern European countries of the period, most Italian states lacked anti-homosexual legislation or had laws which were not enforced (Beccalossi, 2015).

As for the present, since the 1960s gay male travellers have become more visible on the social scene in the Western world, tenaciously demanding recognition of their identity and rights at the global level. From the first and most potent protest staged to secure full citizenship, following the 1969 raid on the Stonewall Inn on Christopher Street in New York, LGBT people have progressively protested against a heteronormative world, making claims for non-discrimination and inclusive spaces, including through their mobility and travel. Following those events, North America – and subsequently many democratic countries around the world – committed to assuring gay citizens equality. This has also led to increasing attention being paid to the specific issues of gay travellers.

An important milestone for the gay community was the depathologization of their identity in the early 1970s, when the American Psychiatric Association removed homosexuality from its list of mental disorders. Much later, in 1990, the World Health Organization also eliminated homosexuality as a mental illness from the *International Classification of Diseases* (Drescher, 2015). Since then, there has been a progressive trend toward ever-wider legal and political opportunities for gender and sexual minorities with the rise of positive social attitudes regarding equal rights for gay people, resulting in socioeconomic benefits in a range of sectors including tourism (e.g., Guaracino and Salvato, 2017). This trend has involved the birth of more effectively managed 'gay-sensitive' tourist activities. For instance, the 1983 founding of the IGLTA served to support the development of gay tourism and highlight its social and economic importance. Today, the IGLTA is the most important organization in the sector of gay tourism and has numerous affiliates in over 70 countries around the world.

However, the field of tourism research still lacks the strong empirical foundation that would be needed to implement more equal policies in the field of gay tourism (Badgett and Crehan, 2017). In fact, the specific formulation of both human and civil rights tends to differ in each destination, just as practices of citizenship and the application of the law vary substantially according to specific historical and social circumstances.

THEORETICAL UNDERPINNINGS

As mentioned above, gay tourism currently represents one of the segments increasingly served by tour operators, travel agencies, cruise lines and airlines around the world. This kind of niche tourism has been growing rapidly and favoured destinations for the people belonging to gender and sexual minorities have emerged, especially in Western European countries and North America (e.g., Hughes, 2006; Lück, 2005; Vorobjovas-Pinta and Hardy, 2014). Recently coined terms such as 'gaycation' (*Collins English Dictionary*, 2014), referring to a version of a vacation that includes a pronounced aspect of gay culture and branding in either the journey or the destination, and DINKs, 'dual income, no kids' (e.g., van Gils and Kraaykamp, 2008) are sociological indicators of this growing segment.

In particular, researchers have focused on studying tourist destinations and other locally rooted tourist consumption–production complexes (e.g., Scott, 2000; Zukin, 1995; Costa and Lopes, 2013), but these phenomena have also come under critique: for instance, the alleged economic benefits of 'gay-friendliness' have given rise to official pink tourism marketing strategies and new segments of (homo)capitalism with mostly white gay men being 'colonized' by the market (e.g., Nast, 2002). Tourism bolsters the homosexual lobby and, embedded in cultural proximity, such travel may even be on its way to displacing heteronormative capitalist patriarchies (e.g., Knopp, 1992).

Certain niche segments such as adventure and extreme, slow- and low-impact or literary tourism have received sufficient research attention, but due to its complexity gay tourism still remains a neglected area of scholarly exploration (e.g., Blichfeldt et al., 2013; Melián-González et al., 2011; Monterrubio, 2018). A glance at existing empirical research on gay people as tourists reveals that a considerable body of literature was published in the 1990s and early 2000s concentrating on issues such as the economic power of gay travellers and their supposed 'pink dollar' spending capacity (e.g., Holcomb and Luongo, 1996), as well as their preferred destinations and motivations for travelling (e.g., Kinnaird et al., 1994; Pritchard et al., 2000; Puar, 2002).

As Hughes (2002) claims, gay travellers carefully evaluate the normative and cultural conditions of a potential destination in relation to homosexuality before organizing a trip, revealing that members of this community give little or no consideration to the idea of visiting areas such as Jamaica, China or countries in Africa or the Middle East. This data aligns with a more recent analysis (CMI, 2019) finding that a slender percentage of members of the gay community (11%) look to countries with anti-homosexual laws (such as Russia, Jamaica or Kenya) as potential destinations. Other themes of social scientific research on gay tourism are sexuality and holiday choices (e.g., Blichfeldt et al., 2011; Casey, 2009), such as the configuration of homosexual leisure spaces (Pritchard et al., 2000). In addition, some scholars have analysed the holiday profiles of older gay men (e.g., Hughes and Deutsch, 2010) and the destinations' competitiveness in the gay tourism segment (e.g., Melián-González et al., 2011), aided by the proliferation of LGBTIQ+ tourism guides.

Since 2013, the issue of destinations for the LGBT community has also been the focus of the Spartacus Gay Travel Index (Spartacus, 2019), which classifies the degree of inclusivity of sexual and gender minorities by destination. According to LonelyPlanet.com (2022), the top ten LGBTIQ+ friendly places in the world are New York (USA), Barcelona (Spain), Auckland, (New Zealand), Puerto Vallarta (Mexico), Sydney (Australia), Amsterdam (the Netherlands), London (England), Palm Springs (California), Toronto (Canada) and Tel Aviv (Israel). While the ongoing policies implemented in these destinations may garner positive attitudes among inbound tourists (e.g., Kama et al., 2019), some scholars have a critical view of the gay-friendliness of certain destinations presented as 'heavens to be colonized' (e.g., Alexander, 2005).

RESEARCH METHODS

Although the demographic, motivational, behavioural and identity-bound features of gay travel must not be taken for granted, as Vorobjovas-Pinta and Hardy (2016) correctly observe, literature on gay tourism requires a revived empirical assessment of the phenomenon and its ongoing changes. In view of this assumption, we conducted an analysis of the most recent literature on tourism and homosexuality. In fact, a great deal of the research on this issue was conducted at a time when gay people around the world did not enjoy the same visibility they do today. The social, cultural and regulatory contexts of many countries was different. Furthermore, until the early 2010s, the scientific literature on the subject proposed a fairly standardized view of the gay travel market (Waitt and Markwell, 2014).

From 2010 onwards, scientific research has increasingly recognized (homo)sexuality as a salient category of difference in travellers' behaviour, and there has been increasing interest in researching LGBT people's lives (Vorobjovas-Pinta, 2021). When paying attention to gay travellers' lives, lifestyles, markets, holiday destinations and scenes, researchers have often focused on either general aspects or on particular communities (e.g., Valentine and Skelton, 2003; Corbisiero, 2016; Sonders and Beach, 2016; Bartoletti and Giannini, 2019). A literature review can thus represent a valuable tool for generalizing and defining elements that might potentially grant local areas the status of a 'sustainable rainbow tourist destination' in the contemporary world.

In particular, considering the tourist needs of gay travellers as reported in the scientific literature of the last 10 years, we outline a multi-dimensional, good-practice model of a rainbow destination that takes into account various factors. The papers analysed in this review were identified via the two main indexing platforms (Web of Science and ProQuest). Once the textual material was collected by means of the data mining software NVivo, we examined the literature points to identify commonalities, recurring themes and main topics. As a result of our analysis, we formulated an ideal–typical heuristic territorial prototype, that is, a conceptual model useful for explaining the characteristics an area should possess to be considered inclusive of its gay citizens (and therefore welcoming to gay tourists). The characteristics the ideal area must possess have been identified through analogical reasoning. In other words, similar elements have been extracted from the scientific papers considered in the review and brought together. Some aspects have thus been selected and others stressed to create an ideal type characterized by more unitary and coherent connections than those found in empirical reality.

FINDINGS

Our construction of the heuristic territorial model of a 'sustainable rainbow tourist destination' has led to the formulation of an ideal prototype comprising six main elements (Figure 30.1), as detailed below. The elements are all independent from one another but closely interconnected. They are not presented in order of importance, although the earlier ones logically precede those that follow.

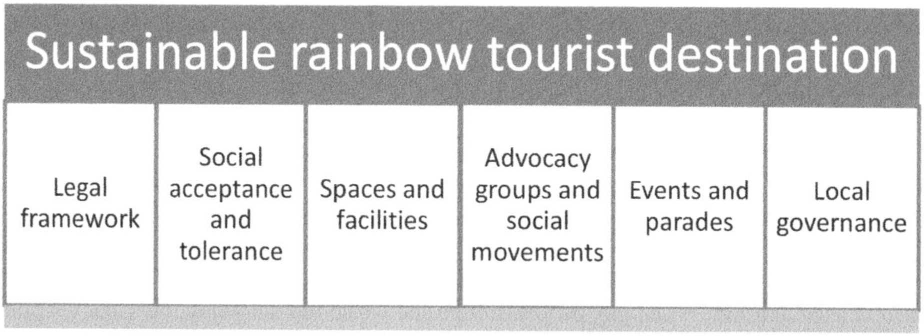

Sustainable rainbow tourist destination					
Legal framework	Social acceptance and tolerance	Spaces and facilities	Advocacy groups and social movements	Events and parades	Local governance

Source: Authors.

Figure 30.1   *Constitutive elements of the ideal type of 'sustainable rainbow tourist destination'*

As indicated above, support for homosexuality has gradually increased in recent decades, mainly in Western societies (Alderson, 2016). Due to major changes in laws, norms and social rules surrounding the issue of sexual and/or gender minority belonging, homosexuality has become more acceptable in society. As is well known, however, in many areas of the world homosexuality is still not fully accepted and, in some cases, even legally condemned. From this analytical angle, it is clear that for many gay people living in hostile areas or places where the legal framework offers them no protection, mobility represents a necessity to escape from repression rather than a choice (e.g., Monaco, 2019c). In many cases, staying at home implies having to hide their sexual orientation, constantly living with the fear of being discovered, accused, or even condemned.

On the basis of these considerations, it is evident that the social and political conditions of local areas represent important elements to be taken into consideration by gay travellers from all over the world. The choice to engage in tourism is therefore limited and conditioned by the geography of inclusiveness. Consequently, one of the first and more important elements characterizing a destination as being inclusive of gay people is its regulatory framework and the level of protection and equality it grants sexual and gender minorities.

It is not sufficient that homosexuality is not punished, therefore; it is also necessary that homophobic acts be condemned by the law. Furthermore, in many countries gay citizens do not fully enjoy the same rights guaranteed to other citizens: unions between same-sex partners are not recognized everywhere, and many countries have set up ad hoc legal institutions (such as civil unions) that limit the rights of same-sex couples (Monaco and Nothdurfter, 2021). Ideally, an open and welcoming territory is a place where all citizens enjoy the same rights and duties, regardless of sexual orientation. A destination where gay residents and tourists can fully experience their citizenship status is a place where they can marry, adopt and access medically assisted reproductive techniques, making rainbow parenting an increasingly common and widespread phenomenon. It is no coincidence that opportunities such as the right to marry, go on a honeymoon, and take advantage of gestational surrogacy or assisted fertilization have already increased the number of gay travellers around the world (Monaco, 2022).

A second element that can characterize a 'sustainable rainbow tourist destination' is the social and cultural context in relation to gender and sexual minorities. Legal protection alone cannot be considered sufficient. A place can be defined as truly inclusive if its inhabitants share a common culture of respect for and appreciation of differences (Jacobs, 1961). On the empirical level, this can be translated, for example, as the absence of homophobic incidents but also awareness-raising and educational initiatives in learning contexts, among others. As indicated in a recent US report (Pew Research Center, 2020), public opinion on the acceptance of homosexuality in society remains sharply divided by country, region and economic development (see Figure 30.2).

It is clear that the prevalent sexual orientation in the context of everyday life is heterosexuality. Consequently, most public and private spaces tend to be heteronormative (Haslop et al., 1998; Provencher, 2007; Scandurra et al., 2021). Over the course of the twentieth century, LGBT people have developed local communities in suburban or rural settings or in ghettos and/or neighbourhoods in (large) cities. These spaces provide their residents with more liveable conditions in larger urban physical settings in which to create and share culture, politics, rituals, sexualities and economies (Corbisiero, 2015). Practices and sites of socialization are a core element of all rainbow spaces and take many forms, from coffee shops to bookstores and other places where homosexual people can gather and express themselves.

Through the use of spaces to express identities and spend time with each other, the community has also generated further spaces such as tourist destinations. Especially in the context of Western gay urban cultures, LGBT neighbourhoods might eventually become zones of lifestyle consumption and tourist attractions for non-homosexuals as well, diluting and eroding

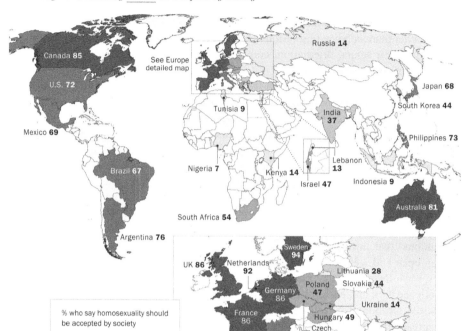

% who say homosexuality should be accepted by society

Source: Spring 2019 Global Attitudes Survey (Pew Research Center, 2020).

Figure 30.2   The global divide in acceptance of homosexuality

gay spaces and identities (Herrera and Scott, 2005; Ruting, 2008; Corbisiero and Monaco, 2017; Monaco, 2019b).

According to Hindle (1994), these spaces represent a concrete and tangible manifestation of the LGBT community in a given city and they aid their users in resisting and escaping from heterosexual oppression. In view of this point, this review underlines that another appealing factor for gay travellers in planning tourist experiences is the existence of specifically dedicated urban spaces, facilities or services in which they can socialize with other members of the community and minimize the risk of falling victim to incidents involving homophobia or prejudice (Figure 30.3).

Gay tourism is certainly one of the main opportunities through which gay people can express their identity, both in democratic parts of the world and in areas where homosexuality is not entirely accepted (Herrera and Scott, 2005; Puar, 2002). Through gay tourism in various countries around the world, social inclusion could be improved and discrimination against sexual minorities eliminated. Sustainable rainbow tourist destinations are places in which the array of tourist options is embedded in a broader social context characterized by inclusivity (Hartal, 2020). The existence of gay clubs or rainbow initiatives is not enough if these factors

Source: Photo by the authors.

Figure 30.3   *New York City: Rainbow Empire State Building*

are not complemented by substantive inclusion policies. Our heuristic territorial model thus also includes advocacy groups and social movements which, in addition to expanding the range of services for LGBT people, also endorse the community in its struggle for social rights (Corbisiero and Monaco, 2020).

Sustainable rainbow tourist destinations, as we are imagining them, are places of social inclusion and, more generally, spaces for promoting civil rights in terms of the recognition and valorization of sexual differences due to locally rooted policies and practices designed to foster integration. Other useful initiatives for attracting gay tourists into the area can include public events and demonstrations. There are now hundreds of film festivals, parades, gay pride weeks and other homosexually themed cultural and artistic events organized throughout the year, both by civic associations and by the public administrations most attentive and sensitive to this issue (see Figure 30.4). Moreover, it is important to stress that grassroots efforts must also be supported at the institutional level. In other words, the good practice model of rainbow tourist destination requires the work of associations, humanitarian organizations, and national and local governments cooperating to guarantee civil rights for all in the framework of virtuous local governance.

CONCLUSION AND IMPLICATIONS

Although it is argued that the gay travel market should not exist at all and sexual orientation should not condition tourist choices (e.g., Fugate, 1993), we recognize gay tourism as an important niche in the travel sector. Furthermore, we argue that there is a clear relationship between a country's progressive policies towards people belonging to gender and sexual minorities and its tourism sector, and that such progressive policies generate greater social benefits as a result of the associated brand image of tolerance, inclusiveness and diversity. Areas capable of presenting themselves as rainbow destinations stand out from others, projecting an image of the entire destination as an inclusive location that welcomes differences.

Figure 30.4   *Napoli gay pride 2017*

The benefits that these localities manage to obtain are not only economic, but also social and cultural.

Indeed, as claimed by Peñaloza (2000), LGBT marketing constitutes an important mediating factor in the encounter between mainstream society and the gay community; however, the most important point is that the influence of rainbow tourism can modify the local structure of the destination, contributing to guaranteeing greater societal participation with equal opportunities for gay people. Thanks in part to tourism options specifically tailored to the homosexual market, decreasing intolerance in relation to homosexuality and improved social inclusion are evident. The evolution of gay tourism around the world is thus closely tied to the development and spread of LGBT rights. In other words, the growth of gay tourism itself is closely connected with societal and political advancements in many areas of the globe.

In Europe, as in other parts of the democratic Western world, there has been a gradual transition in the last few decades from low levels of inclusiveness to greater acceptance and integration of sexual and gender minorities (Corbisiero and Monaco, 2021). The result is that the policy and administrative treatment of LGBT issues is now situated within a gender equality and social equity discourses and dealt with through a rights-based approach in which every person, regardless of sexual orientation and gender identity, has the right to: recognition, legal protection from discrimination, marriage and adoption, healthcare and sexual health services, mobility, tourism and so on. Moreover, the presence of a LGBTIQ+ community in a given local area is taken as a sign of cultural openness, indicating a place where 'different' people and ideas can more easily find space to coexist side by side (Florida, 2002).

On the basis of this sociological analysis, we argue that gay tourism has managed to break free from the confines of exclusively gay spaces to intersect with global tourism. However, we also know that the 'geography of homosexualities' (Browne et al., 2007) remains limited even today and this landscape will have trouble growing if the regulatory frameworks and social and cultural contexts of many countries do not change. It is therefore necessary to hope that the situation of gay people around the world continues to improve and that the countries most inclusive of and progressive in their treatment of sexual minorities will succeed in establishing themselves as models to follow.

Faced with the economic crisis in the wake of the health pandemic of 2020, a welcoming stance towards the gay niche that is not merely symbolic but also substantive, could represent a possible driver for economic recovery in an increasingly global and competitive market. In this sense, gay tourism, in a form comprising all the elements identified in our model, could be considered an opportunity for promoting and bolstering the economic and social development of local areas. The transversal nature of the tourism sector, with its power to enhance production and social change, can also contribute to fostering such development.

The construction of our ideal model of 'sustainable rainbow tourist destination' represents a useful tool to guide and support many countries in this change. More specifically, the fact that this tool can be used to conduct comparisons between an ideal prototype and specific concrete cases could prove useful in encouraging the transformation of local areas and regions, expanding freedom for people of all identities and introducing new practices. On the basis of such a comparison, local political decision-makers can consider and understand how closely their own jurisdiction adheres to the ideal of a rainbow tourist destination or how much it would need to change.

Looking ahead, we conclude that future studies on this topic could apply the proposed heuristic model as a starting point, both to design new and more up-to-date demographic and motivational research on tourism as practised by gay people, and to analyse new data and collected information in a more critical and complete way. In addition, our model indicates directions for future empirical research and calls for a solid theoretical foundation allowing researchers to demonstrate, understand and explain how tourism contributes to social change in specific locations. We have found that the experiences and identities of gay people in non-Western tourism remain an under-studied area of literature (López and Van Broeck, 2010; Visser, 2014; Vorobjovas-Pinta, 2016; Monterrubio, 2018), and the influence of virtual spaces on LGBT people requires investigation (Vorobjovas-Pinta and Hardy; 2016; Monaco, 2019a). These arenas could represent a new direction for social research with an eye to further enriching the understanding of tourism practised by gay people on a global scale.

REFERENCES

Alderson, D. (2016) *Sex, Needs and Queer Culture: From Liberation to the Post-gay*. London: ZED books.

Aldrich, R. (1993) *The Seduction of Mediterranean: Writing, Art and Homosexual Fantasy*. London: Routledge.

Aldrich, R. (2004) Homosexuality and the city: An historical overview. *Urban Studies*, 41, 1719–37.

Alexander, M.J. (2005) *Pedagogies of Crossing*. Durham: Duke University Press.

Badgett, M.V.L. and Crehan, P. (2017) Developing actionable research priorities for LGBTI inclusion. *Journal of Research in Gender Studies*, 7(1), 218–47.

Bartoletti, R. and Giannini, L. (2019) Perché devo dire qual è il mio orientamento sessuale se voglio farmi semplicemente una vacanza? *Fuori Luogo. Rivista di Sociologia del Territorio, Turismo, Tecnologia*, 5(1), 8–18.

Beccalossi C. (2015) *Italian sexualities uncovered, 1789–1914. Genders and sexualities in history.* London: Palgrave Macmillan.

Blichfeldt, B. et al. (2011) It really depends on whether you are in a relationship: A study of gay destinations from a tourist perspective. *Tourism Today*, 3, 7–26.

Blichfeldt, B., Chor, J. and Ballegaard, M.N. (2013) Zoos, sanctuaries and turfs: Enactments and uses of gay spaces during the holidays. *International Journal of Tourism Research*, 15(5), 473–83.

Browne, K. et al. (eds) (2007) *Geographies of Sexualities: Theory, Practices and Politics.* Burlington: Ashgate.

Casey, M. (2009) Tourist gay(ze) or transnational sex: Australian gay men's holiday desires. *Leisure Studies*, 28(2), 157–73.

Clift, S. and Wilkins, J. (1995) Travel, sexual behaviour and gay men. In P. Aggleton, P. Davies and G. Hart (eds) *AIDS: Safety, Sexuality and Risk.* London: Taylor & Francis.

CMI (2019) *CMI's 24st Annual Survey on LGBT Tourism and Hospitality – US Overview Report.* Available at: https://communitymarketinginc.com/documents/temp/CMI_24th-LGBTQ-Travel-Study -Report2019.pdf (accessed 17 August 2020).

Collins English Dictionary (2014) Gaycation. In *Collins English Dictionary – Complete and Unabridged, 12th Edition 2014.* London: HarperCollins Publishers.

Corbisiero, F. (ed.) (2015) *Comunità omosessuali. Le scienze sociali sulla popolazione LGBT.* Milan: Franco Angeli.

Corbisiero, F. (2016) *Sociologia del turismo LGBT.* Milan: Franco Angeli.

Corbisiero, F. and Monaco, S. (2017) *Città arcobaleno. Una mappa della vita omosessuale in Italia.* Rome: Donzelli.

Corbisiero, F. and Monaco, S. (2020) The right to a rainbow city: The Italian homosexual social movements. *Society Register*, 4(4), 69–86.

Corbisiero, F. and Monaco, S. (2021) *Omosessuali Contemporanei. Identità, Culture, Spazi LGBT+.* Milan: Franco Angeli.

Costa, P. and Lopes, R. (2013) Urban design, public space and creative milieus: An international comparative approach to informal dynamics in cultural districts. *Cidades, Comunidades e Territórios*, 26, 40–66.

De Seta, C. (1993) *L'Italia del Grand Tour: da Montaigne a Goethe.* Naples: Electra.

Drescher, J. (2015) Out of DSM: Depathologizing homosexuality. *Behavioral Sciences*, 5(4), 565–75.

Fagiani, M.L. (2010) Turismo LGBT. In E. Marra and E. Ruspini (eds) *Altri turismi – Viaggi, esperienze, emozioni.* Milan: Franco Angeli, 85–100.

Florida, R. (2002) *The rise of the creative class: And how it's transforming work, leisure, community and everyday life.* New York: Basic Books.

Friskopp, A. and Silverstein, S. (1996) *Straight jobs gay lives.* New York: Simon & Schuster.

Fugate, D. (1993) Evaluating the US male homosexual and lesbian population as a viable target market segment. *Journal of Consumer Marketing*, 10(4), 46–57.

Guaracino, J. and Salvato, E. (2017) *Handbook of LGBT tourism and hospitality: A guide for business practice.* New York: Columbia University Press.

Hartal, G. (2020) Touring and obscuring: How sensual, embodied and haptic gay touristic practices construct the geopolitics of pinkwashing. *Social & Cultural Geography*, 1–19.

Haslop, C. et al. (1998) The gay lifestyle-spaces for a subculture of consumption. *Marketing Intelligence & Planning*, 16(5), 318–26.

Herrera, S.L. and Scott, D. (2005) 'We gotta get out of this place!' Leisure travel among gay men living in a small city. *Tourism Review International*, 8(3), 249–62.

Hersant, Y. (1988) *Italies. Anthologies des voyageurs français au XVIII et XIX siècles.* Paris: Robert Laffont.

Hindle, P. (1994) Gay communities and gay space in the city. In S. Whittle (ed.) *The margins of the city: Gay men's urban lives.* Aldershot: Arena.

Holcomb, B. and Luongo, M. (1996) Gay tourism in the United States. *Annals of Tourism Research*, 23(3), 695–726.

Hughes H. (1997) Holidays and homosexual identity. *Tourism Management*, 18(1), 3–7.

Hughes, H. (2002) Gay men's holiday destination choice: A case of risk and avoidance. *International Journal of Travel Research*, 4, 299–312.

Hughes, H. (2006) *Pink tourism: Holidays of gay men and lesbians*. Oxford: Cabi.

Hughes, H. and Deutsch, R. (2010) Holidays of older gay men: Age or sexual orientation as decisive factors? *Tourism Management*, 31, 454–63.

Hughes, H., Monterrubio, C. and Miller, A. (2010) Gay tourists and host community attitudes. *International Journal of Tourism Research*, 12(6), 774–86.

Jacobs, J. (1961) *The death and life of great American cities*. New York: Vintage Books.

Kama, A. et al. (2019) The benefits of an LGBT-inclusive tourist destination. *Journal of Destination Marketing and Management*, 14, 10–16.

Kinnaird, V. et al. (1994) *Tourism: A gender analysis*. Chichester: John Wiley & Sons Ltd.

Knopp, L. (1992) Sexuality and the spatial dynamics of capitalism. *Environment and Planning D: Society and Space*, 10(6), 651–69.

Kotlíková, H. (2013) *Nové trendy v nabídce cestovního ruchu*. Prague: Grada.

Littlewood, I. (2001) *Sultry climates: Travel and sex since the grand tour*. London: John Murray.

Lonely Planet (2022) The 12 Most LGBTIQ+ Friendly Places On Earth: Where to Go for Pride 2022. Available at: https://www.lonelyplanet.com/articles/most-gay-friendly-countries (accessed 15 August 2020).

López, Á. and Van Broeck, A. (2010) Sexual encounters between men in a tourist environment: A comparative study in seven localities in Mexico. In N. Carr and Y. Poria (eds) *Sex and The Sexual during People's Leisure and Tourism Experiences*. Newcastle: Cambridge Scholars Publishing, 119–42.

Lück, M. (2005) *Destination choice and travel behaviour of gay men*. Brock: Brock University Press.

Melián-González, A., Moreno-Gil, S. and Araña, J.E. (2011) Gay tourism in a sun and beach destination. *Tourism Management*, 32(5), 1027–37.

Monaco, S. (2019a) *Sociologia del turismo accessibile. Il diritto alla mobilità e alla libertà di viaggio*. Varrazze: PM Editore.

Monaco, S. (2019b) Quartieri gay. In G. Nuvolati (ed.) *Enciclopedia Sociologica del Luoghi*. Milano: Ledizioni.

Monaco, S. (2019c) Mixed methods e e-research: Frontiere possibili per lo studio delle hidden population. *Sociologia Italiana*, 14, 97–108.

Monaco, S. (2022) Italian same-sex parenting in times of COVID-19: Constructing parenthood on insecure grounds. *Family Relations*, 71(2), 463–74.

Monaco, S. and Nothdurfter, U. (2021) Discovered, made visible, constructed, and left out: LGBT+ parenting in the Italian sociological debate. *Journal of Family Studies*, 1, 1–18.

Monterrubio, C. (2018) Tourism and male homosexual identities: Directions for sociocultural research. *Tourism Review*.

Moreira, M. and Campos, L. (2019) The ritual of ideological interpellation in LGBT Tourism and the impossibility of the desire that moves. *Brazilira magazine of Pesquisa em Turismo*, 13(2), 54–68.

Nast, H.J. (2002) Queer patriarchies, queer racism, international. *Antipode*, 35(5), 874–909.

Novelli, M. (2005) *Niche tourism: Contemporary issues, trends and cases*, Oxford: Butterworth-Heinemann Ltd.

Peñaloza, L. (2000) The commodification of the American West: Marketers' production of cultural meanings at the trade show. *Journal of Marketing*, 64(10), 82–109.

Pew Research Center (2020) *Spring 2019 global attitudes survey*. Washington: Pew Research Center.

Pritchard, A. et al. (2000) Sexuality and holiday choices: Conversations with gay and lesbian tourists. *Leisure Studies*, 19(4), 267–82.

Provencher, D. (2007) Queer French: Globalization, language, and sexual citizenship in France. *Theology & Sexuality*, 15(3), 352–3.

Puar, J.K. (2002) Circuits of queer mobility: Tourism, travel and globalization. *GLQ, A Journal of Lesbian and Gay Studies*, 8(1–2), 101–37.

Rothenberg, T. (1995) And she told two friends: Lesbian creating urban social space. In D. Bell and G. Valentine (eds) *Mapping desire: Geographies of sexualities*. London: Routledge, 165–81.

Ruting, B. (2008) Economic transformations of gay urban spaces: Revisiting Collins' evolutionary gay district model. *Australian Geographer*, 39(3), 259–69.

Scandurra, C., Monaco, S., Dolce, P. and Nothdurfter, U. (2021) Heteronormativity in Italy: psychometric characteristics of the Italian version of the heteronormative attitudes and beliefs scale. *Sexuality Research and Social Policy*, 18, 637–52.

Scott, A.J. (2000) *The cultural economy of cities*. London: Sage.

Sonders and Beach (2016) *Turismo LGBT report*. Milan: Sonders and Beach Italy.

Sosa, K. (2019) The Damron Address Book, a Green Book for gays, kept a generation of men in the know. *Los Angeles Magazine*, 6, 25.

Spartacus (2019) *Spartacus international gay guide*. Berlin: GayGuide UG.

Stuber, M. (2002) Tourism marketing aimed at gay men and lesbians: A business perspective. In S. Clift, M. Luongo and C. Callister (eds) *Gay tourism: Culture, identity and sex*. New York: Continuum, 88–124.

UN (2015) *UN Resolution 70/1: The 2030 agenda*. New York: United Nations General Assembly.

UNWTO (2012) *Global report on LGBT tourism*. Madrid: UN World Travel Organization.

Valentine, G. and Skelton, T. (2003) Finding oneself, losing oneself: The lesbian and gay scene as a paradoxical space. *International Journal of Urban and Regional Research*, 27(4), 849–66.

van Gils, W. and Kraaykamp, G. (2008) The emergence of dual-earner couples. A longitudinal study of the Netherlands. *International Sociology*, 23, 345–66.

Visser, G. (2014) Urban tourism and the de-gaying of Cape Town's De Waterkant. *Urban Forum*, 25(4), 469–82.

Vorobjovas-Pinta, O. (ed.) (2021) *Gay tourism: New perspectives*. Bristol: Channel View Publications.

Vorobjovas-Pinta, O. and Hardy, A. (2014) Rethinking gay tourism: A review of literature. In P.M. Chien (ed.) *CAUTHE 2014: Tourism and hospitality in the contemporary world: Trends, changes and complexity*, Brisbane: The University of Queensland, 635–44.

Vorobjovas-Pinta, O. and Hardy, A. (2016) The evolution of gay travel research. *International Journal of Tourism Research*, 18(4), 409–16.

Waitt, G. and Markwell, K. (2014) *Gay tourism: Culture and context*. New York: Routledge.

Zukin, S. (1995) *The cultures of cities*. Cambridge: Blackwell.

31. The 'albergo diffuso' and tourism revitalization in Southern Italy

Dionisia Russo Krauss

INTRODUCTION

There are a few terms used in the Italian tourism sector that have been around for a number of years now that refer to new forms of tourist accommodation. First and foremost is '*albergo diffuso*', meaning 'scattered hotel'. An albergo diffuso is a kind of horizontal hotel in a historic centre, where the rooms and services are located in different buildings a few hundred metres apart. But there is also the '*paese-albergo*' (hotel–village) and the 'residence diffuso' (scattered residence). The first is a project formulated to enhance a currently inhabited village by offering a network of accommodation facilities, reception services and common spaces for tourists, and having a central booking system, even in the absence of a centralized management system. The second is a central booking system for accommodation in certain houses within a potentially widespread area, but does not include any hotel services (just basic assistance and reception) or centralized management of services (Dall'Ara, 2010).

Albergo diffuso and paese-albergo represent new approaches to tourist accommodation, the aim of which is to reclaim and promote the cultural heritage of smaller towns that can be considered marginal compared to areas which attract major domestic and international tourist flows, because they are not situated on the main communications routes that dictate most tourist itineraries, or because their local histories have a faint echo and are less well known (Mazzetti, 2005). They aim to do so without disfiguring the landscape and in fact create new development opportunities in the areas affected (Russo Krauss, 2007a, 2007b). They are special forms of niche hospitality on offer throughout Italy, representing a real opportunity to rescue the abandoned housing stock, reduce the depopulation of inner regions, and revive the economies of small villages on the Italian peninsula that have a rich history and culture and can boast traditional food and wine specialities, providing them with new opportunities for employment and income (Dall'Ara and Esposto, 2005).

These types of accommodation, which have developed over time, have provided an attractive and sound alternative for a new generation of tourist resistant to the concept of package holidays and eager to immerse themselves in the 'real' Italy, find out more about its history and culture, and discover unspoilt places with authentic values and traditions (Novelli, 2005). The various experiences developed so far have confirmed that, in addition to meeting the specific market requirements, the potential to develop a form of scattered hospitality that respects the local setting also perfectly embodies the aspiration towards a sustainable tourism model based on local resources and specialities. And while regional policies up until a few years ago were still inclined to support the construction of new hotels, tourist villages and 'classic' apartment complexes – in spite of the enormous amount of space they take up and the damage done to the countryside and the landscape itself – the idea of scattered hospitality now seems to have acquired an increasingly powerful presence.

Looking at the initiatives currently in place and the results achieved in Italy so far, scattered hospitality clearly has a number of benefits. It can contribute to the recovery and enhancement of real estate assets of historic centres that are often in an advanced state of disrepair, but without extending the built-up areas to provide accommodation that an increase in tourism often involves (Pollice, 2016). And where it is part of a wider regional regeneration project with the active involvement of local communities, this type of niche accommodation has also proved it can lead to the development of sustainable tourism and is particularly effective in small towns with a dwindling population but good potential to attract visitors.

Rightly defined as a proposition for territorial redevelopment to support and participate in socioeconomic recovery programmes, as well as a business opportunity that is cohesive with the local cultural, environmental and urban context (Cerutti, 2014), the albergo diffuso – which will be the specific theme of this chapter – is therefore an accommodation option that succeeds in combining tradition with innovation (Presenza et al., 2019). Redeveloping an area and its heritage using a model of this kind can combine respect for its historic, cultural and social characteristics with other aspects – economic aspects in particular – connected with business enterprise, the profits of organizations operating in the area and boosting the local economy. In this light, the enhancement of a village is the result of a dialectical process between the territory (culture, history, traditions), businesses (hotels, local authorities and service providers) and tourists, which generates cooperative inter-system relationships between operators (Silvestrelli, 2011).

The aim of this chapter – which is part of a wider research project on human settlements, seismic risk, urban sprawl and socioeconomic revitalization of the inner Campania region in Italy – is to deal with this specific segment of niche hospitality, with an overview of its history and particular characteristics, and a closer look at the first experiments in an area such as Irpinia (i.e., the province of Avellino), which despite its unique cultural and geographical features, abundance of natural and historical interest and good supply of local foods and wines, is still marginal in terms of tourist attractiveness.

The study carried out, which builds on previous studies into scattered hospitality and sustainable development in smaller towns (Russo Krauss, 2004, 2007a, 2007b), was structured in two interrelated stages. One was an analysis of the existing literature on the topic, expanded in recent years by contributions from both geographic and economic–business approaches, focusing mainly on the analysis of case studies or examining particular aspects of the phenomenon (see, among others, Pollice, 2016; Montebelli, 2018; Cucari et al., 2019; Presenza et al., 2019). The other is a direct observation, in the field, in the chosen area (i.e., the area identified as particularly significant within the wider research programme) by visiting villages with existing scattered hospitality projects and establishing contact with both the managers of the structures involved and local authority representatives.

SCATTERED HOSPITALITY AS A SUSTAINABLE STRATEGY TO REVIVE TOURISM

The idea of scattered hospitality, and albergo diffuso in particular, was first spoken of in the post-earthquake reconstruction period in Carnia, Friuli, in the 1980s, when it was speculated that a few deserted villages could be used for tourism purposes, and then in 1989 in the small village of San Leo in the Montefeltro district of Rimini, where the local council developed a tourism project making specific reference to it. The project ran aground when it encountered problems identifying enough homeowners who were interested in the idea, but was later used as the starting point for a tourism development plan by a Mountain Community in the Nuoro area of Sardinia.

It was during the development process for the San Leo project, however, that the basic requirements for the new type of tourist accommodation were identified. The first requirement was a village with an interesting cultural context and an original setting, having both a stock of valuable houses and unoccupied buildings that could be restructured for tourism purposes. The necessity for a host community with a strong sense of identity and a spirit of hospitality was also emphasized (a small village able to facilitate interpersonal relationships being more suitable). The provision of basic services was also considered essential, as were local initiatives aimed at protecting and enhancing the area, and finally, the interest of a hotel operator to experiment with forms of management consistent with the project was required (Dall'Ara, 2002).

Essentially, an albergo diffuso is created by establishing a network of houses in close proximity to each other which became the rooms of a facility offering all the services of a hotel (assistance, catering, common areas for guests); not just a collection of houses but a truly original guest accommodation facility. For rooms it uses houses – prestigious or traditional-style houses within an area of historical and cultural interest, renovated and furnished in such a way as to combine the convenience of services with the originality of the scheme – with one of them serving as the reception. It therefore constitutes a 'horizontal' hotel located in a historic centre with a 'living' host community, which not only provides rooms but offers visitors the chance to immerse themselves in a certain lifestyle, live among the residents and be part of a real neighbourhood for a few days.

So this was how – encouraged by the American experience (these were the boom years of the bed and breakfast-style inn) and bolstered by the Portuguese *pousadas*, the Spanish *paradores* and the French *gîtes ruraux* – hotel–villages and alberghi diffusi popped up practically all over Italy. The number of tourists who prefer facilities of this kind has increased and – demonstrating the leading role Italy has taken in creating an innovative, sustainable and flexible type of accommodation – albergo diffuso has also started to be talked of abroad, using the same Italian expression and recognizing the Italian model as a benchmark that can be replicated in other countries (Romolini et al., 2017).

Today, more than 20 years after the first legislation was passed on the matter (1998 in Sardinia), this form of hospitality has garnered a considerable reputation, which is even more remarkable perhaps when you consider how far it has come, with around 70 facilities across Italy – including '*alberghi diffusi*', '*borghi-albergo*', '*residence diffusi*', '*villaggi-albergo*' and '*alberghi diffusi di campagna*' – forming the National Association of Alberghi Diffusi, active in raising awareness and ensuring compliance with the model on which they are originally based, and with an unspecified number of ideas, attempts and ongoing projects, from networks of houses with a centralized booking system to the broader, more flexible models that come under the classification of hotel–village.

According to the studies carried out and existing literature on the topic, it seems that scattered hospitality has become an effective solution for revitalizing villages in the process of depopulation, many of which are located in the regions of Central and Southern Italy, in particular certain inner areas of Le Marche and Tuscany, parts of Sicily and Sardinia and all over the Southern Apennines (see, for example, the monitoring activity carried out by Villani and Dall'Ara with various tools and observation scales [2015], which confirmed the positive aspects underlying this accommodation model, highlighting among other things how starting up the business in each case triggered a spontaneous process of recovery among property owners in the various villages, which has led to an overall enhancement). The initiatives in place are also evidence that these forms of hospitality can appear on the market as accommodation facilities able to revitalize a territory and prevent it falling prey to 'museumification' or even 'Disneyfication'. Propositions are actually moving in the direction of establishing a recovery of the cultural heritage of smaller centres and demonstrating that they can increase income and employment in these places, as well as counteracting depopulation, by promoting territorial resources and reviving artisan crafts and typical products.

Taking these observations into account, it is natural to agree with those who claim scattered hospitality could be a satisfactory meeting point between the need to protect the territory and its culture and the opportunity to start up a process of local development. It can only happen, however, if the features of the context in question are considered: this is where organizational problems arise and where opportunities to put the idea into operation and the solution to any management issues that could come up must be sought.

It is the responsibility of municipalities and local authorities to put forward concrete proposals to create conditions for developing an attractive tourist destination and support individuals who are willing to invest in such a venture (Valeri and Paoloni, 2017). Scattered hospitality projects, however, should always be part of a broader range of activities designed to protect and enhance the local resources. An albergo diffuso may be a model of sustainable tourism-based territorial development if and insofar as it is not restricted to the facility itself, but extended to the surrounding territory as a constituent part of the offer. In the absence of any intervention specifically designed to revitalize the area and make it more welcoming, there is a risk of a number of isolated facilities being offered in villages, which cannot be competitive on the market (Confalonieri, 2011).

FIRST EXPERIENCES AT AN INNER AREA IN CAMPANIA

Irpinia – a land-locked area extending across the Central–Eastern part of Campania (Figure 31.1) and consisting largely of mountainous and hilly terrain cut through by valleys, with a network of rivers and streams – is still marginal as a tourist attraction and in terms of availability of accommodation. Tourist flows in the Campania region are mainly directed towards the provinces of Naples and Salerno on the coast and are concentrated in Capri, Ischia, Procida, the Sorrento peninsula and the Amalfi and Cilento coasts, as well as the regional capital. Irpinia also comes last in terms of the number of establishments and second-last (before Benevento) in capacity of establishments, providing only 5.6% of the total number of facilities surveyed in Campania and barely 3.2% of the total number of beds available.

In spite of the improvements recorded in recent years (Russo Krauss, 2020), observations and surveys carried out on the current situation still describe a territory that sees a high incidence of hikers and few tourist stays, for short periods and mainly weekends. This was probably due to the few initiatives being fragmented between different players, the scarcity of infrastructures and the difficulty of access to information for visitors, as well as there being no specific image of the territory (Bencardino and Marotta, 2004; Maddaloni and Diana, 2016; Sorrentini, 2018). The area still occupies a marginal position compared to the major tourist

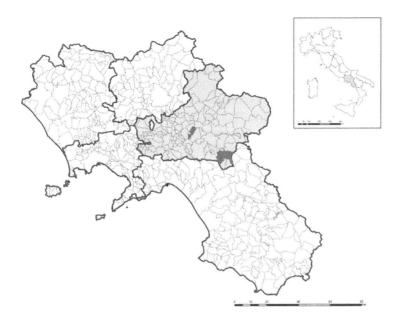

Figure 31.1   Campania region

destinations in the region; in 2018, for example, the province of Avellino contributed only 1.9% (with 117,934 visitors) of the total number of tourists arriving at accommodation establishments in the region, and 1.1% (236,616) of nights spent.

But given its enormous undervalued potential in environmental, historical and cultural resources, tourism constitutes a significant development opportunity in this area, and the recent diversification in tourism practices gives reason to believe that a variety of measures could be taken to utilize the strengths of the region and investigate the possibility of transforming certain disadvantages into competitive advantages. From this point of view then, we can agree with those who recognized that Irpinia – although without great attractors able to move large flows of visitors – could represent, as part of a rebalancing action at regional level, a sort of decompression zone dedicated to niche tourism, offering smaller alternative attractions and responding to the demand for rural and 'plural' tourism, in search of all that encloses and bears witness to the history and identity of a place (Greco, 2010).

At a time like the present, then, and in the situation we are currently (at the time of writing) experiencing with the COVID-19 crisis and the hoped-for recovery, the first that is likely to gain ground as far as the Italian tourism sector is concerned could be precisely these minor destinations rich in resources and peculiar characteristics, the epitome of 'zero kilometre' tourism for discovering less well-known places, uncontaminated landscapes and authentic experiences. Because if it is true, as many believe, that it will take time for confidence to return and that we will feel safer within the confines of our own national boundaries, it is highly likely that proximity will be a key factor. Places that are not too far away and easy to reach by car will be favoured to combine the desire for escape with the search for tranquillity, and lesser-known, niche destinations, smaller but still rich in history, nature and culture, such as villages outside the major tourist circuits, will be preferred. This would be the under-tourism that is widely discussed on TV and in the newspapers, and even by associations such as the Touring Club Italiano: tourism that favours less well-known, less crowded parts of Italy, outdoor activities and slow tourism.

Scattered hospitality is a model that has been under discussion for several years in Irpinia. The programme '*I Villaggi della tradizione*' – which was proposed as far back as 1996 by the Comunità Montana (Mountain Community) Terminio Cervialto with the municipalities of Calabritto, Castelvetere sul Calore, Taurasi and Volturara Irpina – planned for the recovery of these villages by using them as accommodation facilities. So, when the programme was merged with the Borgo Terminio Cervialto PIT – a bottom-up integrated territorial project by a network of local authorities – an attempt was made to start up a new development process using existing properties, aimed at increasing the incidence of tourism in this area. Today, more than 20 years after funding was provided for the first programme and 16 years since the second was given the go-ahead, there are two alberghi diffusi operating in those four municipalities: one in Castelvetere sul Calore ('Borgo di Castelvetere') and the other in Quaglietta hamlet, Calabritto municipality.

Figure 31.2   Borgo di Castelvetere

The first of these, Borgo di Castelvetere (Figure 31.2) reopened in 2013.[1] It comprises 17 accommodation units adapted from former private houses that were damaged in the 1980 earthquake (all restored in the local architectural tradition, equipped with modern conveniences and providing accommodation for between one and five persons), a function room for up to 100 guests, the 'Sapori Diffusi d'Irpinia' tavern (which offers traditional dishes prepared with the finest local produce and excellent DOCG wines) and a shop selling traditional local products and crafts. It is owned by the local council but currently managed by a local entrepreneur, and is part of the National Association of Alberghi Diffusi. It is an integral part of the small village where it is located and provides an excellent opportunity for assessing not just the viability of such a model in this type of setting, but also its potential effects in terms of regenerating the villages involved and repurposing the properties that have been restored.

Figure 31.3   Albergo Diffuso Quaglietta

Following this, the 'Albergo Diffuso Quaglietta' was opened in August 2018 (Figure 31.3). The village from which it takes its name, a small centre of Langobard origin that forms part of the municipality of Calabritto, has been the subject of a redevelopment project that has maintained and restored its mediaeval features, created a series of accommodation units (16 of which are already available and about 20 almost ready), and opened a pub/restaurant called 'Silarus', which altogether constitute a very charming hotel–village. It is run by three young people determined to give substance and continuity to a project that has been realized after years of work, to develop the potential of Quaglietta and turn it into a tourist attraction.

They are convinced it is important to shape a tourist offer made up of various components (including outdoor pursuits and sporting activities, visits to places of religious interest, food and wine tours, health and beauty packages), forming a network of places and virtuous realities from the broader surrounding area and relaunching them. Quaglietta is actually located a short distance from the thermal springs of Contursi in the province of Salerno, the Sanctuary of San Gerardo in Materdomini and the WWF Oasi Valle della Caccia in Senerchia, and could benefit from being integrated into a broader, better-structured tourist offer system.

For Taurasi and Volturara Irpina – the other two villages involved in 'I Villaggi della Tradizione' – nothing done to date has given rise to an albergo diffuso. Two interventions were planned for Taurasi: one to restore the mediaeval village by refurbishing the public buildings and street furniture and the other to restore the castle. These interventions were to be implemented as part of an albergo diffuso programme and would have brought artisan and commercial activities back to the historic centre, involving the local residents. In spite of the intention, however, and the work already completed (the castle, for example, now houses the regional cellar for Irpinia wines and a museum area offering a sensory tour dedicated to wine-making), the scattered hospitality project has never been brought to fruition and there remains within the defensive walls of the castle a series of publicly owned housing units that could usefully be adapted for accommodating visitors. In Volturara Irpina, the restoration of Piazza del Tiglio and the bell tower has been completed and a 12-room hotel has opened, although it is not an albergo diffuso.

There are also other examples of scattered hospitality to be found in Irpinia. One is in Bisaccia, which has an albergo diffuso managed directly by the council and scattered around the various zones of its historic centre, comprising around 20 houses (only a few of which are currently available, however) and five suites inside the castle to be opened shortly. Created as part of a project for the establishment of the Francesco De Sanctis Literary Park and supported by the Patto Territoriale della Baronia (Barony Territorial Pact), the aim of the initiative that brought it to life was always to give the village an original hotel facility that would enhance its status as a local tourist attraction and, at the same time, improve and preserve a minor architectural heritage that would otherwise fall into ruin.

Other ideas put forward are still only at the theoretical stage though, such as the low-environmental-impact hotel-village/scattered hospitality intervention for the old village of Luogosano. This was mentioned in the three-year public works plan for 2014–16 but was abandoned due to a lack of funding. There is also the scattered hospitality programme conceived for Senerchia a few years ago, which has now stalled due to the scarcity of available funds.

CONCLUSION

The research carried out confirms the potential of these types of guest accommodation, which is important in areas like Irpinia that are generally associated with situations of neglect exacerbated by hydrogeological instability, degradation of the agricultural landscape and decaying buildings. Such areas are typically disadvantaged in terms of infrastructure and socioeconomic factors, demographic decline and shortage of essential services, but rich in resources and natural capital, specialities closely linked to the *genius loci* and cultural heritage (Lemmi and Siena Tangheroni, 2015; Marchetti et al., 2017).

Inner areas have been the focus of renewed attention in Italy for a number of years now, especially thanks to the National Strategy for Inner Areas, which embodies the new intervention model with place-based policies aimed at combating depopulation and relaunching the development of these parts of the country. They often see the development of the tourist offer as a means of salvation, a way out of the situation that has always held them back. On the other hand, identifying a variety of more sustainable tourist activities designed to satisfy the demand for unspoilt environments and authentic experiences, along with the success of accommodation facilities created by repurposing existing properties and relying on local forces, can open up new possibilities for them (Meini in Marchetti et al., 2017).

It is too early yet to draw any conclusions from the initiatives carried out to date out in the province of Avellino in terms of results achieved. As examples of participatory planning compatible with the unique identity of the places, however, they can now be recognized as a valid opportunity, considering how this part of inner Campania could be revitalized.

In tourism development planning, Irpinia, along with other inner areas of Italy, is faced with some important and critical issues. These include limitations in analysing the context and difficulty in identifying potential demand; attachment to an often-traditional view of the local cultural heritage, with little attention to improvement and innovation; and difficulties in identifying a management model suited to the characteristics of the local heritage. In view of these difficulties, scattered hospitality offers a real opportunity for development in an economically marginal context, not just in terms of preserving and enhancing the local heritage (although this is essential) but also in terms of developing a wider investment plan for the region. The actual territorial effects on the area under consideration can be assessed more thoroughly as part of further studies.

Again, introducing this type of niche tourism in an effort to regenerate a less well-known area confirms the opportunity to include its cultural heritage in the overall territorial planning and governance processes, in view of a heritage-based development: a development that focuses attention on the specific aspects of the places, maintains and enhances the differences between cultural and environmental systems, and translates into a series of actions that bring out the identity of the place in an overarching territorial project. It is true that communities change over time, but their legacy of local characteristics and values remains constant and it is on this assumption that a process of effective and sustainable change can be founded. The cultural richness of a territory, especially in rural areas that have not suffered any change in their identity, is the key to developing a tourist activity that will complement its production activities (Carta, 1999).

In a region like Campania – where there are a great many contradictory aspects in the way tourism has developed and its environmental, historical, cultural and artistic resources are utilized, and where the structural imbalance between coastal areas and inner areas in terms of the overall accommodation capacity and influx of tourists is immediately evident – the tourist enhancement of historic inner centres (and the consequent development of the surrounding rural areas) is even more desirable. What is more, developments of this kind can be sustained by the strong increase in demand for 'alternative' tourism that focuses more on discovering 'minor' cultural and environmental heritage, rather than on traditional seaside holidays and visits to famous cities of art.

The demand for this type of tourism will probably be augmented in the post-pandemic recovery period as well, by Italians favouring holidays in less well-known places, in small villages and rural areas in their own country, seeking peace and quiet of course, but also seeking the kind of getaway that only micro-destinations can offer. In a small village you often spend less money receiving a more careful welcome, you are in closer contact with nature and can enjoy excellent local products. A stay at an albergo diffuso is also more conducive to observing health and safety restrictions – most of the rooms are in separate apartments and it is easier to practise social distancing in less frequented places which are often surrounded by open spaces where you can walk or engage in sporting activities.

It is no surprise that the Minister of Cultural Heritage and Activities and Tourism, Dario Franceschini, intervened in the ongoing debate on revitalizing the Italian tourism industry, one of the sectors hardest hit by the pandemic, by saying in an interview with the Corriere della Sera on 31 May 2020 that the need to restore and revive small villages should be a priority for intervention. He described them as beautiful but often deserted or neglected places that you see hundreds of along the ridge of the Apennines, and mentioned alberghi diffusi, among other things, as a way of introducing slow, experiential tourism with a journey through tradition (see Guerzoni, 2020).

In conclusion, the protection of property assets and also, of course, the refurbishment and repurposing of them – repurposing that does not require radical transformation of the urban fabric or erosion of its characteristics over time but can, in fact, serve to enhance these features – can help revitalize historic centres by developing tourism and establishing the services it requires (Dall'Ara et al., 2000). And if the desire is to explore an avenue other than mass tourism, scattered hospitality can offer a real alternative in which to invest energy and resources.

For the formula to be truly effective, of course, any project must form part of a broader series of interventions to safeguard and enhance local resources; as mentioned above, albergo diffuso can only be a model for developing sustainable tourism in a region if it is not confined to the structures themselves but includes the surrounding area as an integral part of the offer. Equally important in this respect is the involvement of local communities in drawing up plans and carrying them through, with bottom-up participatory processes and support for those creating systems and networking of the various offerings (Pollice, 2016). Beyond all the simplistic, rhetorical assertions that hold tourism up as a miraculous formula, what is certain is that the overall offer in a geographical area must include both accommodation and access to services, involve well-coordinated planning and investment, and engage the local community as stakeholders in the development of their territory.

NOTE

1.   As Cresta reports [2010], the 'Borgo Antico' albergo diffuso was opened in 2004; it was due to be managed by a joint enterprise charged with enhancing the cultural heritage and local entrepreneurial activities and coordinating the various interventions, as well as providing ongoing training activities for employees in the hospitality sector. The scheme was not without some controversy, however, and the local council decided to appoint third parties to manage it. Closed in September 2009 over a bureaucratic dispute between the council and the hotel manager, the albergo diffuso remained the focus of attention for the Castelvetere administration, which has continued to invest in the idea, trying not to waste that opportunity.

REFERENCES

Bencardino, F. and Marotta, G. (eds) (2004) *Nuovi turismi e politiche di gestione della destinazione. Prospettive di sviluppo per le aree rurali della Campania*. Milano: FrancoAngeli.

Carta, M. (1999) *L'armatura culturale del territorio. Il patrimonio culturale come matrice di identità e strumento di sviluppo*, Milano: FrancoAngeli.

Cerutti, S. (2014) Il ruolo dell'albergo diffuso nello sviluppo turistico dei territori montani: l'esperienza italiana tra tradizione e innovazione. In E. Dai Prà (ed.) *Approcci geo-storici e governo del territorio*. Milano: FrancoAngeli, 108–19.

Confalonieri, M. (2011) A typical Italian phenomenon: The 'albergo diffuso'. *Tourism Management*, 32(3), 685–7.

Cresta, A. (2010) L'albergo diffuso quale risposta alla rivitalizzazione delle comunità e dei territori rurali: il caso di Castelvetere sul Calore. In A. Cresta and I. Greco (eds) *Luoghi e forme del turismo rurale. Evidenze empiriche in Irpinia*. Milano: FrancoAngeli, 153–82.

Cucari, N., Wankowicz, E. and Esposito De Falco, S. (2019) Rural tourism and Albergo Diffuso: A case study for sustainable land-use planning. *Land Use Policy*, 82, 105–19.

Dall'Ara, G. (2002) Albergo diffuso: un'idea che piace. *La Rivista del turismo*, 4(1), 36–40.

Dall'Ara, G. (2010) *Manuale dell'Albergo Diffuso*. Milano: FrancoAngeli.

Dall'Ara, G. and Esposto, M. (eds) (2005) *Il fenomeno degli alberghi diffusi in Italia*. Campobasso: Palladino.

Dall'Ara, G., Di Bartolo, S. and Montaguti, L. (2000) *Modelli originali di ospitalità nelle piccole e medie imprese turistiche*. Milano: FrancoAngeli.

Greco, I. (2010) Il turismo rurale in Irpinia: risorse e peculiarità. In A. Cresta and I. Greco (eds) *Luoghi e forme del turismo rurale. Evidenze empiriche in Irpinia*. Milano: FrancoAngeli, 113–51.

Guerzoni M. (2020) Franceschini: 'Alta velocità e piano per i borghi. Così rilanceremo il turismo al Sud'. *Corriere della Sera*, https://www.corriere.it/politica/20_maggio_31/alta-velocita-piano-borghi-mosse -il-turismo-sud-d6945a08-a2ad-11ea-bc2b-bdd292787b00.shtml

Lemmi, E. and Siena Tangheroni, M. (2015) Il geoitinerario come espressione del turismo postmoderno. In E. Lemmi (ed.) *Turismo e management dei territori: i geoitinerari, fra valori e progettazione turistica*, Bologna: Pàtron, 15–25.

Maddaloni, D. and Diana, P. (2016) Tra stagnazione, crisi e sviluppo locale. L'area irpina secondo i testimoni privilegiati. In G. Basile et al. (eds) *La definizione identitaria di un territorio rurale. Benessere e antichi mestieri nell'Alta Irpinia*. Milano: FrancoAngeli, 29–54.

Marchetti, M., Panunzi, S. and Pazzagli, R. (eds) (2017) *Aree interne. Per una rinascita dei territori rurali e montani*. Soveria Mannelli: Rubbettino.

Mazzetti, E. (2005) Consumo e rigenerazione del paesaggio turistico. *Bollettino della Società Geografica Italiana*, XII(10), 281–93.

Montebelli, S. (2018) Per una rivitalizzazione dei piccoli comuni italiani in disagio insediativo. Il caso dell'albergo diffuso Robur Marsorum a Rovere di Rocca di Mezzo. *Rivista Geografica Italiana*, 125, 63–87.

Novelli, M. (ed.) (2005) *Niche tourism: Contemporary issues, trends and cases*. Oxford: Elsevier.

Pollice, F. (2016) Alberghi di comunità: un modello di empowerment territoriale. *Territori della Cultura*, 25, 82–95.

Presenza, A., Messeni Petruzzelli, A. and Sheehanc, L. (2019) Innovation through tradition in hospitality. The Italian case of Albergo Diffuso. *Tourism Management*, 72, 192–201.

Romolini, A., Fissi, S. and Gori, E. (2017) Integrating territory regeneration, culture and sustainable tourism. The Italian *albergo diffuso* model of hospitality. *Tourism Management Perspectives*, 22, 67–72.

Russo Krauss, D. (2004) Politiche regionali in materia di sviluppo dell'economia turistica e valorizzazione sostenibile di centri minori: il caso della Campania. In Adamo, F. (ed.) *Turismo e territorio in Italia*. Bologna: Pàtron, 579–600.

Russo Krauss, D. (2007a) L'ospitalità diffusa come ipotesi di rianimazione turistica dei centri minori. In Persi, P. (ed.) *Recondita armonia. Il Paesaggio tra progetto e governo del territorio*. Urbino: Università degli studi, Istituto Interfacoltà di Geografia, 480–86.

Russo Krauss, D. (2007b) Ospitalità diffusa, identità locale e turismo sostenibile. Il caso di Giffoni Sei Casali. In Zarrilli, L. (ed.) *Lifescapes. Culture paesaggi identità*. Milano: FrancoAngeli, 175–91.

Russo Krauss, D. (2020), La prospettiva del turismo diffuso per rianimare la Campania interna: esperienze in Irpinia. *Studi e Ricerche socio-territoriali*, 10, 203–27.

Silvestrelli, P. (2011) Valorizzazione del patrimonio culturale e sviluppo dell''albergo diffuso': interdipendenze e sinergie. *Il capitale culturale*, II, 253–74.

Sorrentini, F. (2018) La valorizzazione del turismo nelle aree interne. Alcune riflessioni sulle prospettive di sviluppo locale in Irpinia. *Studi e Ricerche socio-territoriali*, 8, 41–72.

Valeri, M. and Paoloni, P. (2017) Competitiveness and sustainability in tourism industry: The albergo diffuso case study. *International Journal of Business and Management*, 12(12), 107–18.

Villani, T. and Dall'Ara, G. (2015) L'Albergo Diffuso come modello di ospitalità originale e di sviluppo sostenibile dei borghi. *Techne – Journal of Technology for Architecture and Environment*, 10, 169–78.

32. In focus 6 – the 'Wasteland – Graced Land' story of Melkhoutfontein, South Africa

Anthea Rossouw

INTRODUCTION

Founded in 1990, Dreamcatcher South Africa is a non-profit community interest company facilitating social change. It specialises in developing niche tourism experiences that address poverty and social exclusion. Historically, South African tourism focused on package tours to a few tourism 'hotspots' – a monopolistic approach that prevented engagement with communities and inhibited entrepreneurship. With a mantra to 'Go truly local', Dreamcatcher's mission was to disrupt the status quo by developing niche tourism services, owned by local enterprises. Based on micro-niche tourism components (Robinson and Novelli, 2005), Dreamcatcher has pioneered tourism experiences in heritage, culture, education, nature/wildlife, gastronomy, arts/crafts, photography and volunteering. Supported by a network of 'homestay' accommodations, this approach enables local community engagement in ways that are opposed to conventional tourism (Dolezal, 2011). Pollock (2012) highlights the emergence of a 'new conscious consumer'. This tourist segment has been a key market for Dreamcatcher since 2000.

Dreamcatcher's work includes:

- researching opportunities for tourism growth through developing niche tourism products;
- inclusive community enterprise development focusing on women and youth on low incomes;
- social change management which includes challenges to sustainability;
- delivering bespoke local training and mentoring;
- promoting product and tourism service awareness;
- booking service and business channelling.

'WASTELAND – GRACED LAND'

An example of Dreamcatcher's work to facilitate social justice, environmental integrity and economic self-sufficiency is 'Wasteland – Graced Land' in Melkhoutfontein, located on the Garden Route in South Africa. Under Apartheid, the 1960 Group Areas Act removed all residents of colour from the resort town of Stilbaai to Melkhoutfontein, 7 km away. Situated between two dumpsites, poor waste management blighted the community, with waste from surrounding areas openly burned. Melkhoutfontein evolved into one of the most deprived communities in the Western Cape, with high levels of unemployment (Lundahl and Kriel, 1987). Furthermore, the invasive plant species *Acacia cyclops* decimated the natural habitat. DNA testing identified residents as being descendants of the Khoekhoen, the first people known to document their lifestyle through rock art using ochre. Known as 'the forgotten people', the history of the Khoekhoen was erased from history (de Jongh, 2016).

Partnering with the community, Dreamcatcher identified barriers to socioeconomic development and reimagined niche tourism opportunities with them: 'Homestay with Kamamma' (women who carry their children on their backs), followed by 'CookUp with Kamamma', launched in 2000. The latter is an example of gastronomy tourism and involved tourists sharing stories in Kamammas' homes whilst preparing and eating traditional cuisine. Binns and Nel (2002) and Rossouw (2002) document the evolution of these pioneering niche products. Tourists sharing their experiences led to increased bookings, reinforcing market potential. A range of niche tourism experiences followed:

- 'PaintUp With Kamamma' – Heritage Tourism. Melkhoutfontein is graced with murals celebrating important cultural heritage, including that of the Khoekhoen. Collaborating with specialist cultural artist Bruce Rimell, tourists paint alongside locals, enjoying informative, uplifting experiences.
- 'Walkabout Tours' – Educational Tourism. Enterprises empowered to become nationally accredited tour guides offer unique information and stories on walking tours, sharing the transformation of the community from 'Wasteland to Graced land'.
- '*La Bloemen*' – Nature/Wildlife Tourism. This tour focuses on the transformation of a dumpsite into a botanical garden where indigenous species thrive. Tourists join the community to plant, enjoy the fauna and flora and pick and cook organic food.
- 'Waste Its Mine Its Yours' – Arts/Crafts Tourism. Identifying the gap for locally made crafts, the project reuses waste and *Acacia cyclops* wood for crafting. The University of Brighton (UK) and local craft tutors facilitated knowledge exchange and empowered craft enterprises to make and sell crafts.

CHALLENGES

Due to the legacy of Apartheid, transitioning aspiring enterprises from a *servant* mindset to a *service* culture posed a challenge. Due to socialisation norms and discrimination, women were not widely accepted as entrepreneurs or encouraged to have a bank account. Overcoming these challenges required an integrated behavioural change programme with the women, their spouses, elders and the wider community. Over time the tangible impacts and publicity of the niche tourism products changed perceptions. These impacts included increased household income, circulation of money into the community, job creation and socialisation between tourists and locals.

Following the dismantling of Apartheid, communities nominated Dreamcatcher's founder to serve on the national Tourism Transformation Board. Her vision was met with resistance from the mainstream tourism industry, which viewed it as competition and a challenge, rather than an opportunity. This resistance to change can be viewed as a legacy of established tourism practice and a lack of intracultural cohesion. A lack of support remains from tour operators who predominantly continue to follow a 'captured' package tour mindset which inhibits tourists from experiencing the wider South Africa. To overcome this, Dreamcatcher works directly with consumers and has launched its own central booking and business channelling service, eliminating commission to third parties and maximising enterprise income.

SUSTAINABILITY

Dreamcatcher's pluralistic integrated approach encapsulates how niche tourism can contribute to sustainability by:

- empowering disadvantaged and marginalised communities. A new generation of niche tourism providers are part of the tourism supply chain with many of the original enterprises from 2000 still in business;
- enabling social cohesion, collaboration and knowledge exchange between communities and tourists;
- decentralising tourist income stimulating local economic growth;
- addressing environmental challenges – the Wasteland – Graced Land project is now part of the UN-declared Gouritz Biosphere;
- addressing all 17 of the UN Sustainable Development Goals.

OPPORTUNITY

COVID-19 has reinforced the importance of human interaction, self-sufficiency and inclusivity. Dreamcatcher is experiencing unprecedented growth in requests for information from tourism stakeholders aspiring to reinvent/redirect their efforts towards more sustainable practices. There is a growing trend among tourists to seek meaningful human engagement and aspire to personal development whilst addressing inequality. Throughout the COVID-19 pandemic, Dreamcatcher's clients have offered support, vowing to return. This crystalises the impact and potential of niche tourism as a growth sector – as stated by Tomazos (2020: viii): 'Tourism is about being human'.

A clear pathway to niche tourism is appearing. In addition to offering 'stand-alone' experiences, the tourism trends which emerged during the COVID-19 pandemic show that there is an opportunity to reposition the niche tourism experience from a 'contested tourism commodity' (Tomazos, 2020) to one that adds value to mainstream tourism itineraries and packaging. Moreover, niche tourism offers stakeholders in the tourism industry, training institutions and government agencies, as well as funders and investors, an opportunity to reflect on its potential as they aspire to contribute to levelling up society.

Dreamcatcher has spent decades developing niche tourism that delivers tangible economic and social impact in South Africa. Through collective commitment and partnerships, this could be fast tracked. Seize the moment!

REFERENCES

Binns, T. and Nel, E. (2002) Tourism as a local development strategy in South Africa. *The Geographical Journal*, 168(3), 235–47.

de Jongh, M. (2016) *A forgotten first people: The Southern Cape Hessequa*. S.L.: The Watermark Press.

Dolezal, C. (2011) Community-based tourism in Thailand: (Dis-)illusions of authenticity and the necessity for dynamic concepts of culture and power. *Austrian Journal of South-East Asian Studies*, 4(1), 129–38.

Lundahl, P. and Kriel, A. (1987) *A socio-economic overview of the Riversdale District with particular reference to the village of Melkhoutfontein.* Saldru Working Paper No. 67. South Africa Labour and Development Research Unit, Pretoria.

Pollock, A. (2012) Conscious travel: Signposts towards a new Model for tourism. In *UNTWO, Ethics and Tourism Congress*, Quito, Ecuador, 12 September 2012. https://conscioustourism.files.wordpress.com/2011/02/conscious-travel-signposts-towards-a-new-model.pdf

Robinson, M. and Novelli, M. (2005) Niche tourism: An introduction. In Novelli, M. (2005) *Niche tourism: Contemporary issues, trends and cases*, 1–14. Oxford: Butterworth-Heinemann.

Rossouw, A. (2002) *Making Mandela's dream work for tourism* (3rd ed.). Cape Town: Daysign.

Tomazos, K. (2020) *Contested tourism commodities*. Newcastle: Cambridge Scholars Publishing.

PART VII

LATEST DEVELOPMENTS IN NICHE TOURISM

33. South Korean 'one-month stay' travellers
Jaeyeon Choe

INTRODUCTION

South Korea, as the tenth largest economy in the world, is noted for its rapid rise from one of the poorest countries after the Korean War in the 1950s to a highly developed, high-income country (Ahn et al., 2019; Lim, 2004). It remains one of the fastest-growing developed countries in the world and has been recognized for its responsible handling of the pandemic. However, Korea's 'work hard' culture has generated significant social costs. Korea has the highest suicide rate among OECD countries and has the third longest working hours in the OCED (OCED, 2021). Koreans work an average of 1,967 hours per year, while Germans work 1,386 hours and the British work 1,538 hours (OECD, 2021). While the government has brought in limited reforms to reduce working hours, the impact of the fast-paced culture has led to a dramatic fall in fertility rates (Reuters, 2021), as well as causing housing inequality and high living costs (Silva, 2020). Depression is at an all-time high among Korea's youth, and has nearly doubled in the last five years (Yonhap News, 2019).

Outbound travel in Korea is a relatively recent phenomenon and only emerged in the 1980s. After the 1988 Seoul Olympic Games, the government eased outbound travel restrictions, and this resulted in outbound tourism increasing significantly, by 67.3% in 1989 (Ahn et al., 2019). Koreans are now a lucrative outbound and primary source market for many Southeast Asian destinations. While Koreans typically receive only eight days annual leave, the average number of days per trip (for travelling overseas) is 4.79 days per year. Despite the short holiday entitlements, 28.7 million outbound Korean tourists (more than half of the population) spent $34.5 billion abroad in 2019 (Bloomberg, 2020). Significantly, with an average tourists spend of around $1,000 per trip in 2019, Koreans are high spenders while on holiday (Statista, 2021).

The popular method of travel for many Korean tourists has been organized package tours, as these provide psychological shelter (Lee et al., 2015). While packages remain popular for outbound travellers aged 70 and above (Statista, 2020), with the recent developments in information and communication technologies, an increasing number of Koreans are travelling independently (Chung et al., 2017). Several studies indicate that Korean tourists are influenced by social media content and TV shows when choosing tourism destinations (e.g., Kim and Kim, 2020). However, Korean tourists are not a homogenous market. The growth of independent travel has led to various and complex movement patterns and niches based on distinct interests and characteristics (Chung et al., 2017) such as golf tourism (Kim and Lee, 2009) and the emerging 'one-month stay' micro-niche. Unlike traditional backpackers and 'gap year' travellers, the Korean 'one-month stayers' largely visit one destination and stay in one accommodation with the desire of experience living like a local.

Journalists and cultural critics have noted the growth of the YOLO (You Only Live Once) and a 'sohwakhaeng' (small but certain moments of happiness) attitude in Korean society as an antithesis to the prevalent hyper-competitive culture (Chyung, 2018; Park and Lim, 2018). There is also growing disdain for the conventions of social order and collective culture based on Confucianist values among Korea's younger generations (Mitu, 2015; Moon, 2020). Young people are placing more value on individual choices, happiness and work–life balance (Kim, 2019; Kwak and Hong, 2018; Steger and Jung, 2017). This generation is often called the MZ Generation, which pairs two groups – Millennials and Gen Z (born between the 1980s and the early 2000s) (Song and Jang, 2021). They are digitally advanced and active, and they care about social justice, transparency and authenticity. They are avid users of smartphones and social media and favour destinations which have gained popularity through social media, mainstream media, viral marketing and travel snapshots (Lee, 2021).

While Southeast Asian destinations have been popular with one-month stayers as a consequence of the relative low cost of living, relaxing environment and opportunity for online presence (Shin and Choi, 2019), there is also an expanding interest in one-month stays in Europe. While demand for this type and form of travel have been resilient, during the COVID-19 pandemic (still ongoing at the time of writing) it has switched to domestic destinations. Once travel restrictions ease, it is expected that outbound travel demand for this micro-niche will transfer back to the traditional and new tourism destinations abroad. To take advantage of this demand, destinations and tourism-related businesses should understand the socio-demographic characteristics of these micro-niche tourists and their motivations, so as to develop suitable, creative and sustainable tourism programmes, products and services.

As a resilient and self-sustaining micro-niche, the one-month stay also shows potential to grow as a sustainable and responsible niche in comparison to many types of mass tourism (Poon, 1993). One-month stayers often seek to experience and support local cultures by interacting with local people, eating and shopping in locally owned businesses, and staying at homestays and guesthouses rather than international hotels (Shin and Choi, 2019). This has the dual benefit of supporting local economies and being less socially and economically damaging to the destination (Novelli, 2005). These niche characteristics can help contribute to inclusive, safe, resilient and sustainable destinations (SDG 11). One-month stayers' preference for peripheral areas and rural destinations (Ursache, 2015) means the possible creation of new livelihoods as local people respond with the development of new products and services.

While local press and social media have generated public awareness of this micro-niche and the sustainable nature, this chapter seeks to take a scholarly lens to explore those who engage with it, by examining their socio-demographic characteristics, motivations to travel and primary/preferred activities, based on an analysis of 20 blogs and three interviews that were conducted in January and February 2021. This chapter provides insights into this potentially sustainable micro-niche and offers recommendations for small to medium-sized businesses in peripheral areas and rural destinations, and future directions for the niche as travel restrictions ease in the post-COVID-19 period. This chapter also contributes to the niche tourism literature by broadening a culturally and geographically diverse context.

KOREAN ONE-MONTH STAYERS AS A SUSTAINABLE MICRO-NICHE

As the tourism sector becomes increasingly diversified and specialized (Dinis and Krakover, 2015), it is increasingly focusing on providing tourism products and services that serve specialized segments (Novelli, 2005). The growth in niches reflects consumer needs for more sophisticated and meaningful travel (Marson, 2011). Niche tourism is an umbrella term which describes both macro- and micro-tourism segments appealing to a specific group of travellers (Novelli, 2005), and one-month stayers can be framed as a micro-niche. They are a small population, within the context of global tourism and have particular travel motivations, preferences and behaviour. From a demand viewpoint, these tourists participate in special interest practices, experiences, products and services that distinguish and differentiate them, and reflect 'the power, or at least the apparition of power, of the consumer' (Robinson and Novelli, 2005: 1). From a supply perspective, their specific interests have coalesced into a coherent segment, which destinations and businesses can exploit by 'catering to the needs of specific markets by focusing on more diverse tourism products' (Marson, 2011: 9).

As niches are often misidentified, generalized, homogenized and objectified (O' Regan, 2013), niche tourism research often misses the point by applying the concept to behaviours that may be more related to tourist motivation (e.g., wedding tourism) without exploring their psychological needs and shared characteristics. There is a necessity to understand niche tourists' unifying constructs, behaviours and interests, and subsequently identify and develop products that suit those interests. There is also a need to explore whether one-month stayers show a difference in comparison to mass tourism, in regard to their engagement in responsible and sustainable behaviour. The impacts of niche tourists and how this compares to mass tourists remain an unexplored area of research (Weiler and Firth, 2021).

While mass tourism is often seen as a potential threat to environments through its socio-cultural impacts on host communities (Dinis and Krakover, 2015), niche tourism is recognized as a less harmful alternative to mass tourism by some scholars (e.g., Yeoman, 2008). Some niches have been identified as helping to support economic, environmental and social sustainability (e.g., Marson, 2011), by providing opportunities for locally owned businesses and small-scale businesses in remote or rural destinations in particular (Ursache, 2015) and encouraging local participation in tourism (Briedenhann and Wickens, 2004). For example, one-month stayers indicate their preference for local homestays, food and goods (Shin and Choi, 2019). If they behave in a sustainable and responsible manner, this micro-niche can be particularly beneficial for small-scale/locally run tourism businesses in peripheral areas. This could help achieve the social sustainability of tourism in their preferred destinations. Increasing tourist numbers in peripheral areas and communities can lead to increased incomes, new livelihoods and poverty reduction. Such communities also tend to perceive tourism, if sustainable, as 'a panacea for their path to recovery from economic decline and youth outmigration' (Dinis and Krakover, 2015: 3). Further empirical research is needed on the one-month stay niche so as to confirm the niche's characteristics, to explore the factors that supported its emergence and to understand the specific needs, interests, practices and motivations that sustain them. In the COVID-19 context, one-month stayers may have greater desire to stay in quiet locations for their psychological recovery and to allow time and space for reflection on lives, thus there are opportunities for rural destinations to exploit this demand. This is particularly important for rural locations where poverty rates are high in developing countries, and where tourism benefits are not often reached/dispersed.

RESEARCH METHODS

This chapter uses netnography, which is a form of ethnographic research that can be used to collect and analyse online customer information, online cultures and social interaction in contemporary digital communications contexts (Martin and Woodside, 2011). The method is increasingly used for tourism research (Bezzola and Lugosi, 2018; Zhang and Hitchcock, 2017) as a means to understand tourist segments. Blog analysis, in particular, is recognized as a valuable information source for understanding potential visitors and a particular market (Kaufmann et al., 2019; Snee, 2013; Sun et al., 2014). Data were collected from the blogs of 20 Korean one-month stayers, and three of these bloggers were interviewed during January and February 2021.

The research process involved searching for one-month stay blog posts on naver.com, the most popular search portal in Korea (Chung et al., 2017). Keywords such as 'one-month stay travel' were used to search blog posts and narrowed down to: 'one-month stay abroad', 'one-month stay travel in Jeju Island, Korea', 'one-month stay in Asia/Europe' and so on. Each blogger was contacted for their permission to use their blog content as a data source. The blogs were thematically analysed, using a deductive thematic analysis technique (Braun and Clarke, 2006) to understand the writers' motivations, chosen destinations, primary/preferred activities and whether they displayed sustainable practices and behaviours. Three of the bloggers agreed to share more information and stories about their experiences through participating in a semi-structured interview. This also helped to contextualize certain blog entries. All blogs were written between 2018 January and 2020 January.

FINDINGS AND DISCUSSION

Socio-Demographic Characteristics

Based on analysis of blogger posts, one-month stayers largely characterized themselves as single, young and from a professional background. All were college graduates living in urban areas. They were aged between 27 and 36. And 19 blogs out of 20 were written by females. While it is possible to assume that female travellers prefer this form of tourism, female travellers are known to write and engage with blogs more than male travellers (Zhang et al., 2009). Blogging is widespread in the visual and literary media of the travel life of female tourists (Zhang and Hitchcock, 2017); indeed the internet has become an important site for young women to express themselves and to develop a social attitude through dialogue with other young women (Aapola et al., 2005). This possible greater preference of women than men for the micro-niche is supported by the growth in female solo travel across Asia (Yang et al., 2017; Yang et al., 2018), the growth of women's economic power and young women postponing or avoiding marriage (Qian, 2019).

Among 20 bloggers, 19 had quit their jobs and travelled to an overseas destination and the Korean island of Jeju. While the EU Working Time Directive (2003) states that all European countries must offer workers a minimum of four weeks' leave, Koreans have only eight days for annual leave on average, with average overseas trips lasting fewer than five days. A one-month break is considered a large gap in a fast-paced and hyper-competitive society. Despite this constraint, the one male blogger who was a digital nomad (a writer and music critic) explored local music and cultural establishments related to his job during his stay in Poland. While the majority of one-month stayers travel in-between jobs, and during holidays and career breaks, there is a small, but growing number who identify as digital nomads. Another blogger opened her own online travel agency after a one-month stay trip.

Table 33.1   *Profile of 20 bloggers*

Blogger	Year/ month	Destination	Motivation	No. of posts	Type of entry (daily, after events)
1	2020 Nov.	Jeju, Korea	Left a job and taking a break	2	After events
2	2020 Aug.	Jeju	Left a job, healing	5	After events
3	2020 Dec.	Jeju	Left a job and taking a break	17	Daily diary
4	2020 Dec.	Jeju	Left a job and resting	1	After events
5	2018 Apr.	Jeju	Left a job and taking a break	1	After events
6	2019 Feb.	Chiang Mai, Thailand	Left a job and taking a break, relaxing, getting out of routine and recharging	28	Daily diary / daily spending diary
7	2018 May	Chiang Mai	Left a job and taking a break	15	Every other day posting
8	2018 Jun.	Chiang Mai	Left a job and taking a break	14	Every other day / after events
9	2019 April	Chiang Mai	Left a job and taking a break	3	After events
10	2019 Aug.	Bali, Indonesia	Left a job and taking a break	2	After events
11	2019 Mar.	Bali	Left a job and taking a break	5	During / after events
12	2020 Feb.	Bali	Left a job and taking a break	1	After events
13	2018 Aug.	Bali	Left a job and taking a break	5	During / after events
14	2019 Dec.	Bali	Left a job and taking a break	14	Daily diary
15 (male)	2019 Aug.	Several cities in Poland	Digital nomad	30	Daily diary
16	2018 May	Warsaw, Poland	Left a job and drifting	35	Daily diary / after events
17	2019 Oct.	Budapest, Hungary	Left a job and figuring out life	15	Every other day diary
18	2019 Sep.	Budapest	Left a job	30	Daily diary
19	2020 Jan.	Prague, Czech Republic	Left a job and taking a break	22	Daily diary
20	2019 Nov.	Prague	Left a job and taking a break	3	After events

Motivations

The one-month stayers who preferred Southeast Asian destinations chose the region for its climate, inexpensive living costs, perceived friendly local people, perceived safety, food options and short geographic distance to Korea. Bloggers who spent their one-month stay in both Chiang Mai (Thailand) and Bali (Indonesia) admired the friendliness of the local people, their aesthetically pleasing cafes, good food, the relaxing atmosphere and the stunning natural landscapes. Bloggers who chose Eastern Europe were drawn by the inexpensive travel costs (compared to Western Europe), cafe culture, food, architecture, scenery and the local culture and lifestyles.

The primary motivation for all bloggers was a need to take a break from work and seek space to think about what they want to do with their lives. For example:

> Am I living in a right way? If I didn't meet what the society sets for a timeline, is my life wrong? Should I work harder, or should I make myself more relaxed and happier? What do I really want to do with my life? Is my age 30 too late to drift around? I am really not sure if my life is going ok or I am fine […] I needed to get organize my thoughts, so I decided to travel for one month. (Interview 1 – female blogger, aged 31)

Many stated that they were happy that they had fulfilled their dream of taking time out and giving themselves a one-month break. The one-month break was, for bloggers 4 and 6, the 'first time taking a break in life', and they needed to rest and heal their exhausted body and mind. They seemed 'burned out' from working 5–10 years at their first and second full-time jobs. Many of them mentioned that they were 'so consumed' at work, resulting in worsening physical and mental well-being. They believed their lifestyle was not sustainable, and they were unhappy. Some wrote that they wanted to try a one-month stay before it was too late.

The secondary motivation for one-month stay travel was for 'self-healing' and 'to reward myself'. The bloggers sought to cope with burnout through a one-month stay while seeking work–life balance. Given increased mental health concerns among young people in Korea, the one-month niche is cherished by many of the bloggers as a means of relaxation and an opportunity to recover. For example:

> I worked really hard for 6 years at my previous job. After working hard at a company, what's left to me was only bad health and poor well-being. I really needed a break for my well-being. So I quit and left for Jeju Island the very next day. While in Jeju, I ate very well and rested well for one whole month for the first time. I listened to music alone, walked a lot, drove around for the scenery a lot, went to lots of cool places. What I did most was walking and jogging. I had a whole month focusing on myself and reflecting. Why I worked hard till now, why I did that and what I should do later […] I've got a new job now, and I am working hard for another one-month living later! (Interview 2, female blogger, aged 29)

> One-month living in Chiang Mai was enormously meaningful in my life. I did this after working for five years at my previous job. I wanted to give myself a present for having worked extremely hard! For the first time, I had a space to think deeply and honestly about my life and what to do next. After the one-month living, I decided to start my own business. And I just registered as a business owner for my online travel agency! (Interview 3, female blogger, aged 32)

Travelling for self-healing and self-reward can be related to the idea of self-gifts: personal purchases which are distinguished from other purchases by a particular motivation and context – literally, gifts to oneself. Though it is not broadly explored in tourism studies, the self-gift giving concept, which includes holidays, has been recognized as a growing consumer motive in marketing research (Heath et al., 2011). Self-gift giving generally includes motivations such as to 'reward myself', to 'cheer myself up', to 'be nice to myself', to 'relieve stress' (Mick and DeMoss, 1990; Olshavsky and Lee, 1993) and to 'enjoy life' (Heath et al., 2015). While it is more prevalent in North American culture (Norton, 2017), self-gift giving is spreading along with hedonistic values (Kivetz and Simonson, 2002) among young Koreans and around Asia in general. This contrasts with the travel behaviour of older generations, based on 'older values', with research finding the Korean seniors' primary travel constraint was 'to feel guilty' about spending money on themselves (Lee and Tideswell, 2005). The 'self-gift giving' concept is associated with the emotional, symbolic and fantasizing experiences of consumption (Heath et al., 2011). Combined with tourism imaginaries (Salazar, 2012; Salazar and Graburn, 2014), one-month stayers travel to destinations that are perceived to offer relaxation and a slow pace of life, so as to provide a platform for 'healing'. Self-gifts also entail unique, sacred or otherwise rich hedonic experiences (Heath et al., 2015). The one-month stay trip may also act as a therapeutic device (Mick and Faure, 1998) by facilitating 'self-medication' (Sherry et al., 1995) as travellers slow down and engage in healthy/simple activities, allowing for rest and escape. For example, one-month stayers mentioned that 'Watching sunset every evening was my happiness' and 'Getting out of routine, experiencing local culture and focusing on myself were very refreshing'. Self-gifts also serve as a coping strategy to (temporarily) escape negative feelings, and associated emotions (e.g., stress). People pursue therapeutic self-gifts (Mick, 1991) in the context of negative life experiences or a natural disaster (Heath et al., 2015).

Preferred Activities and Sustainable Potential

Accommodation, for 19 out of 20 bloggers, was booked through Airbnb. Important for many was a private space to relax and facilities that would allow them to cook Korean food when homesick. While two bloggers switched back and forth between a Korean guesthouse and Airbnb, most stayed in the same property for their entire time abroad. As most of the bloggers were female, they prioritized safety as a vital factor when deciding where to stay. They chose Airbnb for its perceived safety as a trusted brand. While the bloggers staying in Southeast Asia largely chose studio-type accommodation, those travelling to Europe rented a room in a shared house. Those staying in Asia seemed to be more confident to stay alone given the perceived safety of those destinations, while those in Europe preferred to stay with others due to cultural unfamiliarity and perception of risk.

The choice of accommodation was also impacted by the availability of nearby amenities such as coffee shops. Cafe culture is a strong part of contemporary living and leisure space in Korea (Song, 2014), and cafes were considered by one-month stayers to be a space to hang out, socialize and relax. Many of the bloggers wrote that spending time at a cafe alone helped them feel relaxed and enabled them to slow down, so as to get their thoughts together about their life and future. The relative importance of the cafe for a one-month stayer is evidenced by the fact that all bloggers shared detailed information about the cafes they visited. Besides hanging out at cafes, the majority of bloggers pursued the slow pace of life at their chosen destinations, enjoying the end of long commutes and trialling new pastimes such as nature walks, jogging, cycling, getting a massage and exploring local markets. Some took classes on arts and crafts, English language, yoga and surfing.

Those who were staying in Bali noted that interacting with friendly local people made them happy. This feeling of happiness is exemplified by one blogger, who wrote, 'I stayed in a small village where I enjoyed eco-life and natural setting in rural Bali. I loved the very friendly local people while expecting the "real" Bali. I felt so happy'. Some noted that through this experience, they learned that enjoying life and a good work–life balance is important. The following quote provides examples of this realization of the importance of work–life balance by one-month stayers:

> Bali taught me that 'enjoying' is important part of life. This might have been deep in my heart, and Bali helped brought it out to me. It made me realize the importance of myself, how precious I am, and how I should appreciate myself as who I am. (Blogger 13)

With their engagement with local people and cultures, the one-month stayers exhibited sustainable interests, behaviours and practices. Unlike some, they were interested in learning about 'authentic' local culture through experiences instead of visiting touristy attractions. The focus of many one-month stayers was concentrating on their own recovery, reflection and gaining new perspectives. They enjoyed eating at small local restaurants, street food stalls and local markets. They appreciated the opportunity to interact with local street vendors, shop owners, cafe waiters, drivers and accommodation hosts. One blogger commented on her blog how she enjoyed baking and exploring local food with a host family in Prague. Another blogged about how they liked to go to local churches and attend masses for the cultural experience and contemplation.

The bloggers did not see themselves as privileged. All of the bloggers expressed concern about the cost of accommodation, food, transport and so on. They spent their savings cautiously by taking budget airlines (with a stopover). Unlike 'regular' Korean tourists who travel abroad for less than a week per year, and have high average daily spending rates, the one-month stayers were cautious of cost due to the length of their stay. Savings rates for under 30s are low (Nikkei, 2021; Suzuki, 2021; Yeom et al., 2021), and many of the bloggers had only been working for a few years and had limited accumulated savings. However, compared to 'traditional' backpackers, their behaviour seemed less frugal. For example, they stayed at private apartments (rather than hostels), took classes, ate out every day and hung out at cafes. Most of them diligently published a daily spending diary on their blogs with detailed itinerary information, photos, receipts and reviews of the various places they visited. They also shared tips on how to save money and answered their blog readers' questions about optimizing budgets. Communicating and engaging with their readers/followers by providing exact details of costs is a common practice among Korean bloggers generally, who generally tend to micro-detail their ideas and lifestyles.

CONCLUSIONS

This chapter provides insights into a micro-niche which emerged from Korea and therefore outside the Western context. As Asian outbound markets mature and societies change, there should be more diverse conceptualizations, methodologies, case studies and theoretical development of the niche tourism literature (e.g., Chen, 2016). While many niche tourism studies focus on destinations and tourism products without fully exploring socio-demographic and psychographic profiles (Weiler and Firth, 2021), this chapter contributes to the literature by providing the socio-demographic characteristics of Korean one-month stayers and examining their motivations, interests and potentially more responsible and more sustainable behaviour.

Based on blog and interview analyses, the one-month stay trend seems to be positive for young Koreans' wellness, due to its therapeutic nature. As social, cultural and employment changes caused by the pandemic give rise to feelings of depression, detachment and alienation, the search for a more authentic, truer self is likely to see more individuals seeking the sanctuary of a one-month stay trip. During the COVID-19 period, the one-month stay experience remained a resilient and sustainable micro-niche as it transferred to domestic destinations in Korea. Given its characteristics, the niche will likely bounce back to destinations abroad once COVID-19 is under control and lockdowns ease. While Koreans restarted travelling abroad again in the first quarter of 2021 as European destinations reopened, bookings and travel to more cautious Southeast Asian destinations did not begin until the fourth quarter of 2021. The one-month stay is a fast-growing and potentially lucrative micro-niche for local businesses, and shows the potential to have a considerable positive socio-economic impact on destinations. Such travellers represent a new opportunity for tourism and hospitality businesses to exploit the particular characteristics of the locality, so as to help widen the base of potential travellers interested in this kind of experience. There is also a possibility that one-month stayers might prefer even more remote, quieter locations in the post-pandemic period for their psychological and physical recovery, to provide a space for reflection and to seek meaning in life.

As one-month stayers are active on Korean portals like naver.com, daum.com and other social media platforms (e.g., Naver Blog, Daum Cafe, Instagram), they can also become powerful e-WOM (electronic word-of-mouth) opinion leaders and influencers. There are opportunities for destinations to reach prospective one-month stayers through social media, as it has created strong communities and spaces for dispersed niche tourists (Croy et al., 2021; Dinhopl and Gretzel, 2018; Volgger et al., 2021). The one-month stayers actively use blogs and vlogs to communicate and share information, and inspire others as opinion leaders and influencers. Local authorities and tourism businesses should promote their destinations and tourism programmes, utilizing the online communities and the power of bloggers/vloggers. '[C]ooperative marketing and the harnessing of new media may provide new opportunities not previously available to destinations and businesses to reach special interest tourists and sustain their interest' (Weiler and Firth, 2021: 23). In Korea, for example, after recognizing the opportunity presented by the one-month stay travel trend during the COVID period, Airbnb partnered with a local rural village, Hadong, in order to promote local stays. Korean local authorities also encourage one-month stay programmes and promote long-term stay experiences through social media with sponsored one-month stay marketing campaigns with key bloggers.

Therefore, tourism destinations and small businesses should exploit this emerging micro-niche market in a suitable, creative and sustainable manner, through repositioning their programmes, products and services. Businesses in peripheral areas and rural destinations and small/micro-tourism businesses should add a variety of accommodation types, programmes and services for limited budgets. Identifying the right programme, product and service is important as it can attract governmental support (Dinis and Krakover, 2015). For example, in Korea, local authorities have invested in providing creative one-month stay experience programmes to support rural economies after identifying the niche as a means to support domestic rural destinations during the pandemic. Thus, one-month stay travel trends and demand have attracted government attention as a way to bring support and funding to those rural destinations.

One-month stay travellers are potentially more responsible and sustainable as tourists, as they are keen on experiencing local cultures and living like locals, consuming locally produced food and goods, staying at local apartments or homestays and avoiding touristy establishments. As this kind of purchase behaviour can also aid small businesses to position/

target their products and services, the one-month stay micro-niche has the potential to be more sustainably developed and managed by businesses and communities compared to mass tourism. For example, in Southeast Asia, the benefits of tourism have not been distributed to peripheral destinations. This micro-niche has the potential to positively impact areas such as rural villages by diversifying livelihoods through small-scale tourism businesses and new income sources, leading to social sustainability, cultural resilience and inclusive growth. This niche can beneficially promote inclusive growth in developing economies, and can be supportive of UN Sustainable Development Goal 11: 'Make cities and human settlements inclusive, safe, resilient and sustainable'. Destinations and tourism authorities should exploit this one-month stay trend/demand to revitalize the peripheral/rural areas and cultures in the post-COVID context.

REFERENCES

Aapola, S., Gonick, M. and Harris, A. (2005) *Young femininity girlhood power and social change.* Hampshire, UK: Palgrave Macmillan.

Ahn, Y., Lee, S. and Ahn, Y. (2019) Who are domestic travel agency users and who buys full package trips? A study of Korean outbound travelers. *Journal of Asian Finance, Economics and Business,* 6(4), 147–58.

Bezzola, T. and Lugosi, P. (2018) Negotiating place through food and drink: Experiencing home and away. *Tourist Studies,* 18(4), 486–506.

Bloomberg (2020) Stuck at home South Korean tourists could prop up the economy. *Bloomberg,* 7 August. Available at: https://www.bloombergquint.com/global-economics/stuck-at-home-south -korean-tourists-could-prop-up-the-economy (accessed 10 August 2020).

Braun, V. and Clarke, V. (2006) Using thematic analysis in psychology. *Qualitative Research in Psychology,* 3(2), 77–101.

Briedenhann, J. and Wickens, E. (2004) Tourism routes as a tool for the economic development of rural areas: Vibrant hope or impossible dream? *Tourism Management,* 25(1), 71–9.

Chen, C. (2016) How can Taiwan create a niche in Asia's cruise tourism industry? *Tourism Management,* 55, 173–83.

Chung, H., Chung, N. and Nam, Y. (2017) A social network analysis of tourist movement patterns in blogs: Korean backpackers in Europe. *Sustainability,* 9, 2251.

Chyung, E. (2018) 'Sohwakhaeng' taps into Koreans' desire to find happiness in little things. *Korean Herald,* 29 July. Available at: http://www.koreaherald.com/view.php?ud=20180729000195 (accessed 10 August 2020).

Croy, W. G., Reichenberger, I. and Benjaminet, S. (2021) Film tourist tribes. In C. Pforr, R. Dowling and M. Volgger (eds) *Consumer tribes in tourism: Contemporary perspectives on special-interest tourism.* Singapore: Springer, 53–68.

Dinhopl, A. and Gretzel, U. (2018) The networked neo-tribal gaze. In A. Hardy, A. Bennett, and B. Robards (eds) *Neo-tribes: Consumption, leisure and tourism.* Switzerland: Palgrave, 221–34.

Dinis, A. and Krakover, S. (2015) Niche tourism in small peripheral towns: The case of Jewish heritage in Belmonte, Portugal. *Tourism Planning & Development,* 13(3), 310–32.

Heath, M.T., Tynan, C. and Ennew, C.T. (2011) Self-gift giving: Understanding consumers and exploring brand messages. *Journal of Marketing Communications,* 17(2), 127–44.

Heath, T.P., Tynan, C. and Ennew, C. (2015) Accounts of self-gift giving: Nature, context and emotions. *European Journal of Marketing,* 49(7/8), 1067–86.

Kaufmann, M., Sigfried, P., Huck, L. and Stettler, J. (2019) Analysis of tourism hotspot behaviour based on geolocated travel blog data: The case of Qyer. *International Journal of Geo-Information,* 8, 493–515.

Kim, A. and Lee, Y.S. (2009) Queensland as a golf tourism destination: From South Korean market perspective. *International Journal of Tourism Policy,* 2(1–2), 124–37.

Kim, B. and Kim, J. (2020) The rise of a new tourism destination: How did Vladivostok become the closest Europe for Korean tourists? *Journal of Eurasian Studies*, 11(2), 117–32.

Kim, S. (2019) The 'condescending old people' of South Korea's workforce. *BBC*, 6 August. Available at: https://www.bbc.com/worklife/article/20190726-the-condescending-old-people-of-south-koreas-workforce (accessed 5 January 2020).

Kivetz, R. and Simonson, I. (2002) Earning to right to indulge: Effort as a determinant of customer preferences toward frequency program rewards. *Journal of Marketing Research*, 39(2), 155–70.

Kwak, J. and Hong, J. (2018) An analysis of the YOLO phenomenon using big data: Based on tour consumption. *International Journal of Tourism and Hospitality Research*, 32(2), 21–34.

Lee, S. (2021) Tourism organization reveals travel trends of 2020. *Korea JoongAng Daily*, 22 April. Available at: https://koreajoongangdaily.joins.com/2021/04/22/culture/foodTravel/Korea-Tourism-Organization/20210422201000445.html?detailWord= (accessed 5 May 2021).

Lee, S.H. and Tideswell, C. (2005) Understanding attitudes towards leisure travel and the constraints faced by senior Koreans. *Journal of Vacation Marketing*, 11(3), 249–63.

Lee, Y.S., Prebebsen, N.K. and Chen, J. (2015) Christian spirituality and tourist motivations. *Tourism Analysis*, 20(6), 631–43.

Lim, C. (2004) The major determinants of Korean outbound travel to Australia. *Mathematics and Computers in Simulation*, 64, 477–85.

Marson, D. (2011) From mass tourism to niche tourism. In P. Robinson, S. Heitmann and P. Dieke (eds) *Research themes for tourism*. CABI, 1–15.

Martin, D. and Woodside, A.G. (2011) Storytelling research on international visitors: Interpreting own experiences in Tokyo. *Qualitative Market Research: An International Journal*, 14(1), 27–54.

Mick, D.G. (1991) Giving gifts to ourselves: A Greimassian analysis leading to testable propositions. In H. Larsen, D.G. Mick and C. Alsted (eds) *Marketing and semiotics: Selected papers from the Copenhagen Symposium*. Copenhagen: Copenhagen Business School Press, 142–59.

Mick, D.G. and DeMoss, M. (1990) To me from me: A descriptive phenomenology of self-gifts. In M. E. Goldberg, G. Gorn and R.W. Pollay (eds) *Advances in consumer research, vol. 17*. Provo, UT: Association for Consumer Research, 677–82.

Mick, D.G. and Faure, C. (1998) Consumer self-gifts in achievement contexts: The role of outcomes, attributions, emotions and deservingness. *International Journal of Research in Marketing*, 15(4), 293–307.

Mitu, B. (2015) Confucianism and the contemporary Korean society. *Romanian Journal of Sociological Studies*, 1, 31–38.

Moon, G. (2020) The young Koreans pushing back on a culture of endurance. *BBC*, 9 January. Available at: https://www.bbc.com/worklife/article/20200108-the-young-koreans-pushing-back-on-a-culture-of-endurance (accessed 11 January 2020).

Nikkei (2021) South Korea unemployment rate soars to 21-year high. *Nikkei Asia*, 10 February. Available at: https://asia.nikkei.com/Economy/South-Korea-unemployment-rate-soars-to-21-year-high (accessed 2 March 2021).

Norton, M. (2017) Self-gifting: Marketing and 'treat yourself' culture. *Third Wunder*, 13 October. Available at: https://www.thirdwunder.com/marketing-self-gifting/ (accessed 5 January 2020).

Novelli, M. (2005) *Niche Tourism: Contemporary issues, trends and cases*. Oxford, UK: Elsevier.

OECD (2021) Hours worked (indicator). doi: 10.1787/47be1c78-en (accessed 23 April 2021).

Olshavsky, R.W. and Lee, D.H. (1993) Self-gifts: A metacognition perspective. In L. McAlister and M.L. Rothschild (eds) *Advances in consumer research, vol. 20*. Association for Consumer Research, 547–52.

O'Regan, M. (2013) Framing tourism: Niche tourists. In S. McCabe (ed) *The Routledge Handbook of Tourism Marketing*. London: Routledge, 268–80.

Park and Lim (2018) 공부보다 아이와의 인생 체험 위해 떠난다...엄마표 '한달 살기' 열풍, *DongA*, 26 August. Available at: https://news.v.daum.net/v/20180826151933554 (accessed 18 February 2020).

Poon, A. (1993) *Tourism, technology and competitive strategies*. Wallingford: CAB International.

Qian, Y. (2019) Why young people in South Korea are staying single despite efforts to spark dating. *The Conversation*, 12 February. Available at: https://www.salon.com/2019/02/14/why-young-people

-in-south-korea-are-staying-single-despite-efforts-to-spark-dating_partner/ (accessed 12 December 2020).

Reuters (2021) South Korea's fertility rate falls to lowest in the world. *Reuters*, 24 February. Available at: https://www.reuters.com/business/healthcare-pharmaceuticals/skoreas-fertility-rate-falls-lowest -world-2021-02-24/ (accessed 1 March 2021).

Robinson, M. and Novelli, M. (2005) Niche tourism: An introduction. In M. Novelli (ed.) *Niche tourism: Contemporary issues, trends and cases.* Oxford: Butterworth-Heinemann, 1–14.

Salazar, N.B. (2012) Tourism imaginaries: A conceptual approach. *Annals of Tourism Research*, 39, 863–82.

Salazar, N.B. and Graburn, N. (2014) *Tourism imaginaries: Anthropological approaches.* New York: Berghahn.

Sherry, J.F., Jr., McGrath, M.A. and Levy, S.J. (1995) Monadic giving: Anatomy of gifts to the self. In J. F., Sherry Jr. (ed.) *Contemporary marketing and consumer behavior: An anthropological sourcebook.* Thousand Oaks, CA: SAGE, 399–432.

Shin, I. and Choi. M. (2019) One-month stay in fashion among Korean overseas travellers. *Pulsenews,* 4 March. Available at: https://pulsenews.co.kr/view.php?year=2019&no=129249 (accessed 28 March 2019).

Silva, K. (2020) Less and later marriage in South Korea. *Omnia*, 13 February. Available at: https://omnia .sas.upenn.edu/story/less-and-later-marriage-south-korea (accessed 15 February 2020).

Snee, H. (2013) Framing the other: Cosmopolitanism and the representation of difference in overseas gap year narratives. *British Journal of Sociology*, 64(1), 142–62.

Song, J.E.R. (2014) The soybean paste girl: The cultural and gender politics of coffee consumption in contemporary South Korea. *Journal of Korean Studies*, 19(2), 429–48.

Song, S.M. and Jang, S.H. (2021) An identification of determinants to ambivalent purchase intention of fashion luxury brand expanded cosmetic for MZ generation. *The Journal of the Korea Contents Association*, 21(3), 47–67.

Statista (2020) Average outbound travel days in South Korea 2019, by age group. *Statista Research Department*, 11 August. Available at: https://www.statista.com/statistics/1136314/south-korea -average-foreign-travel-days-by-age-group/ (accessed 1 September 2020).

Statista (2021) Expenditure of tourists from South Korea 2010–2020. *Statista Research Department*, February. Available at: https://www.statista.com/statistics/1143158/south-korea-expenditure-south -korean-tourists/ (accessed 1 March 2021).

Steger, I. and Jung, S. (2017) Exhausted by the herd, single South Koreans are gingerly embracing the 'YOLO' lifestyle. *Quarts*, 3 August. Available at: https://qz.com/1024923/exhausted-by-the-herd -single-south-koreans-are-gingerly-embracing-the-yolo-lifestyle/ (accessed 3 February 2020).

Sun, M., Ryan, C. and Pan, S. (2014) Assessing tourists' perceptions and behaviour through photographic and blog analysis: The case of Chinese bloggers and New Zealand holidays. *Tourism Management Perspectives*, 12, 125–33.

Suzuki, S (2021) South Korea facing worst labor market crisis since 1997. *Nikkei Asia*, 21 February. Available at: https://asia.nikkei.com/Economy/South-Korea-facing-worst-labor-market-crisis-since -19972 (accessed 16 March 2021).

Ursache, M. (2015) Niche tourism markets – Means of enhancing sustainable economic development in EU's Eastern periphery. *CES Working Papers, ISSN 2067-7693, Alexandru Ioan Cuza University of Iasi, Centre for European Studies, Iasi*, 7(2), 648–61.

Volgger, M., Pforr, C. and Ross Dowling, R. (2021) Tribes in tourism: A socio-cultural perspective on special interest tourism consumption. In C. Pforr, R. Dowling and M. Volgger (eds) *Consumer tribes in tourism: Contemporary perspectives on special-interest tourism.* Singapore: Springer, 261–7.

Weiler, B. and Firth, T. (2021) special interest travel: Reflections, rejections and reassertions. In C. Pforr, R. Dowling and M. Volgger (eds) *Consumer tribes in tourism: Contemporary perspectives on special-interest tourism.* Singapore: Springer, 11–26.

Yang, E.C.L., Khoo-Lattimore, C. and Arcodia, C. (2017) A narrative review of Asian female travellers: Looking into the future through the past. *Current Issues in Tourism*, 20(10), 1008–27.

Yang, E.C.L., Khoo-Lattimore, C. and Arcodia, C. (2018) Power and empowerment: How Asian solo female travellers perceive and negotiate risks. *Tourism Management*, 68, 32–45.

Yeom, J.H., Young S.U. and Chea, S. (2021) Greed and desperation drive the young into big stock bets. *JoongAngDaily*, 1 February. Available at: https://koreajoongangdaily.joins.com/2021/02/01/business/finance/stock-kospi-kosdaq/20210201201700642.html (accessed 2 March 2021).

Yeoman, I. (2008) *Tomorrow's tourist: Scenarios and trends*. London: Routledge.

Yonhap News (2019) More youth suffering from depression. *Yonhap News*, 29 November. Available at: https://en.yna.co.kr/view/AEN20191129003700320 (accessed 12 December 2020).

Zhang, K.Z.K., Lee, M.K.O., Cheung C.M.K. and Chen, H. (2009) Understanding the role of gender in bloggers' switching behaviour. *Decision Support Business*, 47, 540–46.

Zhang, Y. and Hitchcock, M.J. (2017) The Chinese female tourist gaze: A netnography of young women's blogs on Macao. *Current Issues in Tourism*, 20(3), 315–30.

34. Unseen Tours' virtual 'Not-in-a-Pub' quizzes: social inclusion and empowerment in times of COVID-19

Claudia Dolezal, Jayni Gudka and Dominic Lapointe

INTRODUCTION

COVID-19 had a devastating impact on the year 2020 in many ways, and especially on the tourism industry. A complete curb on international travel led the tourism industry to come to an immediate standstill, affecting the livelihoods of millions of people working in the tourism sector across urban and rural areas on all continents, experiencing sudden and significant drops in the number of tourist arrivals. Unable to offer the necessary space for social distancing, city spaces have been regarded as particularly risky to live in or move around. As a consequence, many decided to spend their 2020 summer staycationing in the countryside, turning rural areas into the tourism 'winners' of 2020 (Vaishar and Šťastná, 2022).

In cities, the situation has been much more sobering: London, for example, experienced a major tourism downturn with 'spending by tourists in central London [...] set to plummet by £10.9 billion' in 2020, as forecasted in October 2020 by the London Mayor Sadiq Khan (London Government, 2020). However, the sudden drop in tourist arrivals in one of the major urban tourism destinations of the world is not the only issue the city has had to deal with. London has also faced a range of other problems caused by the crisis, including the exacerbation of the longstanding problem of homelessness. With the tourism and hospitality sectors particularly impacted by the crisis and many people losing their jobs and livelihoods as a consequence, homelessness grew significantly in 2020. Statistics show that there were 4,227 rough sleepers in London in April–June 2020, which is a 33% increase on the same period in the previous year (Chain, 2021).

One organization already working with this marginalized group of people was able to continue addressing the problem of homelessness and the loss of livelihoods within their organization through pivoting their business and creating an alternative livelihood with the development of a niche tourism product during this time of crisis. Unseen Tours' virtual 'Not-in-a-pub' quizzes were curated by their formerly homeless and vulnerably housed tour guides in London to offer an alternative income through the lockdown caused by the pandemic.

Unseen Tours is a London-based social enterprise that has been supporting Londoners who have been affected by homelessness. Since 2010 they have been training them to become tour guides and offering alternative tours to tourists who want to see the city from a different angle, or learn about homelessness. Knowing that they were supporting vulnerable adults working in one of the most volatile industries affected by COVID-19, the directors of Unseen Tours had to find an alternative opportunity for their tour guides. The virtual pub quizzes were thus created to make up for the sudden loss in livelihood of those guides, while also keeping the momentum going for future tours and visits of London's 'unseen' spaces.

This chapter discusses Unseen Tours' response to the crisis by analysing their virtual tourism product through the niche tourism lens. Its aim is threefold: firstly, it offers insights into the creation process of a niche product in times of crisis and the motivations behind it; secondly, it demonstrates how niche tourism can support marginalized members of society not just with an alternative livelihood but also a sense of personal empowerment; and thirdly, it shows how virtual niche tourism can offer both tangible and intangible benefits in times of crisis, contributing to sustainable tourism through social change and a greater sense of public responsibility. To arrive at a deeper analysis of the latter, this chapter draws on Young's (2011) social connection model of responsibility.

The key argument this chapter makes is that niche tourism can provide much more than a simple product diversification strategy that responds to the rise of the authenticity-seeking tourist. It has the potential to not only assist vulnerable Londoners economically through crises such as the COVID-19 pandemic, but also offers an opportunity to contribute in a meaningful way. Through the tours, they can turn their stories and knowledge of the city into tourism assets, while also increasing a wider understanding of the issues around homelessness. This chapter therefore adds to Novelli's (2018) call to extend the debate on whether and how niche tourism can be a more sustainable and responsible kind of tourism for the challenges destinations are currently facing, particularly when it comes to poverty eradication in a non-developing country context. It also aims to explore how niche tourism can go further than responsible consumption to address situations of structural injustice, like urban homelessness, through a responsibility justice lens aimed at social transformations (Young, 2011).

VIRTUAL PUB QUIZZES: HOMELESS GUIDES' NICHE TOURISM PRODUCT

In its original form, niche tourism has been conceptualized as an alternative to mass tourism – a stark contrast in the numbers of travellers and their motives (Novelli, 2005). Niche tourism was originally defined from three different stances: the geographical and demographic approach, the product-related approach and the customer-related approach (Robinson and Novelli, 2005). As shown in an earlier publication (Dolezal and Gudka, 2019), Unseen Tours' pre-pandemic offerings fit this conceptualization of niche tourism in all of these three dimensions:

- *The geographical (and demographic) niche*: This becomes obvious when looking at the urban spaces in which Unseen tours take place. While some Unseen tours are situated in well-known tourist areas, others focus on some of the more 'edgy', less frequented and therefore more 'unseen' and remote corners of London.
- *The product-related niche*: Unseen Tours offer a niche product in that the attractions included in the tours are very specific (e.g., street art in London by 'Stik' and 'Banksy' or places of famous movie scenes such as *Bridget Jones' Diary*) and the knowledge that guides communicate is extremely 'niche'.
- *The customer-related niche*: Unseen Tours targets quite a niche market – with earlier research that has argued that the homeless tours 'fulfil tourists' ever-present demands for encountering the "authentic" (Dolezal and Gudka, 2019: 142). The tours therefore cater to those tourists that not only want to see another side of London, far away from the glitzy

image that many tourists might have, but also to those that have an interest to learn more about homelessness and marginalization in an urban context.

The above shows that Unseen Tours' usual product (i.e., tours led by people affected by homelessness) qualifies as a type of niche tourism, particularly within the macro-niche of urban tourism (Robinson and Novelli, 2005) and a micro-niche that could be categorized as 'resident-related social tourism'. The latter is defined as including 'groups into tourism that would otherwise be excluded from it' (Minnaert, 2014: 283). Earlier research showed that tour guiding led by people with experience of homelessness can be seen as a form of social tourism of a city, contributing to societal change in an urban context (Dolezal and Gudka, 2019). However, the question that emerges is whether this is also the case when looking at the virtual products that Unseen Tours offer in times of COVID-19. Could these products still be classified as a kind of social niche tourism?

Before moving on to a terminological debate, it is important to define sustainability and social inclusion in the context of niche tourism. Though niche tourism was originally regarded as the polar opposite to mass forms of tourism, some have argued that many forms of niche tourism have since been commodified to such an extent that they are now aimed at the masses (Marson, 2011; Peeters, 2012). This means that it is difficult to describe niche tourism as 'niche' in the same way in today's context as the boundary between mass and niche tourism becomes more blurred (Novelli, 2018), raising the question of the sustainability of niche tourism in its original form. While its potential 'to offer greater opportunities and a tourism that is more sustainable, less damaging and, importantly, more capable of delivering high-spending tourists' (Robinson and Novelli, 2005: 1) has been discussed quite early on, the sustainability debate has intensified in recent years. Destination management/marketing organizations have begun to use niche tourism to support more sustainable tourism product development, which has also intensified the discussion as to whether and how niche tourism can make the industry better, more sustainable and, above all, more inclusive (Novelli, 2018).

Novelli (2018) has argued that niche tourism's contribution to destinations and people's livelihoods is significant, particularly in some of the most remote parts of the world through 'spreading the benefits into the wider community and inclusive growth by providing a wider set of opportunities for those affected by tourism' (p. 346). Tourism therefore becomes a tool to stimulate inclusive growth, not just through the fostering of SMEs and small businesses, but also due to the power it holds to reach its economic benefits beyond just a small, privileged group of people, towards those operating at the margins (Dinis and Krakover, 2016; Hampton and Jeyacheya, 2013; Novelli, 2018).

In the context of the present research on virtual pub quizzes by those who have experienced homelessness (but also tour guiding if looking at Unseen Tours' activities more broadly), this idea of social inclusion applies. Unseen Tours aims to redistribute some of the economic benefits of the tourism industry to also include those most marginalized in an urban environment.

In this way, this type of niche tourism not only satisfies the destinations' needs in becoming more sustainable and more closely aligned with the UN SDGs, but it also satisfies the consumer's demand for opportunities to become a more conscious traveller – one that makes a difference while looking for more meaningful and authentic experiences when travelling (Novelli, 2018). At the same time though, one has to acknowledge the threat of commodification that is always lurking just around the corner (Marson, 2011). Many of the tourists that go on Unseen tours are not just looking for a more 'authentic' representation of London in a city tour, but are also driven by a desire to act more responsibly when travelling and make sure that they know how their money is spent (i.e., that it is reaching those that do actually work for it) (Tripadvisor, 2019). Beyond the economic dimension, Unseen Tours therefore allow a discursive moment between the guides and the tourist about the experience of the city and of homelessness.

What happens when niche tourism suddenly turns into a virtual form of tourism, taking place online via platforms like Zoom? Can virtual tourism continue to make a positive contribution to a more sustainable and responsible future of tourism for the guides employed by the industry, even when not consumed at the destination? In the first edited volume on niche tourism by Novelli (2005), Arnold (2005) discusses virtual niche tourism as a form of niche tourism that integrates technology into the cultural tourism sector to enhance the tourist experience (e.g., through virtual tours). Without a doubt, virtual tourism has been growing steadily since then, with research focusing on virtual tourism for tourism and destination marketing (Huang et al., 2016; Palmer and McCole, 2000), the perception of authenticity amongst consumers (Mura et al., 2017), virtual and augmented reality (Beck et al., 2019; Yung and Khoo-Lattimore, 2017), and e-tourism to combat destination challenges, such as destination recovery after COVID-19, particularly in developing countries (Chirisa, 2020).

However, few nowadays would refer to virtual tourism or the integration of technology as 'niche', particularly in times of COVID-19 where tourism has significantly shifted to online spaces (Wörndl et al., 2021) and one's virtual life and identity have at times become more important than one's real-life encounters (Riva and Wiederhold, 2020). The crisis has led to various changes in the tourism sector, with one being the increasing virtualization of the tourist product, or rather, future tourism products. Many countries joined the bandwagon of posting promotional videos, creating virtual tours and the like to advertise their destinations for tourists to visit and enjoy in the future – shifting the (presently very limited) tourism experience into the virtual space (Mariano, 2020). Indeed, Yang et al. (2021), in a recent study, found that 360° destination virtual tours can relieve psychological stress during COVID-19 and therefore be a useful substitute for tourism.

Just like travel, much of our social life has transitioned to the virtual world in this time of crisis, with plentiful leisure opportunities thanks to technological progress (Black, 2021). Particularly in a time with significant restrictions on movement, 'the importance of everyday digital technologies for communicating remotely with intimate others' (Watson et al., 2021: 1) has intensified. Previous studies have shown that social media can create virtual intimacy, particularly between friends and family who find themselves distanced geographically (Farci et al., 2017; Longhurst, 2016). However, what was new during the COVID-19 pandemic was a significant shift of leisure and entertainment into virtual spaces. Since March 2020, the world has seen leisure events, work, conferences, coffee chats and family gatherings take place online (Black, 2021; Watson et al., 2021). Even rituals have been amended and moved into the virtual world (Imber-Black, 2020). This seeking of virtual presence with others (particularly when cameras are turned on) (Watson et al., 2021), often led to people being in touch more often and with more people than they would usually (Hacker et al., 2020). COVID-19 has therefore led to new ways of interacting online (Khobra and Gaur, 2020), a 'new virtual togetherness' and solidarity (Hacker et al., 2020), as well as a new 'experience economy upsurge' (Kaur and Kaur, 2020: 239), to which businesses have needed to respond.

Virtual pub quizzes are one of these responses and inventions that were on the rise during the pandemic outbreak, with various London pubs moving their evening entertainment online to 'provide the intellectual stimulation that bored self-distancers are [...] craving' (Brennan, 2020: n.p.). Cartilage (2020) argues that 'it is perhaps [...] a shared sense of anxiety and boredom during lockdown that has led people to find new ways of enacting solidarity to try and alleviate them, such as singing with neighbours, hosting "virtual pub quizzes" or online exercise groups' (p. 18).

Unseen Tours was probably one of the first social enterprises that pivoted its business to live pub quizzes with a social purpose in a time that increasingly demanded solidarity, responsibility and a more conscious way of consumption (Higgins-Desbiolles, 2020; Ioannides and Gyimóthy, 2020; Pardo and Ladeiras, 2020; Stankov et al., 2020). The momentary suspension of tourism caused by COVID-19 provided an opportunity for the sector to 'reorient tourism based on the rights and interests of local communities and local peoples' (Higgins-Desbiolles, 2020: 620) as well as demand a more mindful, conscious and compassionate tourism industry and tourist (Stankov et al., 2020), and one that is more socially inclusive (McCabe and Qiao, 2020; Pardo and Ladeiras, 2020). Virtual pub quizzes generated an opportunity for this, providing a niche (tourism) product with a social purpose, a way, or at least a tool, to stimulate 'resident-related social tourism', while also meeting market demands for a viable virtual tourism experience.

UNSEEN TOURS' VIRTUAL PUB QUIZZES: LONDON'S HOMELESS TOUR GUIDES AT WORK DURING TIMES OF CRISIS

Unseen Tours is a not-for-profit London social enterprise that offers a source of income to people who have experienced homelessness and vulnerable housing situations, through training and employing these individuals as tour guides. These guides take tourists on walking tours through the areas in which they live – both well-known and less well-known to tourists – weaving in their own stories and experiences of homelessness into the tour narrative. The aim of the organization is to make a positive contribution to address the growing problem of homelessness in London, which, over the years, has been steadily rising (Homeless Link, 2021a).

Unseen Tours does this not only by providing meaningful work opportunities for people affected by homelessness, but also by putting them '"back on the map", giving them political power by being responsible for part of the tourism industry in the city' (Dolezal and Gudka, 2019: 157). Given that homeless and vulnerably housed Londoners are often seen as invisible, their contribution to tourism becomes an important tool that renders them visible not just in front of tourists but also the wider society and government (Dolezal and Lapointe, 2020). Furthermore, Unseen Tours seeks to challenge stereotypes surrounding homelessness, which is achieved through conversations with tourists around the topic and having the guides tell their own, very personal stories of homelessness while guiding people around London (Dolezal and Gudka, 2019).

The tours take place in different areas of London (e.g., London Bridge, Brick Lane), usually in areas where the guides have lived or worked. The content of the tours varies, but generally the guides share historical and social knowledge of the area, combined with their experiences of being homeless. The attractions they talk about along the way include well-known and lesser-known attractions and places with a 'niche' interest, such as Bridget Jones' front door in London Bridge. The intention at all times is to give tourists a glimpse of a different kind of

London, to show them 'a historical London with an "unseen" dimension, through the lens of homelessness' (Dolezal and Gudka, 2019: 147) (see Figure 34.1).

Source: Unseen Tours.

Figure 34.1   On a tour with Soho guide Nic

With the global pandemic reaching the UK in March 2020 resulting in a national lockdown, guides were forced to stop their tours without notice, meaning they suddenly lost their source of income. The first 'Not-in-the-Pub' quiz in April was therefore an innovative and creative way to establish a new source of income for the guides (see Figure 34.2). This is illustrated by one of the quotes from Pete, the Brick Lane Tour guide: 'We at Unseen Tours had kept busy in the last few months by organizing our "Not-In-A-Pub" quiz [...] as a way to keep our profile up and, of course, bring in some much-needed cash for us tour guides'. Unseen Tours added: 'We have expanded our product range, but our vision and purpose has remained the same' (Gudka, 2020b).

The quizzes are meant to not only generate an income for guides but to also keep tackling the social stigma surrounding homelessness, by adding an educational dimension in which guides play an active role. The first quiz open to the public took place in April 2020 and was followed by a range of private quizzes for companies and other groups. Guides were involved in the quiz content and question design from the very start, meaning that the first quiz took around three weeks to prepare. The key motivation was to make sure that the guides understood the purpose of the quiz, how it worked so that they could frame their questions better, equipped with their own knowledge of London, so that it could then be marketed successfully to the public.

The quiz questions remained closely linked to the tours that guides were doing in their usual day to day lives. After the first few quizzes, London's lockdown was temporarily lifted in the summer, allowing Unseen Tour guides to resume their tours after completing COVID-19 safety training based on Visit England's guidelines (see Figures 34.3 and 34.4). 'We also decided to start the tours with some social distancing measures to maintain the safety of our customers and ourselves, which included wearing a visor, wearing a portable microphone

Source:　Claudia Dolezal.

Figure 34.2　　*Unseen Tours' 'Not-in-a-Pub' quiz from participants' perspective*

and encouraging that everyone stays the recommended length of 2 metres apart and other measures. Also, during the training for this the Unseen Tours team met for the first time in months and we had a nice picnic'. says Pete, one of the guides (2021). At that time, Unseen Tours received Visit Britain's 'Good to Go' industry standard in recognition of those safety precautions the social enterprise was taking. As stated on the website, 'The label demonstrates that Unseen Tours is adhering to public health guidance as set out by the government, and that we have carried out a Covid-19 risk assessment'. (Unseen Tours, 2020a: n.p.).

METHODOLOGY

The present research is based on a qualitative methodology, which aims to gain insights into guides' and customers' experiences of participating in the virtual quizzes. Participant observations were conducted online, with the authors of the chapter participating in pub quizzes themselves, both in the role of attendees and organizers. It must be noted that the second author participated in all of these, given her involvement in Unseen Tours' work and the organization of the quizzes. A total of four 'Not-in-a-Pub' quizzes were attended over the months of April to June, followed by 12 private Christmas quizzes in the months of November and December. The biggest quiz in summer (the first one, taking place on 25 April) had 67 groups join, with 135 Zoom accounts joining the quiz in total. The biggest one – the Christmas Quiz – had 105 participants from one single company. In terms of the involvement of guides, three guides participated in the curating of questions, a fourth was involved in the video element, while a fifth guide did not want to participate. At least one guide was present at each of the virtual

Source: Unseen Tours (2020a).

Figure 34.3 *Unseen Tours' COVID-19 safety regulations*

Source: Unseen Tours.

Figure 34.4 *On an Unseen Tour with David during the COVID-19 pandemic*

Christmas quizzes, which means that all those four guides that were part of the quizzes were also part of the observations.

Participatory observations were non-intrusive and covert in that the researchers did not reveal their role, given that this was not their only purpose of participating in the quizzes, as this could have affected people's behaviour and hence presented the researchers with an inaccurate account of reality. Observations took place in a non-intrusive way to gain some first insights into people's experience, however, without asking any obvious questions or revealing participants' identities. Ethical considerations were therefore given to issues such as treating data confidentially, making sure no individuals could be identified later on in the research and not asking sensitive questions or impacting on the experience of individuals in the quiz in any kind of way. This research therefore constitutes an exploratory study on the topic, creating the first discussion of some of the emerging issues to then form the basis for future, more in-depth research on the topic.

In addition to participant observations of the quiz, the CEO of the social enterprise, who also is one of the co-authors, was interviewed to share her insights of the pub quizzes, the motivations behind them and how they developed over the months, analysed and written up by the other authors to ensure a more objective stance on the topic. To represent guides' opinions on the quizzes, interviews that Unseen Tours conducted with the guides are drawn on and referenced here.

FROM PUBLIC TO CORPORATE QUIZZES: ADDING A SOCIAL DIMENSION TO VIRTUAL TOURISM

From the very start, the purpose of the virtual 'Not-in-a-Pub' quizzes was to find a way to continue engaging the guides by providing meaningful work opportunities for them, as well as having online dialogues about homelessness. According to the CEO there were a number of reasons behind the virtual pub quizzes. These include the fact that the quizzes:

- constituted an alternative work opportunity through the creation of a niche product;
- responded to a niche gap in the market – as people were looking for interesting social activities to undertake with their friends while maintaining the necessary social distancing measures;
- provided a way for the social enterprise to have a dialogue with the public about homelessness issues, as was usually done on tours, meaning that the virtual quizzes were a way to further Unseen Tours' goal of challenging stereotypes surrounding homelessness;
- were a way for the public to benefit from the guides' niche and expert knowledge on London;
- brought London to people at a time when it was impossible to otherwise discover the city, making it accessible for people with impairments and disabilities, as well as people living abroad. Other research confirms that COVID-19 and the rise in technologies and virtual activities has led to higher participation in events and social inclusion (Hacker et al., 2020);
- became a small revenue stream for the social enterprise. Initially, all money was distributed amongst all the guides who curated the questions for the quiz. For the Christmas Quiz, however, 60% of the profits were distributed amongst the guides as the rest was used to pay for the admin costs/phone costs and marketing which Unseen Tours would have usually covered through the tours, but were unable to because of the lockdown;
- helped to market the tours – many people who came to the quizzes were enchanted by the guides' charisma. Some of these quiz participants proceeded to come on the tour during the summer, when guides were allowed to run some tours after implementing the COVID-19 safety measures, and others said they looked forward to coming in the future.

All the reasons mentioned above resulted in a virtual niche tourism product with a social purpose – linking entertainment aspects of a pub quiz with London as a destination, facilitated with the expert knowledge of the organization's formerly homeless tour guides. The successful implementation of the virtual quizzes also led to Unseen Tours receiving a commendation at the Homeless Link Social Enterprise of the Year Awards for their excellent and innovative work to support guides during the pandemic (Homeless Link, 2021b).

While the first virtual pub quizzes were open to the public, Unseen Tours soon started venturing into the field of corporate quizzes, sold as corporate social responsibility (CSR) partnerships to companies:

> A single quiz can last between one to two hours and also be tailored to corporate needs making them shorter or longer, or even including a specialist subject to make them more relevant and interesting for your staff. At a cost of just £5 per team it's a perfect experience for both small, medium or bigger businesses. Running corporate quizzes on a monthly basis is a great way to continue maintaining the excitement and allowing staff to connect and outside of work-related Zoom calls and webinars. (Unseen Tours, 2020c)

Tapping into this new market was done both as a way to maximize the financial support for guides to keep raising awareness about the homelessness issue, while also filling a gap in the market regarding virtual team building in times of crisis (Gudka, 2020a; Unseen Tours, 2020b). At the same time, the importance of the social impact dimension helped promote the quiz to businesses, especially in the run up to Christmas, with the tagline 'Make a positive social impact with your office Christmas party this year' (Gudka, 2020c; Unseen Tours, 2020d). While the idea of generating a positive social impact as part of companies' CSR has been heavily criticized in the literature (Banerjee, 2008; Newell and Frynas, 2007; Weijo et al., 2014), this chapter argues that the *active* involvement of guides made this virtual niche tourism product a viable livelihood replacement and a suitable product for ethical CSR requirements of companies, while simultaneously fulfilling Unseen Tours' social enterprise ethos:

> With the added benefit of making a positive social impact by raising awareness about homelessness, the tours will stimulate reflection and understanding of local issues, through a gentle combination of facts and personal stories. The quiz will feature a variety of trivia, including history, film, theatre and a very special Christmas music round, and be hosted live by our fabulous Quiz masters. (Gudka, 2020c)

It was particularly the guides' expert knowledge that featured heavily in these quizzes, turning this into both an asset and attraction in a virtual context.

GUIDES WITH EXPERIENCE OF HOMELESSNESS AS VIRTUAL QUIZ CURATORS: VIRTUAL NICHE TOURISM TO EMPOWER MARGINALIZED PEOPLES

From attending and observing the virtual quizzes, it becomes obvious that the content is strongly based on the guides' knowledge of London. However, the CEO also revealed that the way questions were curated varied a lot between guides. All the information in the quizzes comes from guides and their knowledge, however, it took some guides longer than others to be able to contribute questions in a style or format that was suitable for the quiz. Pete, Unseen

Tours' Brick Lane tour guide, for example, said that: 'it was harder than I imagined to think of questions based on my tour, and it took me a while to get the hang of it'. Soho tour guide Nic found it equally challenging:

> Then along came Zoom. An Unseen Tours quiz! Way to go. I was taken aback as to how difficult I found curating questions. I'm not a puzzle person, it doesn't really cross my mind to do a crossword, I'd rather read. Fascinating facts are a doddle to find, but creating a question with three alternative answers?! It was a skill I had to work on. (Nic, 2020)

However, this process of curating questions was refined over the course of the year with the help of the Unseen Tours volunteers who led the virtual quiz initiative. At the beginning, they simply requested facts from the guides and worked with them to transform them into suitable questions. As more quizzes were created and co-hosted by the tour guides in the summer, they became more confident and accustomed to the type of questions that worked well, meaning that the creation of the Christmas quiz was much more streamlined. With a growth in confidence about what was expected, guides also began suggesting suitable quiz rounds, such as a UK Christmas chart number 1s which was curated by David, the London Bridge tour guide, who is a great lover of music.

In terms of the content of the quizzes it also became obvious that the quizzes promoted to the general public taking place at the start of the pandemic were aimed at more regular quiz goers – those who regularly participated in pub quizzes and hence were able to deal with quite challenging questions that required a deeper understanding of London (see Figure 34.5).

Q10   Near the Globe Theatre, there is an old stone seat. Who used to rest here during their work day?

a) Priests
b) Prostitutes
c) Ferrymen
d) Theatre actors

Source: Unseen Tours.

Figure 34.5   *Sample question of an Unseen Tours 'Not-in-a-Pub' quiz*

Gradually, however, and also to make the quizzes more open to the general public and those future travellers living in other countries (rather than only pub quiz enthusiasts with a greater knowledge of London), the questions became easier. For the Christmas quizzes, questions were not only simplified but also made more generic, meaning that they didn't require as much specialist knowledge of London.

Despite the fact that quizzes became a little less 'niche' (both in terms of questions and the market they attracted) and aimed more at the general public, the guides played an essential role at all times. Their expertise forms the basis of the product, with questions ranging from music to street art, demonstrating that niche tourism requires more specialized insight, going beyond the generic knowledge often associated with mass products (Novelli, 2018). Guides therefore had the specialist knowledge of London to add value to the virtual quizzes, and some (i.e., those who felt like attending the quiz live) also used the 'virtual stage' during the quiz by presenting the questions, getting a further sense of empowerment and achievement. Again, as in the tours, guides are empowered by 'shap[ing] the narrative' (Dolezal and Gudka, 2019: 157) and 'sharing their own personal stories, rather than pointing to and sharing those of others' (ibid: 154).

For example, David, the London Bridge tour guide, reflected on his virtual quiz experience:

> I was Quizmaster for my first online quiz, including six of our Unseen Tours Christmas Not-in-a-Pub Quizzes! I have experience of hosting quizzes in the past, but never virtually, and usually just for friends and people at my church.
> My round was the music round. Music is a passion of mine and I have an eclectic taste. When I was 30, I came up with 90 songs that I liked, and that had all been released in the 30 years since I was born (one rule: they couldn't be from the same group or artist!). I played all of these on my 30th birthday, and did the same my 40th and 50th! My favourite artist of all time is Phil Collins – I have a photo of him on the wall that has moved with me through five different homes. The quizzes were a fun opportunity to bring all of this knowledge together and put minds to the test!' (David, 2021)

This quote illustrates the personal connection that guides have to their quiz questions, as well as the sense of achievement they gained through transmitting their knowledge and testing others. Other guides became so engaged in the quizzes that they spoke about how special the quizzes were for them, given that 'The passions and friendships were newly rekindled and life became more bearable once more (when) the "Not-In-A-Pub" quizzes were back on' (Pete, 2021).

When it comes to the participation in the quizzes, guides who curated questions were invited (but, of course, not forced) at all times to actively participate in the live quiz. However, not all guides were comfortable to participate live for numerous reasons: 'Personally I remain on audio during the quiz, I've always avoided cameras where possible. Just me, no deep reason' (Nic, 2020). Other tour guides faced extra obstacles in attending the virtual quizzes, such as being unable to download the necessary mobile apps due to lack of confidence (and skill) in using technology (which Unseen Tours volunteers would usually help them with when they met for regular catch ups). This was perhaps the biggest challenge that the pandemic's lockdown created for the organization – the inability to meet in person to help with tasks such as accessing technology, which was an additional service that the volunteers helped the less technologically confident tour guides with. As Khobra and Gaur (2020) argue, one of the biggest challenges defining the time of the pandemic is that 'the "new normal" is characterized by the privilege of accessibility [and] affordance (virtual and economic)' (p. 5). When guides were unable to join quizzes, Unseen Tours showed a video or audio clip of them introducing their round of questions, and giving thanks to the audience. That way, Unseen Tours ensured that guides could present themselves – either through a video or through their own words live – rather than be introduced by others, which is essential to shape a realistic discourse by those who often find themselves at the margins of society (Monroe and Bishop 2016, about homelessness in this case).

The skills and knowledge that the guides were able to develop through the virtual and utilize in the quizzes therefore elevated them into a position of authority, just like during the tours (Dolezal and Gudka, 2020). Participants regularly show their admiration of guides' knowledge with comments such as 'Amazing Quiz, I never knew so much about the Old Smoke. Definitely going to do some tours about the art and music' (Shah, 2020, pub quiz participant). In return, guides felt proud of their knowledge and highly appreciated the responses they received. Nic, for example, confirmed the personal meaning of the quizzes by arguing that 'The response to the quizzes has been very uplifting though, listening to, and engaging with people, all so very diverse' (Nic, 2020).

CHALLENGING THE PUBLIC'S PERCEPTION OF HOMELESSNESS

The personal stories, pictures and videos, along with the active participation of the guides, is, of course, what brings the quiz to life for many of the participants. By hearing guides' stories and seeing their pictures and videos, participants were able to feel a personal connection with the guides, just as they would have on the tours. These interactions are important because they allow the guides to voice their own opinions and experiences while also developing their skills and confidence.

During the quiz, participants heard about the positive social impact that their joining the quiz had from the tour guides themselves, extending Unseen Tours' social impact further. Unseen Tours as a social enterprise also presented a couple of videos of two of the tour guides, sharing the impact that the organization has had on them over the past decade, creating a synergy between the quiz and tour activities. The videos also emphasized the issues faced when experiencing homelessness. Though this theme was significant in the introduction and promotion of the quiz, it was not the main focus of the quiz. This decision was taken to ensure a fun and uplifting team building activity for corporates, fitting in better with the Christmas quiz theme of goodwill and positivity and creating a fun experience to end the difficult year with, rather than focusing solely on the realities of homelessness which, though important, could bring the mood of the virtual experience down. There was, however, time allocated during the introduction, interval and quiz marking and scoring time for participants to engage guides with questions and conversations about homelessness. This allowed for a carefully balanced experience – enabling Unseen Tours to facilitate a fun experience for groups and corporates, while also allowing themes of homelessness to be approached in a safe and responsible way. It also ensured that the quiz did not reinforce a negative, poverty-porn-driven stereotype of homelessness, demonstrating the value that people who happened to have experienced homelessness brought to the quiz through their expert knowledge instead. In addition, these conversations helped Unseen Tours meet their objective of raising awareness and have conversations about homelessness. The virtual therefore became a useful space not just for entertainment in times of social distancing and lockdown, but also to maintain the conversation surrounding homelessness – a useful replacement for the real-life tours that would usually take place.

It became obvious that many companies regarded the social impact as a key reason to book a quiz. Participants were clearly entertained by an evening with colleagues or friends in a virtual pub quiz, but it also became apparent that a significant motivation for joining the quiz was to help support those whose livelihoods had been negatively impacted by the pandemic. One participant of the Christmas quizzes, for example, posted the following on LinkedIn, referring to his experience of attending the quiz:

> Personally I don't like to participate in flamboyant Christmas parties, on the basis of all wasteful consumption and the relating environmental damage. However, I am proud to be part of this year's Christmas celebration. Fun event, with opportunity to add to our general knowledge, and most importantly with a positive social impact! (Shah, 2020).

After all, niche tourism is not just about making new, authentic, experiences, but also increasingly about making a difference and being a more conscious consumer (Novelli, 2018). In a sense, participants here can be regarded as responsible 'niche consumers' – those that will turn into niche tourists at some point in the future. Particularly in times of the global COVID-19 pandemic, many argue that consumption patterns are essentially changing, paying more attention to buying locally, getting meaningful products and experiences and supporting those that are heavily affected by the crisis (Severo et al., 2021; Stankov et al., 2020). Therefore, niche tourism can, particularly in times of crisis 'play a key role in developing a better (future) tourism that does less harm and more good, if its suppliers and their destinations consciously and conscientiously focus on the desired outcomes and potential inputs and actions' (Novelli, 2018: 353).

KEEPING THE SPARK ALIVE: LINKING THE VIRTUAL TO THE PHYSICAL TOURS TO RESTART TOURISM AFTER THE CRISIS

Most importantly, Unseen Tours, together with the guides, are trying to link the quiz questions to their usual tours through London's boroughs. This helps Unseen Tours in restarting the tours in the future, while also providing a way to assist guides through a time where they miss going on tours:

> Not sure where I'd be without Unseen Tours, a focus for my passion for lives lived in London. I miss giving people a glimpse into another side of different lives, I miss connecting with complete strangers at Tottenham Court Road, yet feeling like we've maybe shared something, a good memory, hopefully. (Nic, 2020)

In summer 2020, the guides had the chance to get back to their usual work for at least a couple of weeks:

> We hosted a few during the summer months and we were complimented on them (i.e., the quizzes) by all our customers, but then it was time to get back to our real work… the best tours in London! We had a few bookings, though of course, the Corona situation had less people travelling to London for holidays, but we managed quite a few. (Pete, 2021)

When lockdown hit again in the autumn of 2020, Unseen Tours shifted back to the virtual quizzes. To create further synergies between the quizzes and the tours, in some of the quizzes video rounds were introduced. One such round was based on Pete's tour of Brick Lane, where people were asked questions based on a short taster experience of his walking tour through five videos about Brick Lane and some of the local history (including Jack the Ripper trivia). It also included a short 90-second mini-tour of Brick Lane's street art, which is a passion of Pete's. Participants were told to keep their eyes and ears open throughout the segment, after which they were asked one question about what they saw and remembered. Another question in this round was 'what does Pete say next?', where Unseen Tours filmed a short extract of his tour, and then stopped the video mid-sentence, so that participants had to guess what they think Pete said next on his tour. This helped bring the tours to life once more, and created intrigue amongst quiz participants, enticing them to join the tour when it restarted.

For the corporate quizzes, an optional prize could also be added – a private tour for the winning team – thus furthering the link to the tours and maintaining consumers' interest in participating in a tour in the future. When asked about the significance of the Christmas quizzes, Pete said:

> Fast forward to November and Unseen Tours started to organize our 'Christmas-Not-In-A-Pub' quizzes and they went down like the New Years Eve fireworks go up… Spectacularly! Winter, and in particular December are our busiest time of year, yeah I know most people presume that summer is our busiest time, but not so. BANG! The 'Christmas-Not-In-A-Pub' blew up! They were fun, interactive and (with a healthy dose of alcohol) also hilarious. One of the 'Christmas-Not-In-A-Pub' quizzes had over 100 participants! WOW! [...] although another shocker was about to be dropped… CHRISTMAS IS CANCELLED! Screamed the tabloids and the internet… hhhhmmmmm… Oh well, I thought, I've not celebrated crimbo for years, so what the heck? I was self-isolating anyway, and during this time Unseen Tours had an online team meeting where we had an internal, just for fun 'Christmas-Not-In-A-Pub' quiz. It was fun, but one of the questions, put by one of our amazing volunteers Jen was, 'What have you learned this year?' I really had to think hard and deeply about my answers. Remembering one of the worst years in living memory, we all had positive things to say in reply to this question. That sums up Unseen Tours emphatically, no matter what the odds there is always a better future that we can influence.

The spaces created through Unseen Tours' virtual pub quizzes have therefore become not just a new way to socialize for the guides, but also a tool to keep their passion for London alive. This is in line with many other experience providers that 'are resorting to innovation in keeping the engagement alive' (Kaur and Kaur, 2020: 241). Guides cannot wait to get back to their usual job, which increases their motivation for the future: 'These quizzes made me hanker to get back to touring around my beloved Brick Lane' (Pete, 2021).

At the same time, participants were inspired by the quizzes to get on a tour in the future. Some that joined the tours in the summer (when the lockdown eased slightly) argued that they:

> loved the quiz, it certainly put us to the test and we were both pretty surprised by how much there was still to learn about the city we'd always called home. As the lockdown was lifted, we took the opportunity to go on the Shoreditch tour, as the area's street art had always been something we'd wanted to explore further. The unexpected outcome of which was that our son is now determined to take up graffiti art too - something that we're not sure about yet, but just goes to show that we all learnt a lot and left the tour feeling inspired in our own individual ways. (Quiz participants and tour attendees from London – 46, male and 47, female)

Others who had not been in London at the time of lockdown had a feeling that they 'felt much more connected again to London, which I hugely miss during this time' (virtual quiz participant from Austria, 32, female).

This heightened sense of longing for certain places might be due to the fact that:

> [q]uarantine is destroying our sense of place. On the one hand, we can no longer go to the places that characterized our daily life and made sense of our identity. On the other, even the home is no longer a place because it has stopped having boundaries for those who live there. (Riva and Wiederhold, 2020: 277)

The discussion of space in this context therefore turns into one of blurring between space and place: 'As such, rather than using video technologies to make them feel more "at home", these devices and media were employed in a way that helped people who were confined to their homes to escape this sense of confinement and isolation' (Watson et al., 2021: 12). The virtual can therefore turn into a refuge for both participants and guides, a space that can, at least temporarily, give us a sense of being away, in the places we usually inhabit and frequent in our day to day lives.

SHARED SOCIAL JUSTICE AND RESPONSIBILITY THROUGH VIRTUAL NICHE TOURISM

Reflecting on the above, it becomes clear that Unseen Tours step away from the usual market-based responsible tourism niche to tackle issues of social justice in a more sustainable manner through their virtual pub quizzes. Indeed, as Iris Marion Young states (1990), social justice goes beyond economic redistribution and should include: '(1): developing and exercising one's capacities and expressing one's experiences, and (2): participating in determining one's actions and the conditions of one's actions' (p. 37). As discussed in this chapter, the virtual quizzes work within this social justice perspective as they are supported by having guides develop questions themselves, expressing their experience of London, of the pandemic and of homelessness, while also working with the social enterprise in determining the conditions of their actions and the building of activities. The combination of those two principles makes the experience and the impacts of homelessness more visible and enables the challenging of stereotypes.

Furthermore, this chapter shows that responsible niche tourism needs to go beyond merely providing responsible consumption options for individuals, towards contributing towards a wider-reaching socially shared responsibility. Oftentimes, responsible niche tourism is limited to the capacity of the individual as the consumer, a form of neoliberal subject, to make choices that are better for self and society. This virtuous consumption seems hard to criticize. After all, it shows the influence that individuals can still have on the political sphere through participating in, and sometimes competing in, the market, even when that responsibility is depoliticized (Lapointe et al., 2018). Unseen Tours' virtual quizzes, however, go beyond these market dynamics to enact the social connection model of responsibility (Young, 2011).

This social connection model postulates that responsibility for social justice is socially shared and negotiated according to differences in power, privileges, interests and collective ability (Young, 2011), and hence will differ between individuals in regards to these factors. Power refers to the capacity of agents over the issues at stake, with privileges at times closely related. To illustrate the role of privileges in responsibility, Young (2011) gives the example of a Western middle-class consumer's privilege that benefits from a large choice of apparel to buy at a reasonable price but at the expense of the injustice generated by sweatshop workers' conditions, whereas the lower class has less privilege to change their habits to act on sweatshop workers' conditions. In an Unseen Tour pub quiz, this privilege in responsibility is seen in the financially better-off quiz participants (who usually have not experienced homelessness themselves) choosing to spend their time and money on a virtual pub quiz instead of, for example, spending the same on a movie streaming platform; the latter may have provided as much entertainment for the participant as the quiz does, but without the positive social impact of the quiz. This also presents a certain privilege to act on one's responsibility, paired with the privilege of the comfort of a home in pandemic times, which most participants share. However, at the same time, one aspect of Unseen Tours' quizzes is that they create the opportunity to reflect on this privilege in pandemic times, thus leading to greater conscientization and understanding on the issue of homelessness.

Young (2011) also stresses the importance of interest, explaining how different agents accept injustice because it either serves their interest or because they have the awareness of the injustice's impact on their interest. The virtual pub quizzes therefore serve to raise awareness of the realities of homelessness in this case, stimulating discussions around the topic in a way that gives agency and power to those who have experienced homelessness to lead the discussions, while explaining how addressing the injustice would be beneficial to the quiz participant and their relationship with the city. After all, the city is a shared space between guides and participants, which, although characterized by invisibility of certain marginalized groups (Dolezal and Lapointe, 2020), is at the same time a common space. It is one that is lost but also desired, and the virtual quiz therefore highlights how the pandemic lockdown took this urban space from both guides and participants, even if the privilege of working comfortably from home is not evenly distributed in the pandemic space (Rose, 2021).

Young (2011), describes the last dimension of her model as collective ability, referring to the capacities of agents of bringing the issues of injustice into the wider public, maybe even political, arena:

> When I name 'collective ability' as a parameter that agents might use to think about what to do about a structural injustice, I have the following in mind. Some agents are in positions where they can draw on resources of already organized entities and use them in new ways for trying to promote change. (Young, 2011: 147)

Here, Young (2011) stresses that shared responsibility is a political responsibility. While the Unseen Tours quizzes are not directly aimed at political activism, they open up a dialogue that raises awareness of the causes and consequences of homelessness. The existence of Unseen Tours and the virtual quizzes are therefore a result of collective abilities of guides and the organization, which further stimulates the collective ability of more affluent participants to use their power and privileges to understand homelessness issues and become a stimulus for change. While our research did not address this dimension directly, participating in these initiatives does open up the possibilities of mobilizing collective abilities to address homelessness through niche tourism.

CONCLUDING REMARKS

This chapter has discussed Unseen Tours' novel virtual tourism product through the niche tourism lens. It has demonstrated that the virtual pub quizzes create alternative livelihoods and empower tour guides to present their specialist knowledge of London on the new virtual 'stage'.

Utilizing the dynamics of the market, the quizzes have become a niche tourism product linked to London's desired but temporarily lost spaces, a viable engine not just to maintain a discussion around the problem of homelessness in the city, but also to develop a greater shared responsibility amongst the public. As argued by Watson et al. (2021), this chapter showed 'the digital and non-digital materialities of sociality and intimacy, and the capacities opened by people's improvisation with the affordances of home-based communication technologies at a time of extended physical isolation' (p. 1). Leisure taking place in a virtual space therefore becomes a tool that offers benefits to a marginalized group of society – above all in an intangible sense. This chapter has demonstrated that the power of these quizzes reaches far beyond the financial benefit it creates for the tour guides. They foster a sense of solidarity that goes beyond individualistic responsibility and might even mobilize collective abilities to stimulate positive social change.

REFERENCES

Arnold, D. (2005) Virtual tourism – a niche in cultural heritage. In M. Novelli (ed.) *Niche tourism: contemporary issues, trends and cases.* Oxford: Butterworth-Heinemann, 223–32.

Banerjee, S. (2008) Corporate social responsibility: the good, the bad and the ugly. *Critical Sociology*, 34(1), 51–79.

Beck, J., Rainoldi, M. and Egger, R. (2019) Virtual reality in tourism: a state-of-the-art review. *Tourism Review*, 74(3), 586–612.

Black, J. (2021) Football is 'the most important of the least important things': the illusion of sport and COVID-19. *Leisure Sciences*, 43(1–2), 97–103.

Brennan, A. (2020) Virtual pub quiz: the pubs, breweries and distilleries hosting online quizzes amid coronavirus lockdown. Available at: https://www.standard.co.uk/reveller/bars/virtual-pub-quiz-coronavirus-lockdown-a4396276.html (accessed 12 February 2021).

Cartlidge, J. (2020) new normal acceleration strategy for Bali tourism destination recovery with e-tourism and special health protocol for the tourism sector. *Biblioteca della libertà*, LV, maggio-agosto, 228.

Chain. 2021. *Rough sleeping in London (CHAIN reports) – London Datastore.* Available at: https://data.london.gov.uk/dataset/chain-reports (accessed 12 February 2021).

Chirisa, I. (2020) Scope for virtual tourism in the times of COVID-19 in select African destinations. *Journal of Social Sciences*, 64(1–3).

David (2021) *The bright-side of 2020.* Unseen Tours. Available at: https://unseentours.org.uk/blog/the-bright-side-of-2020/ (accessed 12 February 2021).

Dinis, A. and Krakover, S. (2016) Niche tourism in small peripheral towns: the case of Jewish Heritage in Belmonte, Portugal. *Tourism Planning & Development*, 13(3), 310–32.

Dolezal, C. and Gudka, J. (2019) London's 'Unseen Tours': slumming or social tourism? In A. Smith and A. Graham (eds) *Destination London*. London: University of Westminster Press, 141–63.

Dolezal, C. and Lapointe, D. (2020) *How a group of homeless and vulnerably housed tour guides reinvented themselves during the pandemic.* The Conversation. Available at: https://theconversation.com/how-a-group-of-homeless-and-vulnerably-housed-tour-guides-reinvented-themselves-during-the-pandemic-139150 (accessed 12 February 2021).

Farci, M., Rossi, L. and Boccia Artieri, G. (2017) Networked intimacy. Intimacy and friendship among Italian Facebook users. *Information, Communication & Society*, 20(5), 784–801.

Gudka, J. (2020a) How to keep your employees engaged online during lockdown. Linkedin. Available at: https://www.linkedin.com/pulse/5-ways-keep-your-employees-engaged-online-during-lockdown-jayni-gudka/ (accessed 12 February 2021).

Gudka, J. (2020b) To pivot? (Or not to pivot?). Linkedin. Available at: https://www.linkedin.com/pulse/pivot-jayni-gudka/ (accessed 12 February 2021).

Gudka, J. (2020c) Make a positive social impact with your office Christmas party this year. Linkedin. Available at: https://www.linkedin.com/pulse/make-positive-social-impact-your-office-christmas-party-jayni-gudka/ (accessed 12 February 2021).

Hacker, J., vom Brocke, J., Handali, J., Otto, M. and Schneider, J. (2020) Virtually in this together – how web-conferencing systems enabled a new virtual togetherness during the COVID-19 crisis. *European Journal of Information Systems*, 29(5), 563–84.

Hampton, M. and Jeyacheya, J. (2013) *Tourism and inclusive growth in small island developing states.* London: Commonwealth Secretariat.

Higgins-Desbiolles, F. (2020) Socialising tourism for social and ecological justice after COVID-19. *Tourism Geographies*, 22(3), 610–23.

Homeless Link (2021a) Rough sleeping – explore the data. Available at: https://www.homeless.org.uk/facts/homelessness-in-numbers/rough-sleeping/rough-sleeping-explore-data (accessed 12 February 2021).

Homeless Link (2021b) Excellence Awards winners revealed at celebratory event. Available at: https://www.homeless.org.uk/connect/blogs/2020/dec/10/excellence-awards-winners-revealed-at-celebratory-event (accessed 12 February 2021).

Huang, Y., Backman, K., Backman, S. and Chang, L. (2016) Exploring the implications of virtual reality technology in tourism marketing: an integrated research framework. *International Journal of Tourism Research*, 18(2), 116–28.

Imber-Black, E. (2020) Rituals in the time of COVID-19: imagination, responsiveness, and the human spirit. *Family process*, 59(3), 912–21.

Ioannides, D. and Gyimothy, S. (2020) The COVID-19 crisis as an opportunity for escaping the unsustainable global tourism path. *Tourism Geographies*, 22(3), 1–9.

Kaur, G. and Kaur, C. (2020) COVID-19 and the rise of the new experience economy. *FIIB Business Review*, 9(4), 239–48.

Khobra, U. and Gaur, R. (2020) Live (life) streaming: virtual interaction, virtual proximity, and streaming everyday life during the COVID-19 pandemic. *Rupkatha Journal on Interdisciplinary Studies in Humanities*, 12(5), 1–6.

Lapointe, D., Sarrasin, B. and Benjamin, C. (2018) Tourism in the sustained hegemonic neoliberal order. *Revista Latino-Americana de Turismologia*, 4(1), 16–33.

London Government (2020) Mayor reveals tourist spending in central London to plummet by £10.9bn. Available at: https://www.london.gov.uk/press-releases/mayoral/central-london-tourist-spending-to-drop-by-109bn (accessed 12 February 2021).

Longhurst, R. (2016) Mothering, digital media and emotional geographies in Hamilton, Aotearoa New Zealand. *Social & Cultural Geography*, 17(1), 120–39.

Mariano, K. (2020) 17 videos from tourism boards that will remind you to 'stay home today and travel tomorrow'. *Travel Daily*. Available at: https://www.traveldailymedia.com/17-videos-from-tourism-boards-that-will-remind-you-to-stay-home-today-and-travel-tomorrow/ (accessed 12 February 2021).

Marson, D. (2011) From mass tourism to niche tourism. In P. Robinson, S. Heitmann and P. Dieke (eds) *Research themes for tourism*. Wallingford: CABI, 1–15.

McCabe, S. and Qiao, G. (2020) A review of research into social tourism: launching the Annals of Tourism Research Curated Collection on Social Tourism. *Annals of Tourism Research*, 85, 103103.

Minnaert, L. (2014) Social tourism participation: the role of tourism inexperience and uncertainty. *Tourism Management*, 40, 282–9.

Monroe, E. and Bishop, P. (2016) Slum tourism: helping to fight poverty…or voyeuristic exploitation? Research Briefing. London: Tourism Concern.

Mura, P., Tavakoli, R. and Pahlevan Sharif, S. (2017) 'Authentic but not too much': exploring perceptions of authenticity of virtual tourism. *Information Technology & Tourism*, 17(2), 145–59.

Newell, P. and Frynas, J. (2007) Beyond CSR? Business, poverty and social justice: an introduction. *Third World Quarterly*, 28(4), 669–81.

Nic (2020) Nic's 2020 reflections. *Unseen Tours*. Available at: https://unseentours.org.uk/blog/nics -2020-reflections/ (accessed 12 February 2021).

Novelli, M. (2005) *Niche tourism: contemporary issues, trends and cases.* Oxford: Butterworth-Heinemann.

Novelli, M. (2018) Niche tourism: past, present and future. In C. Cooper, S. Volo, W. Gartner and N. Scott (eds) *The Sage Handbook of Tourism Management*. London: SAGE Publications, 344–59.

Palmer, A. and McCole, P. (2000) The role of electronic commerce in creating virtual tourism destination marketing organisations. *International Journal of Contemporary Hospitality Management*, 12(3), 198–204.

Pardo, C. and Ladeiras, A. (2020) Covid-19 'tourism in flight mode': a lost opportunity to rethink tourism – towards a more sustainable and inclusive society. *Worldwide Hospitality and Tourism Themes*, 12(6).

Peeters, P. (2012) A clear path towards sustainable mass tourism? Rejoinder to the paper 'Organic, incremental and induced paths to sustainable mass tourism convergence' by David B. Weaver. *Tourism Management*, 33(5), 1038–41.

Pete (2021) A year in review… and WHAT A YEAR! *Unseen Tours*. Available at: https://unseentours .org.uk/2020-a-year-in-review-and-what-a-year/ (accessed 12 February 2021).

Riva, G. and Wiederhold, B. (2020) How cyberpsychology and virtual reality can help us to overcome the psychological burden of coronavirus. *Cyberpsychology, Behavior, and Social Networking*, 23(5), 277–9.

Robinson, M. and Novelli, M. (2005) Niche tourism: an introduction. In M. Novelli (ed.) *Niche tourism: contemporary issues, trends and cases*. Oxford: Butterworth-Heinemann, 1–14.

Rose, J. (2021) Biopolitics, essential labor, and the political-economic crises of COVID-19. *Leisure Sciences*, 43(1–2), 211–17. DOI: 10.1080/01490400.2020.1774004

Severo, E., De Guimarães, J. and Dellarmelin, M. (2021) Impact of the COVID-19 pandemic on environmental awareness, sustainable consumption and social responsibility: evidence from generations in Brazil and Portugal. *Journal of Cleaner Production*, 286, 124947.

Shah, V. (2020) *Personal post*. Linkedin. Available at: https://www.linkedin.com/feed/update/urn:li: activity:6744590650844483584/ (accessed 12 February 2021).

Stankov, U. Filimonau, V. and Vujičić, M.D. (2020) A mindful shift: an opportunity for mindfulness-driven tourism in a post-pandemic world. *Tourism Geographies*, 22(3), 703–12.

Tripadvisor (2019) Unseen Tours. *Tripadvisor*. Available at: https://www.tripadvisor.co.uk/Attraction _Review-g186338-d3850154-Reviews-or75-Unseen_Tours-London_England.html#REVIEWS (accessed 12 February 2021).

Unseen Tours (2020a) We're good to go. *Unseen Tours*. Available at: https://unseentours.org.uk/blog/ were-good-to-go/ (accessed 12 February 2021).

Unseen Tours (2020b) What to expect from our Christmas Quiz – Unseen Tours. *Unseen Tours*. Available at: https://unseentours.org.uk/what-to-expect-from-our-christmas-quiz/ (accessed 12 February 2021).

Unseen Tours (2020c) Why post-pandemic team building matters. *Unseen Tours*. Available at: https:// unseentours.org.uk/why-post-pandemic-team-building-matters/ (accessed 12 February 2021).

Unseen Tours (2020d) Make a positive social impact with your office Christmas party this year. *Unseen Tours*. Available at: https://unseentours.org.uk/make-a-positive-social-impact-with-your-office-christmas -party-this-year/ (accessed 12 February 2021).

Vaishar, A. and Šťastná, M. (2022) Impact of the COVID-19 pandemic on rural tourism in Czechia Preliminary considerations. *Current Issues in Tourism*, 25(2), 167–91. DOI: 10.1080/13683500.2020.1839027

Watson, A., Lupton, D. and Mike, M. (2021) Enacting intimacy and sociality at a distance in the COVID-19 crisis: the sociomaterialities of home-based communication technologies. *Media International Australia*, 178(1). DOI: 10.1177/1329878X20961568

Weijo, H., Martin, D. and Schouten, J. (2014) Against ethics and CSR: a call for a science-based market-holistic approach to sustainability in business. In R.P. Hill and R. Langan (eds) *Handbook of Research on Marketing and Corporate Social Responsibility*. Cheltenham: Edward Elgar Publishing, 135–46.

Wörndl, W., Koo, C. and Stienmetz, J.L. (eds) (2021) *Information and communication technologies in tourism 2021.* Cham: Springer.

Yang, T., Wai, I.K., Fan, Z.B. and Mo, Q.M. (2021) The impact of a 360° virtual tour on the reduction of psychological stress caused by COVID-19. *Technology in Society*, 64.

Young, I.M. (1990) *Justice and the politics of difference.* Princeton University Press.

Young, I.M. (2011) *Responsibility for justice.* Oxford: Oxford University Press.

Yung, R. and Khoo-Lattimore, C. (2017) New realities: a systematic literature review on virtual reality and augmented reality in tourism research. *Current Issues in Tourism*, 22(17), 2056–81.

35. In focus 7 – hot air ballooning in the Czech Republic

Markéta Novotná and Josef Kunc

This case study focuses on hot air ballooning as a new niche in the tourism offer of the Czech Republic. As a new niche tourism product, it has the potential to increase domestic tourism post-COVID-19. The opportunity lies in the ability to satisfy people's need for extraordinary and non-everyday experiences without having to undertake long-distance trips. As Ioannides and Gyimóthy (2020) observed, the COVID-19 pandemic caused a decline in mainstream tourism practices and gave an opportunity to emergent niche activities which could encourage people to explore their own countries.

Ballooning is represented as an outdoor recreational activity (e.g., Cloke and Perkins, 2002; McKay, 2013). It is one of a number of activities carried out in the countryside and involving an aspect of adventure and the participant's interaction with the natural environment (Avan and Güçer, 2019). As Buckley (2000) pointed out, it is possible to observe substantial convergence of ballooning with adventure, outdoor recreation, nature-based tourism and ecotourism. Moreover, the products primarily based on these elements are well differentiated from the mass 3S (sun, sea, sand) packages.

The history of hot air ballooning in the Czech Republic began in the 1980s. The first contemporary Czech hot air balloon was made in Brno in 1983 by the owner of the Kubicek Balloons Company. Ballooning as a tourism niche has been a fairly recent phenomenon. Since 2015, two specialized balloon centres have been established: Balloon Chateau and Balony.eu. Both combine ballooning activities with the provision of accommodation. Alongside flights which include stay packages, night flights, expedition flights or romantic flights, there are other activities provided by the most significant ballooning operators in the Czech Republic. Table 35.1 presents the services offered by the specialized balloon centres and other important operators.

Ballooning has become an activity affordable to a broad range of people. Domestic clients mostly receive a flight as a present in the form of a gift voucher, usually in a high-capacity balloon for 12–24 passengers. Ballooning as a niche tourism activity for international tourism is more often undertaken when using low-capacity balloons of up to eight seats. These low-capacity balloons are popular with foreign clients who want to experience an individual adventure. Similarly, some Czech clients who want to indulge themselves with an extraordinary experience use the form of a private flight. However, such activities are not very frequent.

There is hidden potential for future development or a post-COVID tourism restart in special offers of packages containing flights and accommodation. The opportunity can be perceived with a focus on luxury private flights for affluent domestic clients who prefer tailormade and unique activities. Such unique activities were previously sought during holidays abroad, which have been recently limited due to national pandemic restrictions. This was demonstrated in the summer of 2020 with the rise in domestic tourists, many of whom wanted to indulge themselves with a special experience.

Table 35.1   *Analysis of the balloon flights offer*

	Balony.eu	Balloon Chateau	Promo Air	Balon.cz	Balloon Adventures Prague
Basic sightseeing flight	✓	✓	✓	✓	✓
Customized flights	✓	✗	✓	✓	✓
Private flight for 2 people	✓	✓	✓	✓	✓
Flight with stay package	✓	✓	✗	✗	✗
Night flight	✓	✓	✗	✓	✗
Special gastro flight	✓	✗	✗	✗	✗
Expedition flight	✓	✗	✓	✓	✗
Tethered balloon	✗	✓	✗	✗	✗
Flying a special shaped balloon	✗	✓	✗	✗	✗
Specialization in foreign markets	✗	✗	✗	✗	✓
Specialized balloon centre service	✓	✓	✗	✗	✗
Balloon events organization	✓	✓	✗	✗	✗

Source: Markéta Novotná and Josef Kunc.

One advantage of ballooning lies in the fact that it is an outdoor rather than an indoor activity. Moreover, the setting of ballooning could enhance outdoor recreation activities as a lifestyle because of their relevance to wellbeing (Rice et al., 2020). At present, the real challenge is to find appropriate solutions and anti-COVID-19 measures. The Czech producer of balloons ranked among the top manufacturers in the global market developed various ideas on how to modify balloons to enable protection against COVID-19 infection. These involved not only safety measures but also a marketing campaign to promote the use of face masks and antiseptic tissues by providing these emblazoned with the company logo as a promotional gift for passengers.

With regard to the development of sustainable tourism, seeing the world from a bird's-eye perspective contributes to the promotion of hidden localities. Therefore, this niche represents an opportunity for the promotion of local culture and heritage, enhances diversification of the general tourism offer and promotes a more balanced approach to tourism's growth. Moreover, about fifty companies organizing hot air balloon flights in the Czech market are mainly of a family nature, deeply embedded in their communities.

REFERENCES

Avan, S.K. and Güçer, E. (2019) Determining the leisure satisfaction levels of individuals having hot air balloon ride as an adventurous recreational activity. *Journal of Multidisciplinary Academic Tourism*, 4(2), 63–9. doi: 10.31822/jomat.618715

Buckley, R. (2000) Neat trends: current issues in nature, eco- and adventure tourism. *International Journal of Tourism Research*, 2(6), 437–44. doi: 10.1002/1522-1970(200011/12)

Cloke, P. and Perkins, H.C. (2002) Commodification and adventure in New Zealand tourism. *Current Issues in Tourism*, 5(6), 521–49. doi: 10.1080/13683500208667939

Ioannides, D. and Gyimóthy, S. (2020) The COVID-19 crisis as an opportunity for escaping the unsustainable global tourism path. *Tourism Geographies*, 22(3), 1–9. doi: 10.1080/14616688.2020.1763445

McKay, T. (2013) Adventure tourism: opportunities and management challenges for SADC destinations. *Acta Academica*, 45(3), 30–62.

Rice, W.L., Mateer, T.J., Reigner, N., Newman, P., Lawhon, B. and Taff, B.D. (2020) Changes in recreational behaviors of outdoor enthusiasts during the COVID-19 pandemic: analysis across urban and rural communities. *Journal of Urban Ecology*, 6(1), 1–7. doi: 10.1093/jue/juaa020

36. In focus 8 – flights to nowhere

Martine Bakker

In September 2020, the Australian airline Qantas made international news headlines when it announced a special seven-hour flight over Australia departing and landing in Sydney. The flight on a Dreamliner 787 had 134 tickets for sale and they were sold out in 10 minutes. It promoted great views over the Great Barrier Reef, Uluru and Sydney Harbour, and special meals and onboard entertainment (Mzezewa, 2020). This was not the first time during the COVID-19 pandemic that airlines offered these 'flights to nowhere'. In August of 2020, Brunei Airlines offered a two-hour 'fly and dine' experience and Taiwan-based airline EVA Air offered a special Father's Day flight to nowhere on their Hello Kitty-themed A330 Dream jet. The three-hour sightseeing flight was catered for by a three-star Michelin chef and included Hello Kitty amenities. A month earlier the same airline had offered three half-day tours where passengers got to experience the normal airport procedures of checking in and boarding. These flights did not leave the gate or include a meal. While the 'flights to nowhere' filled a real market demand, critics are concerned about the unnecessary use of fuel.

So, is this a COVID-19-induced new phenomenon and form of niche tourism? Have we seen this before? Flights where aeroplanes depart and land at the same airport with the purpose of sightseeing, also called commercial air tours or scenic airs flights, are not new. When commercial flying really took off in the 1930s, airlines started to offer 'flightseeing' trips. The British airline Imperial Airways operated a series of Afternoon Tea Flights over London where passengers could see the main points of interest of the city while enjoying a cup of tea (Budd, 2009). Since then, flightseeing trips have become a popular way to see major cities or natural sights. Nowadays you can do an air safari or game flights to track and view wild animals from the air on the African continent. Buddha Air in Kathmandu offers daily early morning 50-minute flights where passengers can see Mount Everest from the air from their guaranteed window seat. Antarctica Flights, which had been offering sightseeing flights from Australia to Antarctica (a 12-hour experience), announced in August 2020 they will be chartering a Qantas 787 Dreamliner to carry out the flights during the 2020–21 season (Slotnick, 2020). Then there are helicopter flights, such as those over Manhattan, the Grand Canyon, the coast of Hawaii, the glaciers in New Zealand and other places. Besides sightseeing, these helicopter flights are also often booked to experience the excitement of a (first-time) helicopter ride. Travelling without a destination is not limited to air travel. There are also cruises with no destination. Bradley Rink (2019) studied cruisers in South Africa that go on multi-day cruises to nowhere where the main pastime is partying and eating, while Dallen et al. (2016) discuss so-called 'booze cruises' on ferries between Scandinavian countries where passengers would not get off until they returned to their homeport. Commercial space travel could technically also be considered 'flights to nowhere' if passengers do not leave their space flight during the journey.

How can we explain the interest in flying as a touristic activity in itself, instead of a means to an end? When commercial airlines were still in their infancy, flying was considered an exciting activity as it could provide a 'god-like' view (Budd, 2009). Aeroplanes flew at much lower altitudes than now, and passengers would spend much of their time looking out of the window. Aeroplane pilots would divert and descend to view sights and, on many of the routes, passengers would receive special maps showing the route and all the sights they could spot from the air (Pirie, 2009). For many people, watching the world below from a window seat up in the air is still enjoyable, as the many 'hash tagged' posts on Instagram show. It is not just the sightseeing aspect that attracts people to fly for the sake of flying, it also still has a certain mystique. Elsner (as cited in Millward, 2008: 16) wrote in 1930 that 'one becomes very loose from the earth when flying, and ordinary disappointments fade away almost as quickly as does a city left behind an air liner'. This feeling of being aero-mobile is considered as a special way of interacting with the world. Altitude can provide a third dimension that can be used to detach oneself from what is happening on the ground below and become an 'armchair' spectator. This aero-mobile tourist gaze or 'tourism from above' can also exempt 'its users from the chaos and materiality of the city' below (Rink, 2017: 895). This aero-mobile tourist gaze could explain why people want to leave behind lives that have been disrupted by the COVID-19 pandemic and literally detach themselves from the place below, even if it is just for a few hours. Cohen et al. (2011) identified the phenomenon of tourism air travel behavioural addiction, or binge flying, where people just have the need for excessive air travel, even if they know this has a negative consequence for climate change. This addiction to travelling can explain the popularity of the EVA Air flight which did not even leave the gate but only provided the guests with the experience of navigating the airport and boarding. Flights to nowhere are filling a demand for people who are looking to experience something familiar while at the same time undertake something outside their house that is novel. After many months of being at home and in quarantine with no option to travel to a destination, people were looking for some excitement within the COVID-19 health and safety boundaries. Such individuals are likely to mitigate their concerns about climate change by asserting the need to support their national airlines and staff, as well as pointing out that such flights are still below their normal level of carbon emission associated with extensive flying around the world. However, this is something which may worth further investigation.

REFERENCES

Budd, L. C. S. (2009) The view from the air: The cultural geographies of flight. In P. Vannini (ed.) *The Cultures of Alternative Mobilities: Routes Less Travelled.* London: Routledge.

Cohen, S., Higham, J. E. and Cavaliere, C. T. (2011) Binge flying: Behavioural addiction and climate change. *Annals of Tourism Research*, 38(3), 1070–89.

Dallen, T., Saarinen, J. and Viken, A. (2016) Tourism issues and international borders in the Nordic Region. *Scandinavian Journal of Hospitality and Tourism*, 16(1), 1–13.

Millward, L. (2008) The embodied aerial subject: Gendered mobility in British inter-war air tours. *Journal of Transport History*, 29(1), 5–22.

Mzezewa, T. (2020) The flight goes nowhere. And it's sold out. *The New York Times*, September 19. Available at: https://www.nytimes.com/2020/09/19/travel/airlines-pandemic-flights-to-nowhere.html

Pirie, G. (2009) Incidental tourism: British imperial air travel in the 1930s. *Journal of Tourism History*, 1(1), 49–66.

Rink, B. (2017) The aeromobile tourist gaze: Understanding tourism 'from above'. *Tourism Geographies*, 19(5), 878–96.

Rink, B. (2019) Liminality at-sea: Cruises to nowhere and their metaworlds. *Tourism Geographies*, 22(2), 392–412.

Slotnick, D. (2020) Australia's Qantas is reviving its 12-hour sightseeing flights over Antarctica, which land right back where they started. *Business Insider*. Available at: https://www.businessinsider.nl/qantas-antarctica-flights-sightseeing-coronavirus-2020-8?international=true&r=US

Index

academic tourism 219
adventure tourism 50, 130, 243, 284
Afferni, R. 288
affinity tourism xxii
African arts tourism 232–4
'African school' discourse 350, 352
agriculture, culinary tourism 108
agritourism (agriturismo) 84–98, 102
air travel 'to nowhere' 425–6
Alant, K. 88
Albania
    festivals tourism 124–39
    political context 129–30
albergo diffuso 371–82
Aldrich, R. 357
Ali-Knight, J. 250
Aliaga, B. 225
Allis, T. 175
Almeida, M.V. de 333
ancestral tourism 144–5, 147–9, 151–3
Andriotis, K. 288
Angelo, K.M. 147
Angelou, Maya 266
Apartheid 383–4
Araújo, H.R. 181
archaeological excavations 268
architourism 25–37
Arnold, D. 404
artichoke tourism 99–110
artists, tombstones 268–9
arts tourism 232–4, 384
Ashworth, G. 165
Asian tea tourism 69–83
Aslam, M.S. 80
astro-tourism 2–13, 111–23
astronomical sightseeing 4
Australia 175, 242–3, 246, 425
authentic interaction, local communities 345–6
authenticity
    dark tourism 245, 250, 256
    homeless tour guides 402
    tea tourism 74, 80
    tourism promoting 100
    virtual tourism 404
    visitor experiences 276
Axelsson, T. 251

babymoon, definitions 300
babymoon travel 300–315

backpacker culture 140–142
Balinese pilgrimage 328–9
Ballantyne, R. 250
ballooning 422–4
Balmford, A. 28
Baptista, J.A. 346, 352
battlefield tourism 236–49
Bechmann, P.S. 251
Beeton, S. 42, 115
Belarus 164, 168
Belisle, F.J., *Annals* 100
Benson, A. 61, 317, 325
Benur, A.M. 193
Bertioga, Brazil 334–6, 338–41
beverage-related tourism 69–83, 101
Beyern, B. 265
Bielecki, A. 162
'Big 7' European countries 216
big-bang festivals and events 125
Bilbao effect 25–37
Binns, T. 384
Binthabet, A.A. 27
biodiversity conservation 38–48
Biosphere Reserves 38–48
Biran, A. 250
Bird, G.R. 175–6
blog analysis 391–2, 394–5
Blum, L. 333
Boatto, V. 85, 89
Boekstein, M. 111
Bokhari, A.S. 27
'booze cruises' 425
Borges, V.L.B. 181
Borgo Antico albergo diffuso 380
Botterill, K. 242
Braithwaite, R. 237, 240
Bramwell, B. 193
brand management 174–5
Braun, V. 252–3
Brazil
    railway tourism 172–85
    social tourism 332–44
Bremer, T.S. 287, 289
Brown, G. 87
Brownsword, N. 195
Bruwer, J. 88
Bryman, A. 115
Buckley, R. 422
Buda, D. 158

Printed and bound by CPI Group (UK) Ltd, Croydon, CR0 4YY

16/04/2025

14658495-0004